BOONE COUNTY LIBRARY

2040 9100 823 842 7

SO-AJA-367

B.P.R.D. HELL ON EARTH:
GODS AND MONSTERS

created by MIKE MIGNOLA

BOONE COUNTY PUBLIC LIBRARY
BURLINGTON, KY 41005
www.bcpl.org

FEB   2012

DR. KATE CORRIGAN

Current field director for the B.P.R.D., first brought into active duty by Hellboy. Dr. Corrigan is a former professor at New York University, an authority on folklore and occult history, who now serves as primary liaison between the Bureau and the United Nations.

ABE SAPIEN

Victorian scientist and occult investigator Langdon Everett Caul, transformed into a fish-man while hidden in a stasis chamber beneath a Washington, DC, hospital. The true nature of his transformation remains a mystery, but connections have been suggested between Abe and the recently defeated frog monsters.

JOHANN KRAUS

Medium whose physical form was destroyed while his ectoplasmic projection was out of body. A psychic empath, Johann can create temporary forms for the dead to speak to the living. He briefly inhabited an artificial body, before it was destroyed by former B.P.R.D. team leader Captain Ben Daimio.

LIZ SHERMAN

A fire starter since the age of eleven, when she accidentally burned her entire family to death. A fire she started in the center of the world set off terrible global changes, and she's been in hiding ever since.

PANYA

Ancient Egyptian mummy who returned to life during an unrolling ceremony in the nineteenth century. Panya was rescued by the B.P.R.D. from a century-long imprisonment with the Oannes Society. She has demonstrated psychic abilities, although their precise nature and range remain unknown, as do her motives.

ANDREW DEVON

Former professor in modern and medieval languages from Cambridge. While growing up in St. Louis, Missouri, his interest in the supernatural was piqued when he read Kate Corrigan's case study of a demonic possession in Azerbaijan. His effort to debunk it drew the scholar into a world he never believed existed.

MIKE MIGNOLA'S

B.P.R.D.™
HELL ON EARTH
GODS AND MONSTERS

story by **MIKE MIGNOLA** and **JOHN ARCUDI**

art for *Gods* by **GUY DAVIS**

art for *Monsters* by **TYLER CROOK**

colors by **DAVE STEWART**

letters by **CLEM ROBINS**

cover art by **MIKE MIGNOLA** with **DAVE STEWART**

chapter break art by **RYAN SOOK**

editor **SCOTT ALLIE**

assistant editor **DANIEL CHABON**   collection designer **AMY ARENDTS**

publisher **MIKE RICHARDSON**

DARK HORSE BOOKS® ®

Special thanks to Jason Hvam

Mike Richardson **PRESIDENT AND PUBLISHER** · Neil Hankerson **EXECUTIVE VICE PRESIDENT**
Tom Weddle **CHIEF FINANCIAL OFFICER** · Randy Stradley **VICE PRESIDENT OF PUBLISHING**
Michael Martens **VICE PRESIDENT OF BOOK TRADE SALES** · Anita Nelson **VICE PRESIDENT
OF BUSINESS AFFAIRS** · Micha Hershman **VICE PRESIDENT OF MARKETING** · David Scroggy
VICE PRESIDENT OF PRODUCT DEVELOPMENT · Dale LaFountain **VICE PRESIDENT OF
INFORMATION TECHNOLOGY** · Darlene Vogel **SENIOR DIRECTOR OF PRINT, DESIGN, AND
PRODUCTION** · Ken Lizzi **GENERAL COUNSEL** · Davey Estrada **EDITORIAL DIRECTOR** · Scott
Allie **SENIOR MANAGING EDITOR** · Chris Warner **SENIOR BOOKS EDITOR** · Diana Schutz
EXECUTIVE EDITOR · Cary Grazzini **DIRECTOR OF PRINT AND DEVELOPMENT** · Lia Ribacchi
ART DIRECTOR · Cara Niece **DIRECTOR OF SCHEDULING**

DarkHorse.com   Hellboy.com

B.P.R.D.™ Hell on Earth Volume 2: Gods and Monsters © 2011, 2012 Mike Mignola. Abe Sapien™,
Hellboy™, Johann™, and all other prominently featured characters are trademarks of Mike Mignola.
Dark Horse Books® and the Dark Horse logo are registered trademarks of Dark Horse Comics, Inc.
All rights reserved. No portion of this publication may be reproduced or transmitted, in any form or
by any means, without the express written permission of Dark Horse Comics, Inc. Names, characters,
places, and incidents featured in this publication either are the product of the author's imagination or
are used fictitiously. Any resemblance to actual persons (living or dead), events, institutions, or locales,
without satiric intent, is coincidental.

This book collects the comic-book series *B.P.R.D. Hell on Earth: Gods* #1–#3 and *B.P.R.D. Hell on
Earth: Monsters* #1–#2, all originally published by Dark Horse Comics.

Published by Dark Horse Books
A division of Dark Horse Comics, Inc.
10956 SE Main Street
Milwaukie, OR 97222

First edition: February 2012
ISBN 978-1-59582-822-4

10 9 8 7 6 5 4 3 2 1
Printed at Midas Printing International, Ltd., Huizhou, China

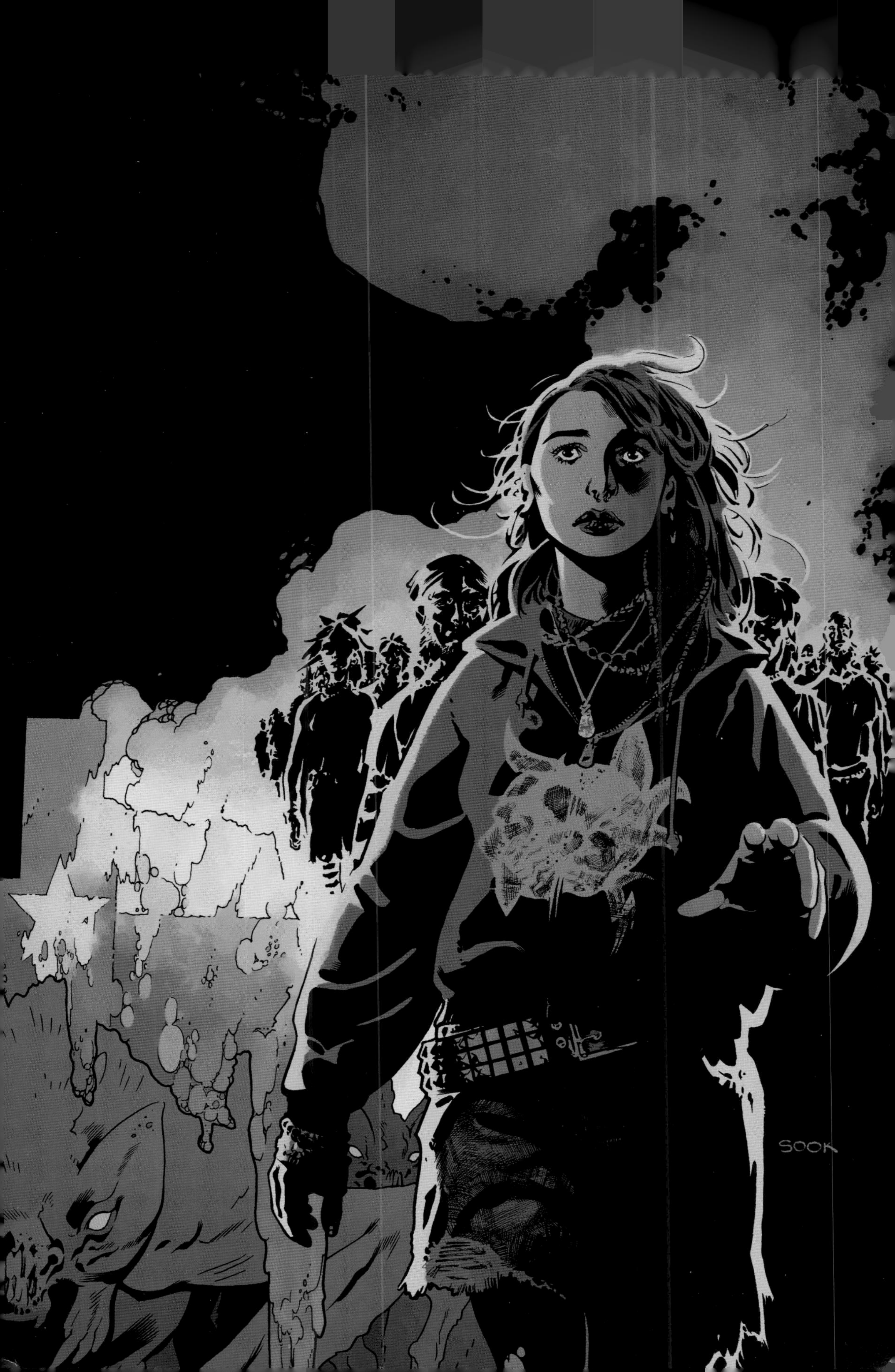
SOOK

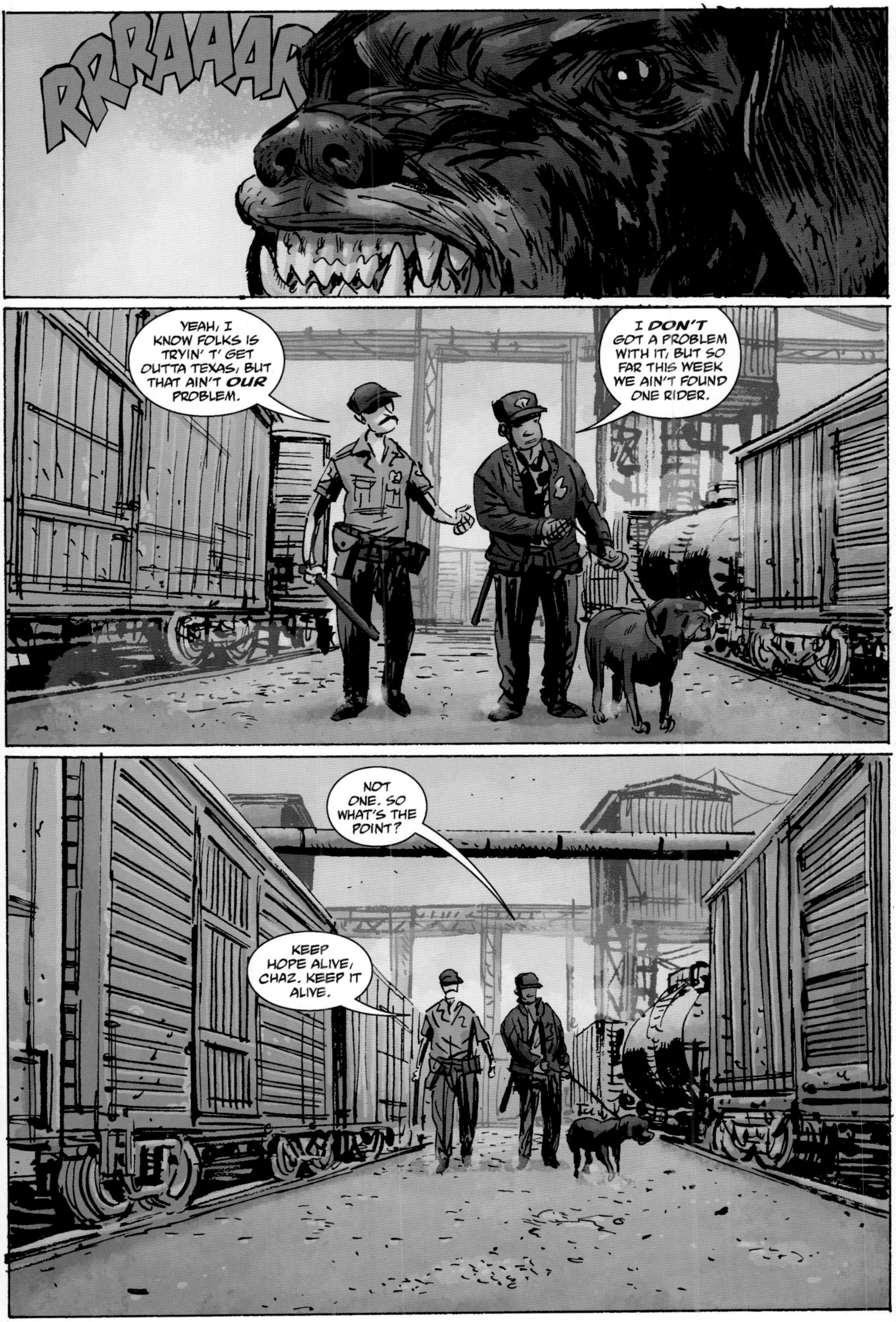
RRRAAAR
YEAH, I KNOW FOLKS IS TRYIN' T' GET OUTTA TEXAS, BUT THAT AIN'T OUR PROBLEM.
I DON'T GOT A PROBLEM WITH IT, BUT SO FAR THIS WEEK WE AIN'T FOUND ONE RIDER.
NOT ONE. SO WHAT'S THE POINT?
KEEP HOPE ALIVE, CHAZ. KEEP IT ALIVE.

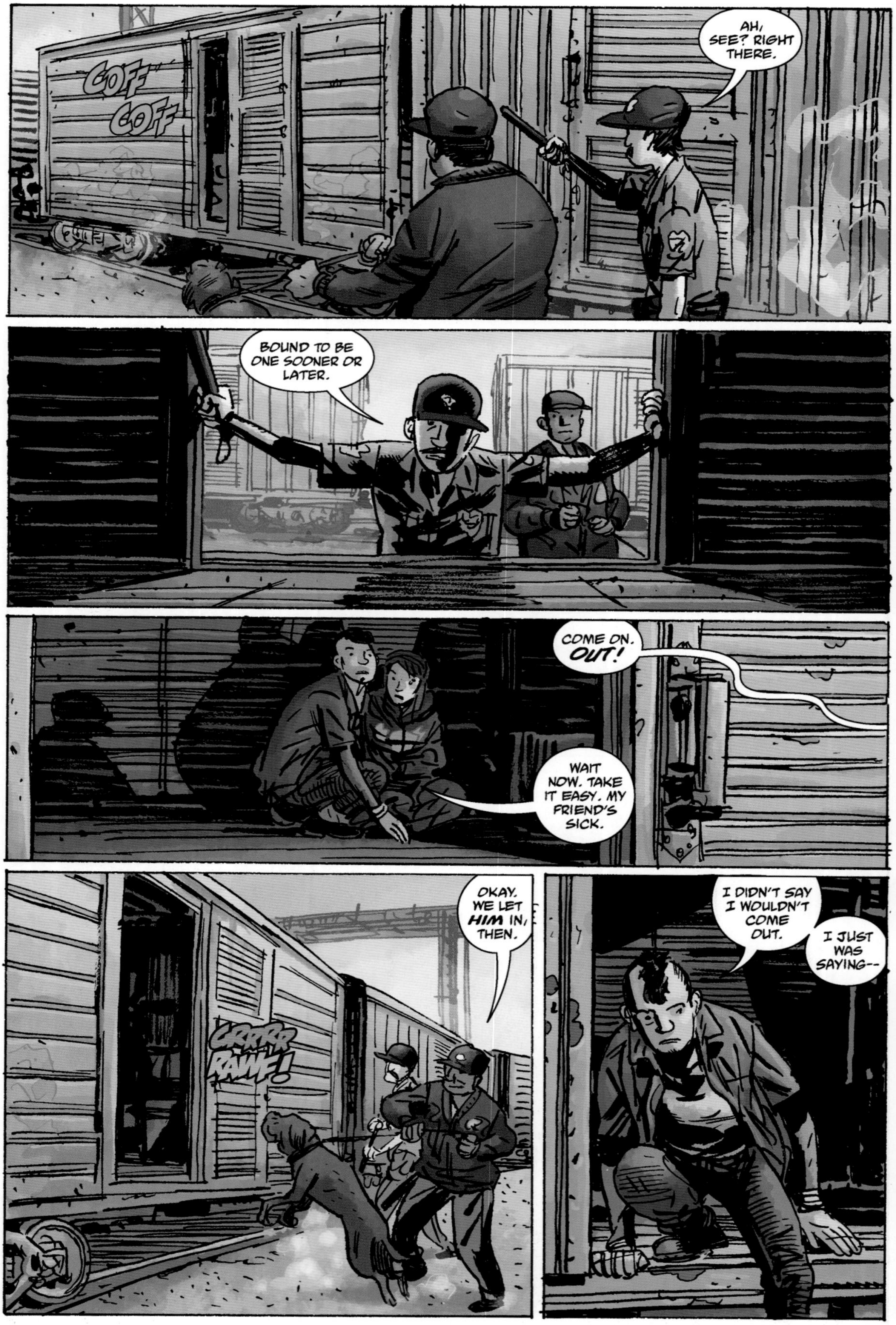
COFF COFF
AH, SEE? RIGHT THERE.
BOUND TO BE ONE SOONER OR LATER.
COME ON. OUT!
WAIT NOW. TAKE IT EASY. MY FRIEND'S SICK.
GRRRR RAWF!
OKAY. WE LET HIM IN, THEN.
I DIDN'T SAY I WOULDN'T COME OUT.
I JUST WAS SAYING--

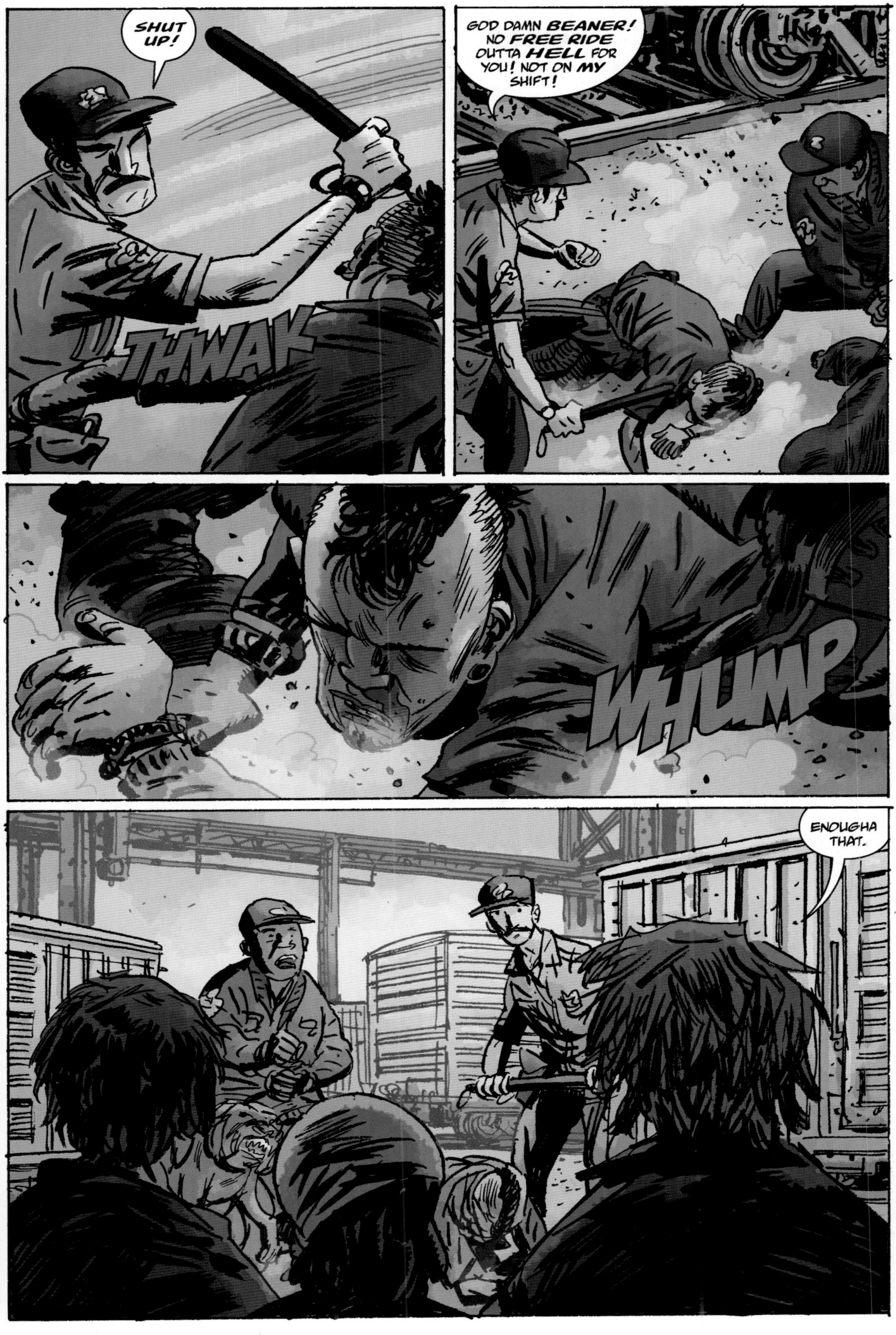
SHUT UP!
THWAK
GOD DAMN BEANER! NO FREE RIDE OUTTA HELL FOR YOU! NOT ON MY SHIFT!
WHUMP
ENOUGHA THAT.

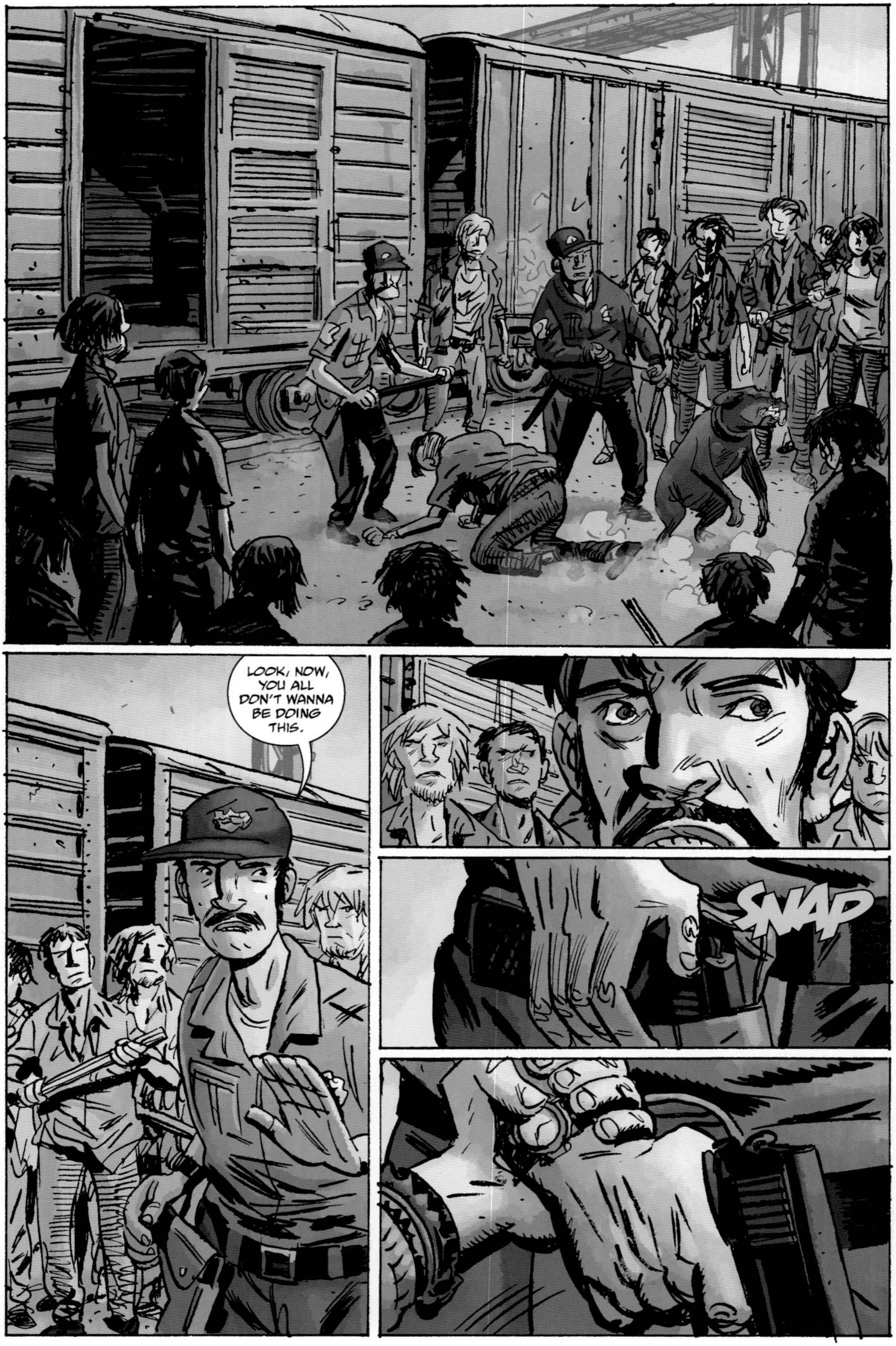
LOOK, NOW, YOU ALL DON'T WANNA BE DOING THIS.
SNAP

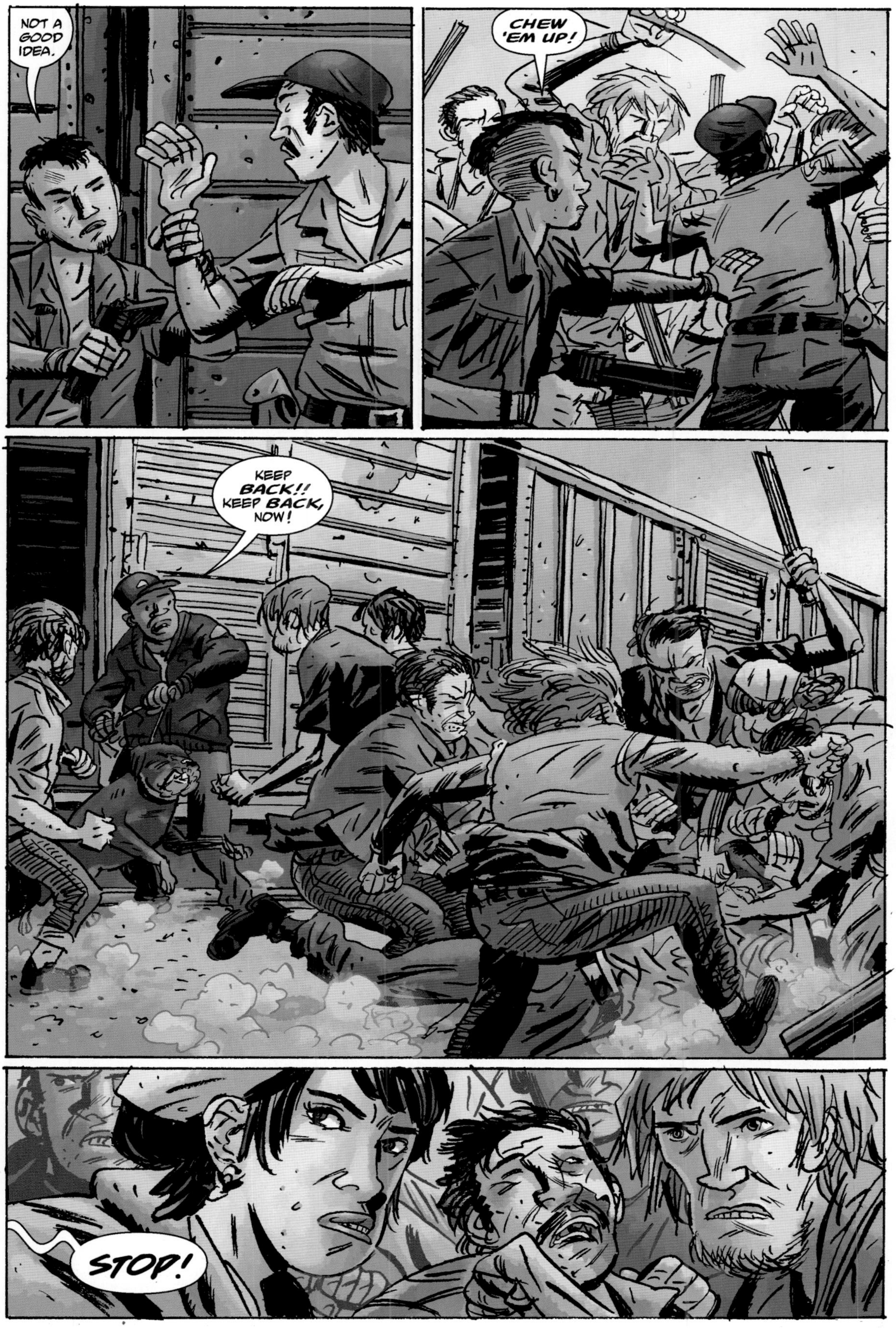
NOT A GOOD IDEA.
CHEW 'EM UP!
KEEP BACK!! KEEP BACK, NOW!
STOP!

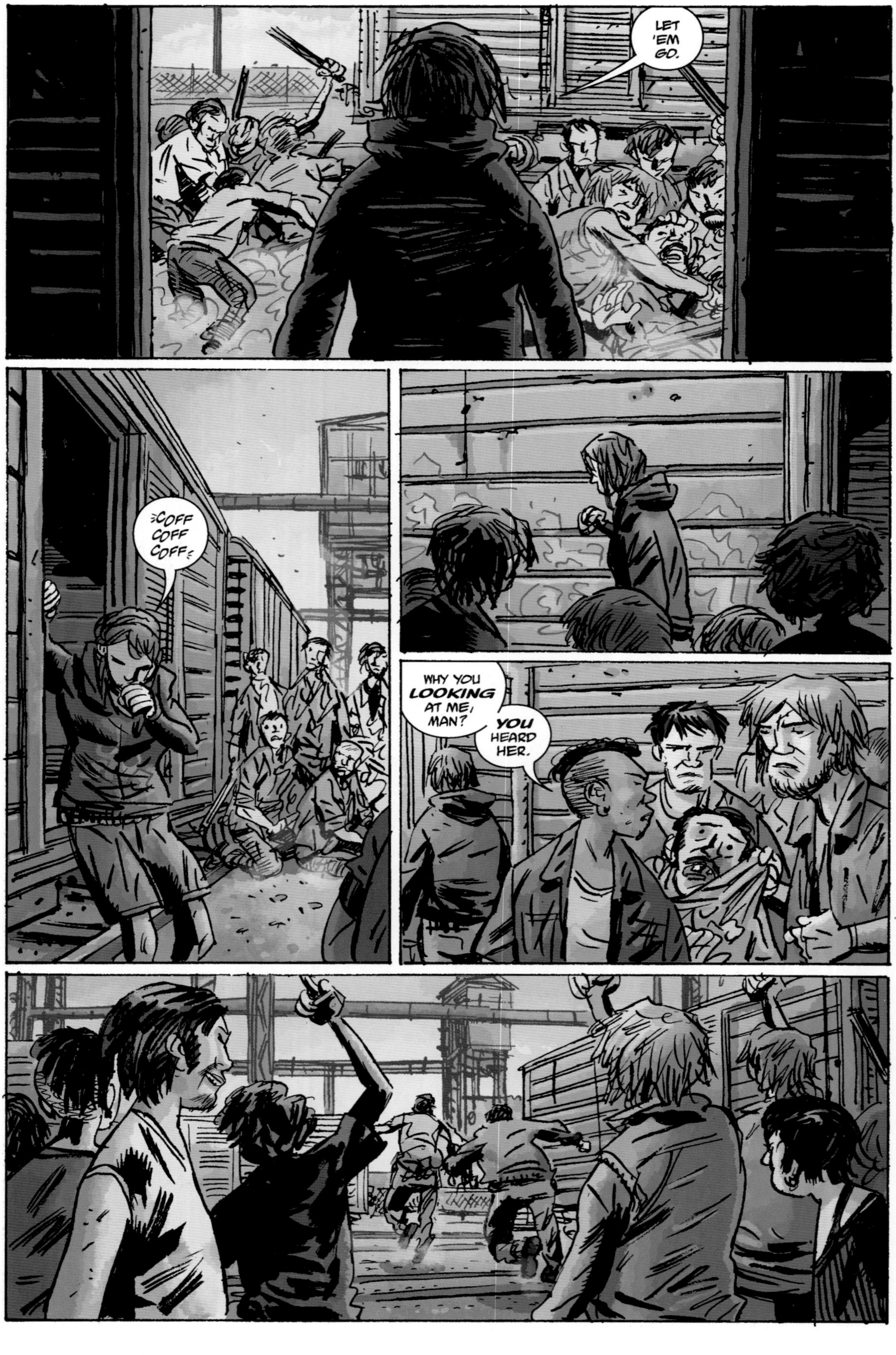
LET 'EM GO.
COFF COFF COFF
WHY YOU **LOOKING** AT ME, MAN?
YOU HEARD HER.

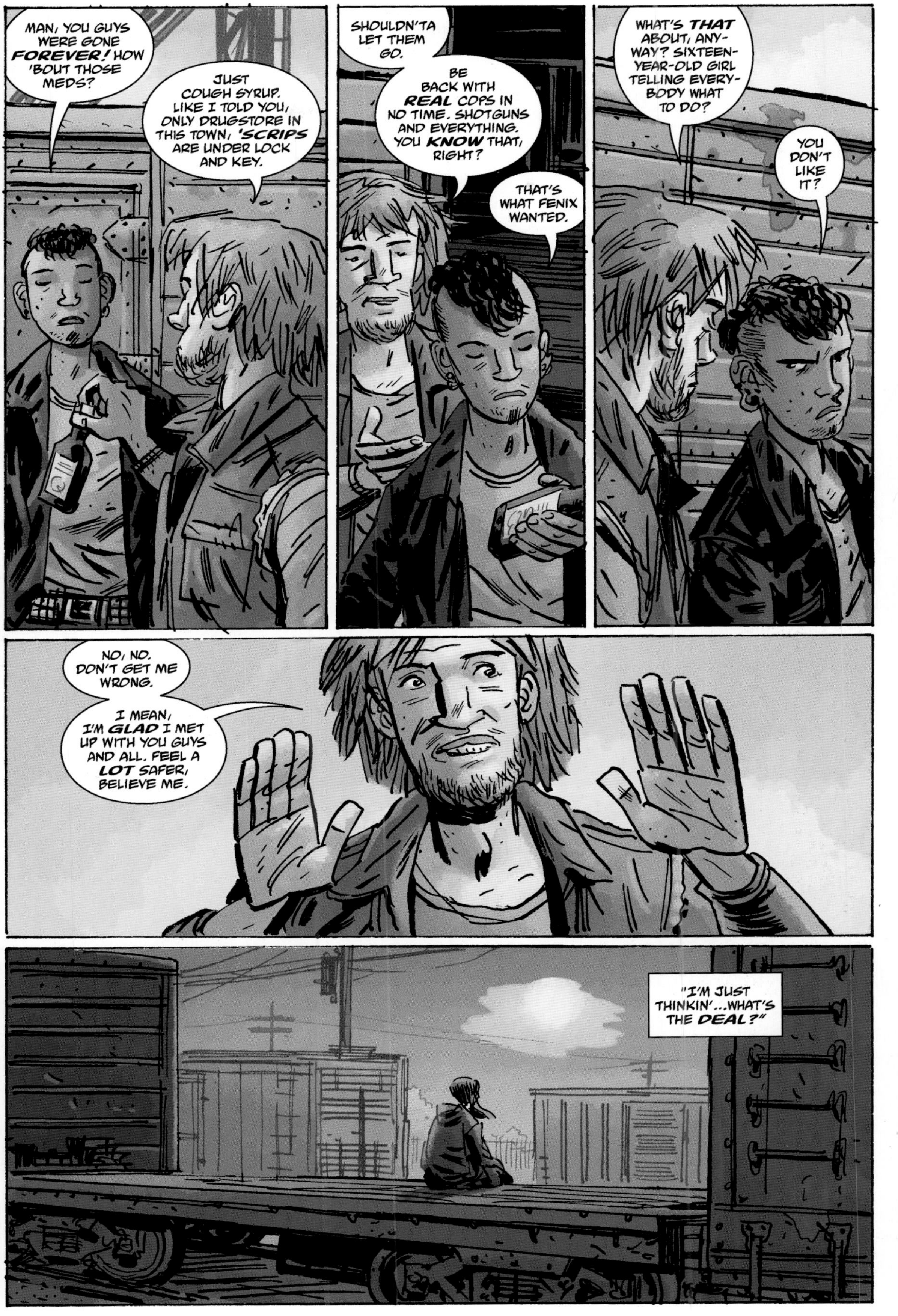
MAN, YOU GUYS WERE GONE FOREVER! HOW 'BOUT THOSE MEDS?
JUST COUGH SYRUP. LIKE I TOLD YOU, ONLY DRUGSTORE IN THIS TOWN, 'SCRIPS ARE UNDER LOCK AND KEY.
SHOULDN'TA LET THEM GO.
BE BACK WITH REAL COPS IN NO TIME. SHOTGUNS AND EVERYTHING. YOU KNOW THAT, RIGHT?
THAT'S WHAT FENIX WANTED.
WHAT'S THAT ABOUT, ANYWAY? SIXTEEN-YEAR-OLD GIRL TELLING EVERYBODY WHAT TO DO?
YOU DON'T LIKE IT?
NO, NO. DON'T GET ME WRONG.
I MEAN, I'M GLAD I MET UP WITH YOU GUYS AND ALL. FEEL A LOT SAFER, BELIEVE ME.
"I'M JUST THINKIN'...WHAT'S THE DEAL?"

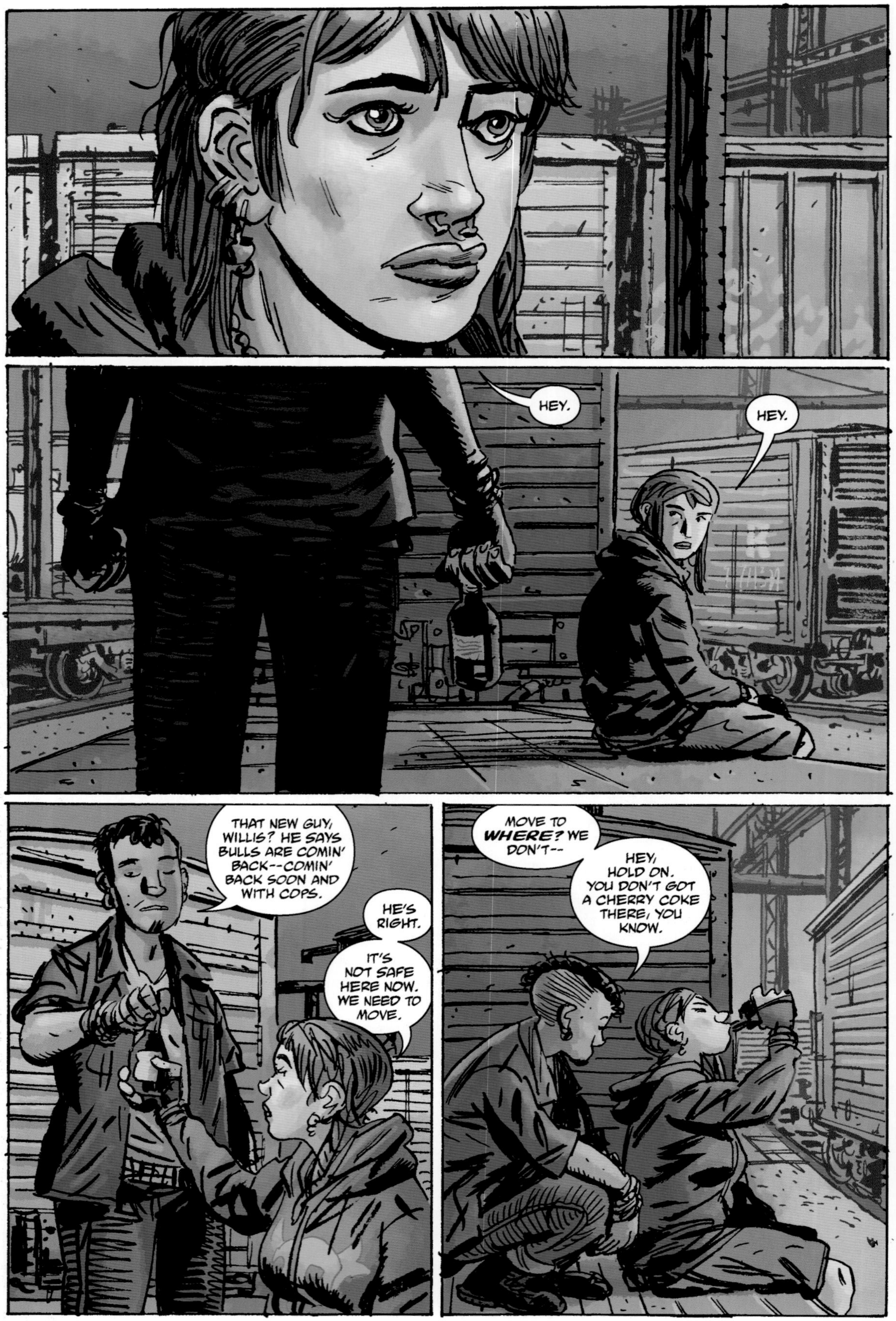
HEY.
HEY.
THAT NEW GUY, WILLIS? HE SAYS BULLS ARE COMIN' BACK--COMIN' BACK SOON AND WITH COPS.
HE'S RIGHT.
IT'S NOT SAFE HERE NOW. WE NEED TO MOVE.
MOVE TO WHERE? WE DON'T--
HEY, HOLD ON. YOU DON'T GOT A CHERRY COKE THERE, YOU KNOW.

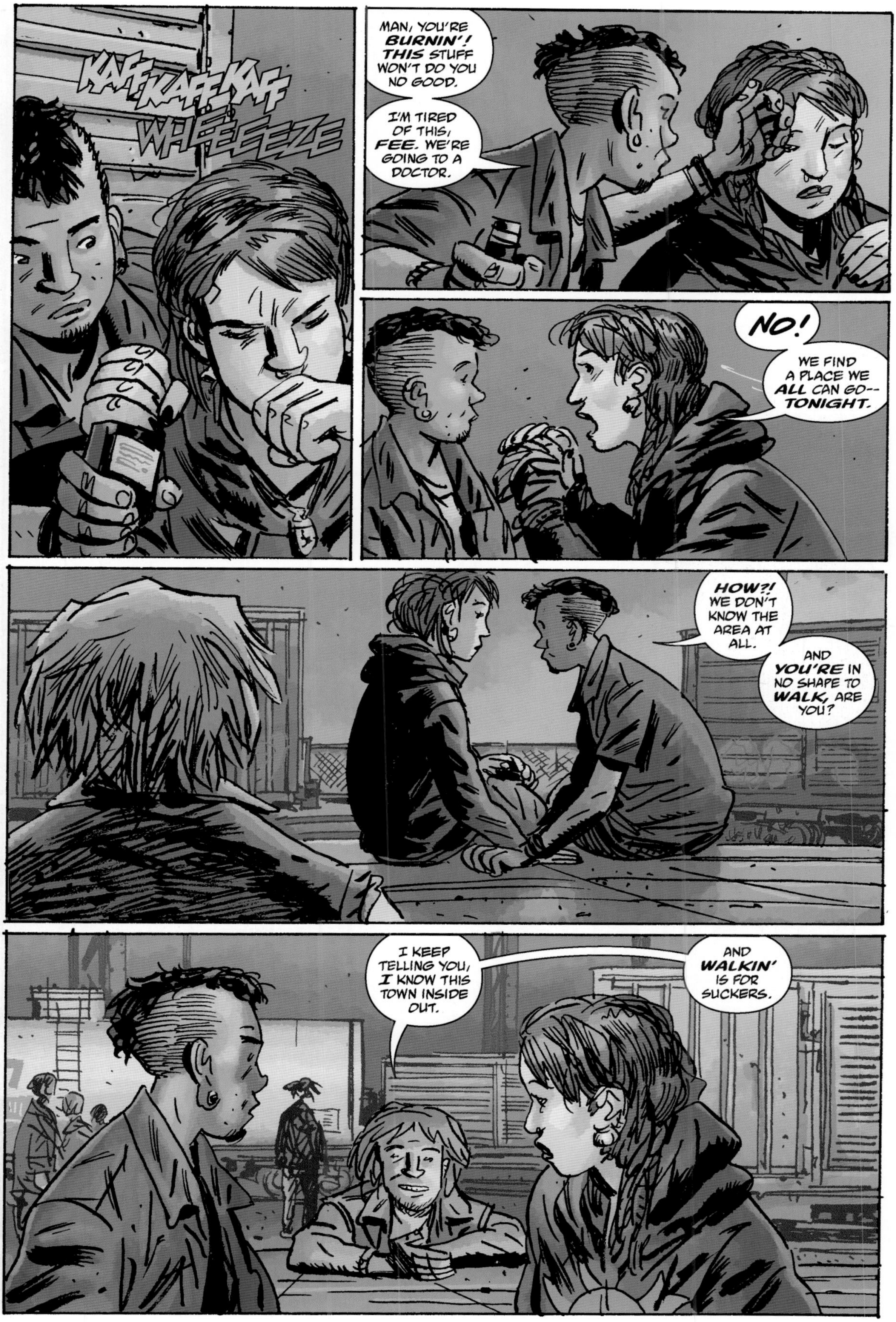

KAFF KAFF KAFF
WHEEEEZE
MAN, YOU'RE **BURNIN'! THIS** STUFF WON'T DO YOU NO GOOD.
I'M TIRED OF THIS, **FEE**. WE'RE GOING TO A DOCTOR.
NO!
WE FIND A PLACE WE **ALL** CAN GO-- **TONIGHT**.
HOW?! WE DON'T KNOW THE AREA AT ALL.
AND **YOU'RE** IN NO SHAPE TO **WALK**, ARE YOU?
I KEEP TELLING YOU, **I** KNOW THIS TOWN INSIDE OUT.
AND **WALKIN'** IS FOR SUCKERS.

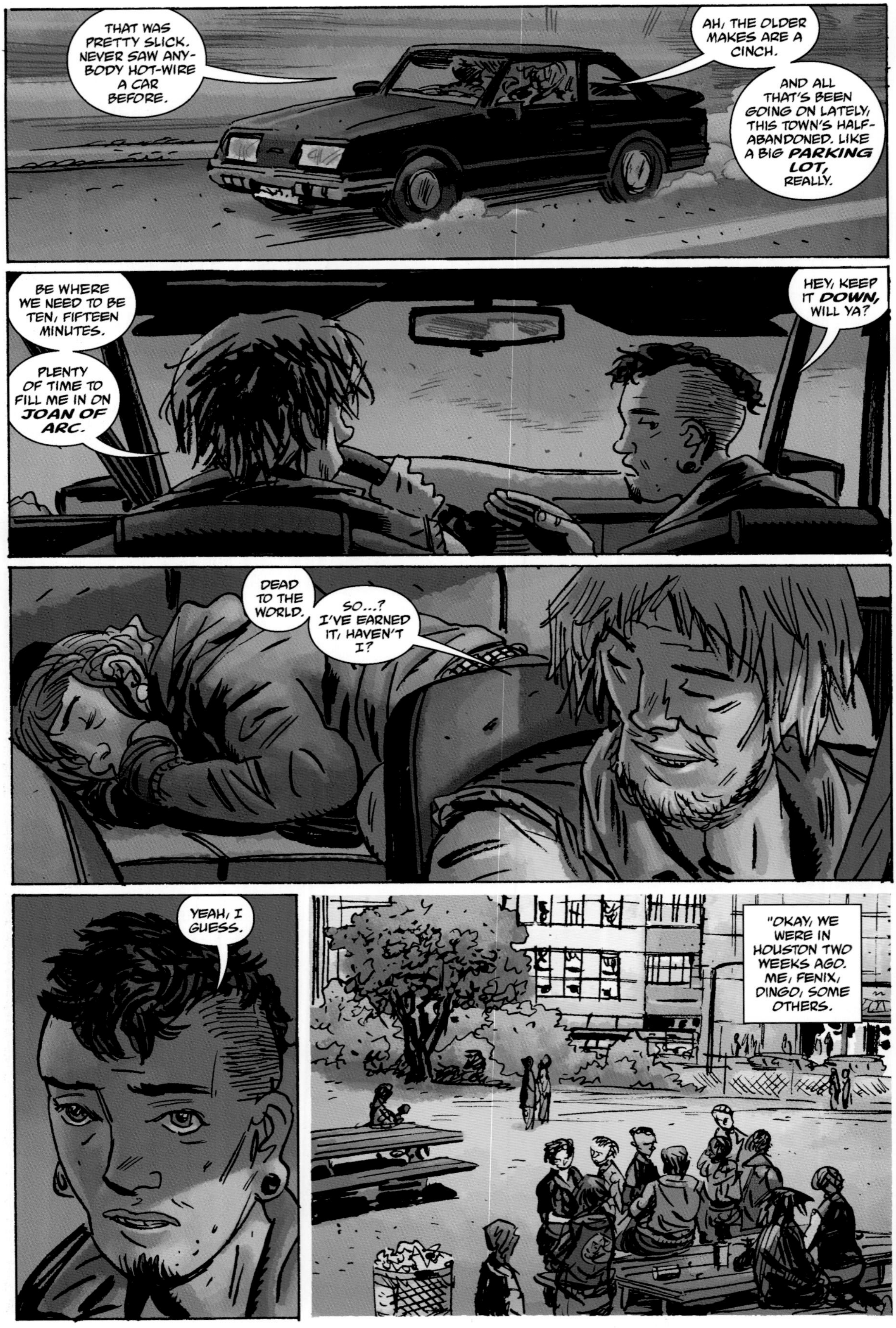
THAT WAS PRETTY SLICK. NEVER SAW ANY-BODY HOT-WIRE A CAR BEFORE.
AH, THE OLDER MAKES ARE A CINCH.
AND ALL THAT'S BEEN GOING ON LATELY, THIS TOWN'S HALF-ABANDONED. LIKE A BIG **PARKING LOT,** REALLY.
BE WHERE WE NEED TO BE TEN, FIFTEEN MINUTES.
PLENTY OF TIME TO FILL ME IN ON **JOAN OF ARC.**
HEY, KEEP IT **DOWN,** WILL YA?
DEAD TO THE WORLD.
SO...? I'VE EARNED IT, HAVEN'T I?
YEAH, I GUESS.
"OKAY, WE WERE IN HOUSTON TWO WEEKS AGO. ME, FENIX, DINGO, SOME OTHERS.

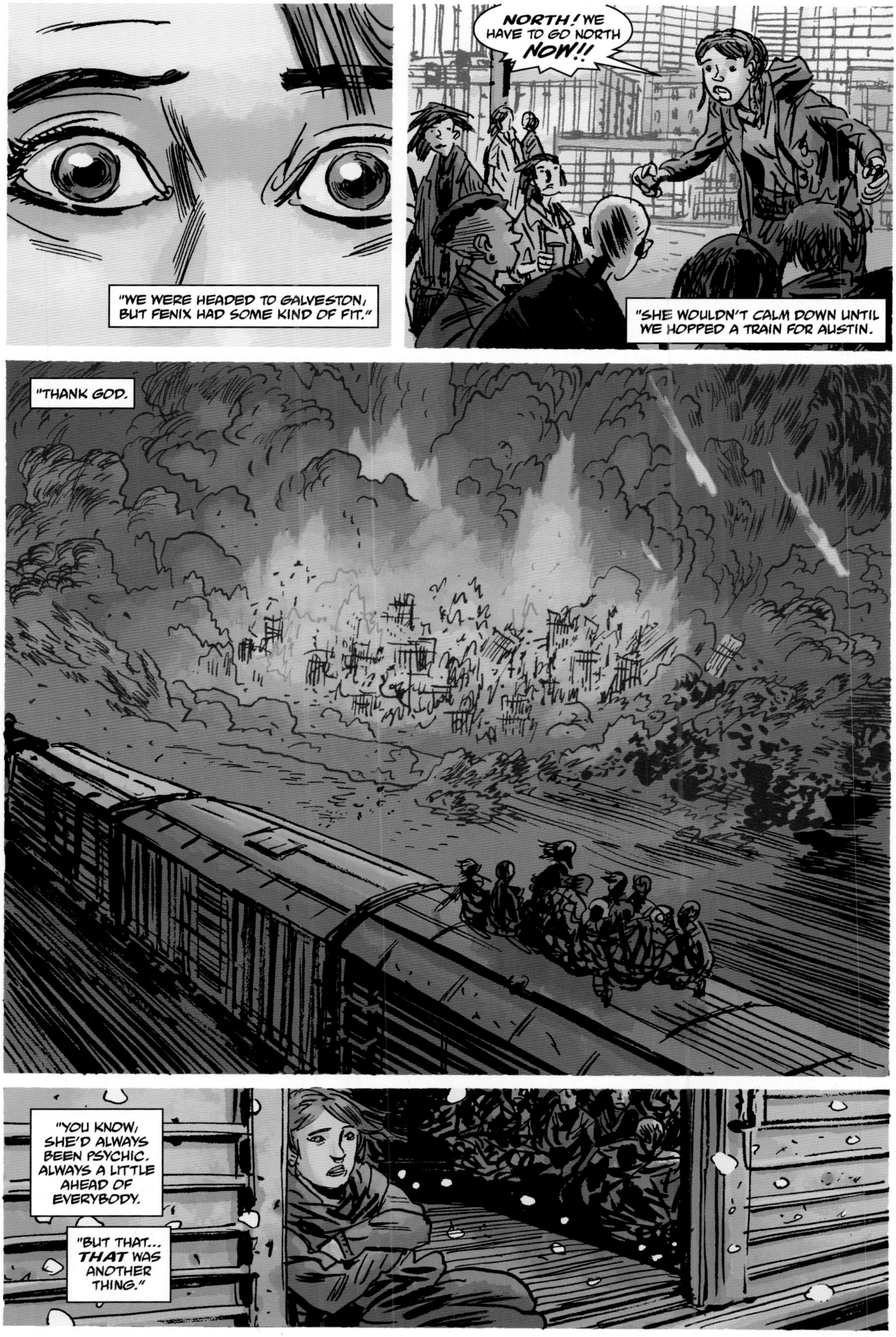
"WE WERE HEADED TO GALVESTON, BUT FENIX HAD SOME KIND OF FIT."
NORTH! WE HAVE TO GO NORTH NOW!!
"SHE WOULDN'T CALM DOWN UNTIL WE HOPPED A TRAIN FOR AUSTIN.
"THANK GOD.
"YOU KNOW, SHE'D ALWAYS BEEN PSYCHIC. ALWAYS A LITTLE AHEAD OF EVERYBODY.
"BUT THAT... THAT WAS ANOTHER THING."

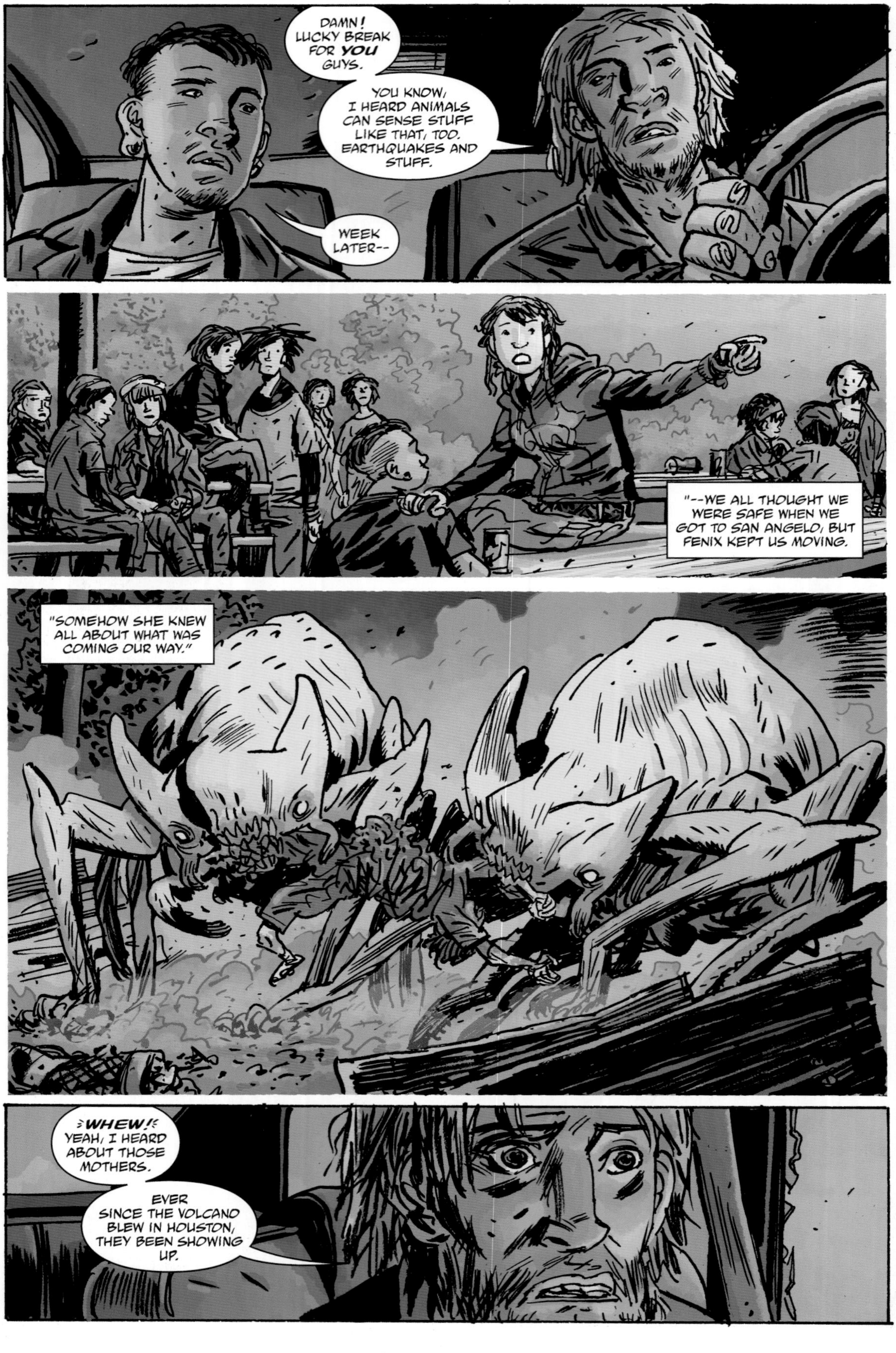
DAMN! LUCKY BREAK FOR *YOU* GUYS.
YOU KNOW, I HEARD ANIMALS CAN SENSE STUFF LIKE THAT, TOO. EARTHQUAKES AND STUFF.
WEEK LATER--
"--WE ALL THOUGHT WE WERE SAFE WHEN WE GOT TO SAN ANGELO, BUT FENIX KEPT US MOVING.
"SOMEHOW SHE KNEW ALL ABOUT WHAT WAS COMING OUR WAY."
WHEW! YEAH, I HEARD ABOUT THOSE MOTHERS.
EVER SINCE THE VOLCANO BLEW IN HOUSTON, THEY BEEN SHOWING UP.

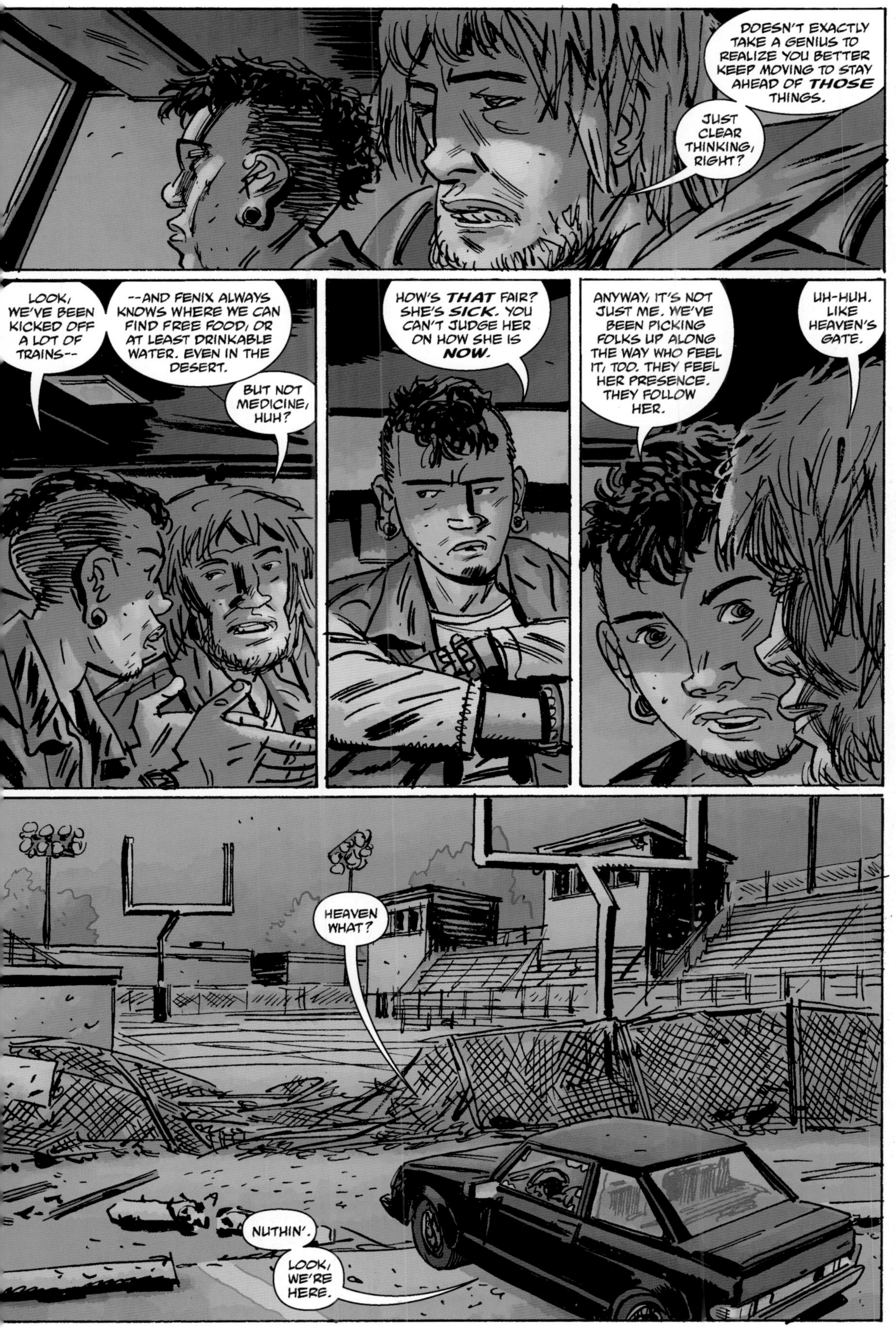
DOESN'T EXACTLY TAKE A GENIUS TO REALIZE YOU BETTER KEEP MOVING TO STAY AHEAD OF **THOSE** THINGS.
JUST CLEAR THINKING, RIGHT?
LOOK, WE'VE BEEN KICKED OFF A LOT OF TRAINS--
--AND FENIX ALWAYS KNOWS WHERE WE CAN FIND FREE FOOD, OR AT LEAST DRINKABLE WATER. EVEN IN THE DESERT.
BUT NOT MEDICINE, HUH?
HOW'S **THAT** FAIR? SHE'S **SICK**. YOU CAN'T JUDGE HER ON HOW SHE IS **NOW**.
ANYWAY, IT'S NOT JUST ME. WE'VE BEEN PICKING FOLKS UP ALONG THE WAY WHO FEEL IT, TOO. THEY FEEL HER PRESENCE. THEY FOLLOW HER.
UH-HUH. LIKE HEAVEN'S GATE.
HEAVEN WHAT?
NUTHIN'.
LOOK, WE'RE HERE.

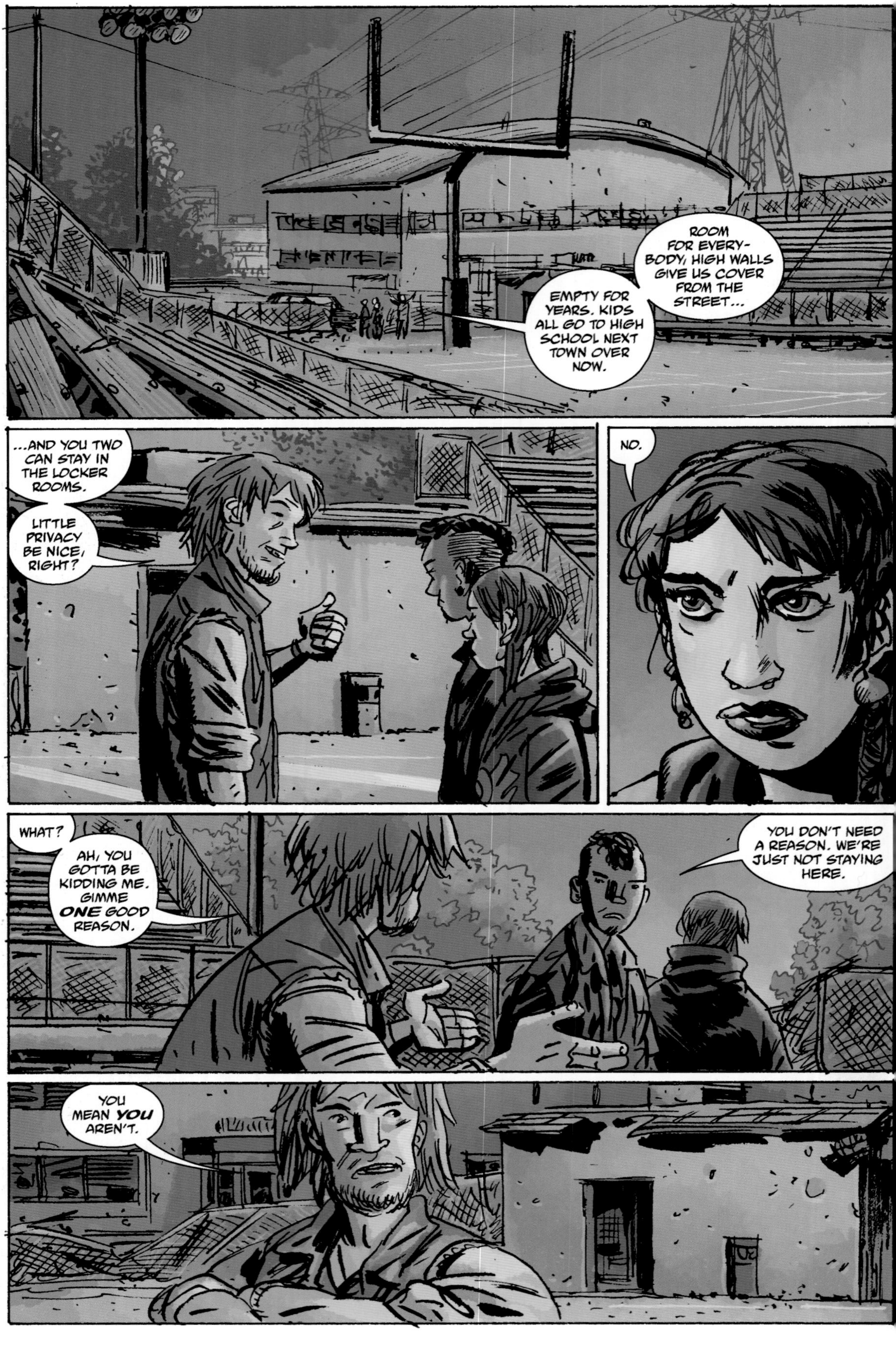
EMPTY FOR YEARS. KIDS ALL GO TO HIGH SCHOOL NEXT TOWN OVER NOW.
ROOM FOR EVERY-BODY, HIGH WALLS GIVE US COVER FROM THE STREET...
...AND YOU TWO CAN STAY IN THE LOCKER ROOMS.
LITTLE PRIVACY BE NICE, RIGHT?
NO.
WHAT?
AH, YOU GOTTA BE KIDDING ME. GIMME ONE GOOD REASON.
YOU DON'T NEED A REASON. WE'RE JUST NOT STAYING HERE.
YOU MEAN YOU AREN'T.

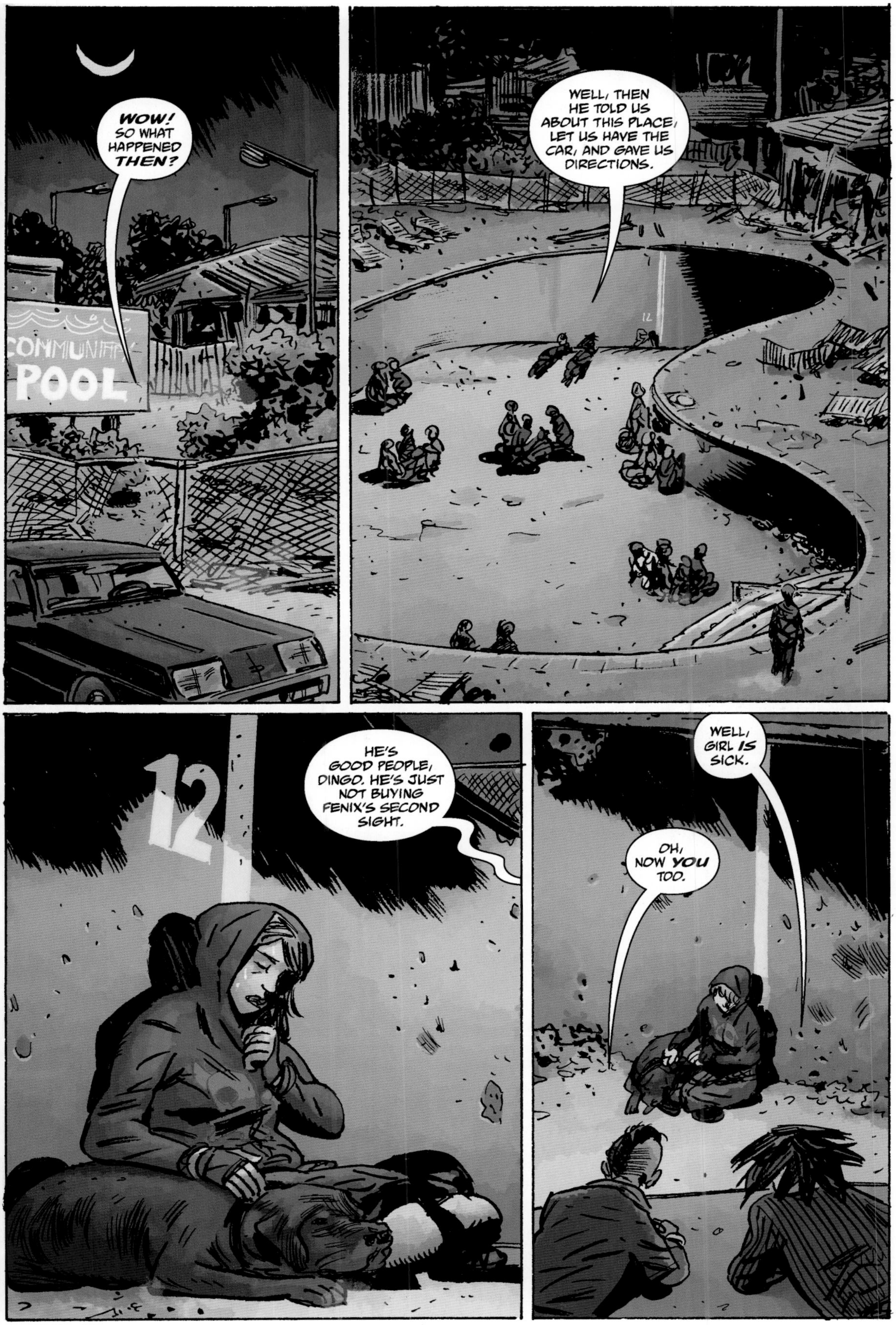
WOW! SO WHAT HAPPENED THEN?
COMMUNITY POOL
WELL, THEN HE TOLD US ABOUT THIS PLACE, LET US HAVE THE CAR, AND GAVE US DIRECTIONS.
12
HE'S GOOD PEOPLE, DINGO. HE'S JUST NOT BUYING FENIX'S SECOND SIGHT.
WELL, GIRL IS SICK.
OH, NOW YOU TOO.

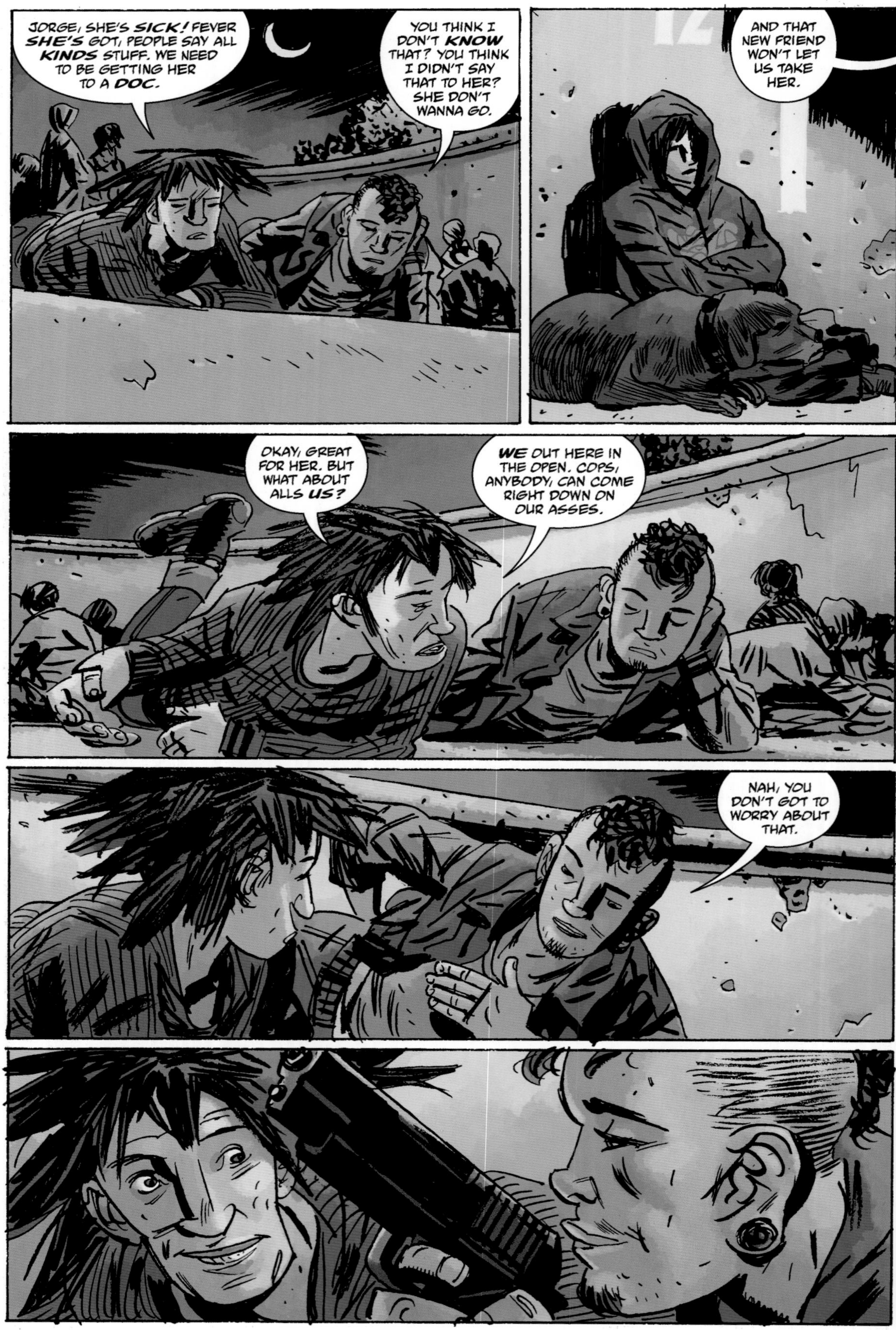
JORGE, SHE'S SICK! FEVER SHE'S GOT, PEOPLE SAY ALL KINDS STUFF. WE NEED TO BE GETTING HER TO A DOC.
YOU THINK I DON'T KNOW THAT? YOU THINK I DIDN'T SAY THAT TO HER? SHE DON'T WANNA GO.
12
AND THAT NEW FRIEND WON'T LET US TAKE HER.
OKAY, GREAT FOR HER. BUT WHAT ABOUT ALLS US?
WE OUT HERE IN THE OPEN. COPS, ANYBODY, CAN COME RIGHT DOWN ON OUR ASSES.
NAH, YOU DON'T GOT TO WORRY ABOUT THAT.

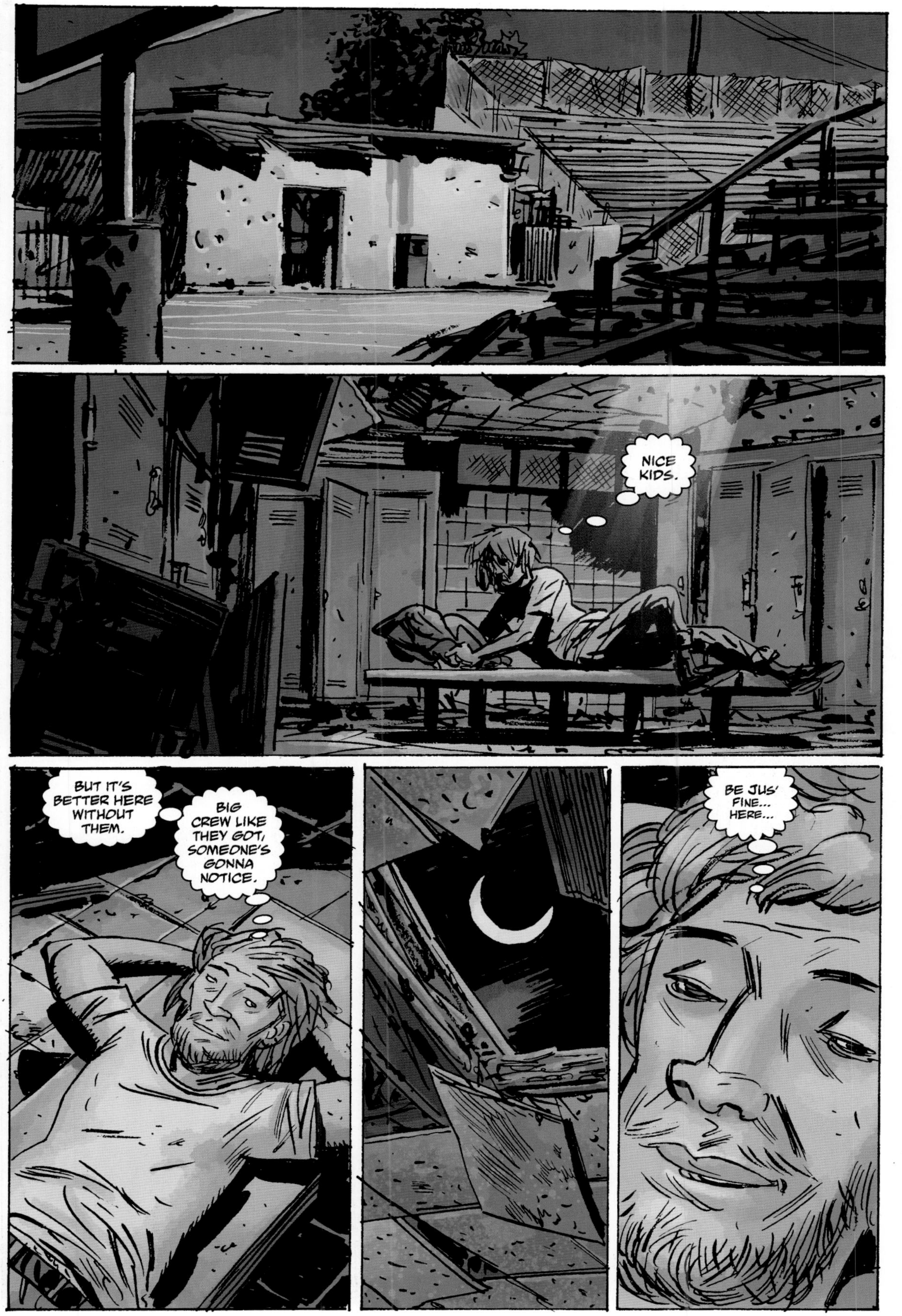
NICE KIDS.
BUT IT'S BETTER HERE WITHOUT THEM.
BIG CREW LIKE THEY GOT, SOMEONE'S GONNA NOTICE.
BE JUS' FINE... HERE...

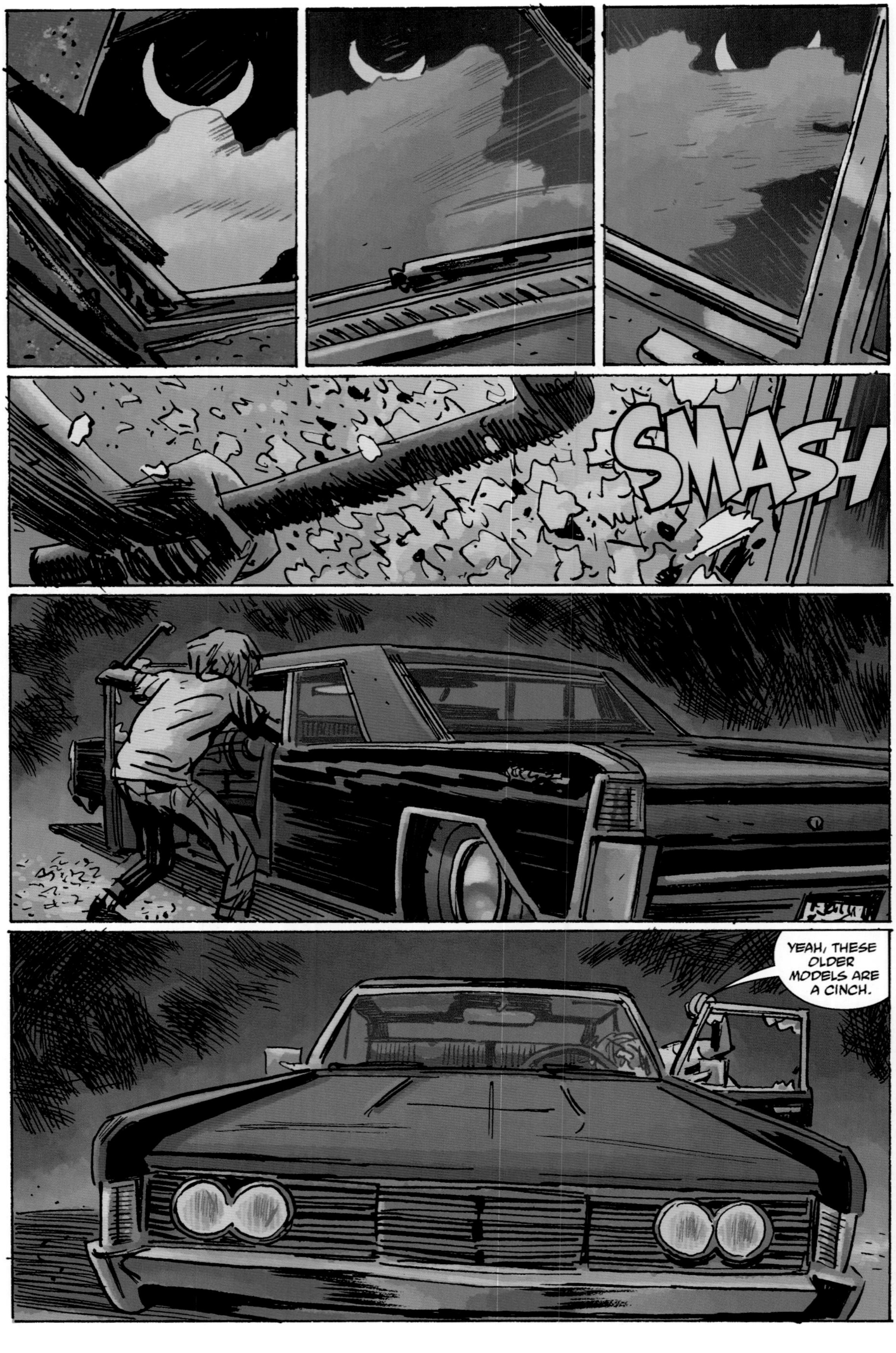
SMASH
YEAH, THESE OLDER MODELS ARE A CINCH.

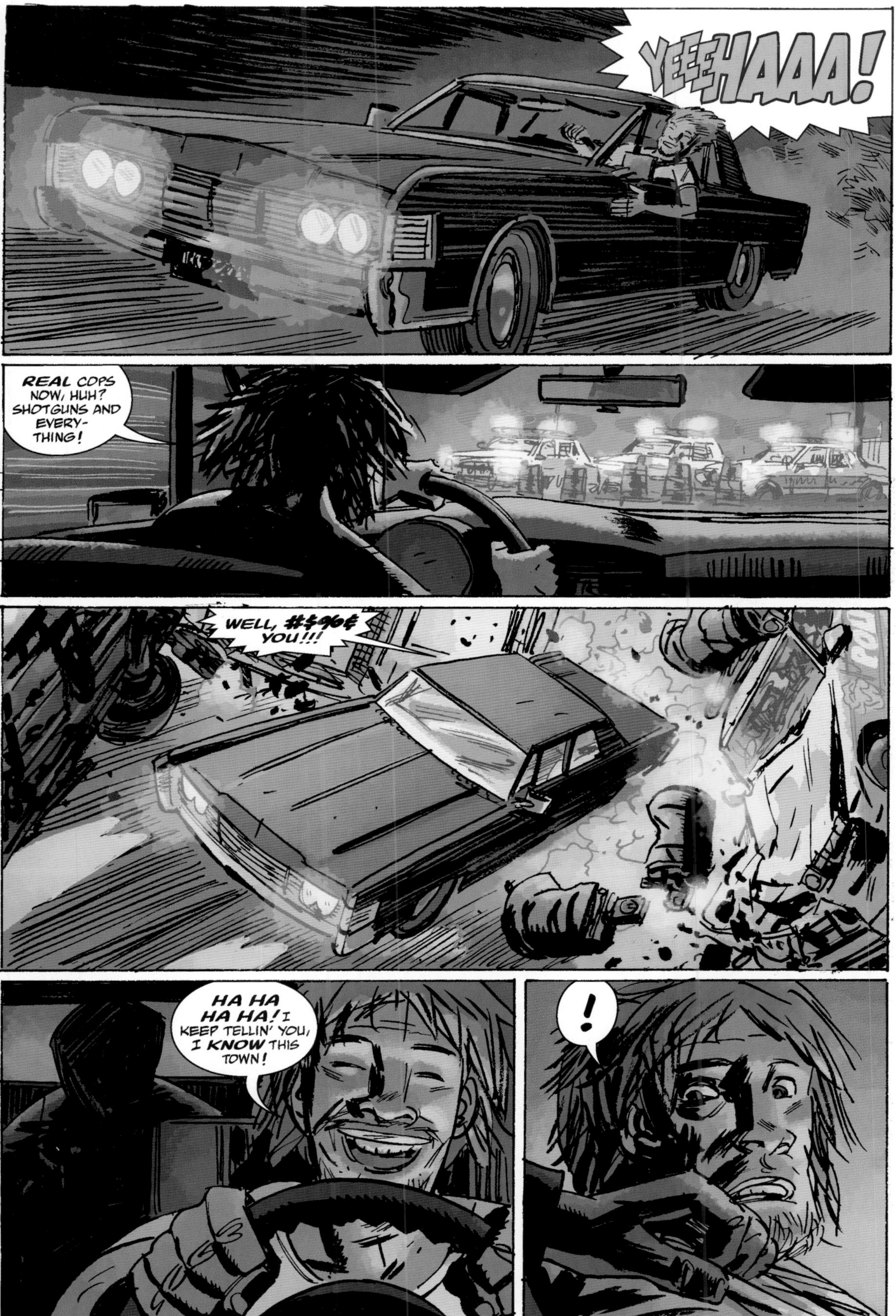
YEEEHAAA!
REAL COPS NOW, HUH? SHOTGUNS AND EVERY- THING!
WELL, #$%¢ YOU!!!
HA HA HA HA! I KEEP TELLIN' YOU, I KNOW THIS TOWN!
!

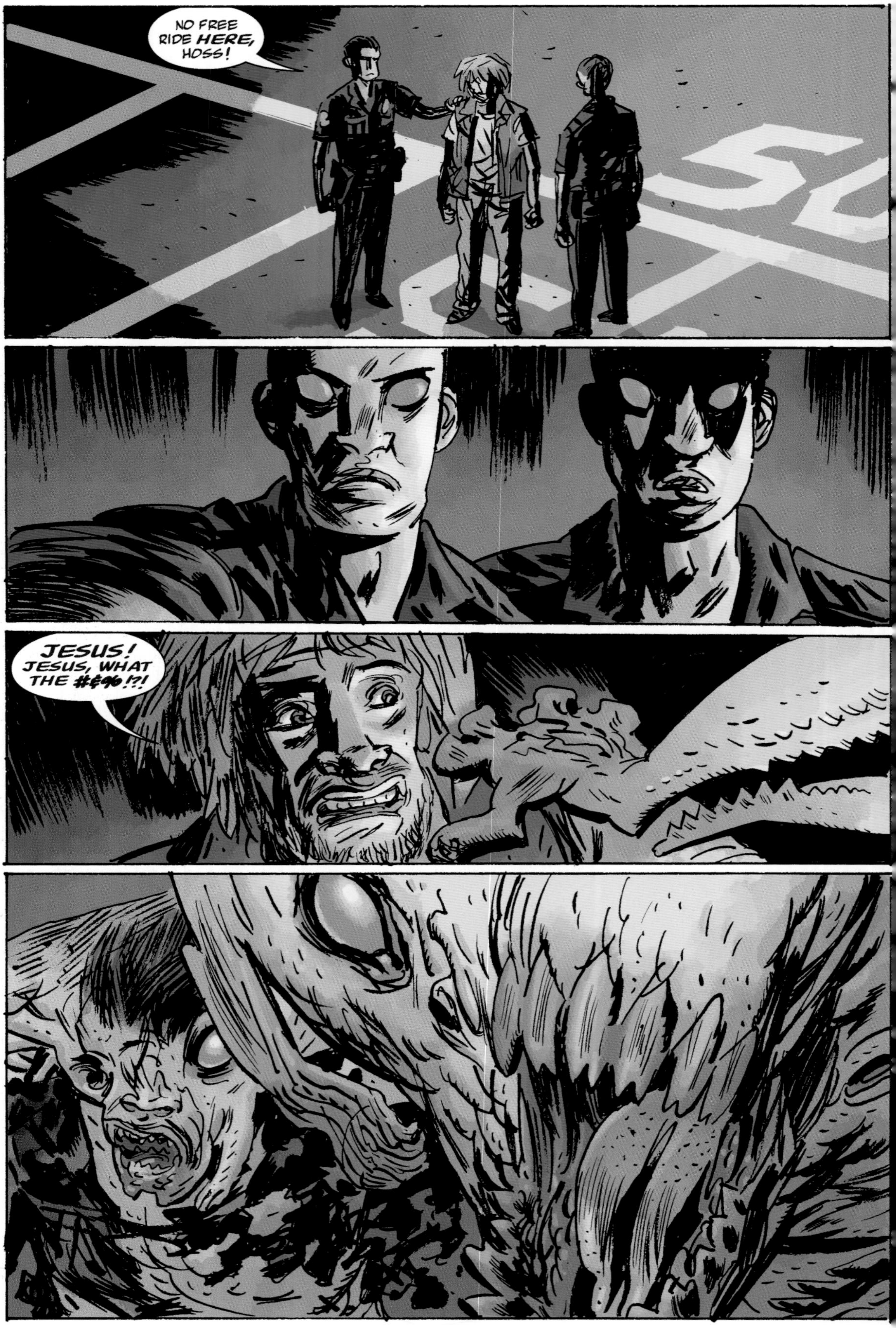
NO FREE RIDE HERE, HOSS!
JESUS! JESUS, WHAT THE #$%!?!

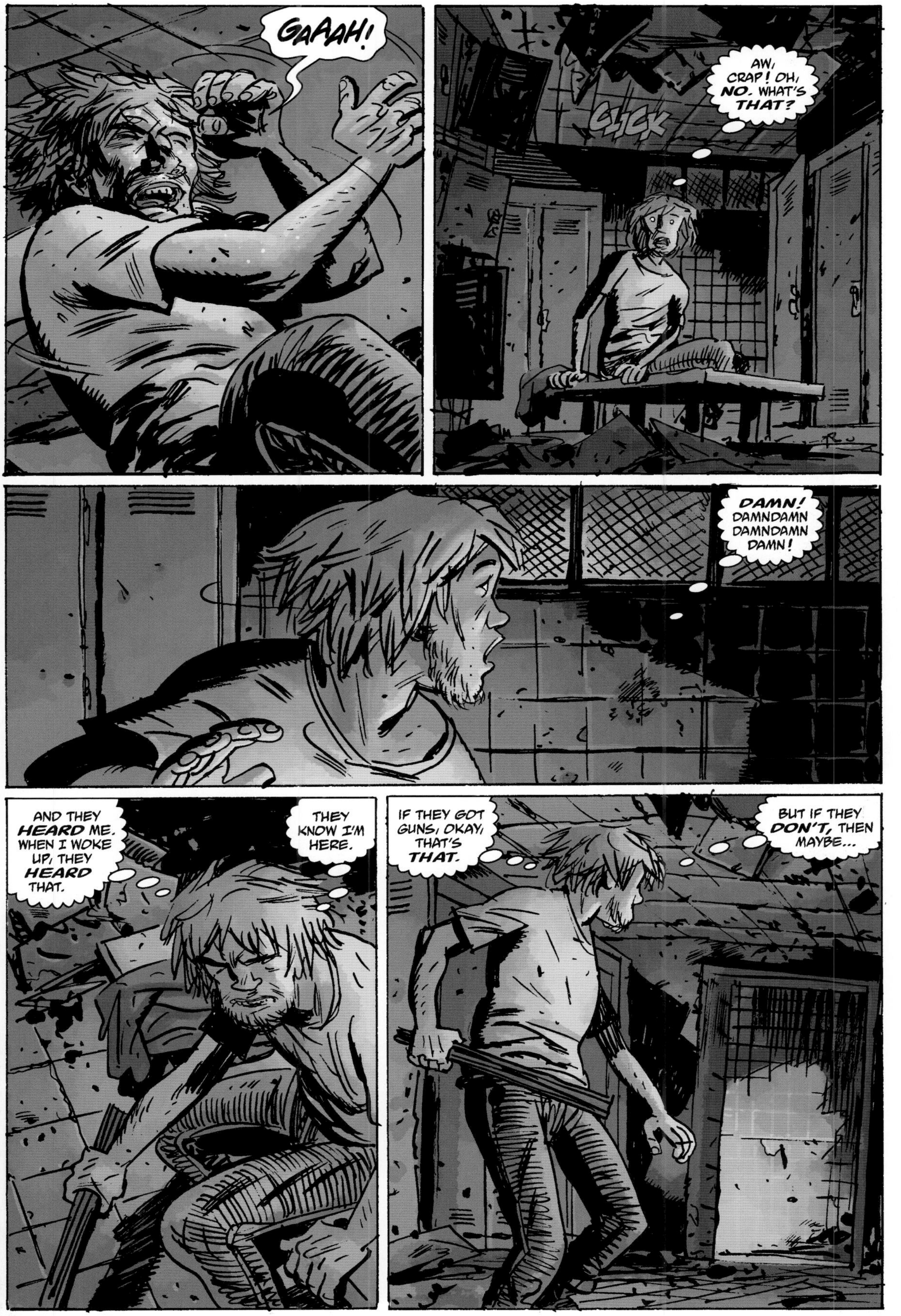
GAAAH!
AW, CRAP! OH, NO. WHAT'S THAT?
CLICK
DAMN! DAMNDAMN DAMNDAMN DAMN!
AND THEY HEARD ME. WHEN I WOKE UP, THEY HEARD THAT.
THEY KNOW I'M HERE.
IF THEY GOT GUNS, OKAY, THAT'S THAT.
BUT IF THEY DON'T, THEN MAYBE...

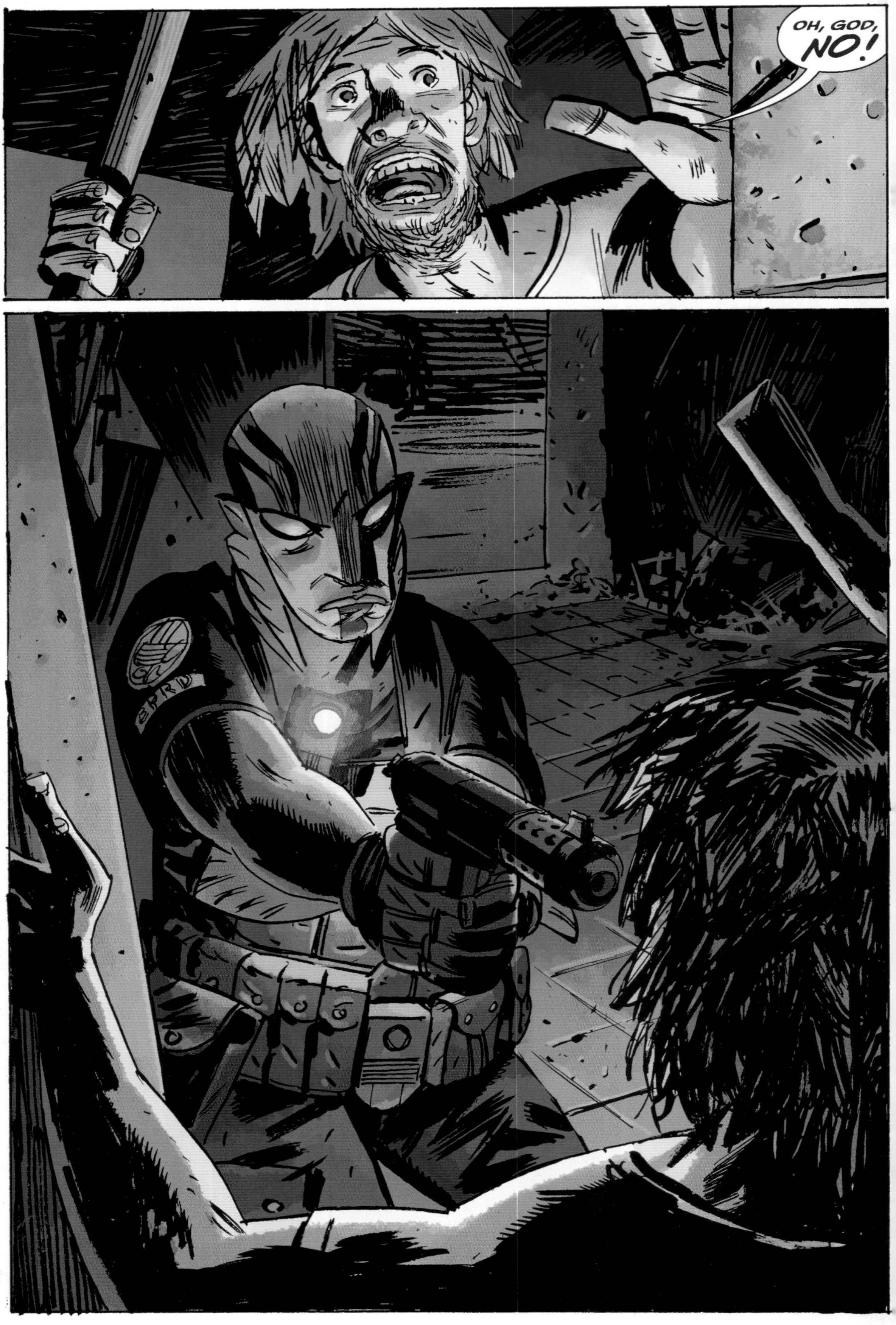
OH, GOD, NO!
BPRD

GODS CHAPTER TWO

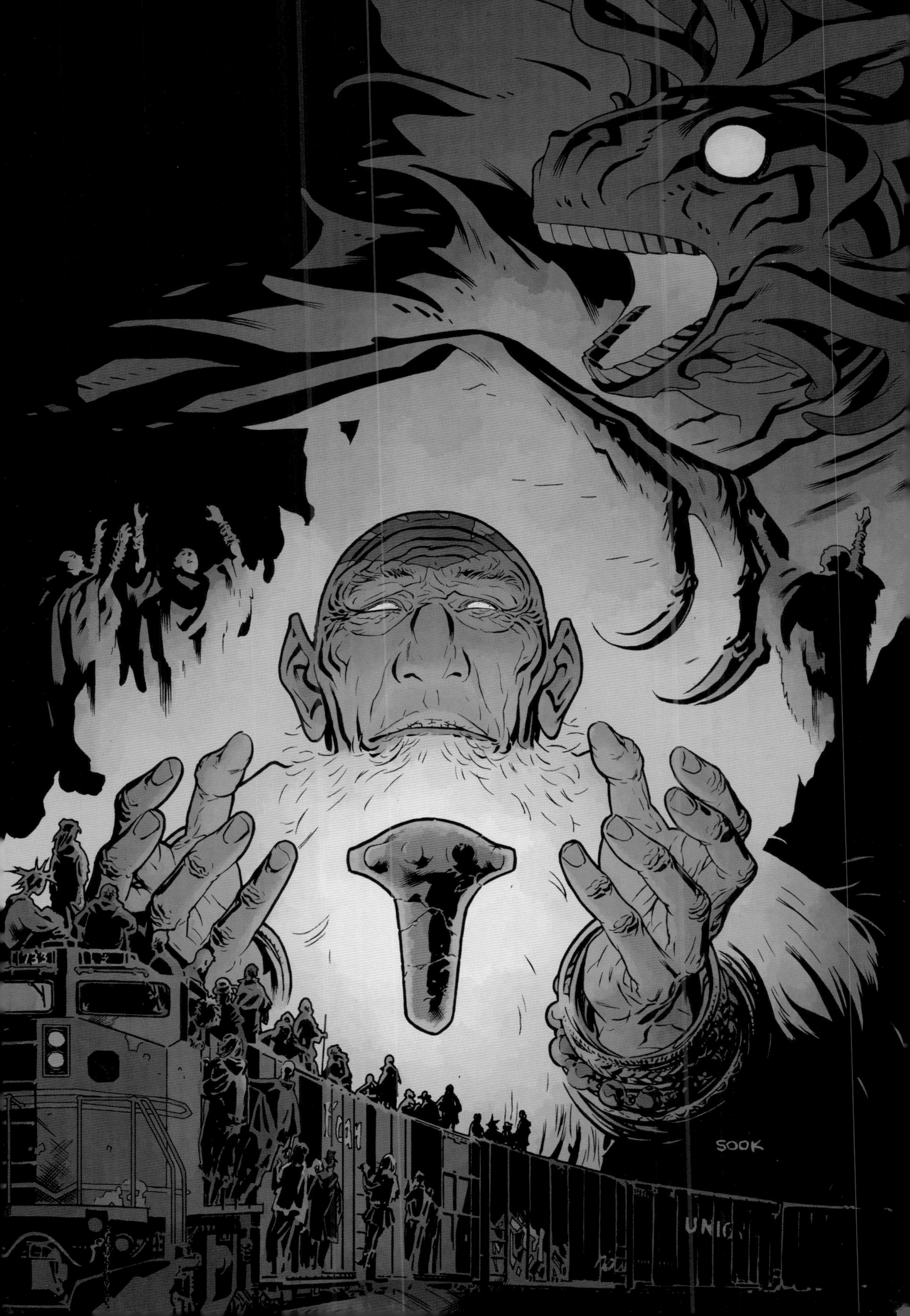
SOOK

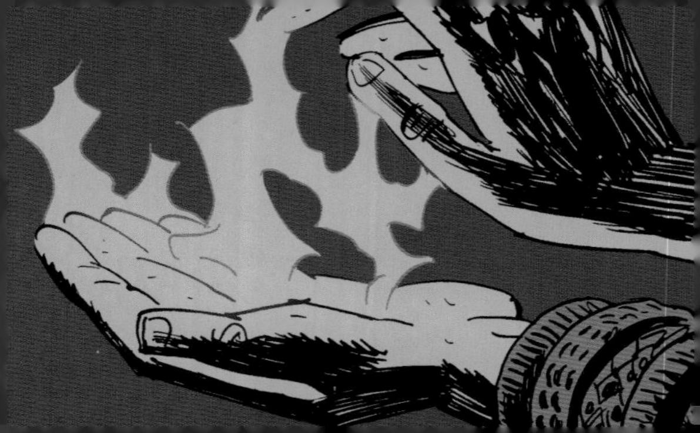

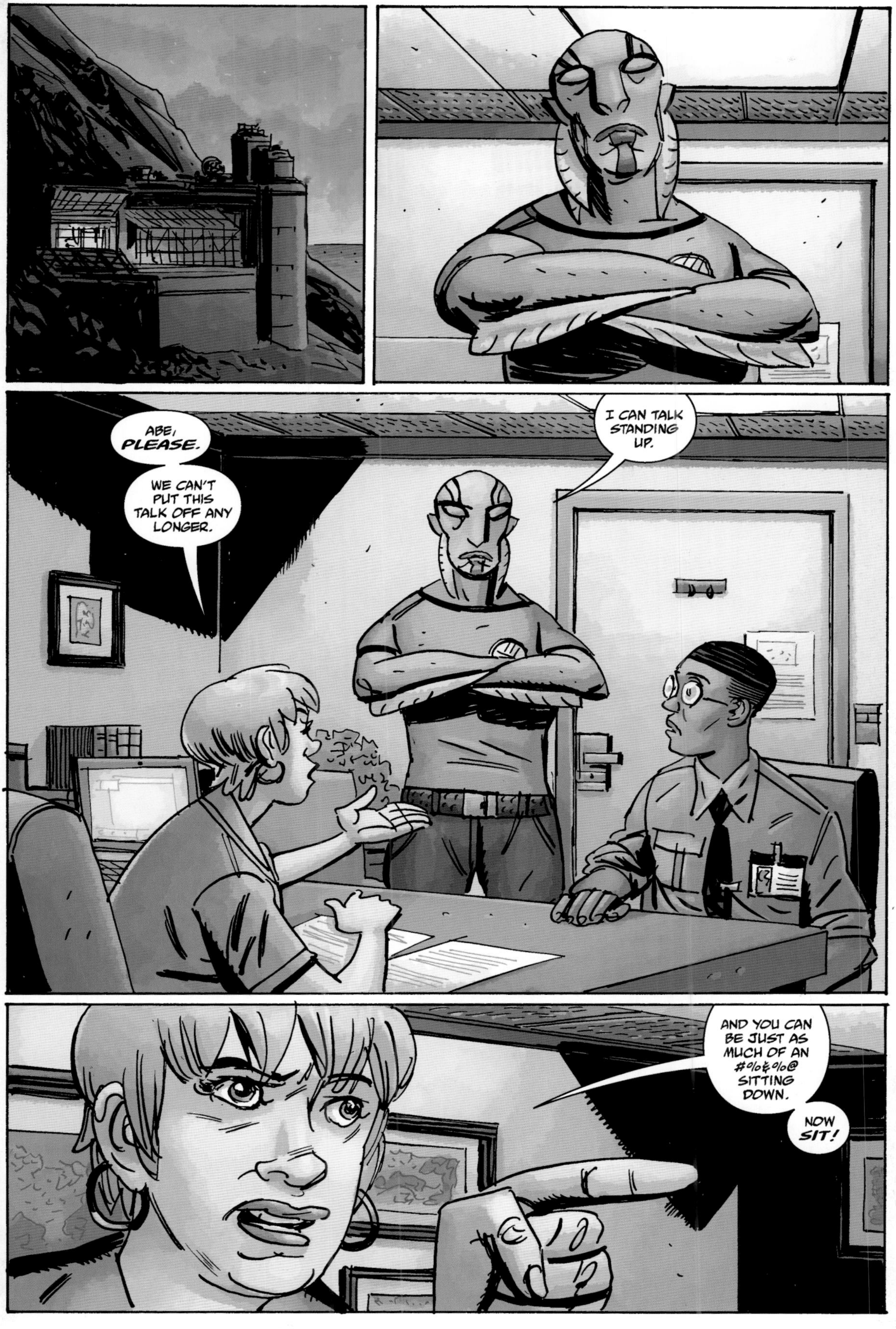

ABE, PLEASE.
WE CAN'T PUT THIS TALK OFF ANY LONGER.
I CAN TALK STANDING UP.
AND YOU CAN BE JUST AS MUCH OF AN #%&%@ SITTING DOWN.
NOW SIT!

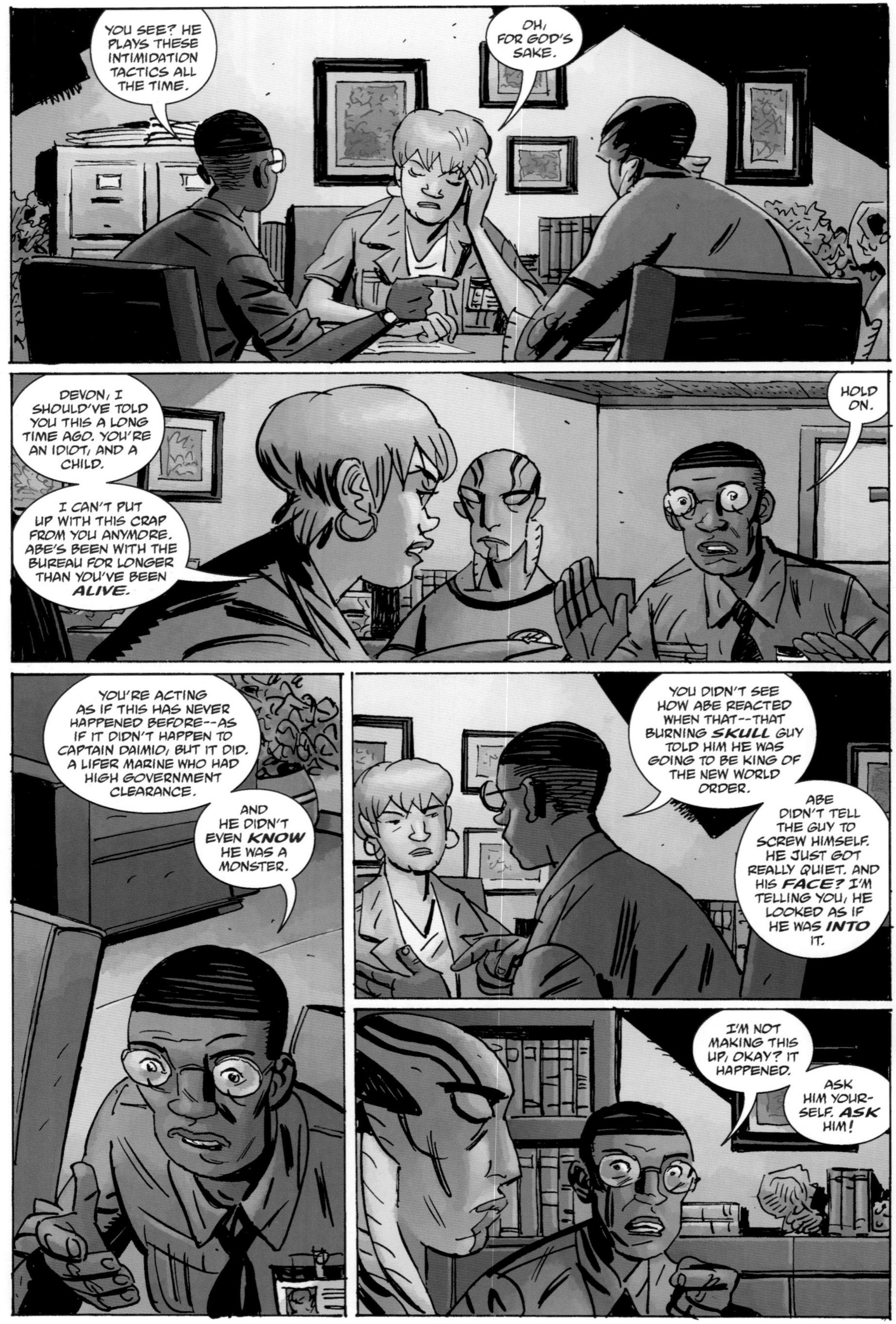
YOU SEE? HE PLAYS THESE INTIMIDATION TACTICS ALL THE TIME.
OH, FOR GOD'S SAKE.
DEVON, I SHOULD'VE TOLD YOU THIS A LONG TIME AGO. YOU'RE AN IDIOT, AND A CHILD.
I CAN'T PUT UP WITH THIS CRAP FROM YOU ANYMORE. ABE'S BEEN WITH THE BUREAU FOR LONGER THAN YOU'VE BEEN ALIVE.
HOLD ON.
YOU'RE ACTING AS IF THIS HAS NEVER HAPPENED BEFORE--AS IF IT DIDN'T HAPPEN TO CAPTAIN DAIMIO, BUT IT DID. A LIFER MARINE WHO HAD HIGH GOVERNMENT CLEARANCE.
AND HE DIDN'T EVEN KNOW HE WAS A MONSTER.
YOU DIDN'T SEE HOW ABE REACTED WHEN THAT--THAT BURNING SKULL GUY TOLD HIM HE WAS GOING TO BE KING OF THE NEW WORLD ORDER.
ABE DIDN'T TELL THE GUY TO SCREW HIMSELF. HE JUST GOT REALLY QUIET. AND HIS FACE? I'M TELLING YOU, HE LOOKED AS IF HE WAS INTO IT.
I'M NOT MAKING THIS UP, OKAY? IT HAPPENED.
ASK HIM YOURSELF. ASK HIM!

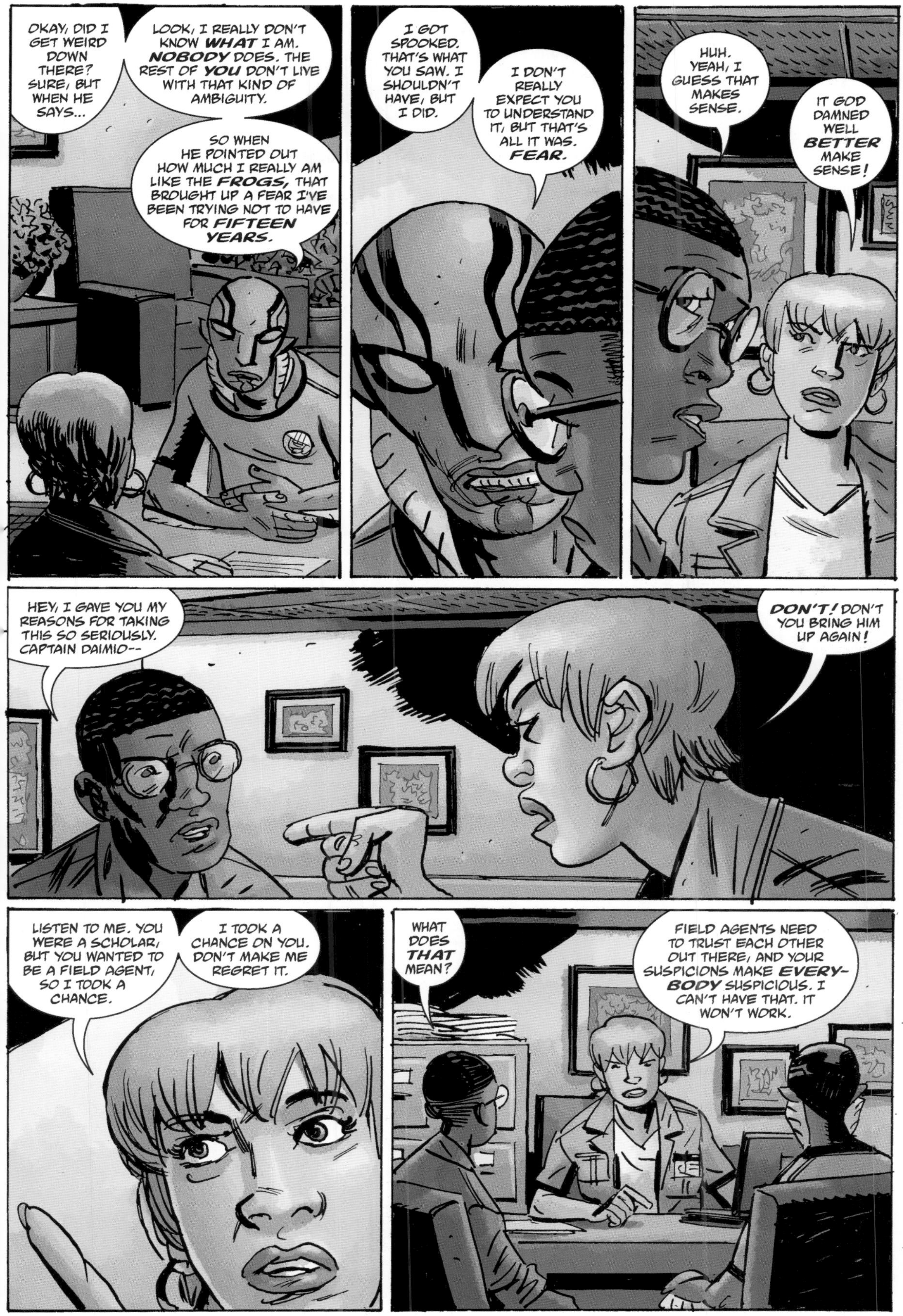
OKAY, DID I GET WEIRD DOWN THERE? SURE, BUT WHEN HE SAYS...
LOOK, I REALLY DON'T KNOW WHAT I AM. NOBODY DOES. THE REST OF YOU DON'T LIVE WITH THAT KIND OF AMBIGUITY.
SO WHEN HE POINTED OUT HOW MUCH I REALLY AM LIKE THE FROGS, THAT BROUGHT UP A FEAR I'VE BEEN TRYING NOT TO HAVE FOR FIFTEEN YEARS.
I GOT SPOOKED. THAT'S WHAT YOU SAW. I SHOULDN'T HAVE, BUT I DID.
I DON'T REALLY EXPECT YOU TO UNDERSTAND IT, BUT THAT'S ALL IT WAS. FEAR.
HUH. YEAH, I GUESS THAT MAKES SENSE.
IT GOD DAMNED WELL BETTER MAKE SENSE!
HEY, I GAVE YOU MY REASONS FOR TAKING THIS SO SERIOUSLY. CAPTAIN DAIMIO--
DON'T! DON'T YOU BRING HIM UP AGAIN!
LISTEN TO ME. YOU WERE A SCHOLAR, BUT YOU WANTED TO BE A FIELD AGENT, SO I TOOK A CHANCE.
I TOOK A CHANCE ON YOU. DON'T MAKE ME REGRET IT.
WHAT DOES THAT MEAN?
FIELD AGENTS NEED TO TRUST EACH OTHER OUT THERE, AND YOUR SUSPICIONS MAKE EVERYBODY SUSPICIOUS. I CAN'T HAVE THAT. IT WON'T WORK.

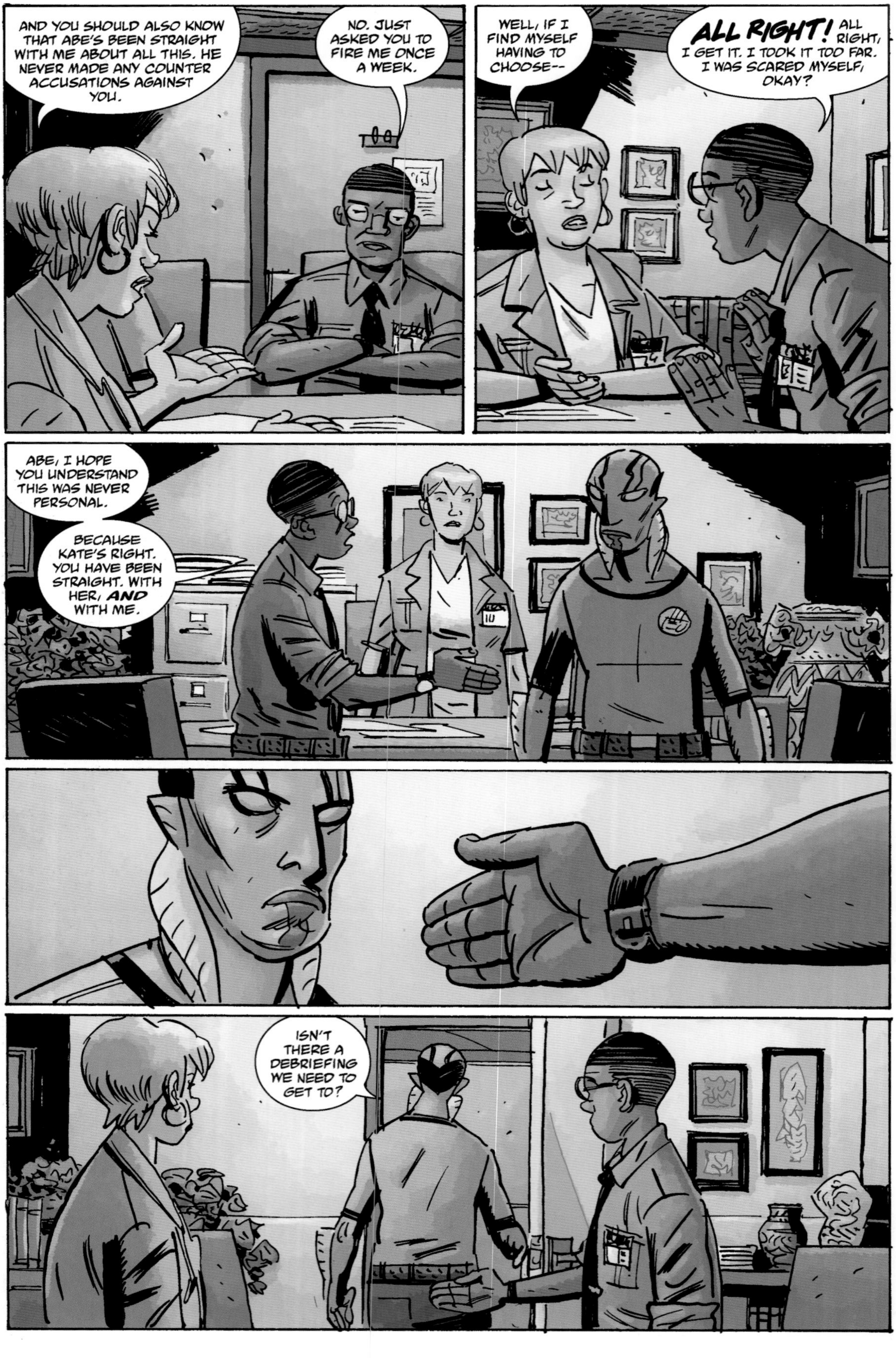
AND YOU SHOULD ALSO KNOW THAT ABE'S BEEN STRAIGHT WITH ME ABOUT ALL THIS. HE NEVER MADE ANY COUNTER ACCUSATIONS AGAINST YOU.
NO. JUST ASKED YOU TO FIRE ME ONCE A WEEK.
WELL, IF I FIND MYSELF HAVING TO CHOOSE--
ALL RIGHT! ALL RIGHT, I GET IT. I TOOK IT TOO FAR. I WAS SCARED MYSELF, OKAY?
ABE, I HOPE YOU UNDERSTAND THIS WAS NEVER PERSONAL.
BECAUSE KATE'S RIGHT. YOU HAVE BEEN STRAIGHT. WITH HER, AND WITH ME.
ISN'T THERE A DEBRIEFING WE NEED TO GET TO?

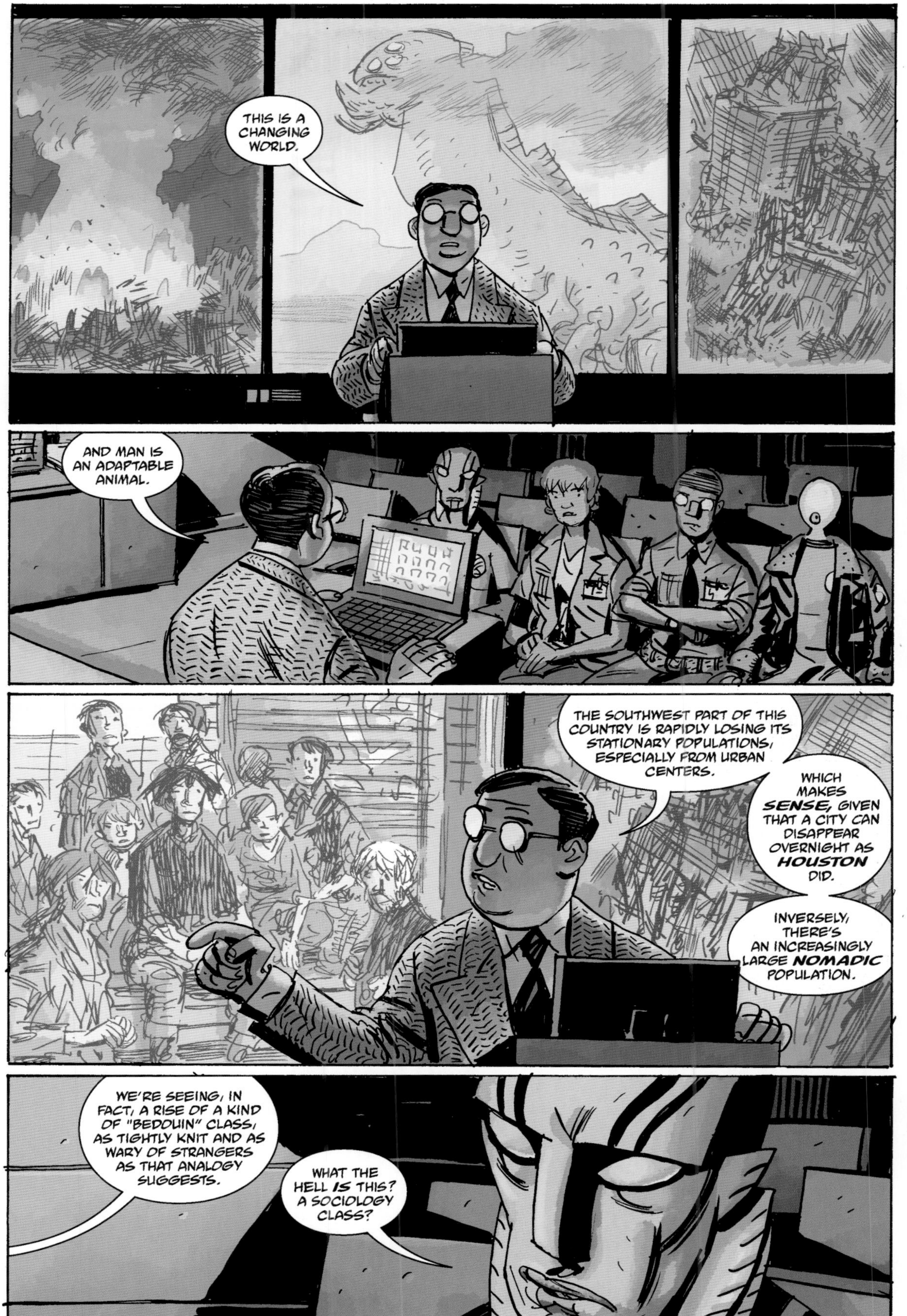
THIS IS A CHANGING WORLD.
AND MAN IS AN ADAPTABLE ANIMAL.
THE SOUTHWEST PART OF THIS COUNTRY IS RAPIDLY LOSING ITS STATIONARY POPULATIONS, ESPECIALLY FROM URBAN CENTERS.
WHICH MAKES SENSE, GIVEN THAT A CITY CAN DISAPPEAR OVERNIGHT AS HOUSTON DID.
INVERSELY, THERE'S AN INCREASINGLY LARGE NOMADIC POPULATION.
WE'RE SEEING, IN FACT, A RISE OF A KIND OF "BEDOUIN" CLASS, AS TIGHTLY KNIT AND AS WARY OF STRANGERS AS THAT ANALOGY SUGGESTS.
WHAT THE HELL IS THIS? A SOCIOLOGY CLASS?

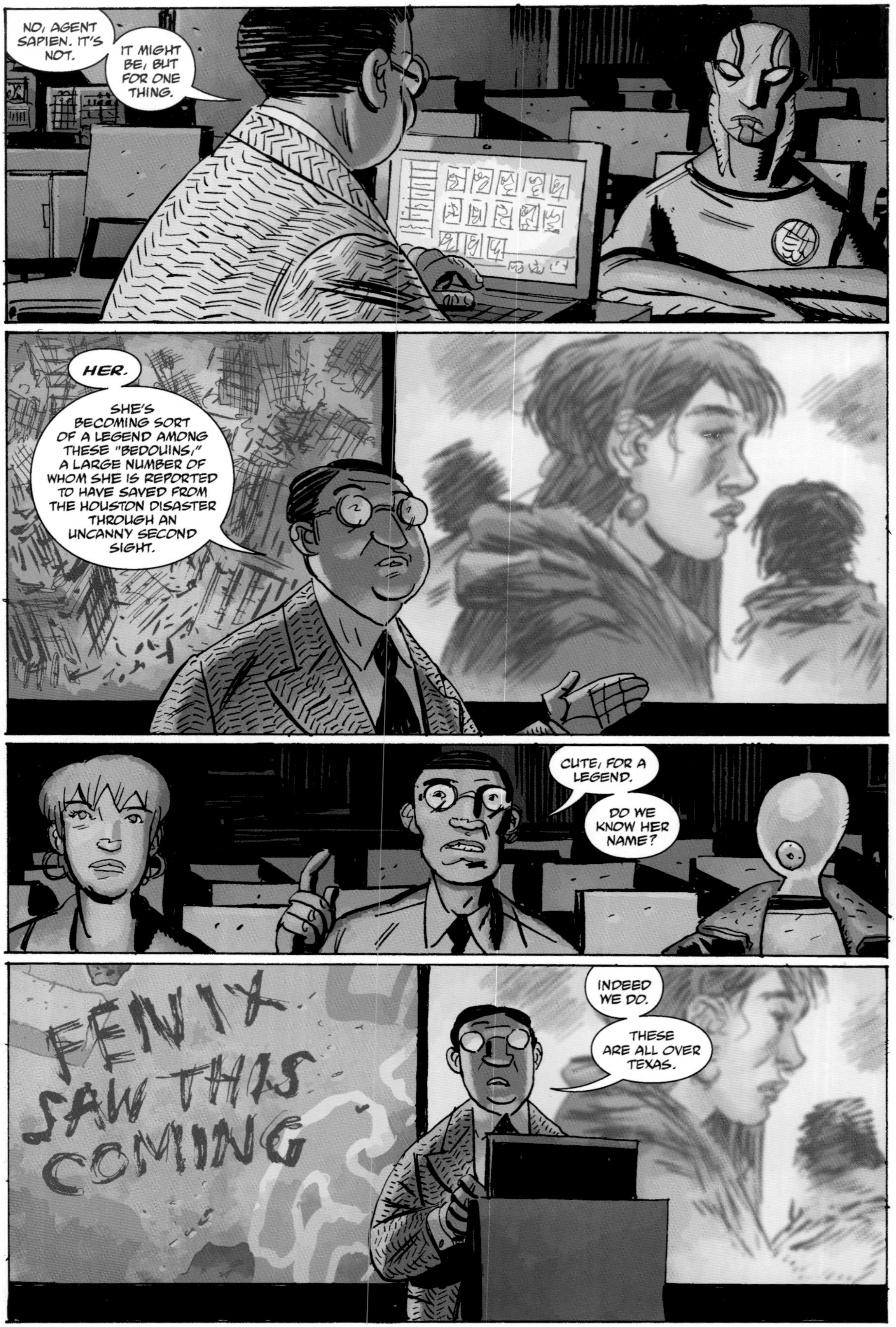
NO, AGENT SAPIEN. IT'S NOT.
IT MIGHT BE, BUT FOR ONE THING.
HER.
SHE'S BECOMING SORT OF A LEGEND AMONG THESE "BEDOUINS," A LARGE NUMBER OF WHOM SHE IS REPORTED TO HAVE SAVED FROM THE HOUSTON DISASTER THROUGH AN UNCANNY SECOND SIGHT.
CUTE, FOR A LEGEND.
DO WE KNOW HER NAME?
INDEED WE DO.
THESE ARE ALL OVER TEXAS.
FENIX SAW THIS COMING

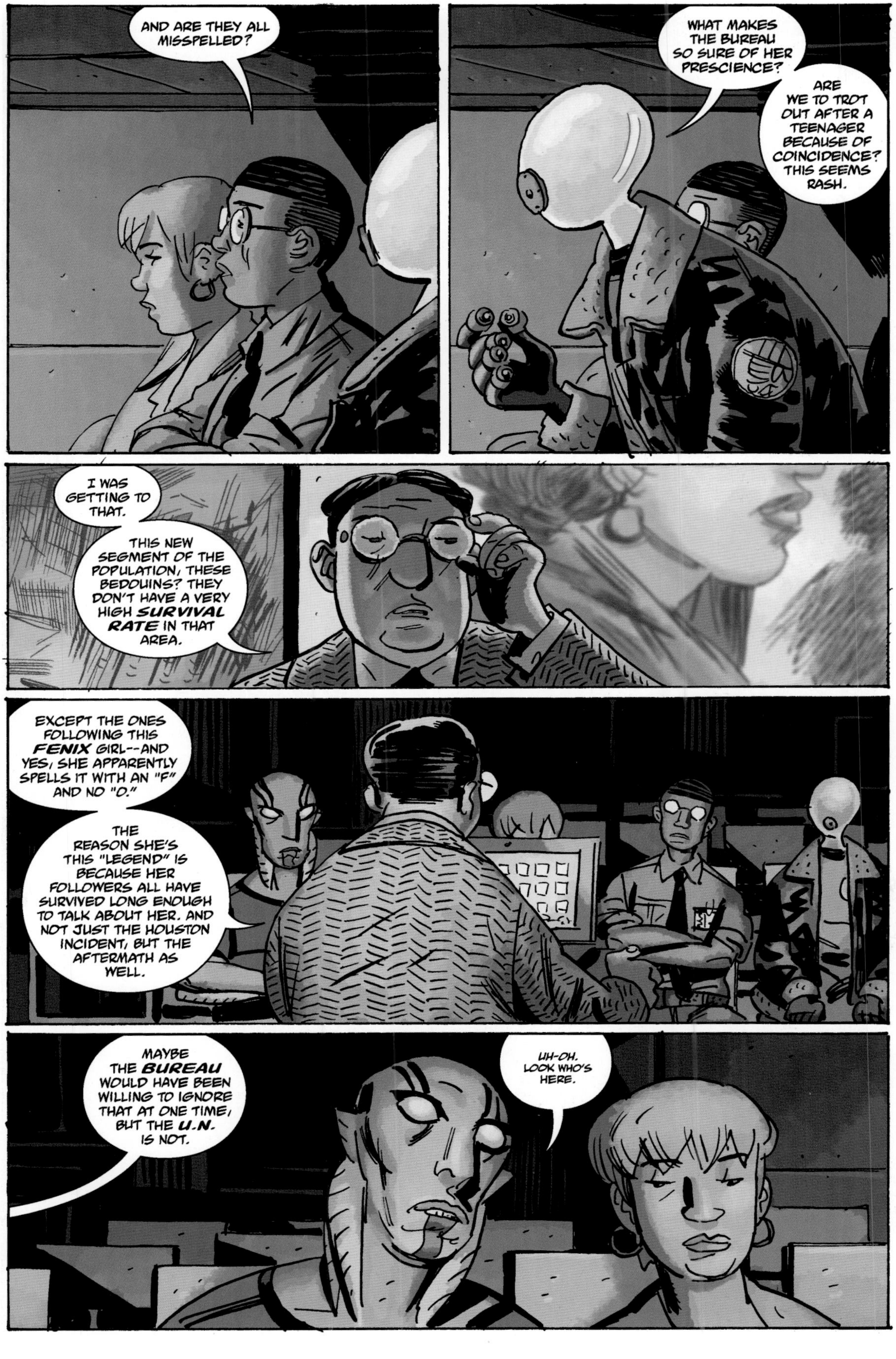
AND ARE THEY ALL MISSPELLED?
WHAT MAKES THE BUREAU SO SURE OF HER PRESCIENCE?
ARE WE TO TROT OUT AFTER A TEENAGER BECAUSE OF COINCIDENCE? THIS SEEMS RASH.
I WAS GETTING TO THAT.
THIS NEW SEGMENT OF THE POPULATION, THESE BEDOUINS? THEY DON'T HAVE A VERY HIGH SURVIVAL RATE IN THAT AREA.
EXCEPT THE ONES FOLLOWING THIS FENIX GIRL--AND YES, SHE APPARENTLY SPELLS IT WITH AN "F" AND NO "O."
THE REASON SHE'S THIS "LEGEND" IS BECAUSE HER FOLLOWERS ALL HAVE SURVIVED LONG ENOUGH TO TALK ABOUT HER. AND NOT JUST THE HOUSTON INCIDENT, BUT THE AFTERMATH AS WELL.
MAYBE THE BUREAU WOULD HAVE BEEN WILLING TO IGNORE THAT AT ONE TIME, BUT THE U.N. IS NOT.
UH-OH. LOOK WHO'S HERE.

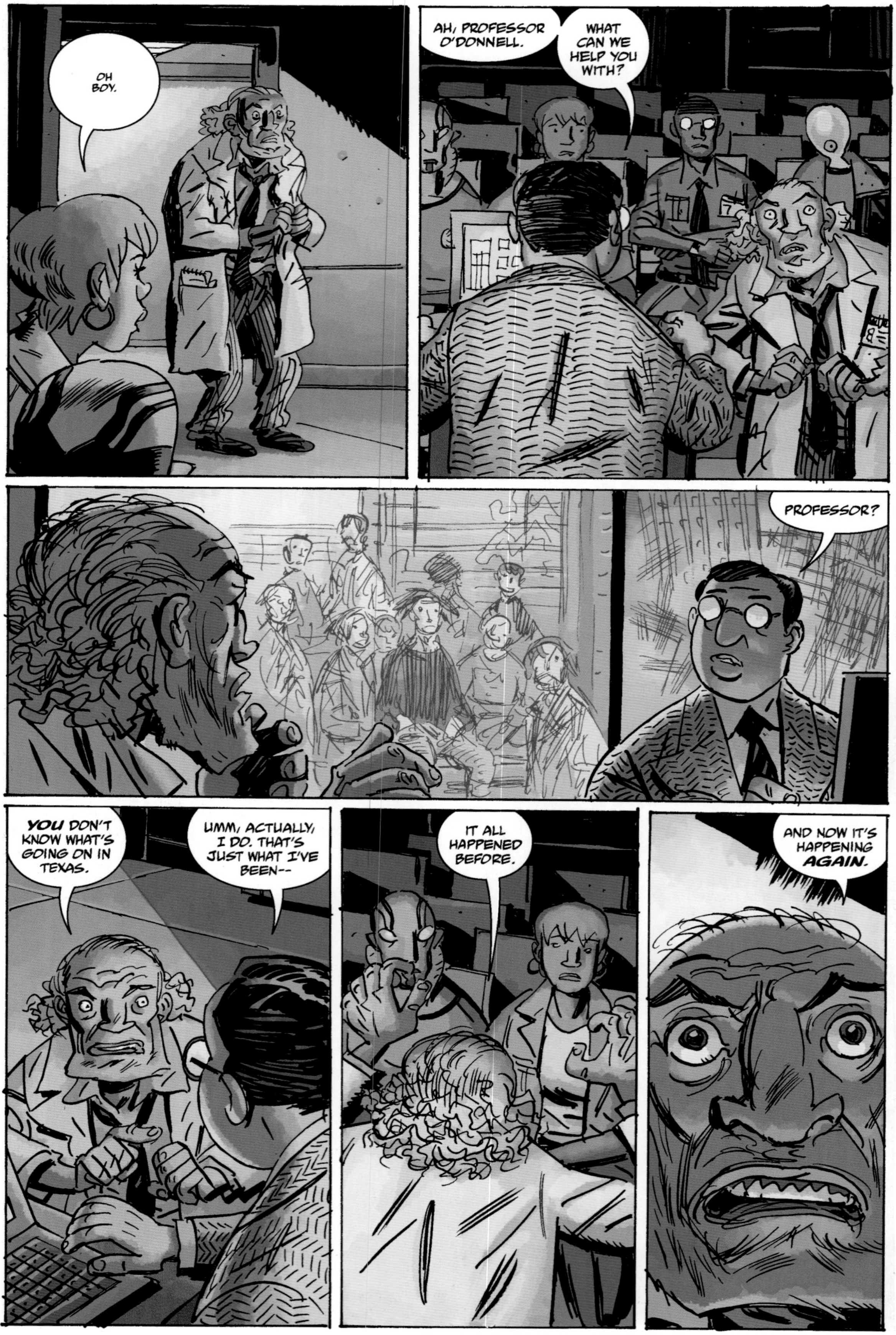
OH BOY.
AH, PROFESSOR O'DONNELL.
WHAT CAN WE HELP YOU WITH?
PROFESSOR?
YOU DON'T KNOW WHAT'S GOING ON IN TEXAS.
UMM, ACTUALLY, I DO. THAT'S JUST WHAT I'VE BEEN--
IT ALL HAPPENED BEFORE.
AND NOW IT'S HAPPENING AGAIN.

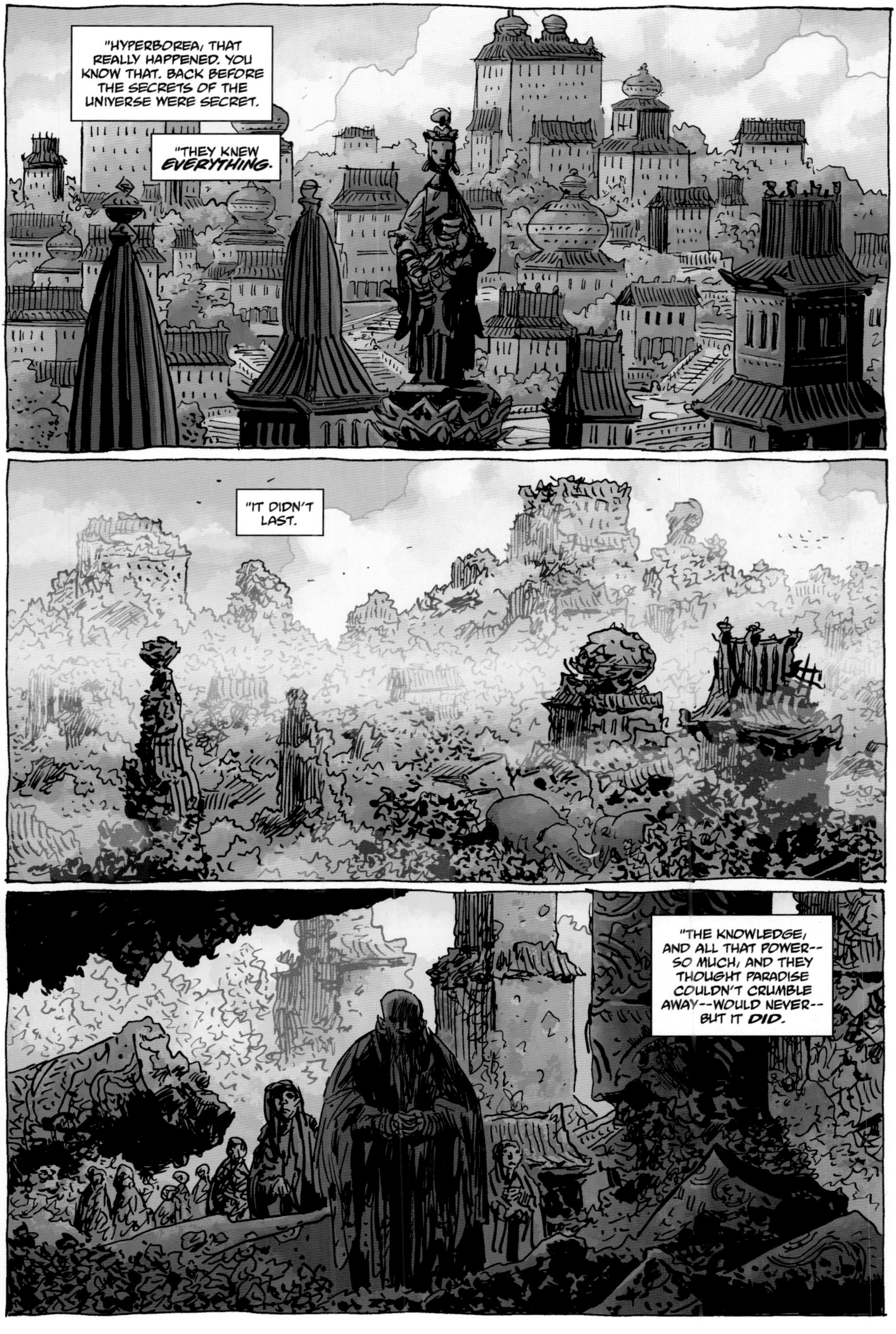
"HYPERBOREA, THAT REALLY HAPPENED. YOU KNOW THAT. BACK BEFORE THE SECRETS OF THE UNIVERSE WERE SECRET.
"THEY KNEW *EVERYTHING*.
"IT DIDN'T LAST.
"THE KNOWLEDGE, AND ALL THAT POWER-- SO MUCH, AND THEY THOUGHT PARADISE COULDN'T CRUMBLE AWAY--WOULD NEVER-- BUT IT *DID*.

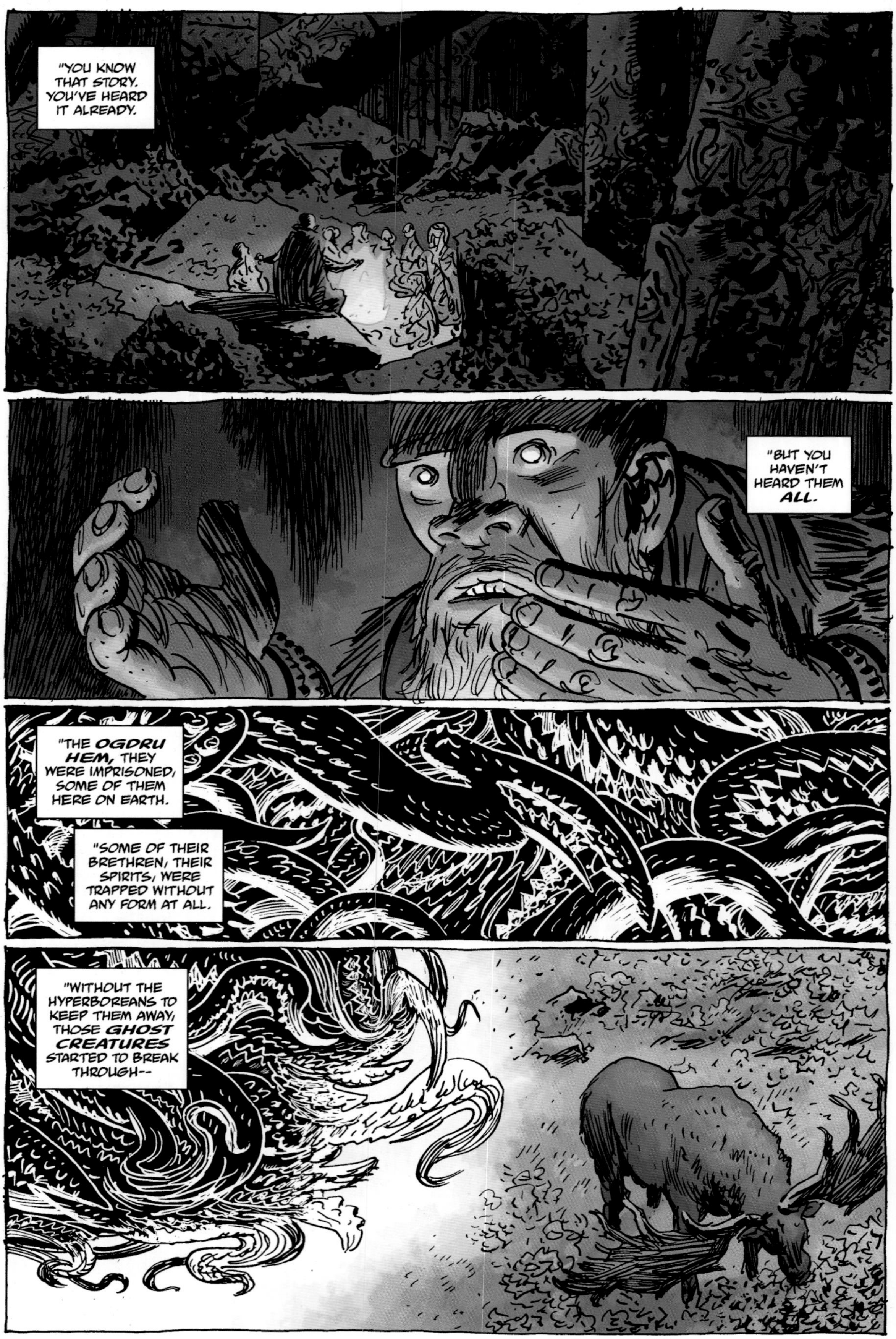
"YOU KNOW THAT STORY. YOU'VE HEARD IT ALREADY.
"BUT YOU HAVEN'T HEARD THEM ALL.
"THE OGDRU HEM, THEY WERE IMPRISONED, SOME OF THEM HERE ON EARTH.
"SOME OF THEIR BRETHREN, THEIR SPIRITS, WERE TRAPPED WITHOUT ANY FORM AT ALL.
"WITHOUT THE HYPERBOREANS TO KEEP THEM AWAY, THOSE GHOST CREATURES STARTED TO BREAK THROUGH--

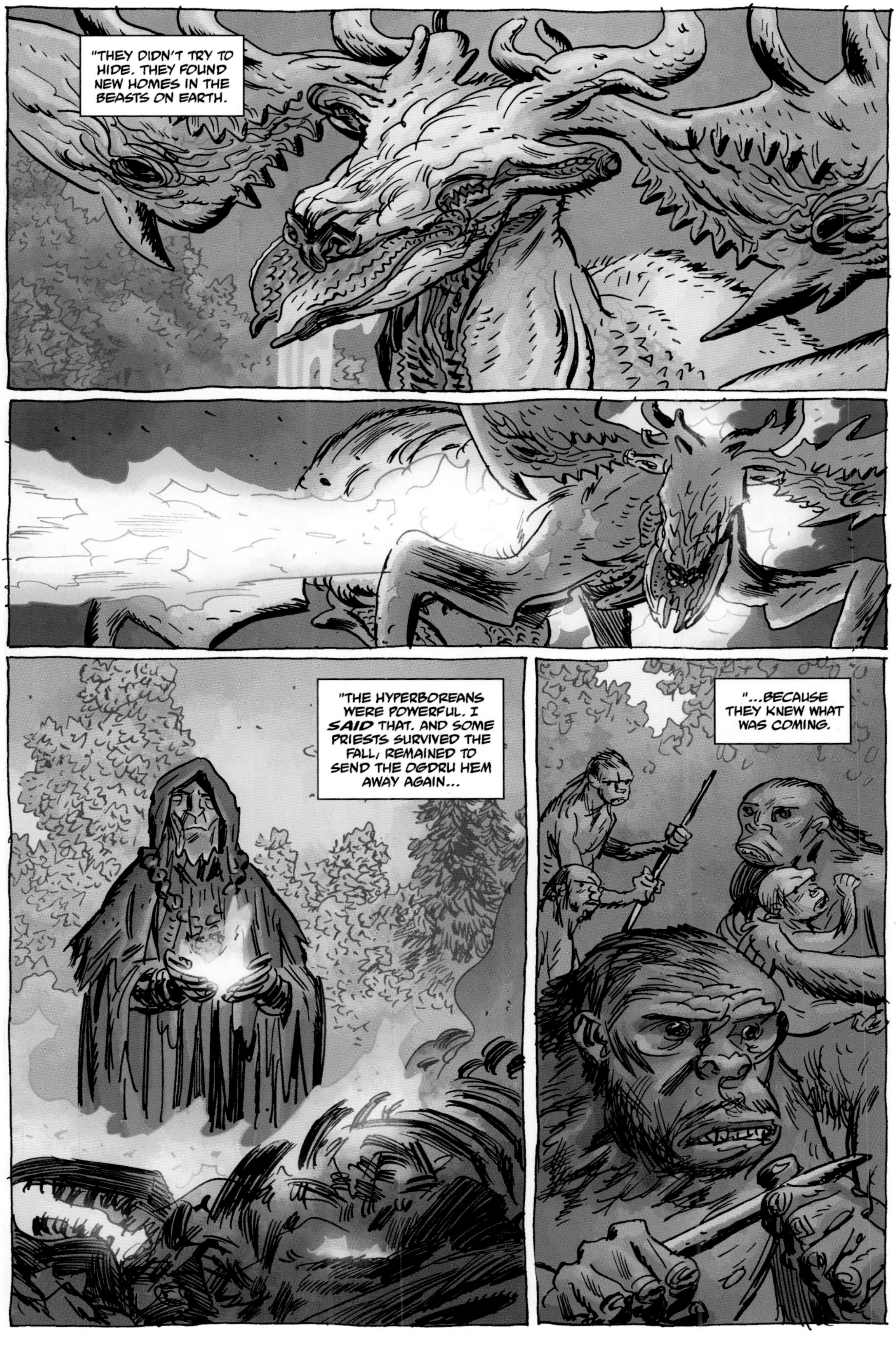
"THEY DIDN'T TRY TO HIDE. THEY FOUND NEW HOMES IN THE BEASTS ON EARTH.
"THE HYPERBOREANS WERE POWERFUL. I SAID THAT. AND SOME PRIESTS SURVIVED THE FALL, REMAINED TO SEND THE OGDRU HEM AWAY AGAIN...
"...BECAUSE THEY KNEW WHAT WAS COMING.

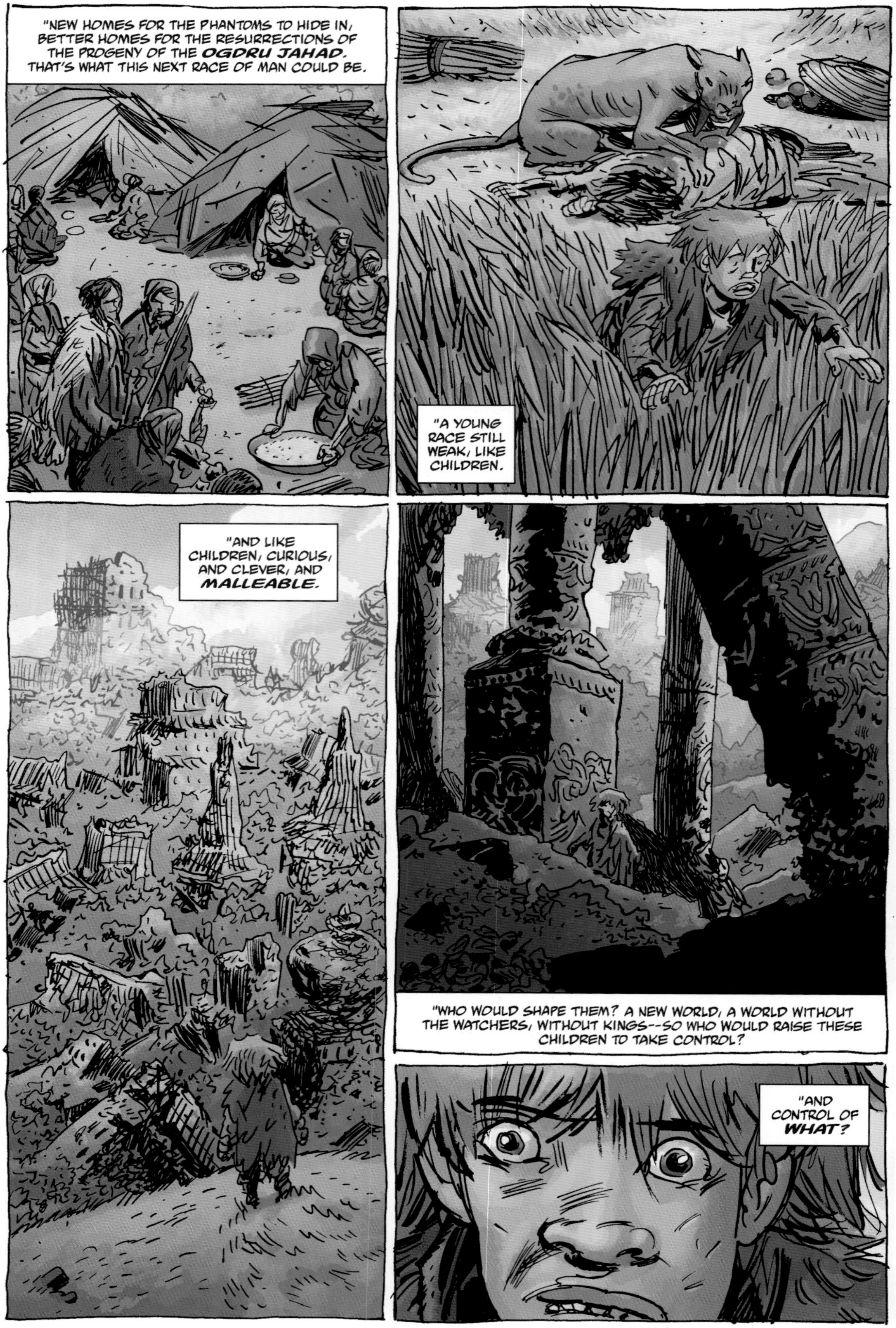
"NEW HOMES FOR THE PHANTOMS TO HIDE IN, BETTER HOMES FOR THE RESURRECTIONS OF THE PROGENY OF THE OGDRU JAHAD. THAT'S WHAT THIS NEXT RACE OF MAN COULD BE.
"A YOUNG RACE STILL WEAK, LIKE CHILDREN.
"AND LIKE CHILDREN, CURIOUS, AND CLEVER, AND MALLEABLE.
"WHO WOULD SHAPE THEM? A NEW WORLD, A WORLD WITHOUT THE WATCHERS, WITHOUT KINGS--SO WHO WOULD RAISE THESE CHILDREN TO TAKE CONTROL?
"AND CONTROL OF WHAT?

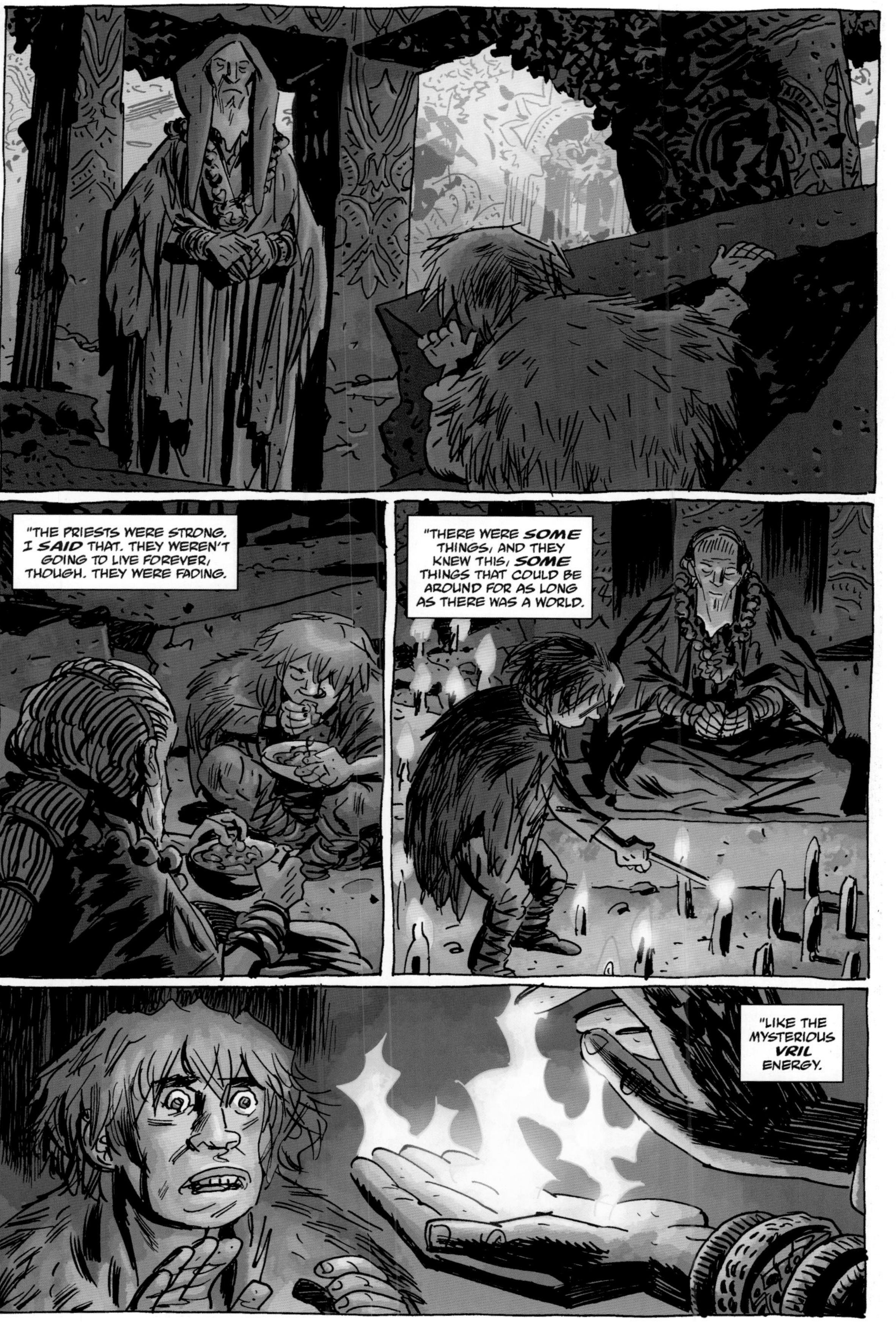
"THE PRIESTS WERE STRONG. I SAID THAT. THEY WEREN'T GOING TO LIVE FOREVER, THOUGH. THEY WERE FADING.
"THERE WERE SOME THINGS, AND THEY KNEW THIS, SOME THINGS THAT COULD BE AROUND FOR AS LONG AS THERE WAS A WORLD.
"LIKE THE MYSTERIOUS VRIL ENERGY.

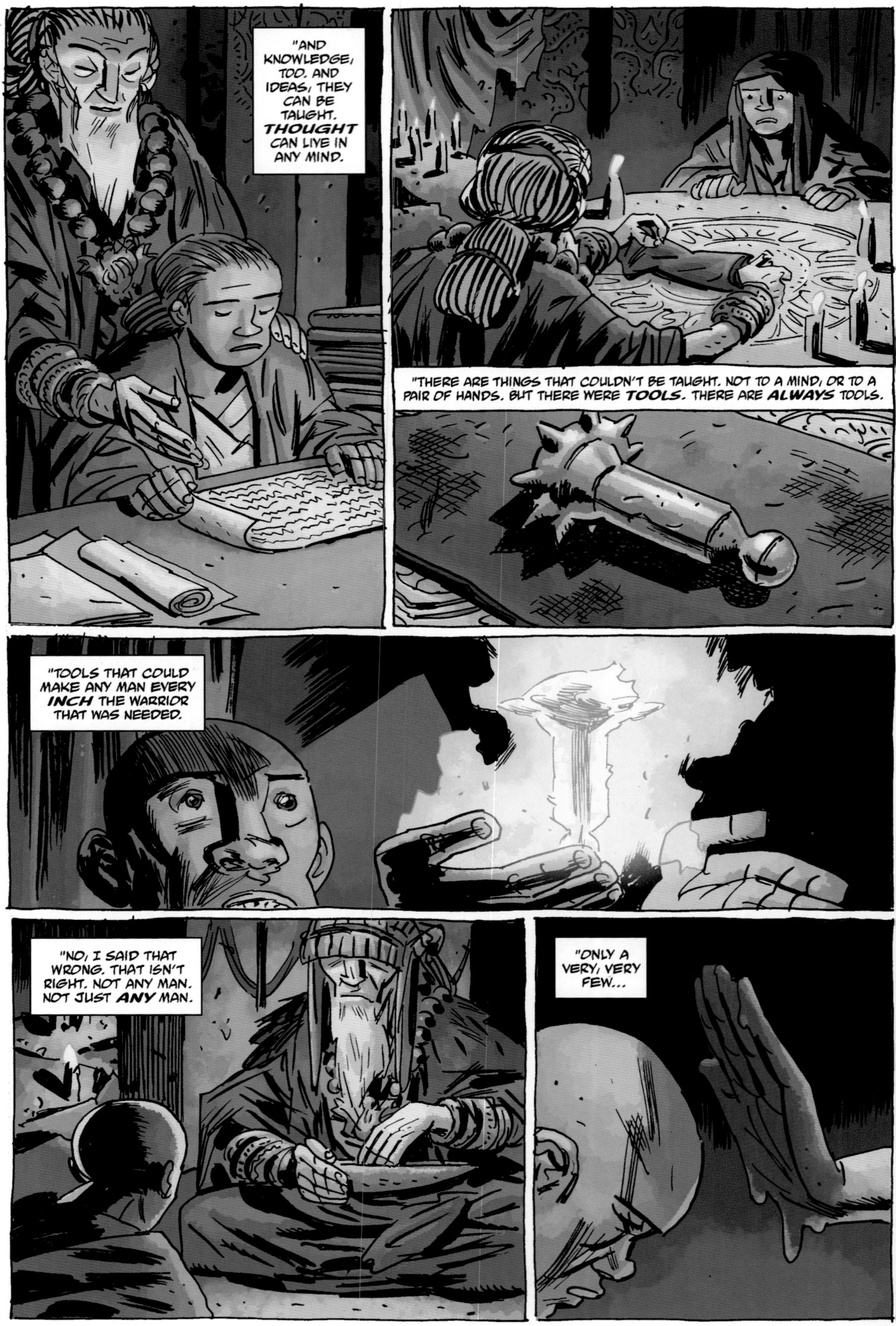
"AND KNOWLEDGE, TOO. AND IDEAS, THEY CAN BE TAUGHT. THOUGHT CAN LIVE IN ANY MIND.
"THERE ARE THINGS THAT COULDN'T BE TAUGHT. NOT TO A MIND, OR TO A PAIR OF HANDS. BUT THERE WERE TOOLS. THERE ARE ALWAYS TOOLS.
"TOOLS THAT COULD MAKE ANY MAN EVERY INCH THE WARRIOR THAT WAS NEEDED.
"NO, I SAID THAT WRONG. THAT ISN'T RIGHT. NOT ANY MAN. NOT JUST ANY MAN.
"ONLY A VERY, VERY FEW...

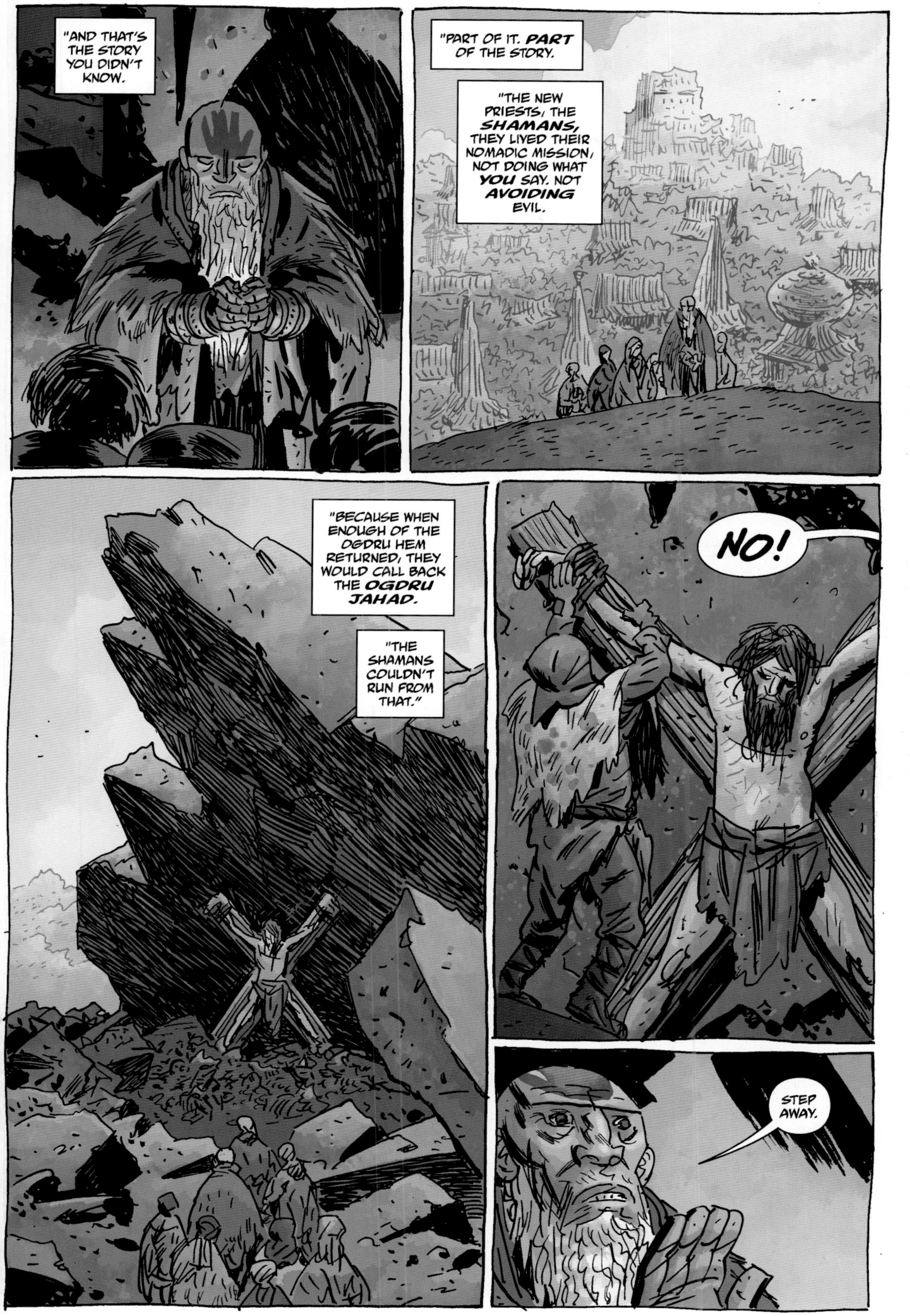
"AND THAT'S THE STORY YOU DIDN'T KNOW.
"PART OF IT. PART OF THE STORY.
"THE NEW PRIESTS, THE SHAMANS, THEY LIVED THEIR NOMADIC MISSION, NOT DOING WHAT YOU SAY. NOT AVOIDING EVIL.
"BECAUSE WHEN ENOUGH OF THE OGDRU HEM RETURNED, THEY WOULD CALL BACK THE OGDRU JAHAD.
"THE SHAMANS COULDN'T RUN FROM THAT."
NO!
STEP AWAY.

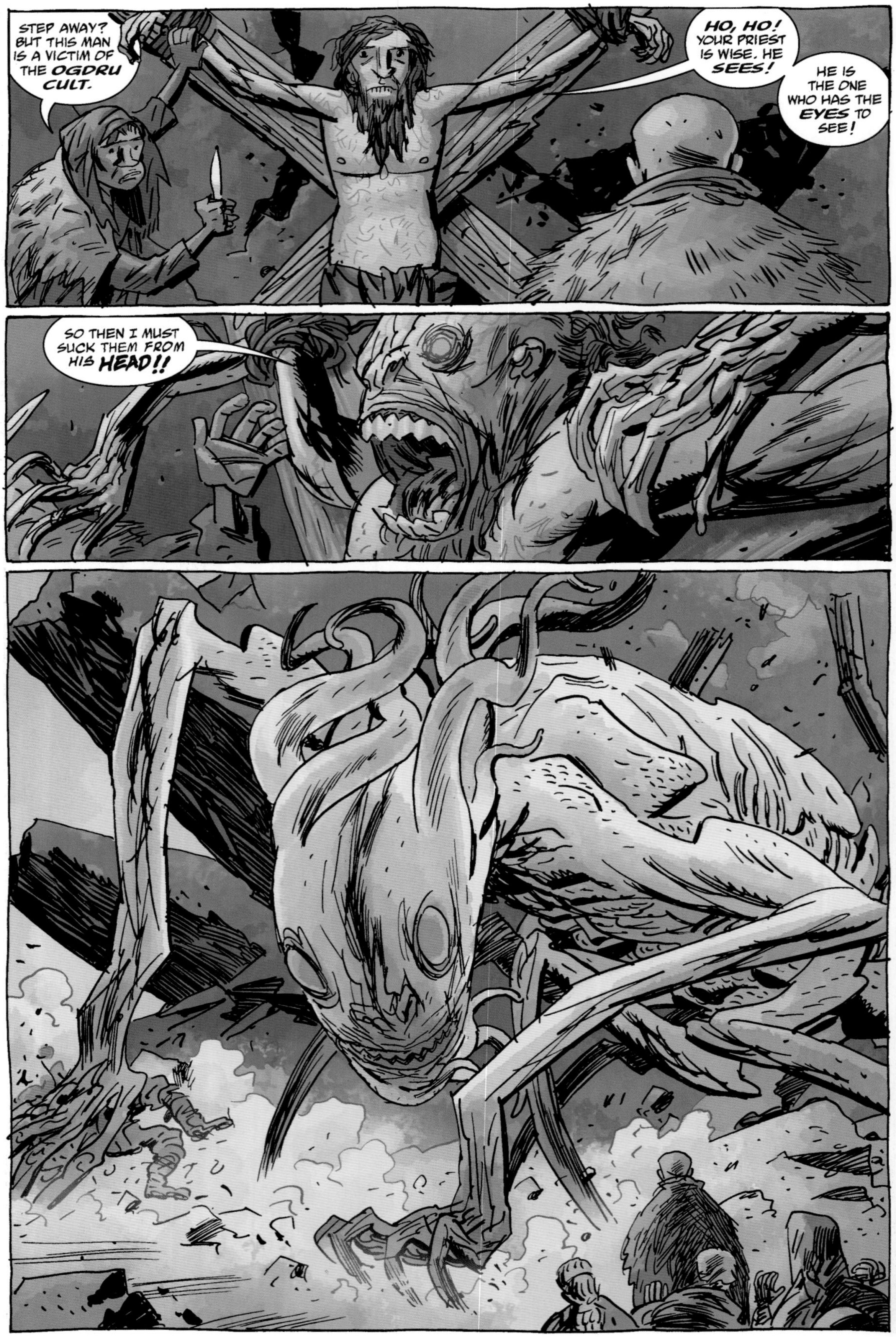
STEP AWAY? BUT THIS MAN IS A VICTIM OF THE OGDRU CULT.
HO, HO! YOUR PRIEST IS WISE. HE SEES!
HE IS THE ONE WHO HAS THE EYES TO SEE!
SO THEN I MUST SUCK THEM FROM HIS HEAD!!

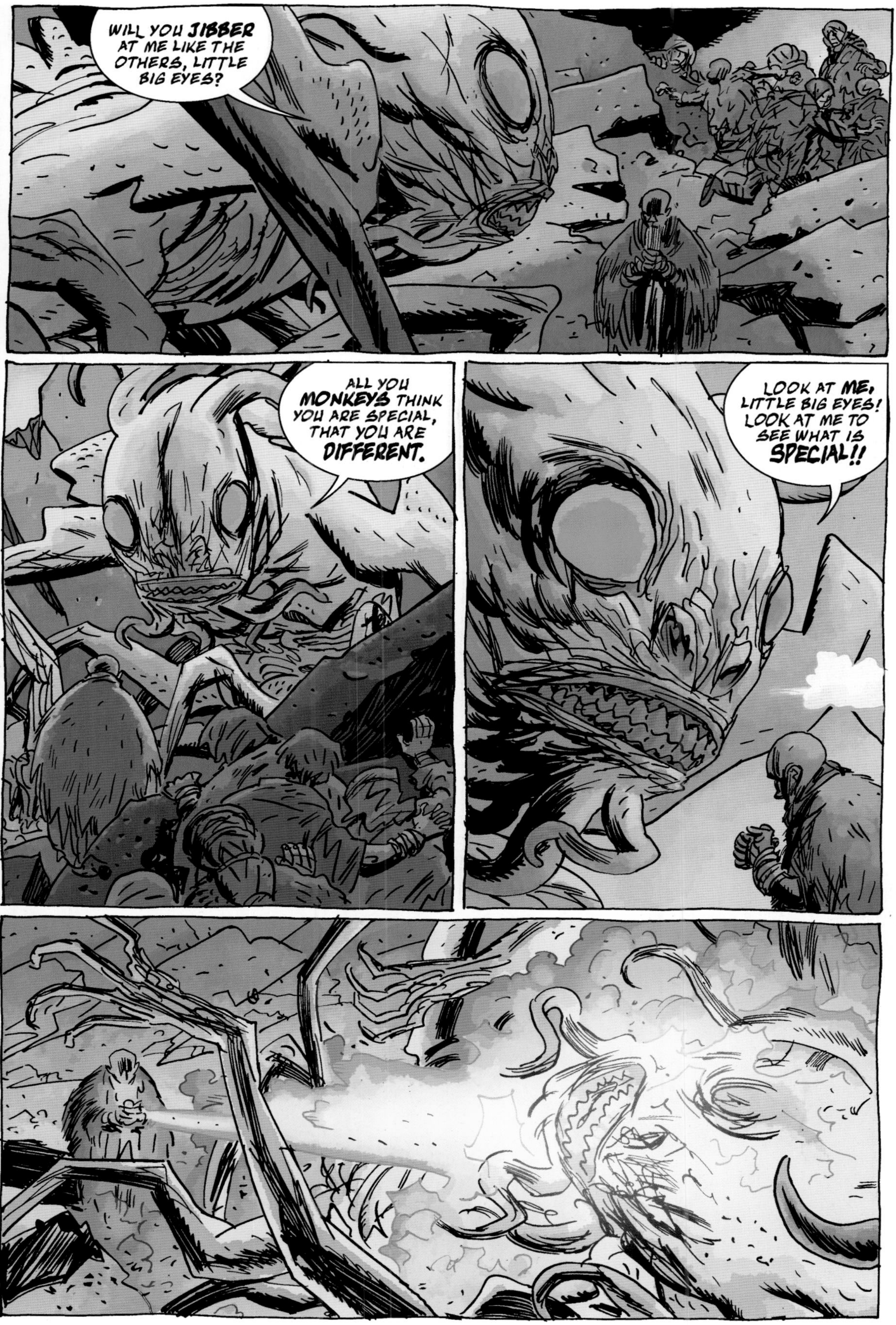
WILL YOU JIBBER AT ME LIKE THE OTHERS, LITTLE BIG EYES?
ALL YOU MONKEYS THINK YOU ARE SPECIAL, THAT YOU ARE DIFFERENT.
LOOK AT ME, LITTLE BIG EYES! LOOK AT ME TO SEE WHAT IS SPECIAL!!

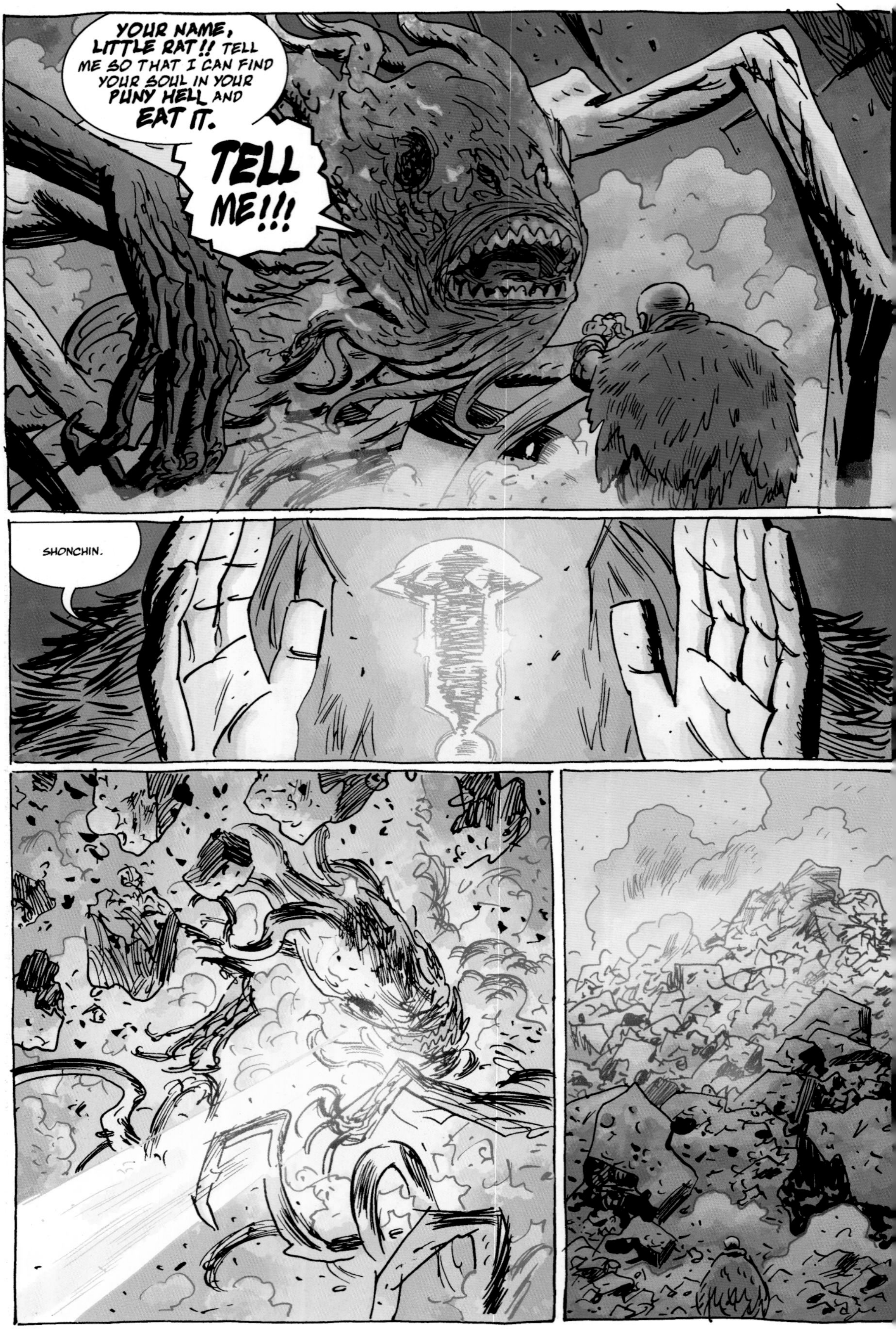
YOUR NAME, LITTLE RAT!! TELL ME SO THAT I CAN FIND YOUR SOUL IN YOUR PUNY HELL AND EAT IT.
TELL ME!!!
SHONCHIN.

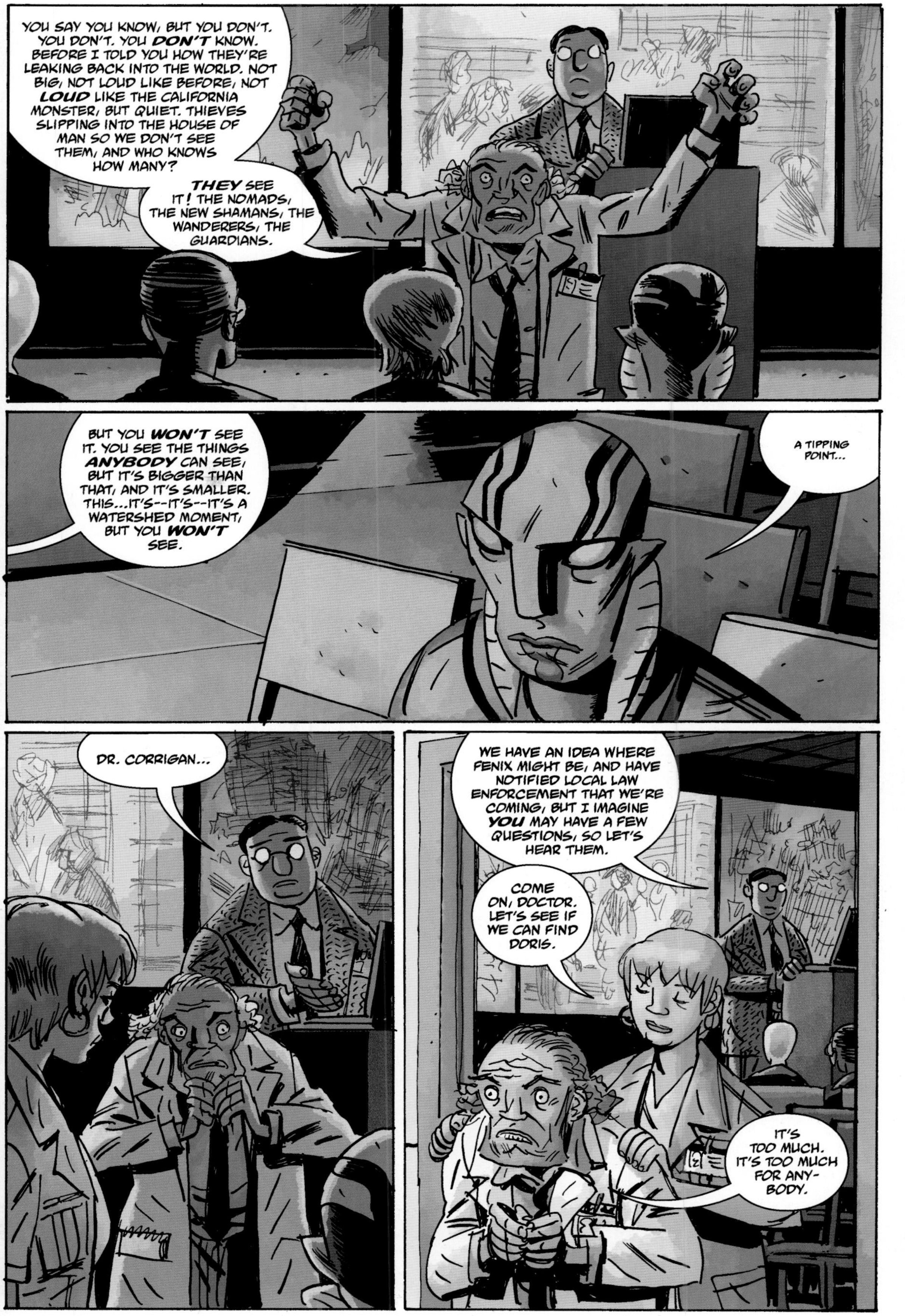
YOU SAY YOU KNOW, BUT YOU DON'T. YOU DON'T. YOU **DON'T** KNOW. BEFORE I TOLD YOU HOW THEY'RE LEAKING BACK INTO THE WORLD. NOT BIG, NOT LOUD LIKE BEFORE, NOT **LOUD** LIKE THE CALIFORNIA MONSTER, BUT QUIET. THIEVES SLIPPING INTO THE HOUSE OF MAN SO WE DON'T SEE THEM, AND WHO KNOWS HOW MANY?
THEY SEE IT! THE NOMADS, THE NEW SHAMANS, THE WANDERERS, THE GUARDIANS.
BUT YOU **WON'T** SEE IT. YOU SEE THE THINGS **ANYBODY** CAN SEE, BUT IT'S BIGGER THAN THAT, AND IT'S SMALLER. THIS...IT'S--IT'S--IT'S A WATERSHED MOMENT, BUT YOU **WON'T** SEE.
A TIPPING POINT...
DR. CORRIGAN...
WE HAVE AN IDEA WHERE FENIX MIGHT BE, AND HAVE NOTIFIED LOCAL LAW ENFORCEMENT THAT WE'RE COMING, BUT I IMAGINE **YOU** MAY HAVE A FEW QUESTIONS, SO LET'S HEAR THEM.
COME ON, DOCTOR. LET'S SEE IF WE CAN FIND DORIS.
IT'S TOO MUCH. IT'S TOO MUCH FOR ANY-BODY.

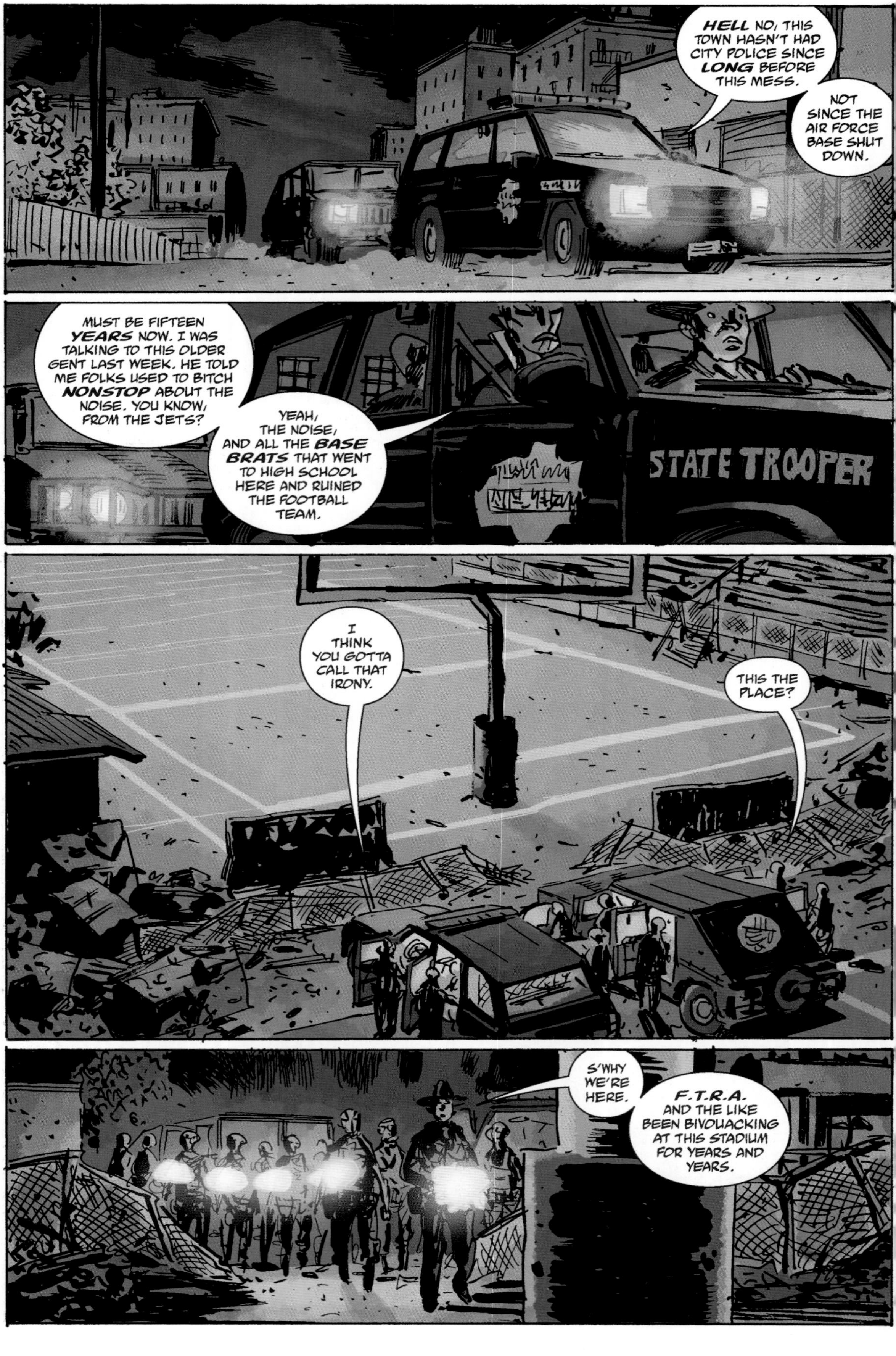
HELL NO, THIS TOWN HASN'T HAD CITY POLICE SINCE LONG BEFORE THIS MESS.
NOT SINCE THE AIR FORCE BASE SHUT DOWN.
MUST BE FIFTEEN YEARS NOW. I WAS TALKING TO THIS OLDER GENT LAST WEEK. HE TOLD ME FOLKS USED TO BITCH NONSTOP ABOUT THE NOISE. YOU KNOW, FROM THE JETS?
YEAH, THE NOISE, AND ALL THE BASE BRATS THAT WENT TO HIGH SCHOOL HERE AND RUINED THE FOOTBALL TEAM.
STATE TROOPER
I THINK YOU GOTTA CALL THAT IRONY.
THIS THE PLACE?
S'WHY WE'RE HERE.
F.T.R.A. AND THE LIKE BEEN BIVOUACKING AT THIS STADIUM FOR YEARS AND YEARS.

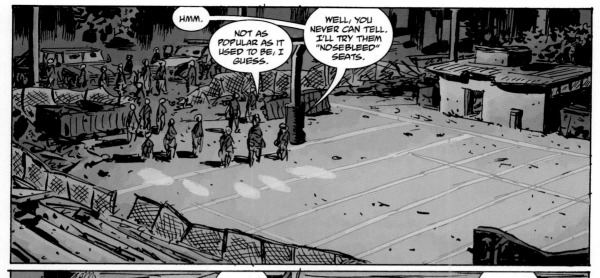

HMM.

NOT AS POPULAR AS IT USED TO BE, I GUESS.

WELL, YOU NEVER CAN TELL. I'LL TRY THEM "NOSEBLEED" SEATS.

I DON'T REALLY SEE THE POINT.

WELL, WE *ARE* ONLY LOOKING FOR ONE GIRL.

NO, WE'RE LOOKING FOR A GIRL WITH A WHOLE ARMY OF FOLLOWERS. IF IT TURNS OUT SHE'S HERE ALL ALONE, THEN SHE'S *NOT* WHO WE THINK SHE IS.

GAAAH!

HOLD ON. THE TROOPER KNOWS THIS WRECK BETTER THAN WE DO. LET'S GET HIM.

OKAY, YOU GET HIM.

MEAN-WHILE, I'LL DO MY JOB.

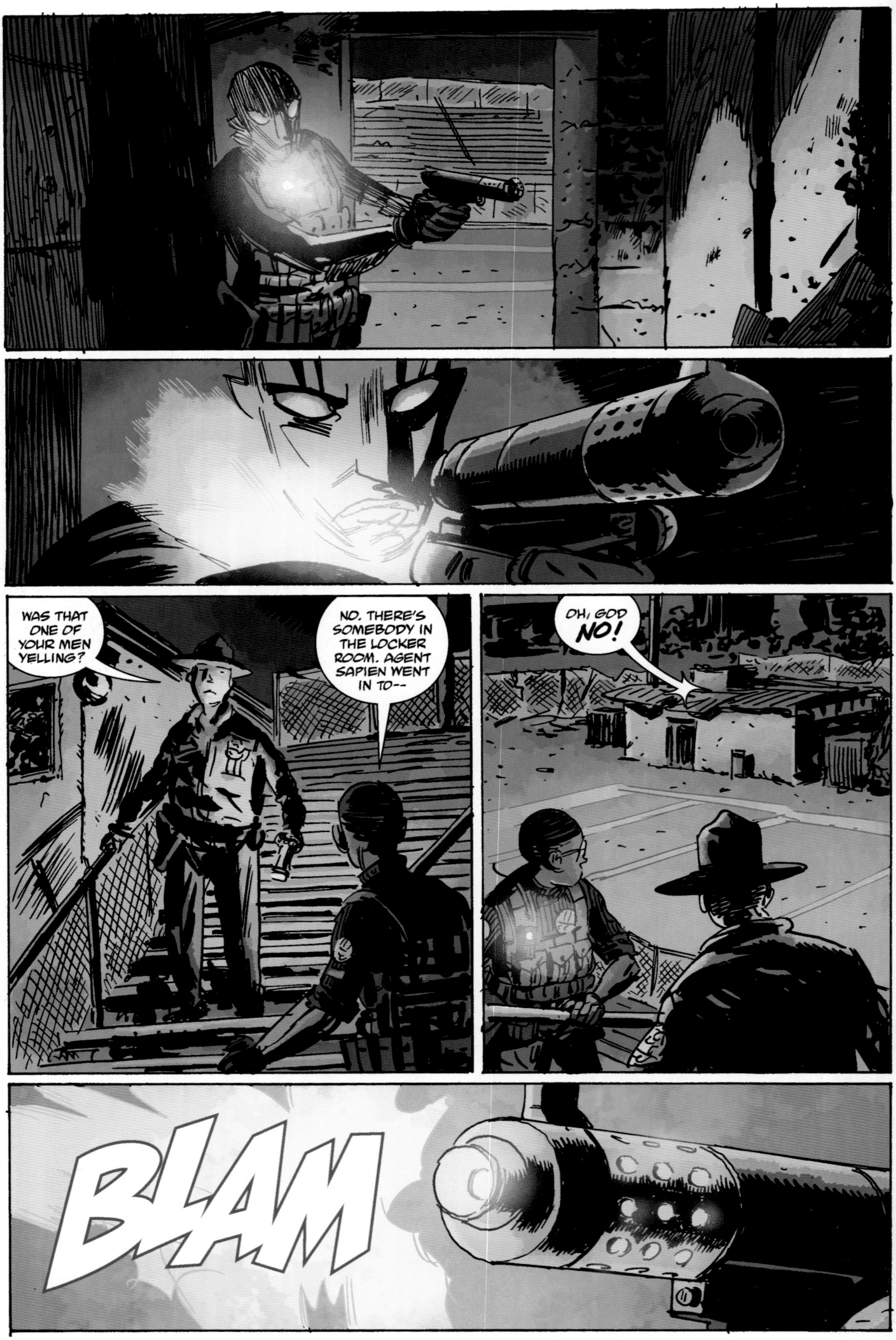

WAS THAT ONE OF YOUR MEN YELLING?
NO. THERE'S SOMEBODY IN THE LOCKER ROOM. AGENT SAPIEN WENT IN TO--
OH, GOD NO!
BLAM

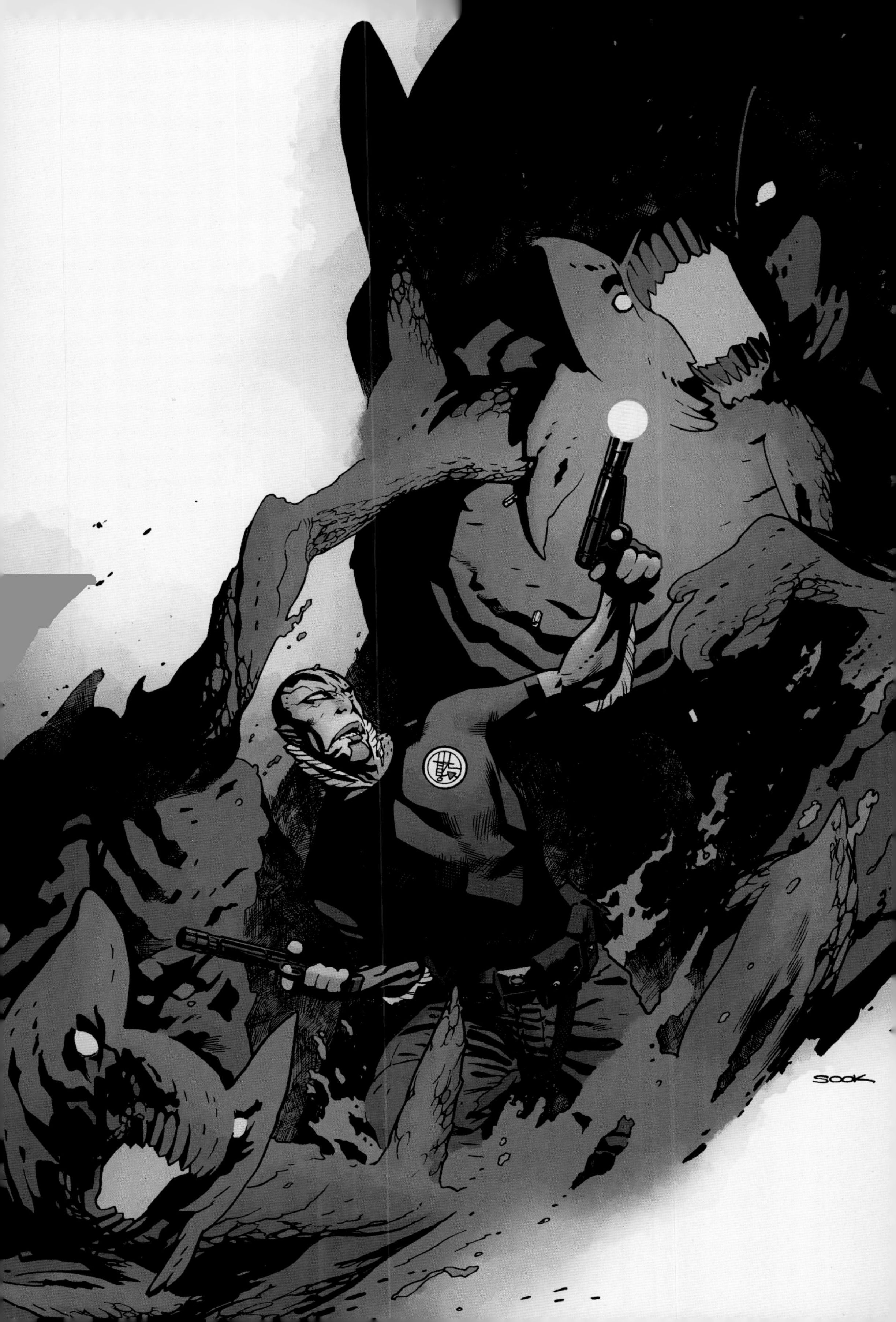
SOOK

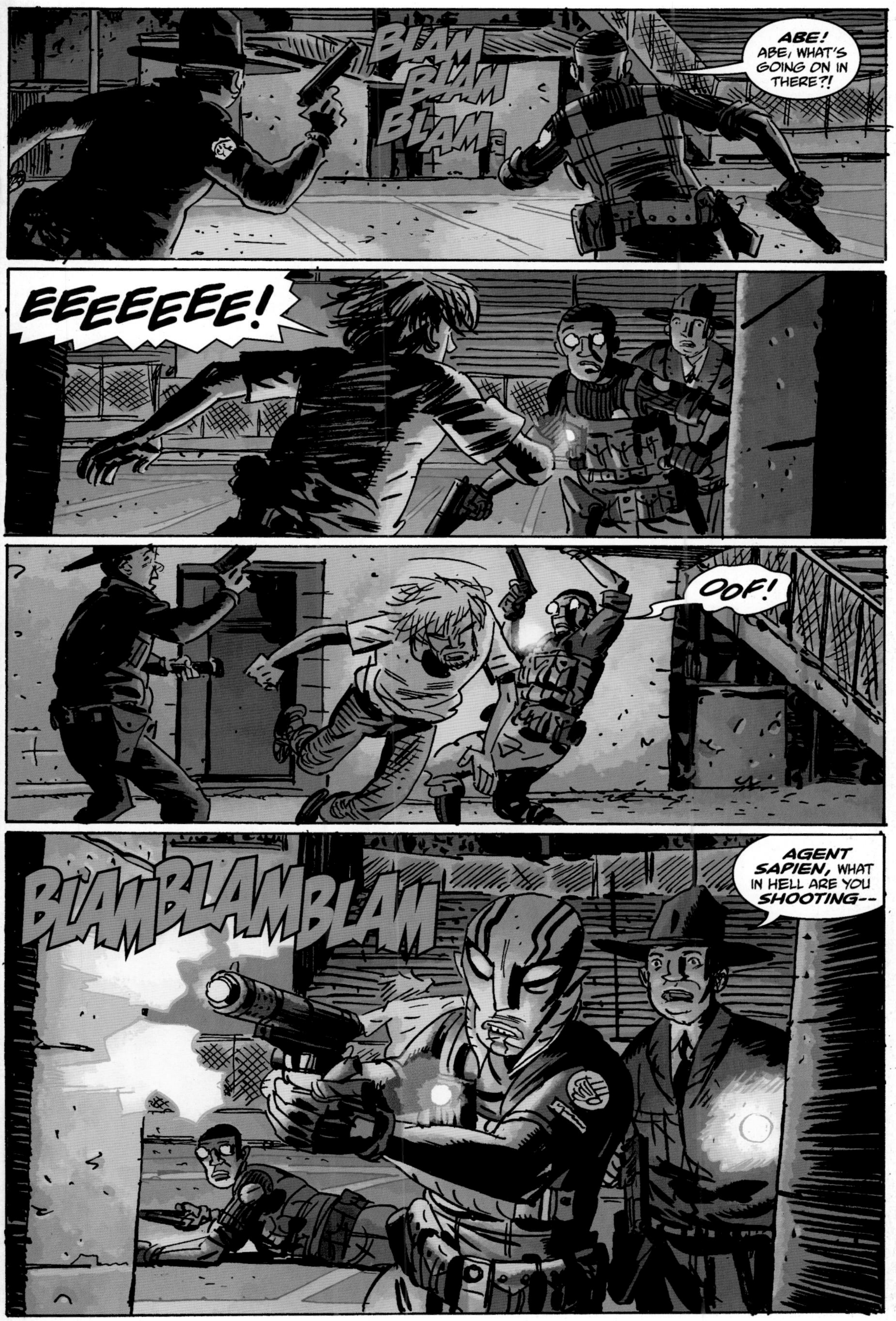
BLAM BLAM BLAM
ABE! ABE, WHAT'S GOING ON IN THERE?!
EEEEEEEE!
OOF!
BLAMBLAMBLAM
AGENT SAPIEN, WHAT IN HELL ARE YOU SHOOTING--

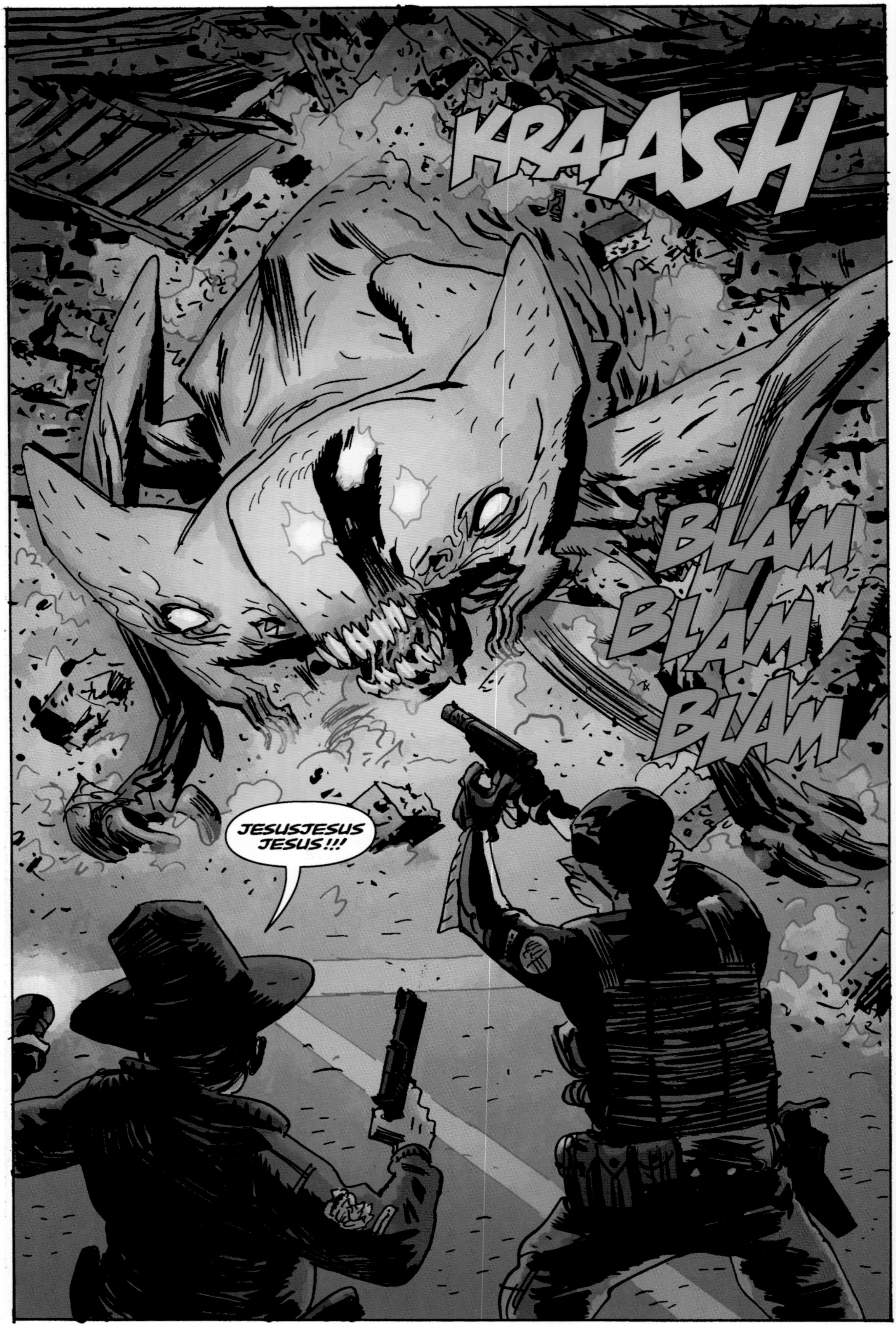
KRA-ASH
BLAM
BLAM
BLAM
JESUSJESUS JESUS!!!

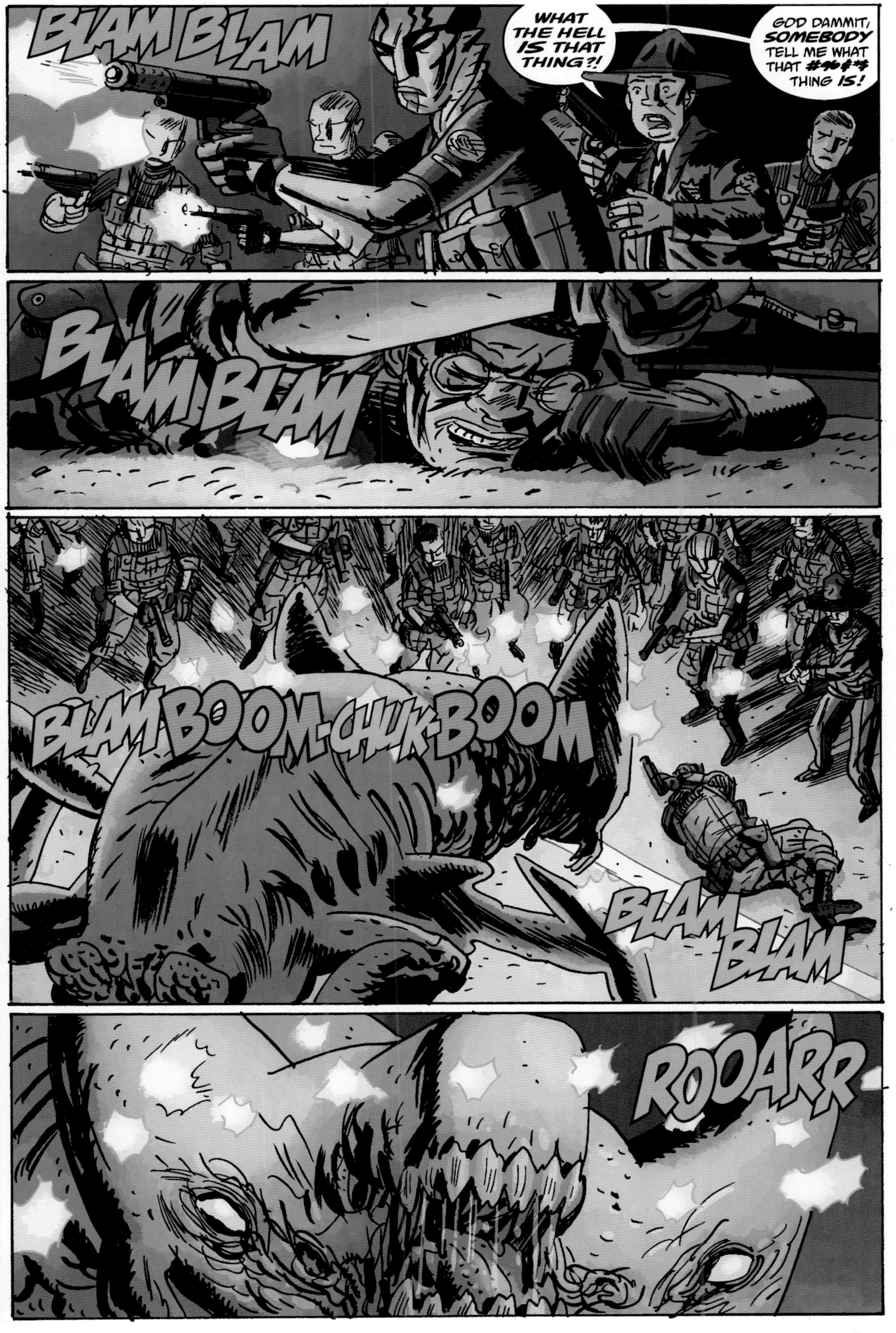
BLAM BLAM
WHAT THE HELL IS THAT THING?!
GOD DAMMIT, SOMEBODY TELL ME WHAT THAT #%¢*$ THING IS!
BLAM BLAM
BLAM BOOM-CHUK-BOOM
BLAM BLAM
ROOARR

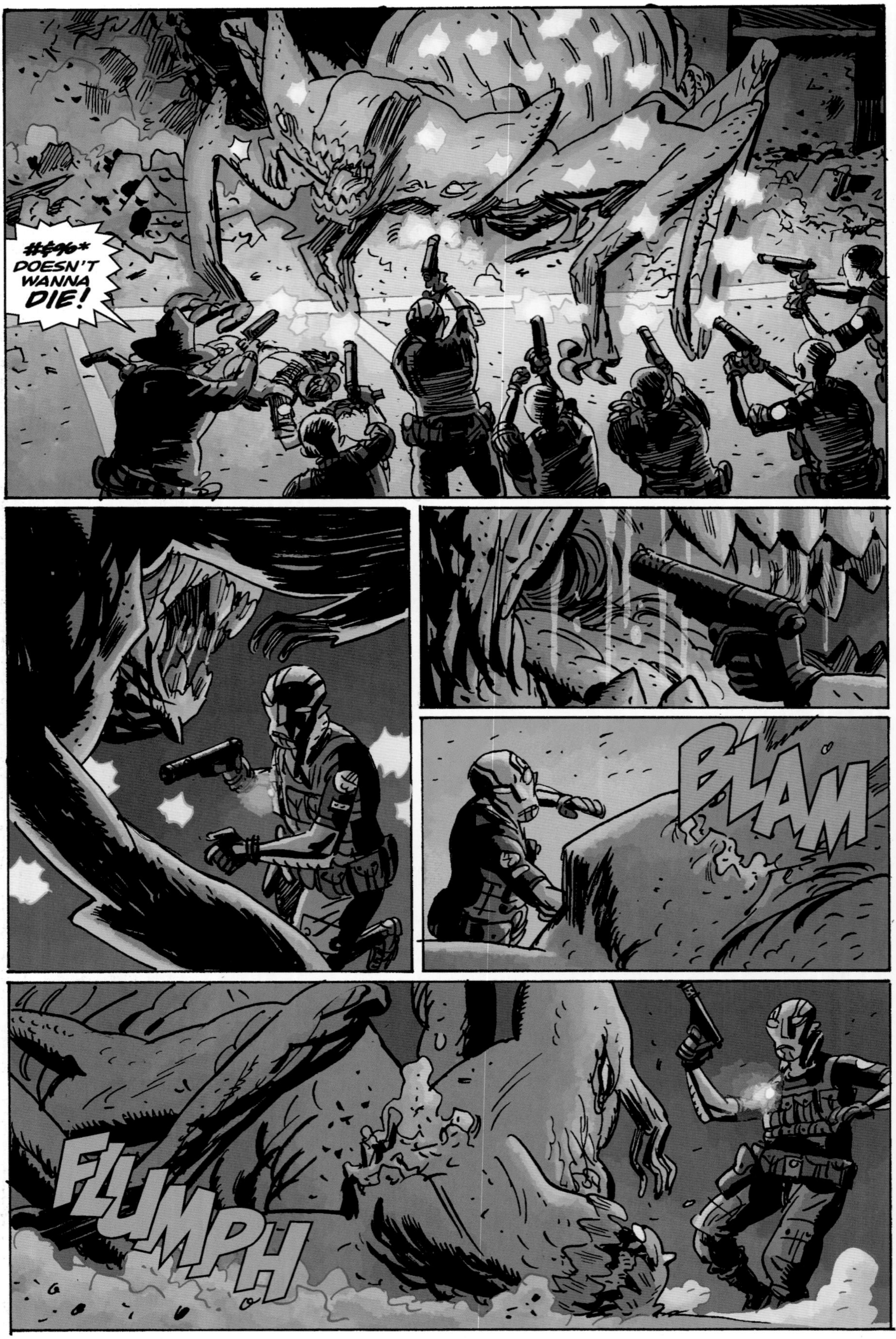
#$%* DOESN'T WANNA DIE!
BLAM
FLUMPH

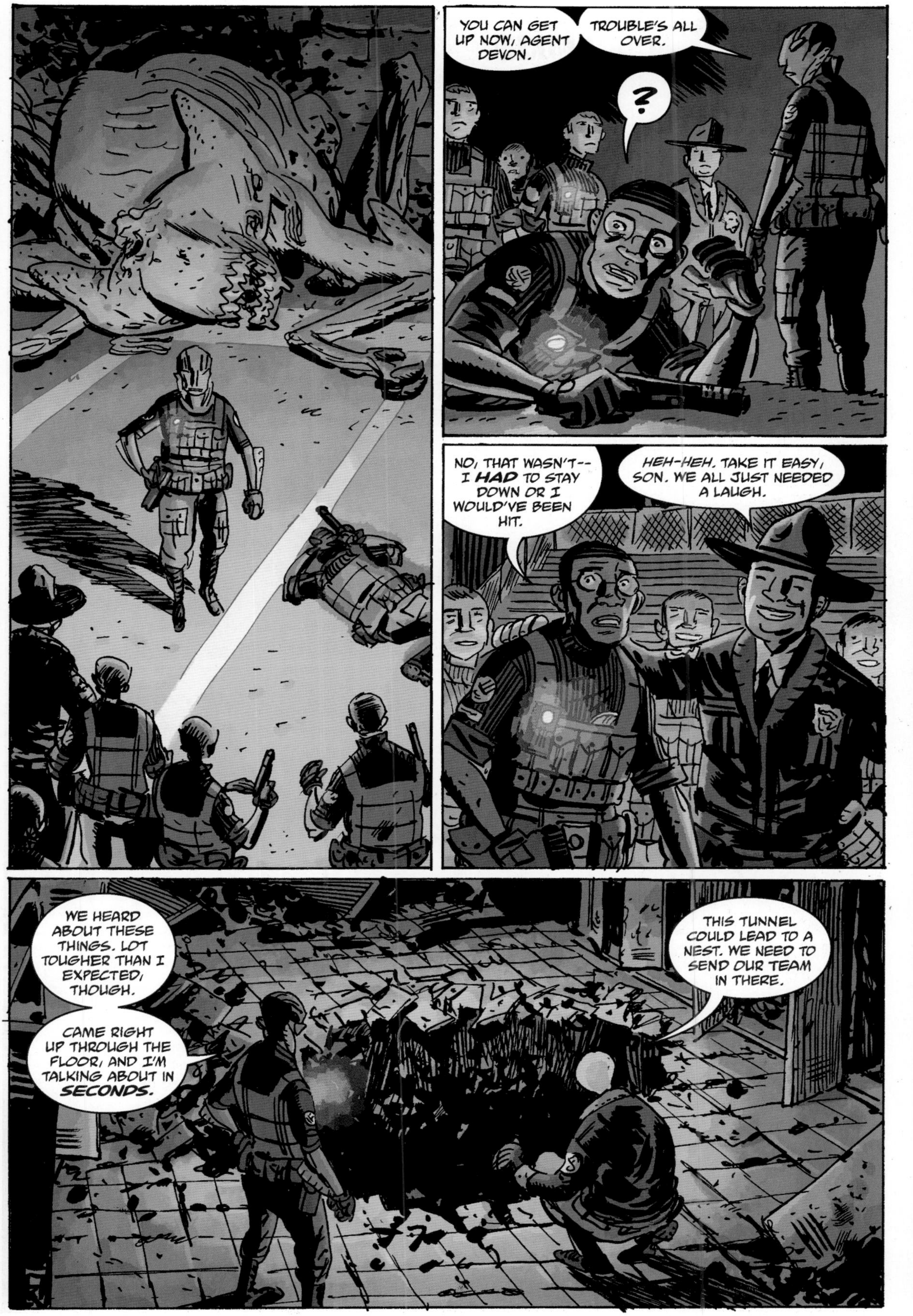
YOU CAN GET UP NOW, AGENT DEVON.
TROUBLE'S ALL OVER.
?
NO, THAT WASN'T-- I HAD TO STAY DOWN OR I WOULD'VE BEEN HIT.
HEH-HEH. TAKE IT EASY, SON. WE ALL JUST NEEDED A LAUGH.
WE HEARD ABOUT THESE THINGS. LOT TOUGHER THAN I EXPECTED, THOUGH.
CAME RIGHT UP THROUGH THE FLOOR, AND I'M TALKING ABOUT IN SECONDS.
THIS TUNNEL COULD LEAD TO A NEST. WE NEED TO SEND OUR TEAM IN THERE.

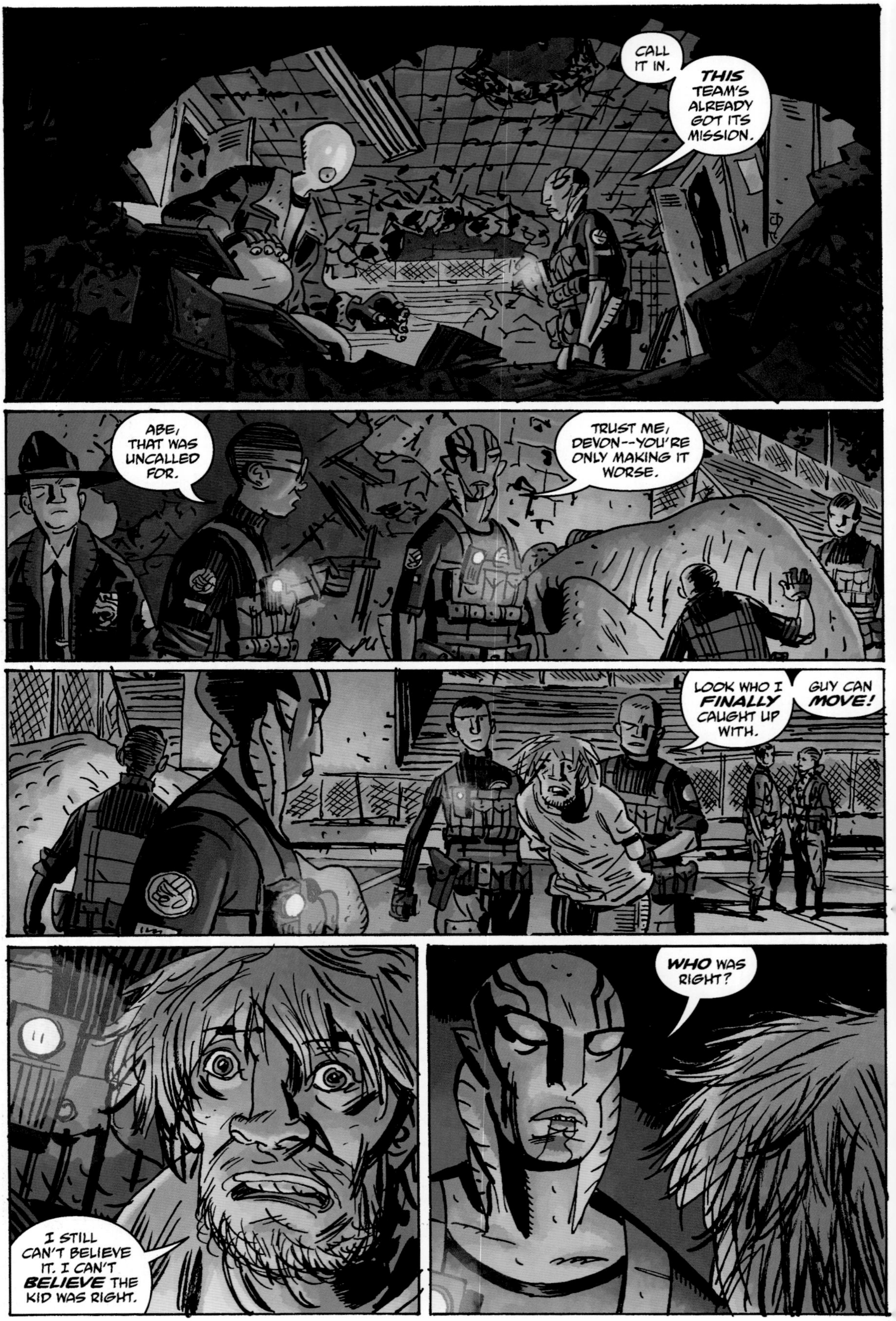
CALL IT IN.
THIS TEAM'S ALREADY GOT ITS MISSION.
ABE, THAT WAS UNCALLED FOR.
TRUST ME, DEVON--YOU'RE ONLY MAKING IT WORSE.
LOOK WHO I FINALLY CAUGHT UP WITH.
GUY CAN MOVE!
I STILL CAN'T BELIEVE IT. I CAN'T BELIEVE THE KID WAS RIGHT.
WHO WAS RIGHT?

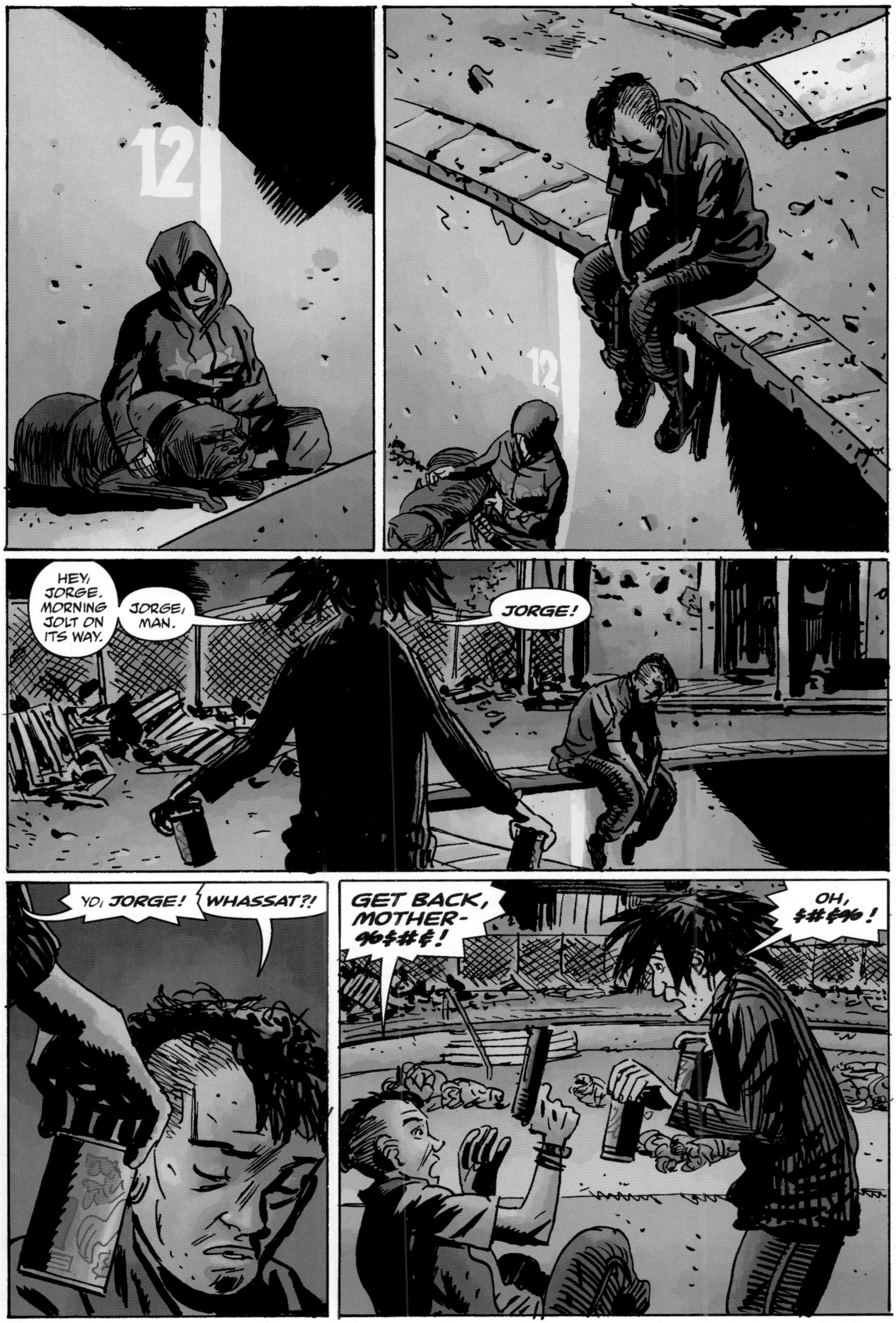
HEY, JORGE. MORNING JOLT ON ITS WAY.
JORGE, MAN.
JORGE!
YO, JORGE!
WHASSAT?!
GET BACK, MOTHER-%$#&!
OH, $#&%!

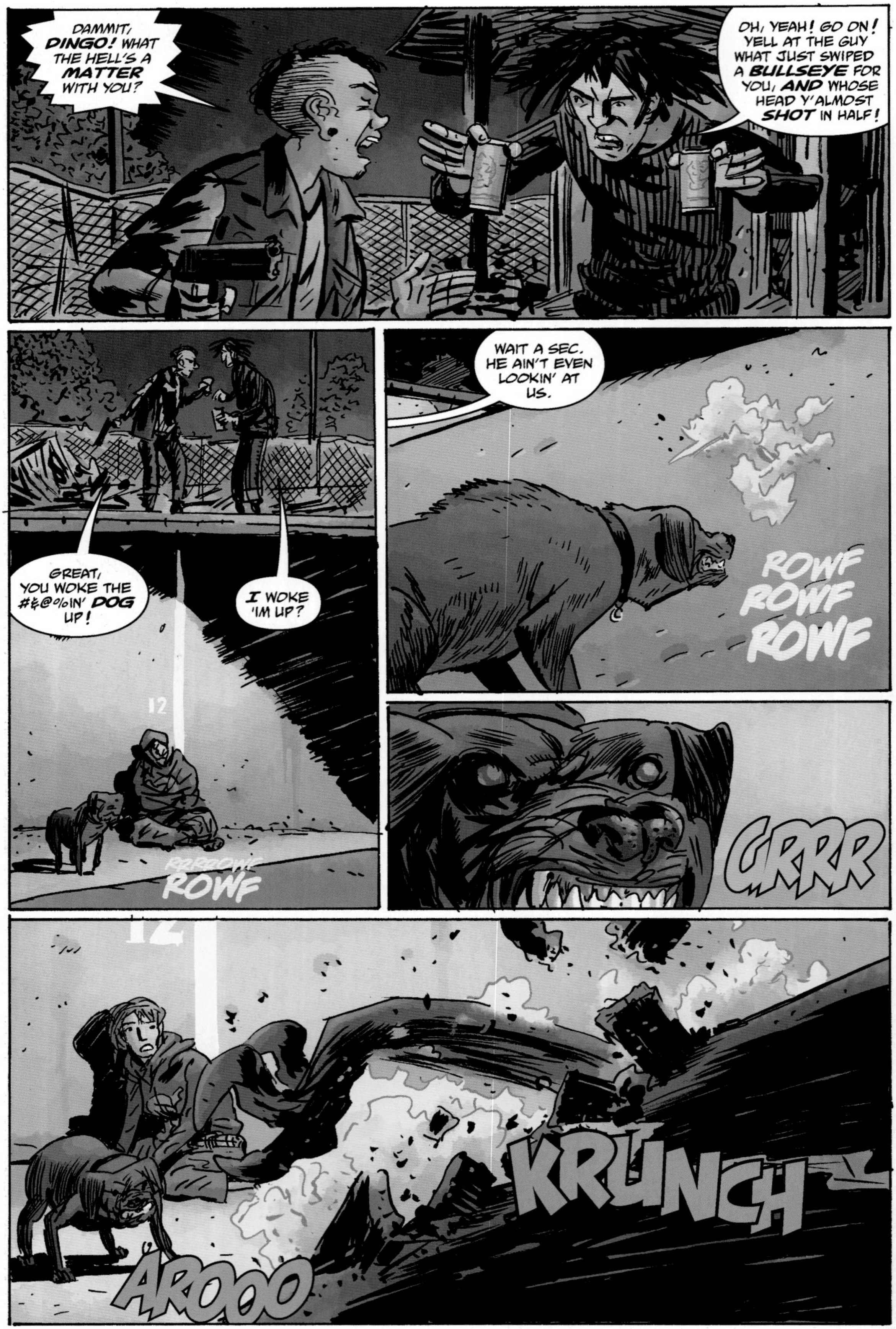

DAMMIT, DINGO! WHAT THE HELL'S A MATTER WITH YOU?
OH, YEAH! GO ON! YELL AT THE GUY WHAT JUST SWIPED A BULLSEYE FOR YOU, AND WHOSE HEAD Y'ALMOST SHOT IN HALF!
GREAT, YOU WOKE THE #&@%IN' DOG UP!
I WOKE 'IM UP?
12
RRRROWF ROWF
WAIT A SEC. HE AIN'T EVEN LOOKIN' AT US.
ROWF ROWF ROWF
GRRR
12
KRUNCH
AROOO

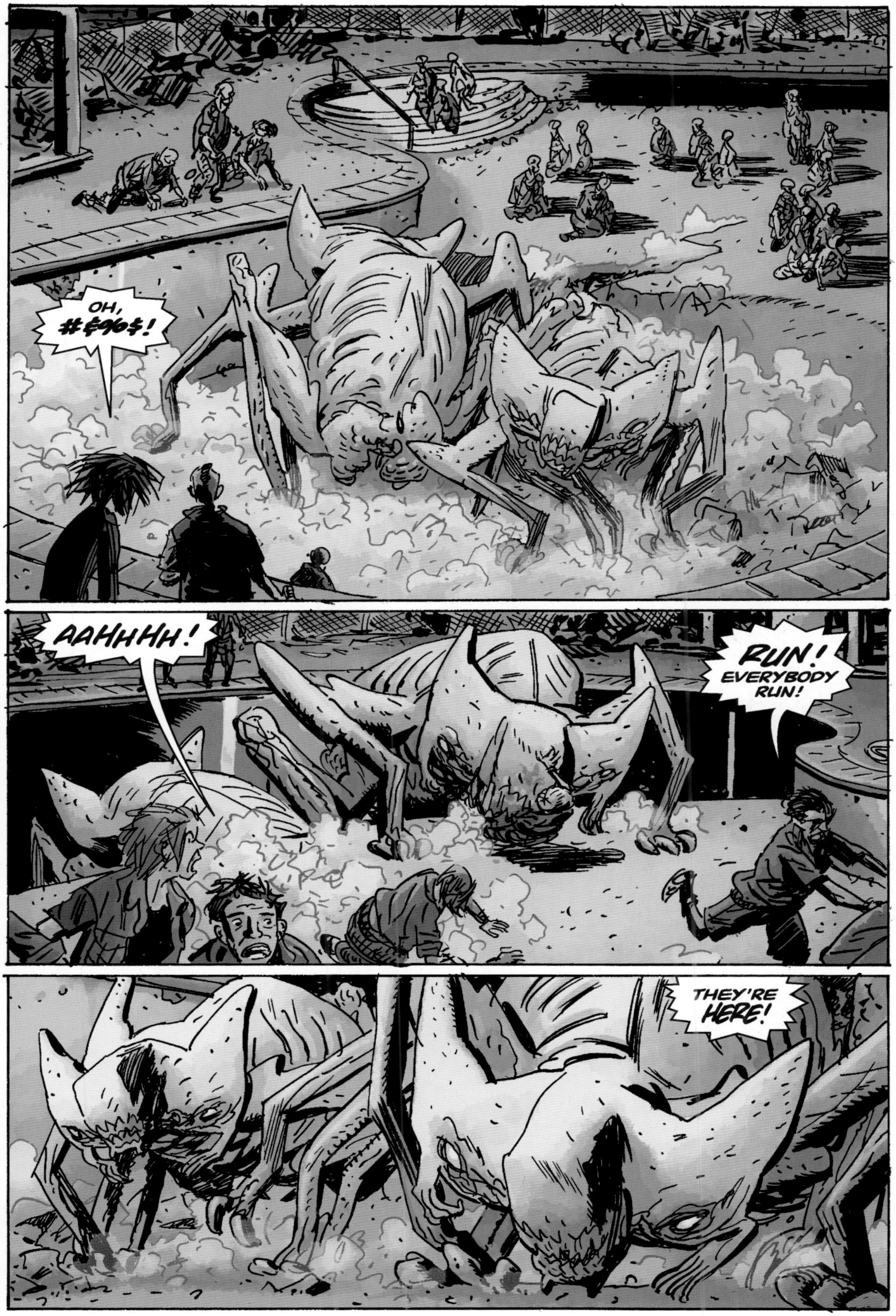
OH, #&%$!
AAHHHH!
RUN! EVERYBODY RUN!
THEY'RE HERE!

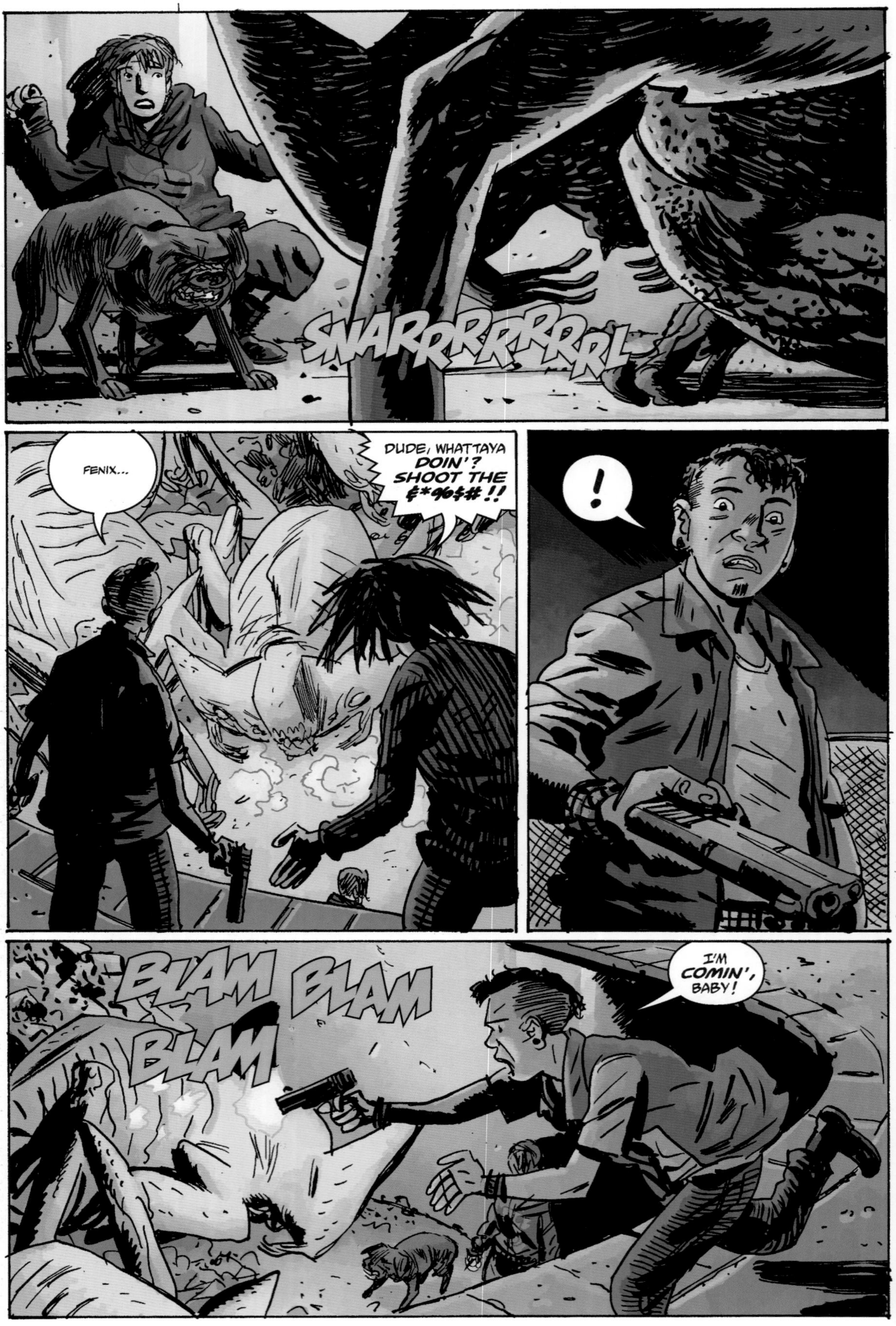
SNARRRRRRRRL
FENIX...
DUDE, WHATTAYA DOIN'? SHOOT THE &*%$#!!
!
BLAM BLAM
BLAM
I'M COMIN', BABY!

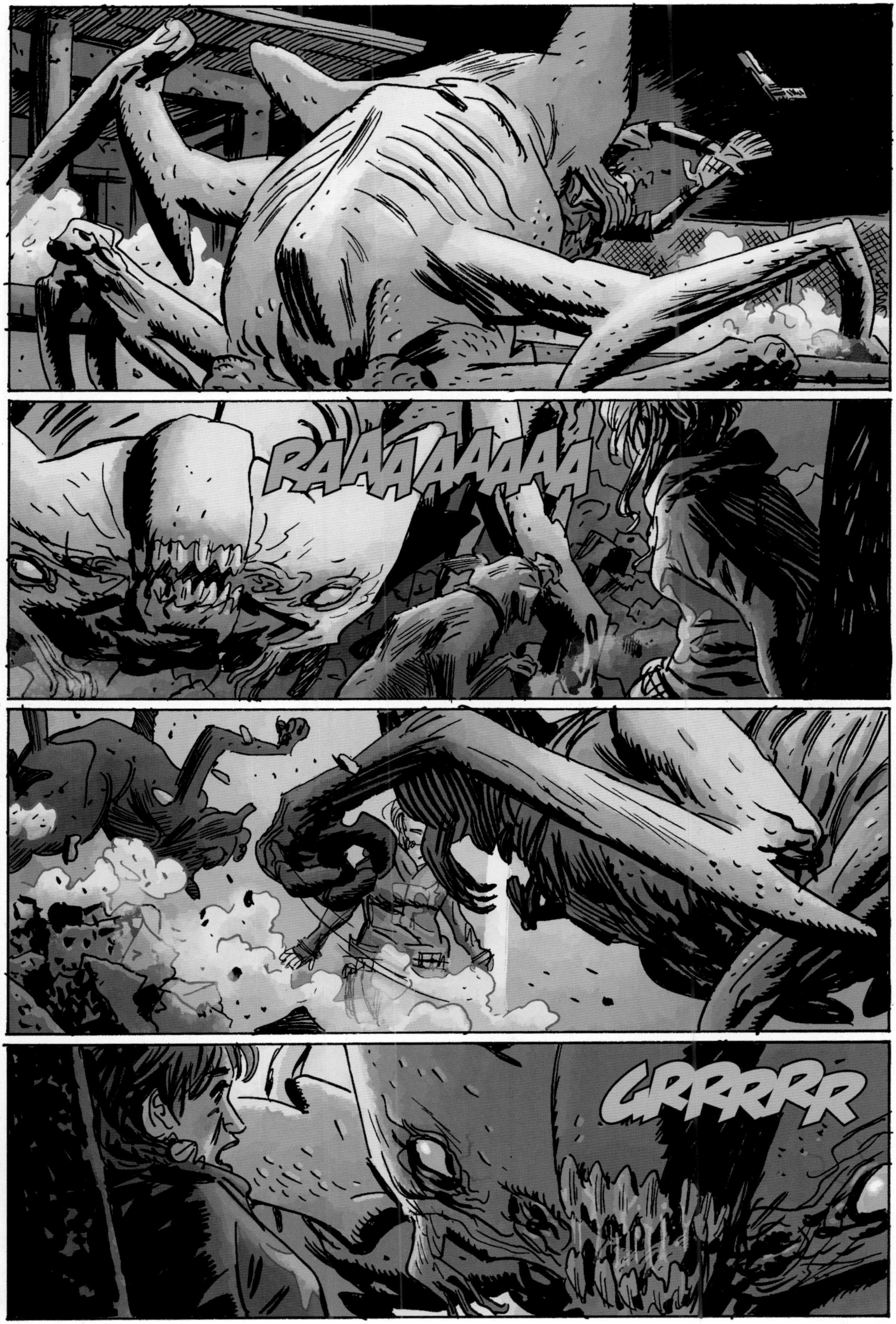
RAAAAAAAA
GRRRRR

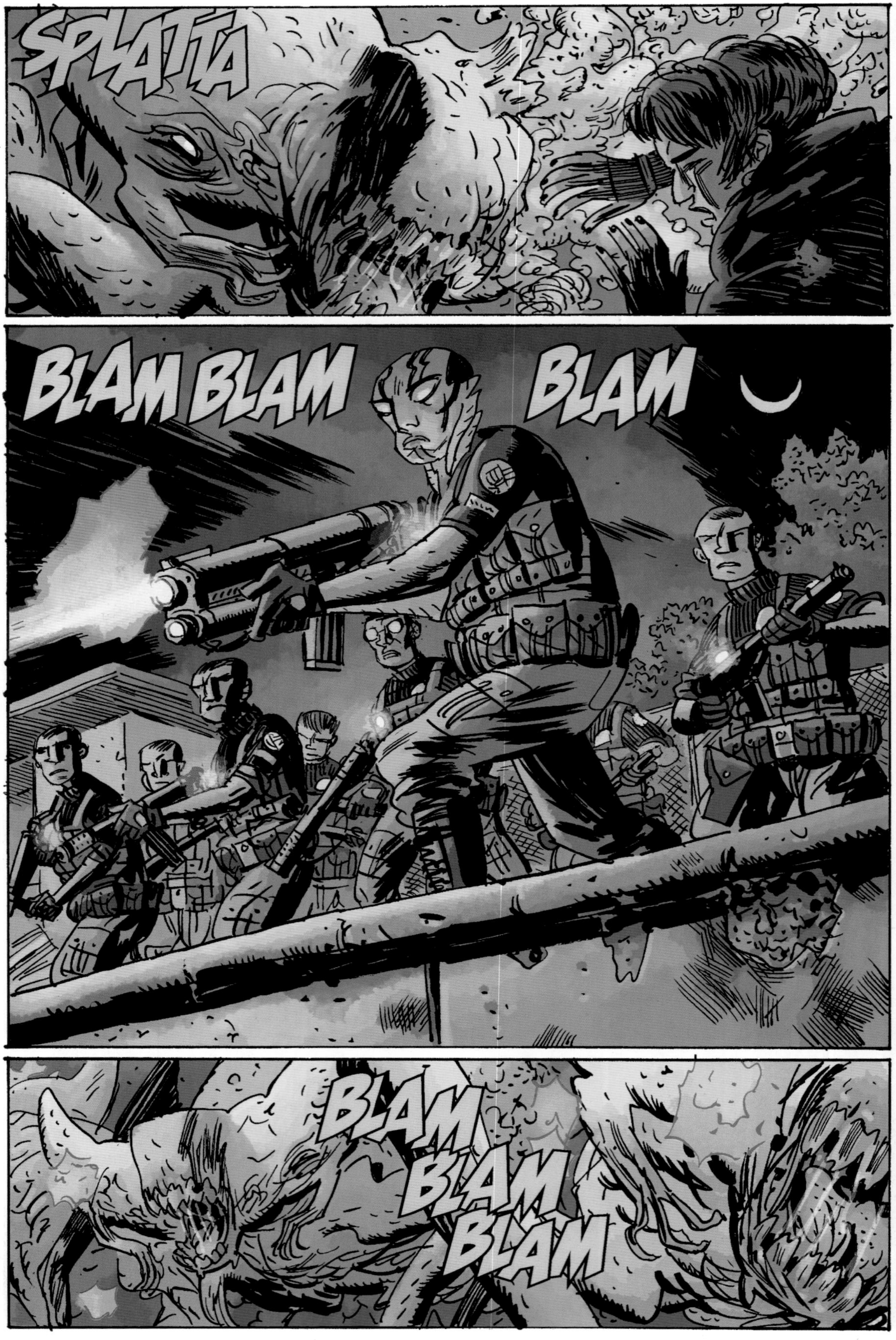
SPLATTA
BLAM BLAM
BLAM
BLAM
BLAM
BLAM

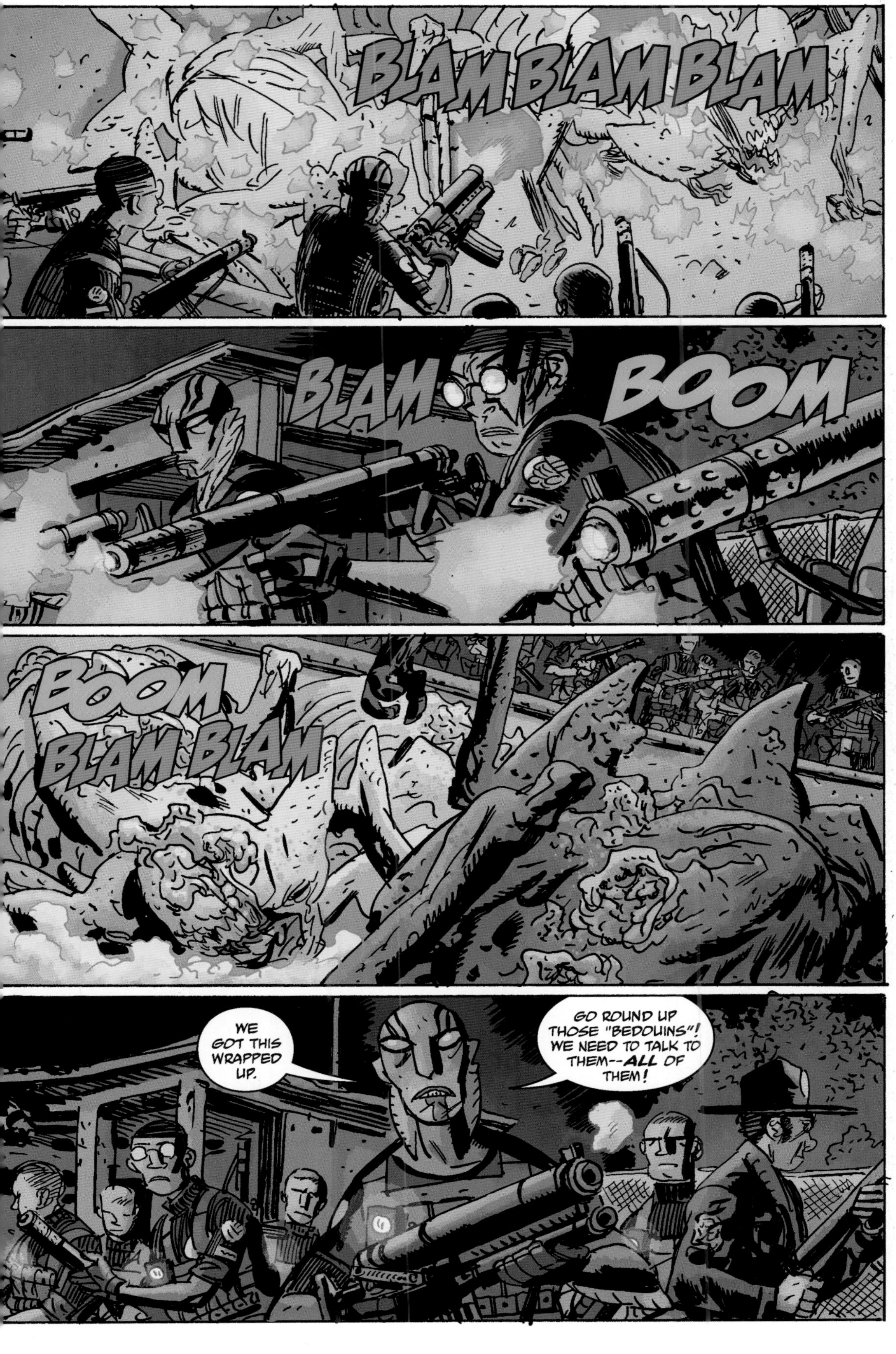
BLAM BLAM BLAM
BLAM
BOOM
BOOM
BLAM BLAM
WE GOT THIS WRAPPED UP.
GO ROUND UP THOSE "BEDOUINS"! WE NEED TO TALK TO THEM--ALL OF THEM!

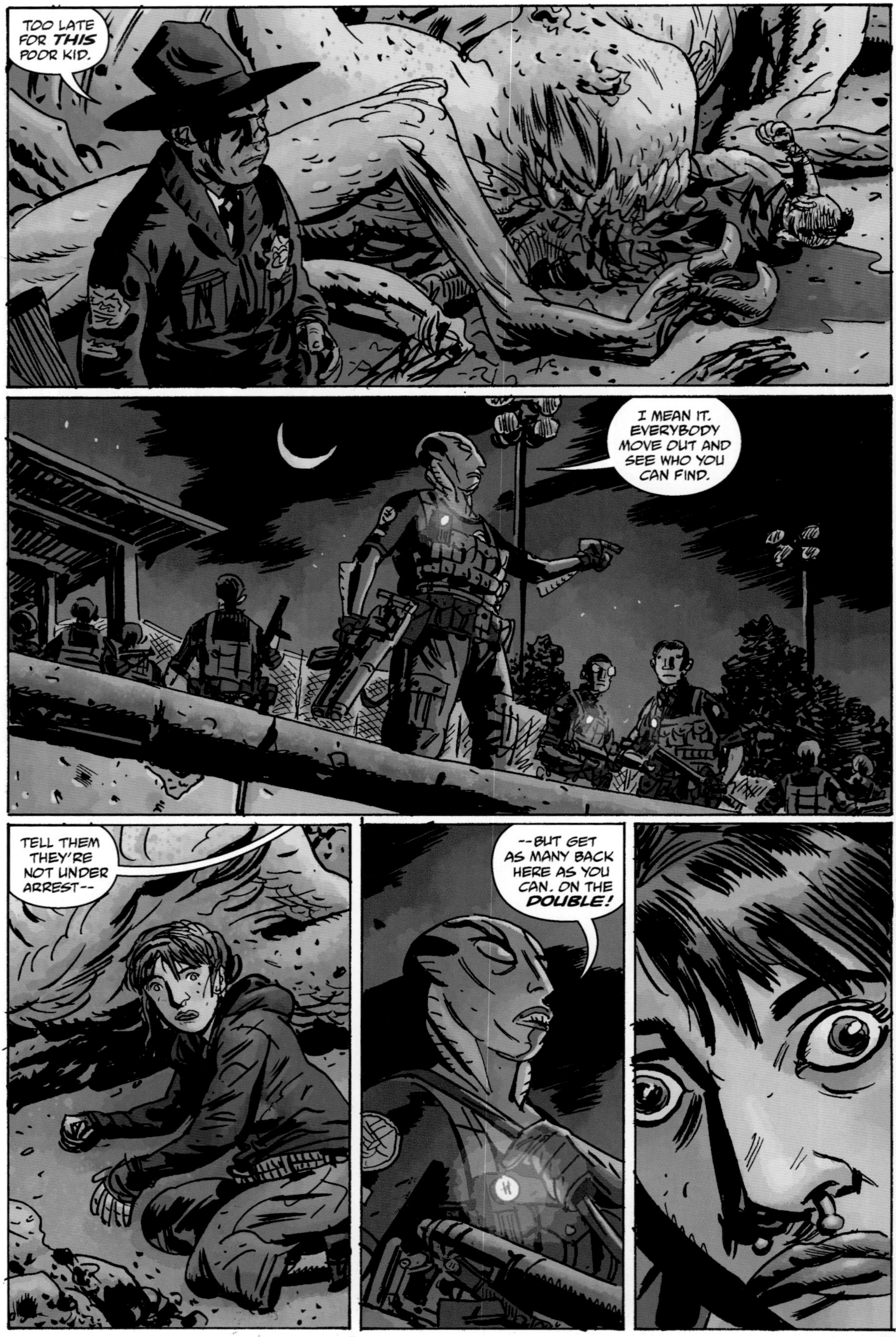
TOO LATE FOR THIS POOR KID.
I MEAN IT. EVERYBODY MOVE OUT AND SEE WHO YOU CAN FIND.
TELL THEM THEY'RE NOT UNDER ARREST--
--BUT GET AS MANY BACK HERE AS YOU CAN. ON THE DOUBLE!

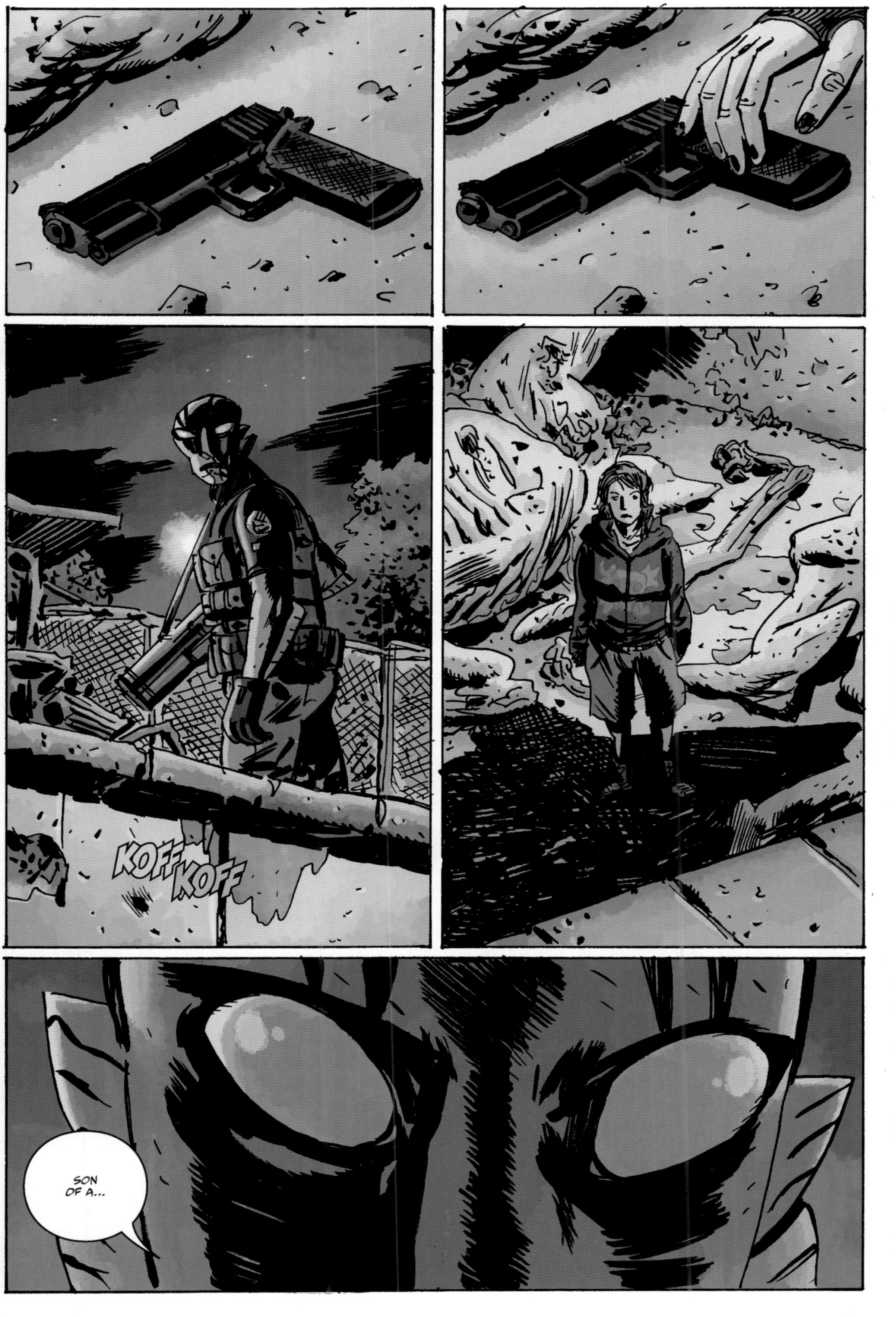
KOFF KOFF
SON OF A...

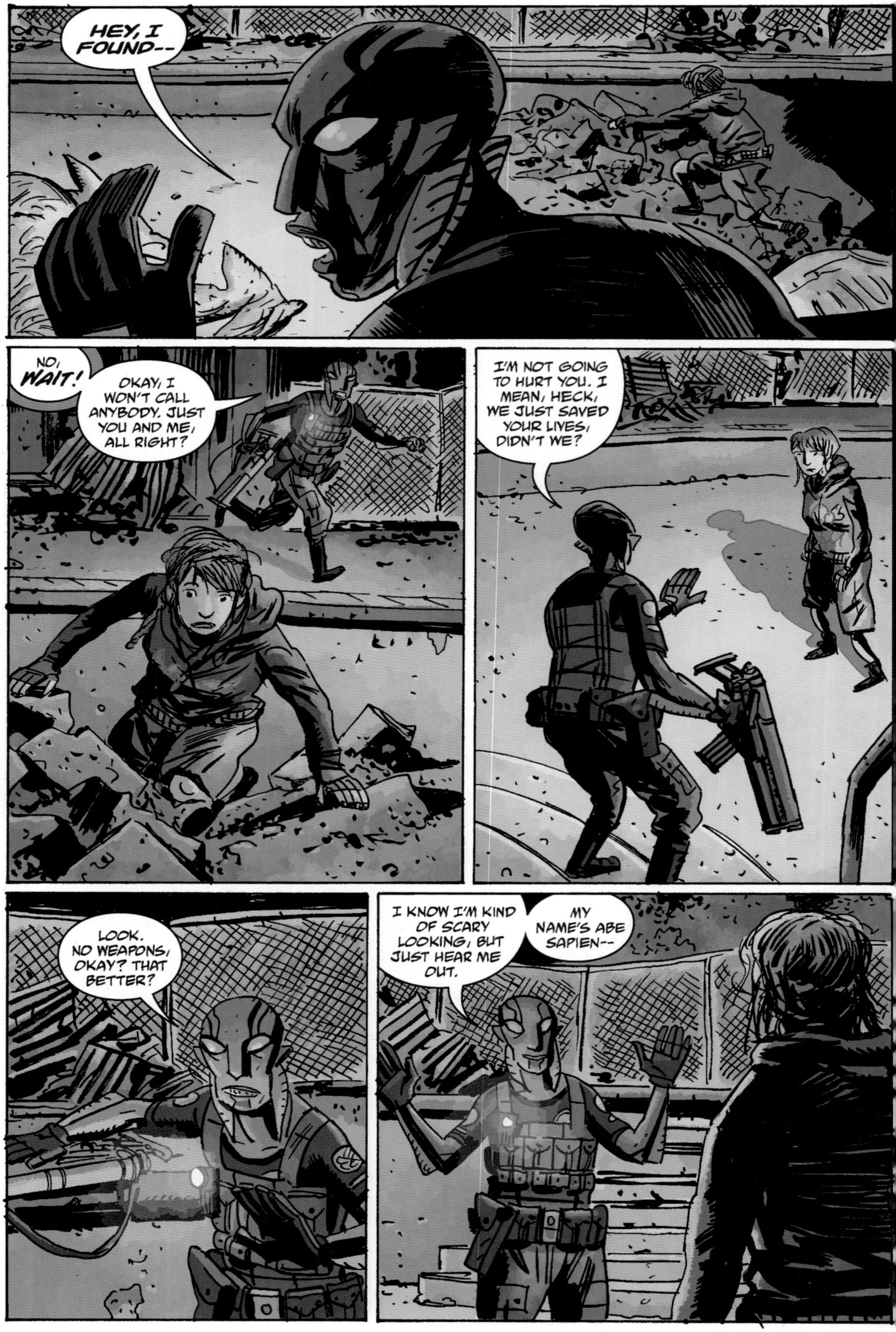
HEY, I FOUND--
NO, WAIT!
OKAY, I WON'T CALL ANYBODY. JUST YOU AND ME, ALL RIGHT?
I'M NOT GOING TO HURT YOU. I MEAN, HECK, WE JUST SAVED YOUR LIVES, DIDN'T WE?
LOOK. NO WEAPONS, OKAY? THAT BETTER?
I KNOW I'M KIND OF SCARY LOOKING, BUT JUST HEAR ME OUT.
MY NAME'S ABE SAPIEN--

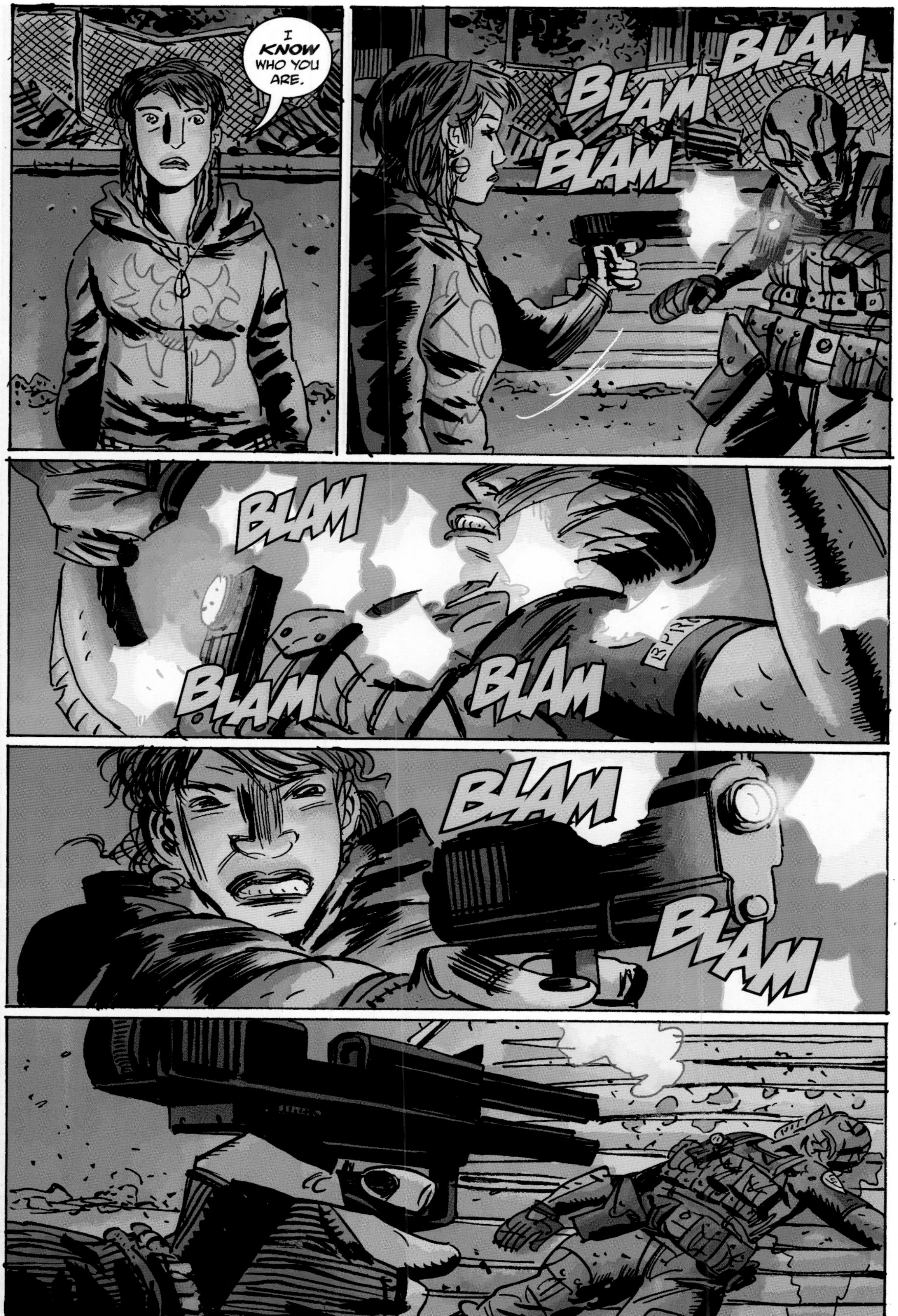
I KNOW WHO YOU ARE.
BLAM
BLAM
BLAM
BLAM
BLAM
BLAM
BLAM
BLAM
BPRD

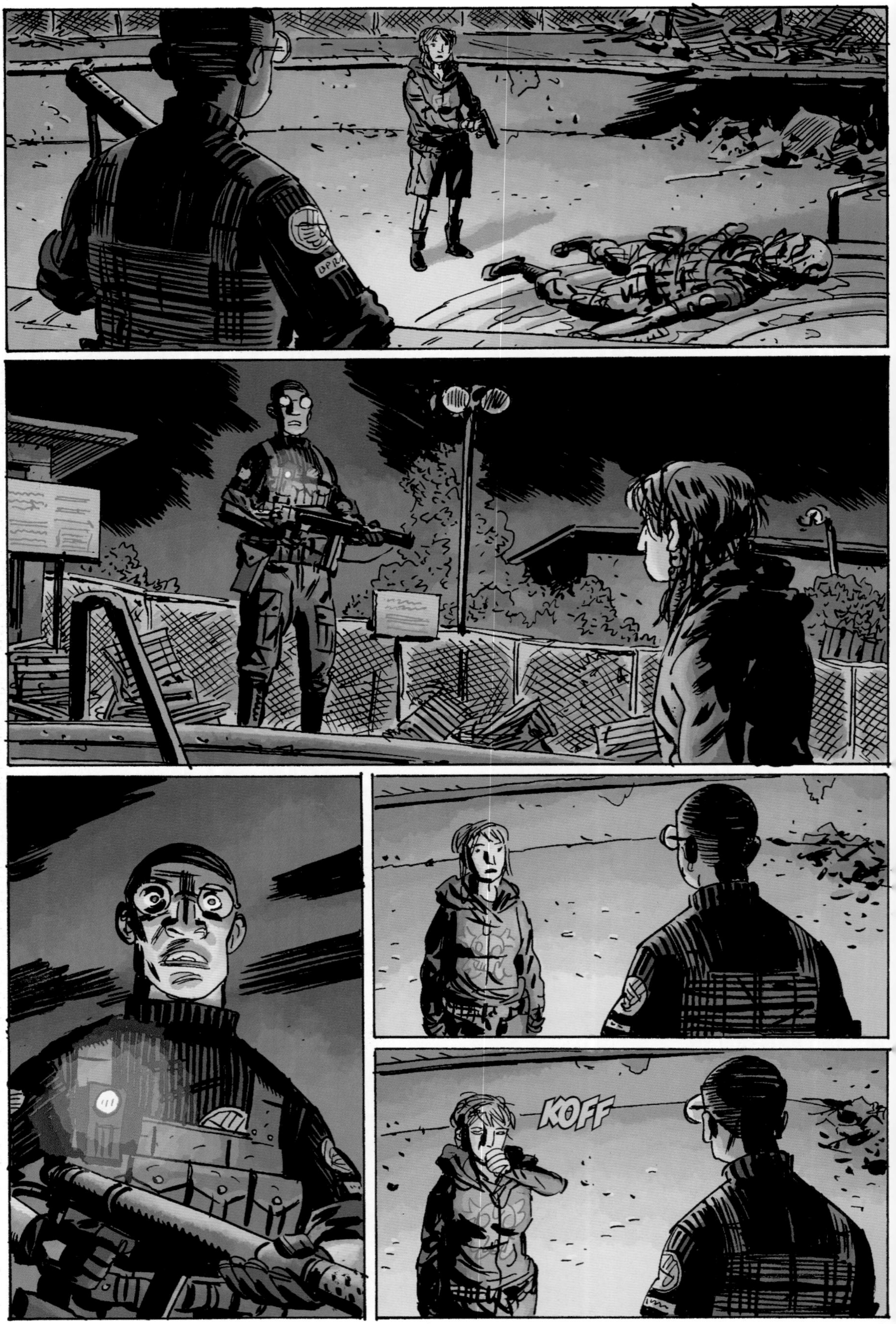
KOFF

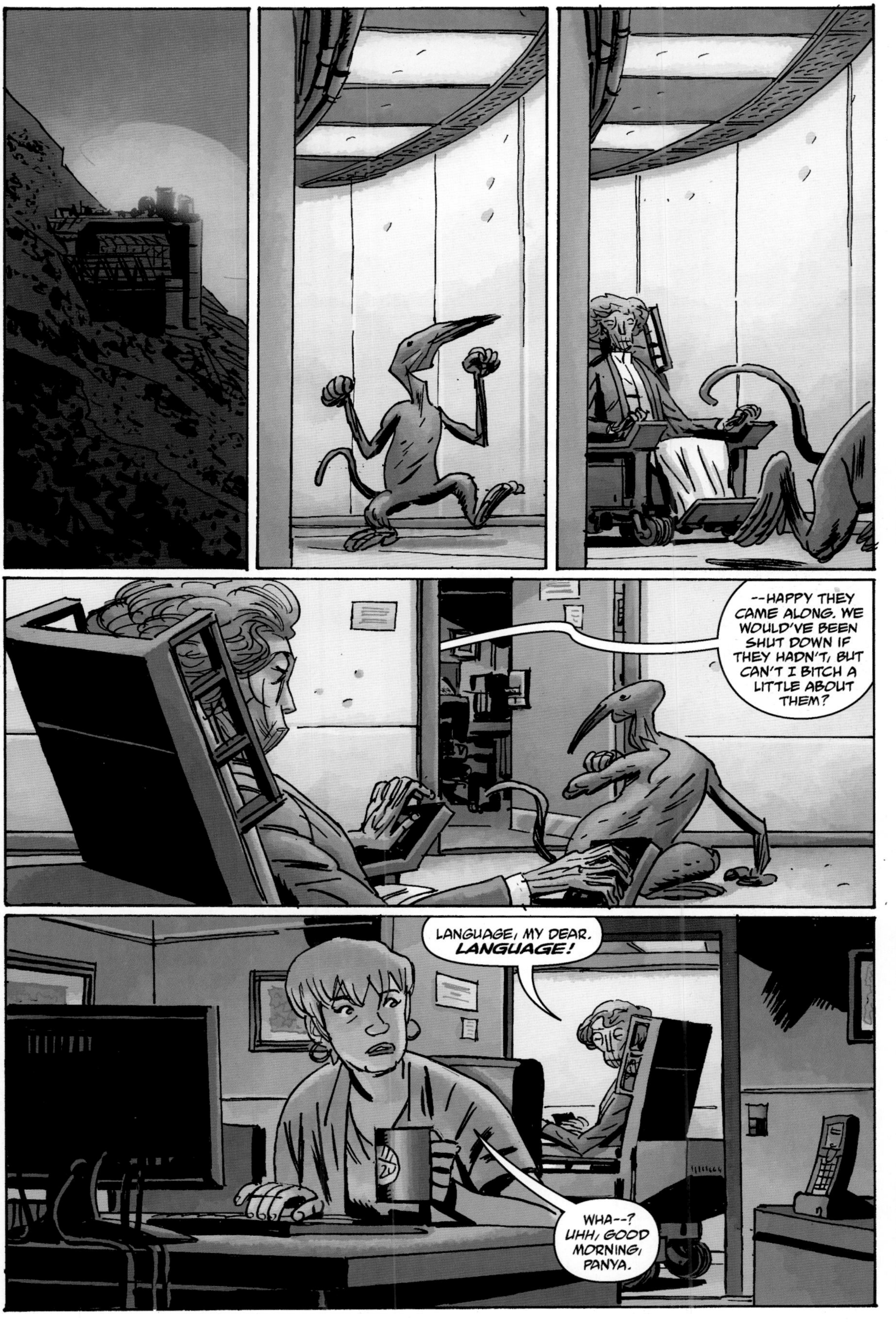
--HAPPY THEY CAME ALONG. WE WOULD'VE BEEN SHUT DOWN IF THEY HADN'T, BUT CAN'T I BITCH A LITTLE ABOUT THEM?
LANGUAGE, MY DEAR. LANGUAGE!
WHA--? UHH, GOOD MORNING, PANYA.

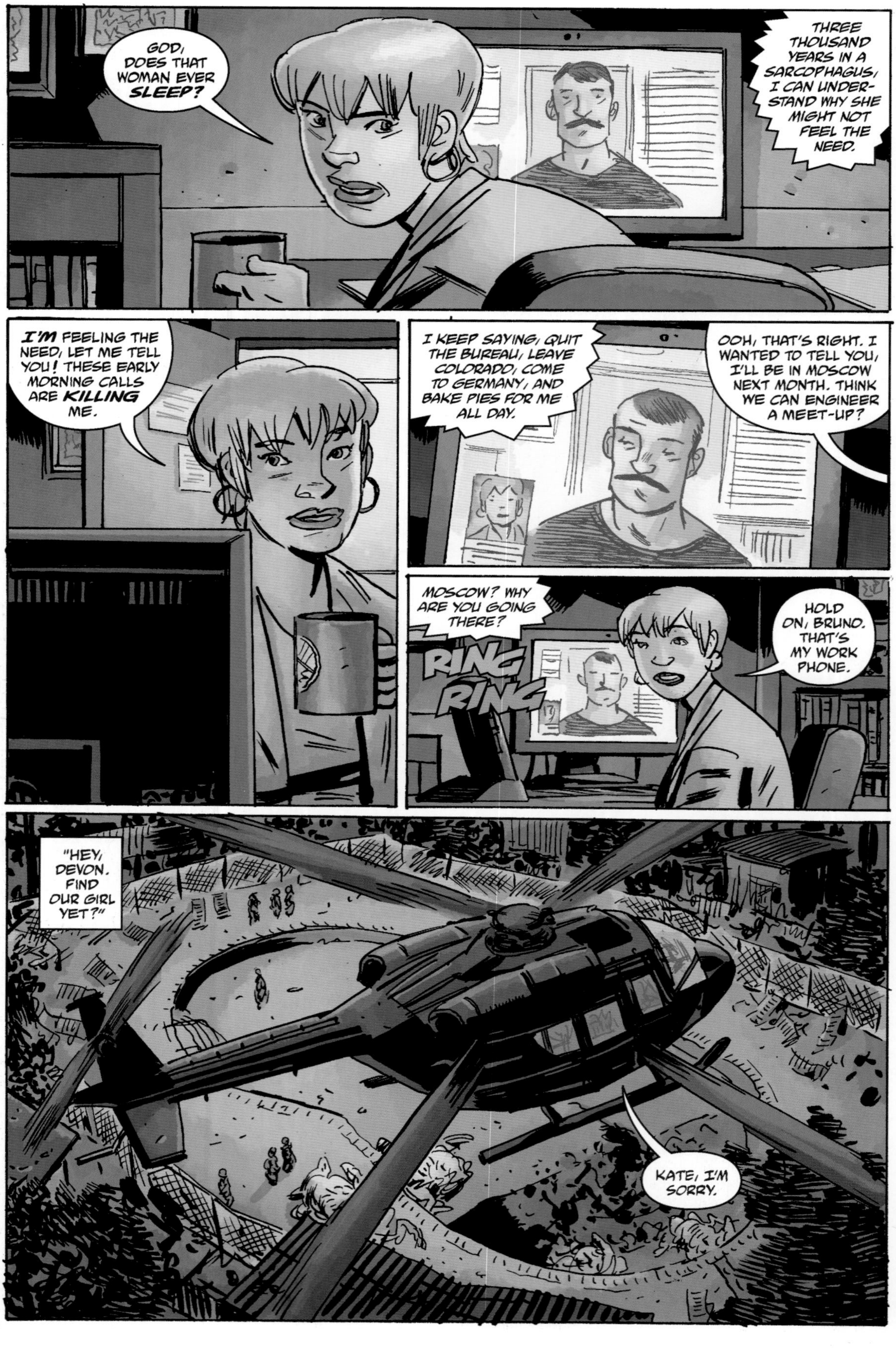
GOD, DOES THAT WOMAN EVER SLEEP?
THREE THOUSAND YEARS IN A SARCOPHAGUS, I CAN UNDER-STAND WHY SHE MIGHT NOT FEEL THE NEED.
I'M FEELING THE NEED, LET ME TELL YOU! THESE EARLY MORNING CALLS ARE KILLING ME.
I KEEP SAYING, QUIT THE BUREAU, LEAVE COLORADO, COME TO GERMANY, AND BAKE PIES FOR ME ALL DAY.
OOH, THAT'S RIGHT. I WANTED TO TELL YOU, I'LL BE IN MOSCOW NEXT MONTH. THINK WE CAN ENGINEER A MEET-UP?
MOSCOW? WHY ARE YOU GOING THERE?
RING RING
HOLD ON, BRUNO. THAT'S MY WORK PHONE.
"HEY, DEVON. FIND OUR GIRL YET?"
KATE, I'M SORRY.

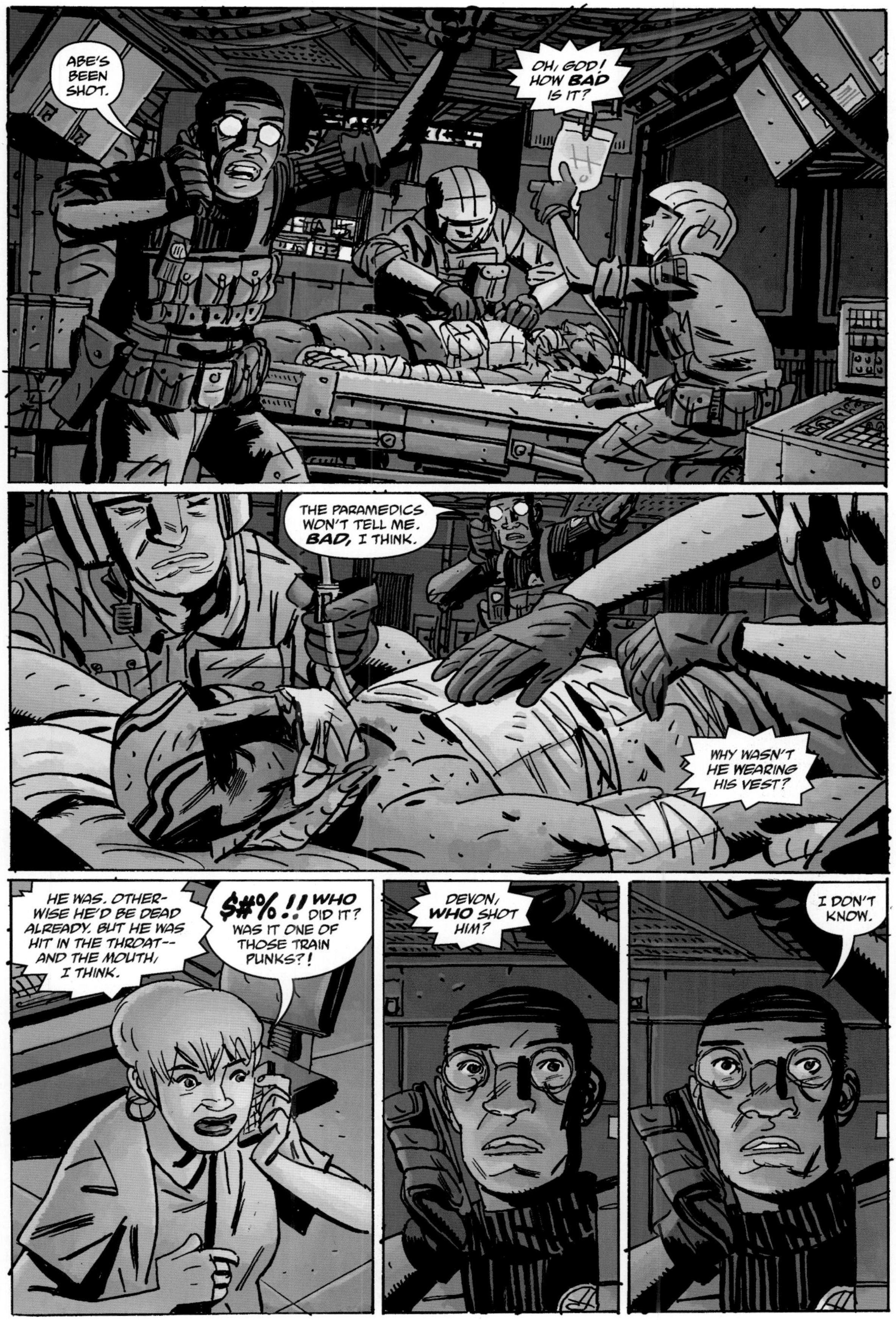
ABE'S BEEN SHOT.
OH, GOD! HOW BAD IS IT?
THE PARAMEDICS WON'T TELL ME. BAD, I THINK.
WHY WASN'T HE WEARING HIS VEST?
HE WAS. OTHERWISE HE'D BE DEAD ALREADY. BUT HE WAS HIT IN THE THROAT-- AND THE MOUTH, I THINK.
$#%!! WHO DID IT? WAS IT ONE OF THOSE TRAIN PUNKS?!
DEVON, WHO SHOT HIM?
I DON'T KNOW.

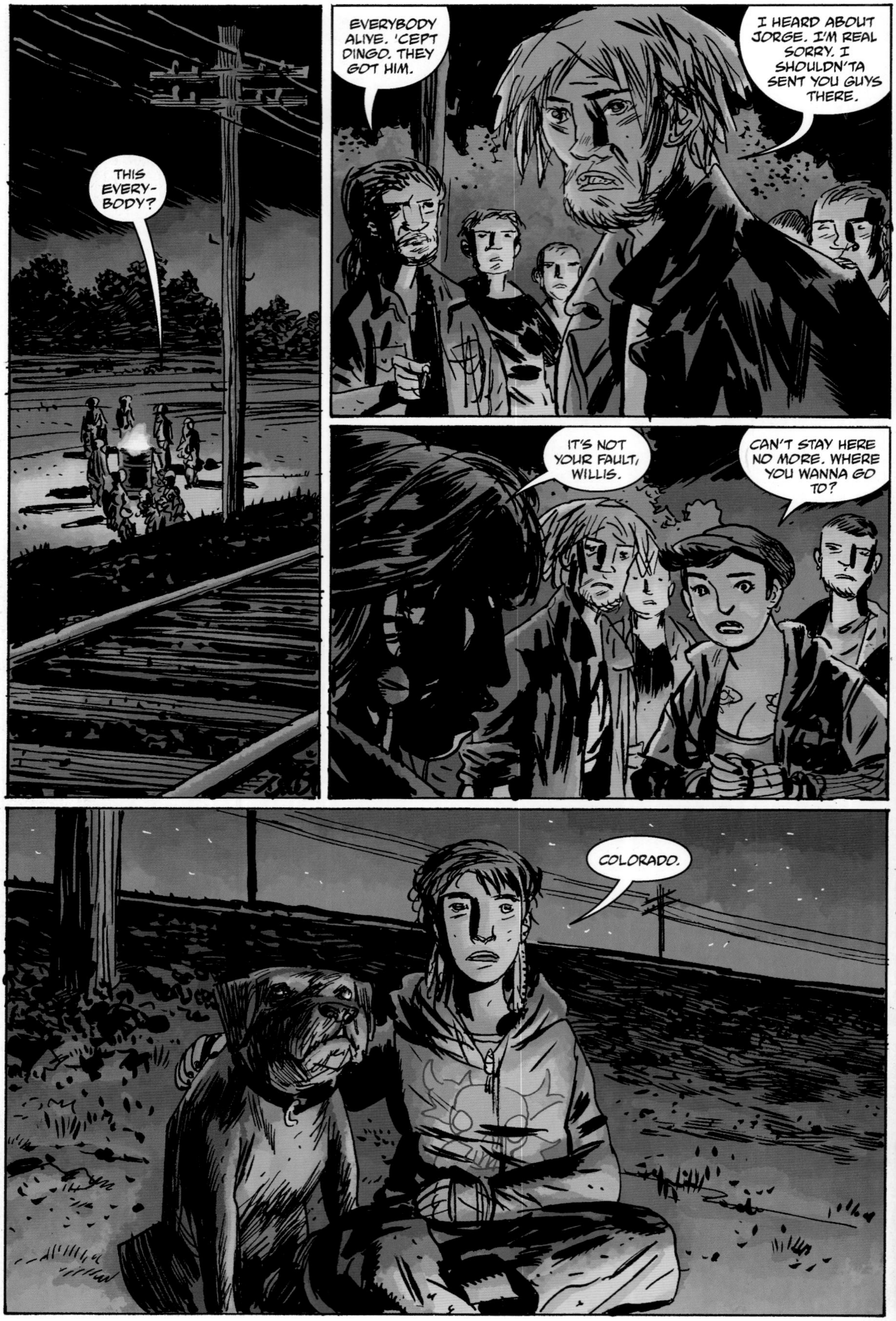
THIS EVERY-BODY?
EVERYBODY ALIVE. 'CEPT DINGO. THEY GOT HIM.
I HEARD ABOUT JORGE. I'M REAL SORRY. I SHOULDN'TA SENT YOU GUYS THERE.
IT'S NOT YOUR FAULT, WILLIS.
CAN'T STAY HERE NO MORE. WHERE YOU WANNA GO TO?
COLORADO.

MONSTERS CHAPTER ONE

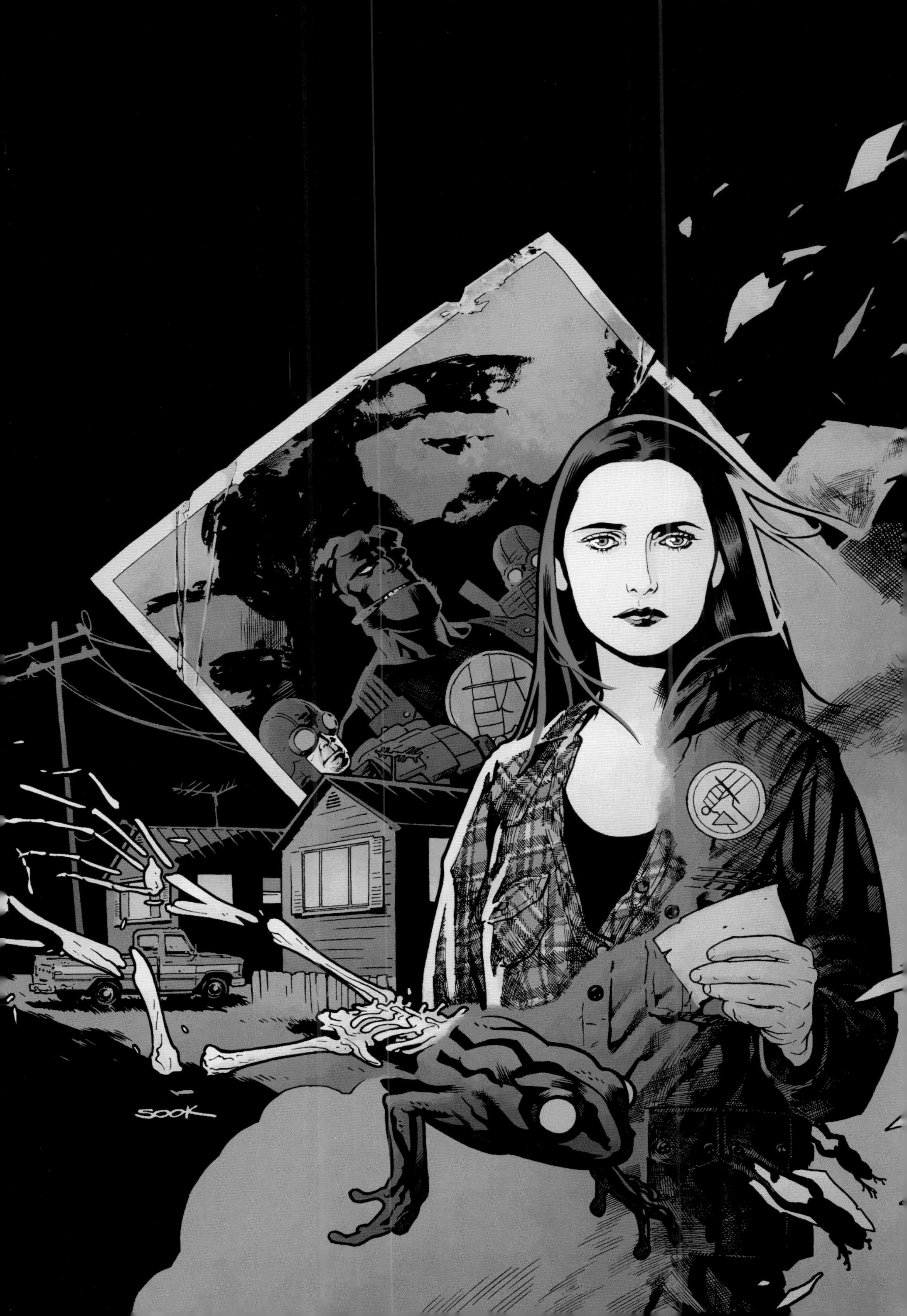
SOOK

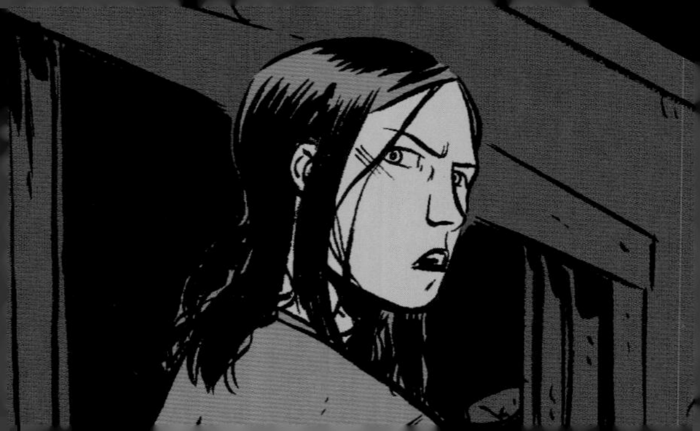

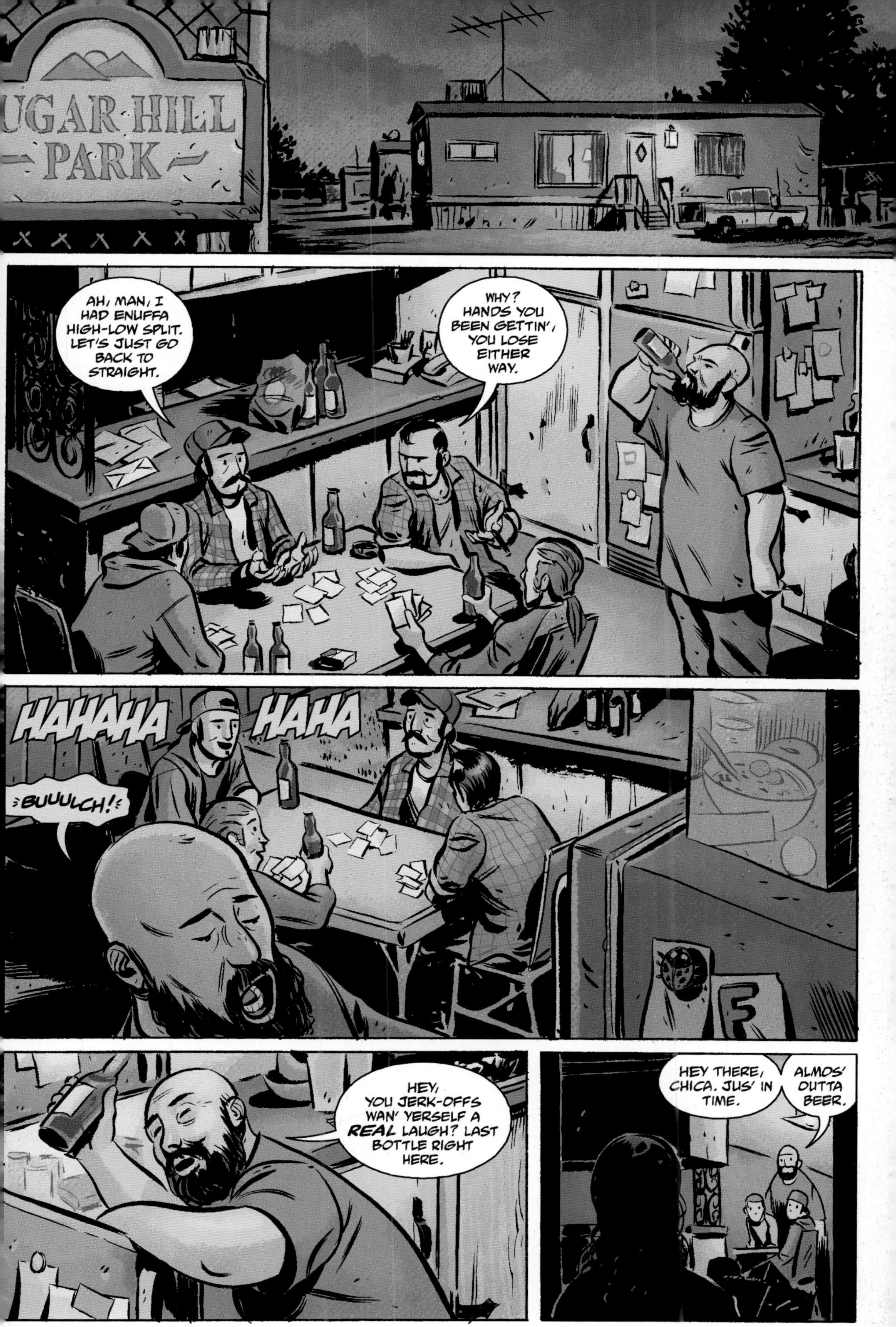
UGAR HILL
PARK
AH, MAN, I HAD ENUFFA HIGH-LOW SPLIT. LET'S JUST GO BACK TO STRAIGHT.
WHY? HANDS YOU BEEN GETTIN', YOU LOSE EITHER WAY.
HAHAHA
HAHA
BUUULCH!
HEY, YOU JERK-OFFS WAN' YERSELF A REAL LAUGH? LAST BOTTLE RIGHT HERE.
HEY THERE, CHICA. JUS' IN TIME.
ALMOS' OUTTA BEER.

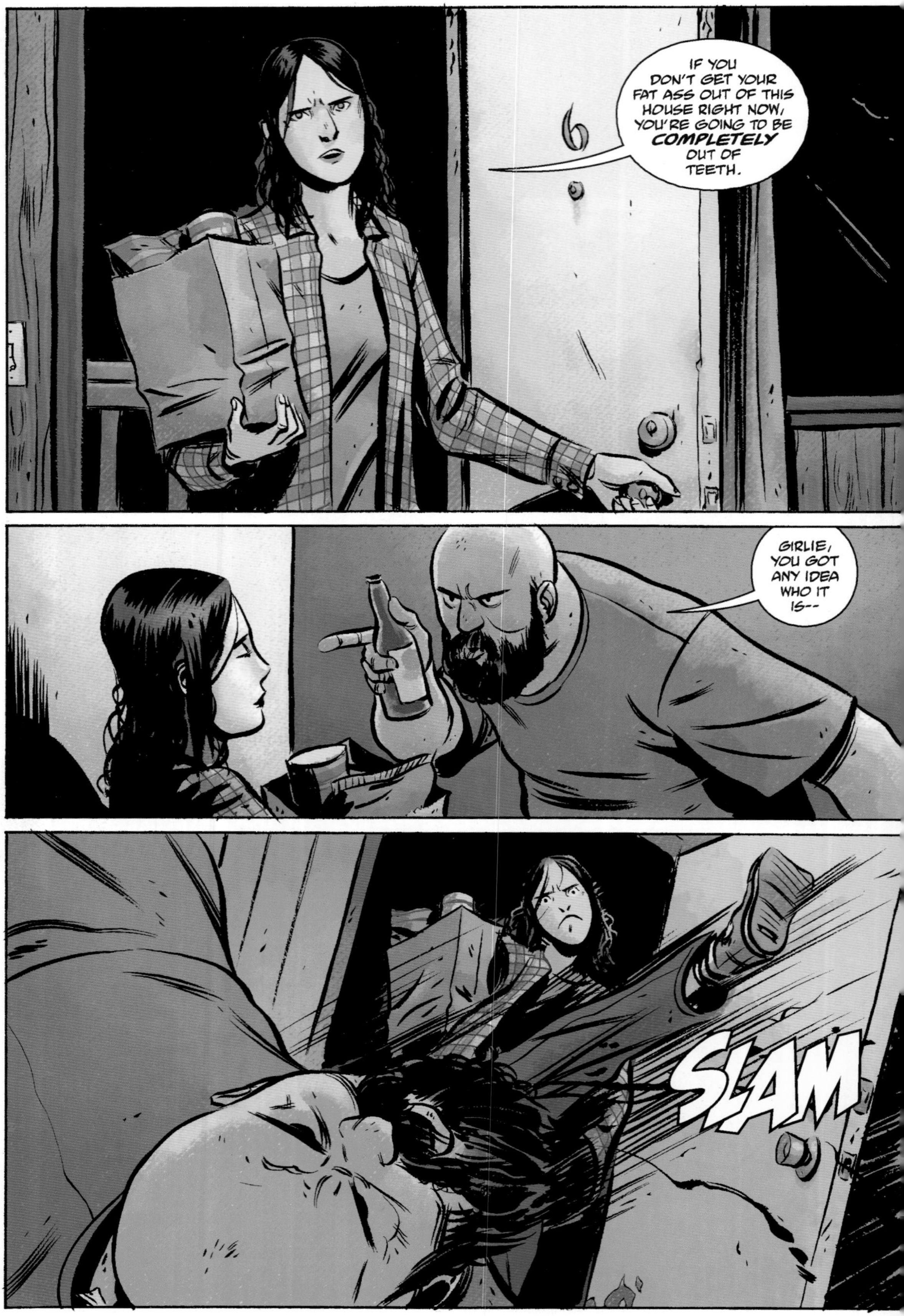
IF YOU DON'T GET YOUR FAT ASS OUT OF THIS HOUSE RIGHT NOW, YOU'RE GOING TO BE *COMPLETELY* OUT OF TEETH.
GIRLIE, YOU GOT ANY IDEA WHO IT IS--
SLAM

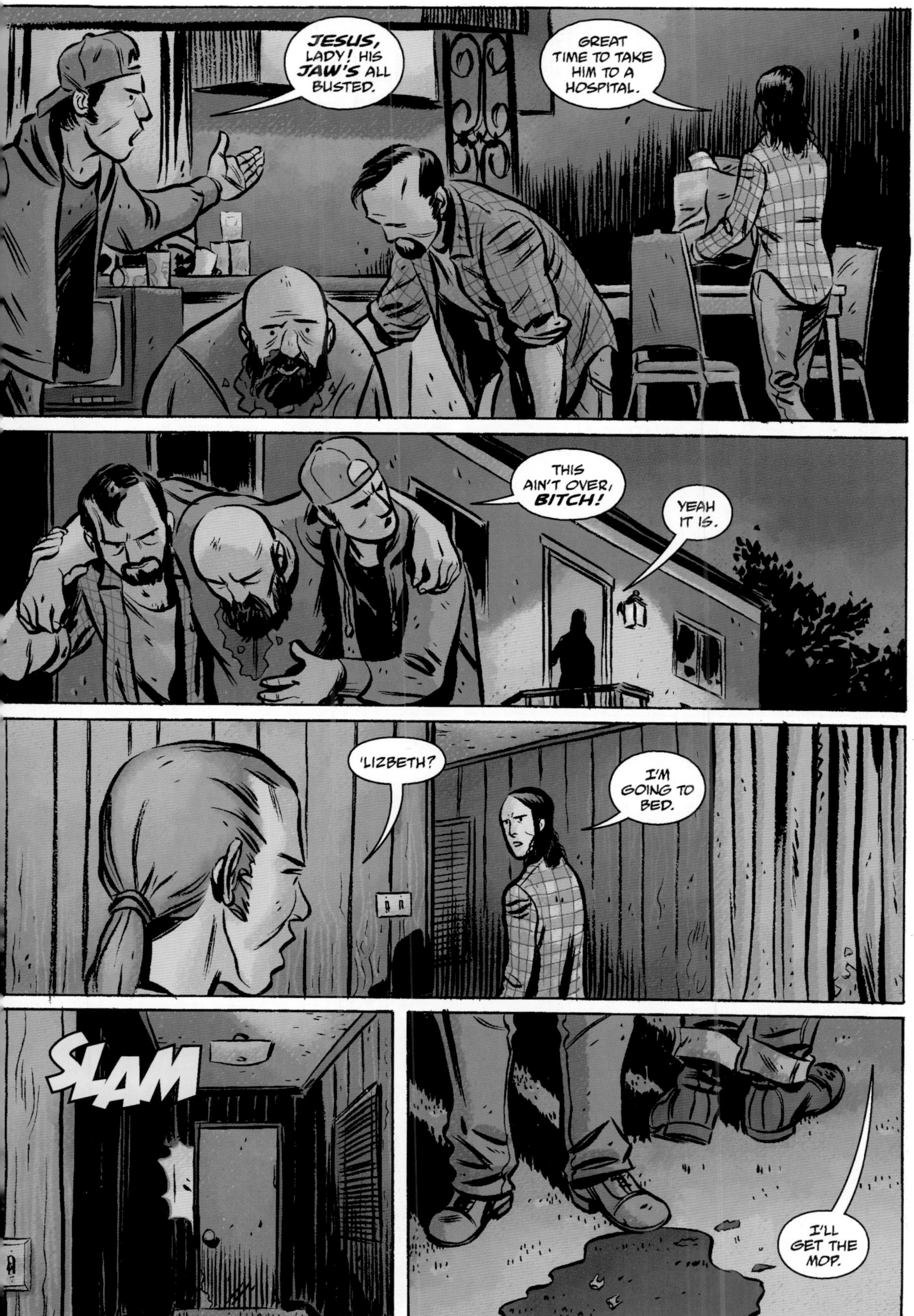
JESUS, LADY! HIS JAW'S ALL BUSTED.
GREAT TIME TO TAKE HIM TO A HOSPITAL.
THIS AIN'T OVER, BITCH!
YEAH IT IS.
'LIZBETH?
I'M GOING TO BED.
SLAM
I'LL GET THE MOP.

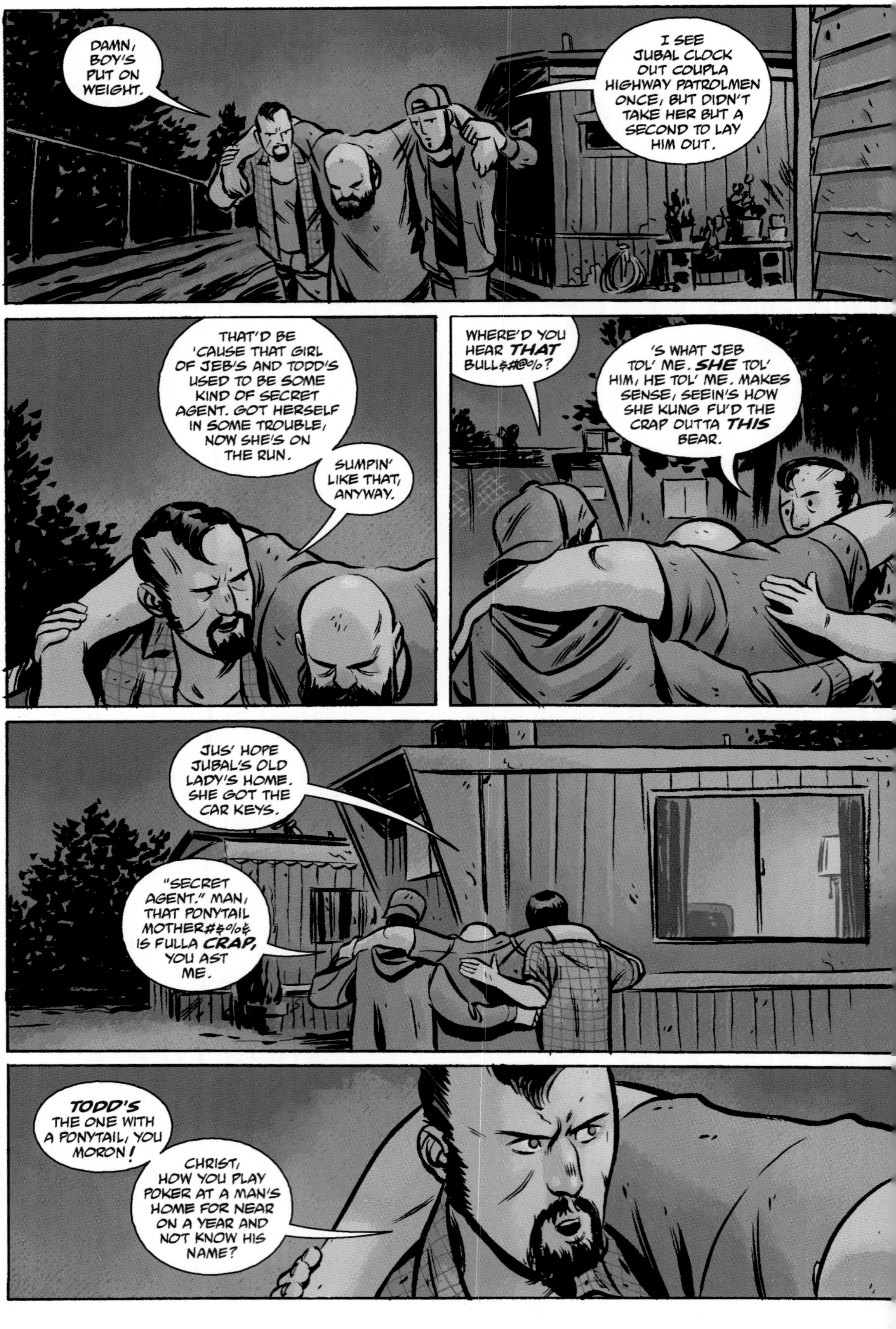
DAMN, BOY'S PUT ON WEIGHT.
I SEE JUBAL CLOCK OUT COUPLA HIGHWAY PATROLMEN ONCE, BUT DIDN'T TAKE HER BUT A SECOND TO LAY HIM OUT.
THAT'D BE 'CAUSE THAT GIRL OF JEB'S AND TODD'S USED TO BE SOME KIND OF SECRET AGENT. GOT HERSELF IN SOME TROUBLE, NOW SHE'S ON THE RUN.
SUMPIN' LIKE THAT, ANYWAY.
WHERE'D YOU HEAR THAT BULL$#@%?
'S WHAT JEB TOL' ME. SHE TOL' HIM, HE TOL' ME. MAKES SENSE, SEEIN'S HOW SHE KUNG FU'D THE CRAP OUTTA THIS BEAR.
JUS' HOPE JUBAL'S OLD LADY'S HOME. SHE GOT THE CAR KEYS.
"SECRET AGENT." MAN, THAT PONYTAIL MOTHER#$%& IS FULLA CRAP, YOU AST ME.
TODD'S THE ONE WITH A PONYTAIL, YOU MORON!
CHRIST, HOW YOU PLAY POKER AT A MAN'S HOME FOR NEAR ON A YEAR AND NOT KNOW HIS NAME?

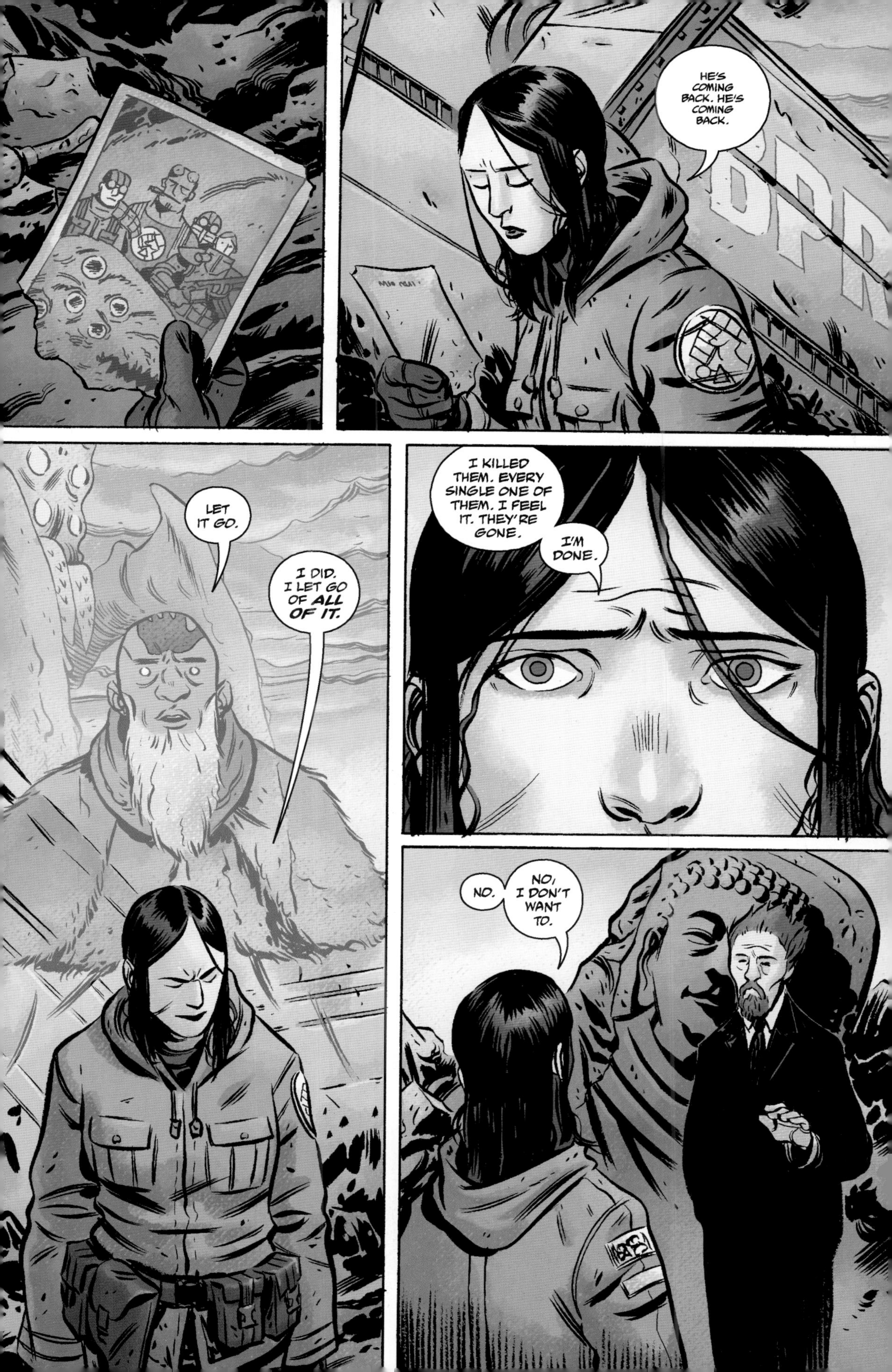
HE'S COMING BACK. HE'S COMING BACK.
LET IT GO.
I DID. I LET GO OF **ALL OF IT.**
I KILLED THEM. EVERY SINGLE ONE OF THEM. I FEEL IT. THEY'RE GONE.
I'M DONE.
NO.
NO, I DON'T WANT TO.

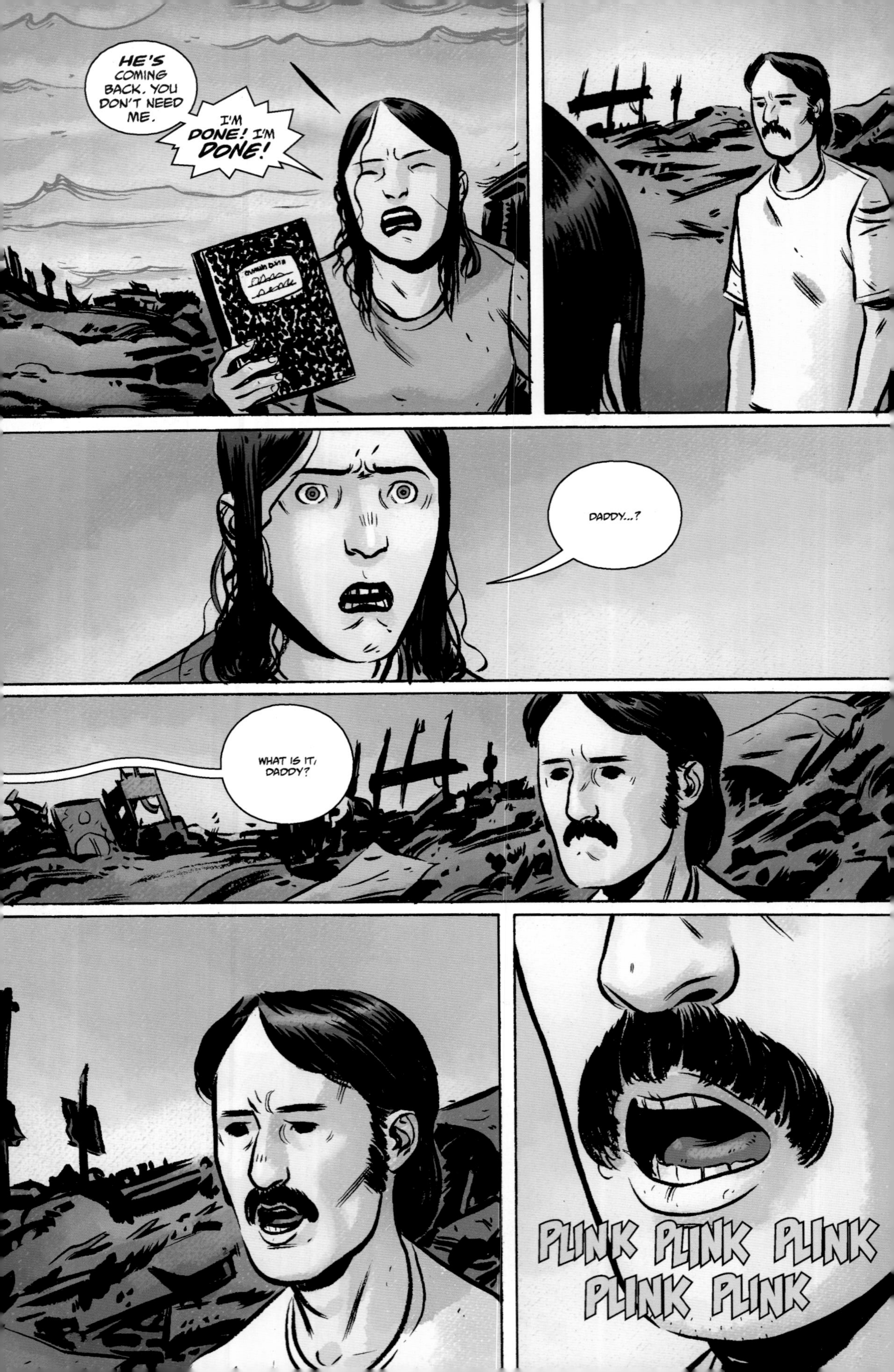
HE'S COMING BACK. YOU DON'T NEED ME.
I'M DONE! I'M DONE!
DADDY...?
WHAT IS IT, DADDY?
PLINK PLINK PLINK
PLINK PLINK

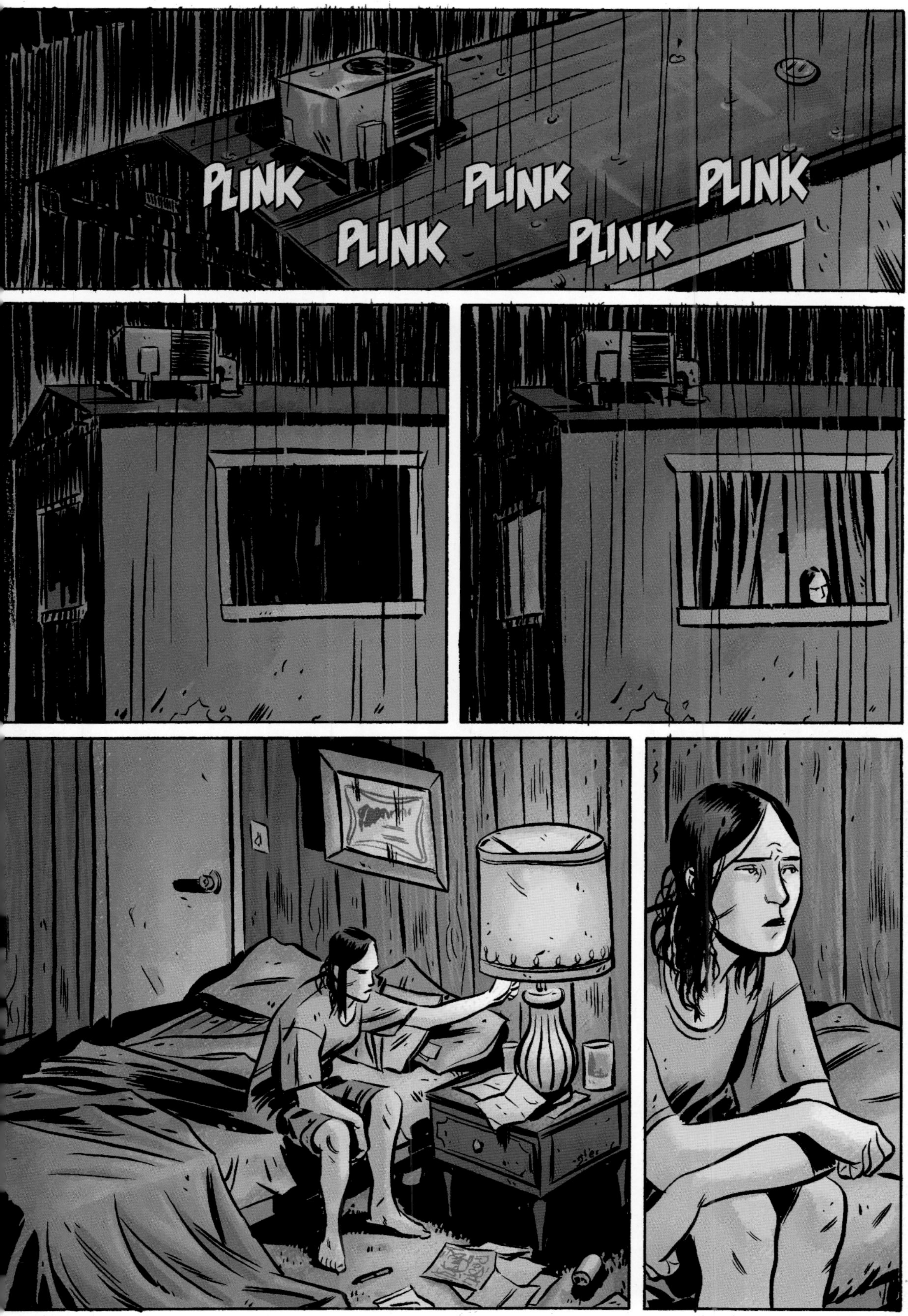
PLINK
PLINK
PLINK
PLINK
PLINK

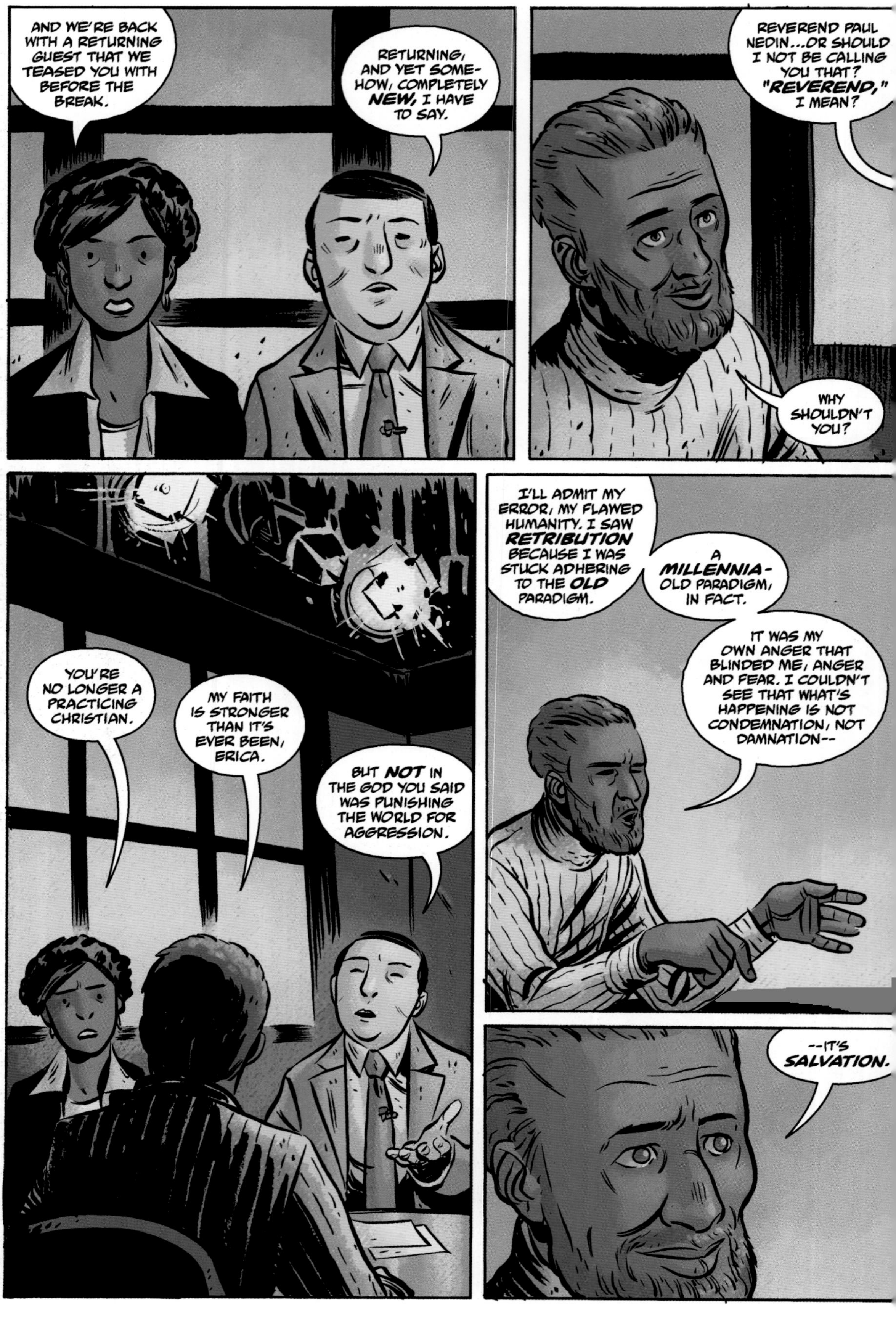
AND WE'RE BACK WITH A RETURNING GUEST THAT WE TEASED YOU WITH BEFORE THE BREAK.
RETURNING, AND YET SOME-HOW, COMPLETELY NEW, I HAVE TO SAY.
REVEREND PAUL NEDIN...OR SHOULD I NOT BE CALLING YOU THAT? "REVEREND," I MEAN?
WHY SHOULDN'T YOU?
YOU'RE NO LONGER A PRACTICING CHRISTIAN.
MY FAITH IS STRONGER THAN IT'S EVER BEEN, ERICA.
BUT NOT IN THE GOD YOU SAID WAS PUNISHING THE WORLD FOR AGGRESSION.
I'LL ADMIT MY ERROR, MY FLAWED HUMANITY. I SAW RETRIBUTION BECAUSE I WAS STUCK ADHERING TO THE OLD PARADIGM.
A MILLENNIA-OLD PARADIGM, IN FACT.
IT WAS MY OWN ANGER THAT BLINDED ME, ANGER AND FEAR. I COULDN'T SEE THAT WHAT'S HAPPENING IS NOT CONDEMNATION, NOT DAMNATION--
--IT'S SALVATION.

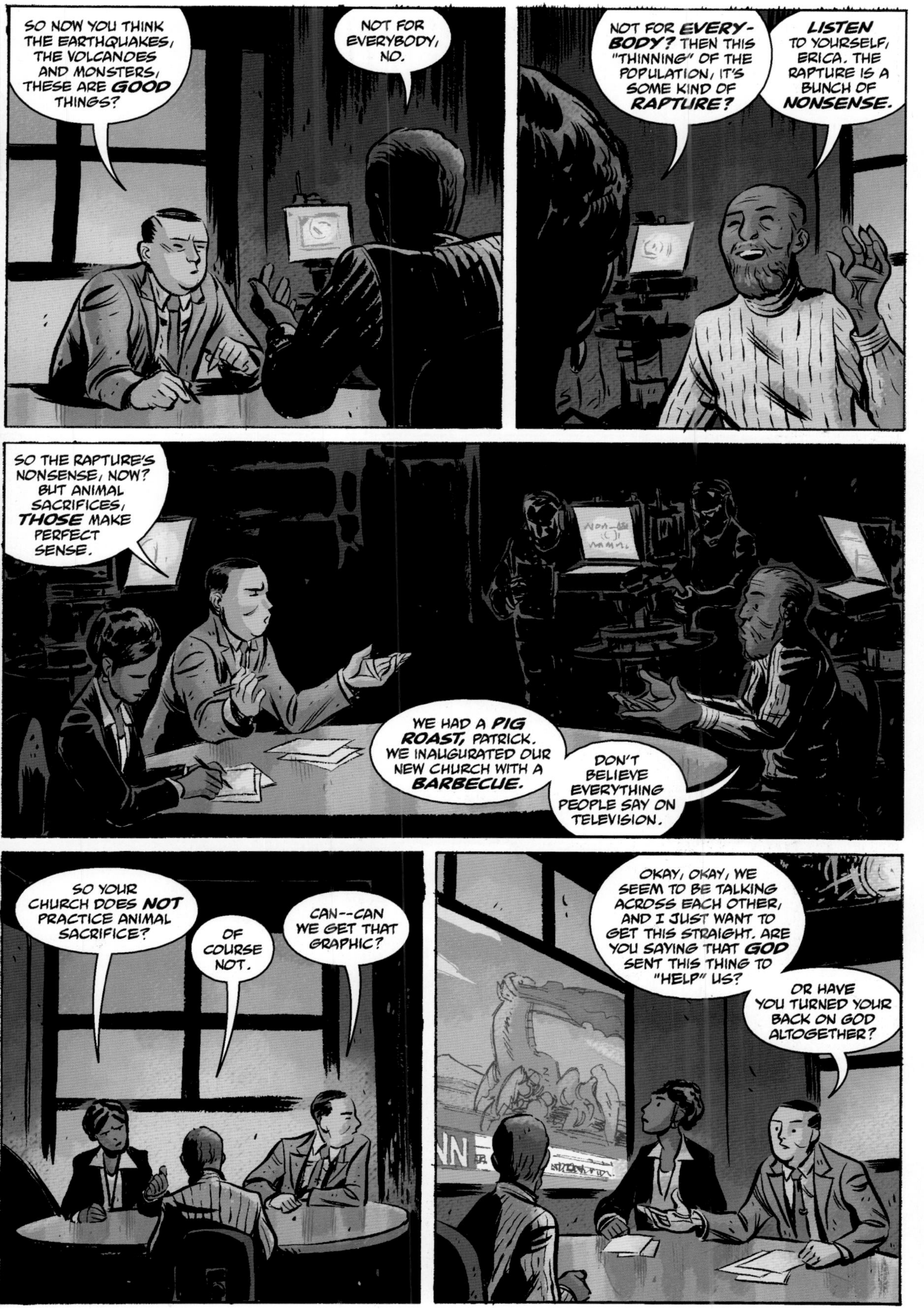
SO NOW YOU THINK THE EARTHQUAKES, THE VOLCANOES AND MONSTERS, THESE ARE GOOD THINGS?
NOT FOR EVERYBODY, NO.
NOT FOR EVERY-BODY? THEN THIS "THINNING" OF THE POPULATION, IT'S SOME KIND OF RAPTURE?
LISTEN TO YOURSELF, ERICA. THE RAPTURE IS A BUNCH OF NONSENSE.
SO THE RAPTURE'S NONSENSE, NOW? BUT ANIMAL SACRIFICES, THOSE MAKE PERFECT SENSE.
WE HAD A PIG ROAST, PATRICK. WE INAUGURATED OUR NEW CHURCH WITH A BARBECUE.
DON'T BELIEVE EVERYTHING PEOPLE SAY ON TELEVISION.
SO YOUR CHURCH DOES NOT PRACTICE ANIMAL SACRIFICE?
OF COURSE NOT.
CAN--CAN WE GET THAT GRAPHIC?
OKAY, OKAY, WE SEEM TO BE TALKING ACROSS EACH OTHER, AND I JUST WANT TO GET THIS STRAIGHT. ARE YOU SAYING THAT GOD SENT THIS THING TO "HELP" US?
OR HAVE YOU TURNED YOUR BACK ON GOD ALTOGETHER?

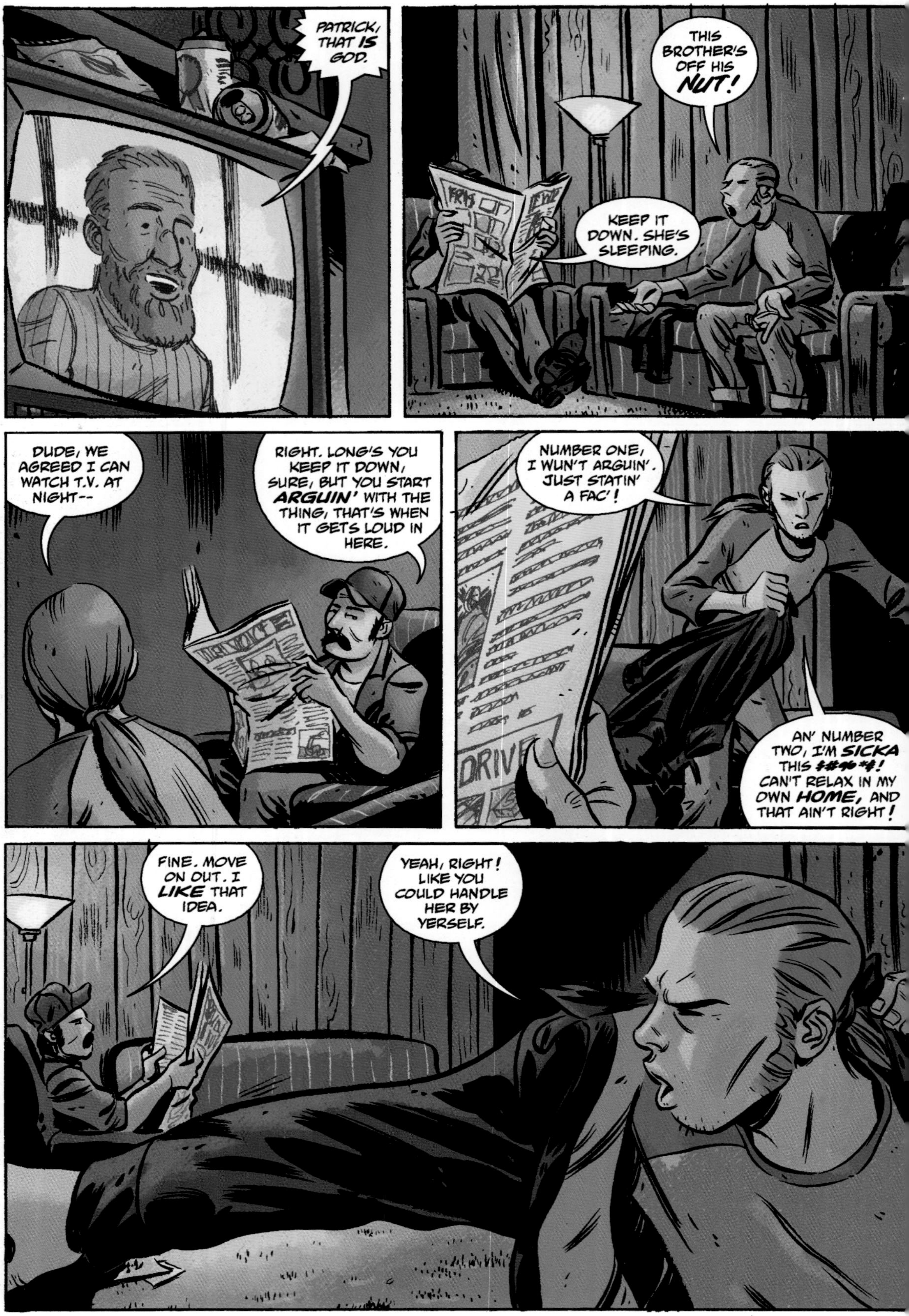
PATRICK, THAT IS GOD.
THIS BROTHER'S OFF HIS NUT!
KEEP IT DOWN. SHE'S SLEEPING.
DUDE, WE AGREED I CAN WATCH T.V. AT NIGHT--
RIGHT. LONG'S YOU KEEP IT DOWN, SURE, BUT YOU START ARGUIN' WITH THE THING, THAT'S WHEN IT GETS LOUD IN HERE.
NUMBER ONE, I WUN'T ARGUIN'. JUST STATIN' A FAC'!
AN' NUMBER TWO, I'M SICKA THIS $#%*#! CAN'T RELAX IN MY OWN HOME, AND THAT AIN'T RIGHT!
FINE. MOVE ON OUT. I LIKE THAT IDEA.
YEAH, RIGHT! LIKE YOU COULD HANDLE HER BY YERSELF.

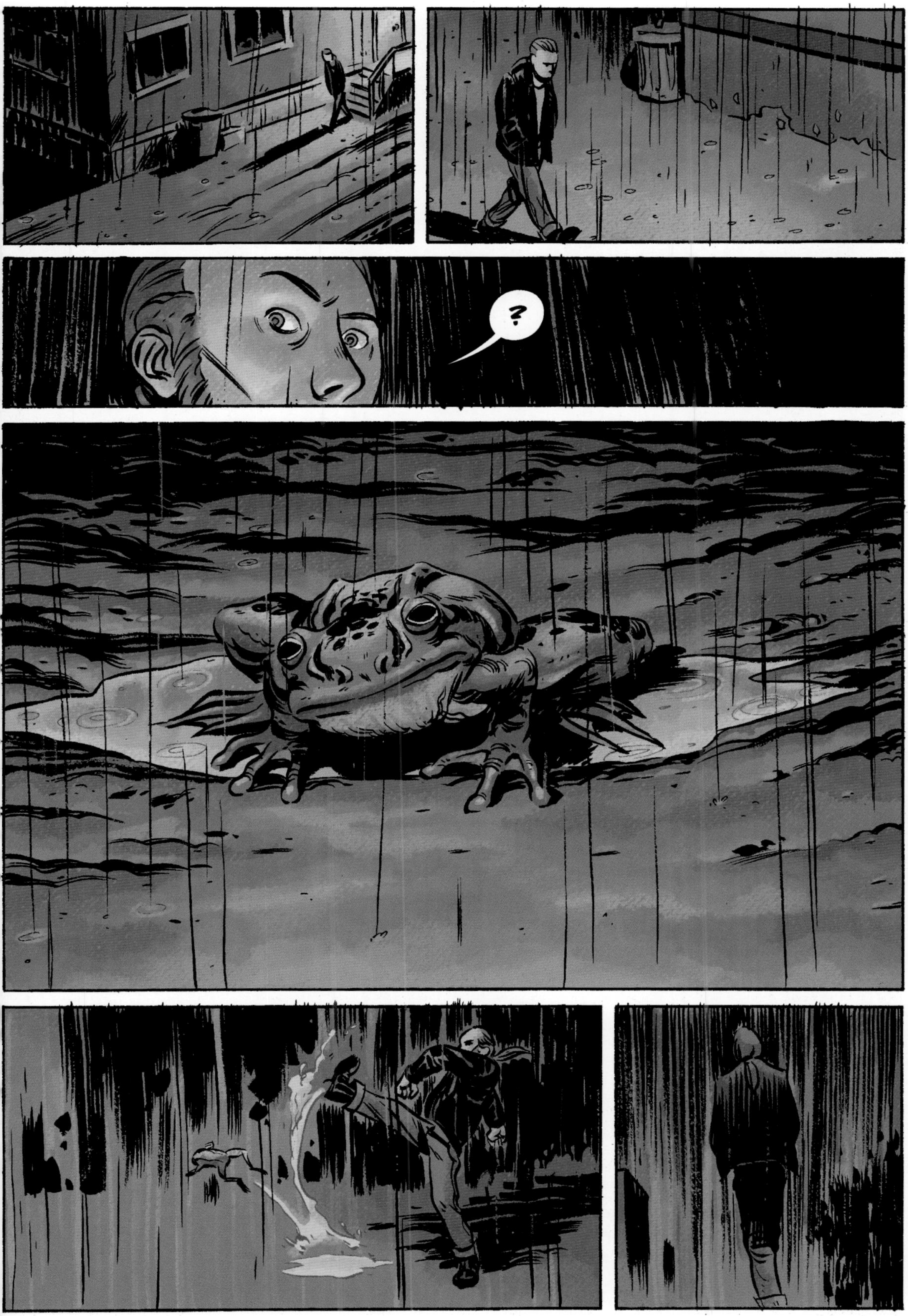
?

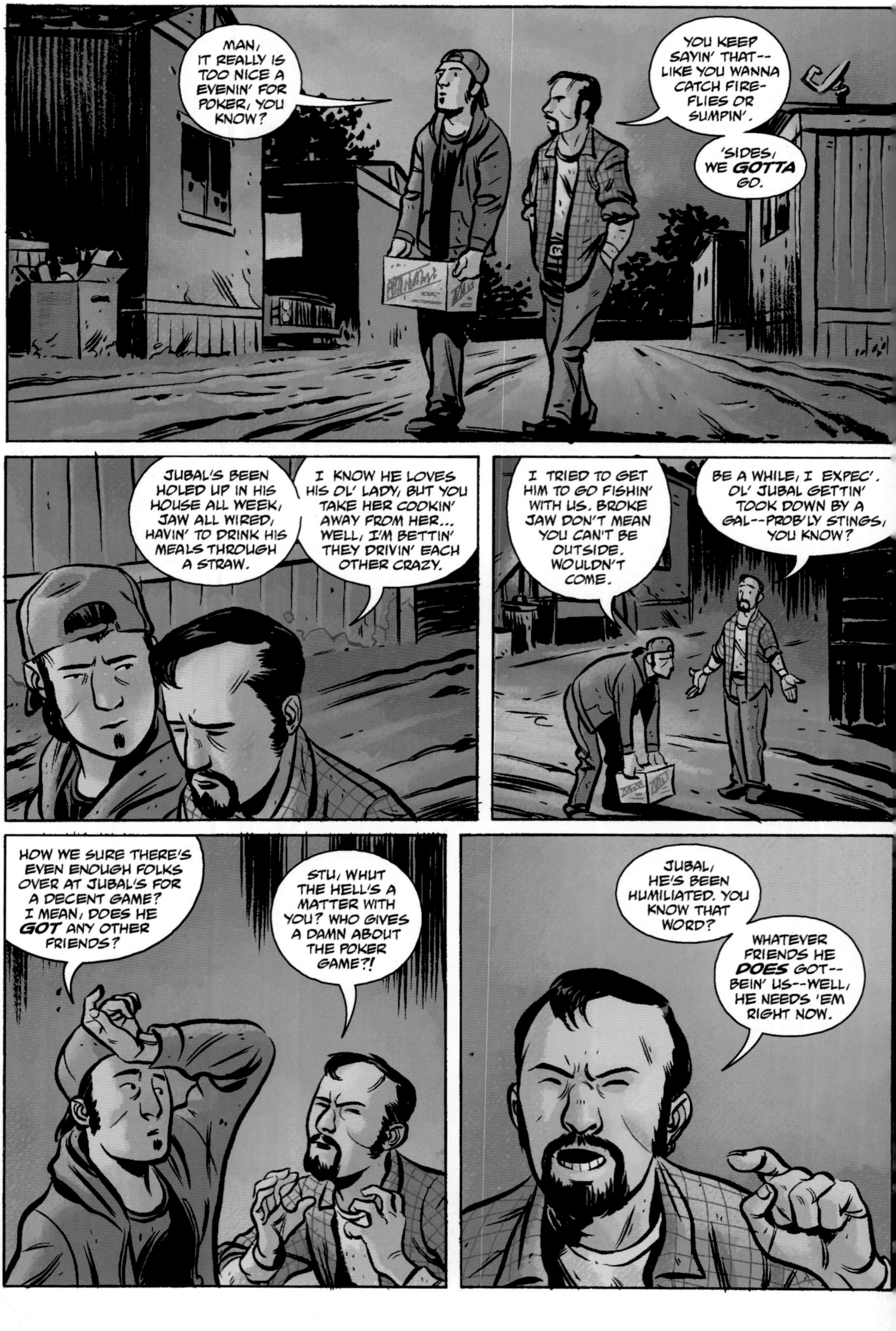
MAN, IT REALLY IS TOO NICE A EVENIN' FOR POKER, YOU KNOW?
YOU KEEP SAYIN' THAT--LIKE YOU WANNA CATCH FIRE-FLIES OR SUMPIN'.
'SIDES, WE GOTTA GO.
JUBAL'S BEEN HOLED UP IN HIS HOUSE ALL WEEK, JAW ALL WIRED, HAVIN' TO DRINK HIS MEALS THROUGH A STRAW.
I KNOW HE LOVES HIS OL' LADY, BUT YOU TAKE HER COOKIN' AWAY FROM HER... WELL, I'M BETTIN' THEY DRIVIN' EACH OTHER CRAZY.
I TRIED TO GET HIM TO GO FISHIN' WITH US. BROKE JAW DON'T MEAN YOU CAN'T BE OUTSIDE. WOULDN'T COME.
BE A WHILE, I EXPEC'. OL' JUBAL GETTIN' TOOK DOWN BY A GAL--PROB'LY STINGS, YOU KNOW?
HOW WE SURE THERE'S EVEN ENOUGH FOLKS OVER AT JUBAL'S FOR A DECENT GAME? I MEAN, DOES HE GOT ANY OTHER FRIENDS?
STU, WHUT THE HELL'S A MATTER WITH YOU? WHO GIVES A DAMN ABOUT THE POKER GAME?!
JUBAL, HE'S BEEN HUMILIATED. YOU KNOW THAT WORD?
WHATEVER FRIENDS HE DOES GOT--BEIN' US--WELL, HE NEEDS 'EM RIGHT NOW.

COME ON, YOU DUMBASS!

I KNOW WHAT "HUMILIATED" MEANS.

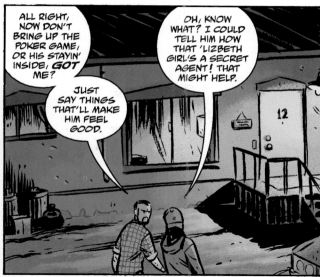

ALL RIGHT, NOW DON'T BRING UP THE POKER GAME, OR HIS STAYIN' INSIDE, *GOT* ME?

JUST SAY THINGS THAT'LL MAKE HIM FEEL GOOD.

OH, KNOW WHAT? I COULD TELL HIM HOW THAT 'LIZBETH GIRL'S A SECRET AGENT! THAT MIGHT HELP.

I GOT A BETTER IDEA. HOW 'BOUT YOU LEAVE THE TALKIN'...

¢#!%...

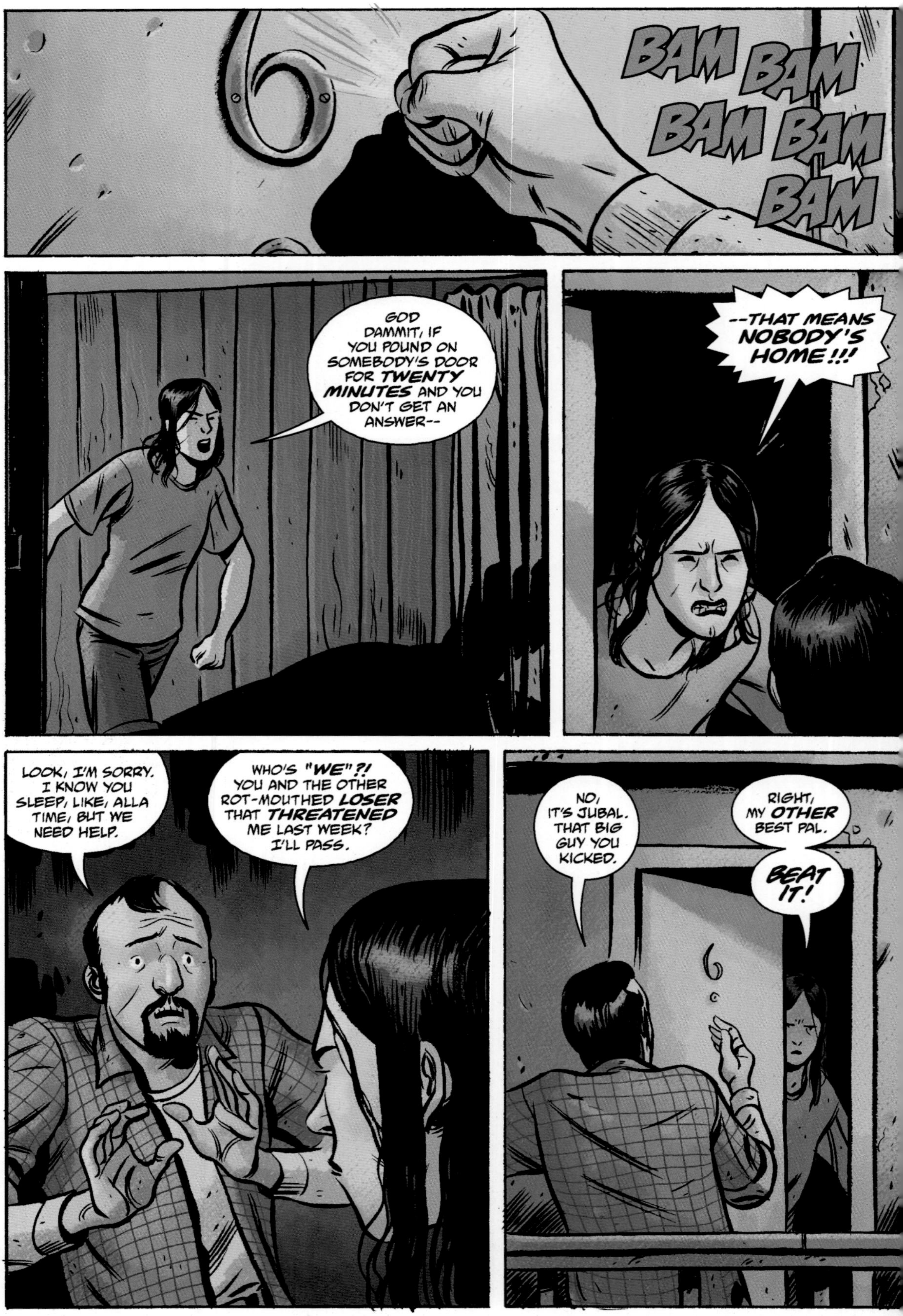
BAM BAM BAM BAM BAM
GOD DAMMIT, IF YOU POUND ON SOMEBODY'S DOOR FOR TWENTY MINUTES AND YOU DON'T GET AN ANSWER--
--THAT MEANS NOBODY'S HOME!!!
LOOK, I'M SORRY. I KNOW YOU SLEEP, LIKE, ALLA TIME, BUT WE NEED HELP.
WHO'S "WE"?! YOU AND THE OTHER ROT-MOUTHED LOSER THAT THREATENED ME LAST WEEK? I'LL PASS.
NO, IT'S JUBAL. THAT BIG GUY YOU KICKED.
RIGHT, MY OTHER BEST PAL.
BEAT IT!

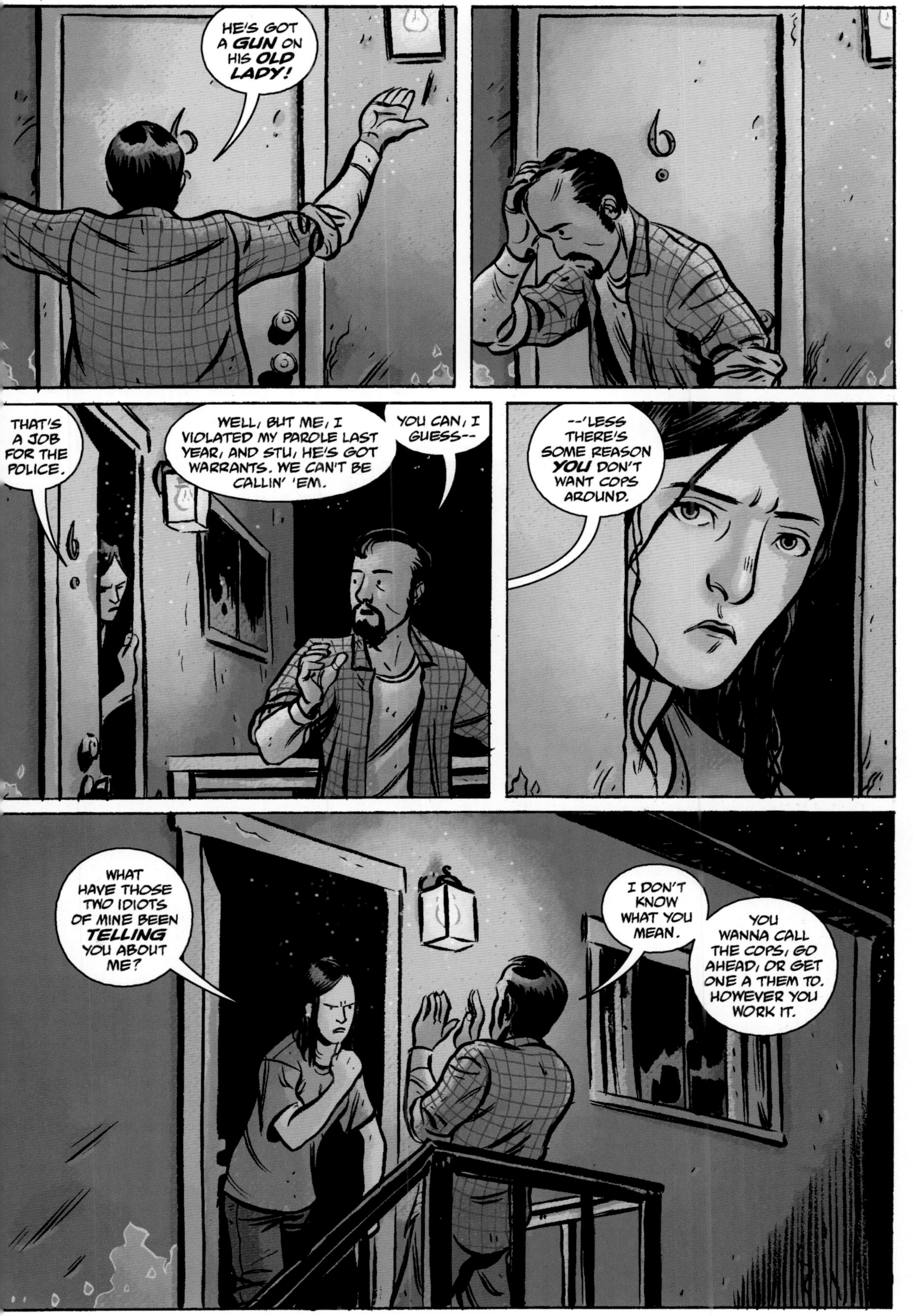
HE'S GOT A GUN ON HIS OLD LADY!
THAT'S A JOB FOR THE POLICE.
WELL, BUT ME, I VIOLATED MY PAROLE LAST YEAR, AND STU, HE'S GOT WARRANTS. WE CAN'T BE CALLIN' 'EM.
YOU CAN, I GUESS--
--'LESS THERE'S SOME REASON YOU DON'T WANT COPS AROUND.
WHAT HAVE THOSE TWO IDIOTS OF MINE BEEN TELLING YOU ABOUT ME?
I DON'T KNOW WHAT YOU MEAN.
YOU WANNA CALL THE COPS, GO AHEAD, OR GET ONE A THEM TO. HOWEVER YOU WORK IT.

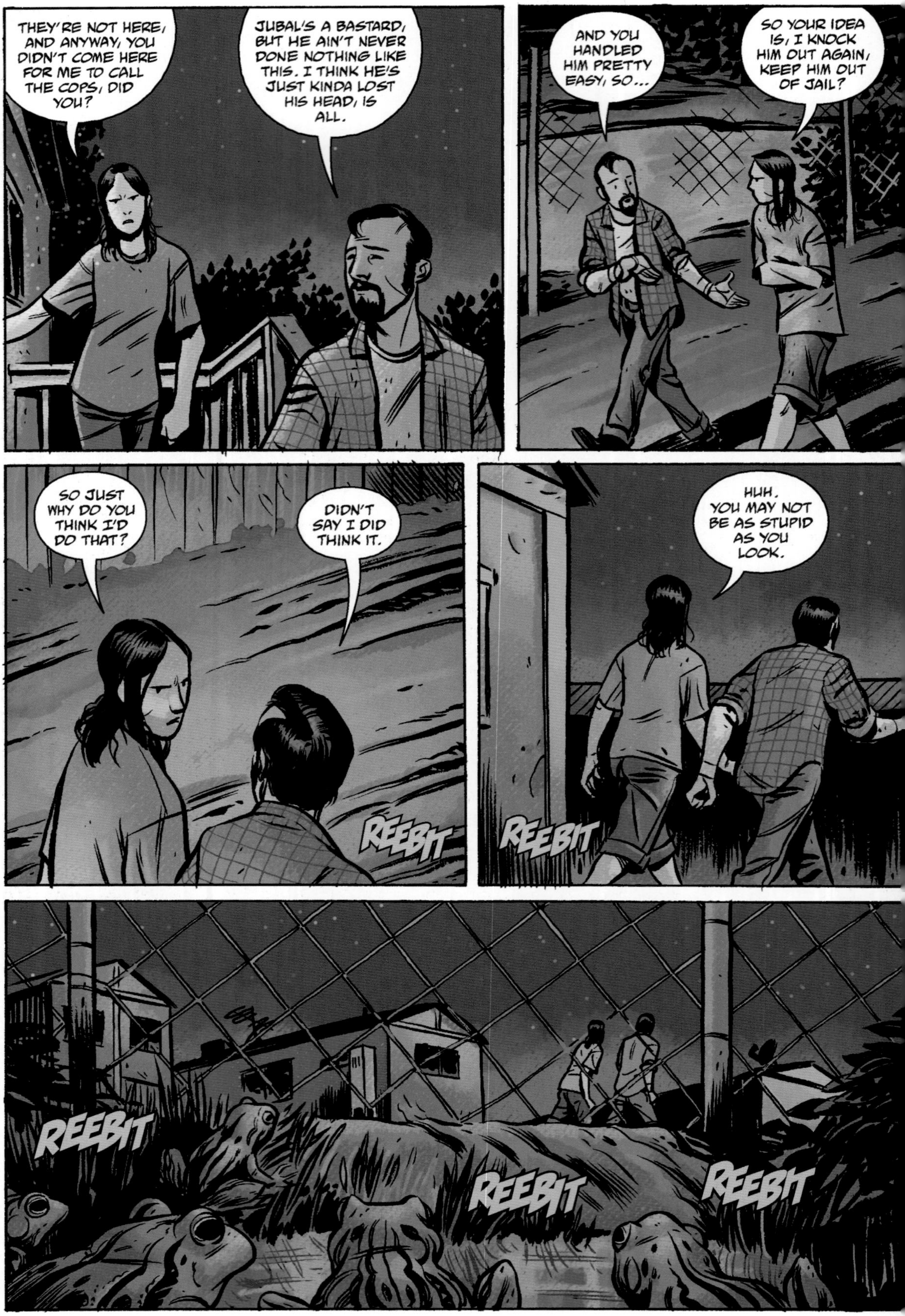
THEY'RE NOT HERE, AND ANYWAY, YOU DIDN'T COME HERE FOR ME TO CALL THE COPS, DID YOU?
JUBAL'S A BASTARD, BUT HE AIN'T NEVER DONE NOTHING LIKE THIS. I THINK HE'S JUST KINDA LOST HIS HEAD, IS ALL.
AND YOU HANDLED HIM PRETTY EASY, SO...
SO YOUR IDEA IS, I KNOCK HIM OUT AGAIN, KEEP HIM OUT OF JAIL?
SO JUST WHY DO YOU THINK I'D DO THAT?
DIDN'T SAY I DID THINK IT.
REEBIT
HUH. YOU MAY NOT BE AS STUPID AS YOU LOOK.
REEBIT
REEBIT
REEBIT
REEBIT

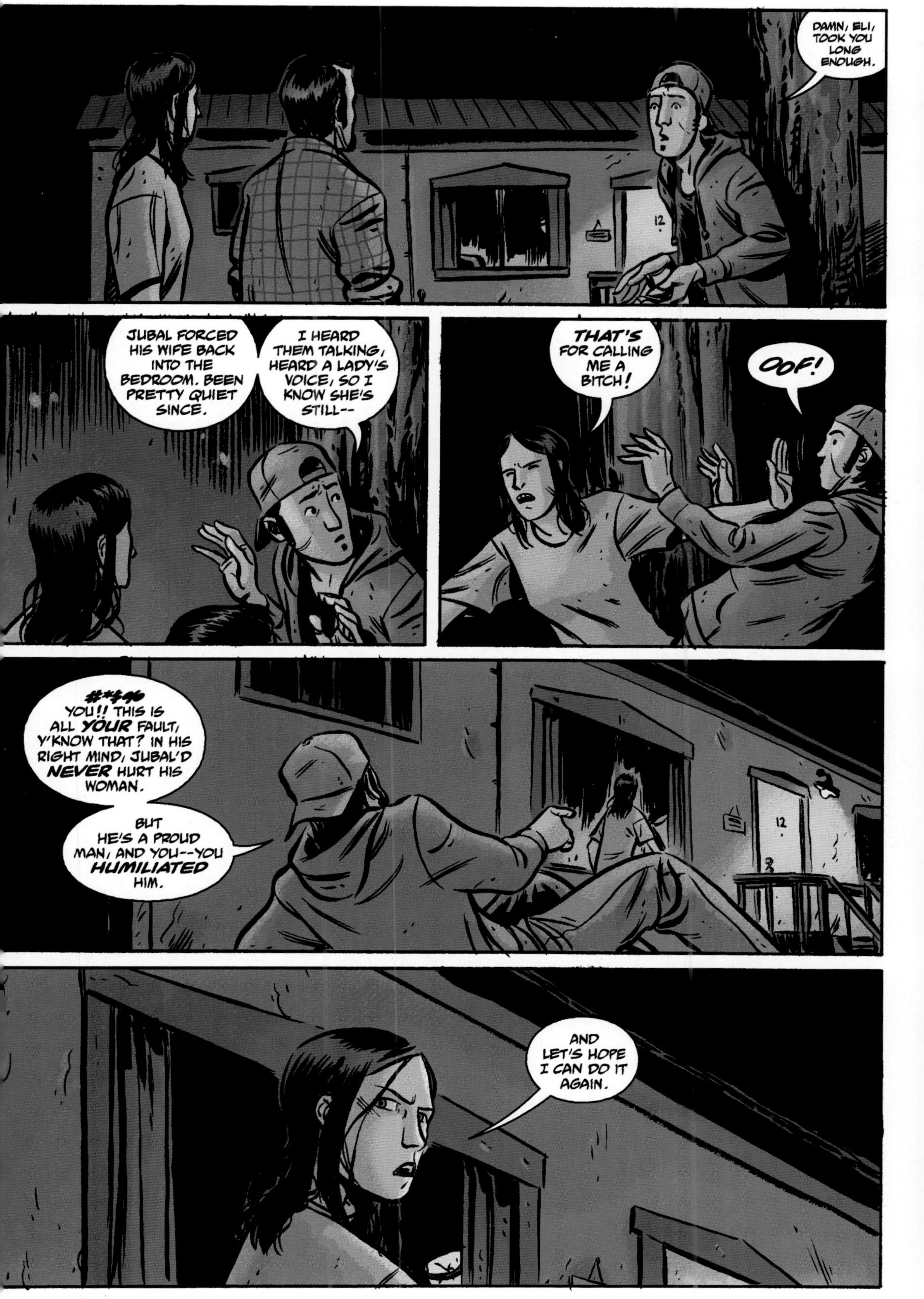
DAMN, ELI, TOOK YOU LONG ENOUGH.
12
JUBAL FORCED HIS WIFE BACK INTO THE BEDROOM. BEEN PRETTY QUIET SINCE.
I HEARD THEM TALKING, HEARD A LADY'S VOICE, SO I KNOW SHE'S STILL--
THAT'S FOR CALLING ME A BITCH!
OOF!
#*$%
YOU!! THIS IS ALL YOUR FAULT, Y'KNOW THAT? IN HIS RIGHT MIND, JUBAL'D NEVER HURT HIS WOMAN.
BUT HE'S A PROUD MAN, AND YOU--YOU HUMILIATED HIM.
12
AND LET'S HOPE I CAN DO IT AGAIN.

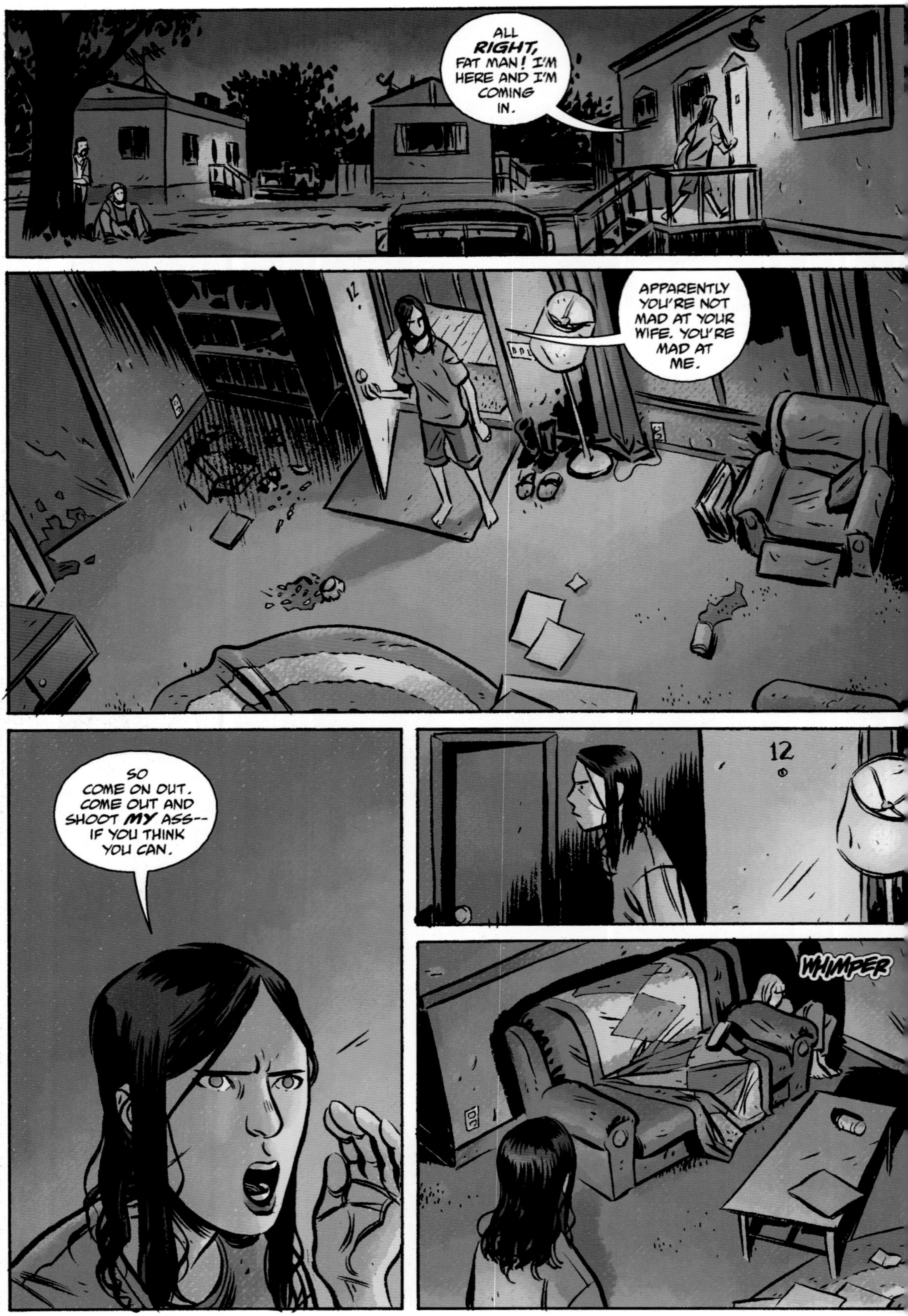
ALL RIGHT, FAT MAN! I'M HERE AND I'M COMING IN.
APPARENTLY YOU'RE NOT MAD AT YOUR WIFE. YOU'RE MAD AT ME.
SO COME ON OUT. COME OUT AND SHOOT MY ASS-- IF YOU THINK YOU CAN.
12
WHIMPER

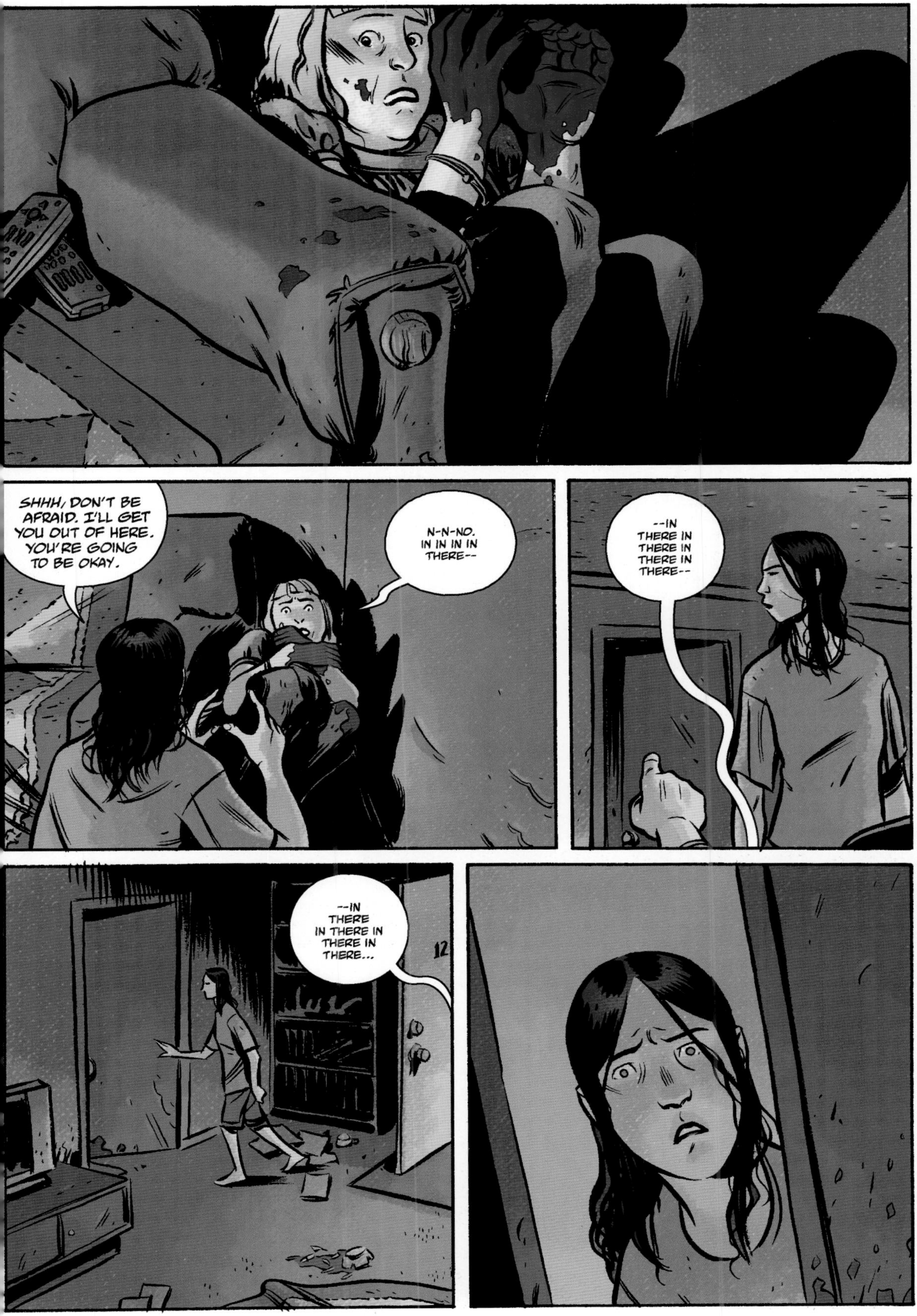
SHHH, DON'T BE AFRAID. I'LL GET YOU OUT OF HERE. YOU'RE GOING TO BE OKAY.
N-N-NO. IN IN IN IN THERE--
--IN THERE IN THERE IN THERE IN THERE--
--IN THERE IN THERE IN THERE IN THERE...
12

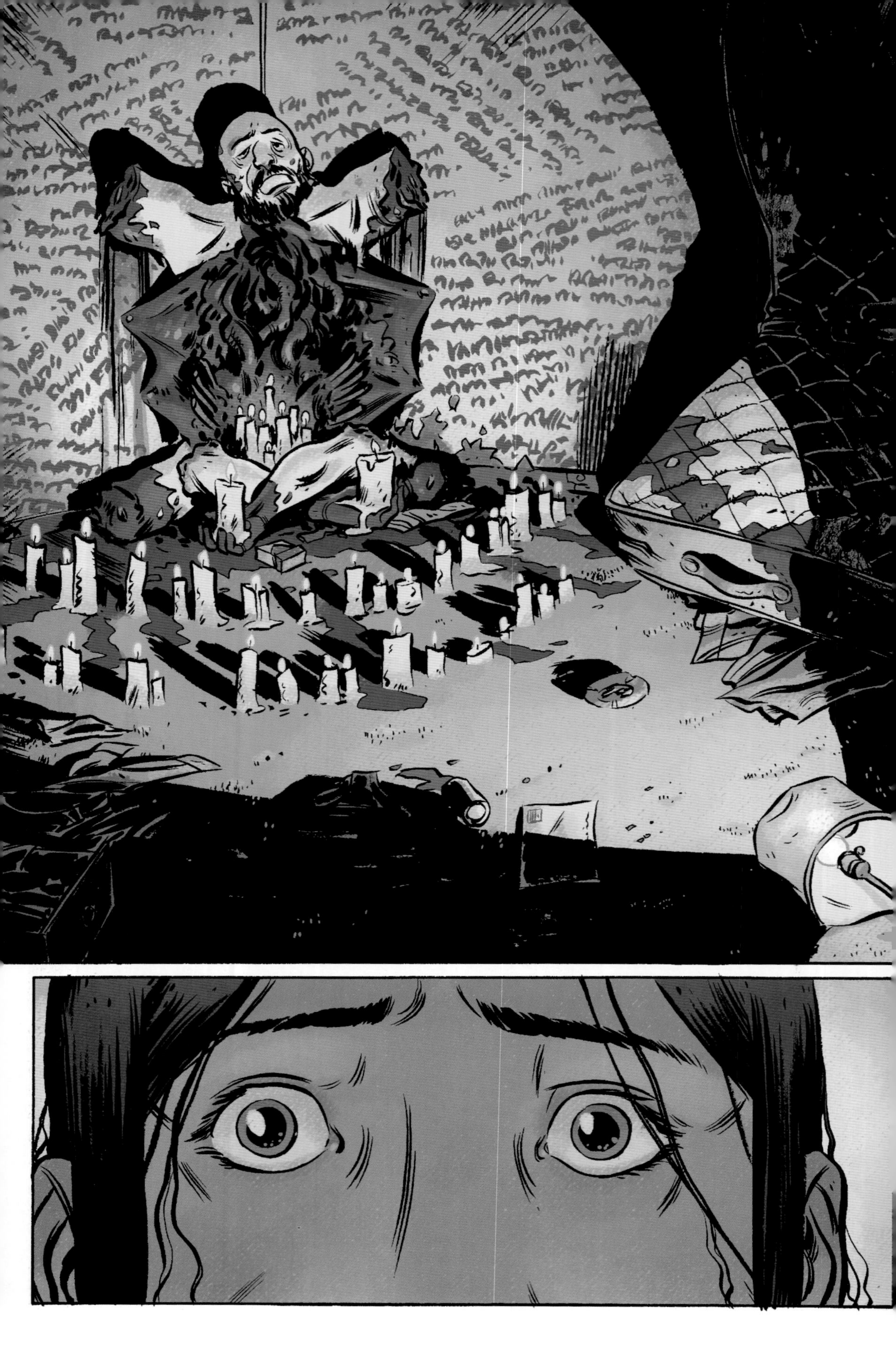

ONLY TIME OF THE AWAKENING WHEN DEVOTION OF THE CHOSEN NUMBER TO GIVE UP THE PASSING WORLD OF THIS

ONLY TIME O WHEN DEVOTIO NUMBER TO GIV

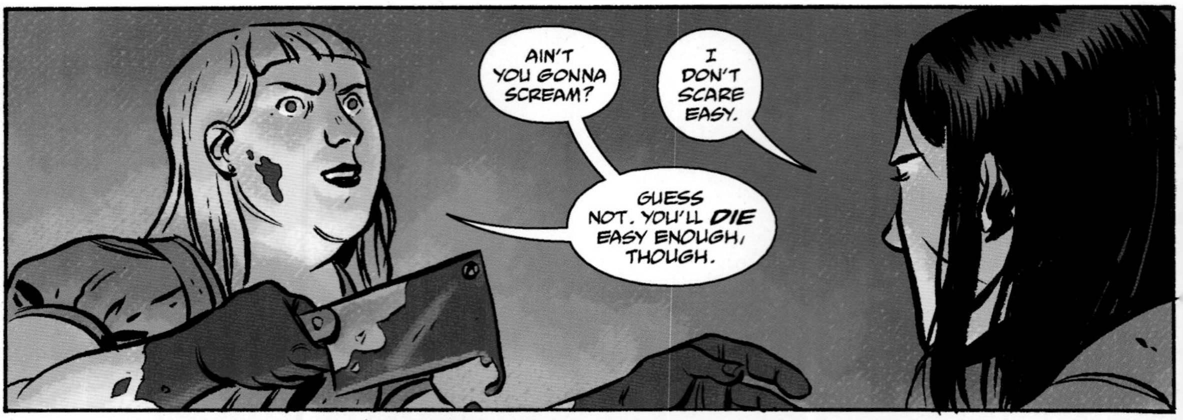
AIN'T YOU GONNA SCREAM?
I DON'T SCARE EASY.
GUESS NOT. YOU'LL DIE EASY ENOUGH, THOUGH.

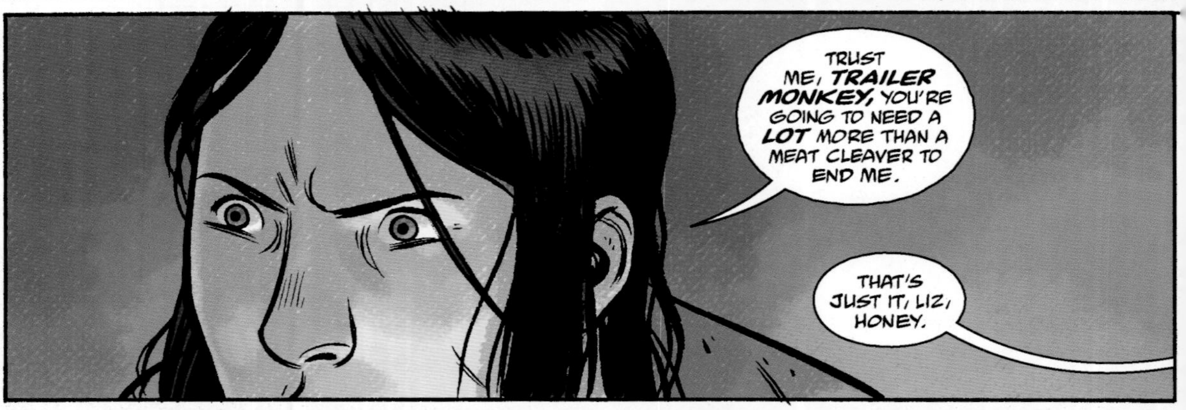
TRUST ME, TRAILER MONKEY, YOU'RE GOING TO NEED A LOT MORE THAN A MEAT CLEAVER TO END ME.
THAT'S JUST IT, LIZ, HONEY.

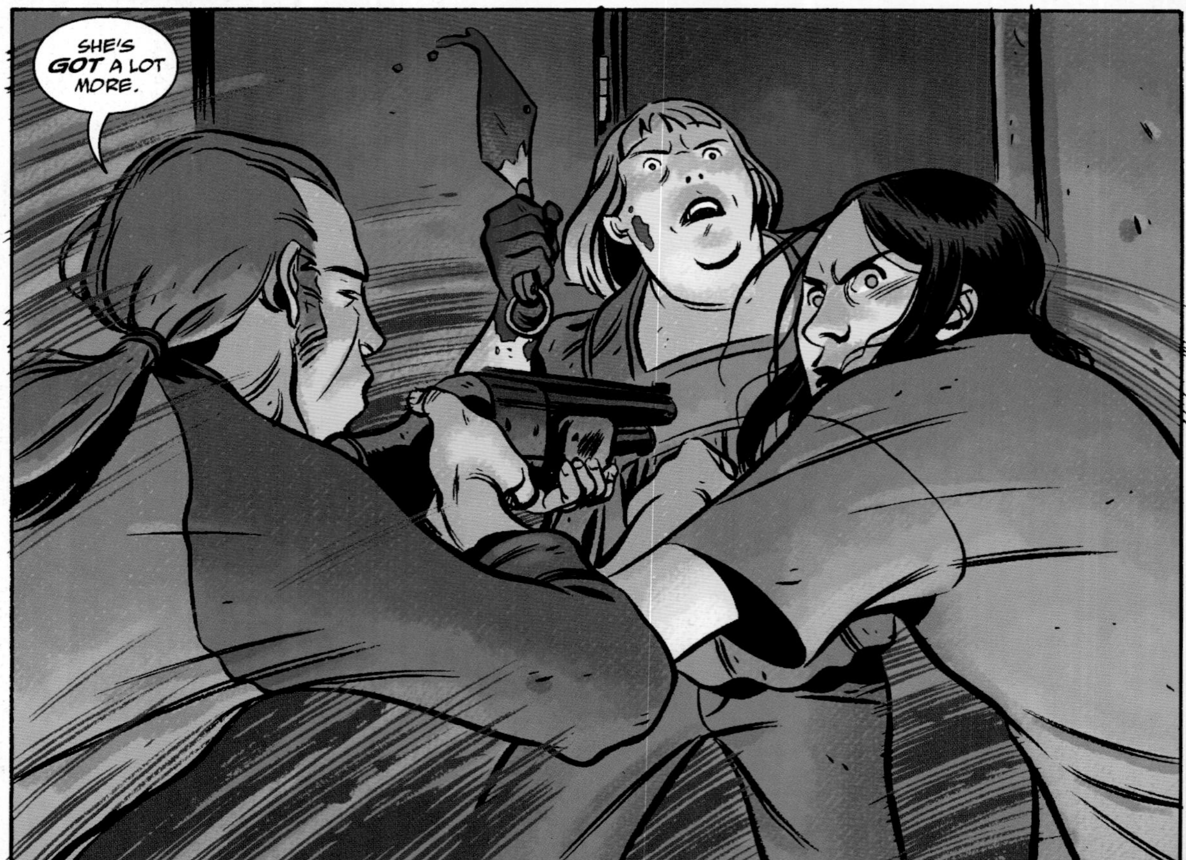
SHE'S GOT A LOT MORE.

MONSTERS CHAPTER TWO

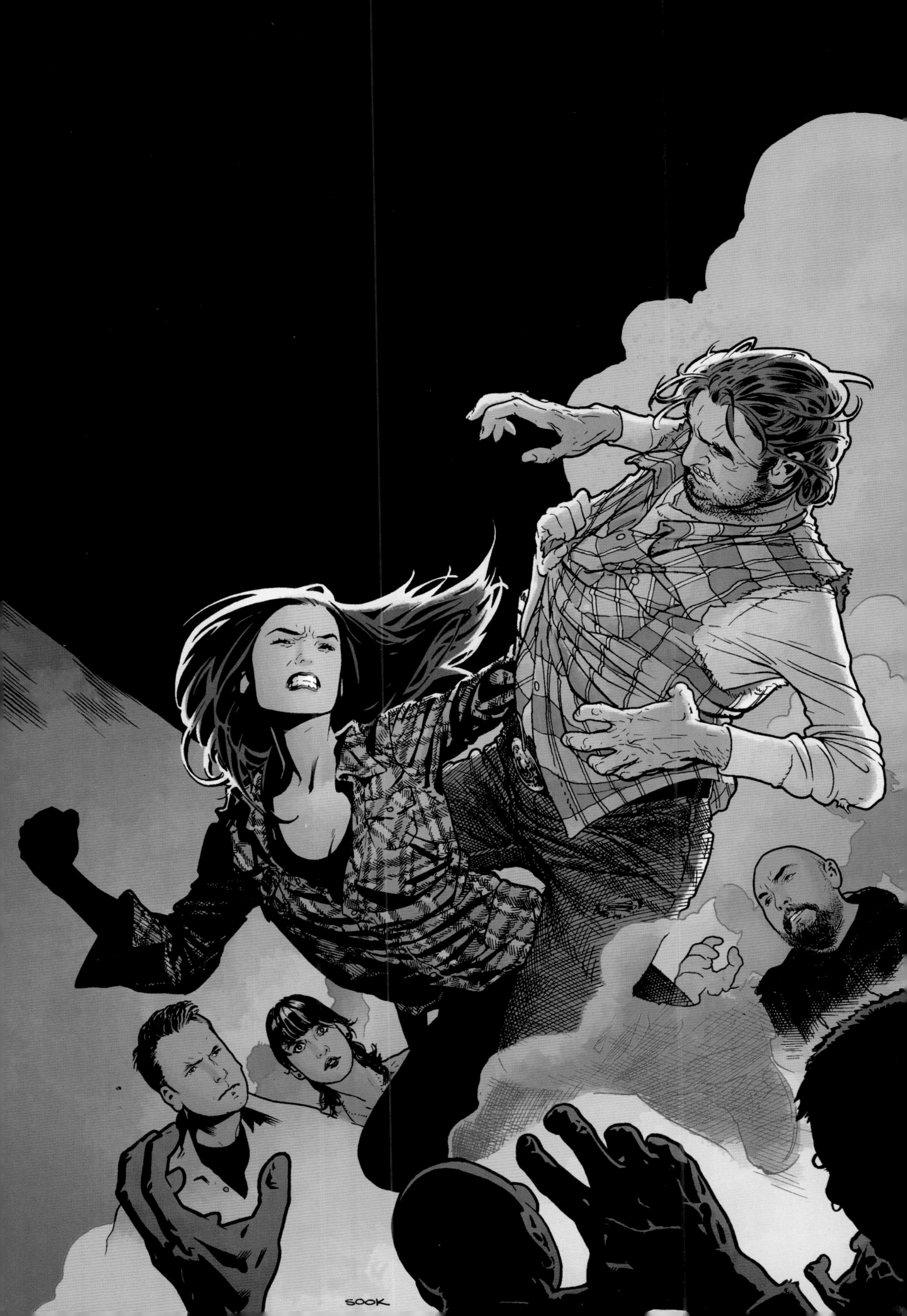
SOOK

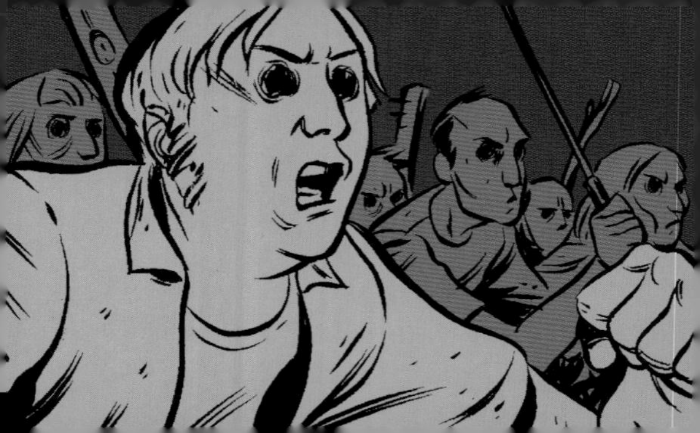

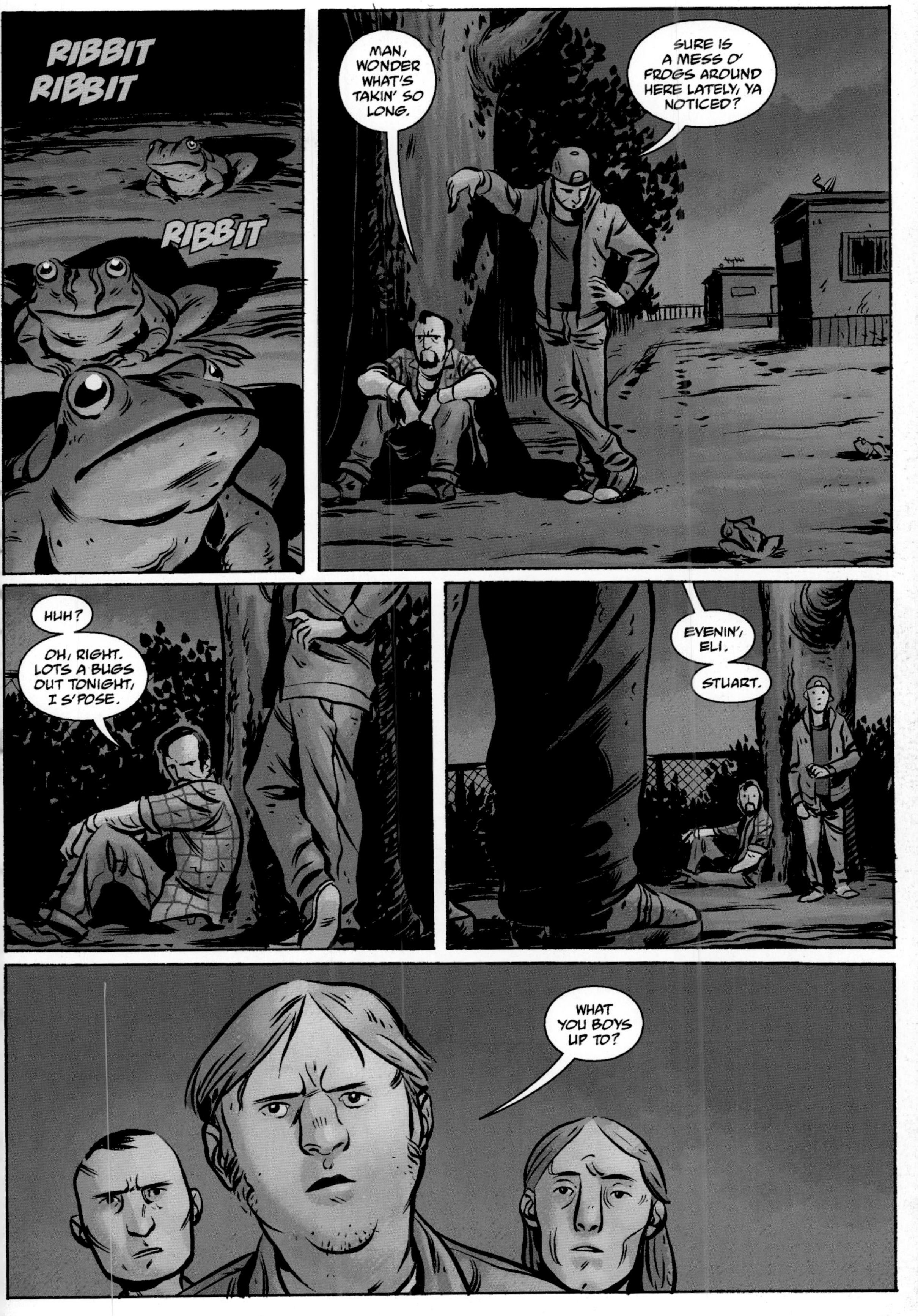
RIBBIT
RIBBIT
RIBBIT
MAN, WONDER WHAT'S TAKIN' SO LONG.
SURE IS A MESS O' FROGS AROUND HERE LATELY, YA NOTICED?
HUH?
OH, RIGHT. LOTS A BUGS OUT TONIGHT, I S'POSE.
EVENIN', ELI.
STUART.
WHAT YOU BOYS UP TO?

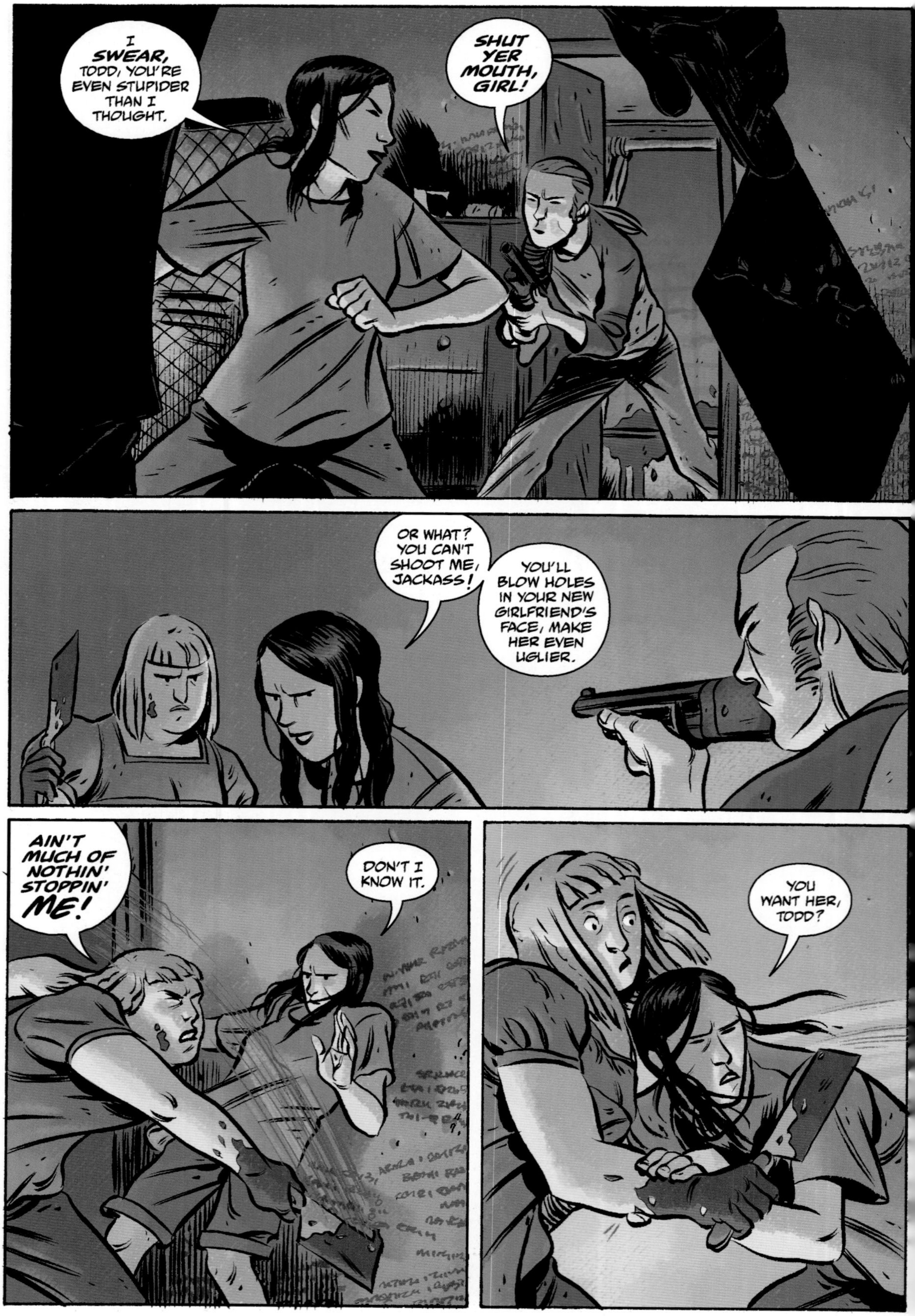
I SWEAR, TODD, YOU'RE EVEN STUPIDER THAN I THOUGHT.
SHUT YER MOUTH, GIRL!
OR WHAT? YOU CAN'T SHOOT ME, JACKASS!
YOU'LL BLOW HOLES IN YOUR NEW GIRLFRIEND'S FACE, MAKE HER EVEN UGLIER.
AIN'T MUCH OF NOTHIN' STOPPIN' ME!
DON'T I KNOW IT.
YOU WANT HER, TODD?

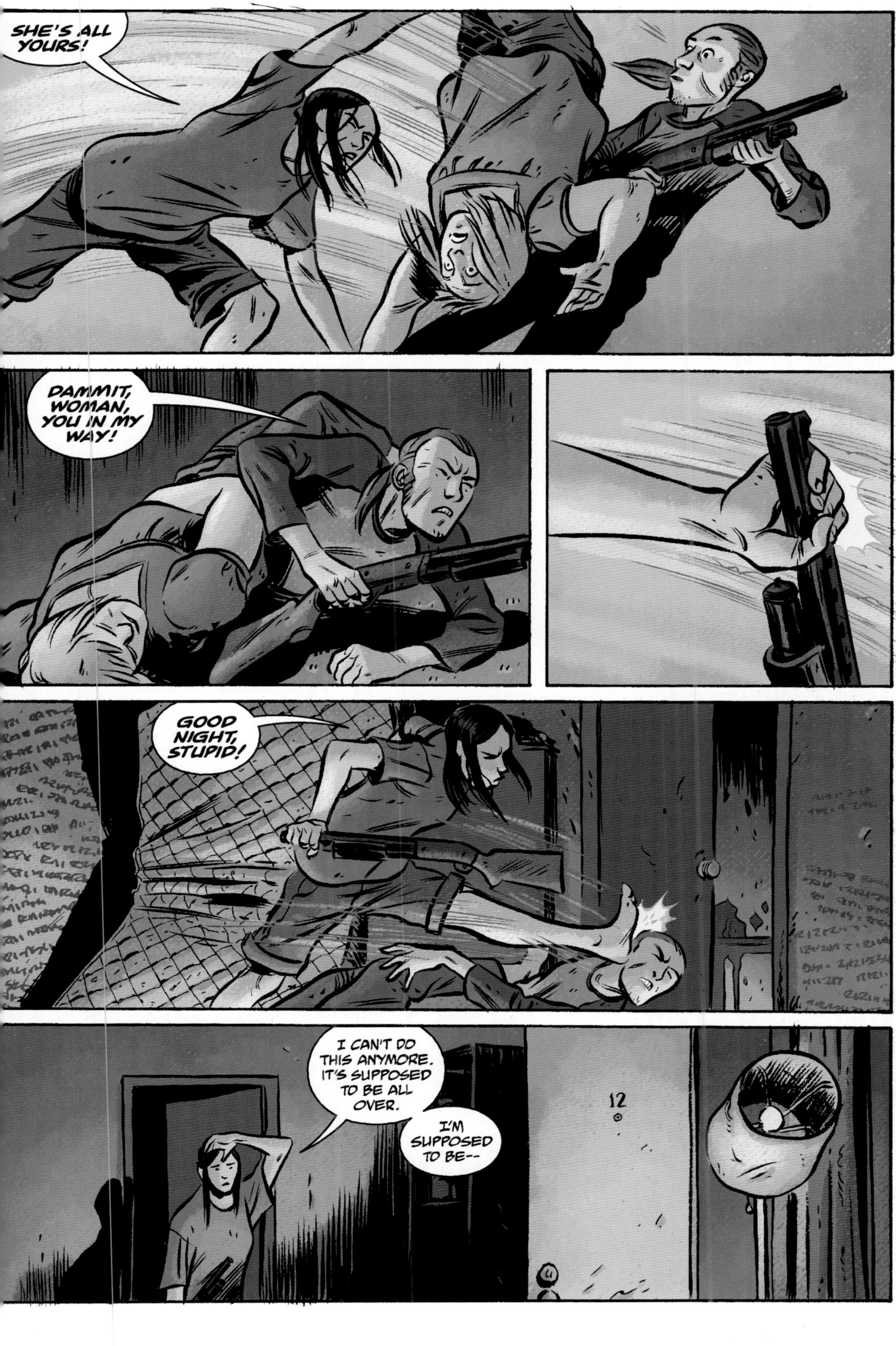
SHE'S ALL YOURS!
DAMMIT, WOMAN, YOU IN MY WAY!
GOOD NIGHT, STUPID!
I CAN'T DO THIS ANYMORE. IT'S SUPPOSED TO BE ALL OVER.
I'M SUPPOSED TO BE--
12

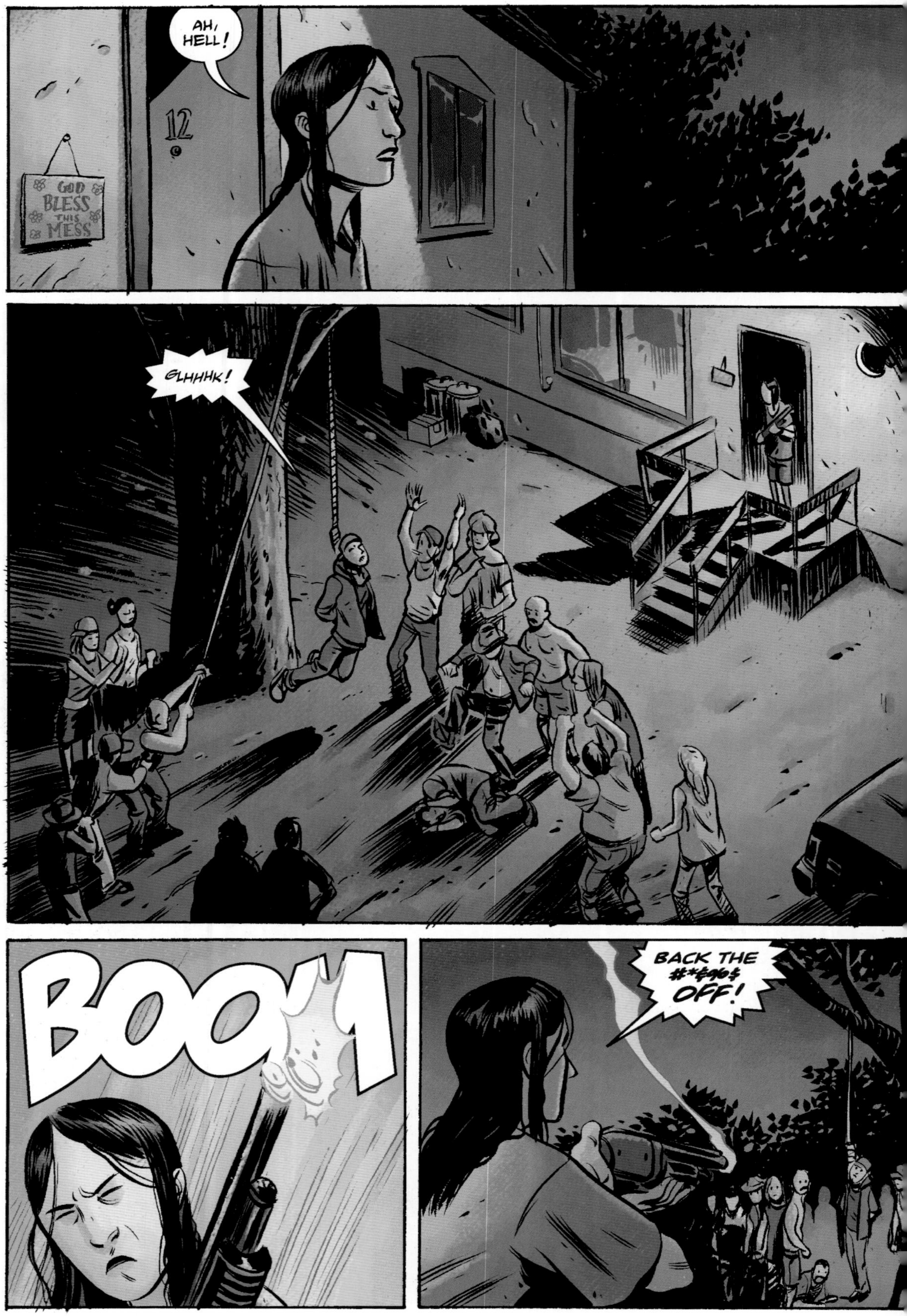
GOD BLESS THIS MESS
12
AH, HELL!
GLHHHK!
BOOM
BACK THE #*$%$ OFF!

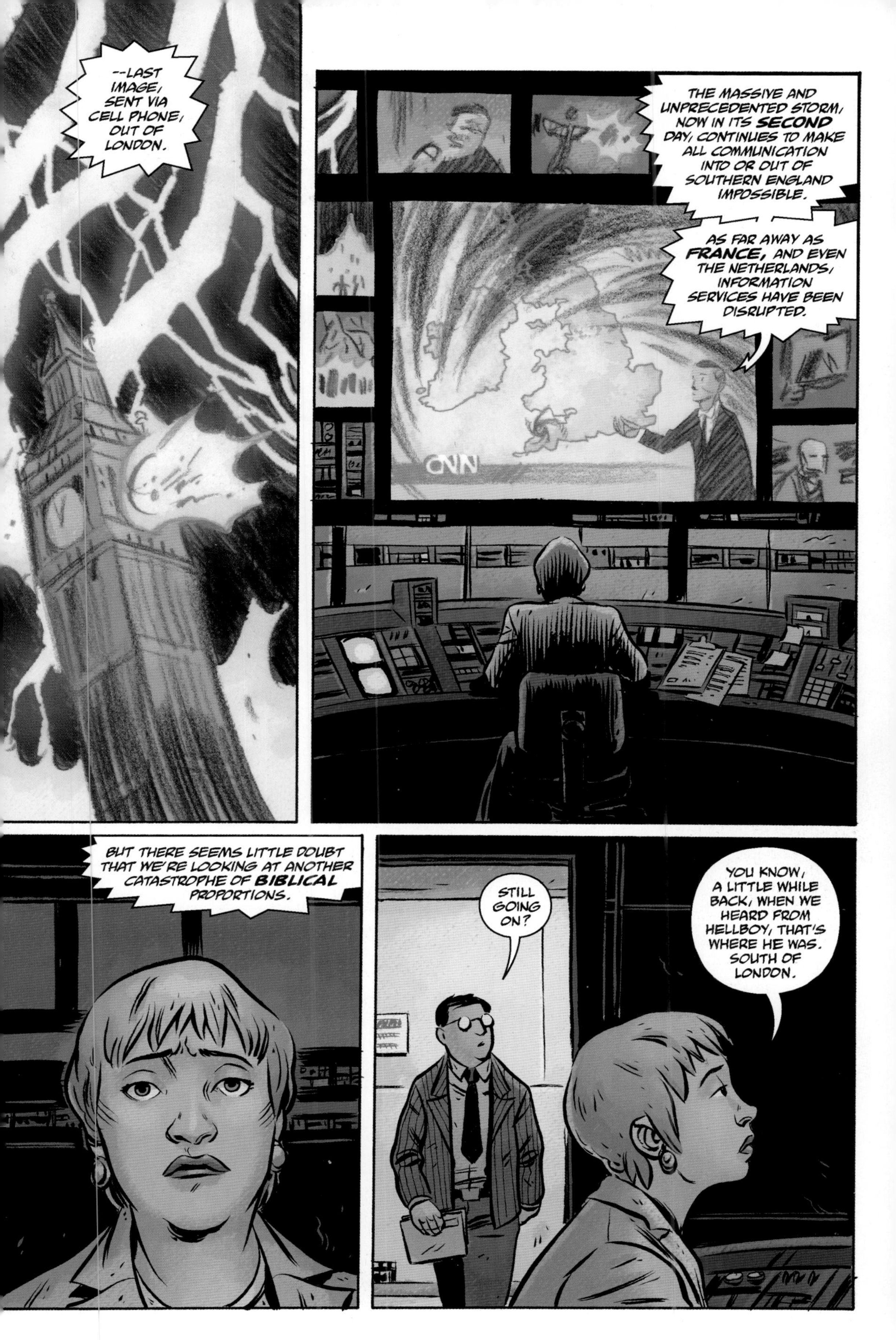
--LAST IMAGE, SENT VIA CELL PHONE, OUT OF LONDON.
THE MASSIVE AND UNPRECEDENTED STORM, NOW IN ITS SECOND DAY, CONTINUES TO MAKE ALL COMMUNICATION INTO OR OUT OF SOUTHERN ENGLAND IMPOSSIBLE.
AS FAR AWAY AS FRANCE, AND EVEN THE NETHERLANDS, INFORMATION SERVICES HAVE BEEN DISRUPTED.
CNN
BUT THERE SEEMS LITTLE DOUBT THAT WE'RE LOOKING AT ANOTHER CATASTROPHE OF BIBLICAL PROPORTIONS.
STILL GOING ON?
YOU KNOW, A LITTLE WHILE BACK, WHEN WE HEARD FROM HELLBOY, THAT'S WHERE HE WAS. SOUTH OF LONDON.

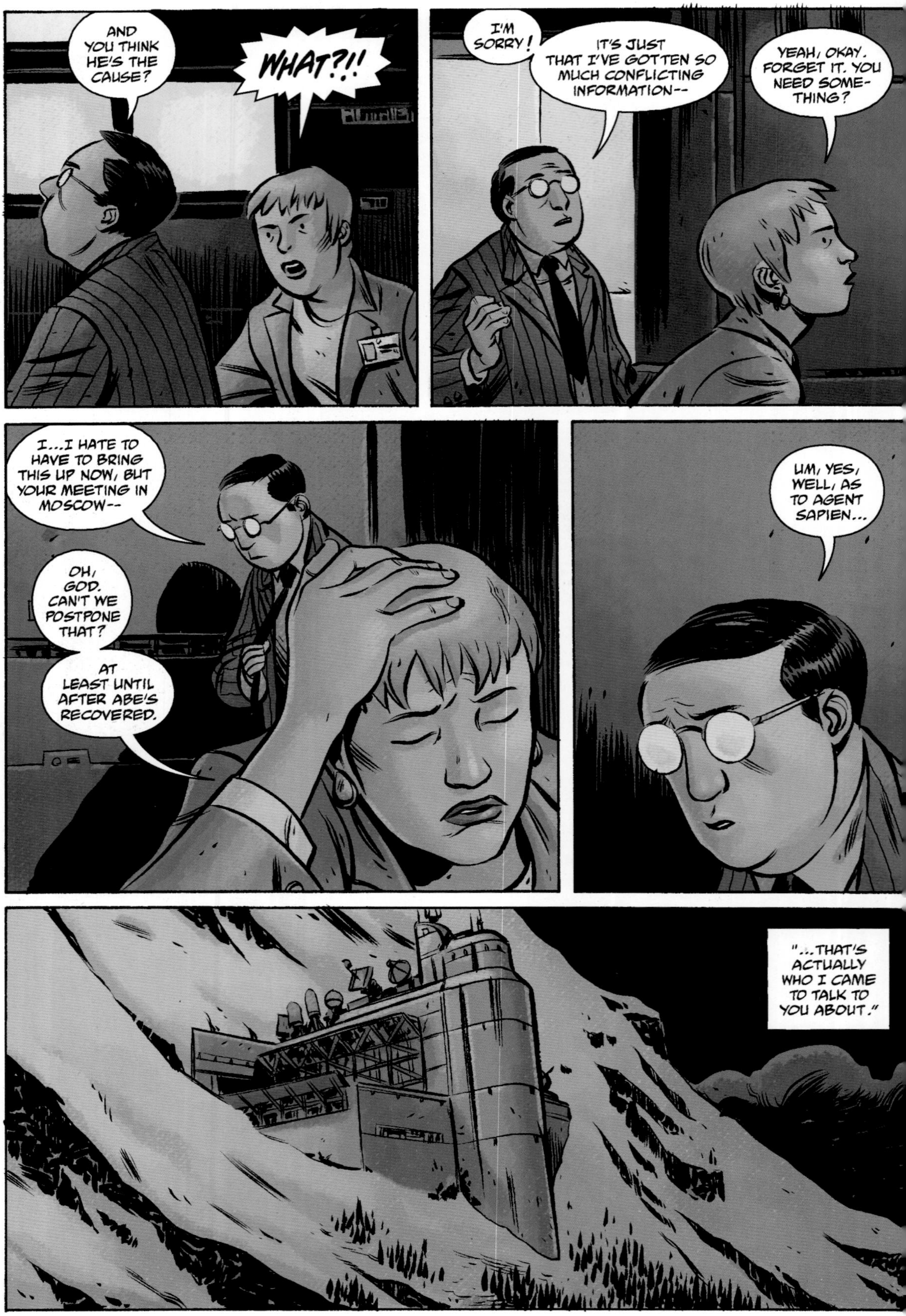
AND YOU THINK HE'S THE CAUSE?
WHAT?!!
I'M SORRY!
IT'S JUST THAT I'VE GOTTEN SO MUCH CONFLICTING INFORMATION--
YEAH, OKAY. FORGET IT. YOU NEED SOME-THING?
I...I HATE TO HAVE TO BRING THIS UP NOW, BUT YOUR MEETING IN MOSCOW--
OH, GOD. CAN'T WE POSTPONE THAT?
AT LEAST UNTIL AFTER ABE'S RECOVERED.
UM, YES, WELL, AS TO AGENT SAPIEN...
"...THAT'S ACTUALLY WHO I CAME TO TALK TO YOU ABOUT."

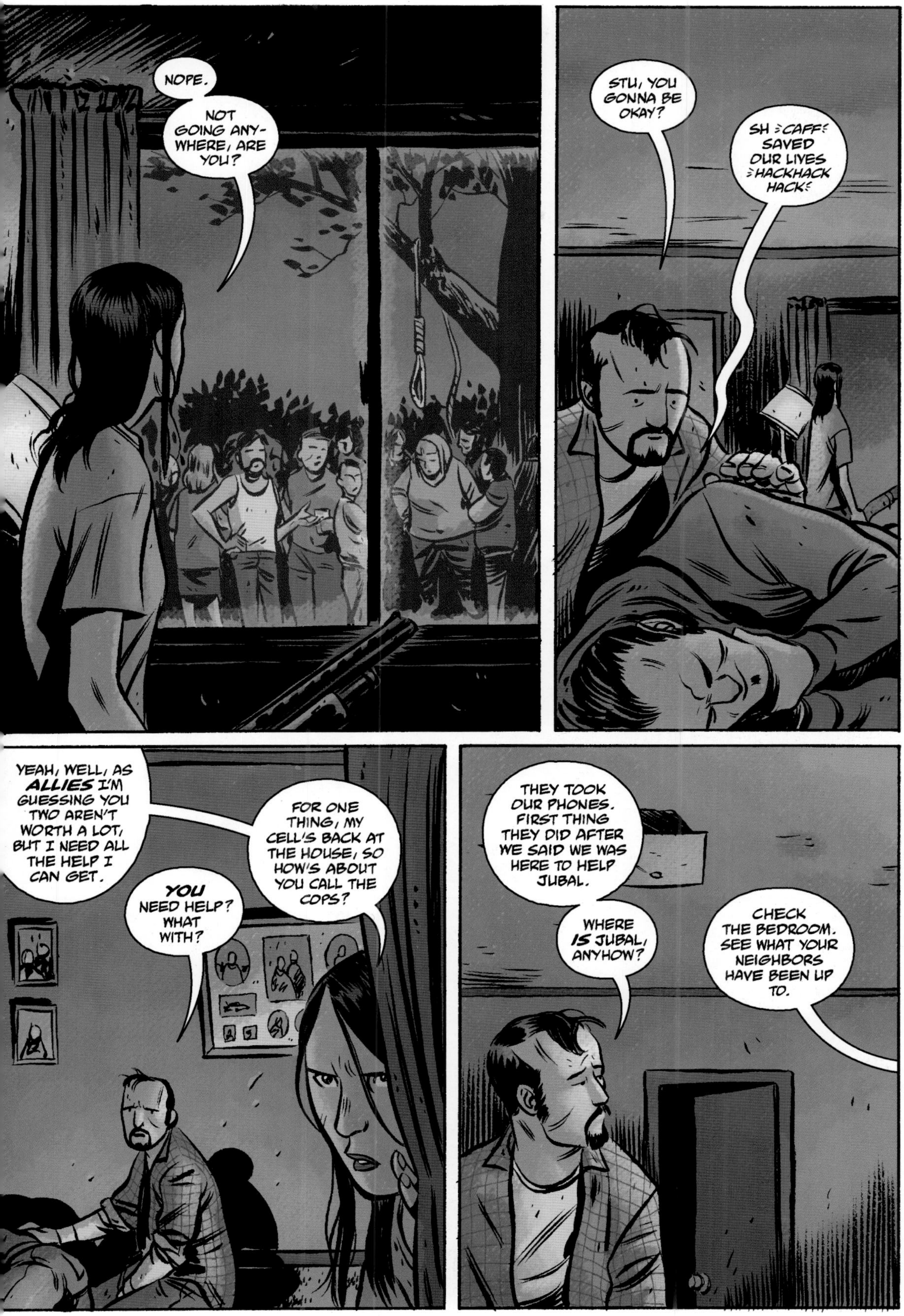
NOPE.
NOT GOING ANYWHERE, ARE YOU?
STU, YOU GONNA BE OKAY?
SH ≈CAFF≈ SAVED OUR LIVES ≈HACKHACK HACK≈
YEAH, WELL, AS ALLIES I'M GUESSING YOU TWO AREN'T WORTH A LOT, BUT I NEED ALL THE HELP I CAN GET.
YOU NEED HELP? WHAT WITH?
FOR ONE THING, MY CELL'S BACK AT THE HOUSE, SO HOW'S ABOUT YOU CALL THE COPS?
THEY TOOK OUR PHONES. FIRST THING THEY DID AFTER WE SAID WE WAS HERE TO HELP JUBAL.
WHERE IS JUBAL, ANYHOW?
CHECK THE BEDROOM. SEE WHAT YOUR NEIGHBORS HAVE BEEN UP TO.

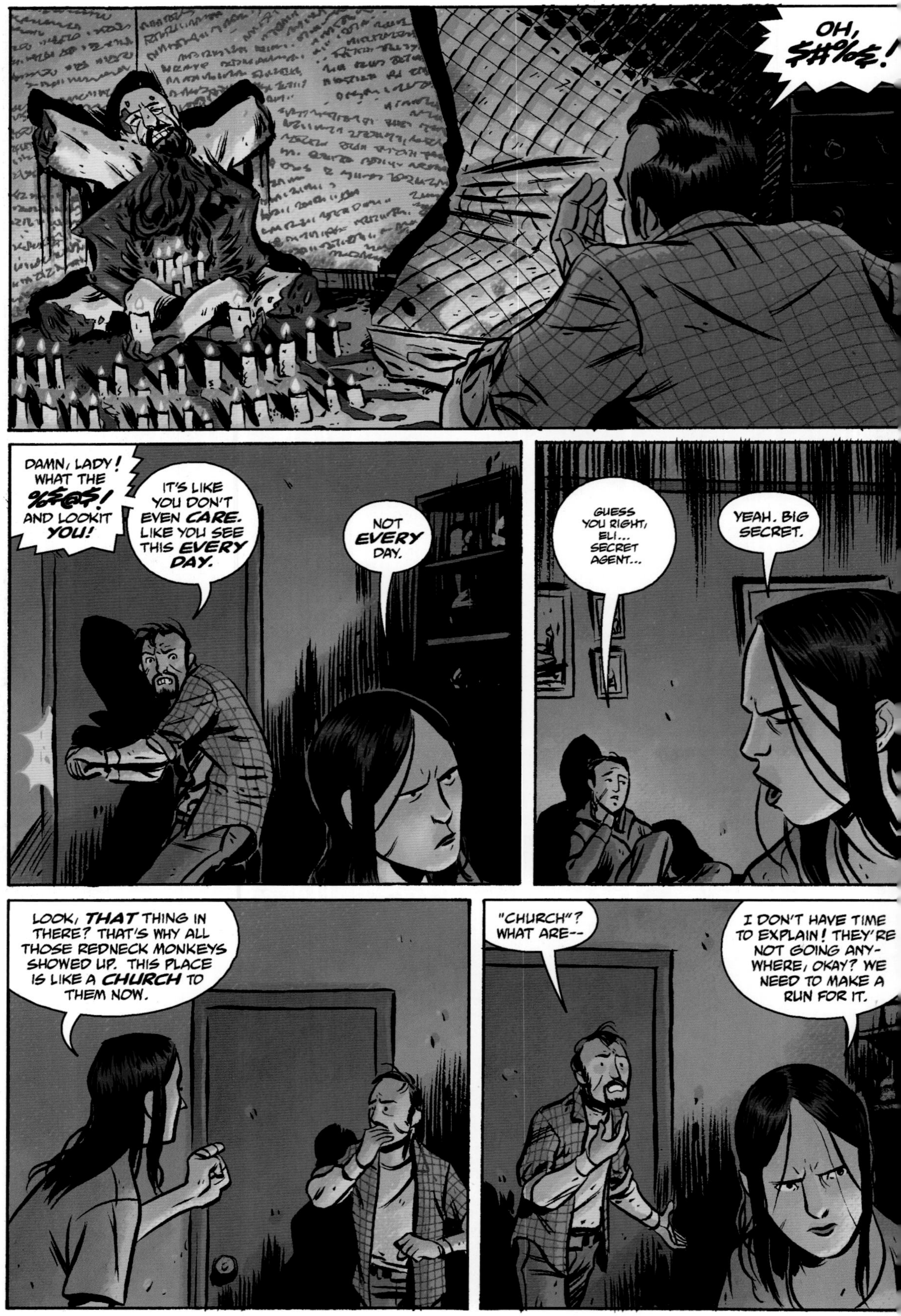
OH, $#%&!
DAMN, LADY! WHAT THE %$@$! AND LOOKIT YOU!
IT'S LIKE YOU DON'T EVEN CARE. LIKE YOU SEE THIS EVERY DAY.
NOT EVERY DAY.
GUESS YOU RIGHT, ELI... SECRET AGENT...
YEAH. BIG SECRET.
LOOK, THAT THING IN THERE? THAT'S WHY ALL THOSE REDNECK MONKEYS SHOWED UP. THIS PLACE IS LIKE A CHURCH TO THEM NOW.
"CHURCH"? WHAT ARE--
I DON'T HAVE TIME TO EXPLAIN! THEY'RE NOT GOING ANYWHERE, OKAY? WE NEED TO MAKE A RUN FOR IT.

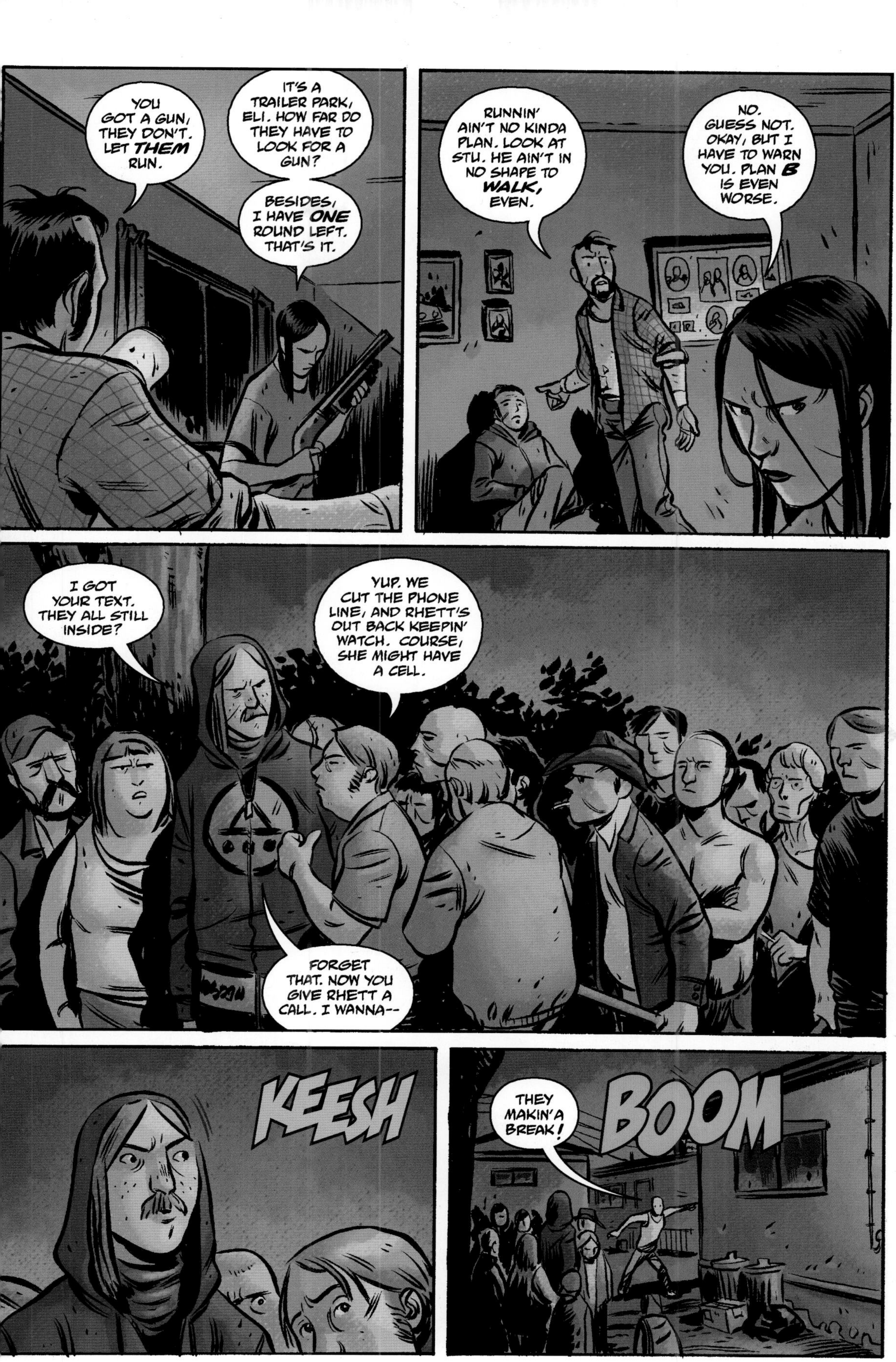
YOU GOT A GUN, THEY DON'T. LET THEM RUN.
IT'S A TRAILER PARK, ELI. HOW FAR DO THEY HAVE TO LOOK FOR A GUN?
BESIDES, I HAVE ONE ROUND LEFT. THAT'S IT.
RUNNIN' AIN'T NO KINDA PLAN. LOOK AT STU. HE AIN'T IN NO SHAPE TO WALK, EVEN.
NO. GUESS NOT. OKAY, BUT I HAVE TO WARN YOU. PLAN B IS EVEN WORSE.
I GOT YOUR TEXT. THEY ALL STILL INSIDE?
YUP. WE CUT THE PHONE LINE, AND RHETT'S OUT BACK KEEPIN' WATCH. COURSE, SHE MIGHT HAVE A CELL.
FORGET THAT. NOW YOU GIVE RHETT A CALL. I WANNA--
KEESH
BOOM
THEY MAKIN'A BREAK!

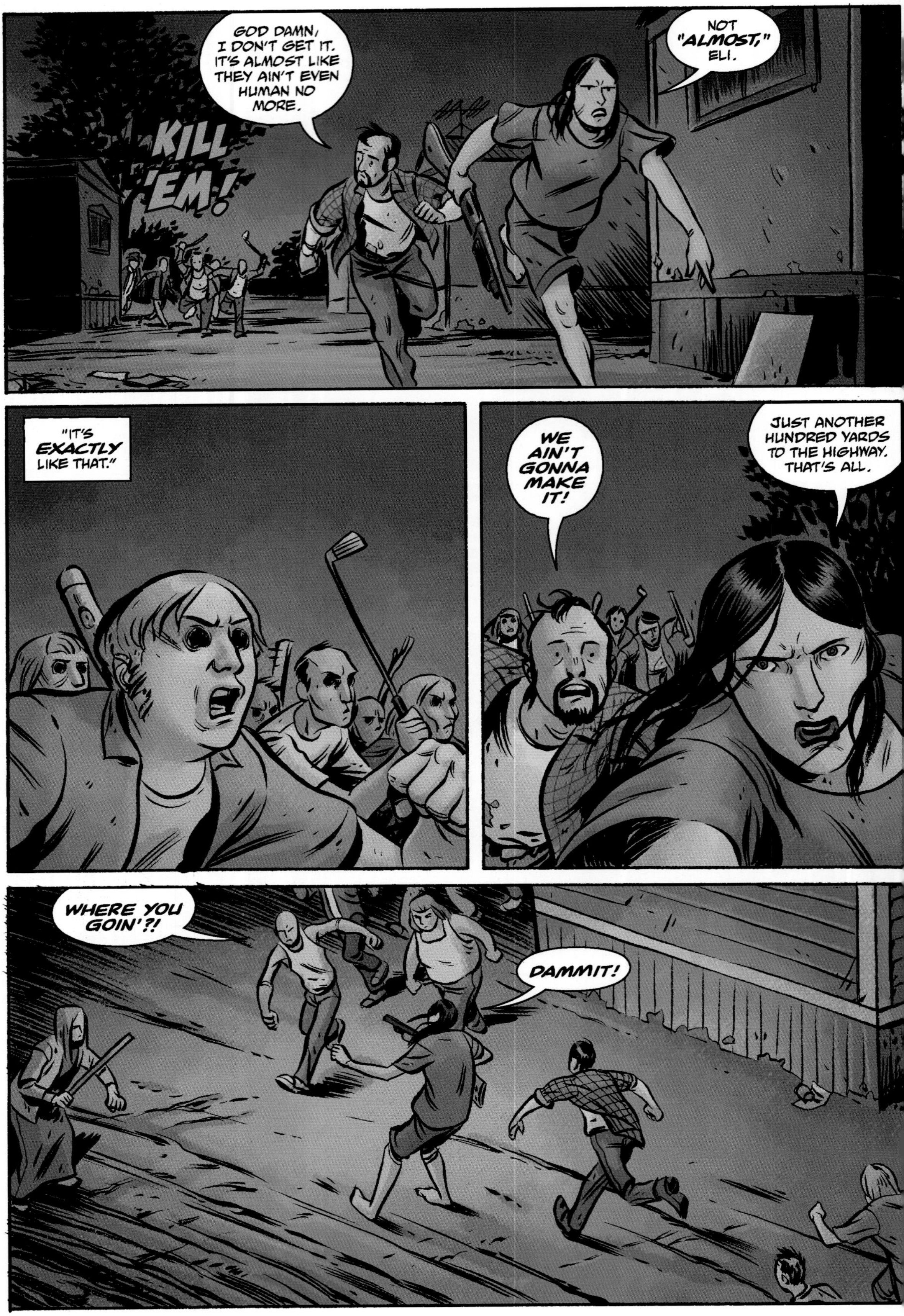
KILL 'EM!
GOD DAMN, I DON'T GET IT. IT'S ALMOST LIKE THEY AIN'T EVEN HUMAN NO MORE.
NOT "ALMOST," ELI.
"IT'S EXACTLY LIKE THAT."
WE AIN'T GONNA MAKE IT!
JUST ANOTHER HUNDRED YARDS TO THE HIGHWAY. THAT'S ALL.
WHERE YOU GOIN'?!
DAMMIT!

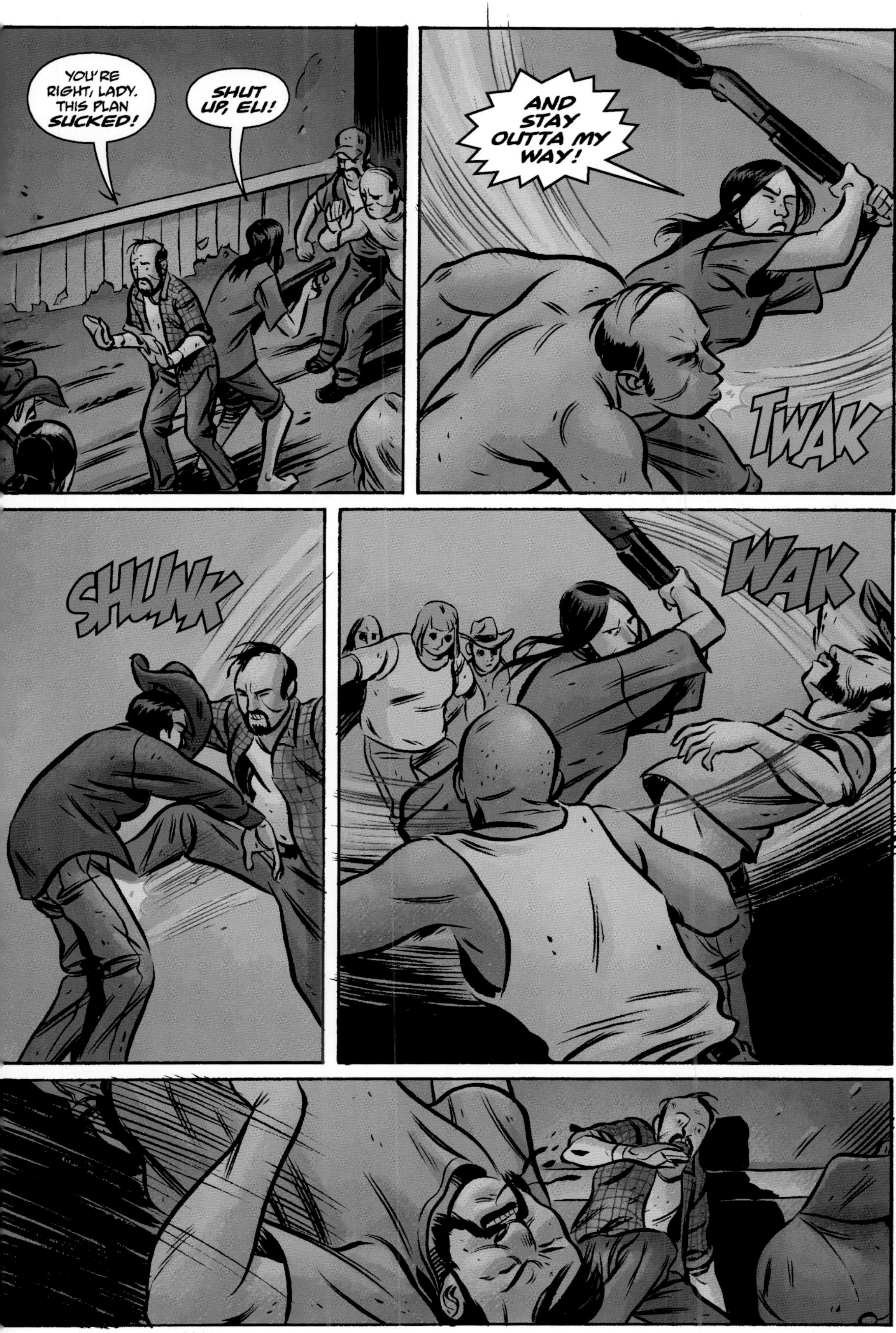
YOU'RE RIGHT, LADY. THIS PLAN SUCKED!
SHUT UP, ELI!
AND STAY OUTTA MY WAY!
TWAK
SHUNK
WAK

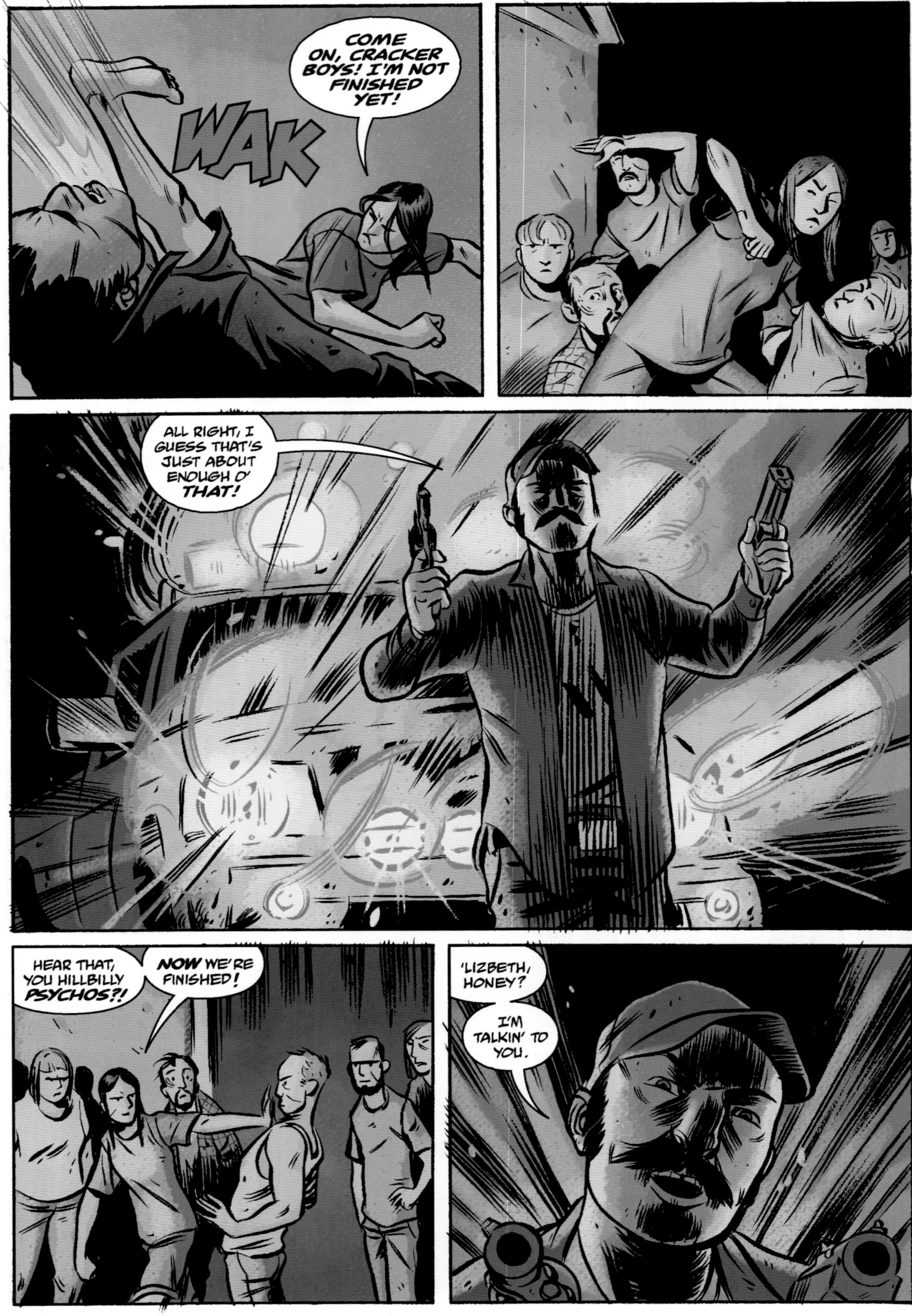
COME ON, CRACKER BOYS! I'M NOT FINISHED YET!
WAK
ALL RIGHT, I GUESS THAT'S JUST ABOUT ENOUGH O' THAT!
HEAR THAT, YOU HILLBILLY PSYCHOS?!
NOW WE'RE FINISHED!
'LIZBETH, HONEY?
I'M TALKIN' TO YOU.

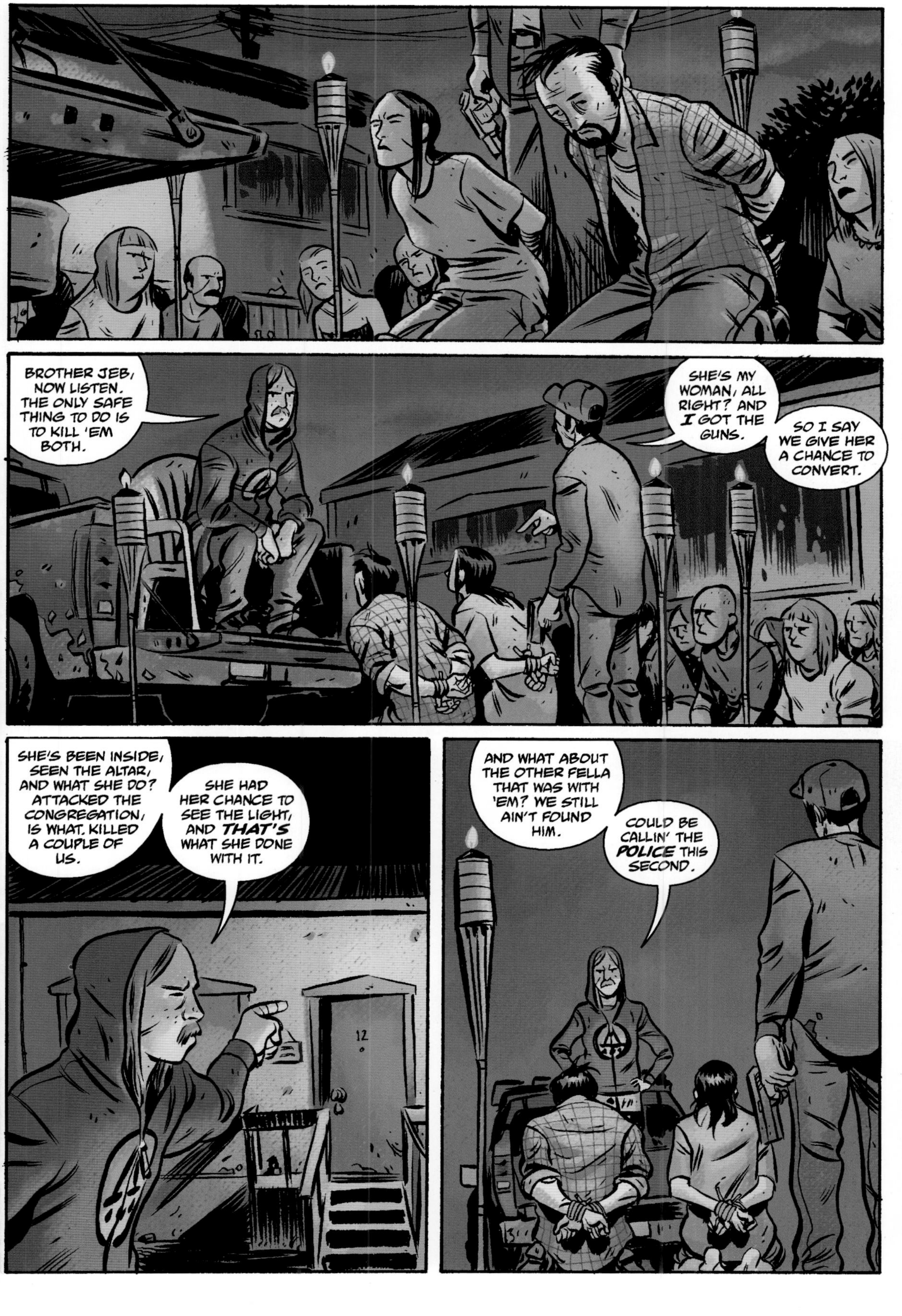
BROTHER JEB, NOW LISTEN. THE ONLY SAFE THING TO DO IS TO KILL 'EM BOTH.
SHE'S MY WOMAN, ALL RIGHT? AND I GOT THE GUNS.
SO I SAY WE GIVE HER A CHANCE TO CONVERT.
SHE'S BEEN INSIDE, SEEN THE ALTAR, AND WHAT SHE DO? ATTACKED THE CONGREGATION, IS WHAT. KILLED A COUPLE OF US.
SHE HAD HER CHANCE TO SEE THE LIGHT, AND THAT'S WHAT SHE DONE WITH IT.
AND WHAT ABOUT THE OTHER FELLA THAT WAS WITH 'EM? WE STILL AIN'T FOUND HIM.
COULD BE CALLIN' THE POLICE THIS SECOND.

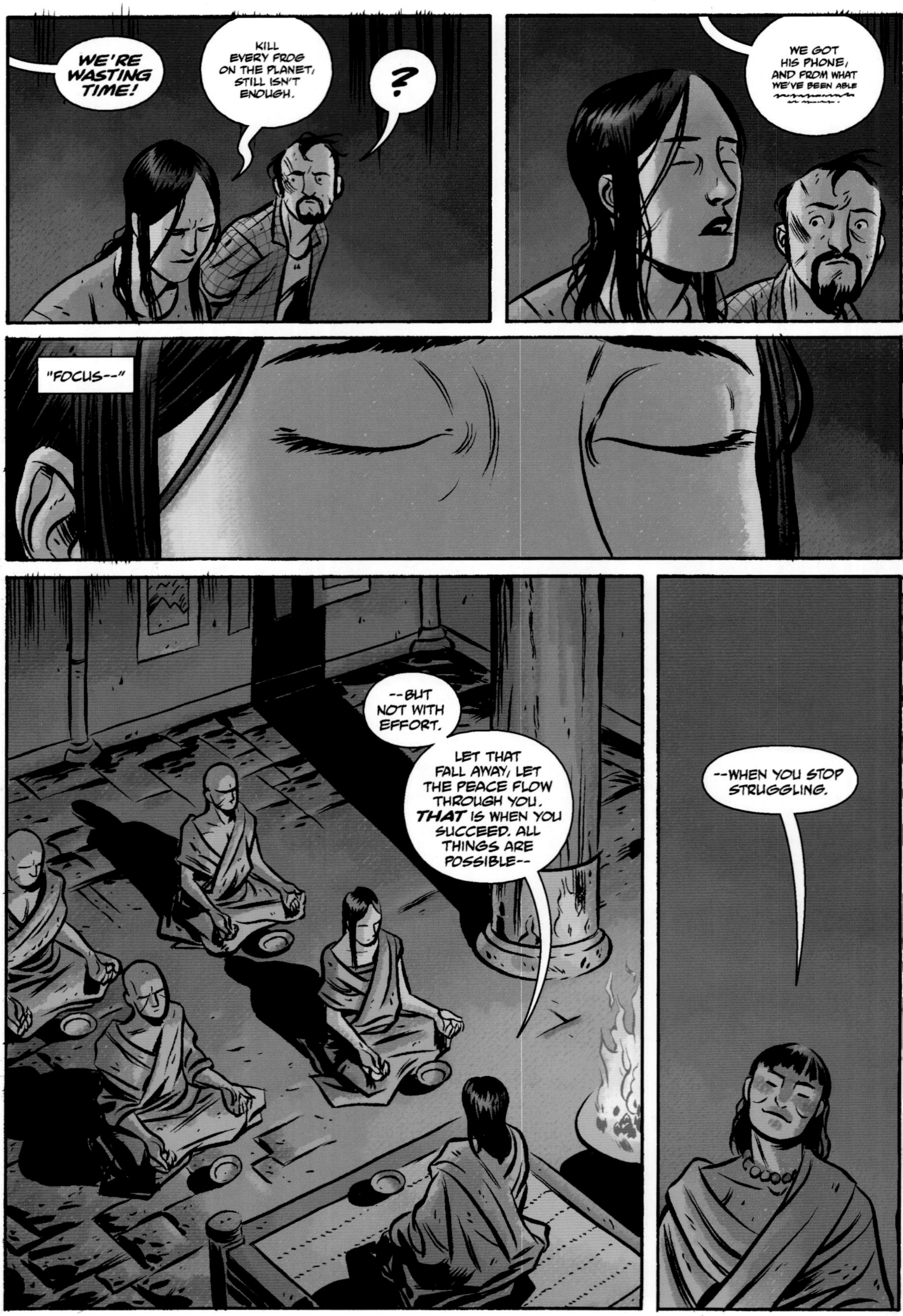
WE'RE WASTING TIME!
KILL EVERY FROG ON THE PLANET, STILL ISN'T ENOUGH.
?
WE GOT HIS PHONE, AND FROM WHAT WE'VE BEEN ABLE
"FOCUS--"
--BUT NOT WITH EFFORT.
LET THAT FALL AWAY, LET THE PEACE FLOW THROUGH YOU. THAT IS WHEN YOU SUCCEED. ALL THINGS ARE POSSIBLE--
--WHEN YOU STOP STRUGGLING.

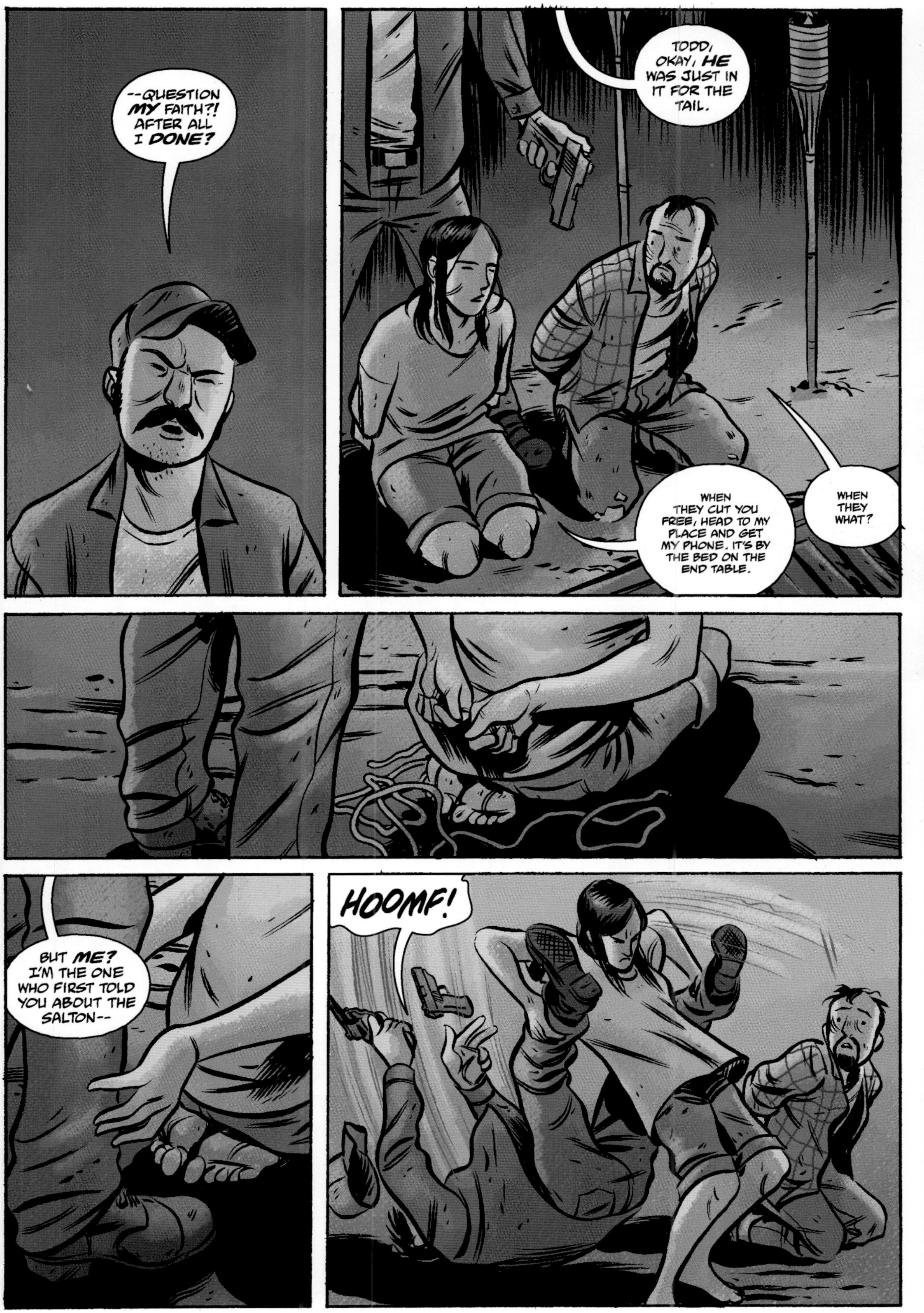
--QUESTION MY FAITH?! AFTER ALL I DONE?
TODD, OKAY, HE WAS JUST IN IT FOR THE TAIL.
WHEN THEY CUT YOU FREE, HEAD TO MY PLACE AND GET MY PHONE. IT'S BY THE BED ON THE END TABLE.
WHEN THEY WHAT?
BUT ME? I'M THE ONE WHO FIRST TOLD YOU ABOUT THE SALTON--
HOOMF!

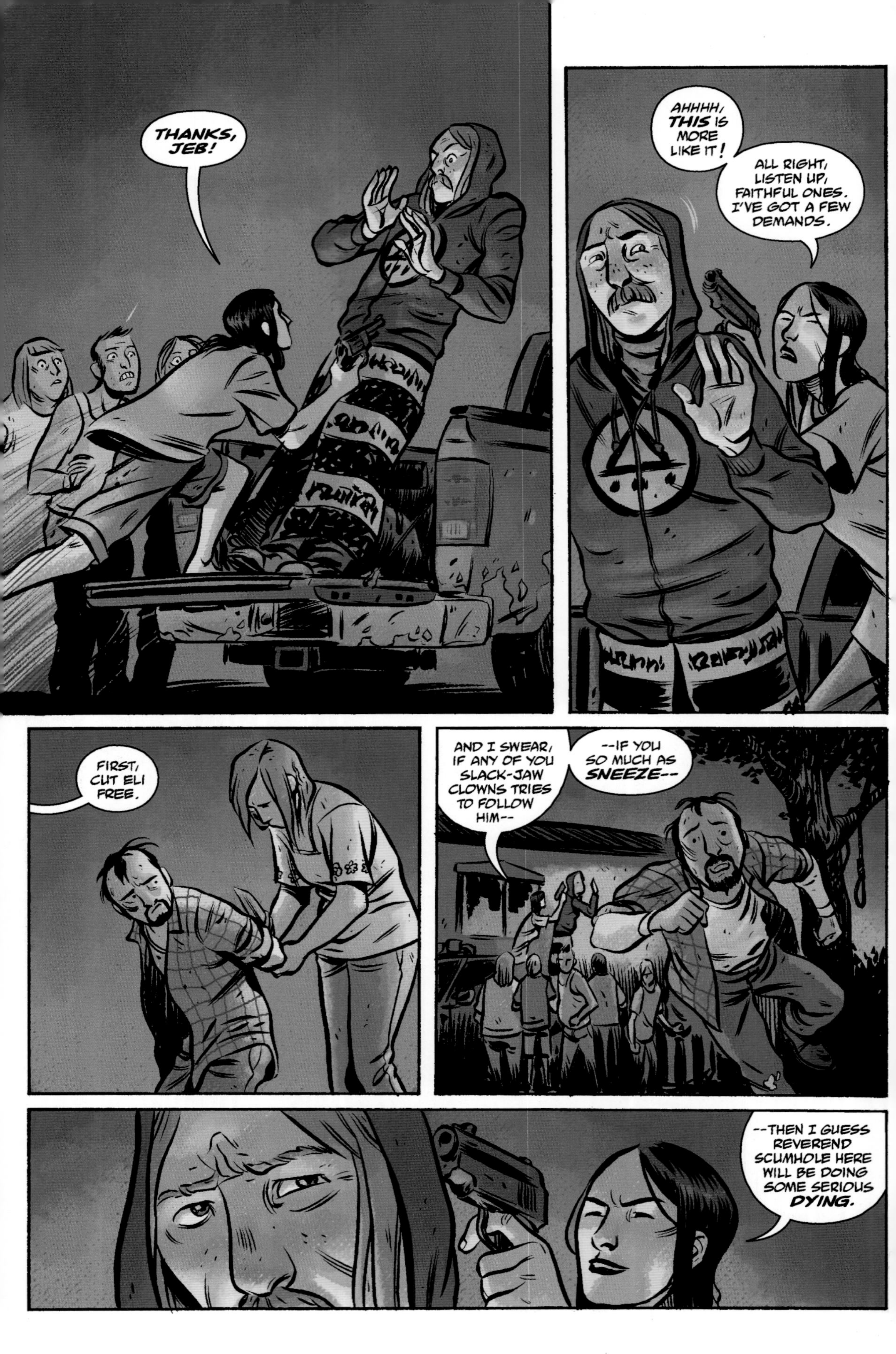
THANKS, JEB!
AHHHH, THIS IS MORE LIKE IT!
ALL RIGHT, LISTEN UP, FAITHFUL ONES. I'VE GOT A FEW DEMANDS.
FIRST, CUT ELI FREE.
AND I SWEAR, IF ANY OF YOU SLACK-JAW CLOWNS TRIES TO FOLLOW HIM--
--IF YOU SO MUCH AS SNEEZE--
--THEN I GUESS REVEREND SCUMHOLE HERE WILL BE DOING SOME SERIOUS DYING.

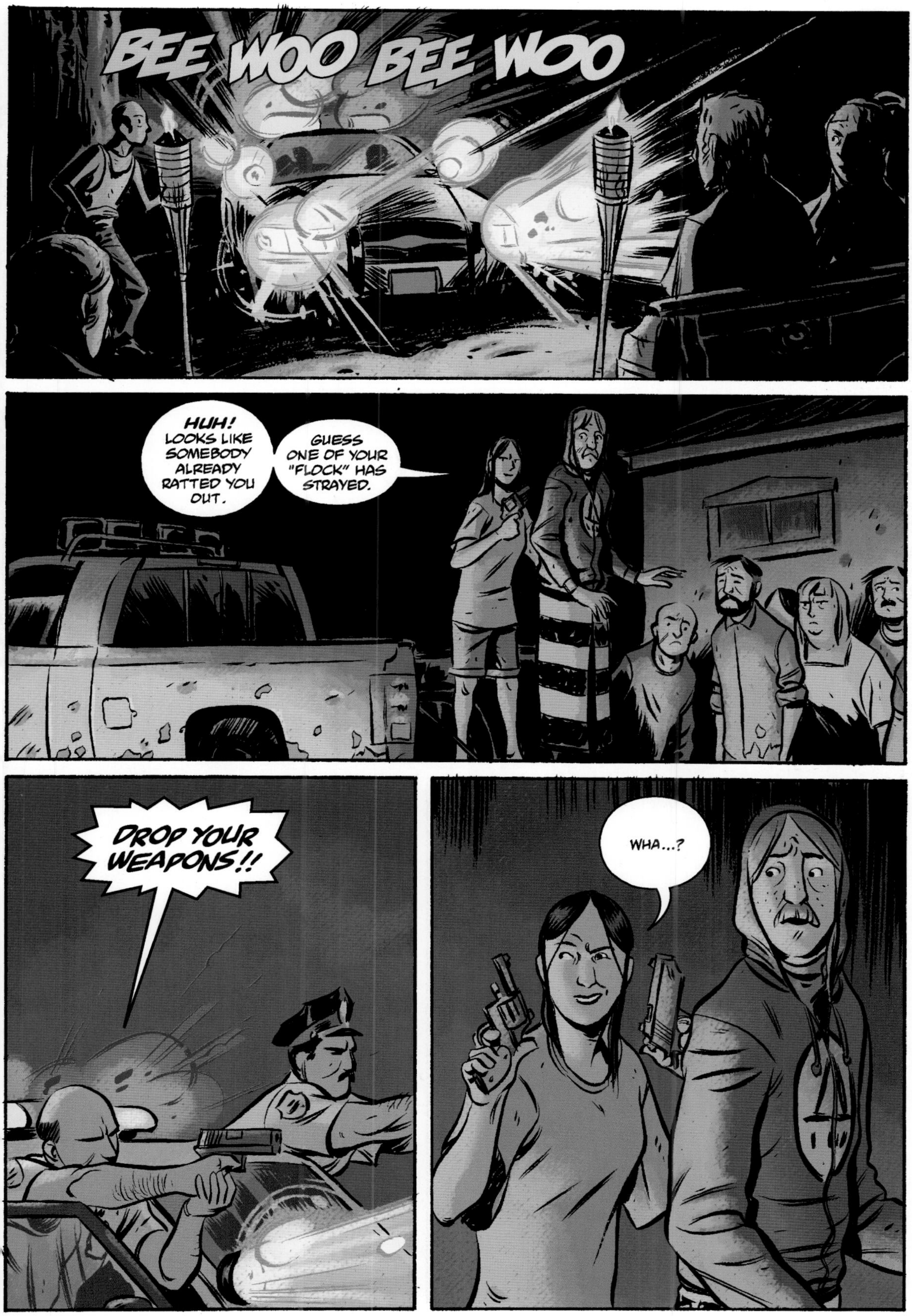
BEE WOO BEE WOO
HUH! LOOKS LIKE SOMEBODY ALREADY RATTED YOU OUT.
GUESS ONE OF YOUR "FLOCK" HAS STRAYED.
DROP YOUR WEAPONS!!
WHA...?

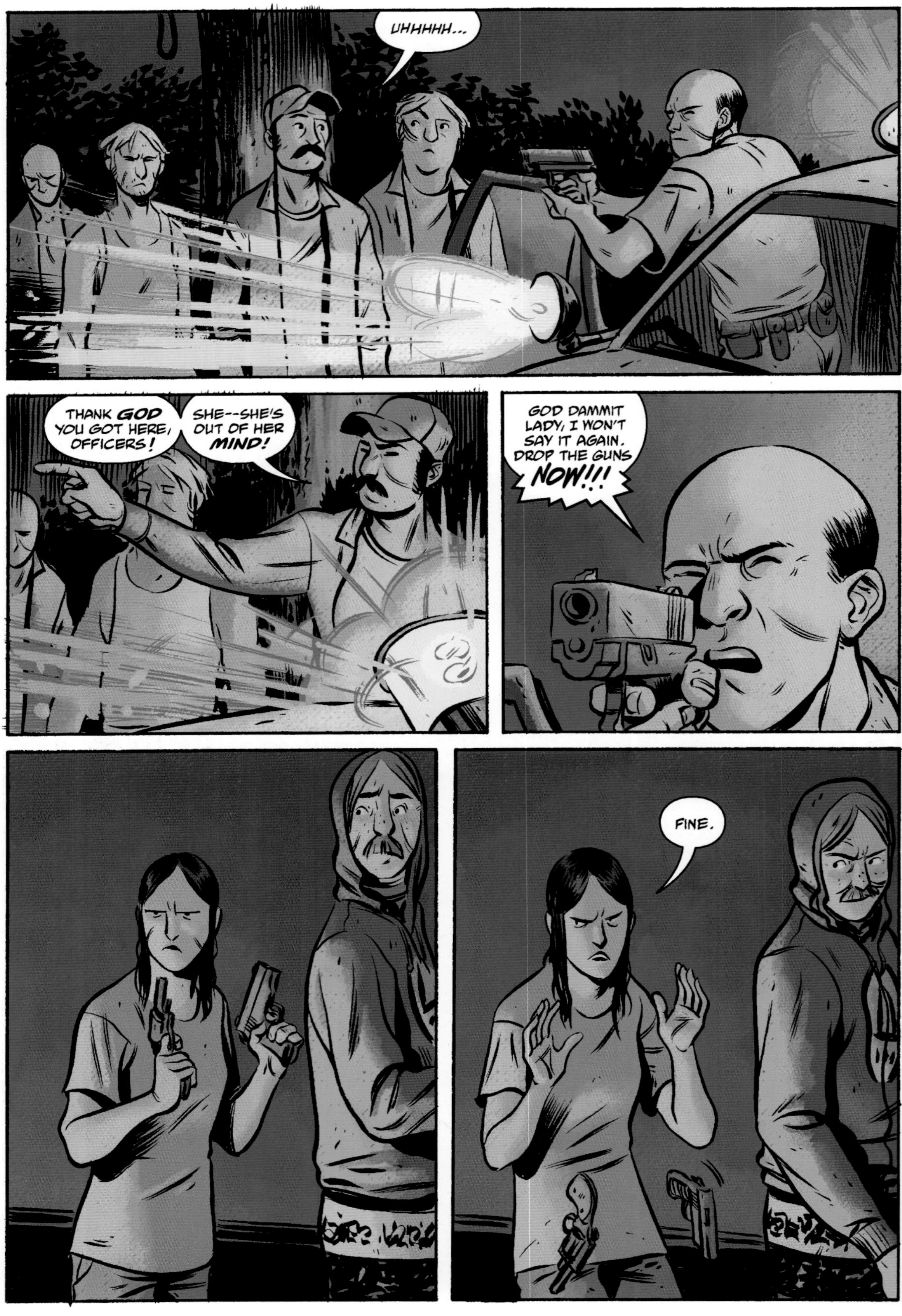
UHHHHH...
THANK GOD YOU GOT HERE, OFFICERS!
SHE--SHE'S OUT OF HER MIND!
GOD DAMMIT LADY, I WON'T SAY IT AGAIN. DROP THE GUNS NOW!!!
FINE.

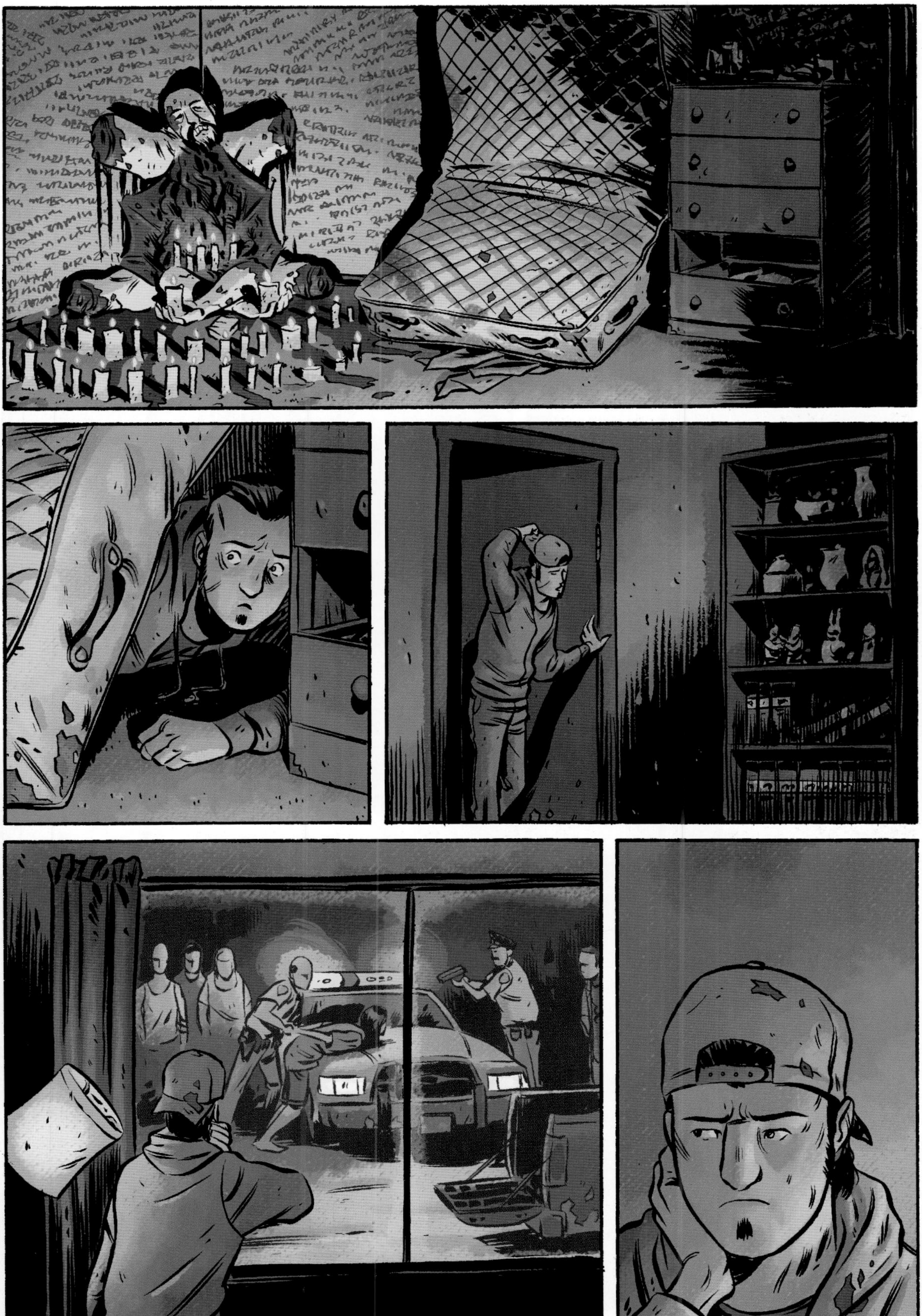

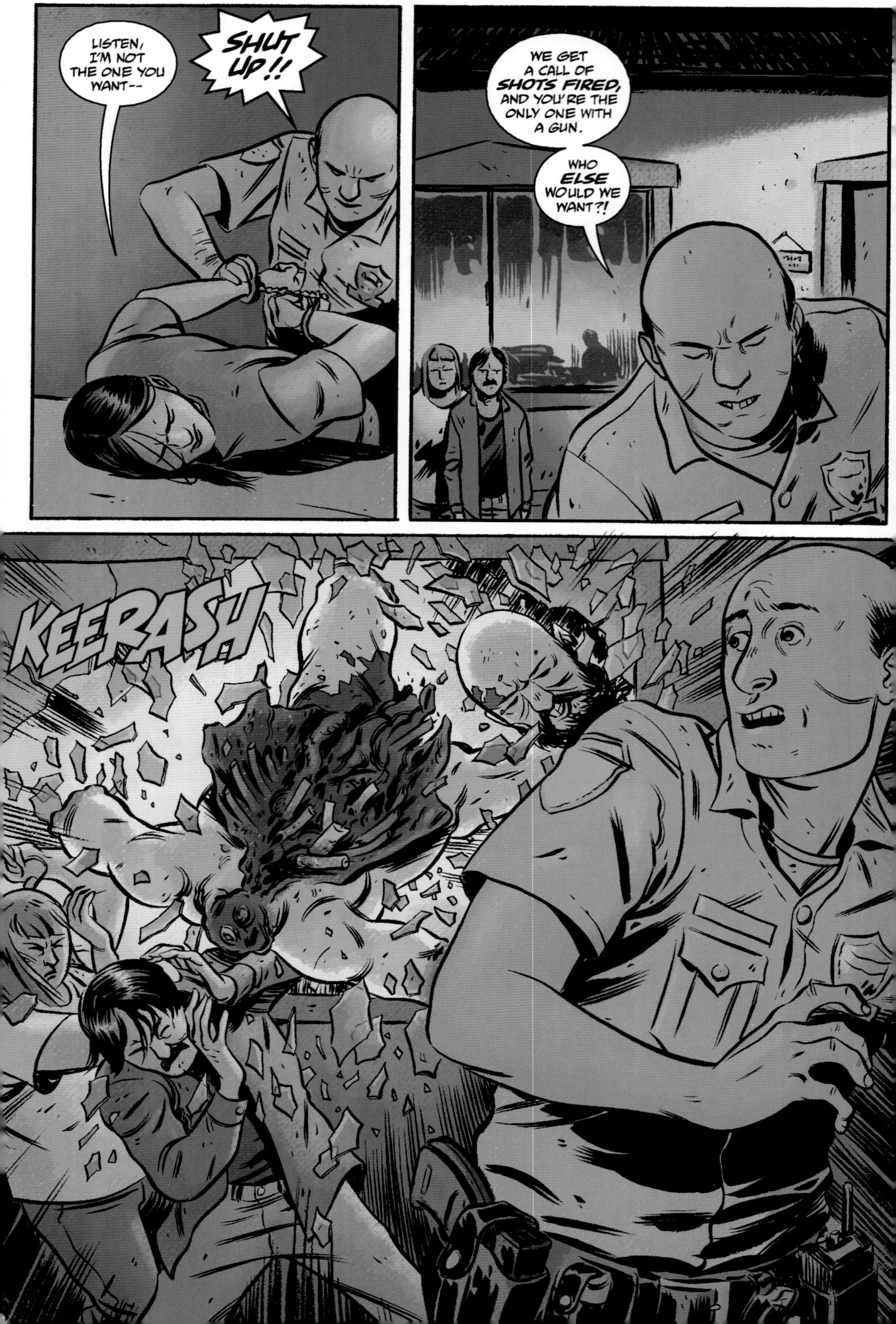
LISTEN, I'M NOT THE ONE YOU WANT--
SHUT UP!!
WE GET A CALL OF SHOTS FIRED, AND YOU'RE THE ONLY ONE WITH A GUN.
WHO ELSE WOULD WE WANT?!
KEERASH

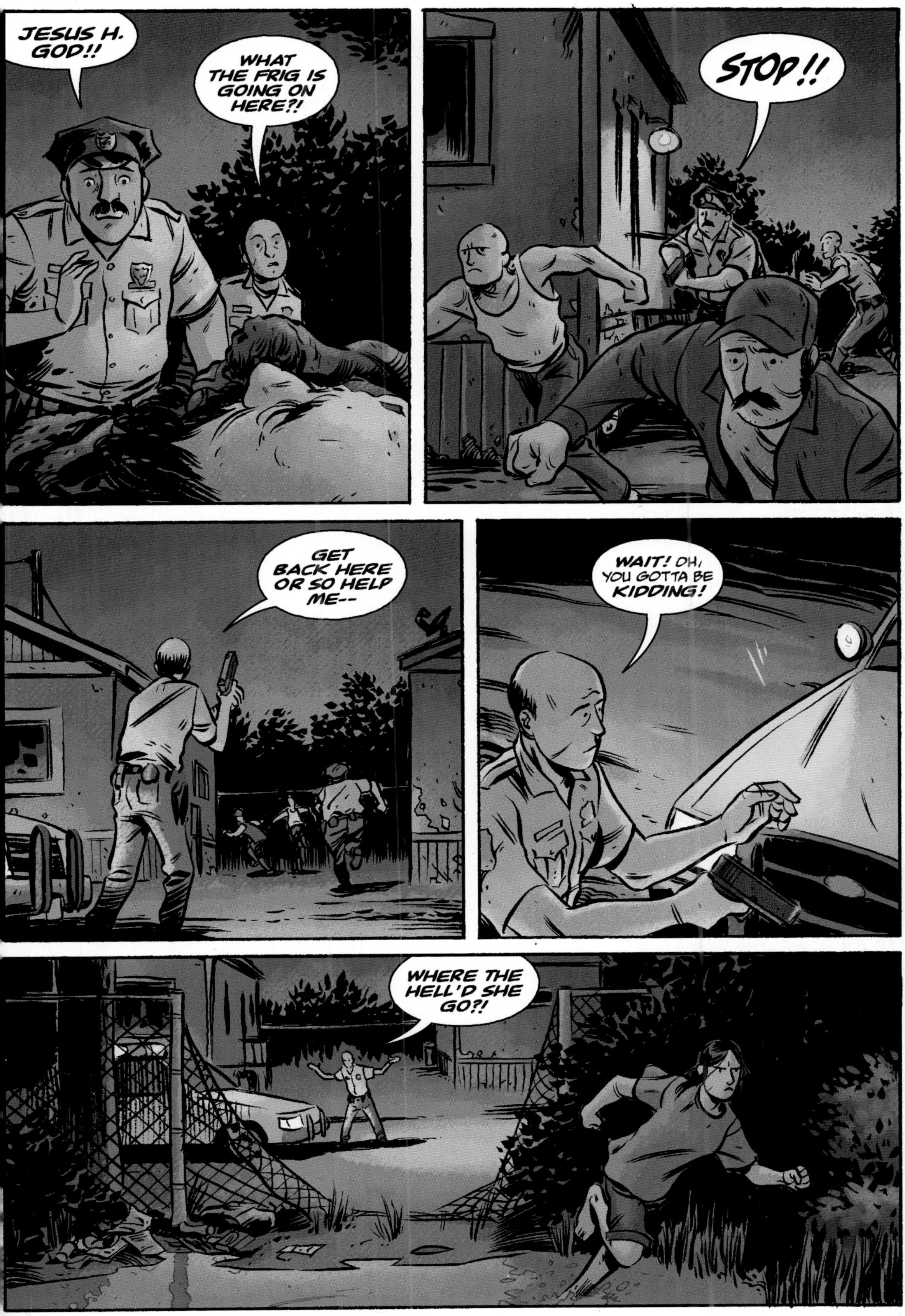
JESUS H. GOD!!
WHAT THE FRIG IS GOING ON HERE?!
STOP!!
GET BACK HERE OR SO HELP ME--
WAIT! OH, YOU GOTTA BE KIDDING!
WHERE THE HELL'D SHE GO?!

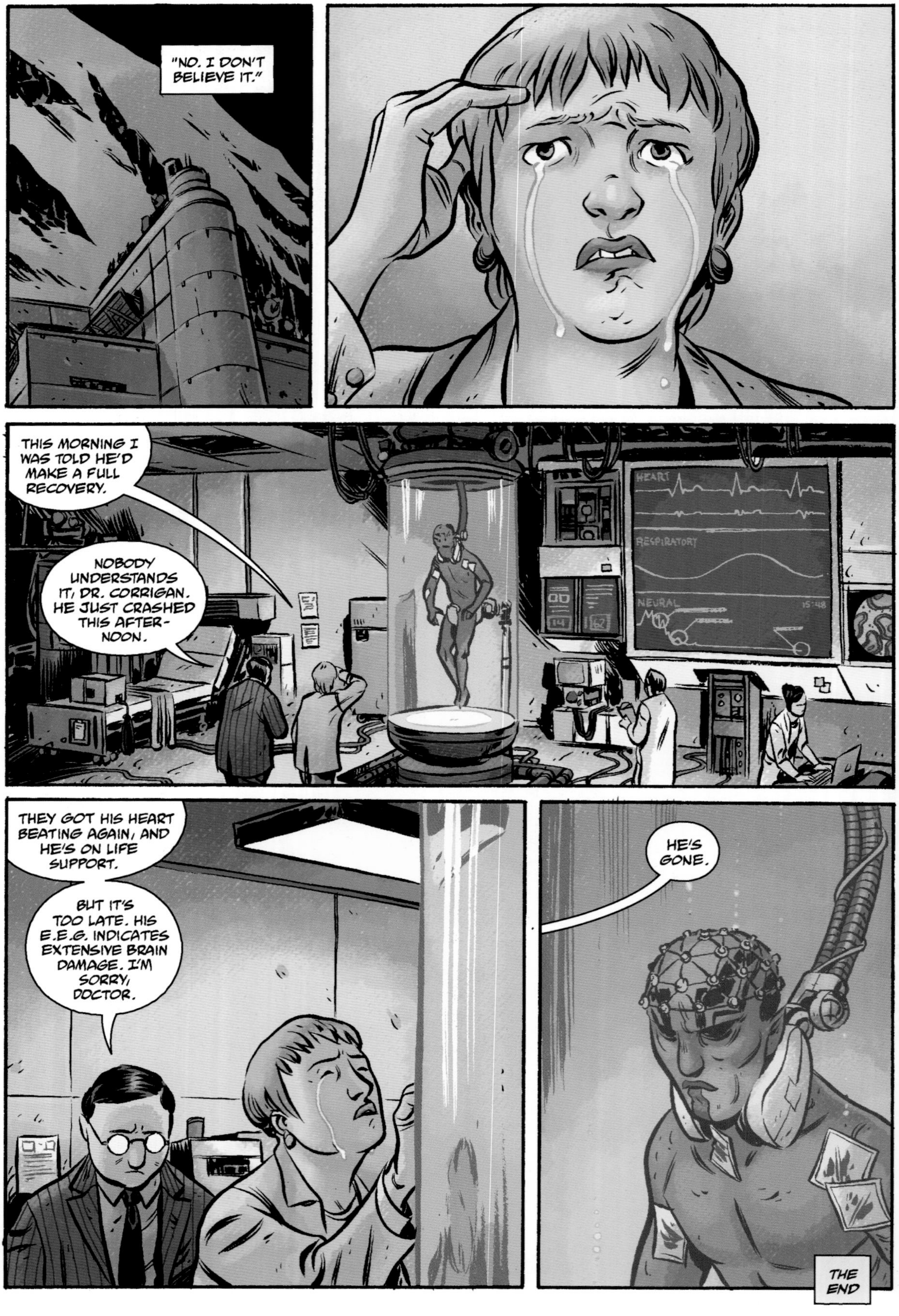
"NO. I DON'T BELIEVE IT."
THIS MORNING I WAS TOLD HE'D MAKE A FULL RECOVERY.
NOBODY UNDERSTANDS IT, DR. CORRIGAN. HE JUST CRASHED THIS AFTER-NOON.
HEART
RESPIRATORY
NEURAL
15:48
THEY GOT HIS HEART BEATING AGAIN, AND HE'S ON LIFE SUPPORT.
BUT IT'S TOO LATE. HIS E.E.G. INDICATES EXTENSIVE BRAIN DAMAGE. I'M SORRY, DOCTOR.
HE'S GONE.
THE END

B.P.R.D.™

SKETCHBOOK

Notes by Scott Allie

The character of Fenix had been kicking around John Arcudi's head for a while and had come up in conversations with his good friend and former *B.P.R.D.* artist Ryan Sook. We enlisted Ryan to do the covers for this arc in large part so he could use them to define Fenix—but also because he's a tremendously talented cover artist we'd long wanted to bring back into the mix. He put extra effort into getting her face just right, as well as the design on her hoodie.

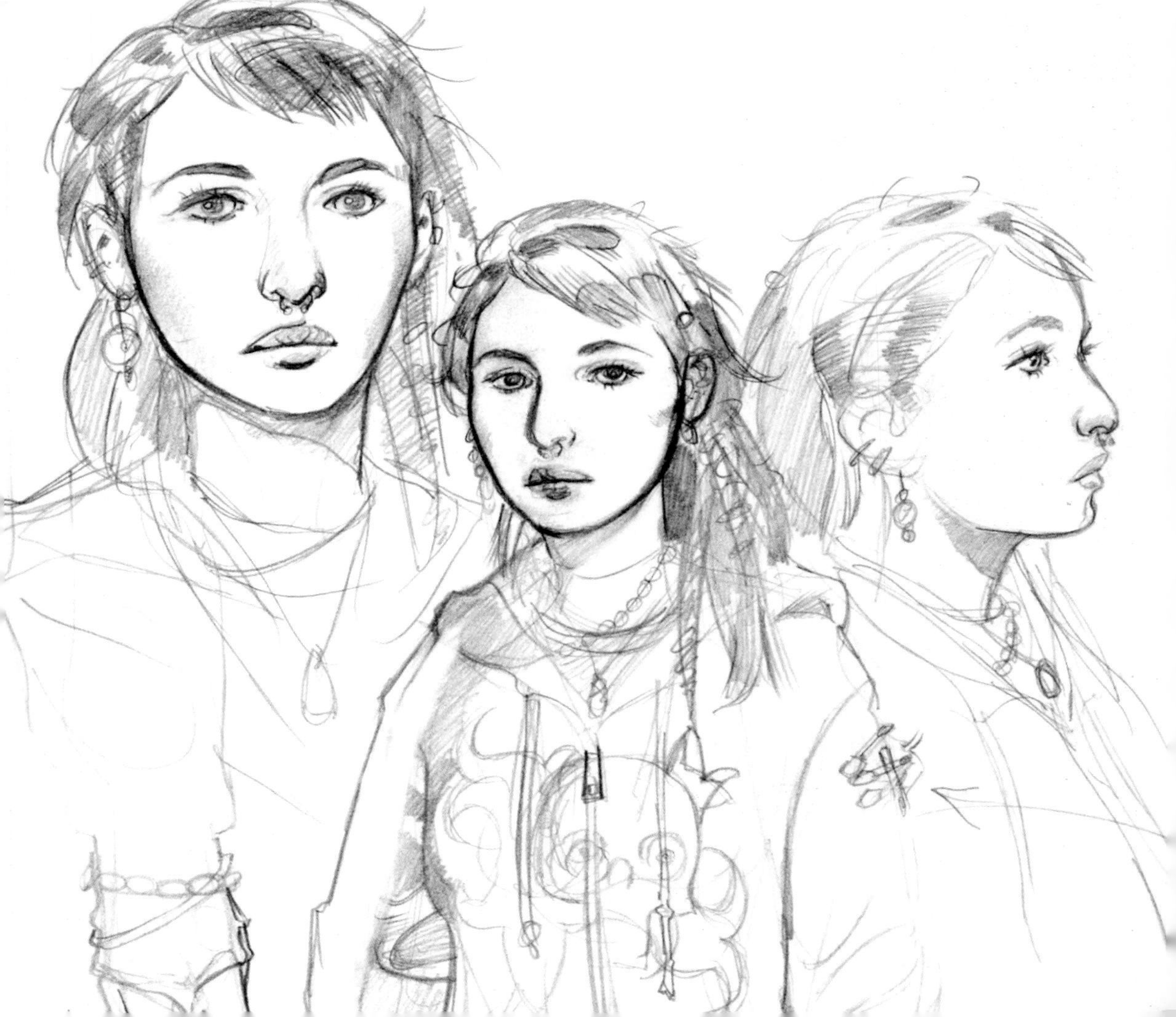

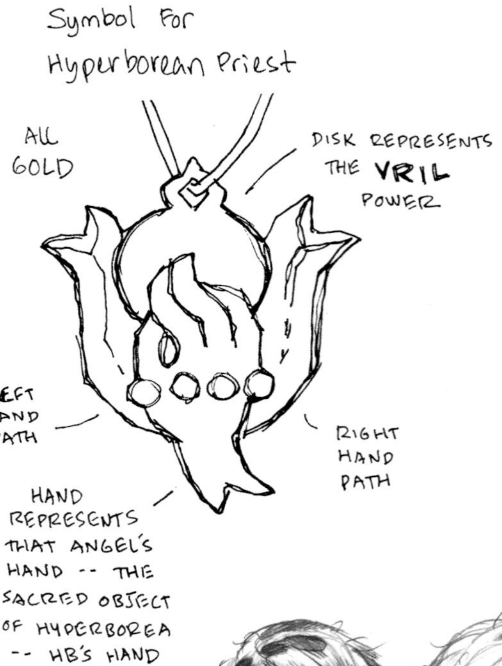
Symbol For
Hyperborean Priest
ALL
GOLD
DISK REPRESENTS
THE VRIL
POWER
LEFT
HAND
PATH
RIGHT
HAND
PATH
HAND
REPRESENTS
THAT ANGEL'S
HAND -- THE
SACRED OBJECT
OF HYPERBOREA
-- HB'S HAND

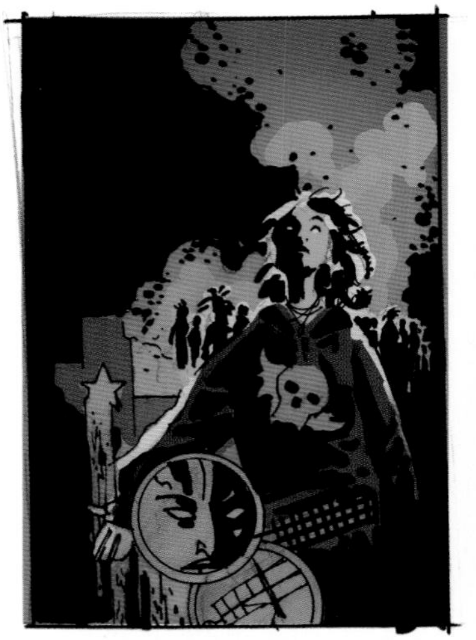

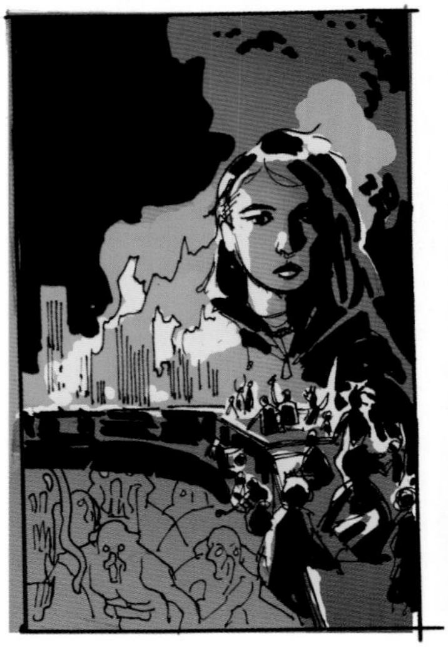

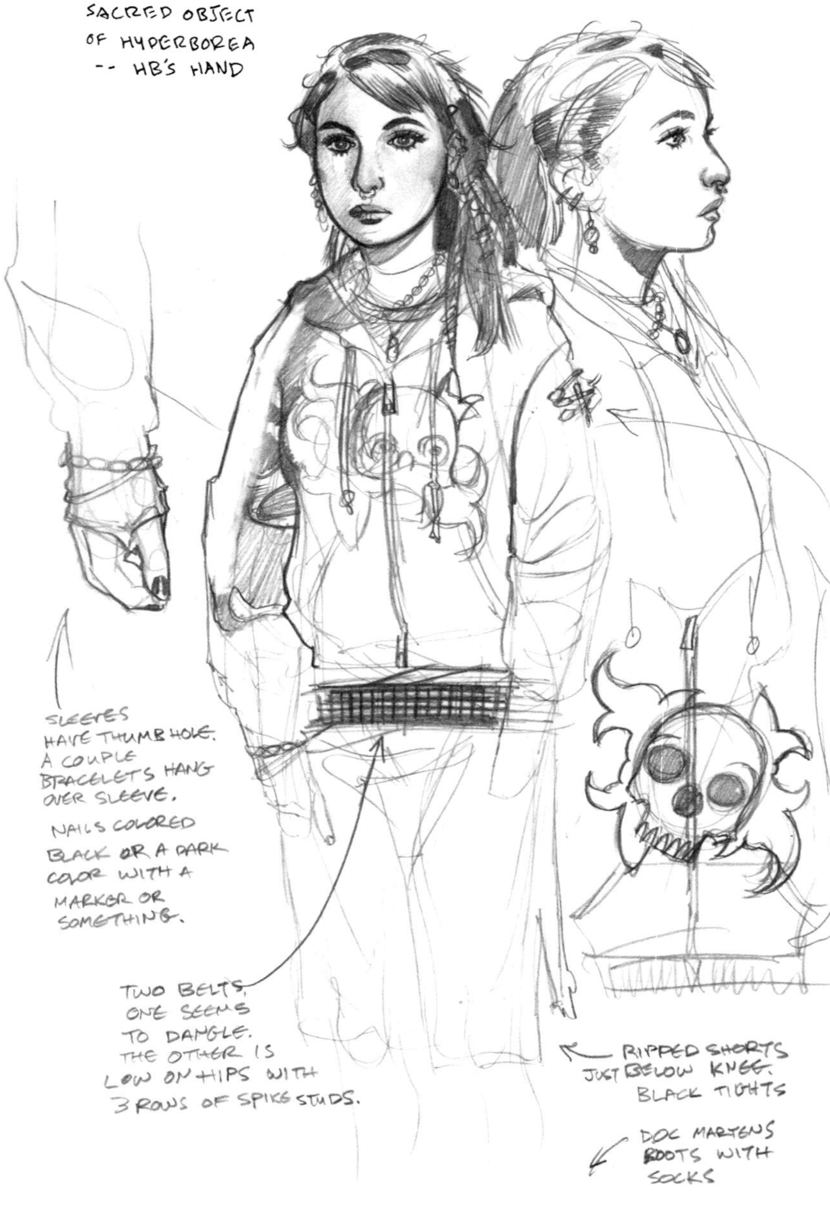
SAFETY PINS
HOLD SWEATSHIRT
SLEEVE TOGETHER.
SLEEVES
HAVE THUMB HOLE.
A COUPLE
BRACELETS HANG
OVER SLEEVE.
NAILS COLORED
BLACK OR A DARK
COLOR WITH A
MARKER OR
SOMETHING.
SWEAT SHIRT
EMBLEM SOMETHING
LIKE THIS. SKULL
IS SPLIT BY
ZIPPER.
TWO BELTS,
ONE SEEMS
TO DANGLE.
THE OTHER IS
LOW ON HIPS WITH
3 ROWS OF SPIKE STUDS.
RIPPED SHORTS
JUST BELOW KNEE.
BLACK TIGHTS
DOC MARTENS
BOOTS WITH
SOCKS

Facing, top left: Mignola's design for the priest's amulet. Top right: Ryan's sketches for the *Gods* #1 cover.

This page: His study for Fenix for the cover. Compare to page 5 of this volume.

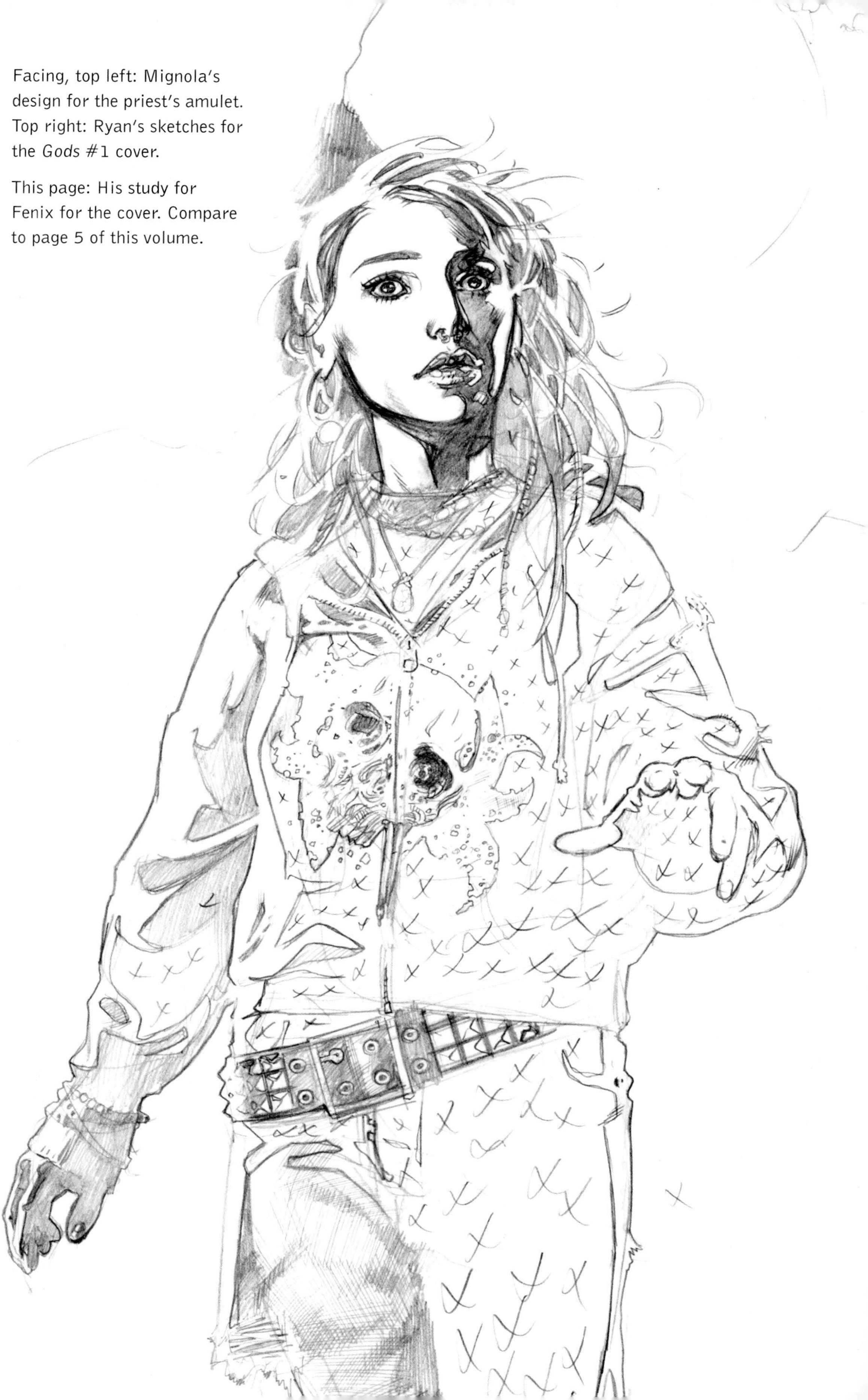

We were asked to create a variant cover for *Gods* #1 and wanted to do something unusual and meaningful. This cover wound up being one of the most collaborative single pieces of art we've created, with everyone on the team throwing in ideas, but of course most of the hard work fell to Guy. The cover signals major changes for Abe Sapien, starting in this volume. The lettering layer got Clem on the cover for the first time.

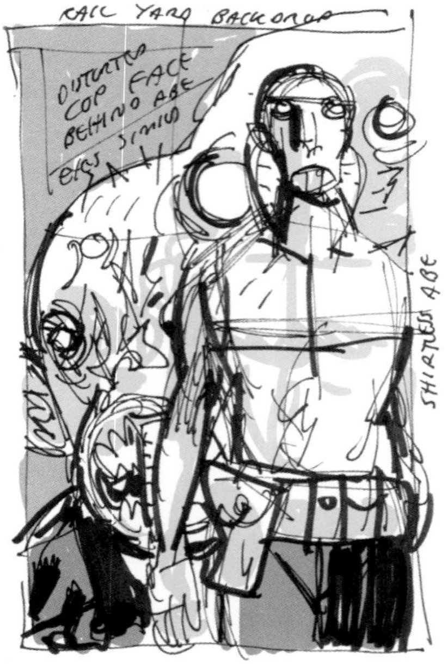
RAIL YARD BACKDROP
COP FACE
BEHIND ABE
SHIRTLESS ABE

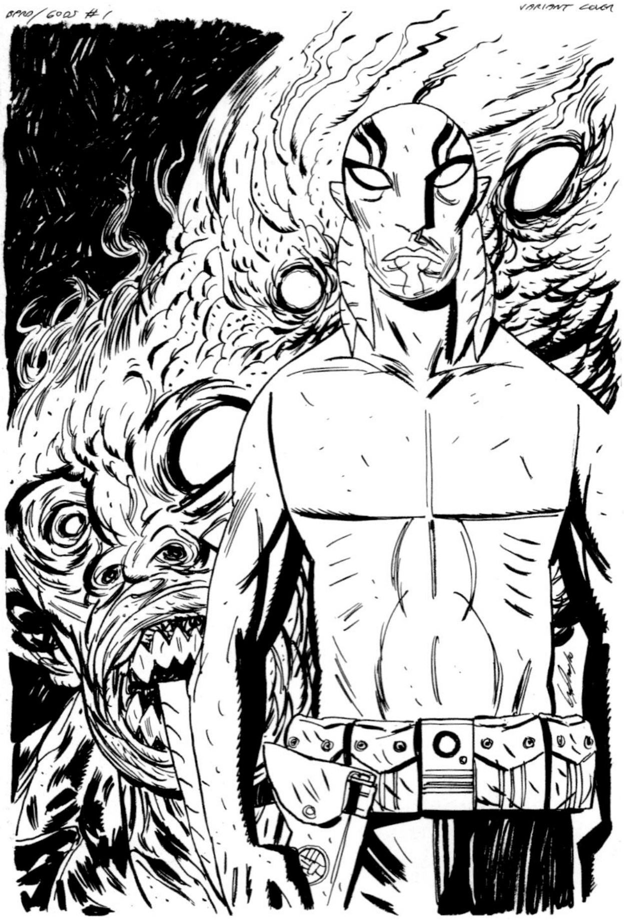
BPRD/GODS #1
VARIANT COVER

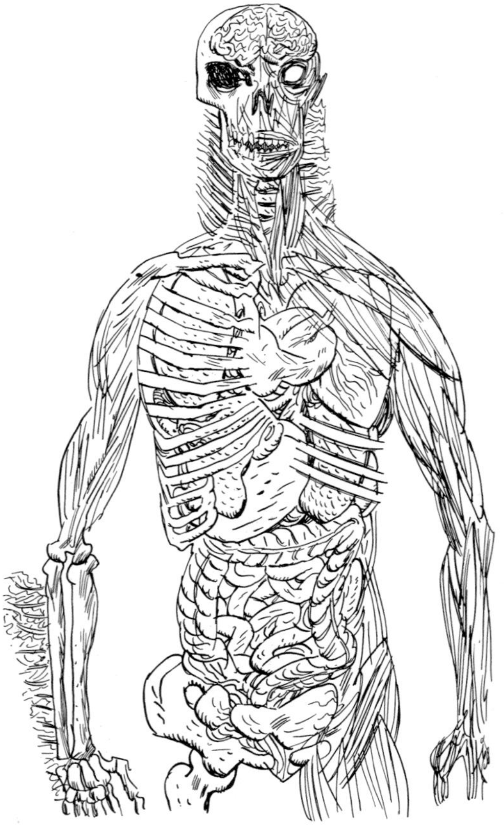

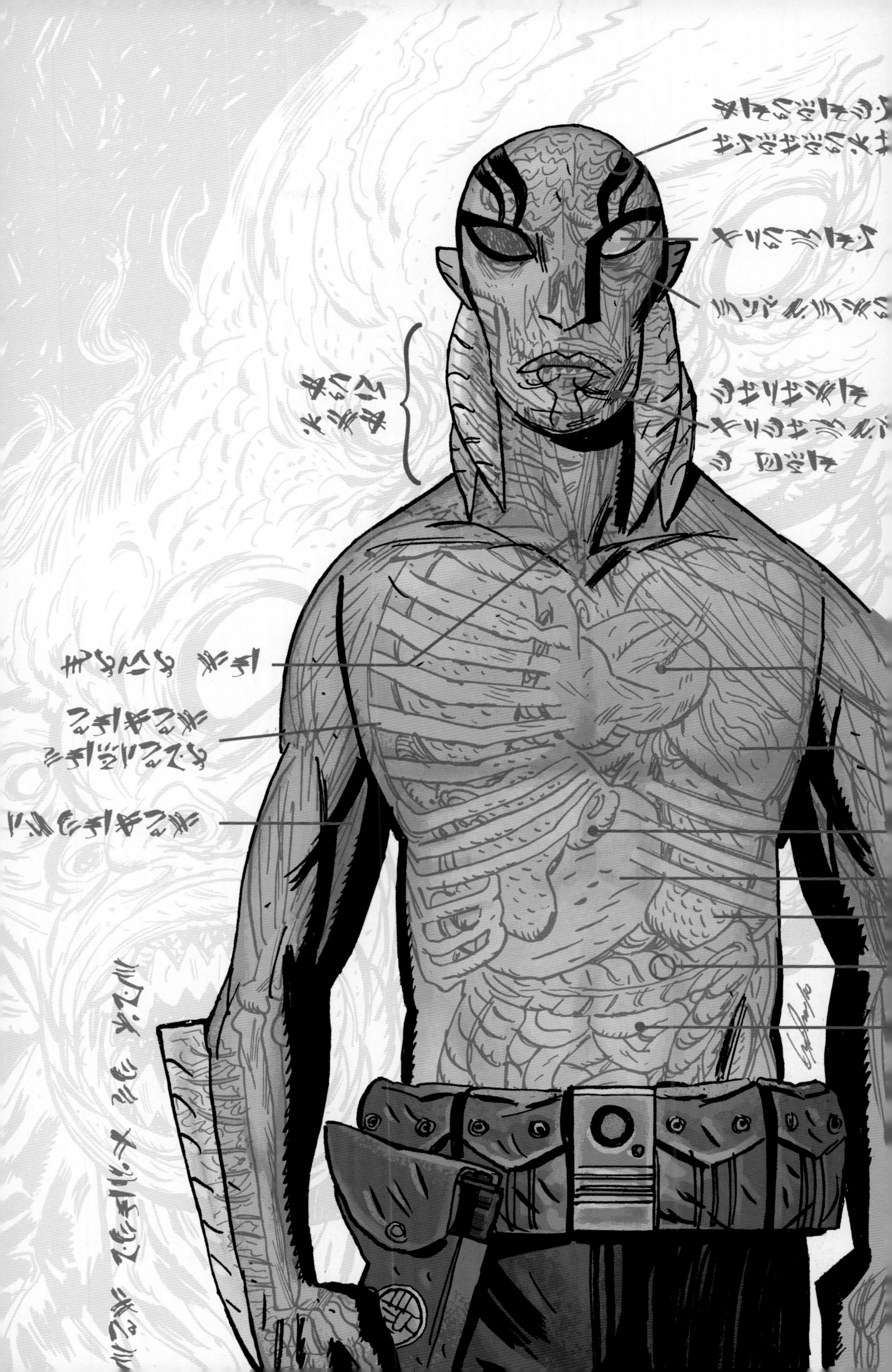

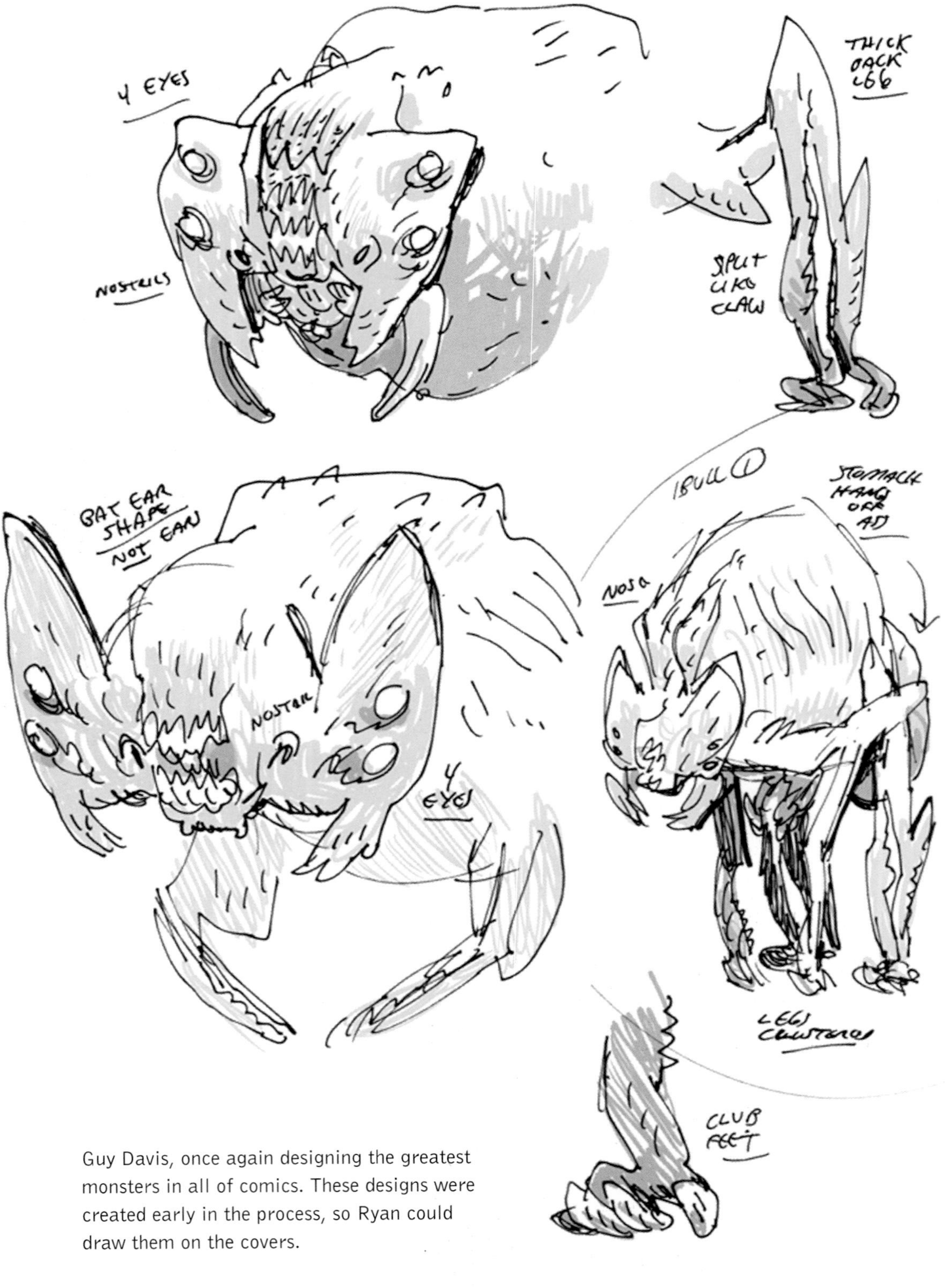
4 EYES
NOSTRILS
SPLIT LIKE CLAW
BAT EAR SHAPE
NOT EAR
4 EYES
NOSE
CLUB FEET

Guy Davis, once again designing the greatest monsters in all of comics. These designs were created early in the process, so Ryan could draw them on the covers.

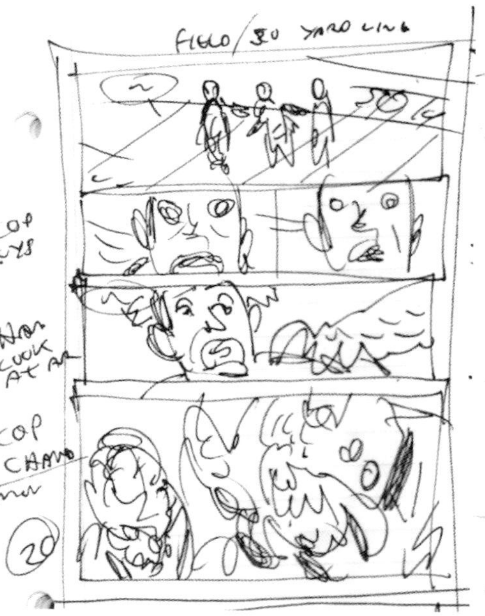

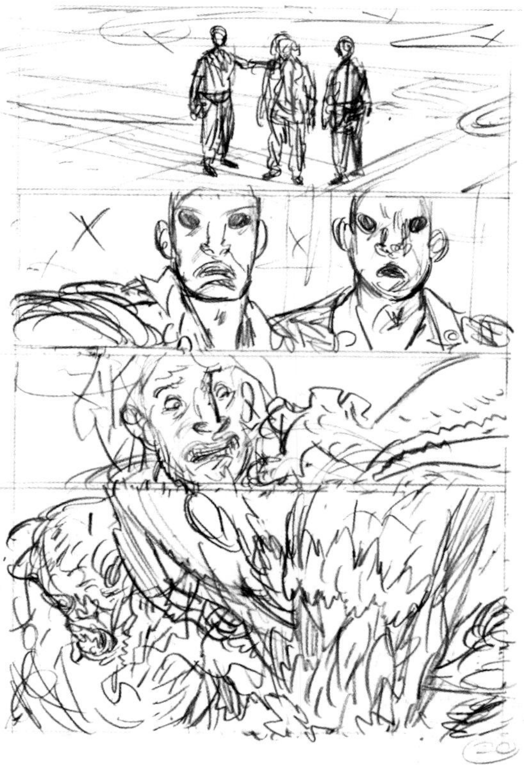

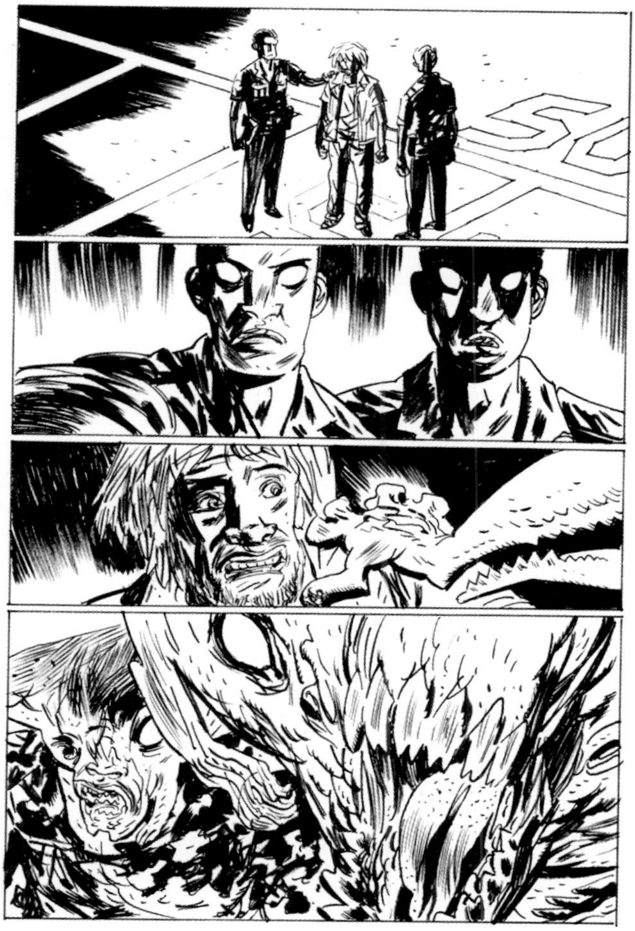

From *Gods*, chapter 1 (page 26 of this volume): layouts, pencils, and inks from Guy Davis.

Sketch, studies, and (facing page) final pencils for Ryan's *Monsters* #1 cover. Compare to page 77 of this volume.

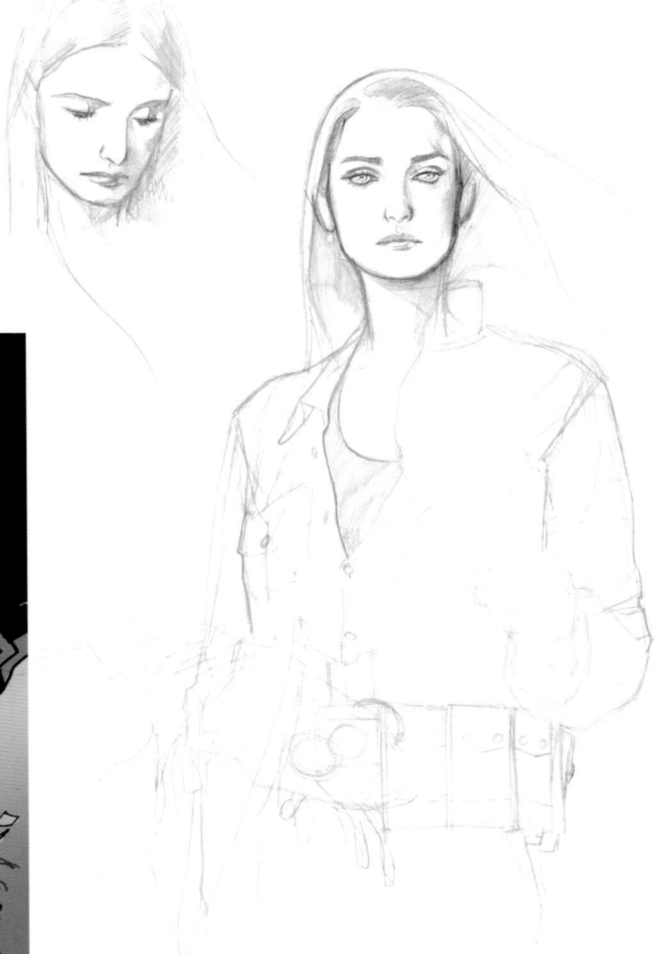

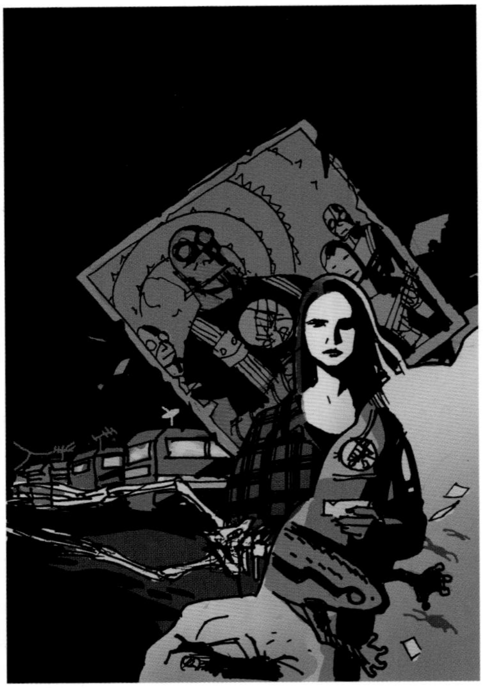

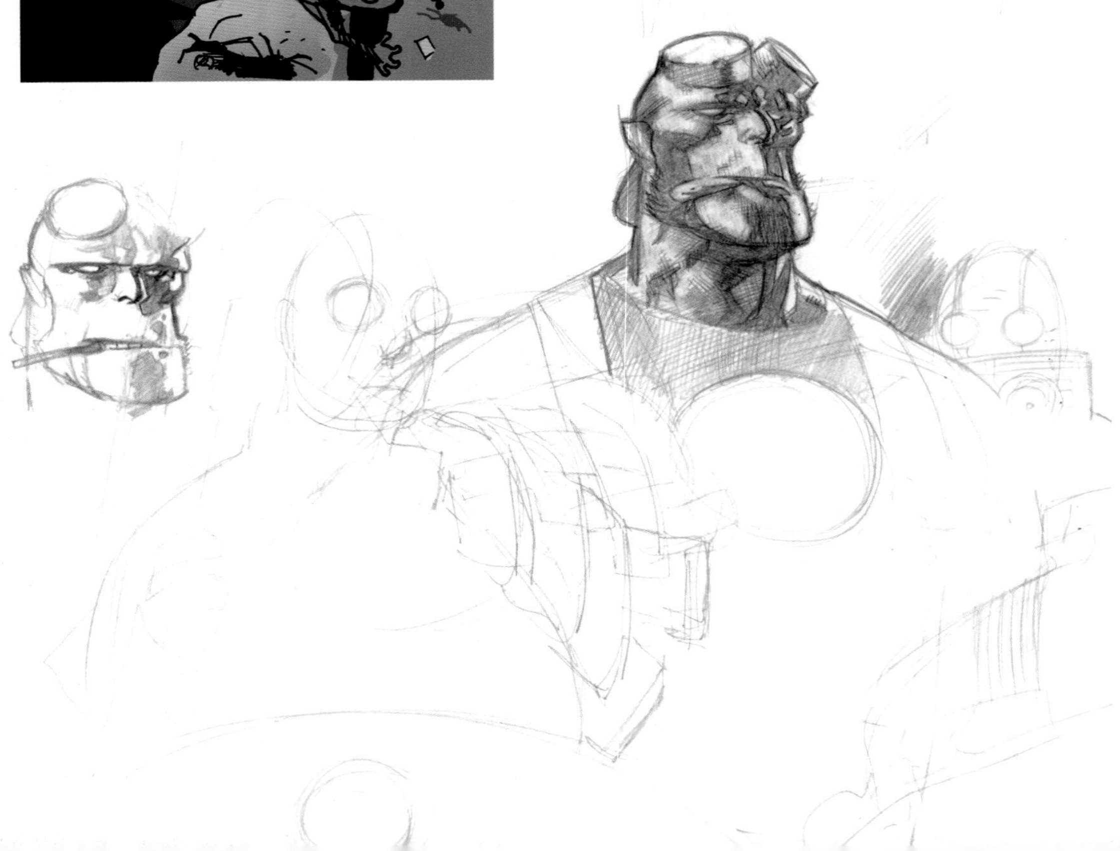

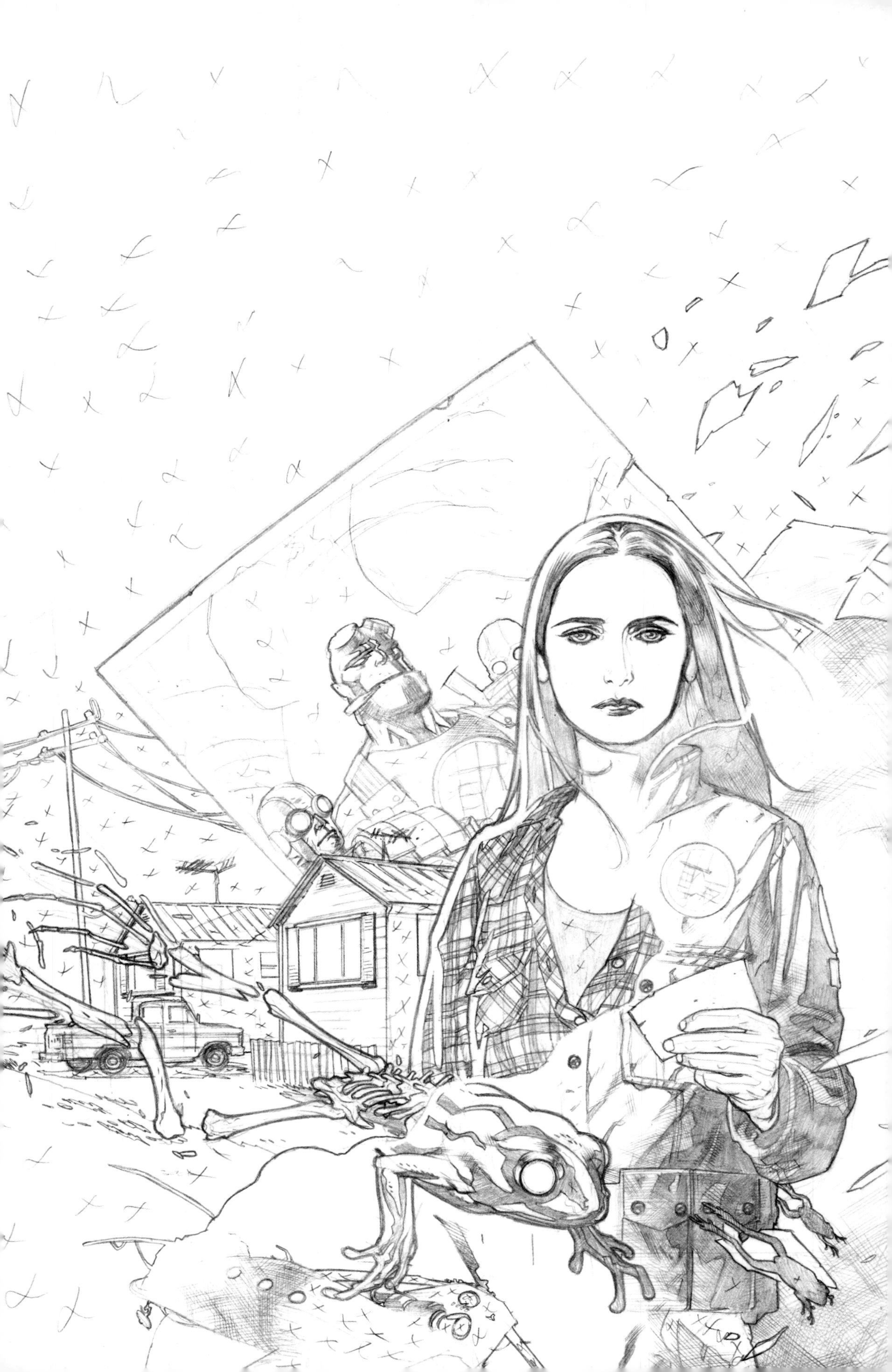

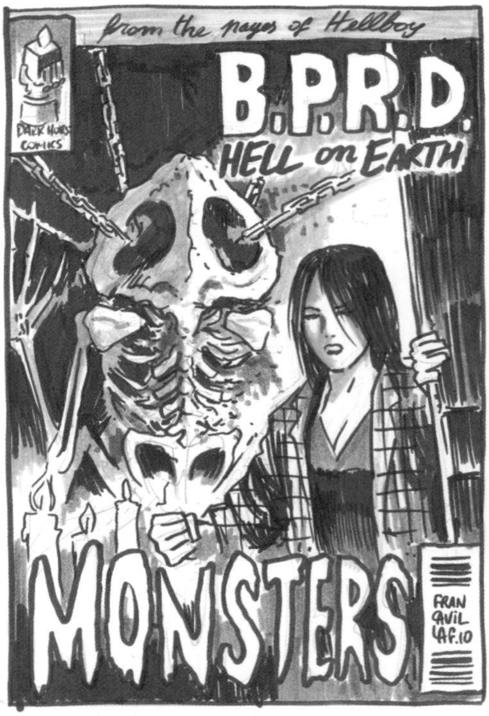
from the pages of Hellboy
DARK HORSE COMICS
B.P.R.D.
HELL on EARTH
MONSTERS
FRAN CAVIL LA F.10

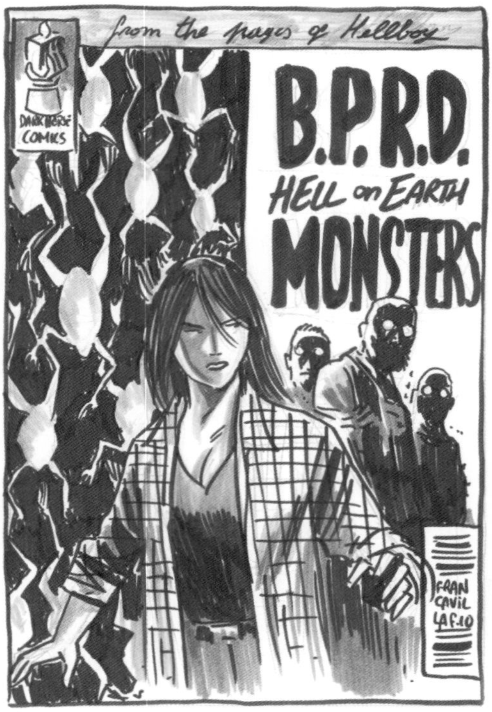
from the pages of Hellboy
DARK HORSE COMICS
B.P.R.D.
HELL on EARTH
MONSTERS
FRAN CAVIL LA F.10

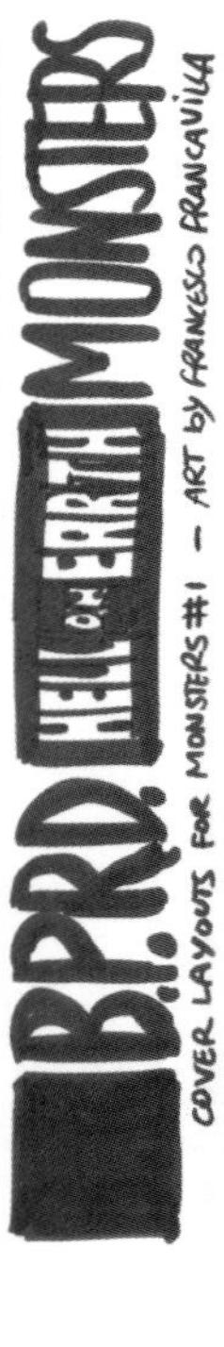
B.P.R.D. HELL on EARTH MONSTERS
COVER LAYOUTS FOR MONSTERS #1 — ART by FRANCESCO FRANCAVILLA

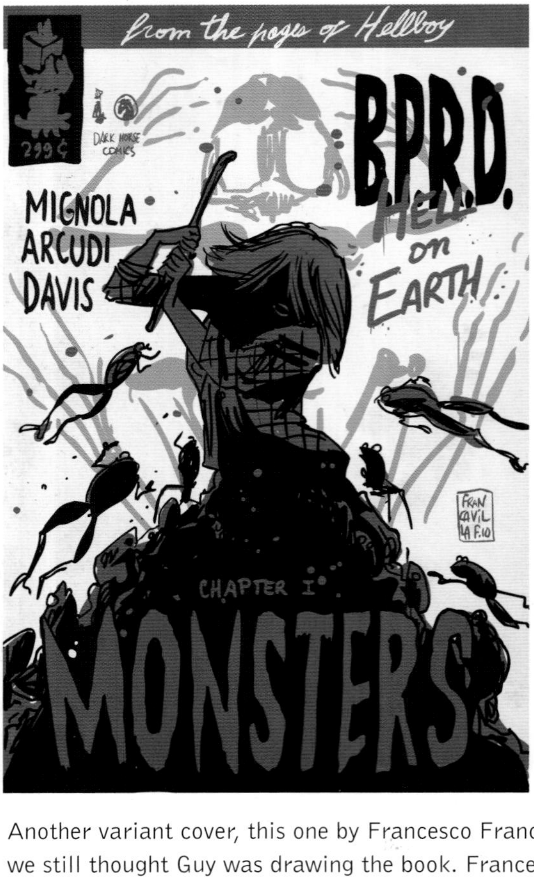
from the pages of Hellboy
299¢
DARK HORSE COMICS
B.P.R.D.
HELL on EARTH
MIGNOLA
ARCUDI
DAVIS
FRAN CAVIL LA F.10
CHAPTER I
MONSTERS

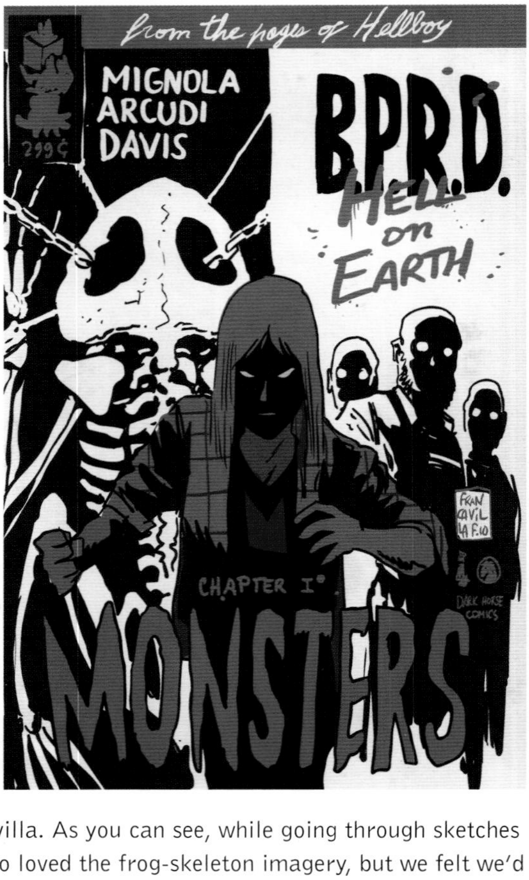
from the pages of Hellboy
299¢
MIGNOLA
ARCUDI
DAVIS
B.P.R.D.
HELL on EARTH
FRAN CAVIL LA F.10
DARK HORSE COMICS
CHAPTER I
MONSTERS

Another variant cover, this one by Francesco Francavilla. As you can see, while going through sketches we still thought Guy was drawing the book. Francesco loved the frog-skeleton imagery, but we felt we'd already used it up on Ryan's covers, so we replaced it with the B.P. R.D. symbol. We specifically asked for the action pose in the third sketch, but realized the more static pose was more effective.

Facing page: The final cover.

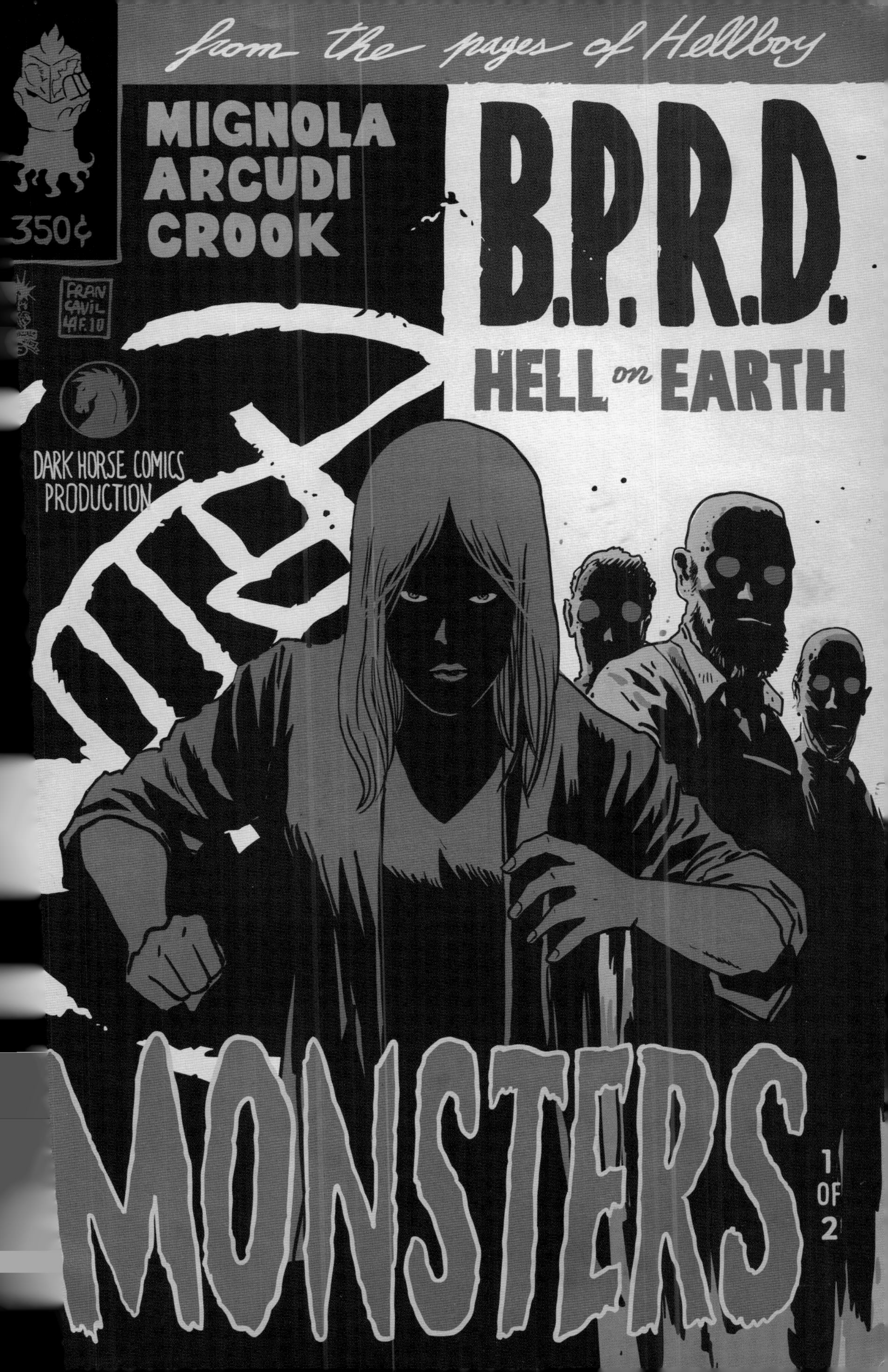
from the pages of Hellboy
MIGNOLA
ARCUDI
CROOK
350¢
B.P.R.D.
HELL on EARTH
DARK HORSE COMICS
PRODUCTION
FRAN CAVIL 14F.10
MONSTERS
1 OF 2

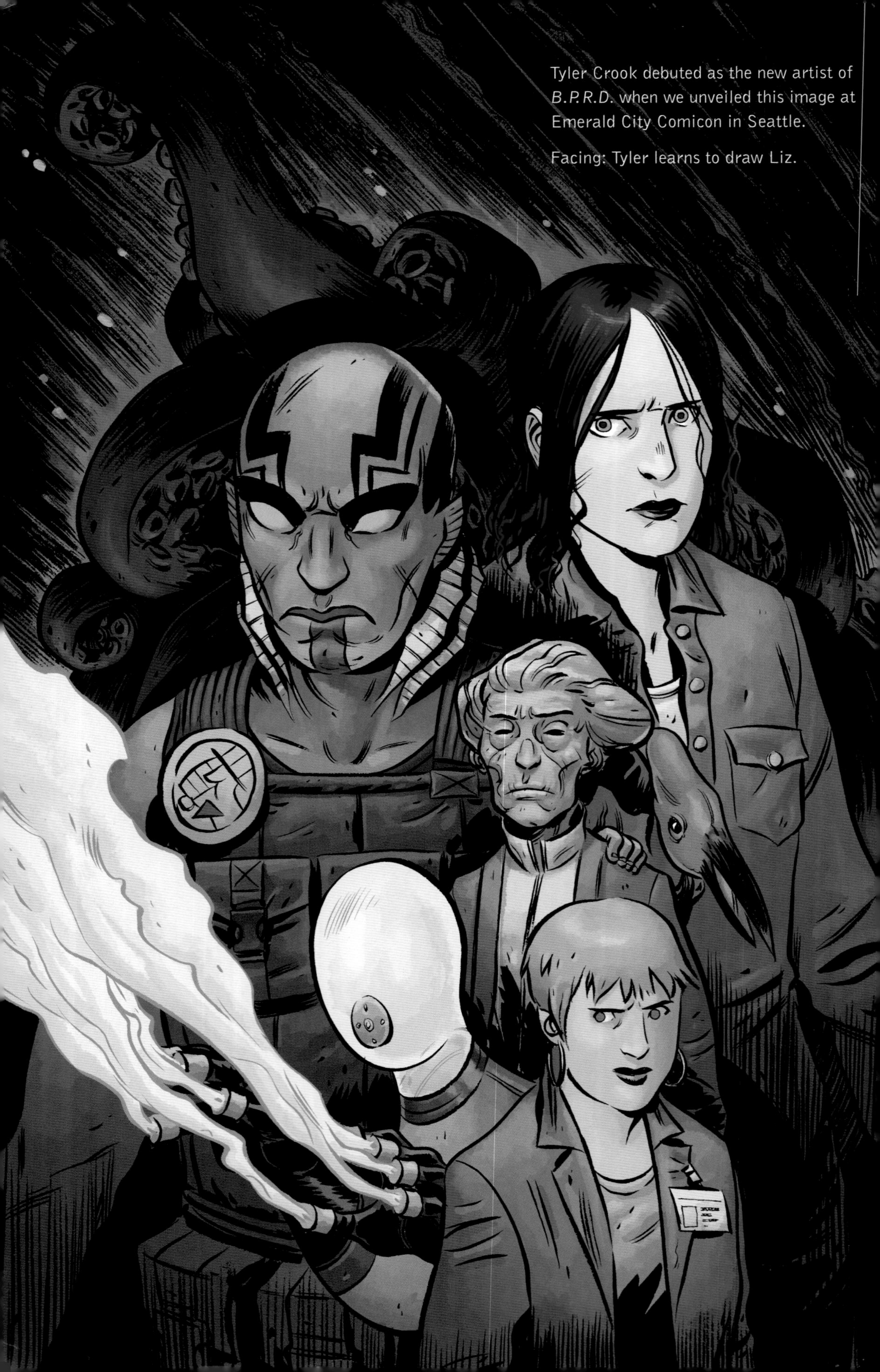

Tyler Crook debuted as the new artist of *B.P.R.D.* when we unveiled this image at Emerald City Comicon in Seattle.

Facing: Tyler learns to draw Liz.

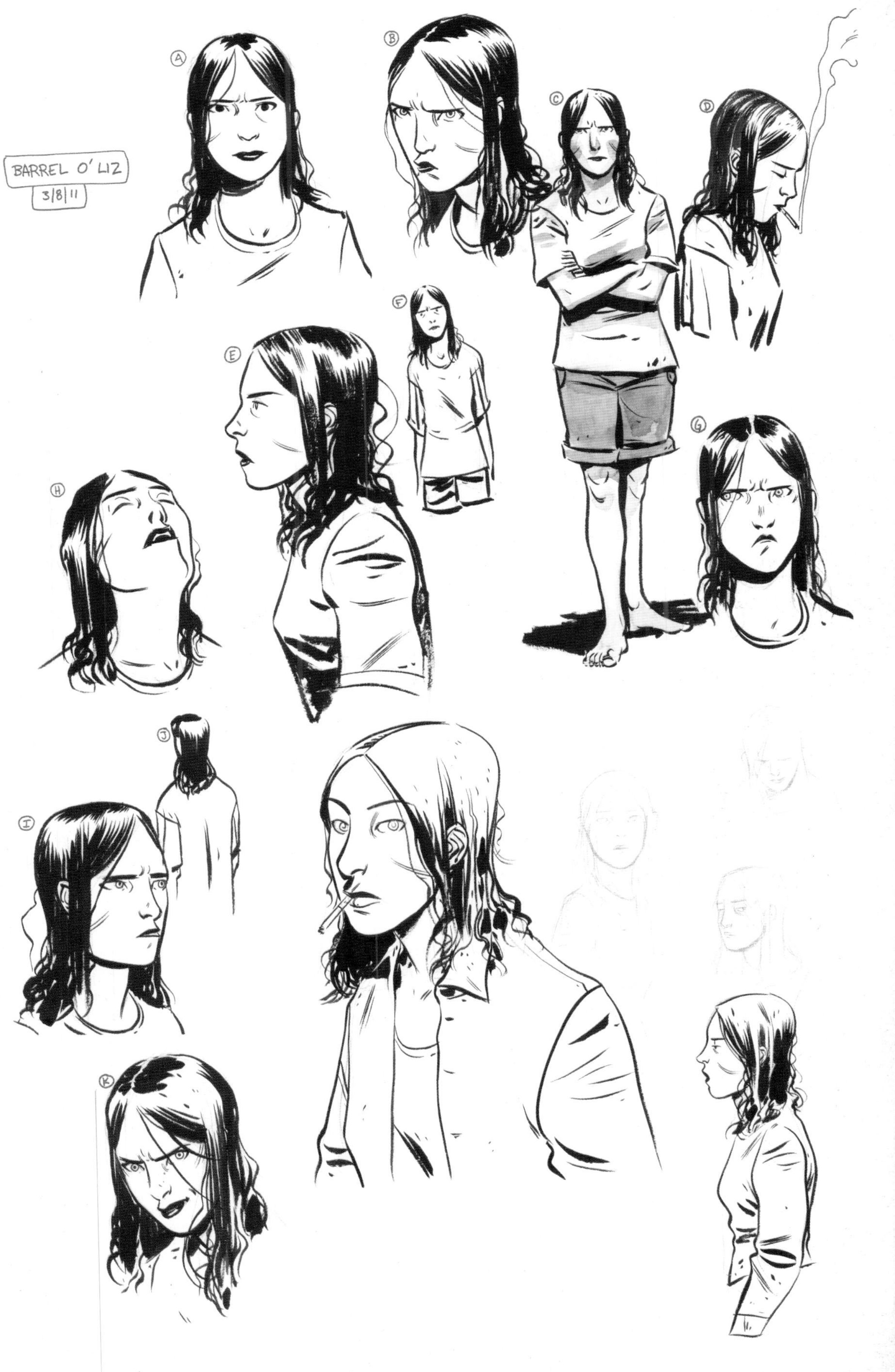

BARREL O' LIZ
3/8/11
A
B
C
D
E
F
G
H
I
J
K

DARK HORSE COMICS ART BOARD

TITLE BPRD ISSUE — ARTIST MISTER CROOK PAGE —

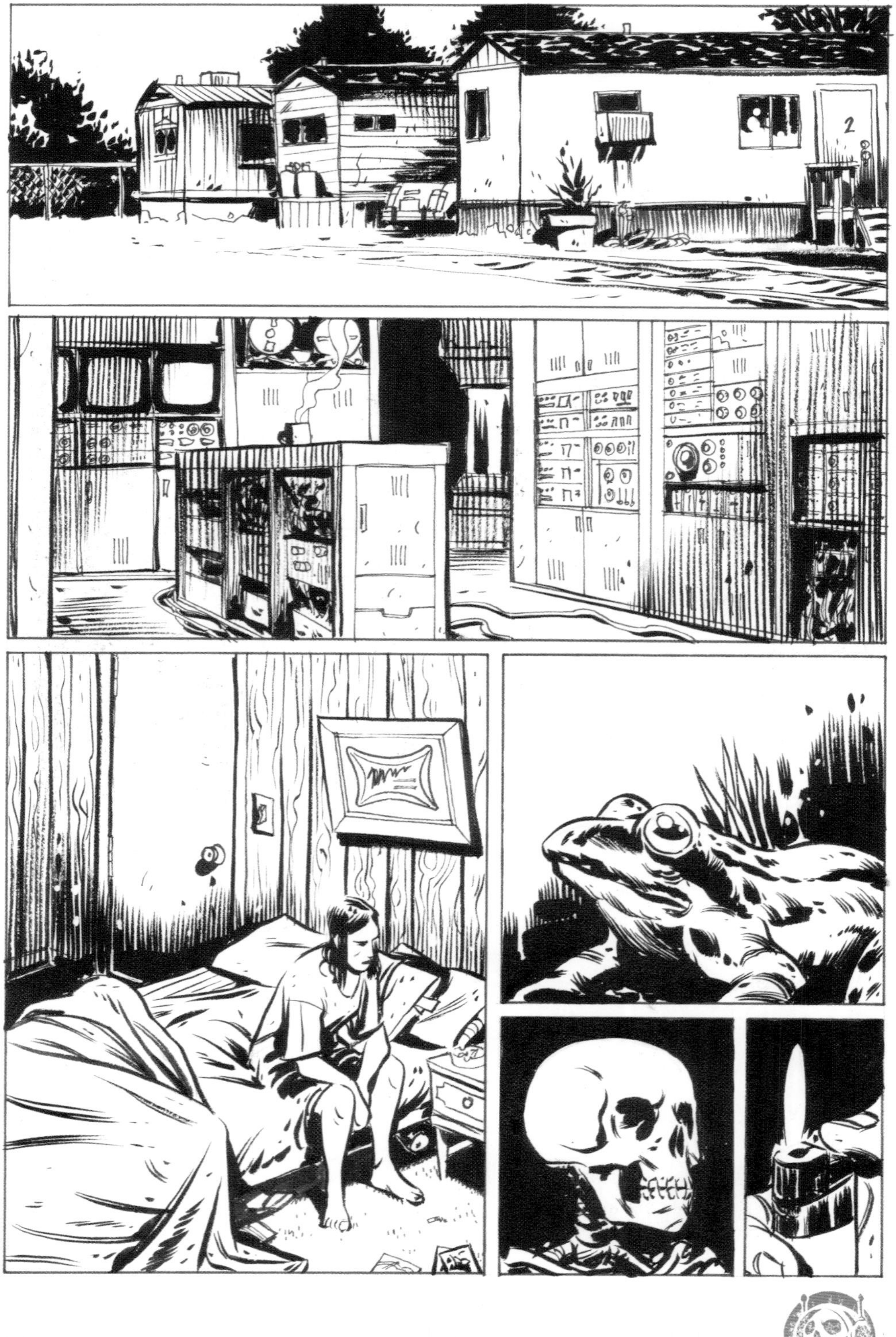
2

FOR ART THAT WILL BE REPRODUCED FROM PENCIL ONLY, DRAW ON THE REVERSE SIDE OF THIS BOARD AND INK IN TRIM MARKS IN BLACK.

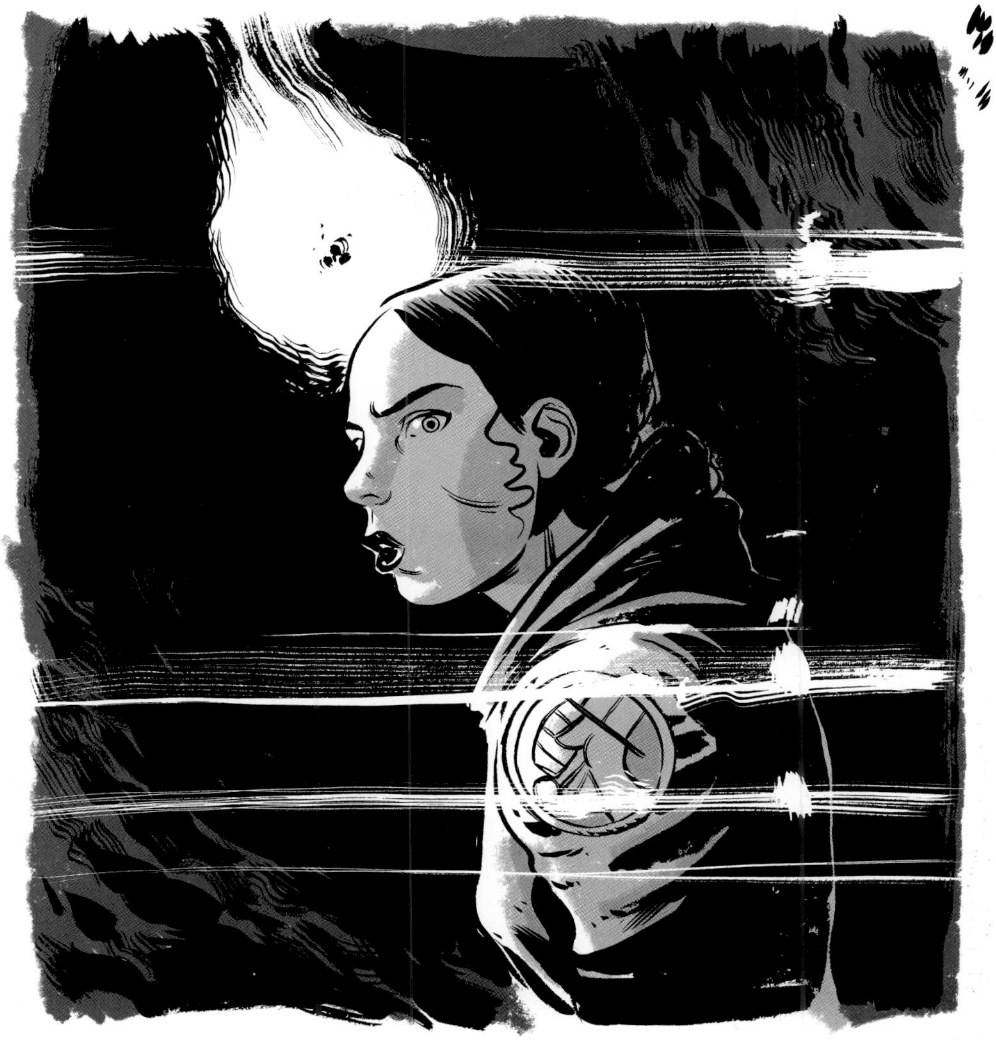

Top: Tyler's art for the inside cover of the *Monsters* comics. Right, and following two pages: Tyler's first original character designs for *B.P.R.D.*

Facing: Tyler warming up. This was never intended to be a page in the book, but it was the start of him bringing the world to life. *Monsters* wound up being an easy arc for him to start on, with only one main character, and a setting firmly rooted in reality. The next arc, *Russia*, would push him into the deep end of the *B.P.R.D.* world.

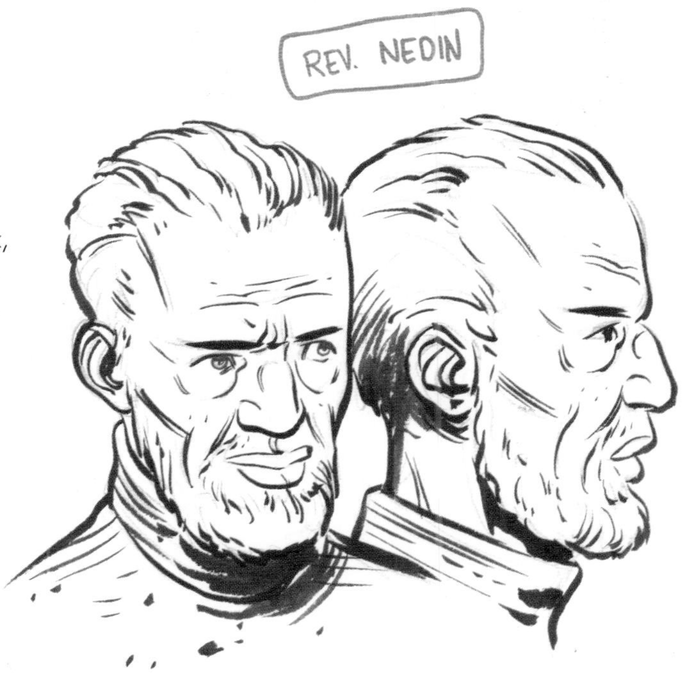
REV. NEDIN

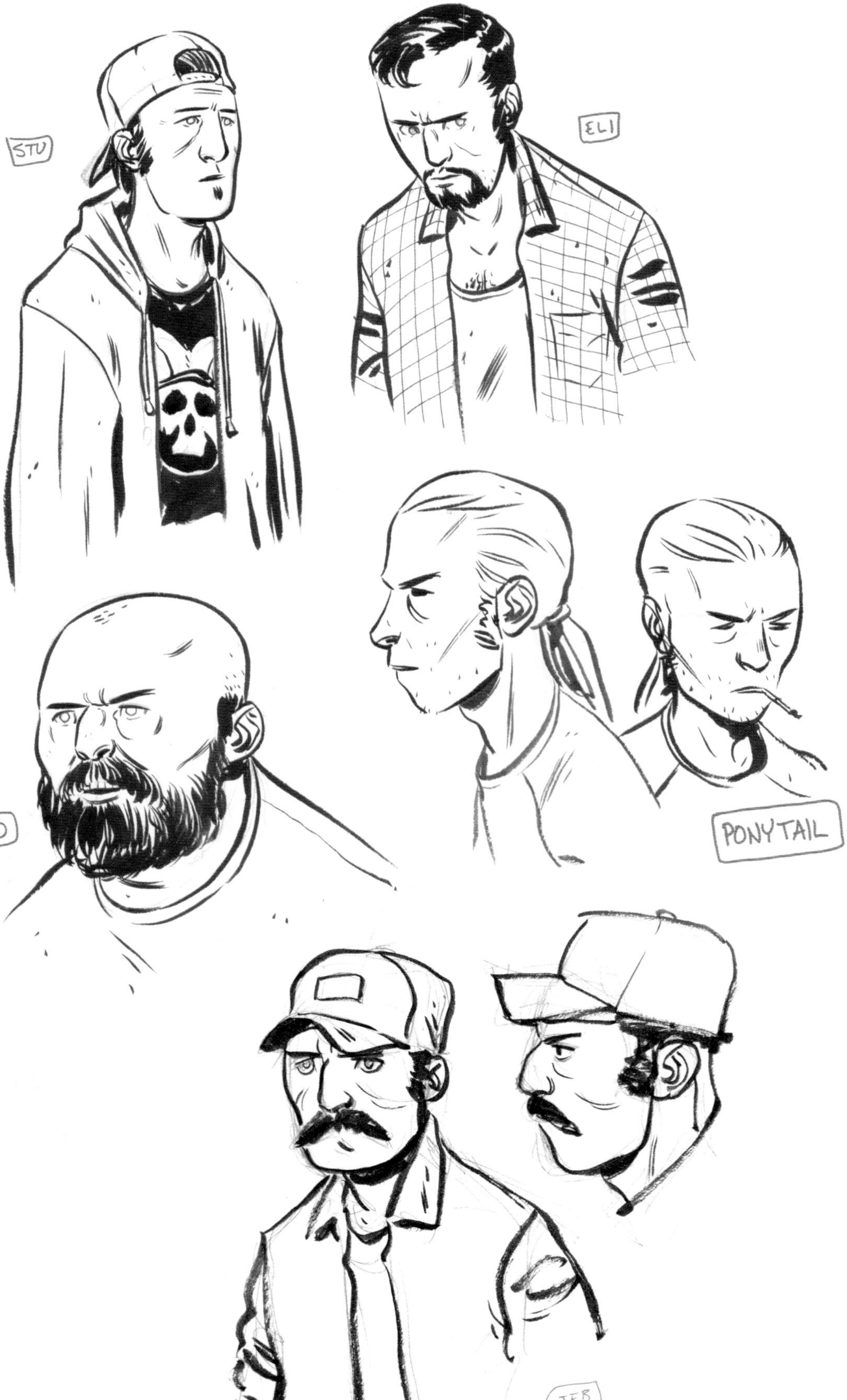
STU
ELI
BEARD
PONYTAIL
JEB

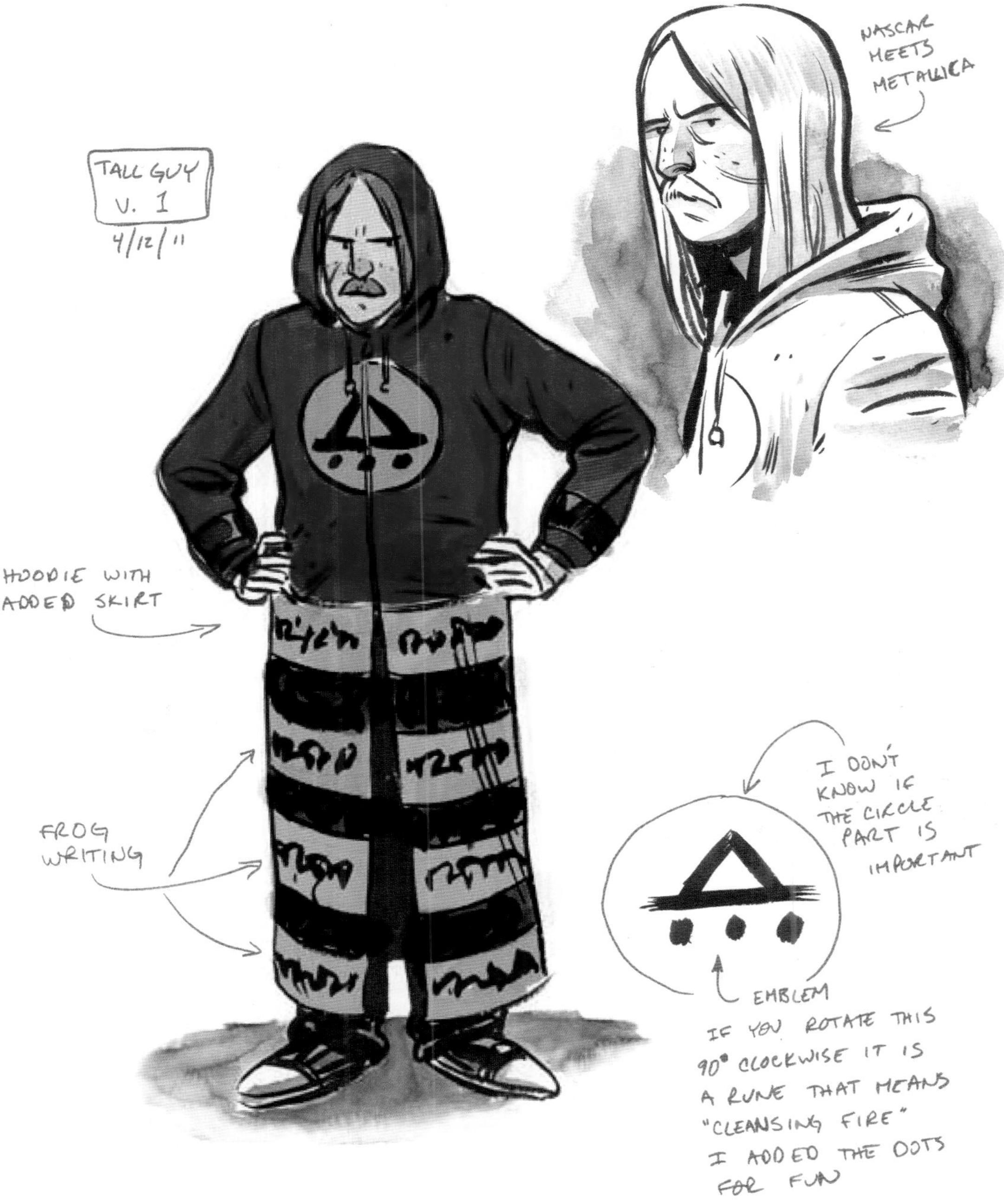
TALL GUY
V. 1
4/12/11
NASCAR MEETS METALLICA
HOODIE WITH ADDED SKIRT
FROG WRITING
I DON'T KNOW IF THE CIRCLE PART IS IMPORTANT
EMBLEM
IF YOU ROTATE THIS 90° CLOCKWISE IT IS A RUNE THAT MEANS "CLEANSING FIRE"
I ADDED THE DOTS FOR FUN

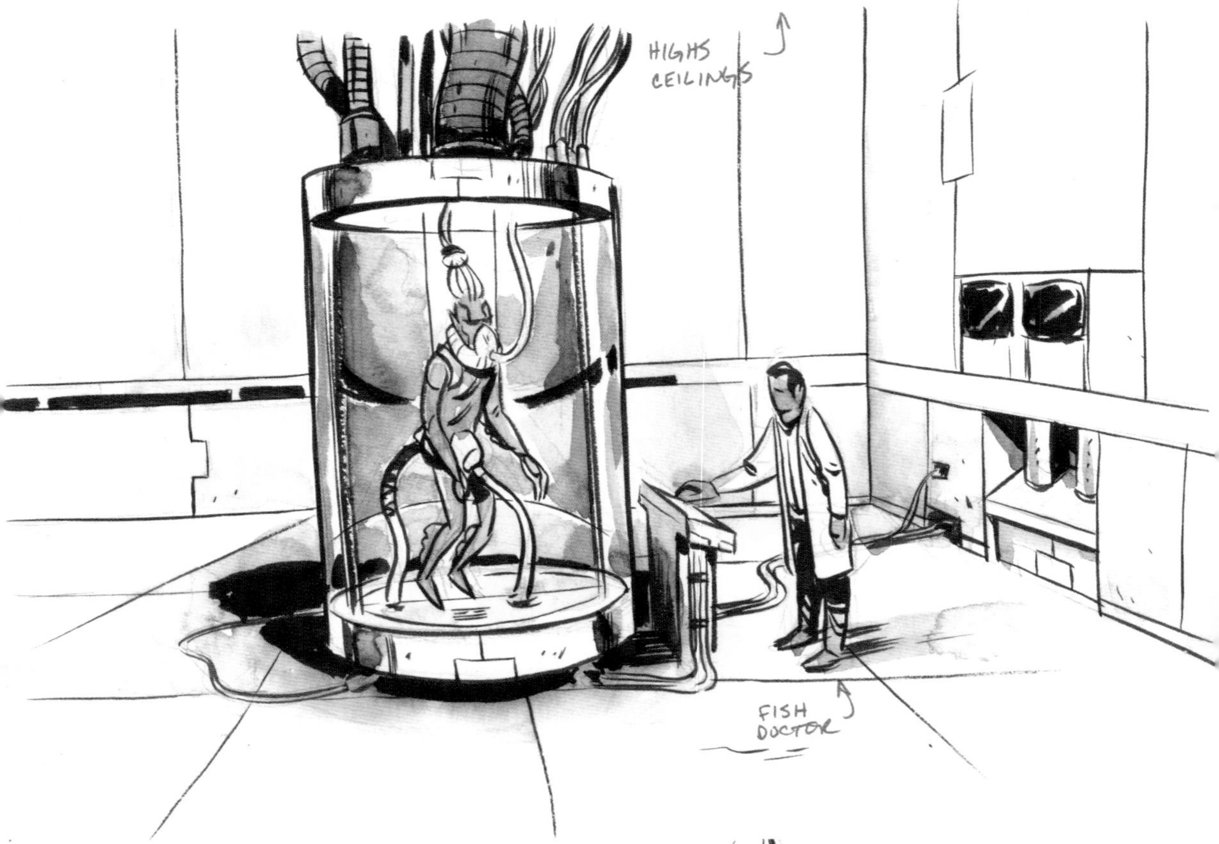
HIGHS CEILINGS
FISH DOCTOR
POOR ABE
4/12/11
V. 1

A lot of work went into designing Abe's tank, making sure Tyler's tech synced up with how Guy designed Bureau settings, and also making sure it all would work with scenes planned for upcoming issues.

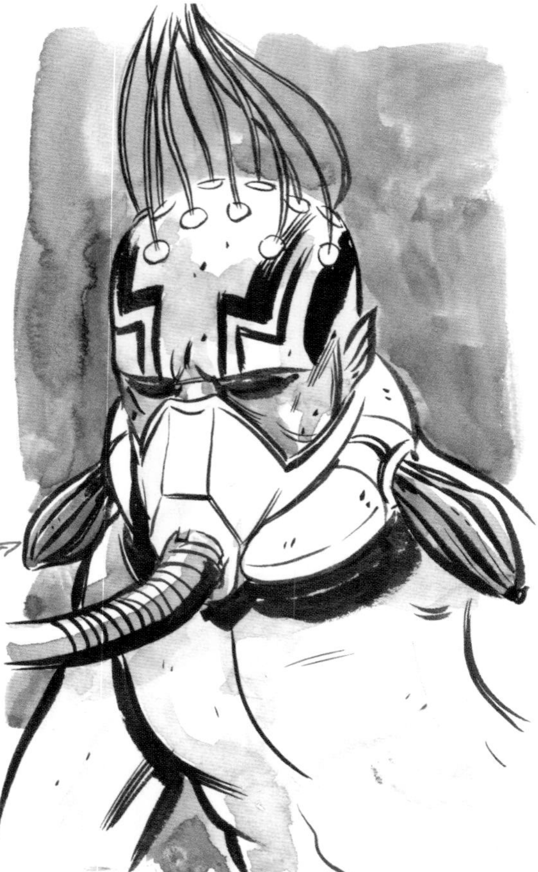
THESE LITTLE BAGS WOULD INFLATE IF HE WAS BREATHING.

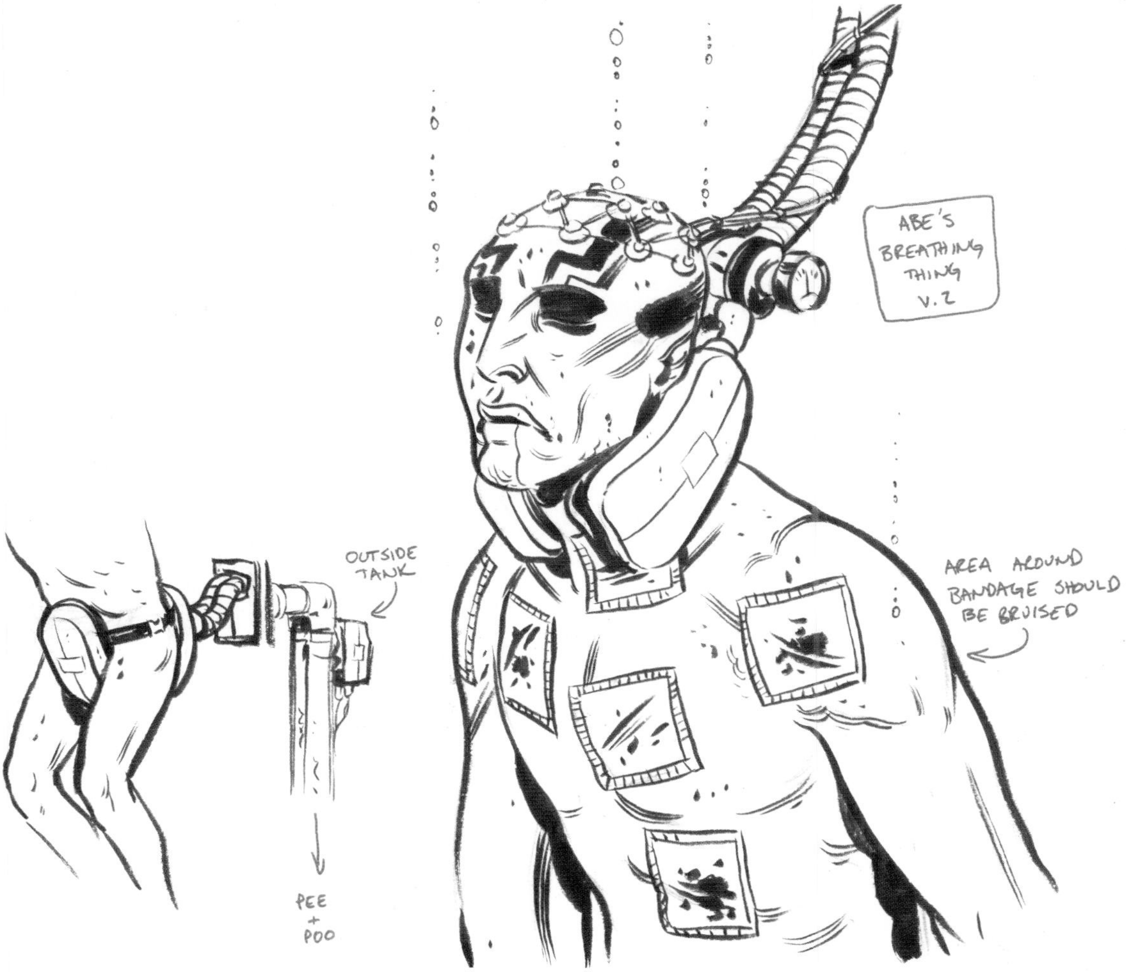
ABE'S BREATHING THING V.2
OUTSIDE TANK
AREA AROUND BANDAGE SHOULD BE BRUISED
PEE + POO

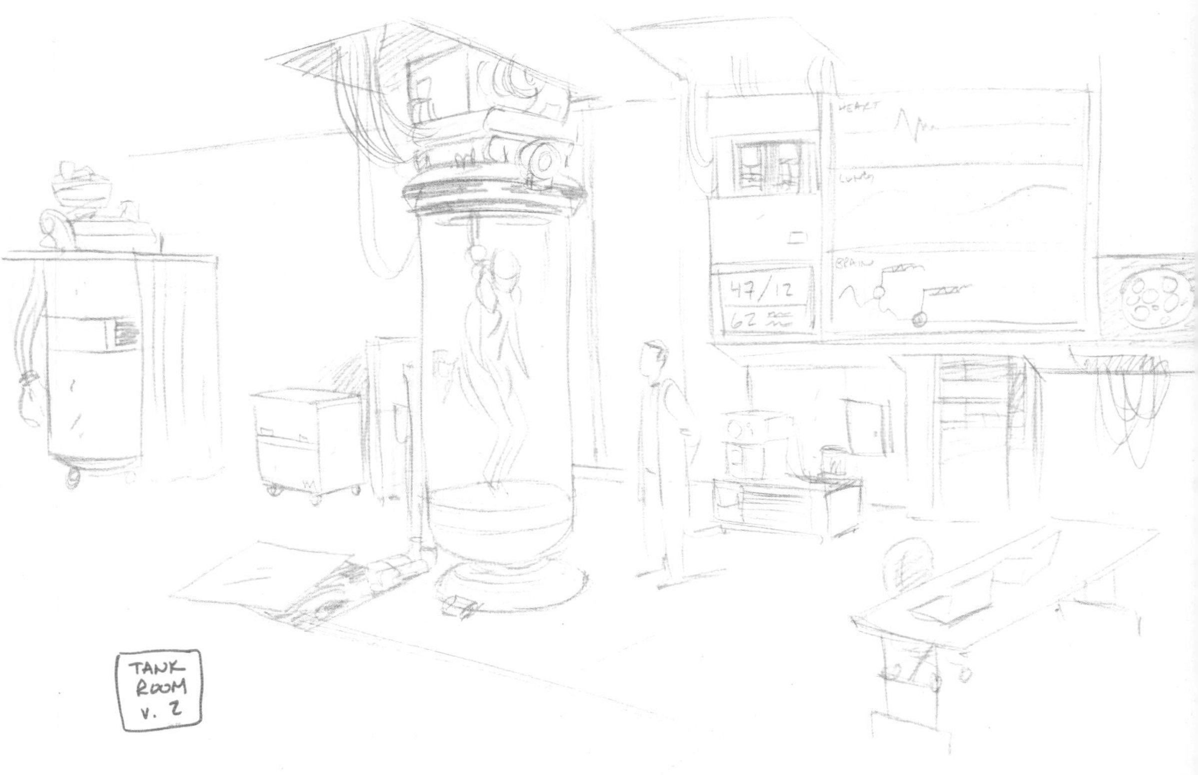
47/12
TANK ROOM V. 2

HELLBOY™

by MIKE MIGNOLA

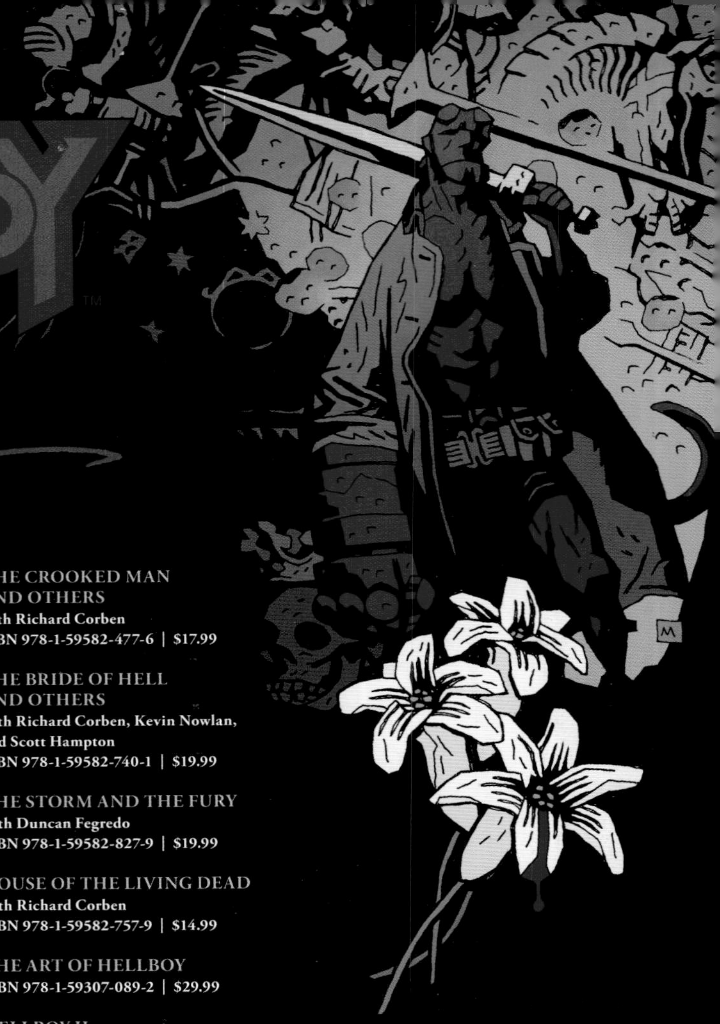

HELLBOY LIBRARY EDITION VOLUME 1:
Seed of Destruction and Wake the Devil
ISBN 978-1-59307-910-9 | $49.99

HELLBOY LIBRARY EDITION VOLUME 2:
The Chained Coffin and The Right Hand of Doom
ISBN 978-1-59307-989-5 | $49.99

HELLBOY LIBRARY EDITION VOLUME 3:
Conqueror Worm and Strange Places
ISBN 978-1-59582-352-6 | $49.99

HELLBOY LIBRARY EDITION VOLUME 4:
The Crooked Man and The Troll Witch
with Richard Corben and others
ISBN 978-1-59582-658-9 | $49.99

SEED OF DESTRUCTION
with John Byrne
ISBN 978-1-59307-094-6 | $17.99

WAKE THE DEVIL
ISBN 978-1-59307-095-3 | $17.99

THE CHAINED COFFIN AND OTHERS
ISBN 978-1-59307-091-5 | $17.99

THE RIGHT HAND OF DOOM
ISBN 978-1-59307-093-9 | $17.99

CONQUEROR WORM
ISBN 978-1-59307-092-2 | $17.99

STRANGE PLACES
ISBN 978-1-59307-475-3 | $17.99

THE TROLL WITCH AND OTHERS
ISBN 978-1-59307-860-7 | $17.99

DARKNESS CALLS
with Duncan Fegredo
ISBN 978-1-59307-896-6 | $19.99

THE WILD HUNT
with Duncan Fegredo
ISBN 978-1-59582-352-6 | $19.99

THE CROOKED MAN AND OTHERS
with Richard Corben
ISBN 978-1-59582-477-6 | $17.99

THE BRIDE OF HELL AND OTHERS
with Richard Corben, Kevin Nowlan, and Scott Hampton
ISBN 978-1-59582-740-1 | $19.99

THE STORM AND THE FURY
with Duncan Fegredo
ISBN 978-1-59582-827-9 | $19.99

HOUSE OF THE LIVING DEAD
with Richard Corben
ISBN 978-1-59582-757-9 | $14.99

THE ART OF HELLBOY
ISBN 978-1-59307-089-2 | $29.99

HELLBOY II: THE ART OF THE MOVIE
ISBN 978-1-59307-964-2 | $24.99

HELLBOY: THE COMPANION
ISBN 978-1-59307-655-9 | $14.99

HELLBOY: WEIRD TALES
VOLUME 1
ISBN 978-1-56971-622-9 | $17.99
VOLUME 2
ISBN 978-1-56971-953-4 | $17.99

HELLBOY: MASKS AND MONSTERS
with James Robinson and Scott Benefiel
ISBN 978-1-59582-567-4 | $17.99

NOVELS

HELLBOY: EMERALD HELL
By Tom Piccirilli
ISBN 978-1-59582-141-6 | $12.99

HELLBOY: THE ALL-SEEING EYE
By Mark Morris
ISBN 978-1-59582-141-6 | $12.99

HELLBOY: THE FIRE WOLVES
By Tim Lebbon
ISBN 978-1-59582-204-8 | $12.99

HELLBOY: THE ICE WOLVES
By Mark Chadbourn
ISBN 978-1-59582-205-5 | $12.99

SHORT STORIES

Illustrated by Mike Mignola

HELLBOY: ODD JOBS
By Poppy Z. Brite, Greg Rucka, and others
ISBN 978-1-56971-440-9 | $14.99

HELLBOY: ODDER JOBS
By Frank Darabont, Guillermo del Toro, and others
ISBN 978-1-59307-226-1 | $14.99

HELLBOY: ODDEST JOBS
By Joe R. Lansdale, China Miéville, and others
ISBN 978-1-59307-944-4 | $14.99

AVAILABLE AT YOUR LOCAL COMICS SHOP OR BOOKSTORE! • To find a comics shop in your area, call 1-888-266-4226.
For more information or to order direct visit DarkHorse.com or call 1-800-862-0052 Mon.–Fri. 9 AM to 5 PM Pacific Time.
Prices and availability subject to change without notice.

BOONE COUNTY LIBRARY

2040 9100 352 884 5

S0-AJA

WITHDRAWN

Mike Mignola's

WEIRD TALES

Volume One

BOONE COUNTY PUBLIC LIBRARY
21 S. MAIN
WALTON, KY 41094
JUN 10 2004

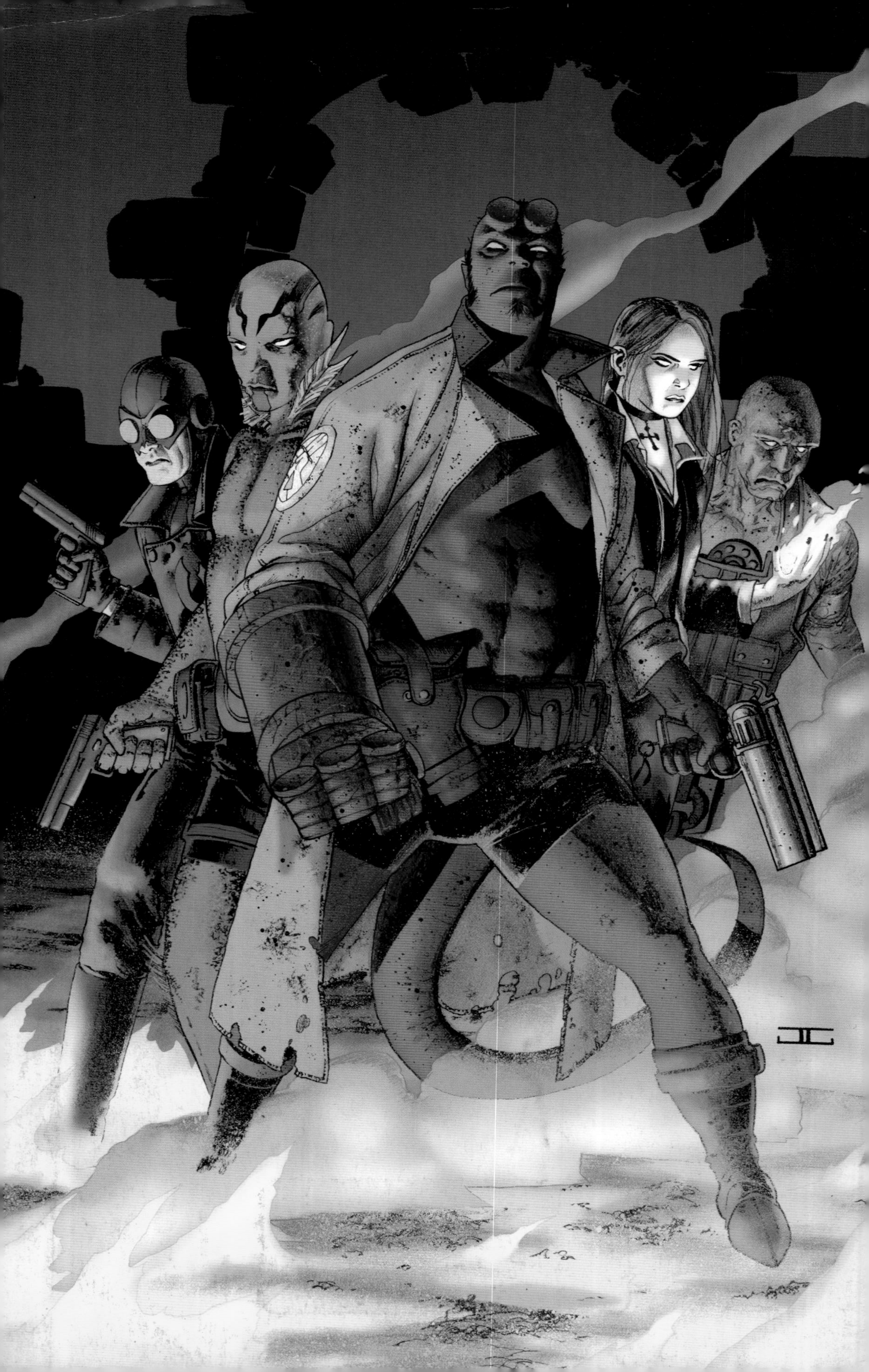

MIKE MIGNOLA'S

WEIRD TALES
Volume One

JOHN ARCUDI, JOE CASEY, JOHN CASSADAY,

RICK CORTES, TYRUBEN ELLINGSON, BOB FINGERMAN,

MATT HOLLINGSWORTH, SEUNG KIM, ROGER LANGRIDGE,

STEVE LIEBER, ALEX MALEEV, OVI NEDELCU, FABIAN NICIEZA,

STEVE PARKHOUSE, JASON PEARSON, ERIC POWELL, STEFANO

RAFFAELE, MARK RICKETTS, SARA RYAN, TOM SNIEGOSKI,

GALEN SHOWMAN, RANDY STRADLEY, WILLIAM STOUT,

ANDI WATSON, ERIC WIGHT & LEINIL FRANCIS YU

✠

Cover art by MIKE MIGNOLA

Cover colors by DAVE STEWART

Edited by SCOTT ALLIE *with* MATT DRYER

Collection designed by LIA RIBACCHI

Published by MIKE RICHARDSON

DARK HORSE BOOKS™

NEIL HANKERSON ✠ executive vice president

TOM WEDDLE ✠ vice president of finance

RANDY STRADLEY ✠ vice president of publishing

CHRIS WARNER ✠ senior books editor

SARA PERRIN ✠ vice president of marketing

MICHAEL MARTENS ✠ vice president of business development

ANITA NELSON ✠ vice president of sales & licensing

DAVID SCROGGY ✠ vice president of product development

DALE LaFOUNTAIN ✠ vice president of information technology

DARLENE VOGEL ✠ director of purchasing

KEN LIZZI ✠ general counsel

Published by Dark Horse Books
a division of Dark Horse Comics, Inc.
10956 SE Main Street
Milwaukie, OR 97222

First edition: November 2003
ISBN: 1-56971-622-6

Hellboy™: Weird Tales, Volume 1, November 2003. Hellboy™, Lobster Johnson™, BPRD™, and all related characters are trademarks of Michael Mignola. Weird Tales ® Victor Dricks, Inc. Used with Permission. Dark Horse Books™ is a trademark of Dark Horse Comics, Inc. Dark Horse Comics® is a trademark of Dark Horse Comics, Inc., registered in various categories and countries. All rights reserved. No portion of this publication may be reproduced or transmitted, in any form or by any means, without the express written permission of Dark Horse Comics, Inc. Names, characters, places, and incidents featured in this publication either are the product of the author's imagination or are used fictitiously. Any resemblance to actual persons (living, dead, or undead), events, institutions, or locales, without satiric intent, is entirely coincidental.

This volume collects issues one through four of the Dark Horse
comic-book series, *Hellboy: Weird Tales.*

1 3 5 7 9 10 2 4 6 8

Printed in China

INTRODUCTION

by SCOTT ALLIE

Since superheroes first appeared, it's always been the iconic characters to whom we're most drawn in comics, more so even than the stories themselves. We identify with them, and we expect them to continue in their adventures throughout our lives, or at least our adolescences. And usually they do, unchanged. And since these are comics, we commune with them, as children, by drawing the characters ourselves. It's actually fun to lay down those tedious lines which make up Spider-man's costume, to have that feeling that we're bringing the character to life with our own hands. This affection for the characters themselves goes on to motivate a good number of the artists who draw the books. We want to contribute, or just have fun playing around with the characters who got us interested in comics, and as often as not, reading in the first place.

From my own very subjective vantage point, I believe that of all the new heroes who popped up in such great numbers in the 1990s, none inspire comic-book artists more than Mike Mignola's little red creation, Hellboy. At a recent convention, I met a young writer who'd walked the hall floor getting people to fill his Hellboy sketchbook; everyone from Jim Lee to Jim Mahfood—sadly absent from these pages—offered up beautiful takes on the character. This isn't even the first sketchbook of its kind. Similar sketchbooks have been kicking around for years. People love to draw Hellboy. Whether this is a tribute to the brilliant, asymmetrical, post-Kirby character design, to the stories themselves, or simply to the excitement that Mike's drawing style has created in the industry, I do believe that the effect of this character on other artists is unparalleled in modern comics.

Over the years, Mike and I have heard from a lot of our favorite artists asking for the chance to draw Hellboy. When Gary Gianni stopped running

comics, a lot of people stepped up asking to fill that space with their own Hellboy stories. As it happened, Mike decided to move in on that prime real estate to make his own stories longer, as well as to occasionally introduce a new character, like 1930s crime-fighting weirdo Lobster Johnson.

There just wasn't any room for these other guys, so we had to make room. This book owes its existence to John Cassaday, Scott Morse, Alex Maleev, and a handful of others who pushed and prodded and nagged us to give them space to draw their own Hellboy stories. Since Mike's art so defines what Hellboy is, we chose to make this book very artist driven, with some of these intensely talented artists taking their first shot at writing their own stories, just as Hellboy was how Mike first developed his own writing chops.

The title, *Weird Tales*, comes, of course, from the most famous of the pulp magazines, the one with which we associate Lovecraft and Conan and so much of the fiction which continues to inspire today's comics artists, none more so than Mike himself. When we were trawling around for a title, *Weird Tales* seemed to say exactly what we were trying to do, to the point where we could consider no other option. For the use of the title, we thank Victor Dricks and Pamela Bruce, who made it possible for us to permanently connect Hellboy with a tradition to which we owe so much.

And these are weird tales, a bizarre collection, and a mixed bag. Some artists gave us terrific variations on Mike's odd little occult mysteries, and others, like Bob Fingerman and Andi Watson, delivered stories in their own unique voices, taking the characters places Mike never dreamt of and never would have gone to on his own. In an anthology, variety is the point, and I think we've delivered that, along with great art from the stars of the mainstream, to the geniuses of independent comics, to some fantastic talents from the world of animation.

CONTENTS

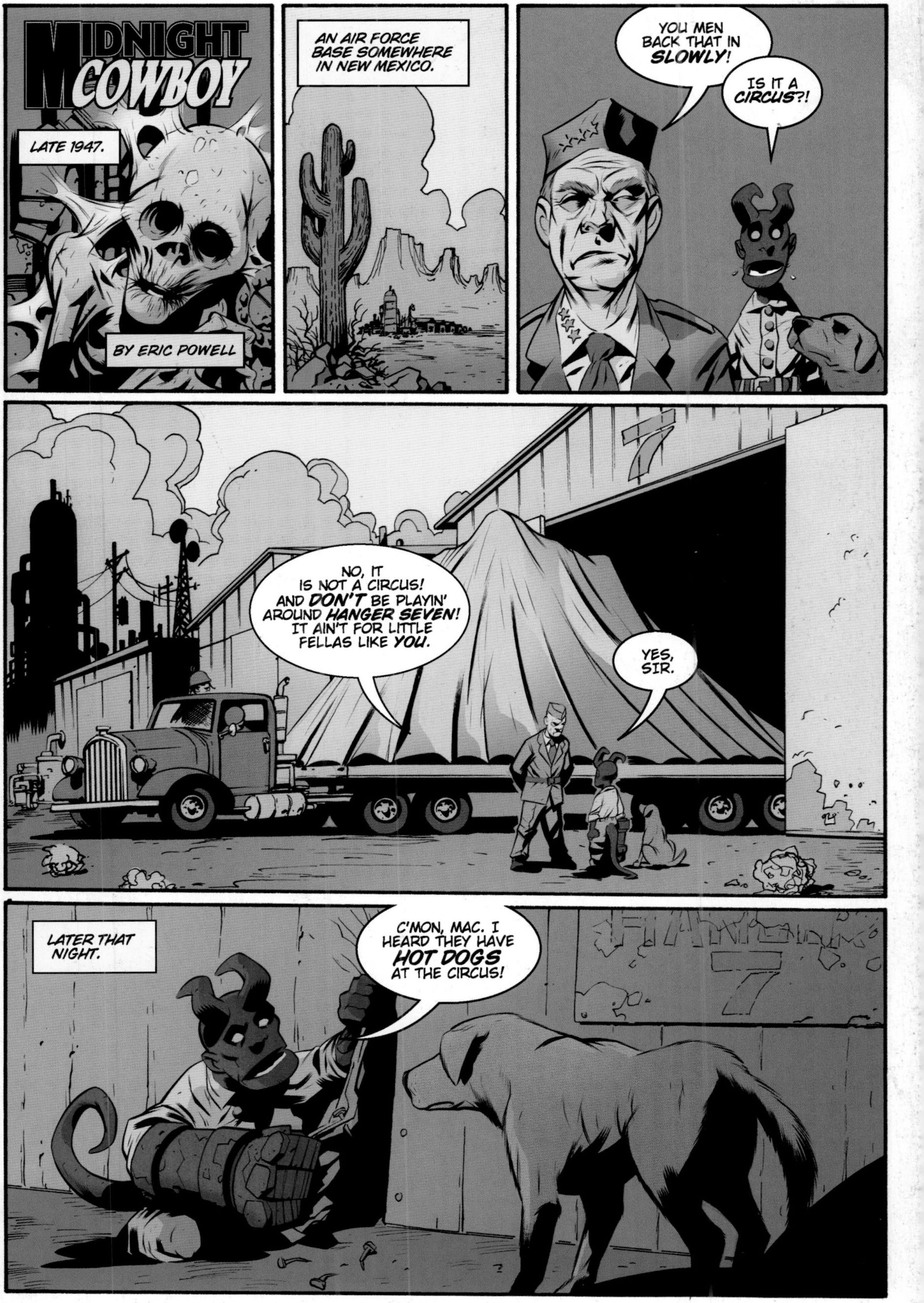
MIDNIGHT COWBOY
LATE 1947.
BY ERIC POWELL
AN AIR FORCE BASE SOMEWHERE IN NEW MEXICO.
YOU MEN BACK THAT IN SLOWLY!
IS IT A CIRCUS?!
NO, IT IS NOT A CIRCUS! AND DON'T BE PLAYIN' AROUND HANGER SEVEN! IT AIN'T FOR LITTLE FELLAS LIKE YOU.
YES, SIR.
LATER THAT NIGHT.
C'MON, MAC. I HEARD THEY HAVE HOT DOGS AT THE CIRCUS!

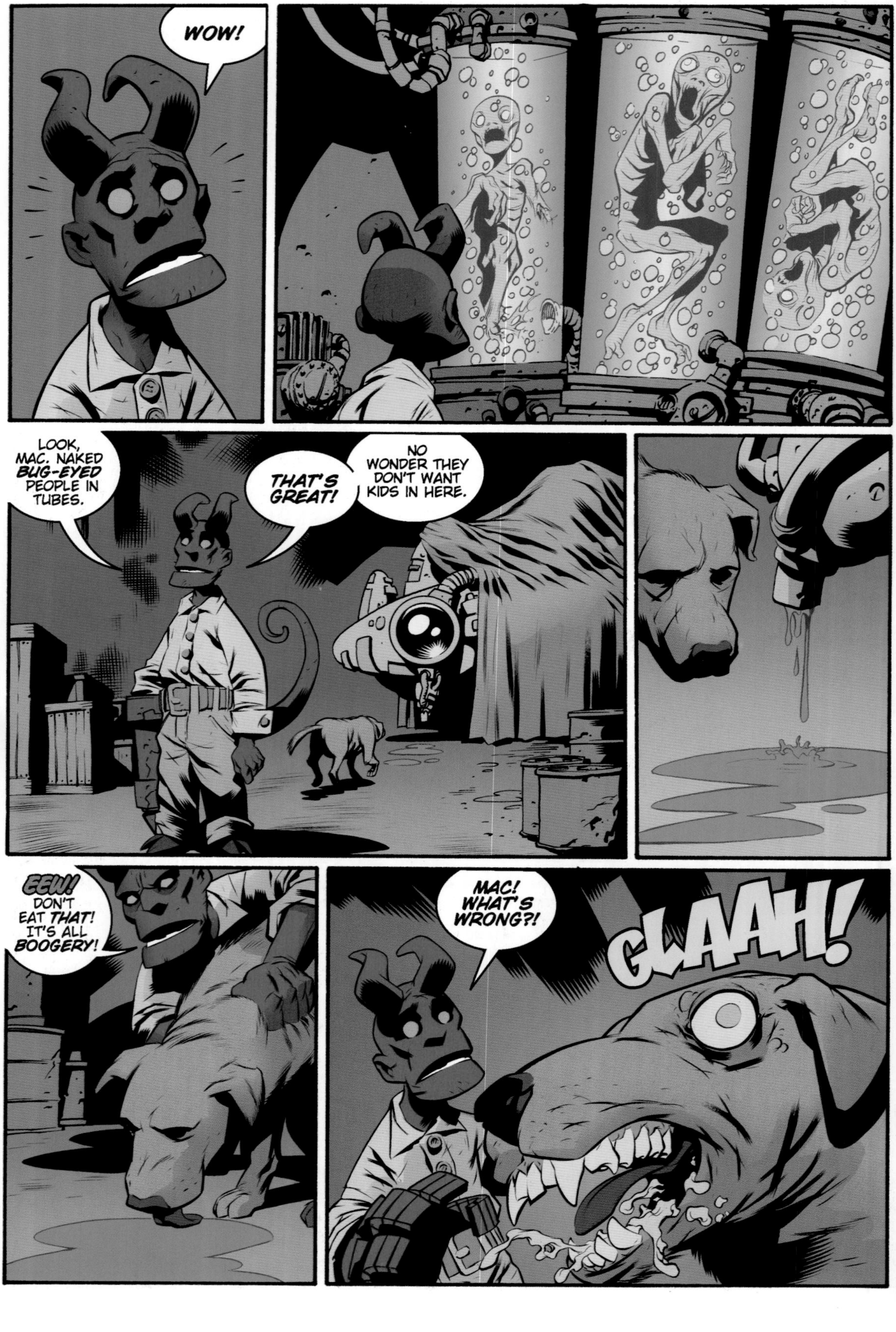
WOW!
LOOK, MAC. NAKED BUG-EYED PEOPLE IN TUBES.
THAT'S GREAT!
NO WONDER THEY DON'T WANT KIDS IN HERE.
EEW! DON'T EAT THAT! IT'S ALL BOOGERY!
MAC! WHAT'S WRONG?!
GLAAH!

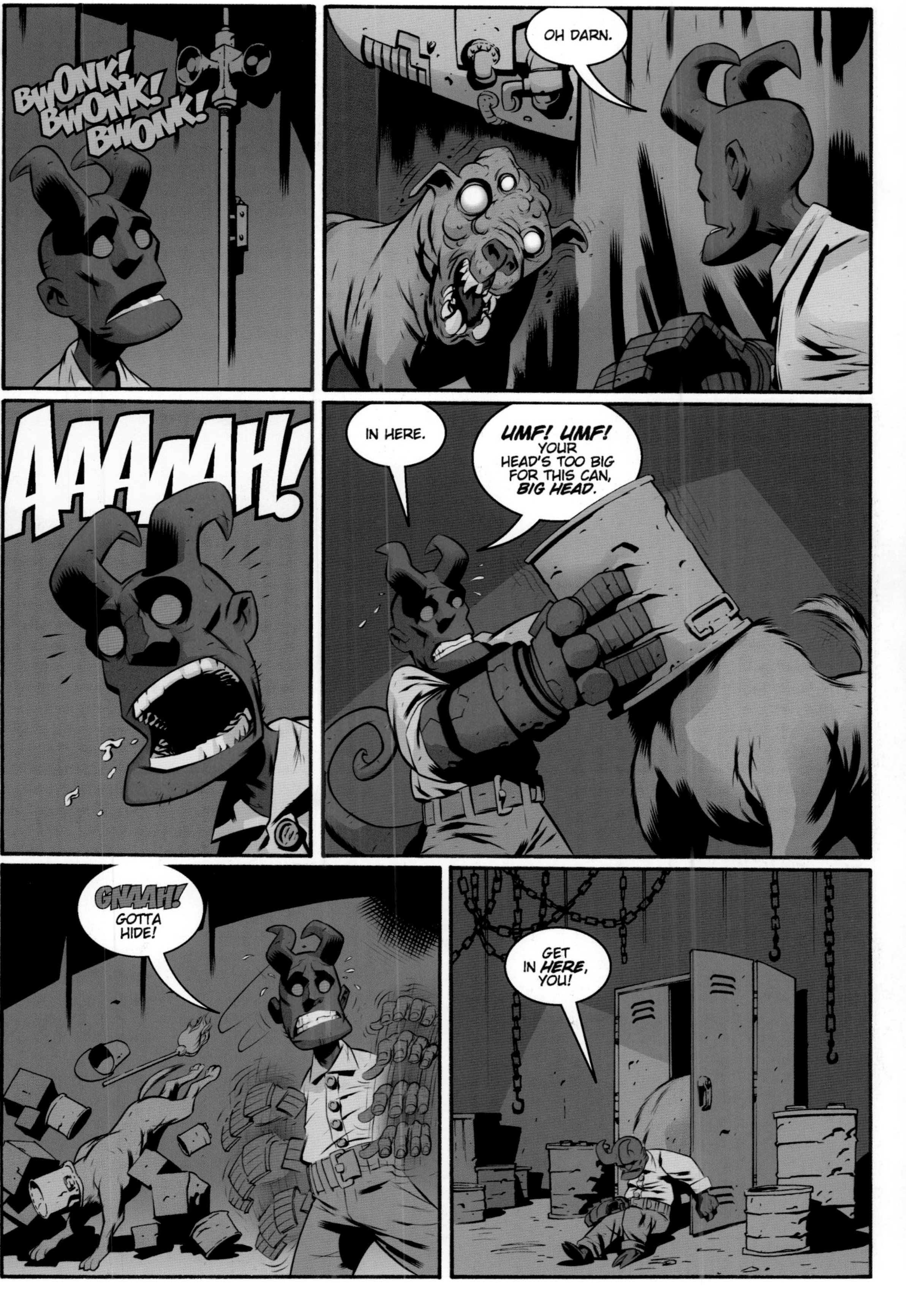
BWONK! BWONK! BWONK!
OH DARN.
AAAAAH!
IN HERE.
UMF! UMF! YOUR HEAD'S TOO BIG FOR THIS CAN, BIG HEAD.
GNAAH! GOTTA HIDE!
GET IN HERE, YOU!

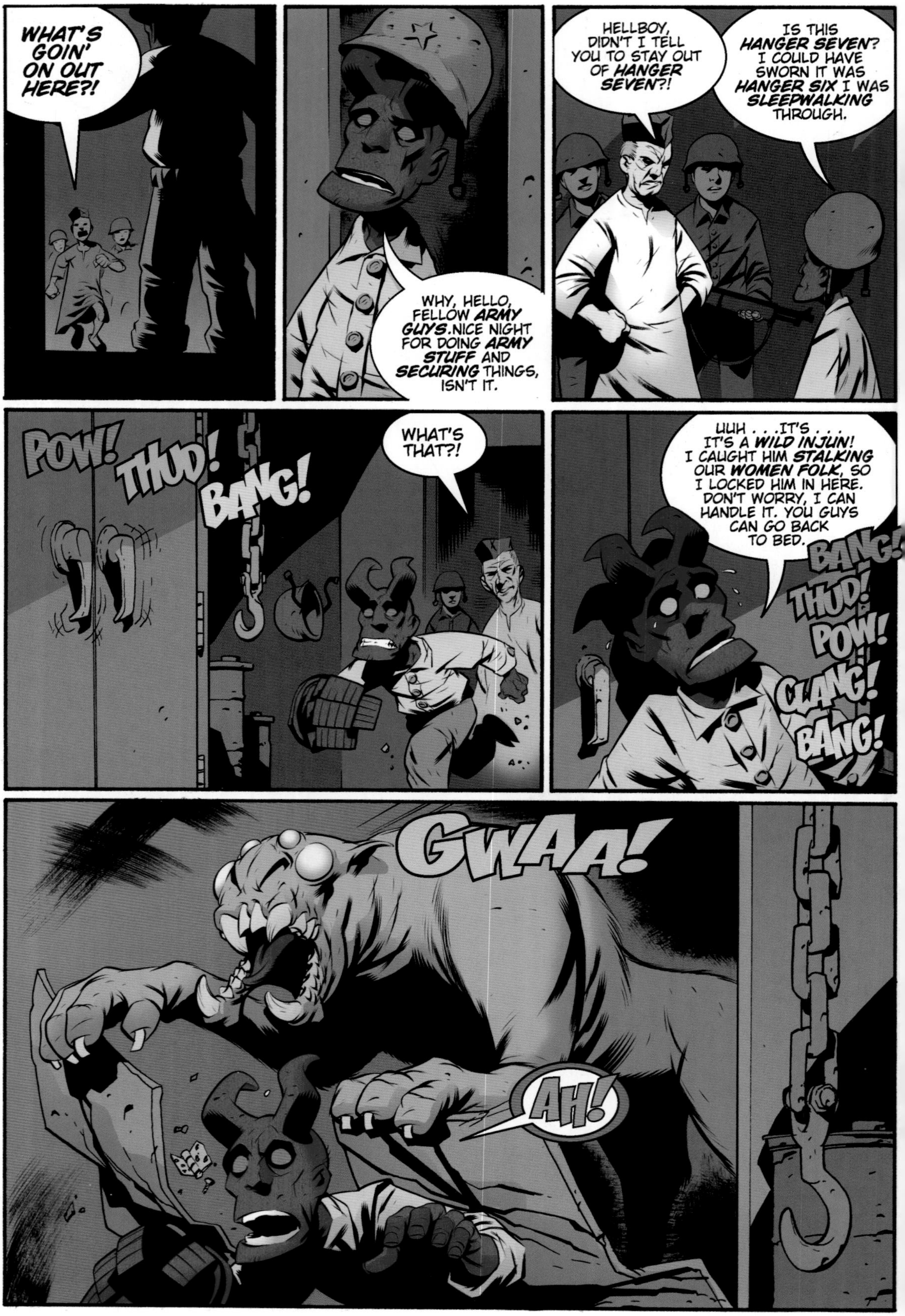

WHAT'S GOIN' ON OUT HERE?!
WHY, HELLO, FELLOW ARMY GUYS. NICE NIGHT FOR DOING ARMY STUFF AND SECURING THINGS, ISN'T IT.
HELLBOY, DIDN'T I TELL YOU TO STAY OUT OF HANGER SEVEN?!
IS THIS HANGER SEVEN? I COULD HAVE SWORN IT WAS HANGER SIX I WAS SLEEPWALKING THROUGH.
POW! THUD! BANG!
WHAT'S THAT?!
UUH . . .IT'S . . . IT'S A WILD INJUN! I CAUGHT HIM STALKING OUR WOMEN FOLK, SO I LOCKED HIM IN HERE. DON'T WORRY, I CAN HANDLE IT. YOU GUYS CAN GO BACK TO BED.
BANG! THUD! POW! CLANG! BANG!
GWAAA!
AH!

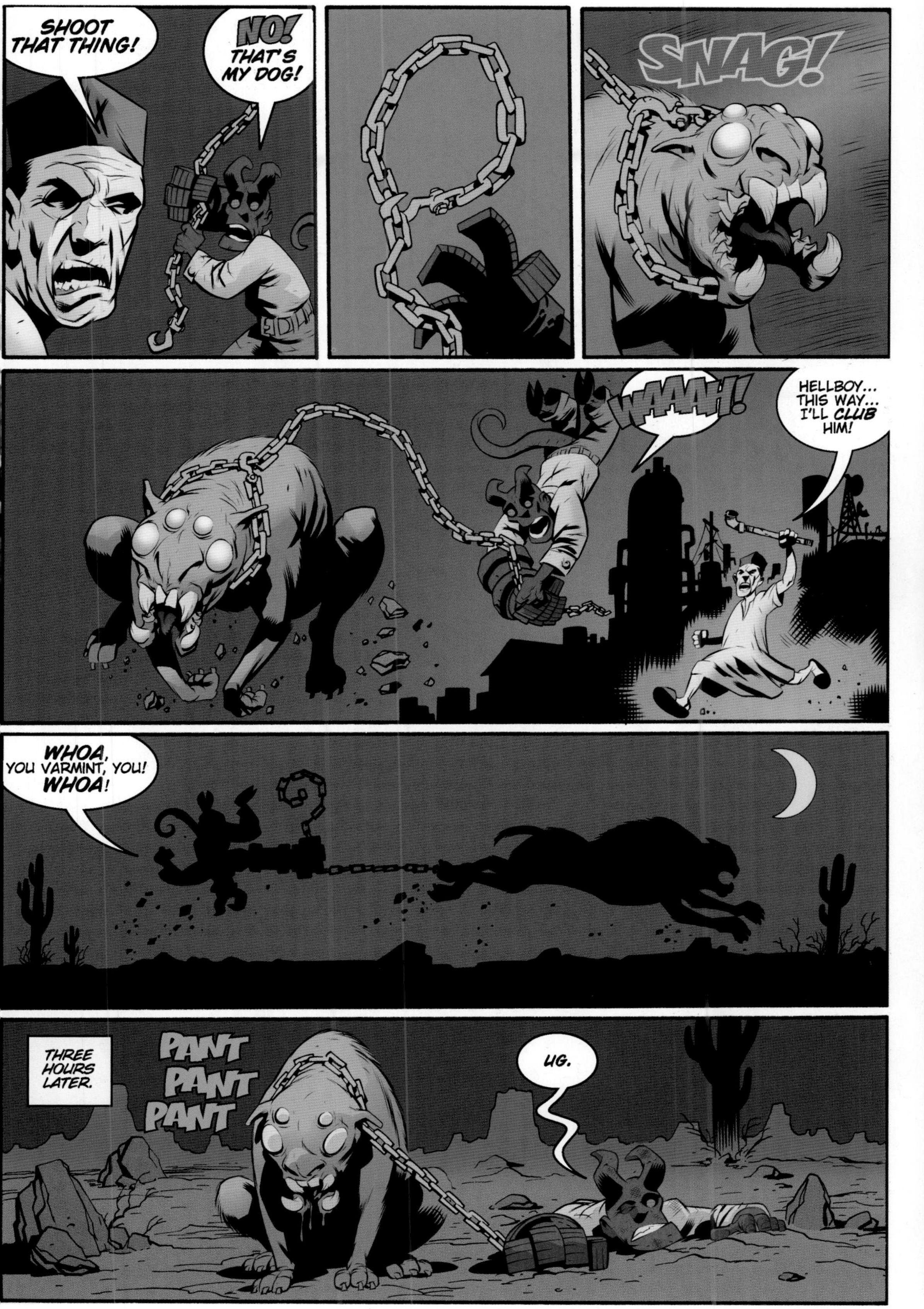
SHOOT THAT THING!
NO! THAT'S MY DOG!
SNAG!
WAAAH!
HELLBOY... THIS WAY... I'LL CLUB HIM!
WHOA, YOU VARMINT, YOU! WHOA!
THREE HOURS LATER.
PANT PANT PANT
UG.

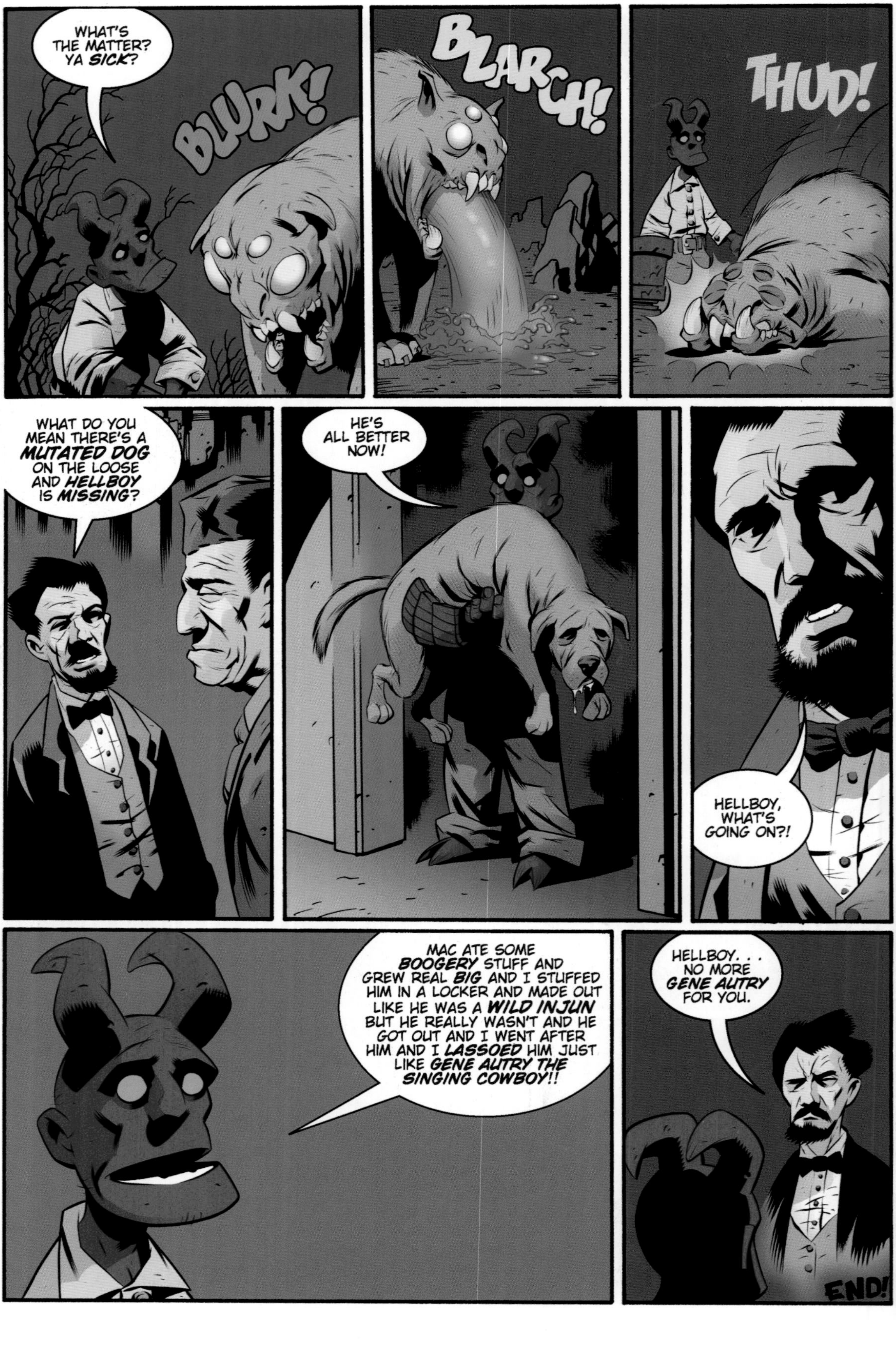
WHAT'S THE MATTER? YA SICK?
BLURK!
BLARCH!
THUD!
WHAT DO YOU MEAN THERE'S A MUTATED DOG ON THE LOOSE AND HELLBOY IS MISSING?
HE'S ALL BETTER NOW!
HELLBOY, WHAT'S GOING ON?!
MAC ATE SOME BOOGERY STUFF AND GREW REAL BIG AND I STUFFED HIM IN A LOCKER AND MADE OUT LIKE HE WAS A WILD INJUN BUT HE REALLY WASN'T AND HE GOT OUT AND I WENT AFTER HIM AND I LASSOED HIM JUST LIKE GENE AUTRY THE SINGING COWBOY!!
HELLBOY. . . NO MORE GENE AUTRY FOR YOU.
END!

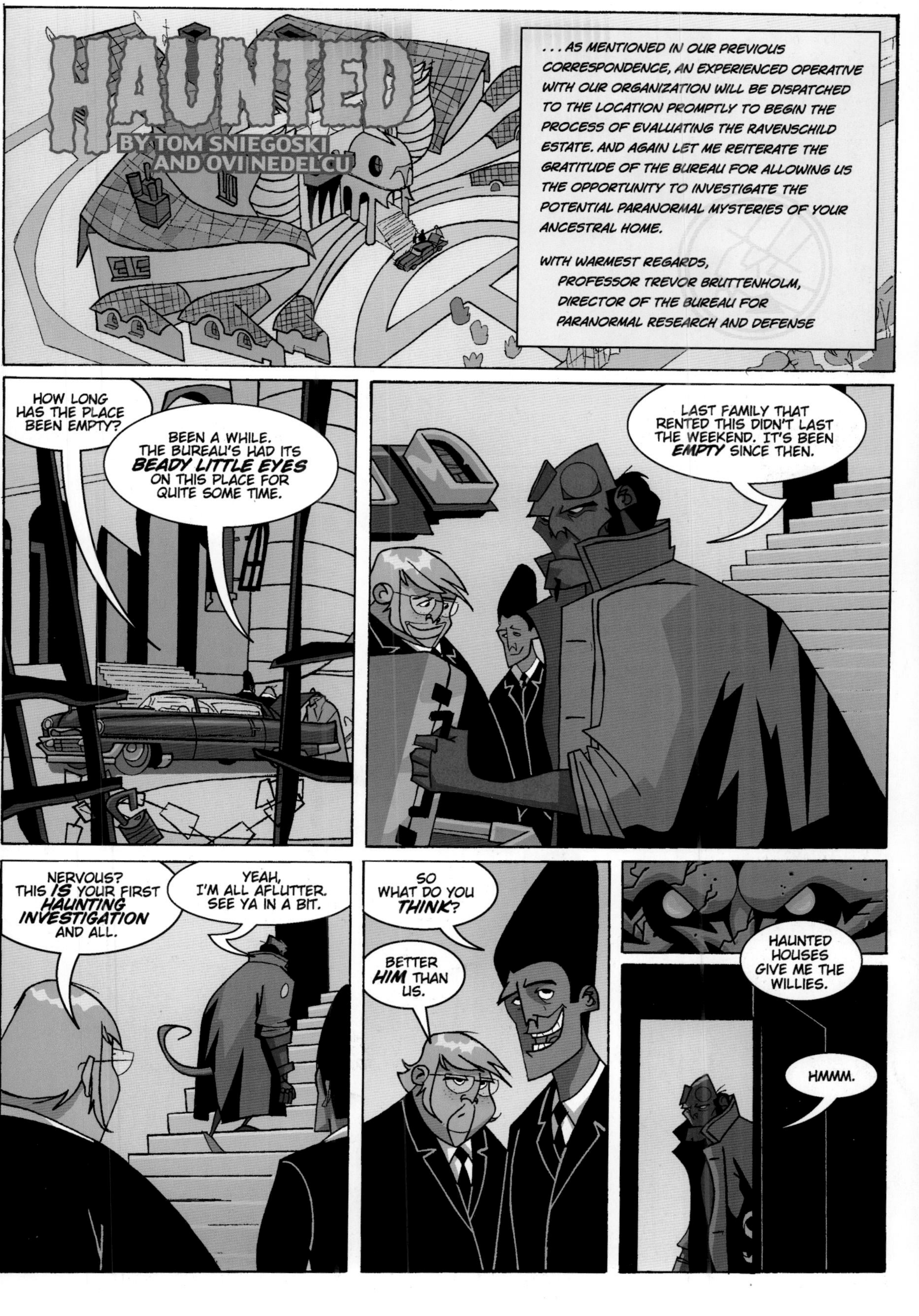
HAUNTED
BY TOM SNIEGOSKI AND OVI NEDELCU
. . . AS MENTIONED IN OUR PREVIOUS CORRESPONDENCE, AN EXPERIENCED OPERATIVE WITH OUR ORGANIZATION WILL BE DISPATCHED TO THE LOCATION PROMPTLY TO BEGIN THE PROCESS OF EVALUATING THE RAVENSCHILD ESTATE. AND AGAIN LET ME REITERATE THE GRATITUDE OF THE BUREAU FOR ALLOWING US THE OPPORTUNITY TO INVESTIGATE THE POTENTIAL PARANORMAL MYSTERIES OF YOUR ANCESTRAL HOME.
WITH WARMEST REGARDS, PROFESSOR TREVOR BRUTTENHOLM, DIRECTOR OF THE BUREAU FOR PARANORMAL RESEARCH AND DEFENSE
HOW LONG HAS THE PLACE BEEN EMPTY?
BEEN A WHILE. THE BUREAU'S HAD ITS BEADY LITTLE EYES ON THIS PLACE FOR QUITE SOME TIME.
LAST FAMILY THAT RENTED THIS DIDN'T LAST THE WEEKEND. IT'S BEEN EMPTY SINCE THEN.
NERVOUS? THIS IS YOUR FIRST HAUNTING INVESTIGATION AND ALL.
YEAH, I'M ALL AFLUTTER. SEE YA IN A BIT.
SO WHAT DO YOU THINK?
BETTER HIM THAN US.
HAUNTED HOUSES GIVE ME THE WILLIES.
HMMM.

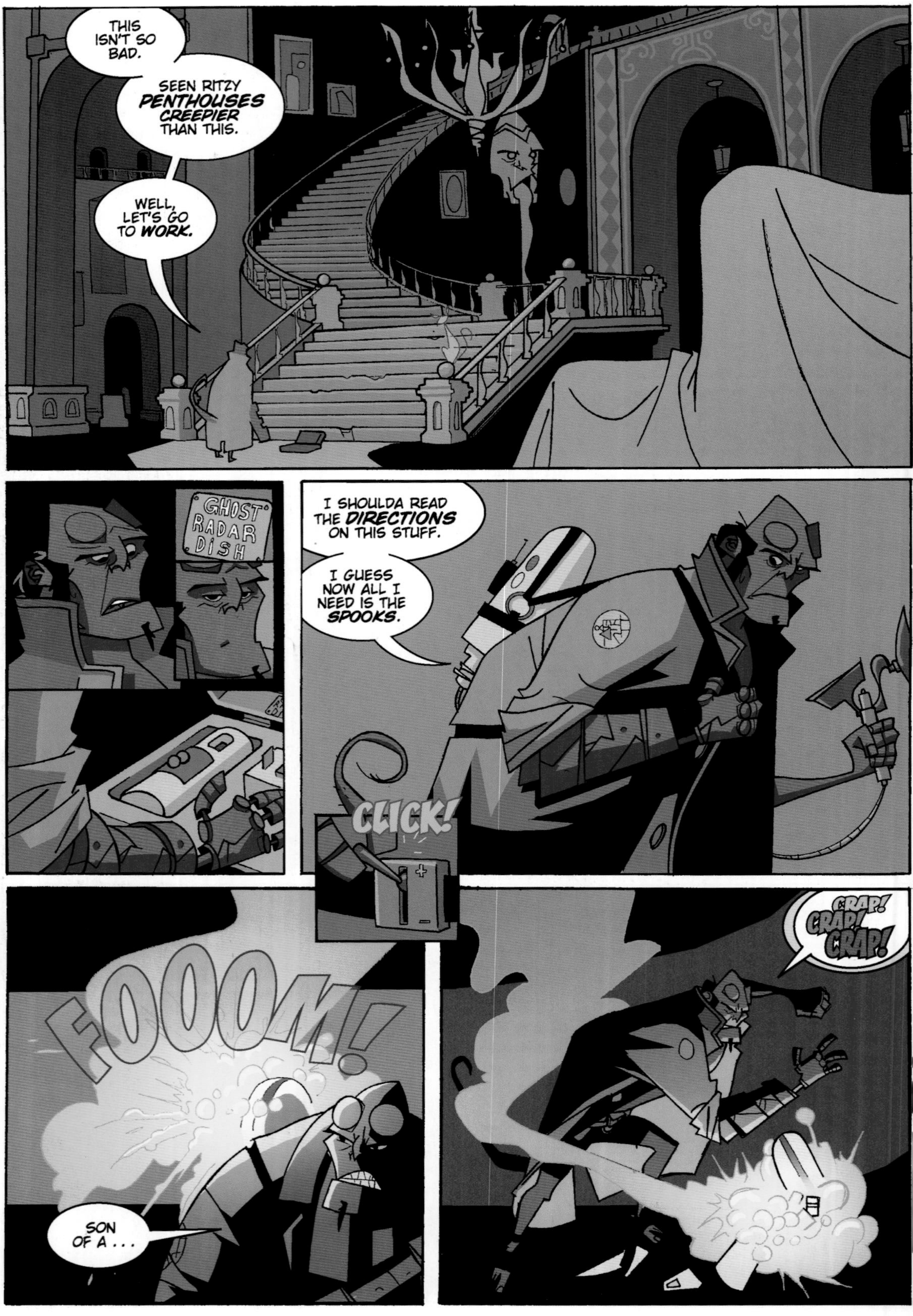
THIS ISN'T SO BAD.
SEEN RITZY PENTHOUSES CREEPIER THAN THIS.
WELL, LET'S GO TO WORK.
GHOST RADAR DISH
I SHOULDA READ THE DIRECTIONS ON THIS STUFF.
I GUESS NOW ALL I NEED IS THE SPOOKS.
CLICK!
FOOOM!
SON OF A . . .
CRAP! CRAP! CRAP!

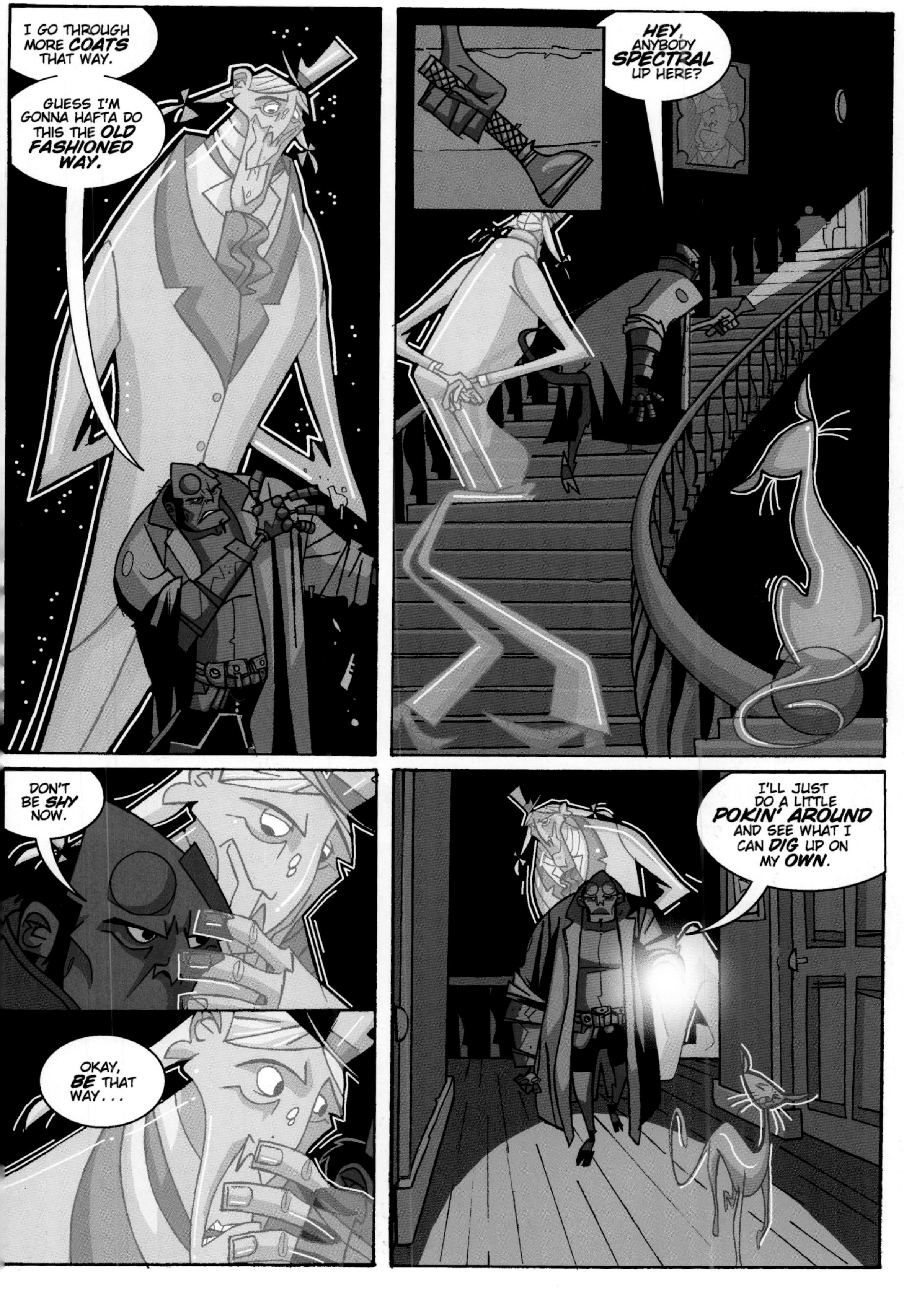
I GO THROUGH MORE COATS THAT WAY.
GUESS I'M GONNA HAFTA DO THIS THE OLD FASHIONED WAY.
HEY, ANYBODY SPECTRAL UP HERE?
DON'T BE SHY NOW.
OKAY, BE THAT WAY...
I'LL JUST DO A LITTLE POKIN' AROUND AND SEE WHAT I CAN DIG UP ON MY OWN.

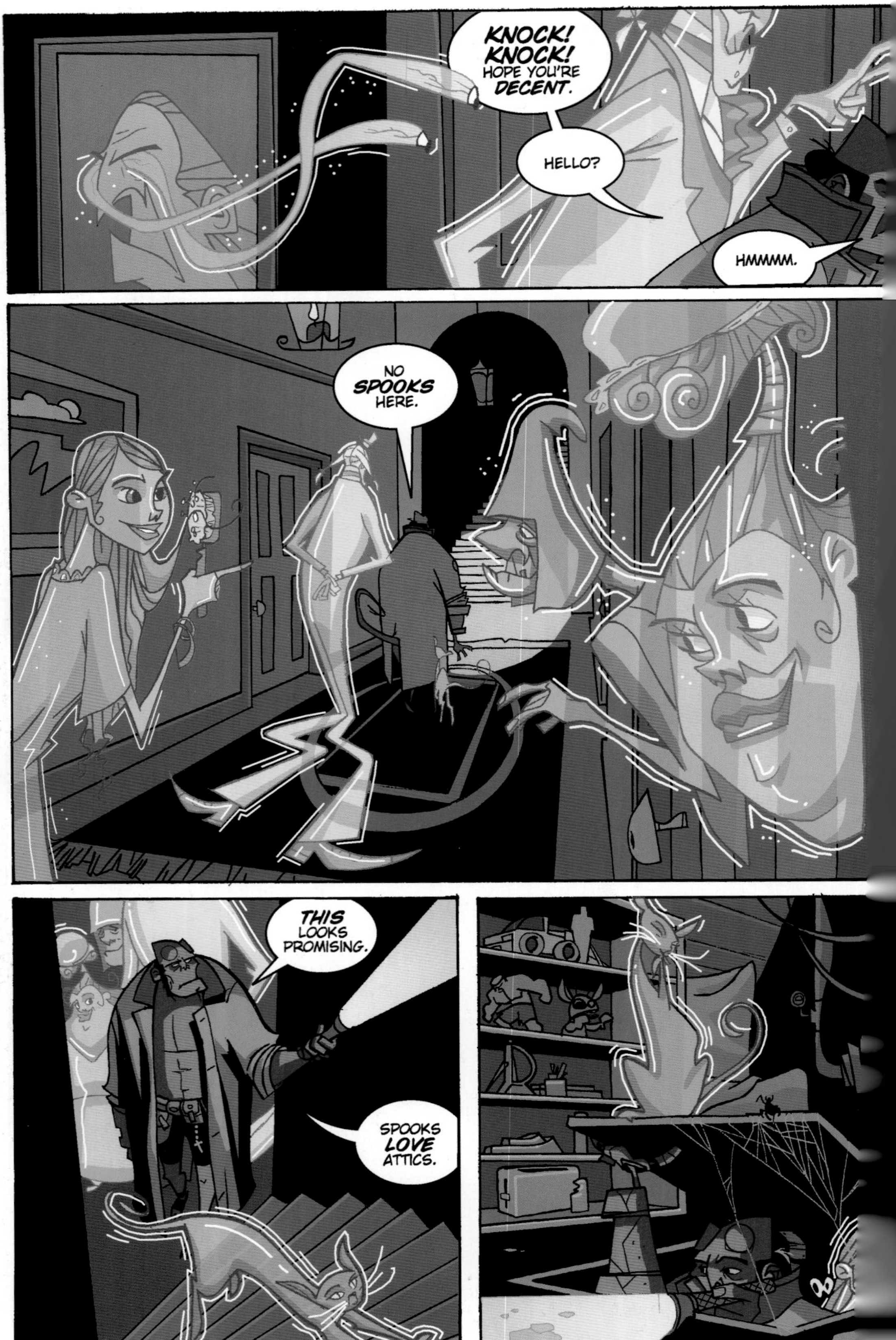
KNOCK! KNOCK! HOPE YOU'RE DECENT.
HELLO?
HMMMM.
NO SPOOKS HERE.
THIS LOOKS PROMISING.
SPOOKS LOVE ATTICS.

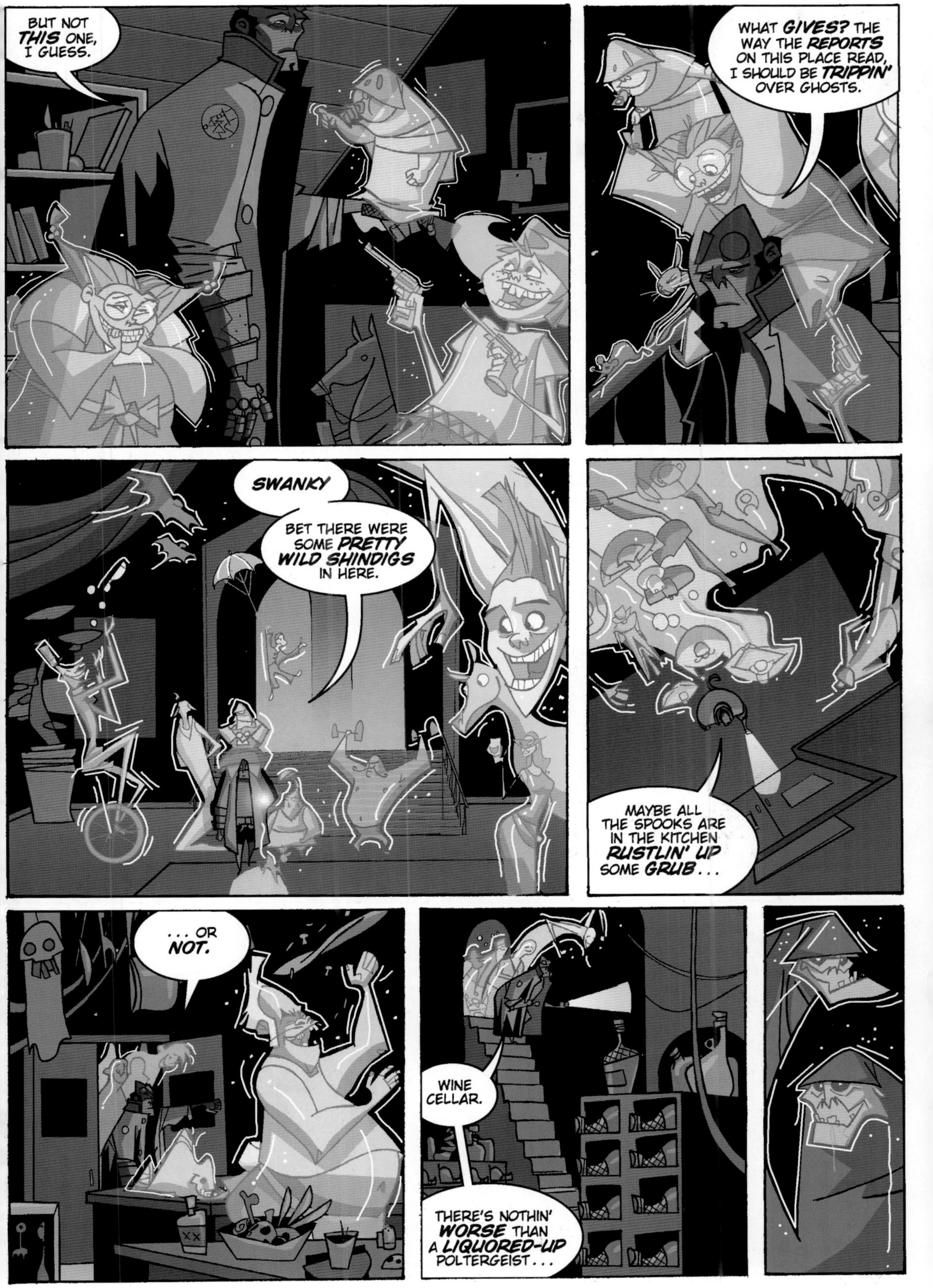
BUT NOT THIS ONE, I GUESS.
WHAT GIVES? THE WAY THE REPORTS ON THIS PLACE READ, I SHOULD BE TRIPPIN' OVER GHOSTS.
SWANKY
BET THERE WERE SOME PRETTY WILD SHINDIGS IN HERE.
MAYBE ALL THE SPOOKS ARE IN THE KITCHEN RUSTLIN' UP SOME GRUB...
...OR NOT.
WINE CELLAR.
THERE'S NOTHIN' WORSE THAN A LIQUORED-UP POLTERGEIST...

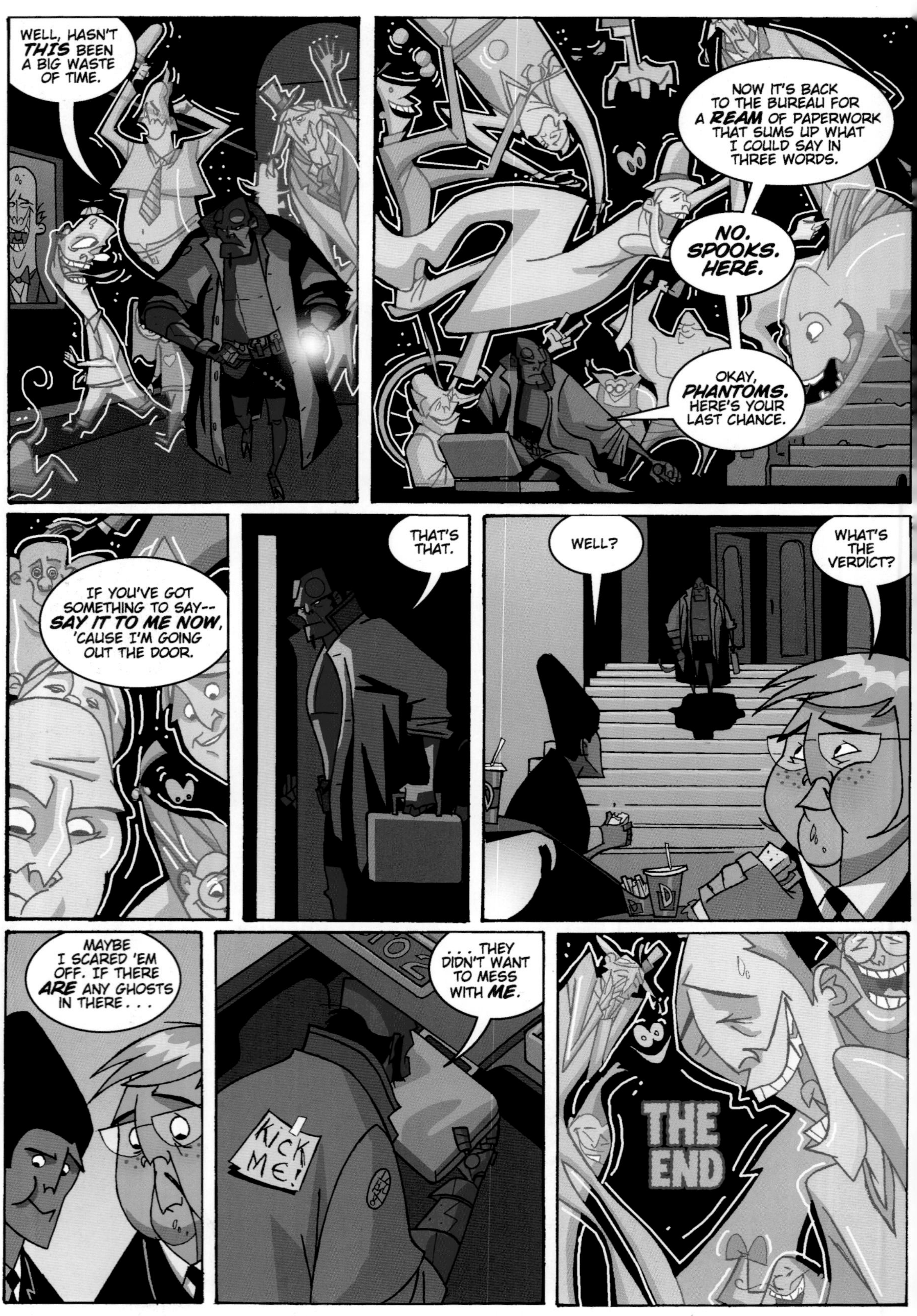
WELL, HASN'T THIS BEEN A BIG WASTE OF TIME.
NOW IT'S BACK TO THE BUREAU FOR A REAM OF PAPERWORK THAT SUMS UP WHAT I COULD SAY IN THREE WORDS.
NO. SPOOKS. HERE.
OKAY, PHANTOMS. HERE'S YOUR LAST CHANCE.
IF YOU'VE GOT SOMETHING TO SAY-- SAY IT TO ME NOW, 'CAUSE I'M GOING OUT THE DOOR.
THAT'S THAT.
WELL?
WHAT'S THE VERDICT?
MAYBE I SCARED 'EM OFF. IF THERE ARE ANY GHOSTS IN THERE . . .
. . . THEY DIDN'T WANT TO MESS WITH ME.
KICK ME!
THE END

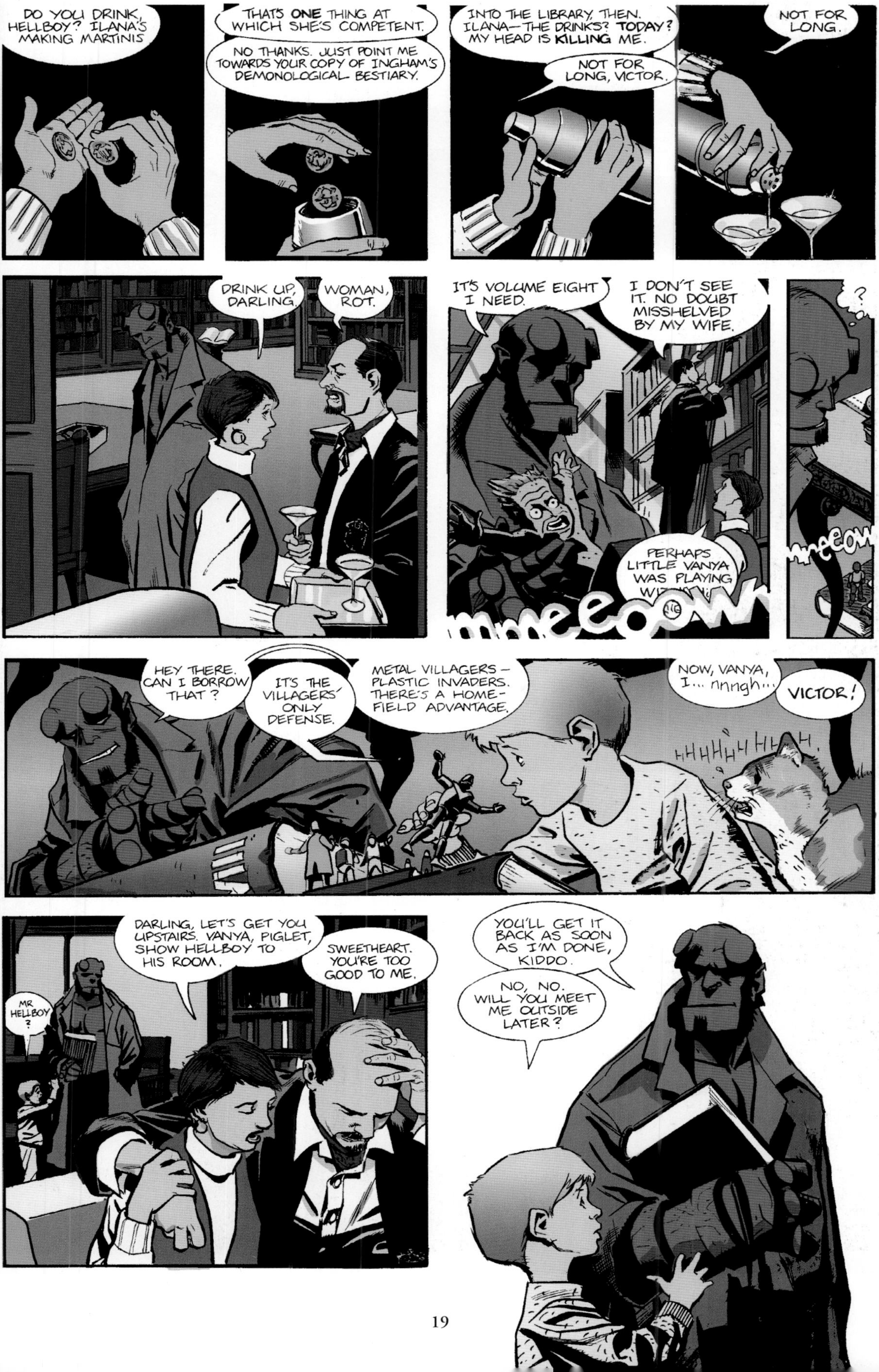
DO YOU DRINK, HELLBOY? ILANA'S MAKING MARTINIS
THAT'S **ONE** THING AT WHICH SHE'S COMPETENT.
NO THANKS. JUST POINT ME TOWARDS YOUR COPY OF INGHAM'S DEMONOLOGICAL BESTIARY.
INTO THE LIBRARY, THEN. ILANA—THE DRINKS? **TODAY**? MY HEAD IS **KILLING** ME.
NOT FOR LONG, VICTOR.
NOT FOR LONG.
DRINK UP, DARLING.
WOMAN, ROT.
IT'S VOLUME EIGHT I NEED.
I DON'T SEE IT. NO DOUBT MISSHELVED BY MY WIFE.
PERHAPS LITTLE VANYA WAS PLAYING
mmeeow
?
mmeeow
HEY THERE. CAN I BORROW THAT?
IT'S THE VILLAGERS' ONLY DEFENSE.
METAL VILLAGERS—PLASTIC INVADERS. THERE'S A HOME-FIELD ADVANTAGE.
NOW, VANYA, I... nnngh...
VICTOR!
HHHHHH HHH
DARLING, LET'S GET YOU UPSTAIRS. VANYA, PIGLET, SHOW HELLBOY TO HIS ROOM.
SWEETHEART. YOU'RE TOO GOOD TO ME.
MR HELLBOY?
YOU'LL GET IT BACK AS SOON AS I'M DONE, KIDDO.
NO, NO. WILL YOU MEET ME OUTSIDE LATER?

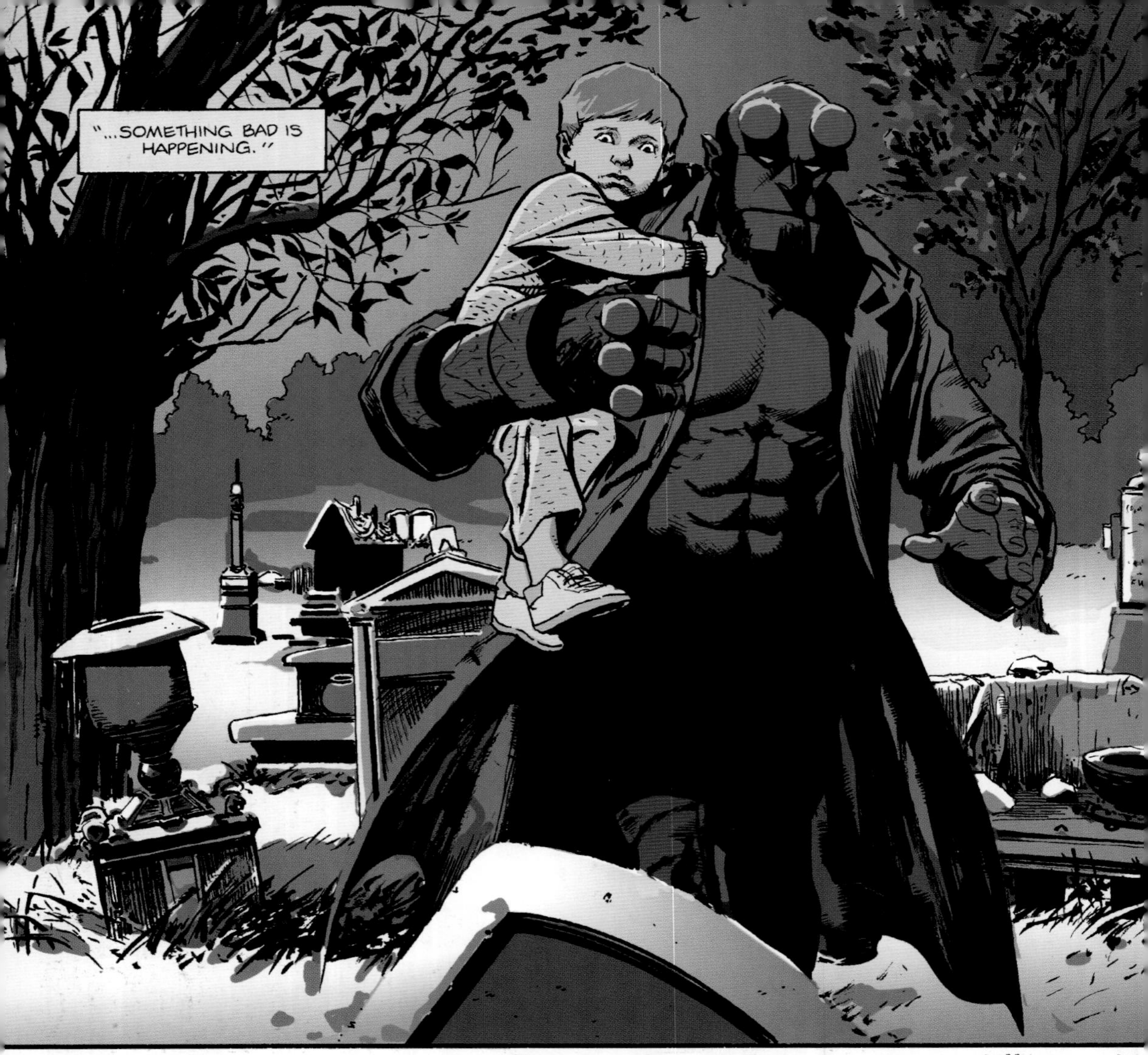
"...SOMETHING BAD IS HAPPENING."

FAMILY STORY

written and illustrated by Sara Ryan and Steve Lieber

Colored by Jeff Parker

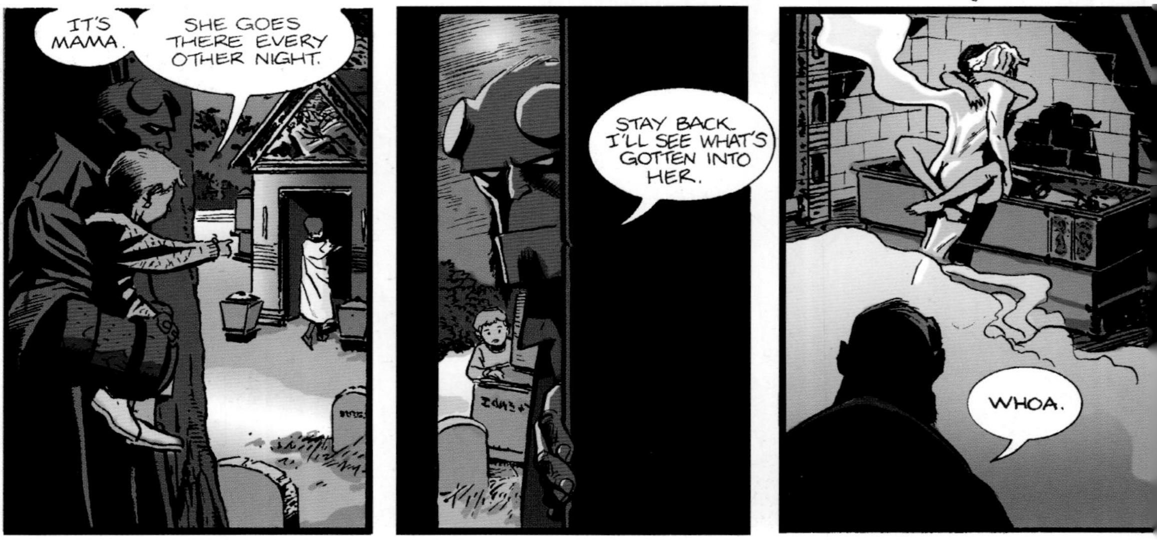
IT'S MAMA.
SHE GOES THERE EVERY OTHER NIGHT.
STAY BACK. I'LL SEE WHAT'S GOTTEN INTO HER.
WHOA.

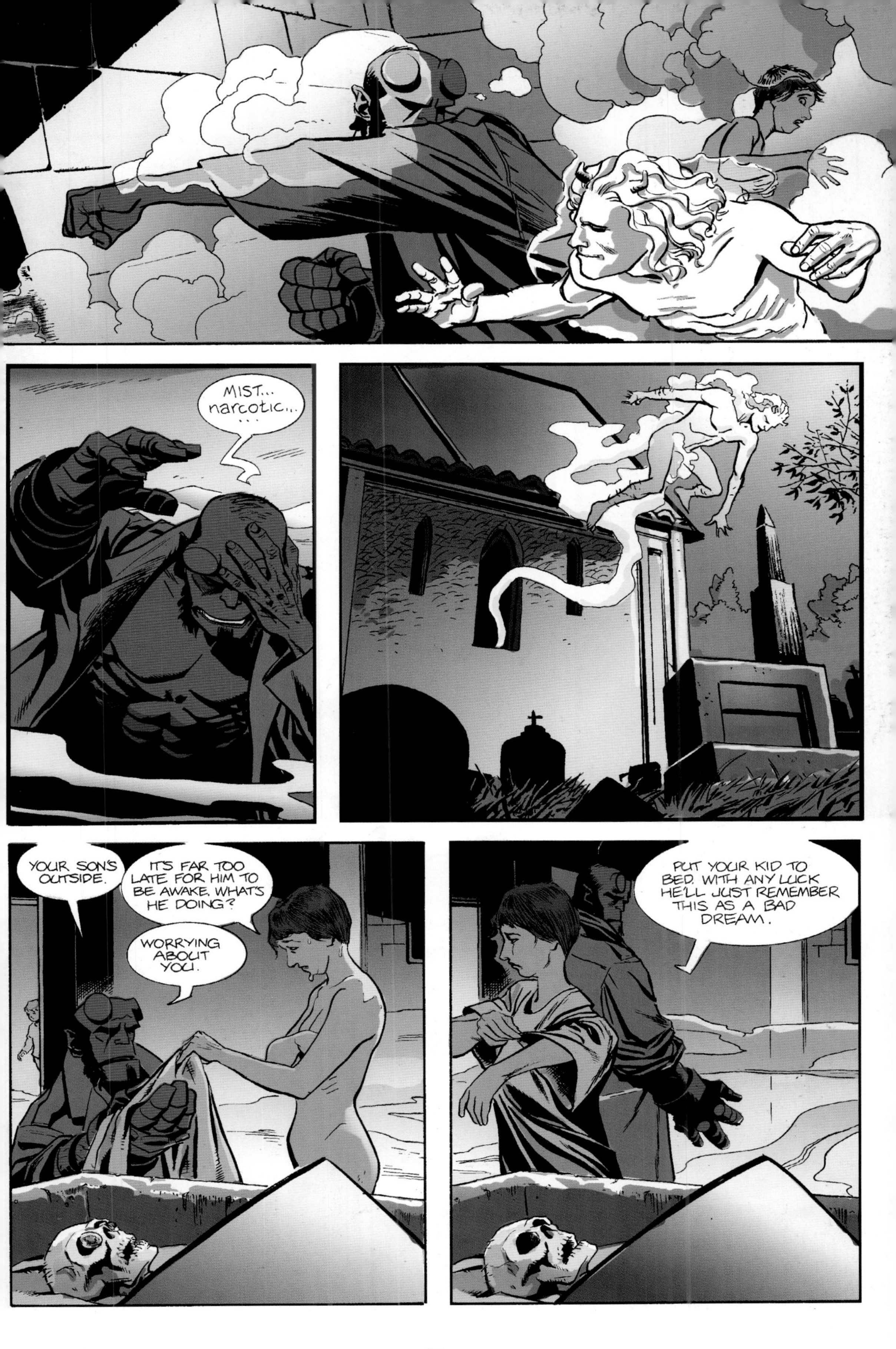
MIST...
narcotic...
...
YOUR SON'S OUTSIDE.
IT'S FAR TOO LATE FOR HIM TO BE AWAKE. WHAT'S HE DOING?
WORRYING ABOUT YOU.
PUT YOUR KID TO BED. WITH ANY LUCK HE'LL JUST REMEMBER THIS AS A BAD DREAM.

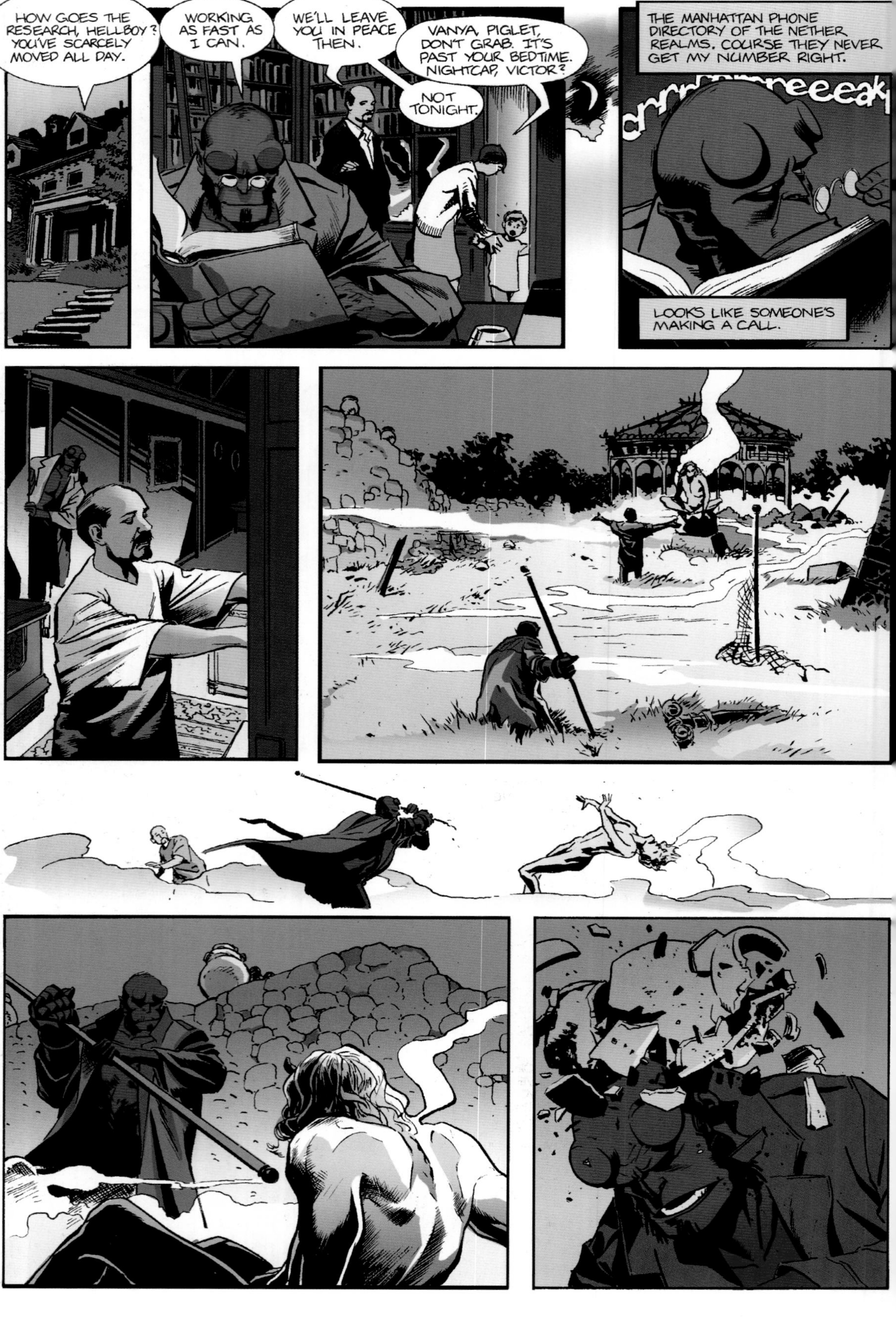
HOW GOES THE RESEARCH, HELLBOY? YOU'VE SCARCELY MOVED ALL DAY.
WORKING AS FAST AS I CAN.
WE'LL LEAVE YOU IN PEACE THEN.
VANYA, PIGLET, DON'T GRAB. IT'S PAST YOUR BEDTIME. NIGHTCAP, VICTOR?
NOT TONIGHT.
THE MANHATTAN PHONE DIRECTORY OF THE NETHER REALMS. COURSE THEY NEVER GET MY NUMBER RIGHT.
crrrrreeeeak
LOOKS LIKE SOMEONE'S MAKING A CALL.

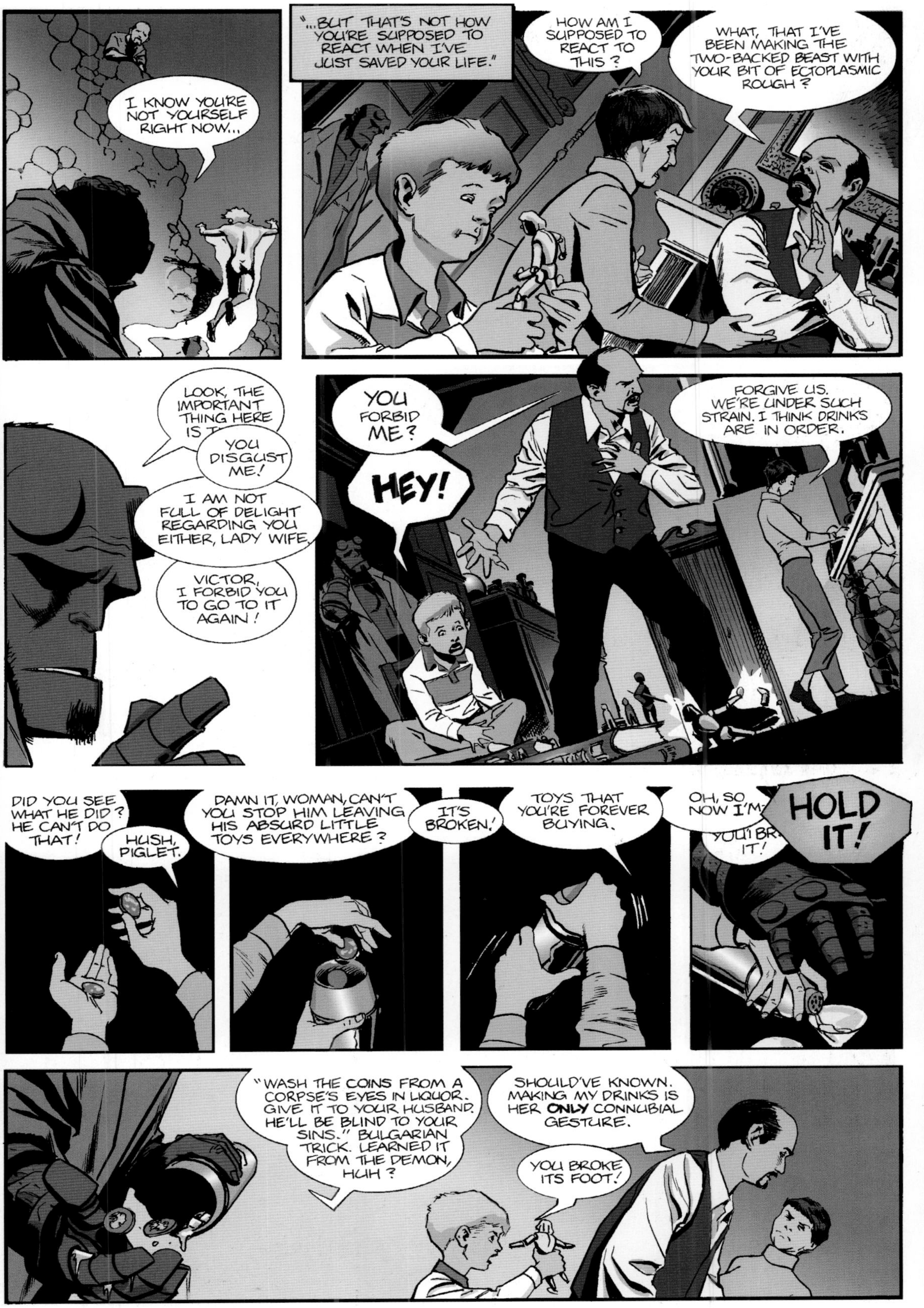
I KNOW YOU'RE NOT YOURSELF RIGHT NOW...
"...BUT THAT'S NOT HOW YOU'RE SUPPOSED TO REACT WHEN I'VE JUST SAVED YOUR LIFE."
HOW AM I SUPPOSED TO REACT TO THIS?
WHAT, THAT I'VE BEEN MAKING THE TWO-BACKED BEAST WITH YOUR BIT OF ECTOPLASMIC ROUGH?
LOOK, THE IMPORTANT THING HERE IS T
YOU DISGUST ME!
I AM NOT FULL OF DELIGHT REGARDING YOU EITHER, LADY WIFE.
VICTOR, I FORBID YOU TO GO TO IT AGAIN!
YOU FORBID ME?
HEY!
FORGIVE US. WE'RE UNDER SUCH STRAIN. I THINK DRINKS ARE IN ORDER.
DID YOU SEE WHAT HE DID? HE CAN'T DO THAT!
HUSH, PIGLET.
DAMN IT, WOMAN, CAN'T YOU STOP HIM LEAVING HIS ABSURD LITTLE TOYS EVERYWHERE?
IT'S BROKEN!
TOYS THAT YOU'RE FOREVER BUYING.
OH, SO, NOW I'M
YOU BR IT!
HOLD IT!
"WASH THE COINS FROM A CORPSE'S EYES IN LIQUOR. GIVE IT TO YOUR HUSBAND. HE'LL BE BLIND TO YOUR SINS." BULGARIAN TRICK. LEARNED IT FROM THE DEMON, HUH?
SHOULD'VE KNOWN. MAKING MY DRINKS IS HER ONLY CONNUBIAL GESTURE.
YOU BROKE ITS FOOT!

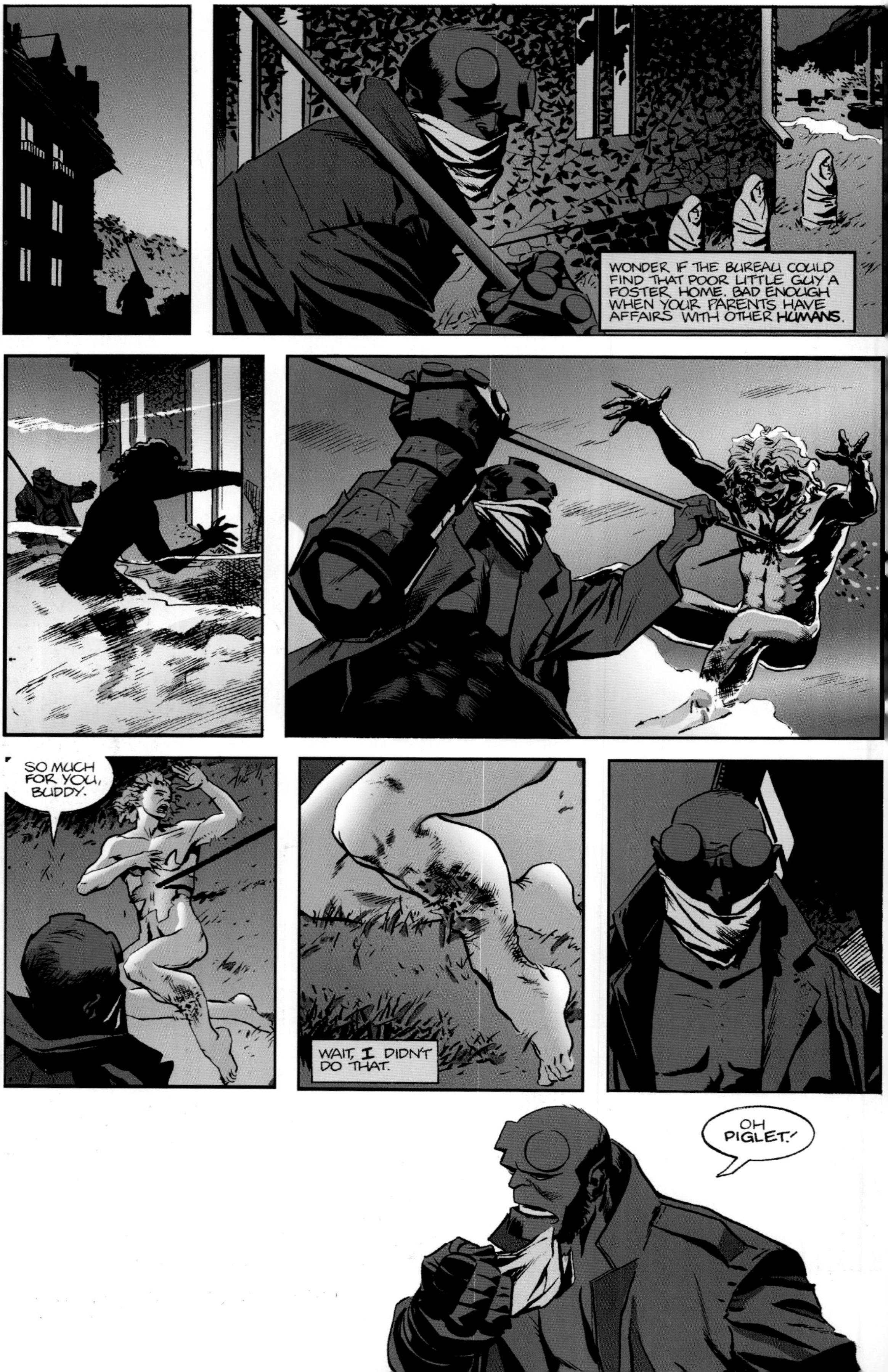
WONDER IF THE BUREAU COULD FIND THAT POOR LITTLE GUY A FOSTER HOME. BAD ENOUGH WHEN YOUR PARENTS HAVE AFFAIRS WITH OTHER HUMANS.
SO MUCH FOR YOU, BUDDY.
WAIT, I DIDN'T DO THAT.
OH PIGLET!

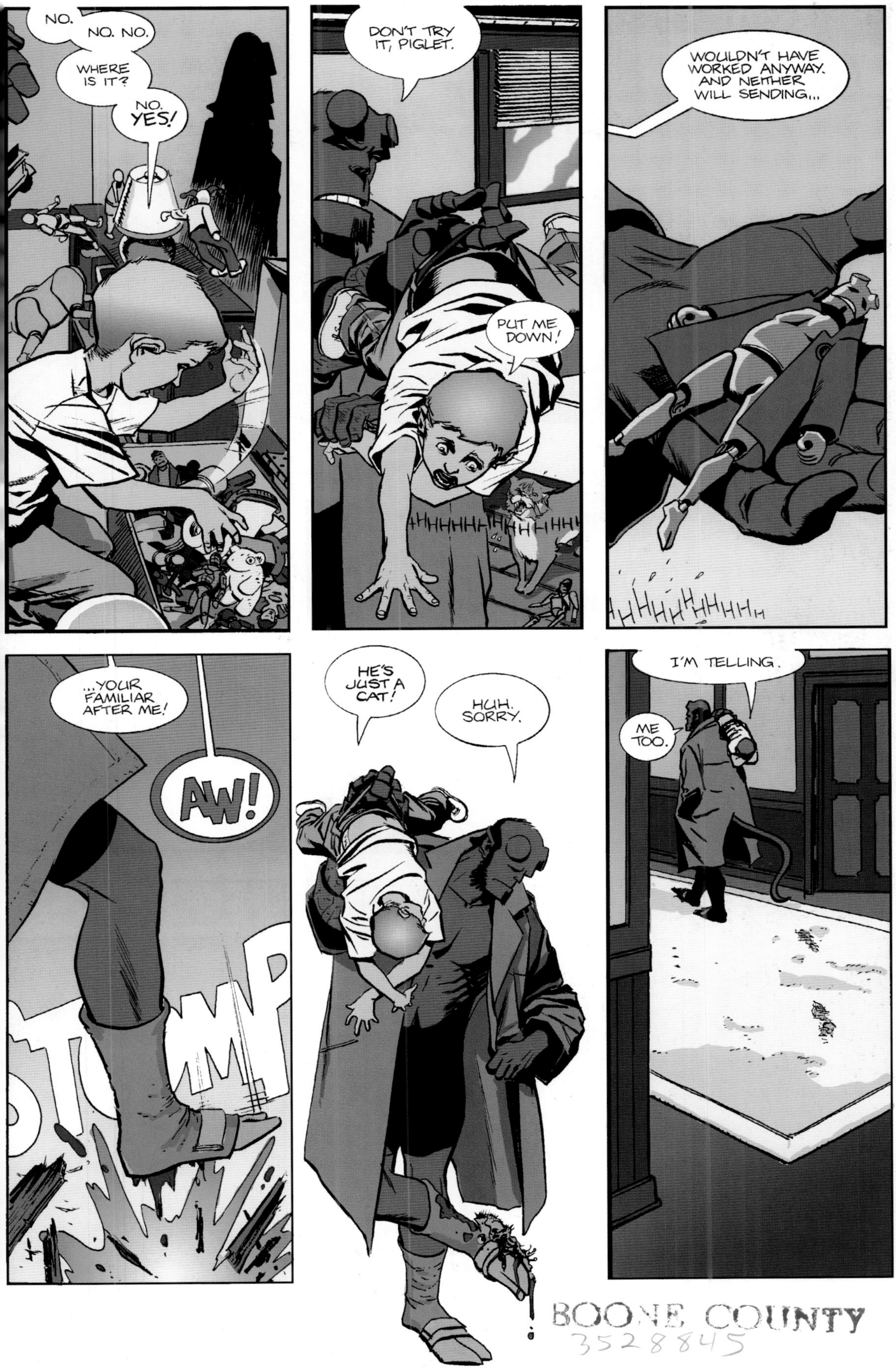

NO.
NO. NO.
WHERE IS IT?
NO. YES!
DON'T TRY IT, PIGLET.
PUT ME DOWN!
HHHHHHHHHHHHHHH
WOULDN'T HAVE WORKED ANYWAY. AND NEITHER WILL SENDING...
HHHHHHHHHHH
...YOUR FAMILIAR AFTER ME!
AW!
STOMP
HE'S JUST A CAT!
HUH. SORRY.
I'M TELLING.
ME TOO.

PIGLET HERE IS WHAT THEY CALL A GIFTED CHILD. PRECOCIOUS, GOOD WITH HIS HANDS, ABLE TO APPLY WHAT HE'S READ.

HE FIGURED OUT THAT IF YOU TWO WERE SUFFICIENTLY, UH, DISTRACTED, HE COULD GET AWAY WITH ANYTHING. INCLUDING BECOMING A RICH ORPHAN.

NOT TO KNOCK YOUR PARENTING SKILLS, BUT I WOULDN'T BUY HIM ANY MORE TOYS.

WHAT WILL HE DO ALL DAY?

START A COIN COLLECTION.

DON'T BE PETTY.

AND I HATE TO ASK, BUT I'M NOWHERE NEAR DONE WITH THE BESTIARY.

TAKE IT. TAKE THE WHOLE LIBRARY.

THOSE BOOKS AREN'T YOURS! YOU CAN'T EVEN RESHELVE THEM PROPERLY!

HE KILLED MY CAT! AREN'T YOU GOING TO DO ANYTHING?

MAY I REMIND YO OF THE STATE O YOUR "LIBRARY I MOVED IN? TE PILES OF BOOKS, MOULDERING, F TOPP

HUSH

OH, DEA AS WELL

FO

I FU IS TA!

AND THEN WITH THE TCHOTCHKE! EVERY SU COVERED WITH THE RIDIC CURIC

THAT'S ENOUGH OF THAT.

CAT

MY FAMILY'S L TREASURES ARE NOT TCHOTCHKE

HE KILLED MY CAT!

SHU YOUR RET LITTL MOU YOU

OH AND SUCH TREA THEY ARE TOO — THE CHINA EGG THE IKONS OF SAINTS YOU NEITH BELIEVE IN CAN PRON

CAN FINE FINE

THE TUREE AND THE URNS, AN SUCH LO

PAY ATTEN ION!? RATHER TAKE FILTHY, WRETCHED.

MOTHER WAS ANOTHE UNLIKELY T BE ACCEPT

THE ONLY DECENT MEMBER OF THAT FAMILY IS ALL OVER MY FOOT.

THE END

26

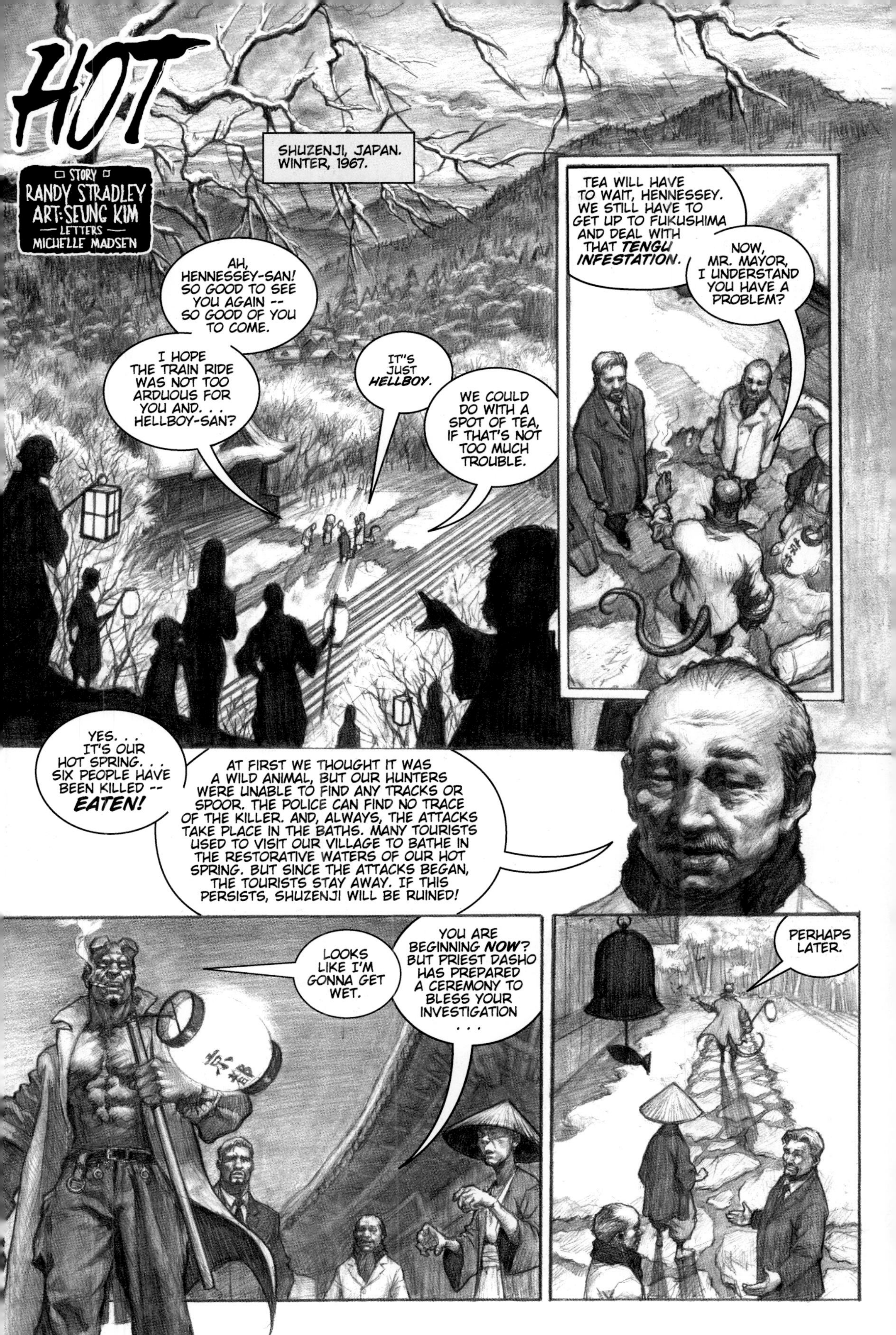

HOT
STORY RANDY STRADLEY
ART: SEUNG KIM
LETTERS MICHELLE MADSEN
SHUZENJI, JAPAN. WINTER, 1967.
AH, HENNESSEY-SAN! SO GOOD TO SEE YOU AGAIN -- SO GOOD OF YOU TO COME.
I HOPE THE TRAIN RIDE WAS NOT TOO ARDUOUS FOR YOU AND. . . HELLBOY-SAN?
IT'S JUST HELLBOY.
WE COULD DO WITH A SPOT OF TEA, IF THAT'S NOT TOO MUCH TROUBLE.
TEA WILL HAVE TO WAIT, HENNESSEY. WE STILL HAVE TO GET UP TO FUKUSHIMA AND DEAL WITH THAT TENGU INFESTATION.
NOW, MR. MAYOR, I UNDERSTAND YOU HAVE A PROBLEM?
YES. . . IT'S OUR HOT SPRING. . . SIX PEOPLE HAVE BEEN KILLED -- EATEN!
AT FIRST WE THOUGHT IT WAS A WILD ANIMAL, BUT OUR HUNTERS WERE UNABLE TO FIND ANY TRACKS OR SPOOR. THE POLICE CAN FIND NO TRACE OF THE KILLER. AND, ALWAYS, THE ATTACKS TAKE PLACE IN THE BATHS. MANY TOURISTS USED TO VISIT OUR VILLAGE TO BATHE IN THE RESTORATIVE WATERS OF OUR HOT SPRING. BUT SINCE THE ATTACKS BEGAN, THE TOURISTS STAY AWAY. IF THIS PERSISTS, SHUZENJI WILL BE RUINED!
LOOKS LIKE I'M GONNA GET WET.
YOU ARE BEGINNING NOW? BUT PRIEST DASHO HAS PREPARED A CEREMONY TO BLESS YOUR INVESTIGATION . . .
PERHAPS LATER.

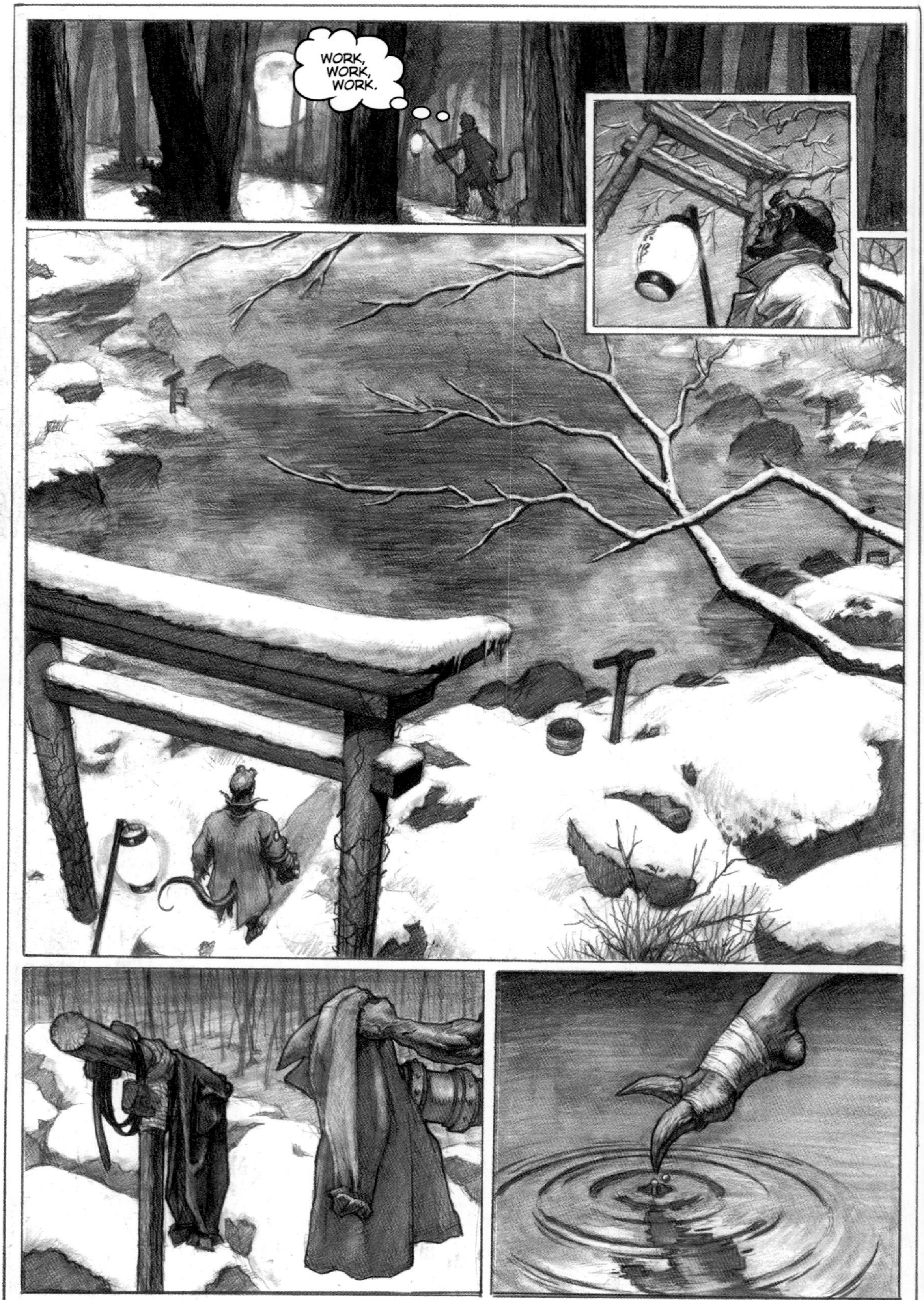
WORK, WORK, WORK.

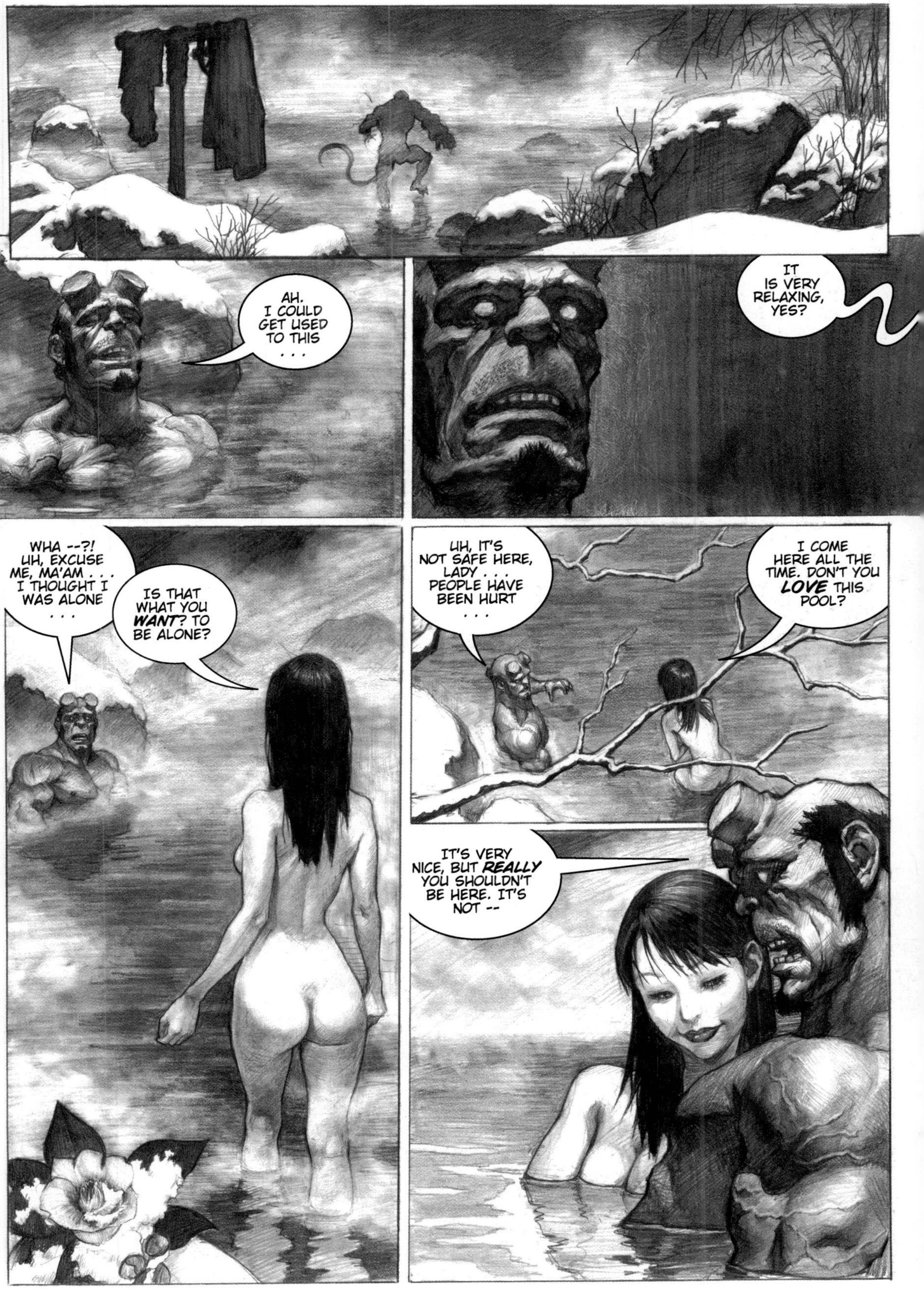
AH. I COULD GET USED TO THIS . . .
IT IS VERY RELAXING, YES?
WHA --?! UH, EXCUSE ME, MA'AM . . . I THOUGHT I WAS ALONE . . .
IS THAT WHAT YOU *WANT*? TO BE ALONE?
UH, IT'S NOT SAFE HERE, LADY . . . PEOPLE HAVE BEEN HURT . . .
I COME HERE ALL THE TIME. DON'T YOU *LOVE* THIS POOL?
IT'S VERY NICE, BUT *REALLY* YOU SHOULDN'T BE HERE. IT'S NOT --

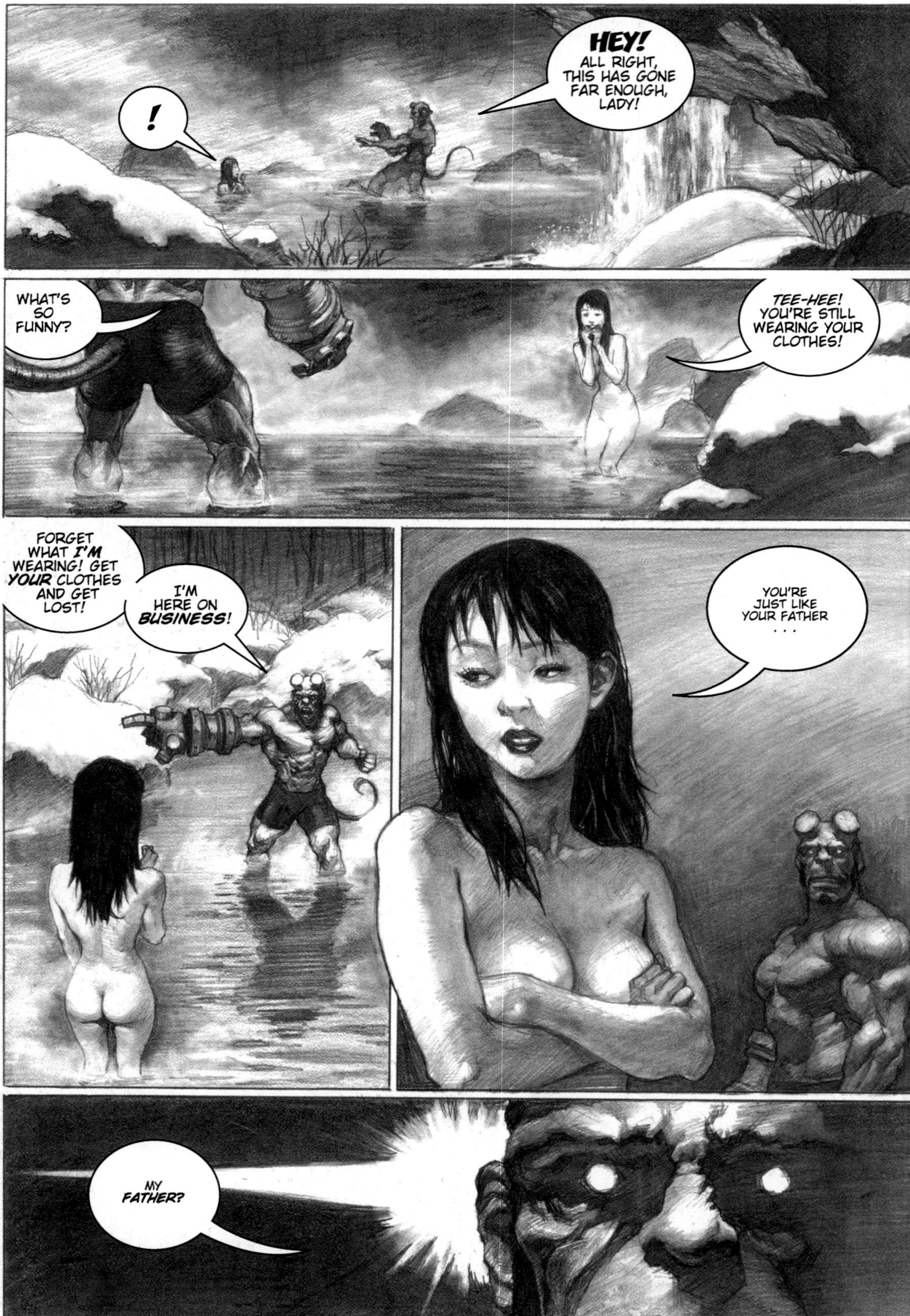
!
HEY! ALL RIGHT, THIS HAS GONE FAR ENOUGH, LADY!
WHAT'S SO FUNNY?
TEE-HEE! YOU'RE STILL WEARING YOUR CLOTHES!
FORGET WHAT I'M WEARING! GET YOUR CLOTHES AND GET LOST!
I'M HERE ON BUSINESS!
YOU'RE JUST LIKE YOUR FATHER . . .
MY FATHER?

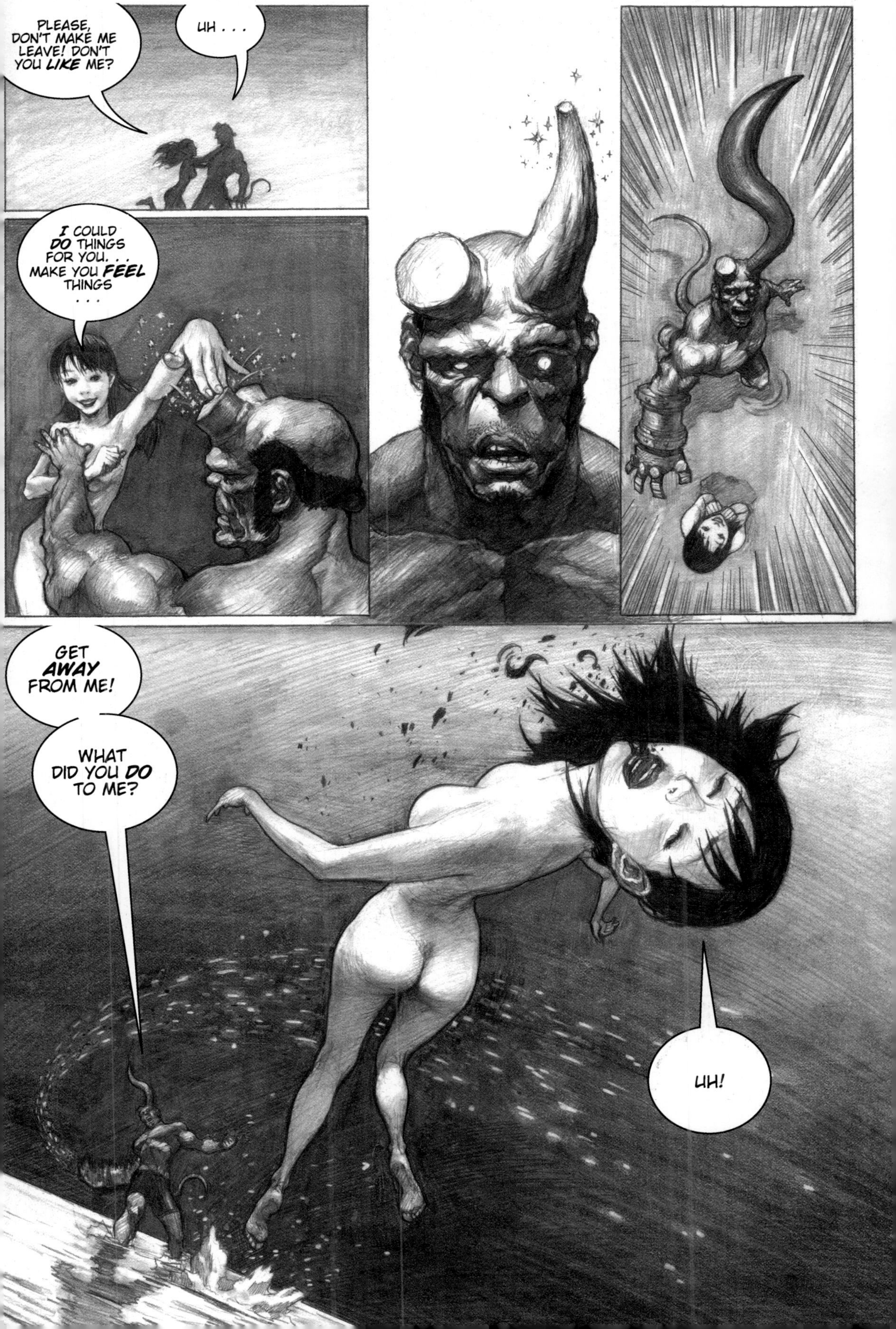
PLEASE, DON'T MAKE ME LEAVE! DON'T YOU LIKE ME?
UH . . .
I COULD DO THINGS FOR YOU. . . MAKE YOU FEEL THINGS . . .
GET AWAY FROM ME!
WHAT DID YOU DO TO ME?
UH!

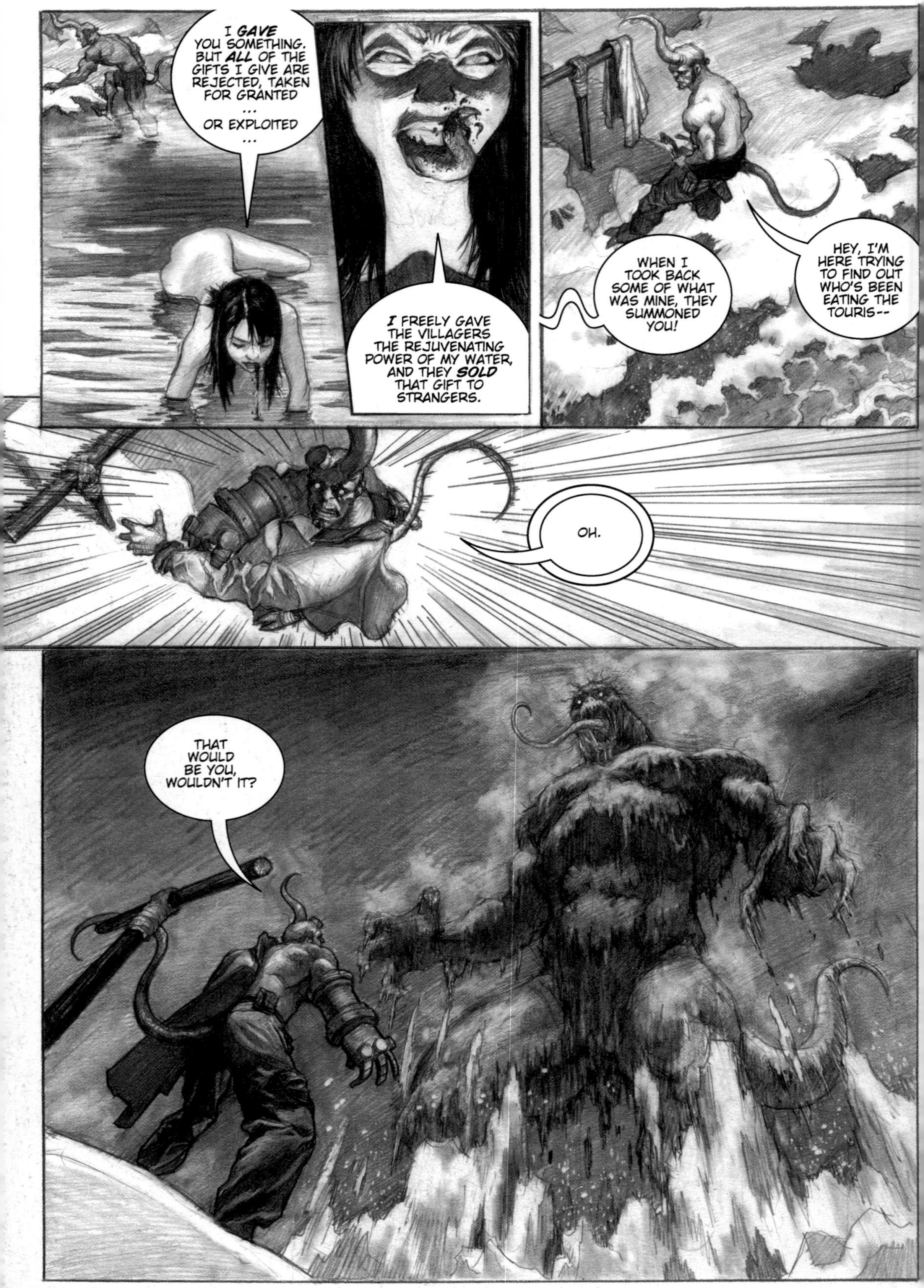
I GAVE YOU SOMETHING. BUT ALL OF THE GIFTS I GIVE ARE REJECTED, TAKEN FOR GRANTED ... OR EXPLOITED ...
I FREELY GAVE THE VILLAGERS THE REJUVENATING POWER OF MY WATER, AND THEY SOLD THAT GIFT TO STRANGERS.
WHEN I TOOK BACK SOME OF WHAT WAS MINE, THEY SUMMONED YOU!
HEY, I'M HERE TRYING TO FIND OUT WHO'S BEEN EATING THE TOURIS--
OH.
THAT WOULD BE YOU, WOULDN'T IT?

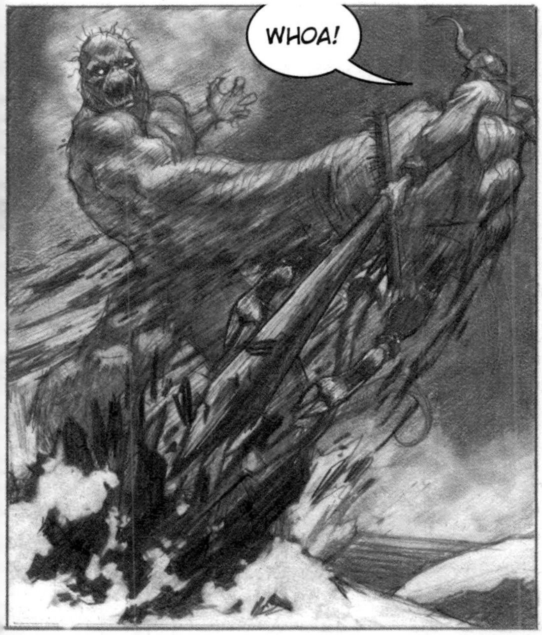
WHOA!

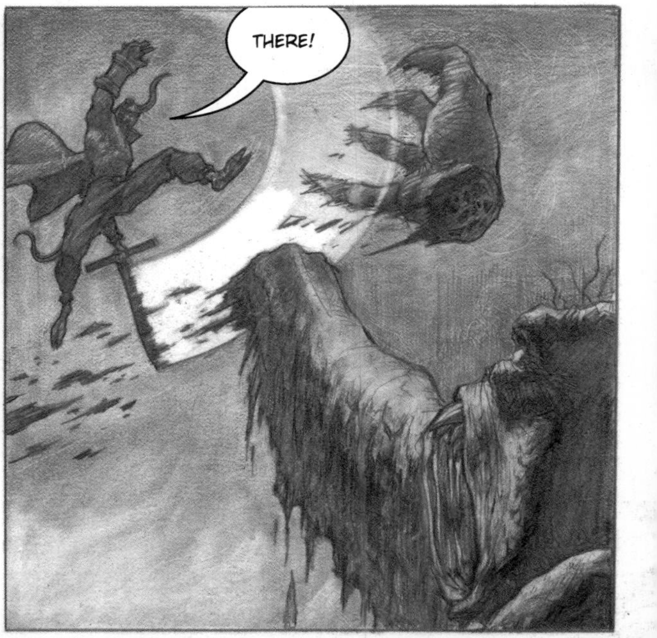
THERE!

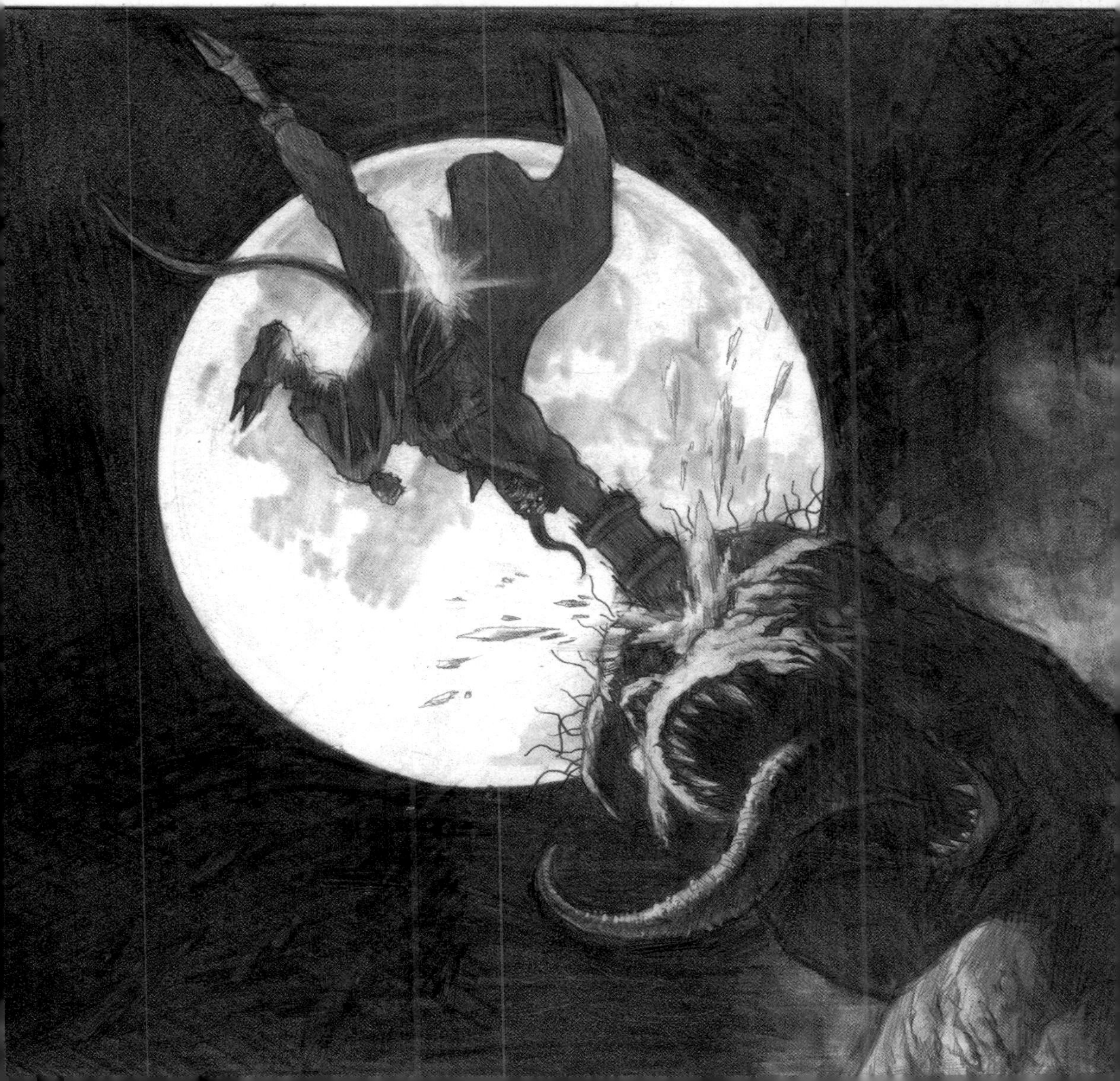

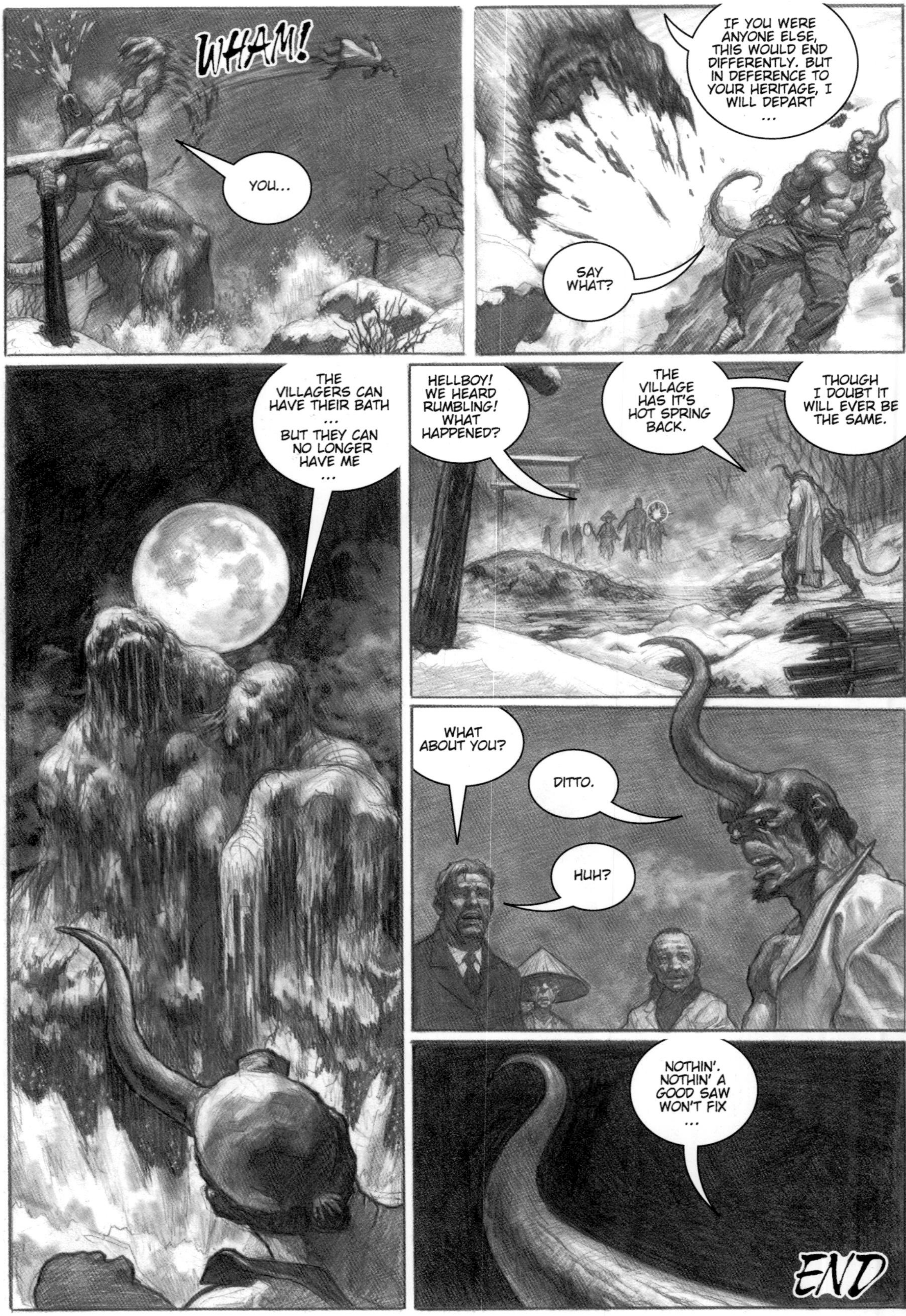
WHAM!
YOU...
IF YOU WERE ANYONE ELSE, THIS WOULD END DIFFERENTLY. BUT IN DEFERENCE TO YOUR HERITAGE, I WILL DEPART ...
SAY WHAT?
THE VILLAGERS CAN HAVE THEIR BATH ... BUT THEY CAN NO LONGER HAVE ME ...
HELLBOY! WE HEARD RUMBLING! WHAT HAPPENED?
THE VILLAGE HAS IT'S HOT SPRING BACK.
THOUGH I DOUBT IT WILL EVER BE THE SAME.
WHAT ABOUT YOU?
DITTO.
HUH?
NOTHIN'. NOTHIN' A GOOD SAW WON'T FIX ...
END

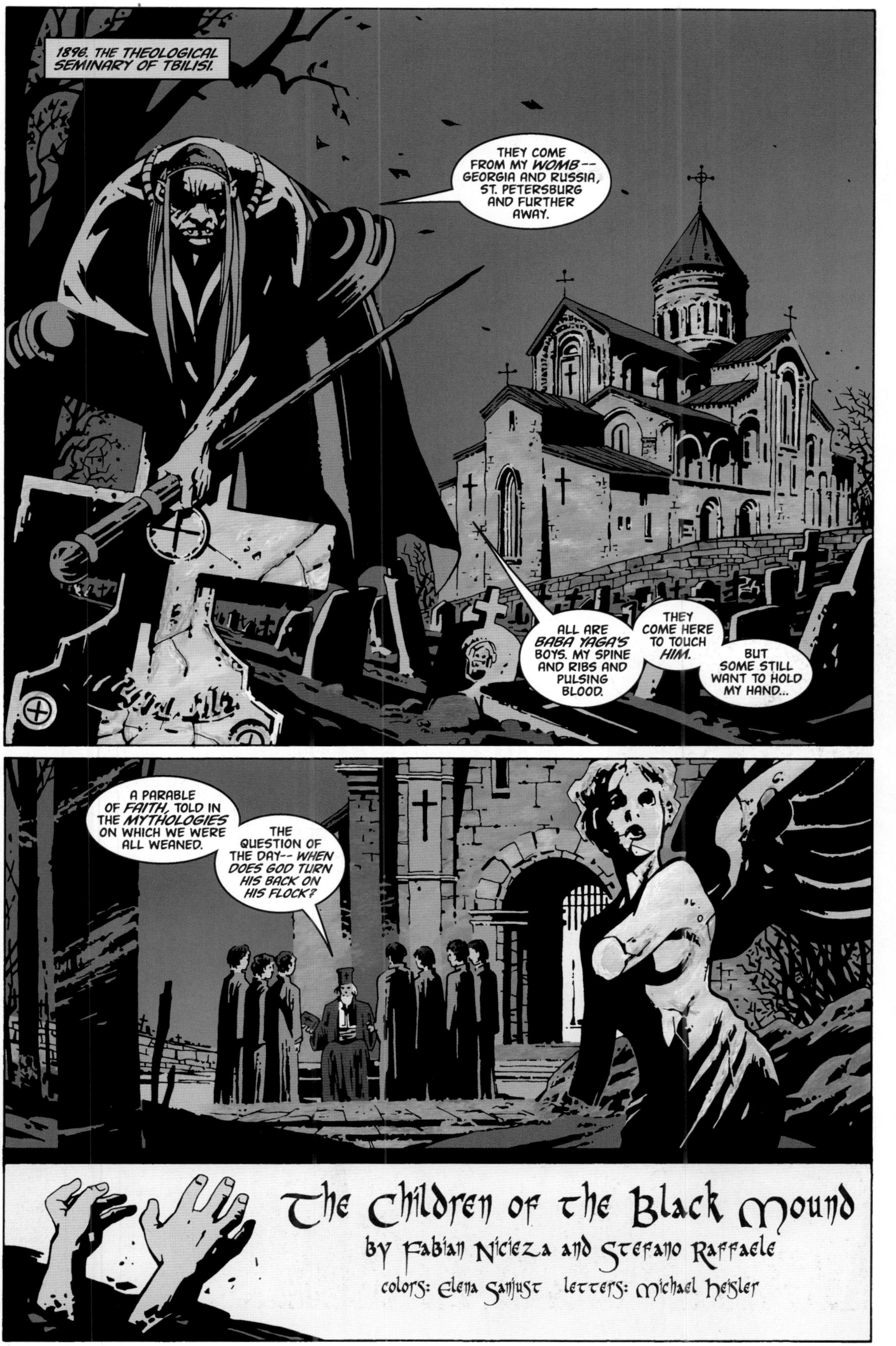
1896. THE THEOLOGICAL SEMINARY OF TBILISI.
THEY COME FROM MY WOMB-- GEORGIA AND RUSSIA, ST. PETERSBURG AND FURTHER AWAY.
ALL ARE BABA YAGA'S BOYS. MY SPINE AND RIBS AND PULSING BLOOD.
THEY COME HERE TO TOUCH HIM.
BUT SOME STILL WANT TO HOLD MY HAND...
A PARABLE OF FAITH, TOLD IN THE MYTHOLOGIES ON WHICH WE WERE ALL WEANED.
THE QUESTION OF THE DAY-- WHEN DOES GOD TURN HIS BACK ON HIS FLOCK?
The Children of the Black Mound
by Fabian Nicieza and Stefano Raffaele
colors: Elena Sanjust letters: Michael Heisler

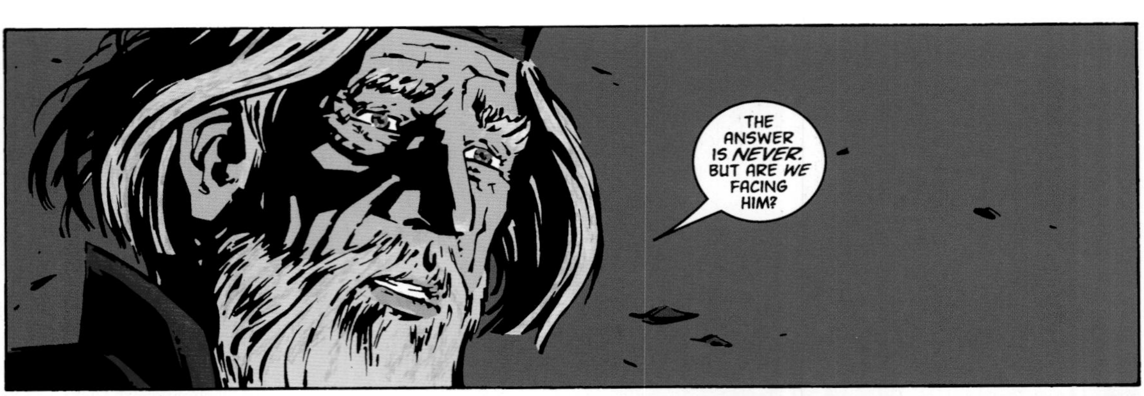
THE ANSWER IS NEVER. BUT ARE WE FACING HIM?

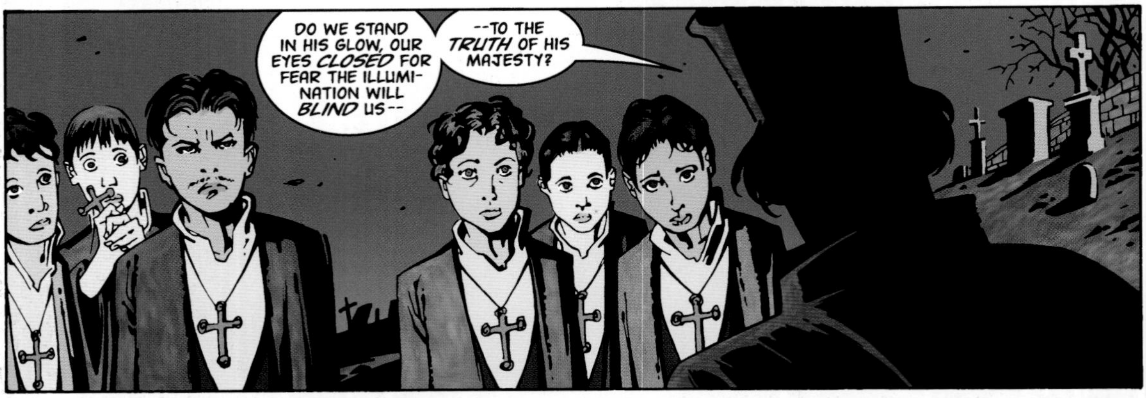
DO WE STAND IN HIS GLOW, OUR EYES CLOSED FOR FEAR THE ILLUMINATION WILL BLIND US--
--TO THE TRUTH OF HIS MAJESTY?

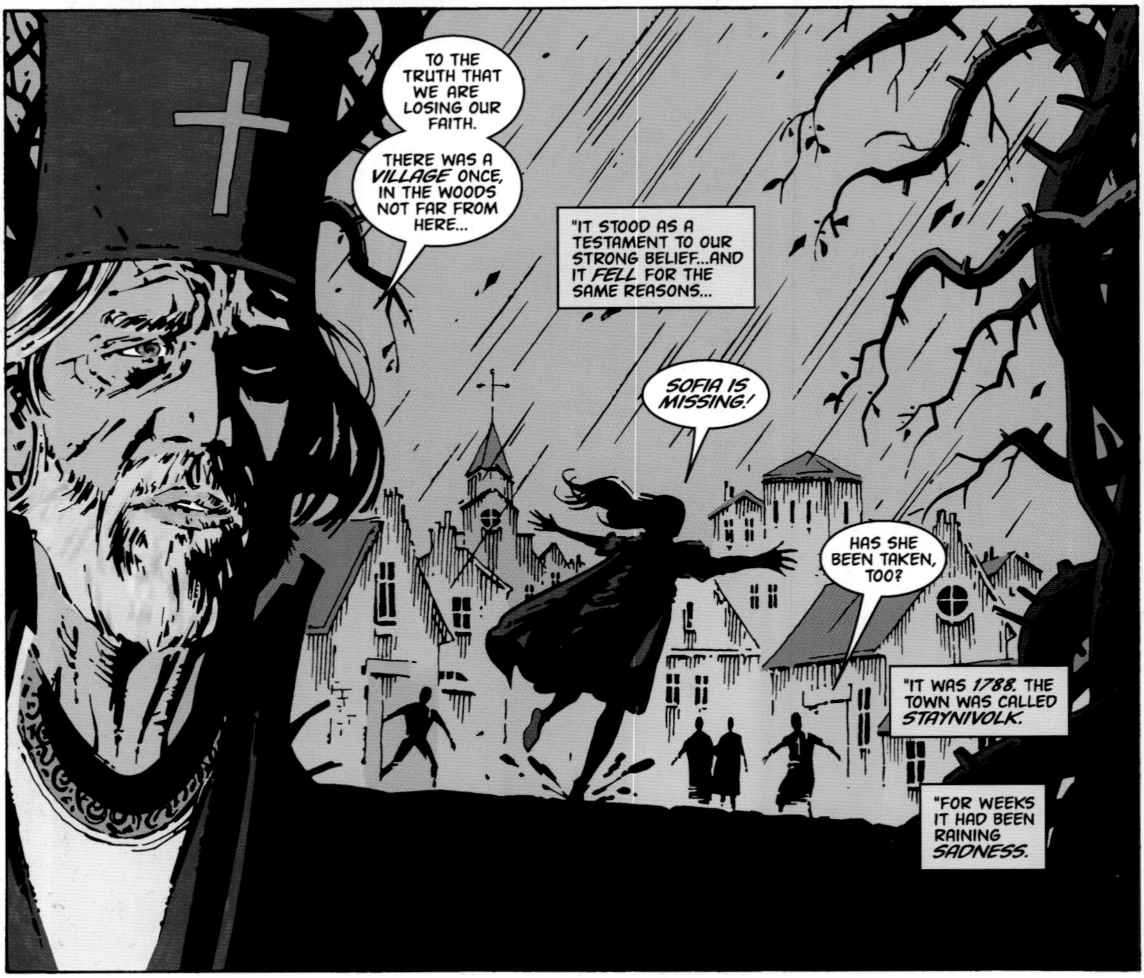
TO THE TRUTH THAT WE ARE LOSING OUR FAITH.
THERE WAS A VILLAGE ONCE, IN THE WOODS NOT FAR FROM HERE...
"IT STOOD AS A TESTAMENT TO OUR STRONG BELIEF...AND IT FELL FOR THE SAME REASONS...
SOFIA IS MISSING!
HAS SHE BEEN TAKEN, TOO?
"IT WAS 1788. THE TOWN WAS CALLED STAYNIVOLK.
"FOR WEEKS IT HAD BEEN RAINING SADNESS.

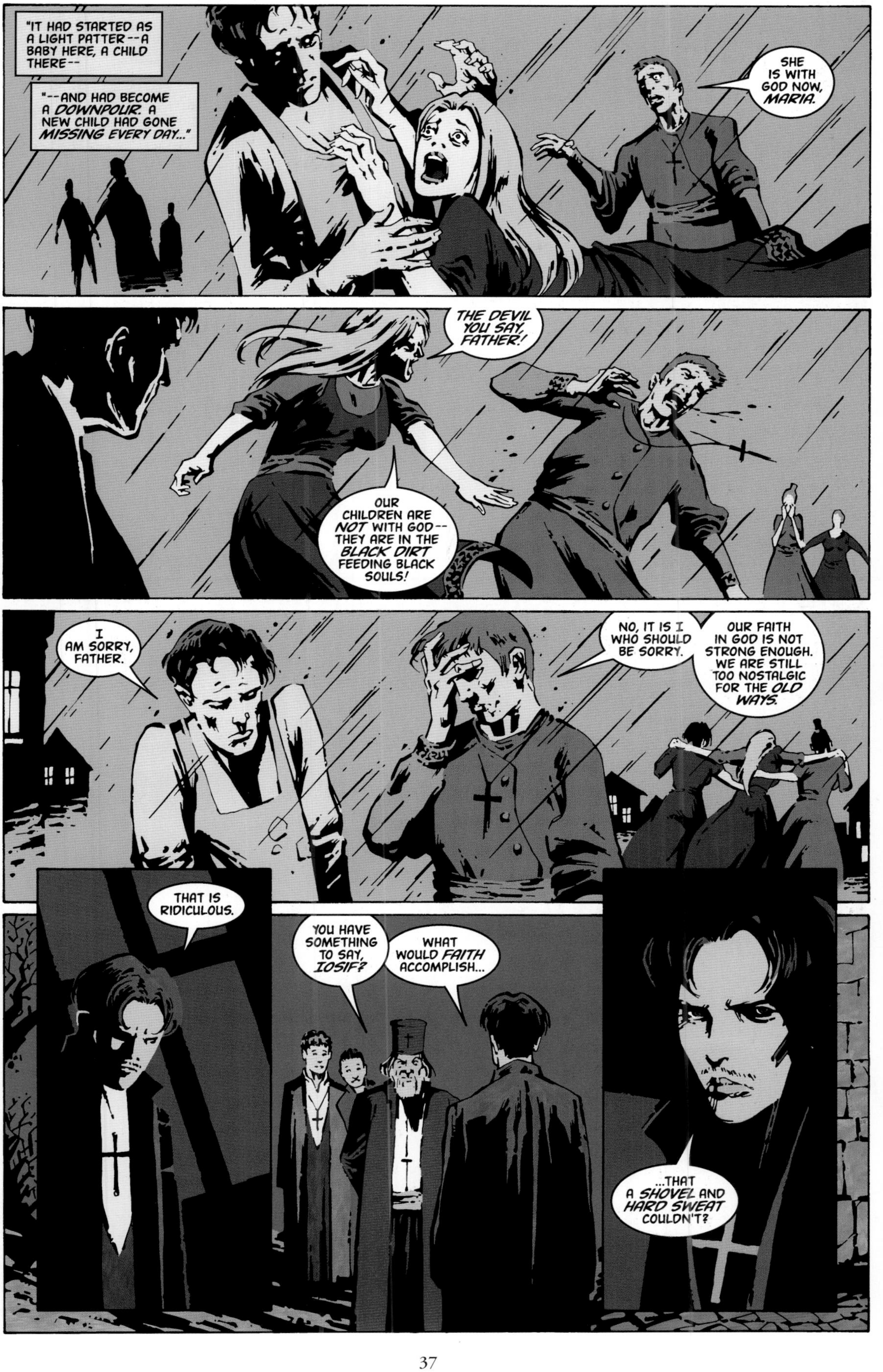
"IT HAD STARTED AS A LIGHT PATTER--A BABY HERE, A CHILD THERE--
"--AND HAD BECOME A DOWNPOUR. A NEW CHILD HAD GONE MISSING EVERY DAY..."
SHE IS WITH GOD NOW, MARIA.
THE DEVIL YOU SAY, FATHER!
OUR CHILDREN ARE NOT WITH GOD-- THEY ARE IN THE BLACK DIRT FEEDING BLACK SOULS!
I AM SORRY, FATHER.
NO, IT IS I WHO SHOULD BE SORRY.
OUR FAITH IN GOD IS NOT STRONG ENOUGH. WE ARE STILL TOO NOSTALGIC FOR THE OLD WAYS.
THAT IS RIDICULOUS.
YOU HAVE SOMETHING TO SAY, IOSIF?
WHAT WOULD FAITH ACCOMPLISH...
...THAT A SHOVEL AND HARD SWEAT COULDN'T?

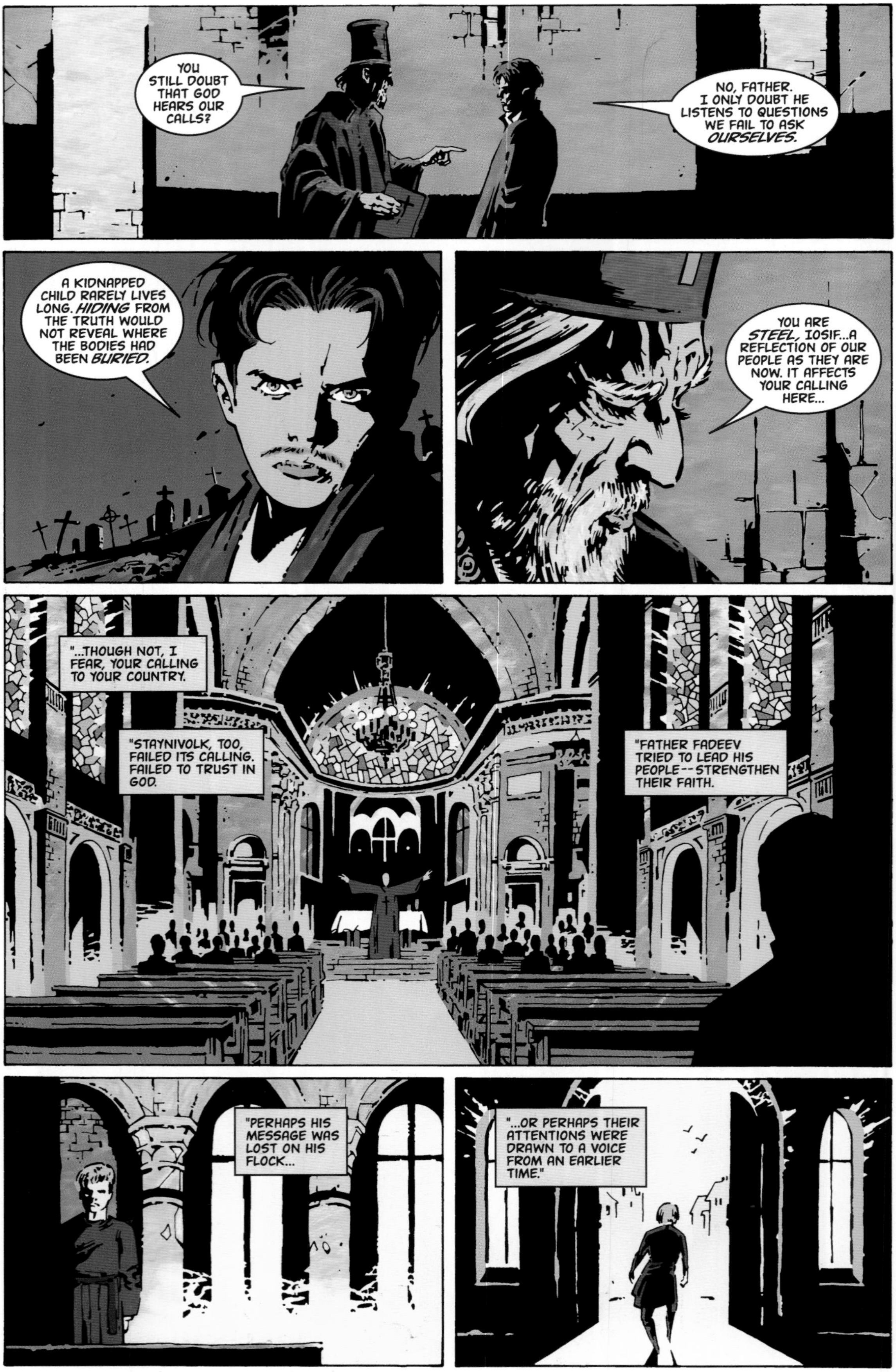
YOU STILL DOUBT THAT GOD HEARS OUR CALLS?
NO, FATHER. I ONLY DOUBT HE LISTENS TO QUESTIONS WE FAIL TO ASK *OURSELVES.*
A KIDNAPPED CHILD RARELY LIVES LONG. *HIDING* FROM THE TRUTH WOULD NOT REVEAL WHERE THE BODIES HAD BEEN *BURIED.*
YOU ARE *STEEL,* IOSIF...A REFLECTION OF OUR PEOPLE AS THEY ARE NOW. IT AFFECTS YOUR CALLING HERE...
"...THOUGH NOT, I FEAR, YOUR CALLING TO YOUR COUNTRY.
"STAYNIVOLK, TOO, FAILED ITS CALLING. FAILED TO TRUST IN GOD.
"FATHER FADEEV TRIED TO LEAD HIS PEOPLE--STRENGTHEN THEIR FAITH.
"PERHAPS HIS MESSAGE WAS LOST ON HIS FLOCK...
"...OR PERHAPS THEIR ATTENTIONS WERE DRAWN TO A VOICE FROM AN EARLIER TIME."

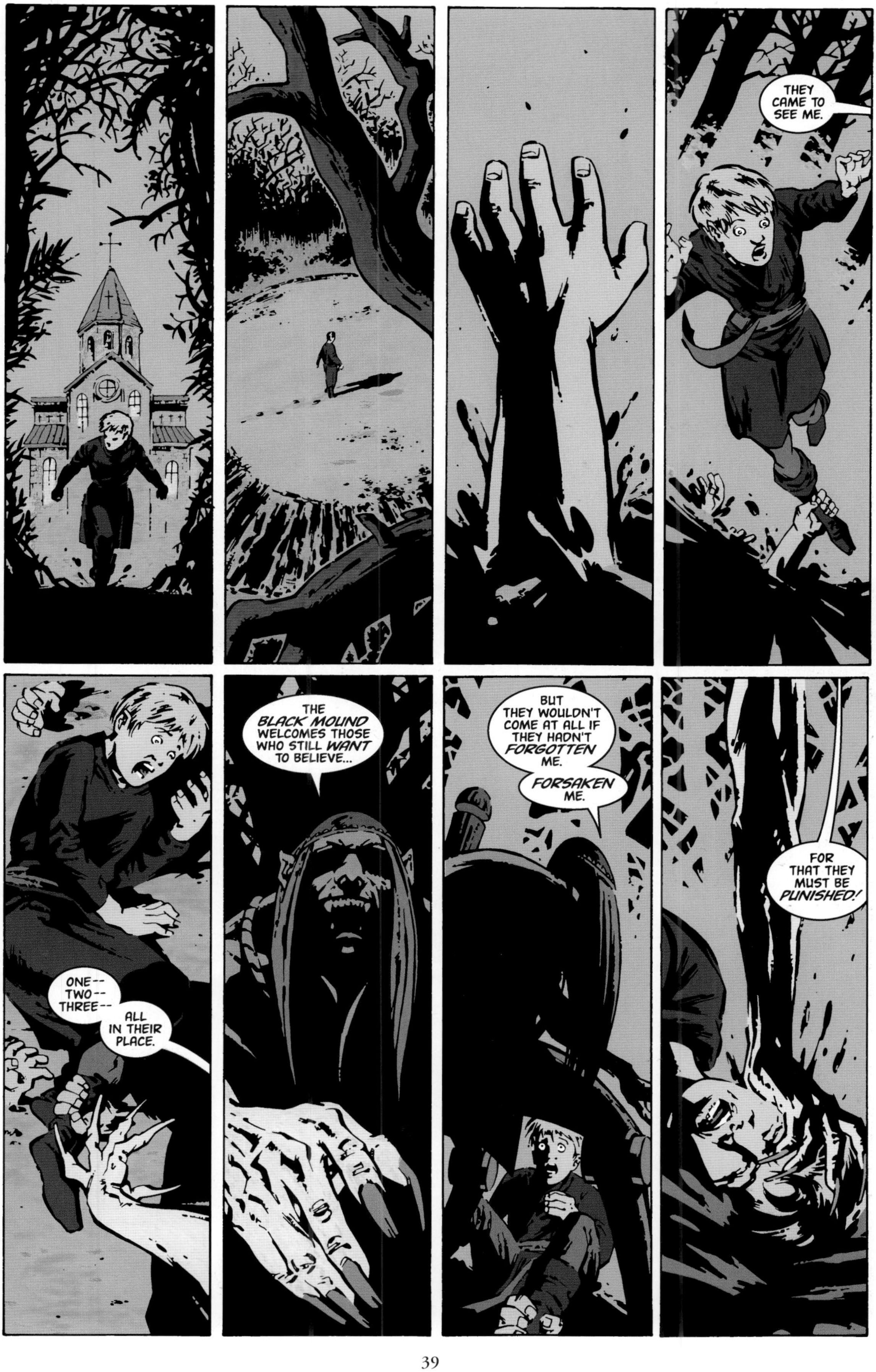
THEY CAME TO SEE ME.
THE BLACK MOUND WELCOMES THOSE WHO STILL WANT TO BELIEVE...
BUT THEY WOULDN'T COME AT ALL IF THEY HADN'T FORGOTTEN ME.
FORSAKEN ME.
FOR THAT THEY MUST BE PUNISHED!
ONE--
TWO--
THREE--
ALL IN THEIR PLACE.

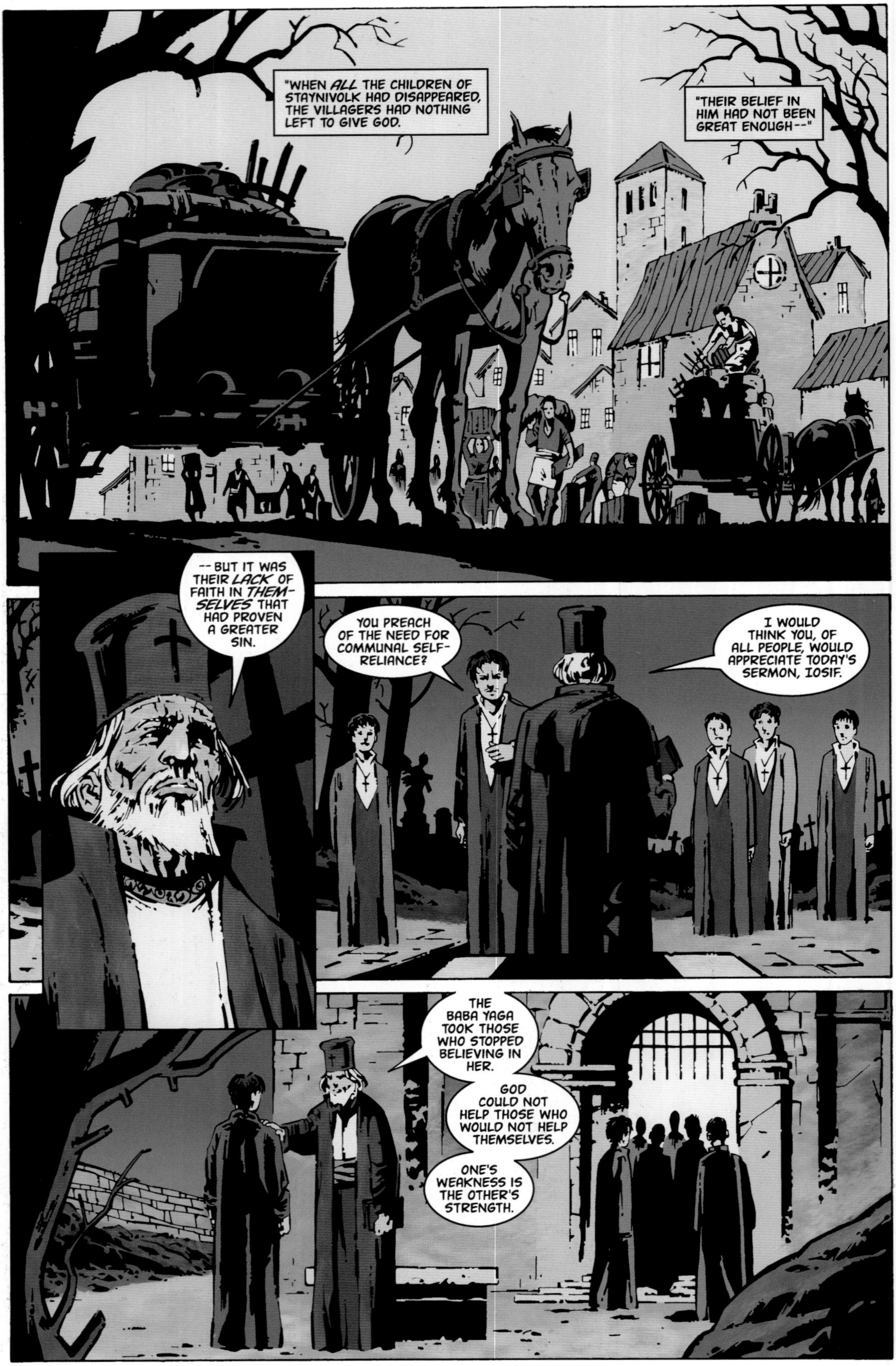
"WHEN ALL THE CHILDREN OF STAYNIVOLK HAD DISAPPEARED, THE VILLAGERS HAD NOTHING LEFT TO GIVE GOD.
"THEIR BELIEF IN HIM HAD NOT BEEN GREAT ENOUGH--"
--BUT IT WAS THEIR LACK OF FAITH IN THEMSELVES THAT HAD PROVEN A GREATER SIN.
YOU PREACH OF THE NEED FOR COMMUNAL SELF-RELIANCE?
I WOULD THINK YOU, OF ALL PEOPLE, WOULD APPRECIATE TODAY'S SERMON, IOSIF.
THE BABA YAGA TOOK THOSE WHO STOPPED BELIEVING IN HER.
GOD COULD NOT HELP THOSE WHO WOULD NOT HELP THEMSELVES.
ONE'S WEAKNESS IS THE OTHER'S STRENGTH.

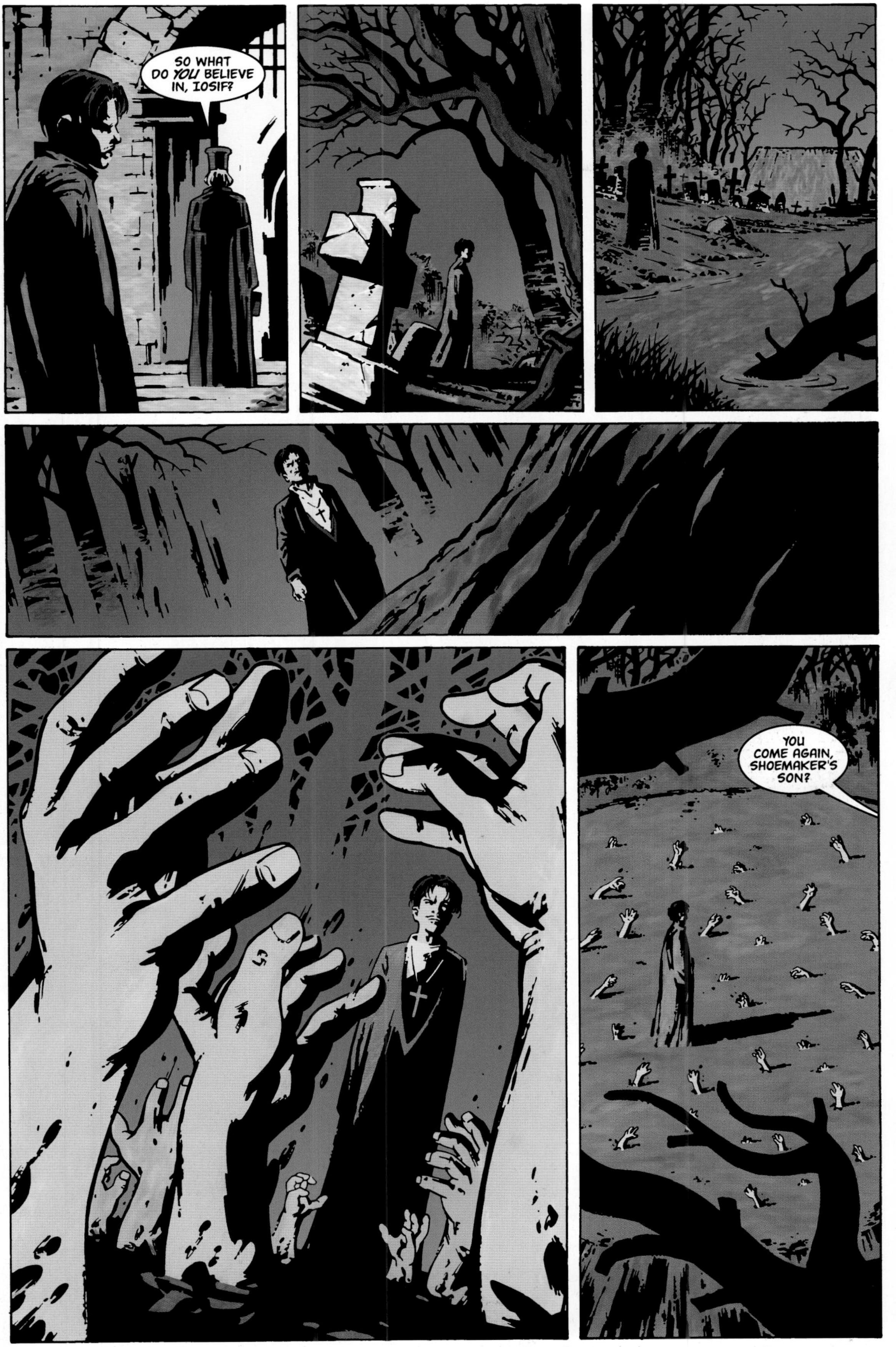
SO WHAT DO YOU BELIEVE IN, IOSIF?
YOU COME AGAIN, SHOEMAKER'S SON?

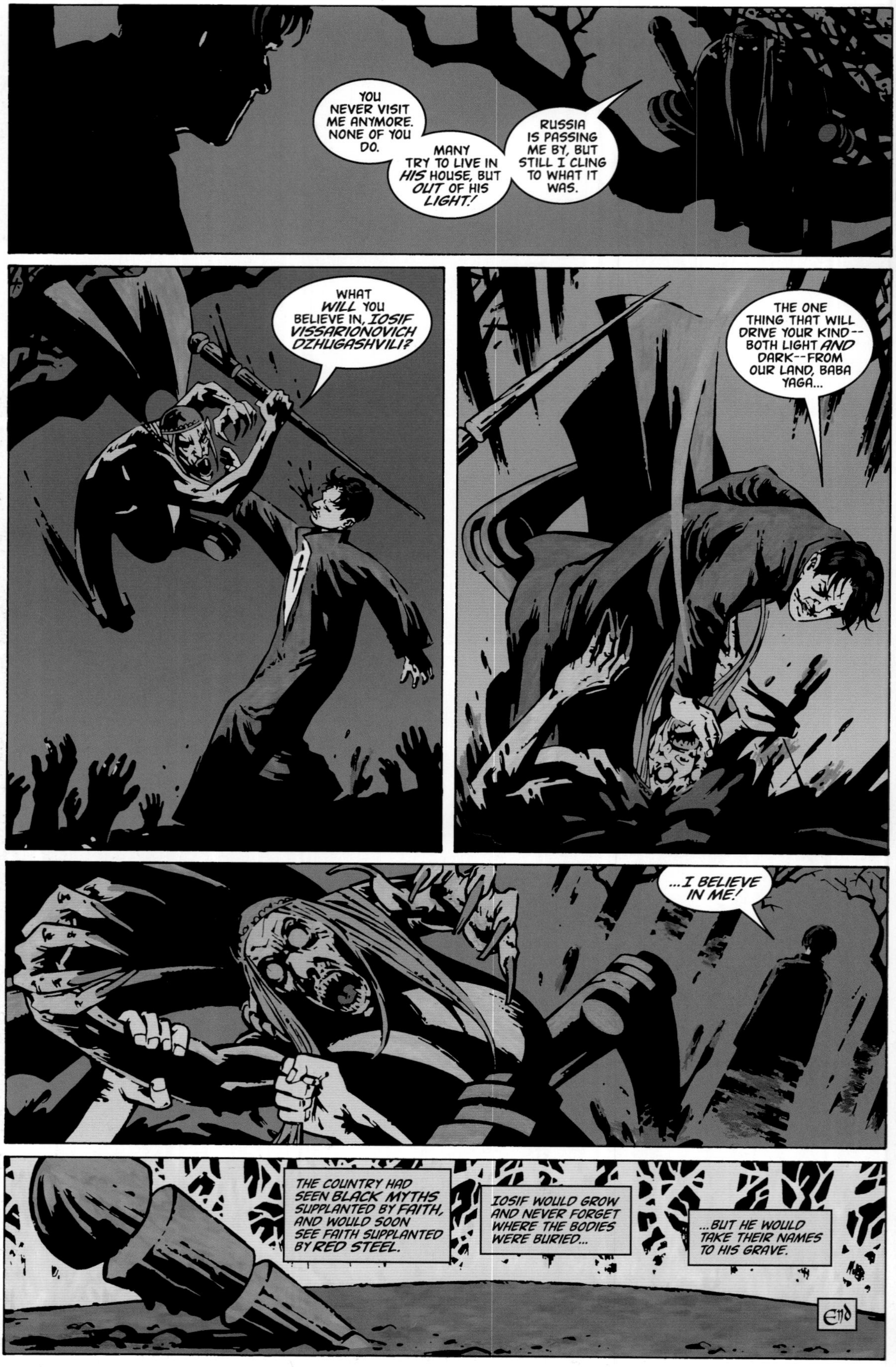
YOU NEVER VISIT ME ANYMORE. NONE OF YOU DO.
MANY TRY TO LIVE IN HIS HOUSE, BUT OUT OF HIS LIGHT!
RUSSIA IS PASSING ME BY, BUT STILL I CLING TO WHAT IT WAS.
WHAT WILL YOU BELIEVE IN, IOSIF VISSARIONOVICH DZHUGASHVILI?
THE ONE THING THAT WILL DRIVE YOUR KIND--BOTH LIGHT AND DARK--FROM OUR LAND, BABA YAGA...
...I BELIEVE IN ME!
THE COUNTRY HAD SEEN BLACK MYTHS SUPPLANTED BY FAITH, AND WOULD SOON SEE FAITH SUPPLANTED BY RED STEEL.
IOSIF WOULD GROW AND NEVER FORGET WHERE THE BODIES WERE BURIED...
...BUT HE WOULD TAKE THEIR NAMES TO HIS GRAVE.
END

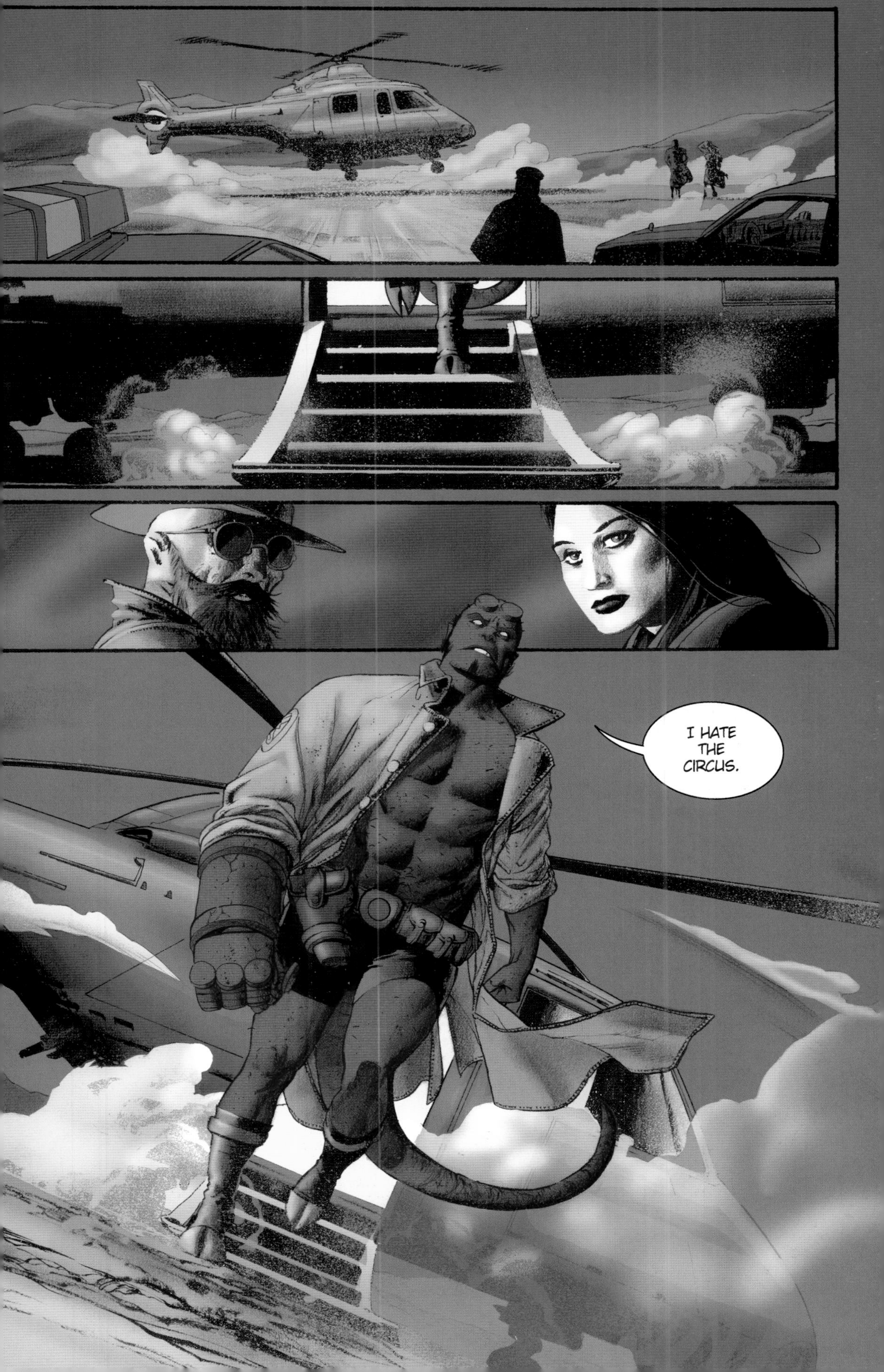
I HATE THE CIRCUS.

Big-Top-Hell-Boy

BY JOHN CASSADAY
COLORS AND LETTERS BY
DAN JACKSON

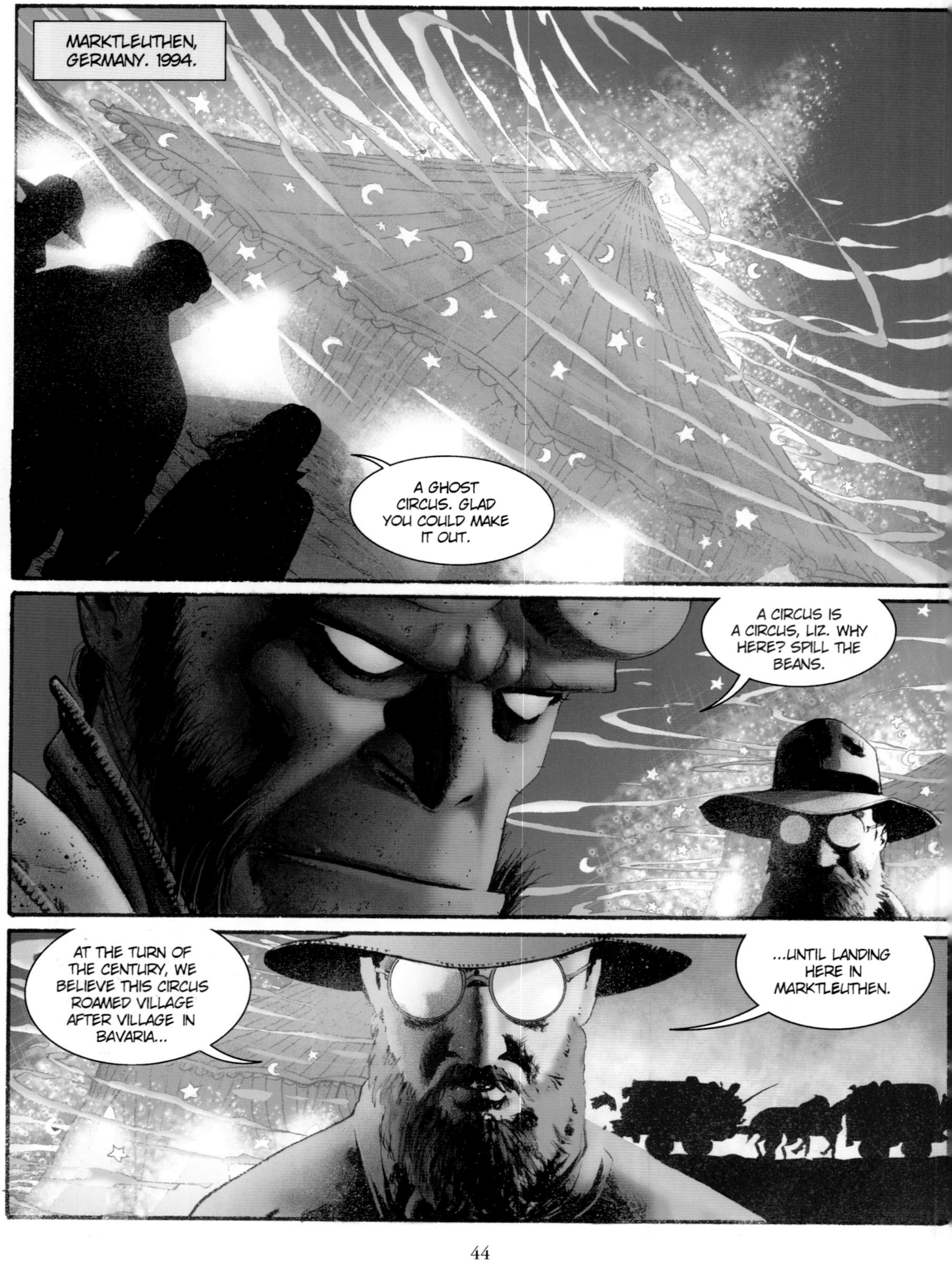
MARKTLEUTHEN, GERMANY. 1994.
A GHOST CIRCUS. GLAD YOU COULD MAKE IT OUT.
A CIRCUS IS A CIRCUS, LIZ. WHY HERE? SPILL THE BEANS.
AT THE TURN OF THE CENTURY, WE BELIEVE THIS CIRCUS ROAMED VILLAGE AFTER VILLAGE IN BAVARIA...
...UNTIL LANDING HERE IN MARKTLEUTHEN.

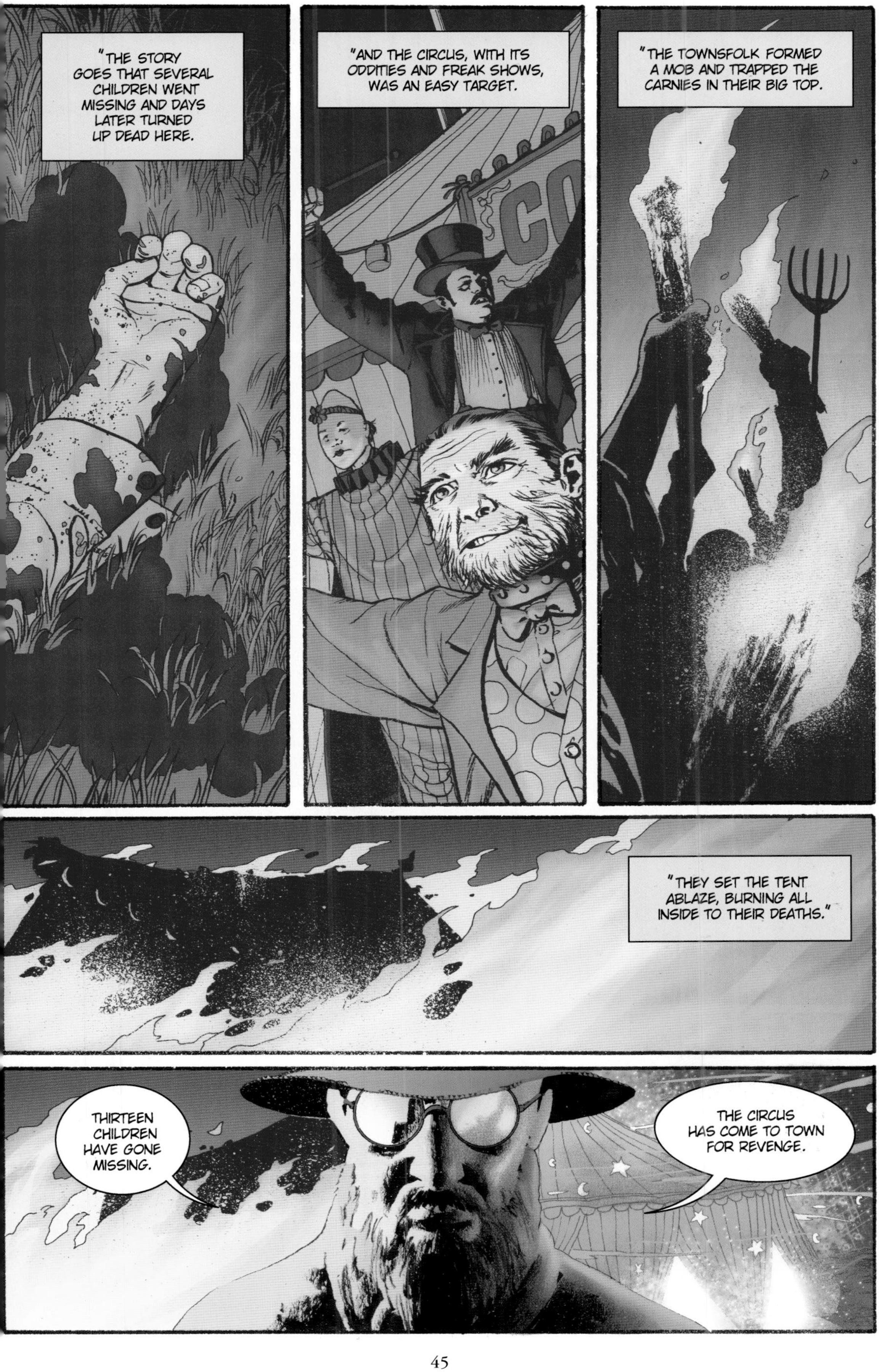
"THE STORY GOES THAT SEVERAL CHILDREN WENT MISSING AND DAYS LATER TURNED UP DEAD HERE.
"AND THE CIRCUS, WITH ITS ODDITIES AND FREAK SHOWS, WAS AN EASY TARGET.
"THE TOWNSFOLK FORMED A MOB AND TRAPPED THE CARNIES IN THEIR BIG TOP.
"THEY SET THE TENT ABLAZE, BURNING ALL INSIDE TO THEIR DEATHS."
THIRTEEN CHILDREN HAVE GONE MISSING.
THE CIRCUS HAS COME TO TOWN FOR REVENGE.

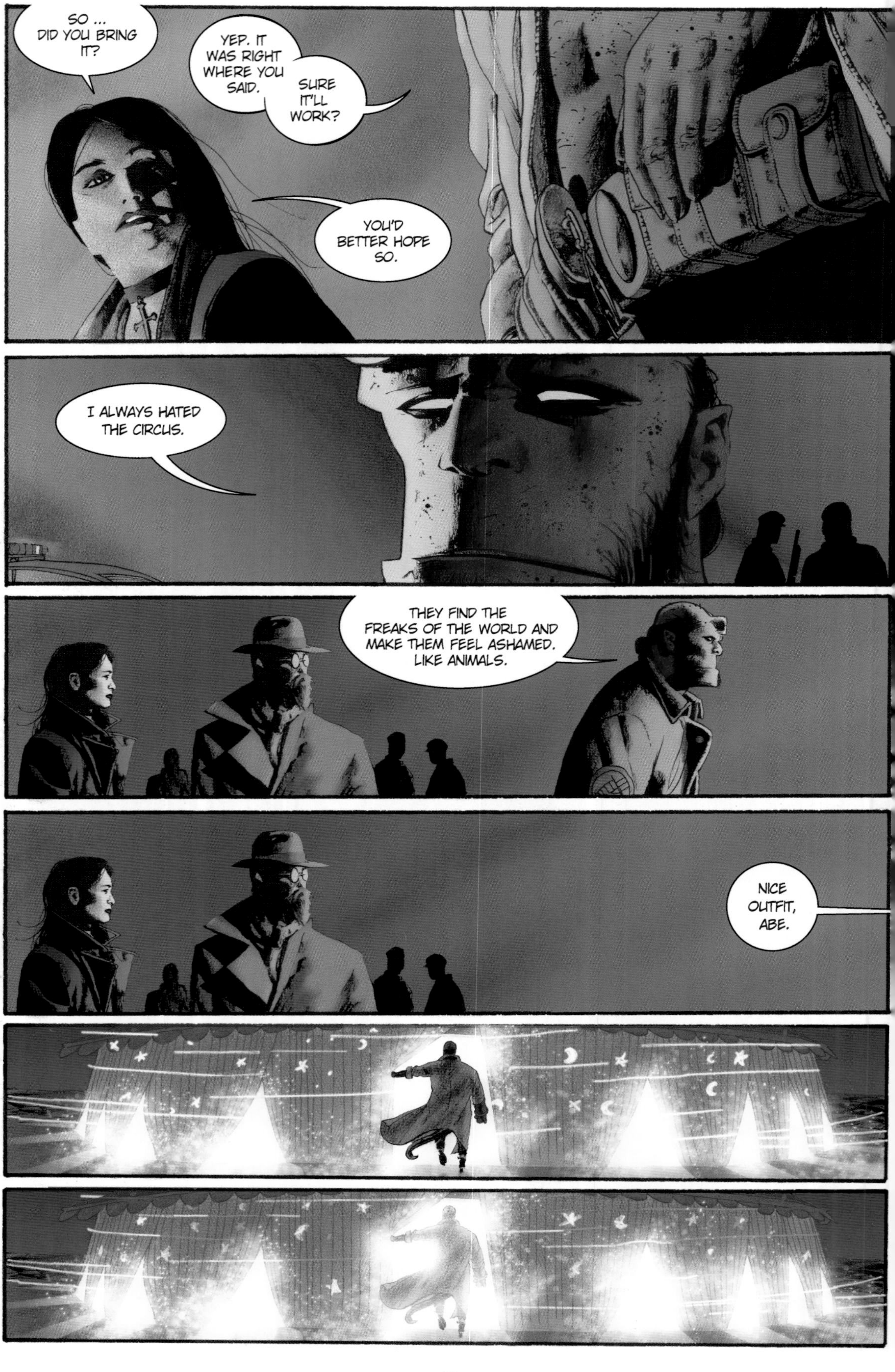
SO ... DID YOU BRING IT?
YEP. IT WAS RIGHT WHERE YOU SAID.
SURE IT'LL WORK?
YOU'D BETTER HOPE SO.
I ALWAYS HATED THE CIRCUS.
THEY FIND THE FREAKS OF THE WORLD AND MAKE THEM FEEL ASHAMED. LIKE ANIMALS.
NICE OUTFIT, ABE.

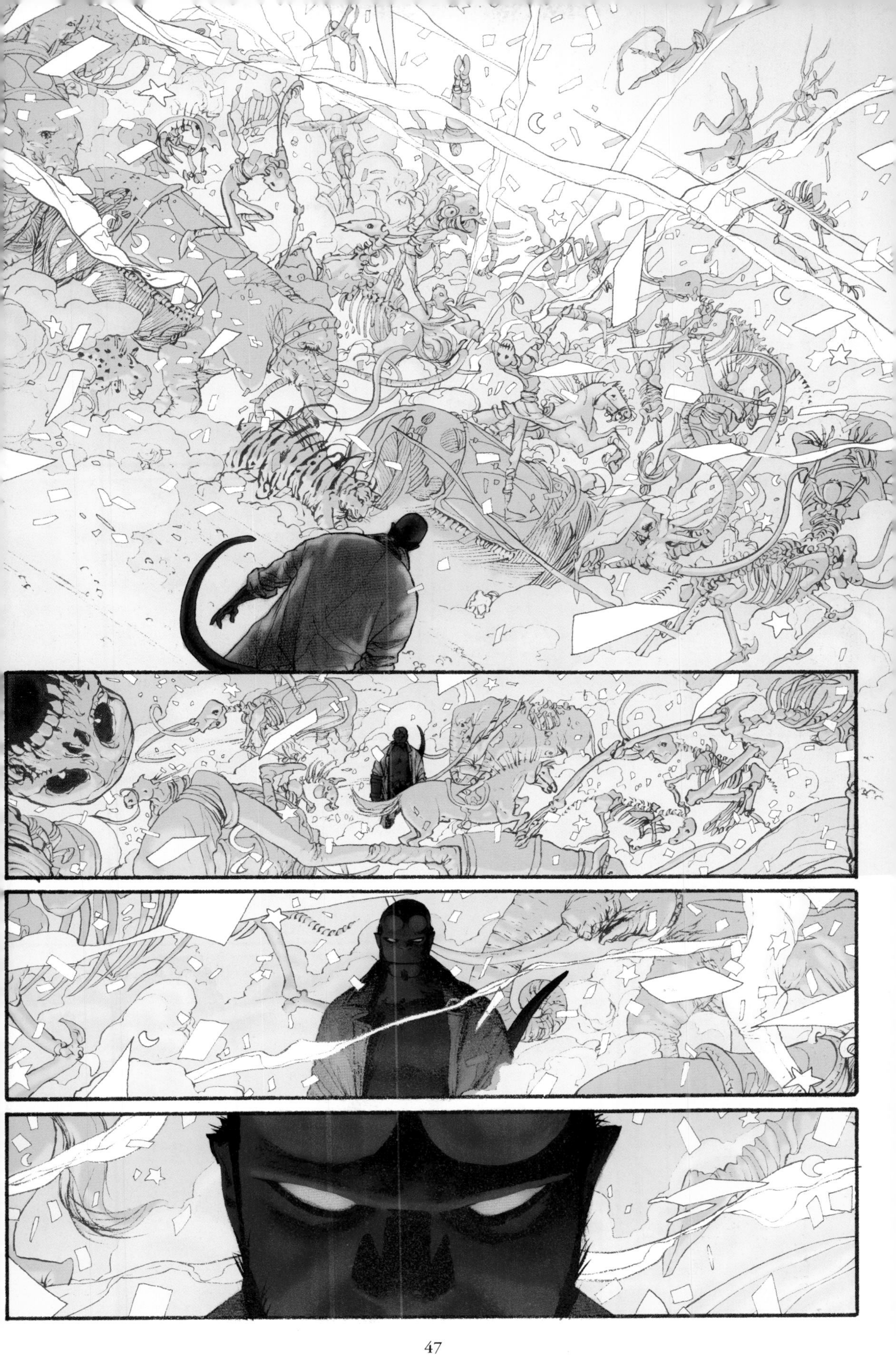

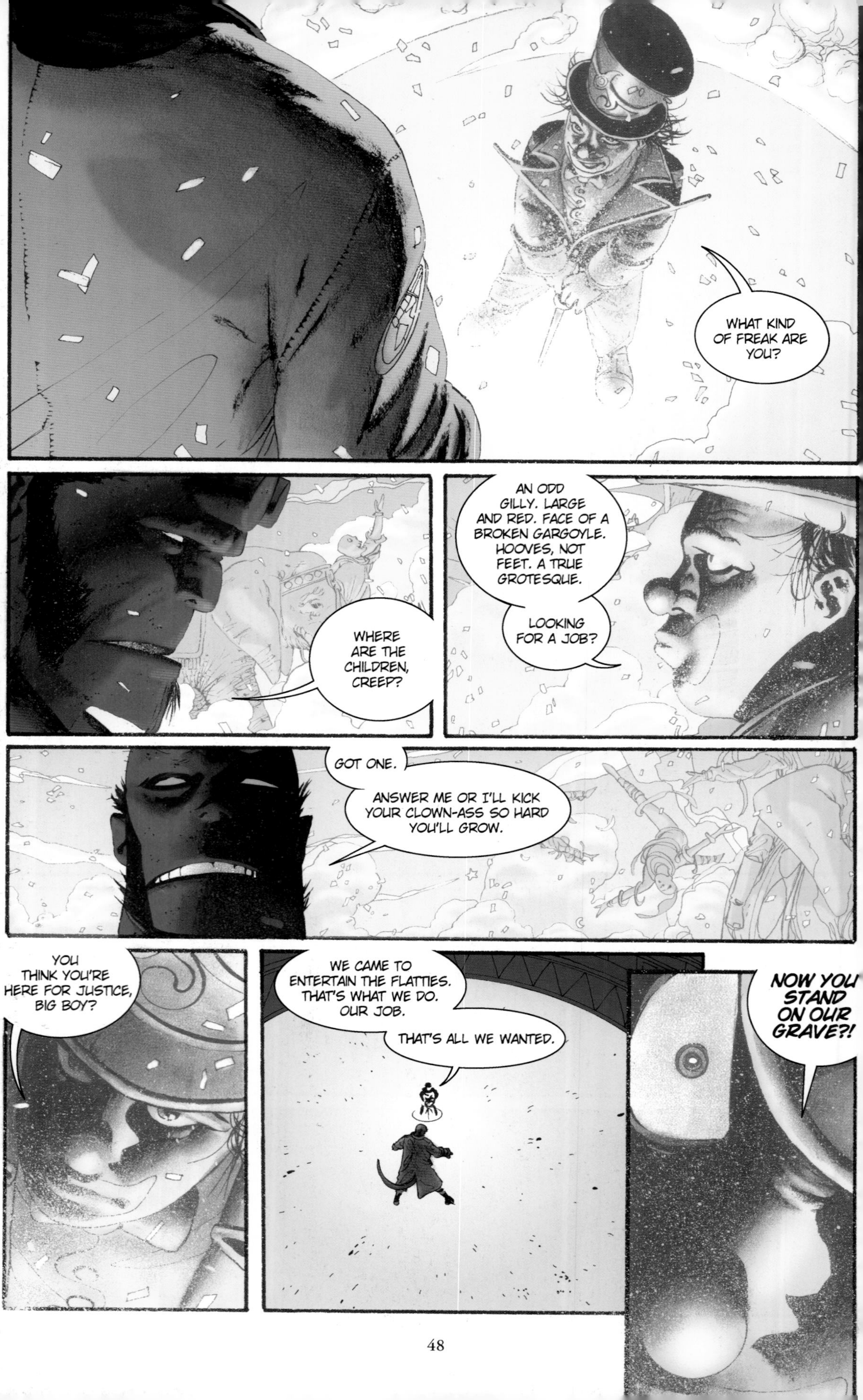
WHAT KIND OF FREAK ARE YOU?
WHERE ARE THE CHILDREN, CREEP?
AN ODD GILLY. LARGE AND RED. FACE OF A BROKEN GARGOYLE. HOOVES, NOT FEET. A TRUE GROTESQUE.
LOOKING FOR A JOB?
GOT ONE.
ANSWER ME OR I'LL KICK YOUR CLOWN-ASS SO HARD YOU'LL GROW.
YOU THINK YOU'RE HERE FOR JUSTICE, BIG BOY?
WE CAME TO ENTERTAIN THE FLATTIES. THAT'S WHAT WE DO. OUR JOB.
THAT'S ALL WE WANTED.
NOW YOU STAND ON OUR GRAVE?!

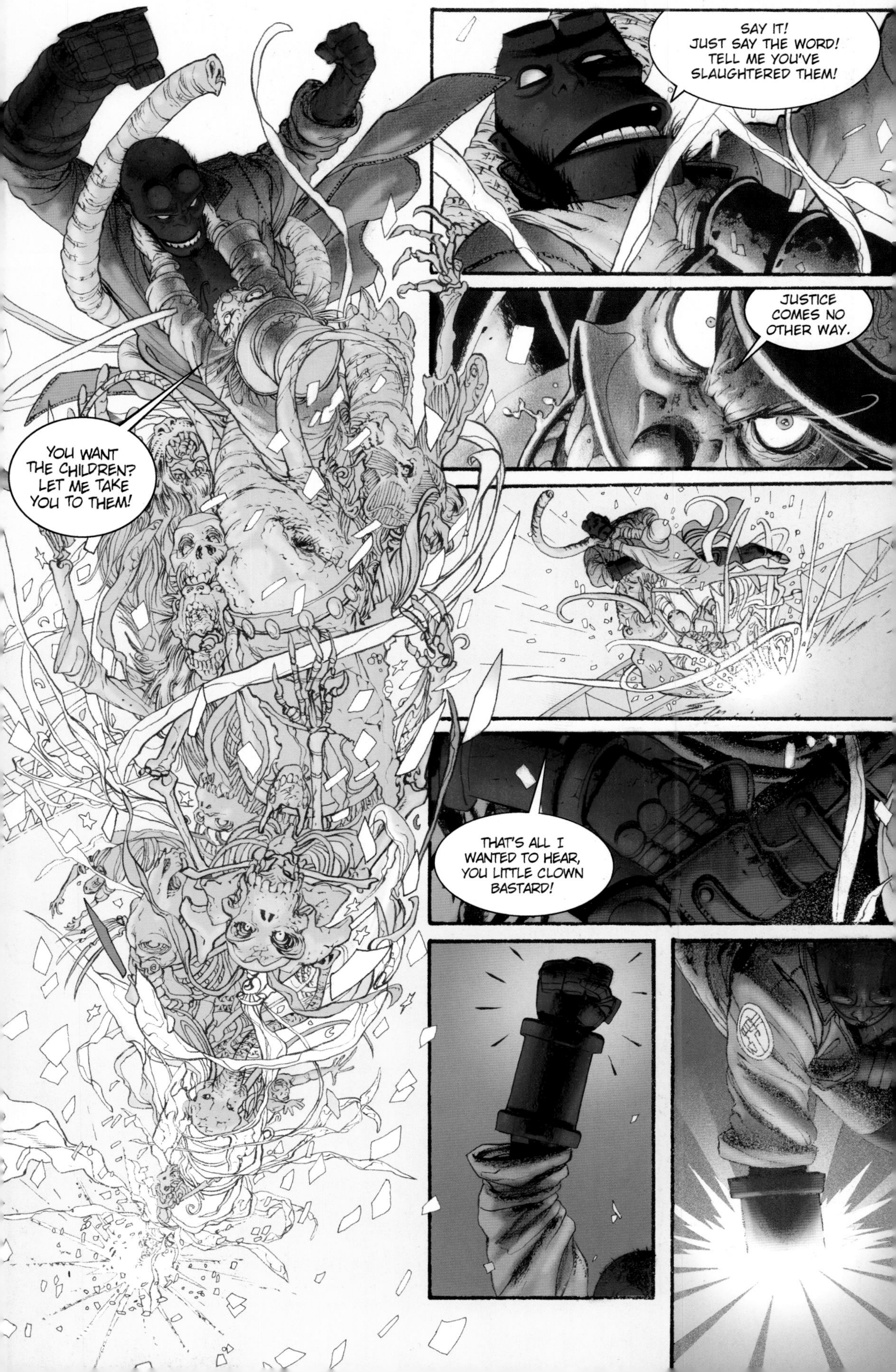
SAY IT! JUST SAY THE WORD! TELL ME YOU'VE SLAUGHTERED THEM!
JUSTICE COMES NO OTHER WAY.
YOU WANT THE CHILDREN? LET ME TAKE YOU TO THEM!
THAT'S ALL I WANTED TO HEAR, YOU LITTLE CLOWN BASTARD!

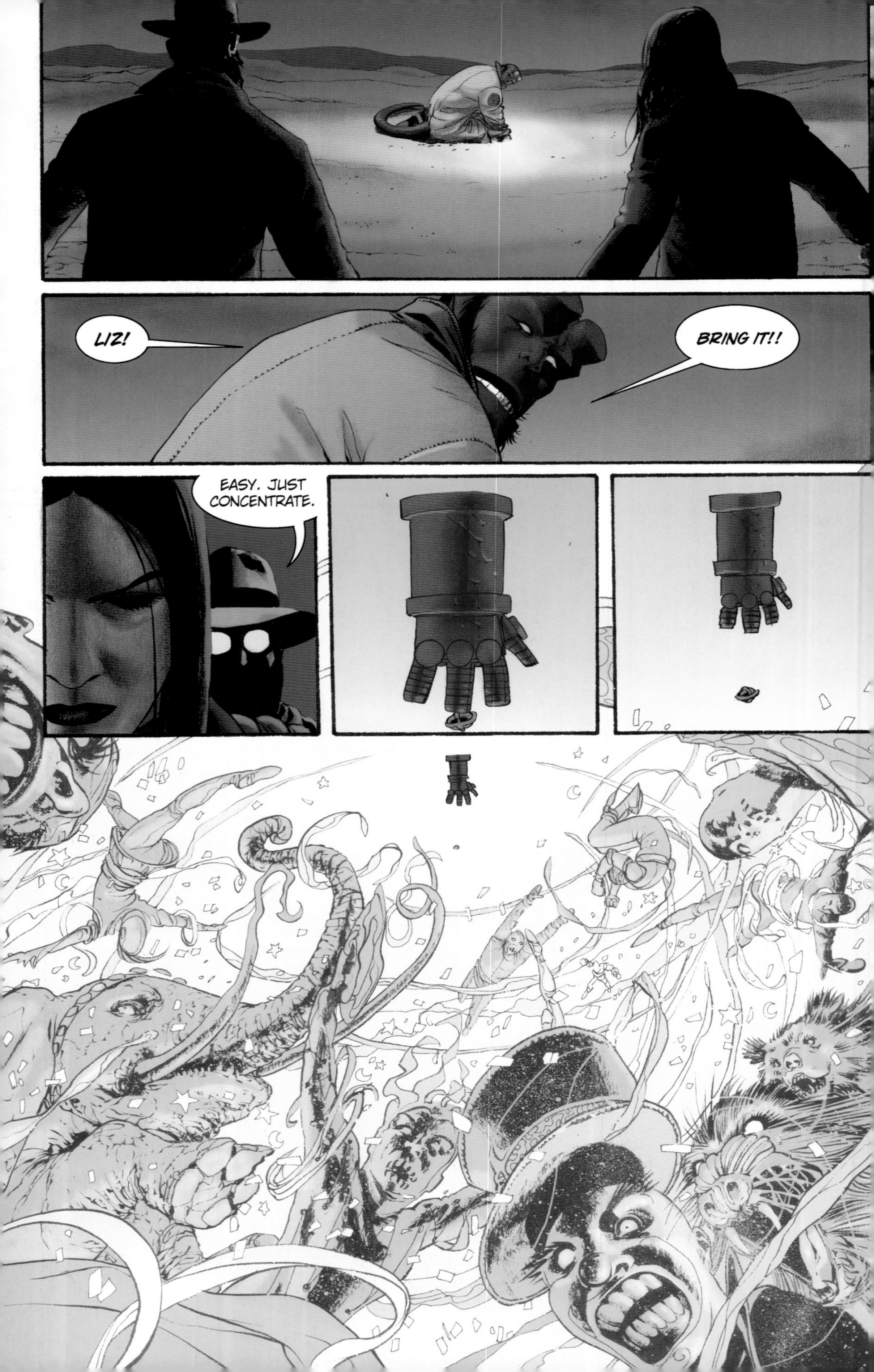
LIZ!
BRING IT!!
EASY. JUST CONCENTRATE.

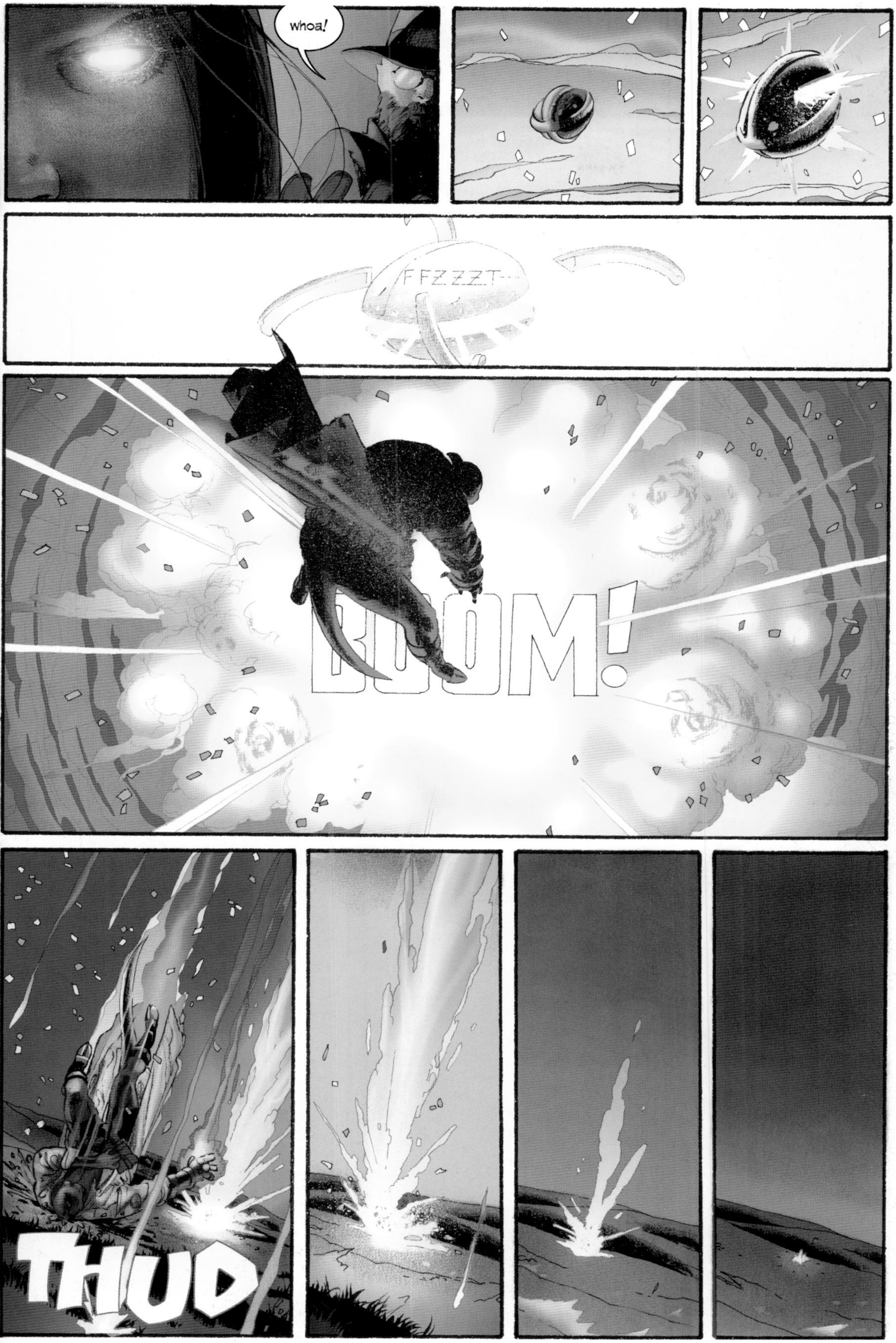
whoa!
FFZZZT--
BOOM!
THUD

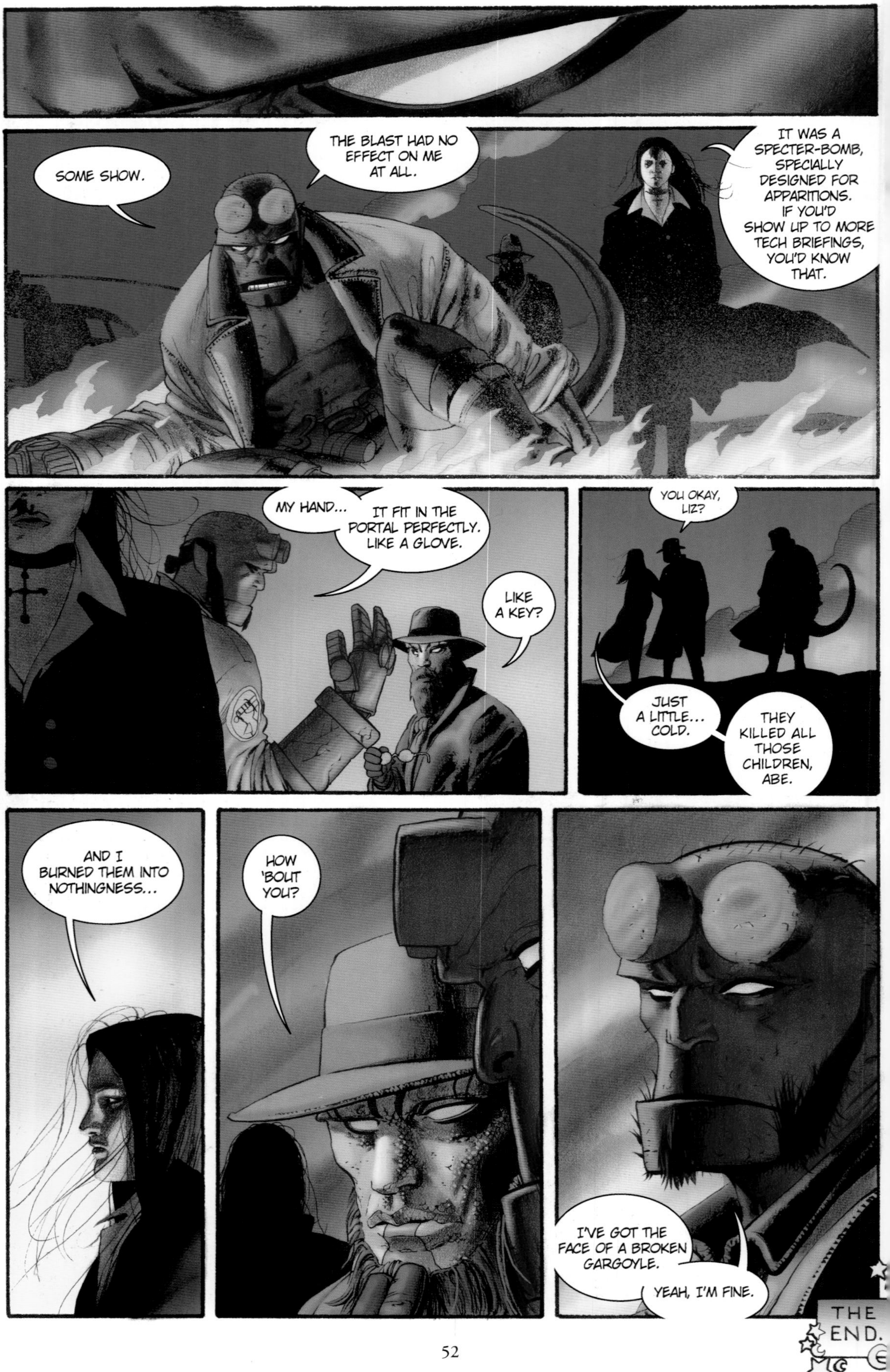
SOME SHOW.
THE BLAST HAD NO EFFECT ON ME AT ALL.
IT WAS A SPECTER-BOMB, SPECIALLY DESIGNED FOR APPARITIONS. IF YOU'D SHOW UP TO MORE TECH BRIEFINGS, YOU'D KNOW THAT.
MY HAND...
IT FIT IN THE PORTAL PERFECTLY. LIKE A GLOVE.
LIKE A KEY?
YOU OKAY, LIZ?
JUST A LITTLE... COLD.
THEY KILLED ALL THOSE CHILDREN, ABE.
AND I BURNED THEM INTO NOTHINGNESS...
HOW 'BOUT YOU?
I'VE GOT THE FACE OF A BROKEN GARGOYLE.
YEAH, I'M FINE.
THE END.

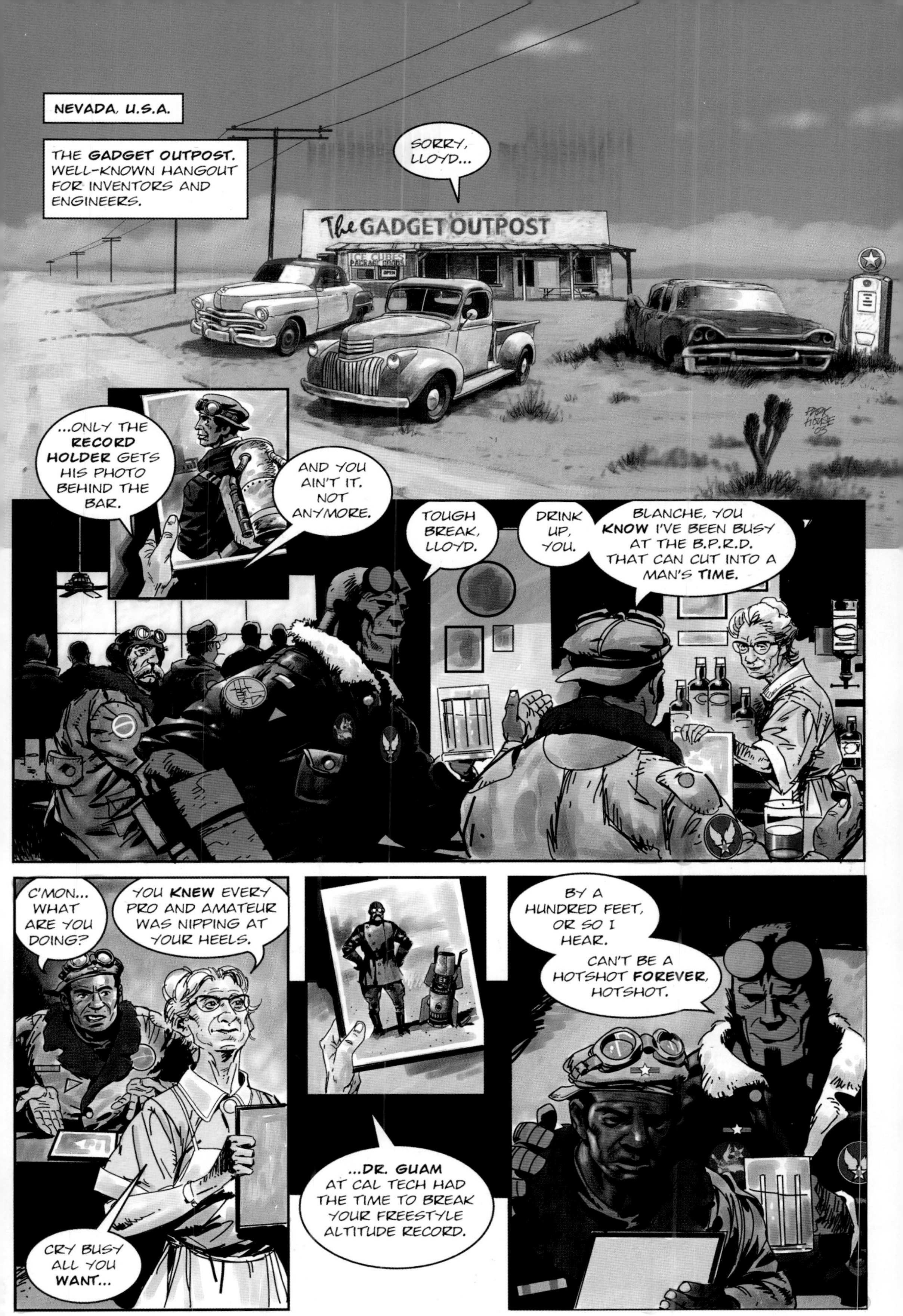
NEVADA, U.S.A.
THE GADGET OUTPOST. WELL-KNOWN HANGOUT FOR INVENTORS AND ENGINEERS.
SORRY, LLOYD...
The GADGET OUTPOST
ICE CUBES
OPEN
...ONLY THE RECORD HOLDER GETS HIS PHOTO BEHIND THE BAR.
AND YOU AIN'T IT. NOT ANYMORE.
TOUGH BREAK, LLOYD.
DRINK UP, YOU.
BLANCHE, YOU KNOW I'VE BEEN BUSY AT THE B.P.R.D. THAT CAN CUT INTO A MAN'S TIME.
C'MON... WHAT ARE YOU DOING?
YOU KNEW EVERY PRO AND AMATEUR WAS NIPPING AT YOUR HEELS.
CRY BUSY ALL YOU WANT...
...DR. GUAM AT CAL TECH HAD THE TIME TO BREAK YOUR FREESTYLE ALTITUDE RECORD.
BY A HUNDRED FEET, OR SO I HEAR.
CAN'T BE A HOTSHOT FOREVER, HOTSHOT.

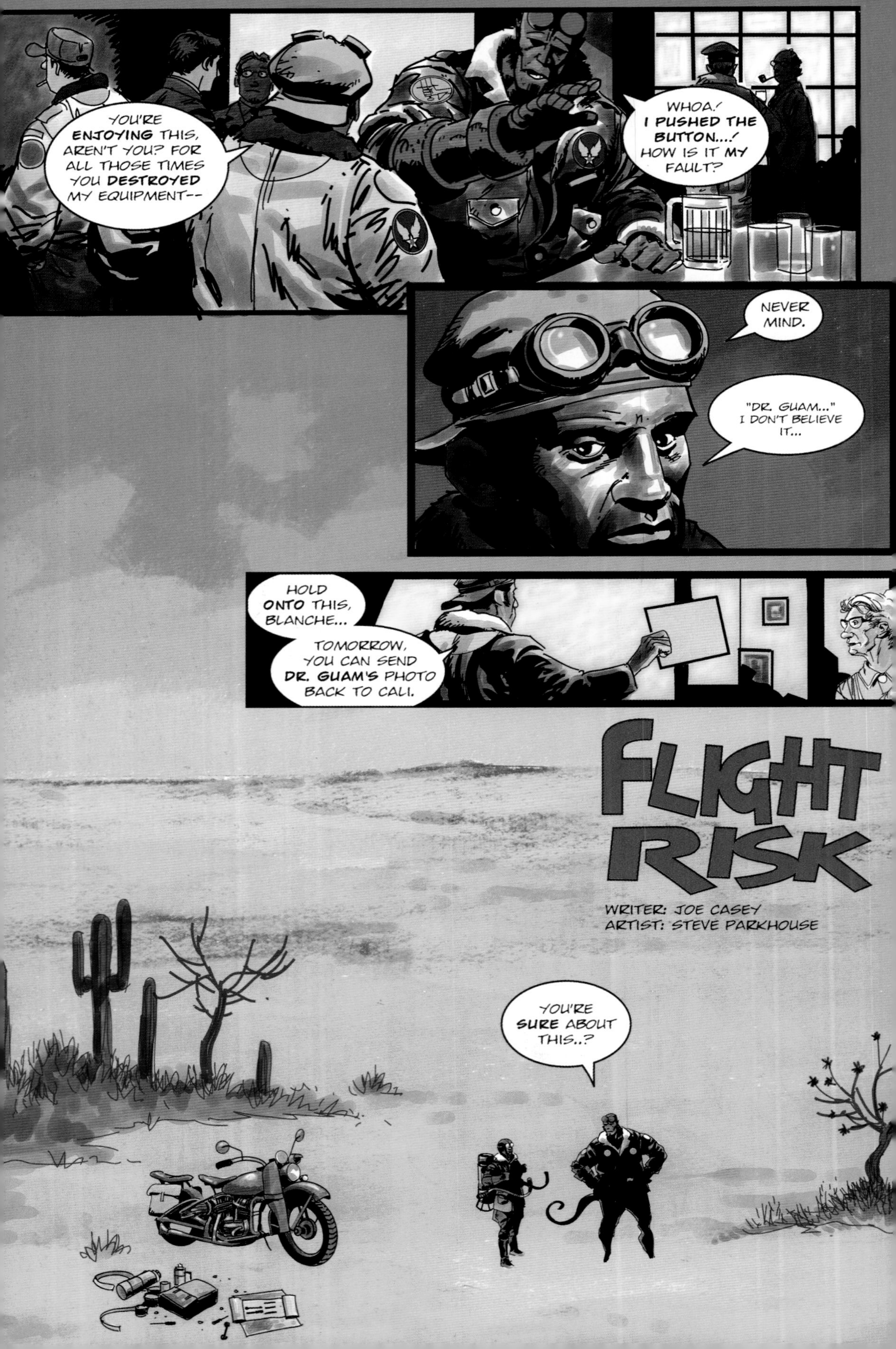
YOU'RE ENJOYING THIS, AREN'T YOU? FOR ALL THOSE TIMES YOU DESTROYED MY EQUIPMENT--
WHOA! I PUSHED THE BUTTON...! HOW IS IT MY FAULT?
NEVER MIND.
"DR. GUAM..." I DON'T BELIEVE IT...
HOLD ONTO THIS, BLANCHE...
TOMORROW, YOU CAN SEND DR. GUAM'S PHOTO BACK TO CALI.
FLIGHT RISK
WRITER: JOE CASEY
ARTIST: STEVE PARKHOUSE
YOU'RE SURE ABOUT THIS..?

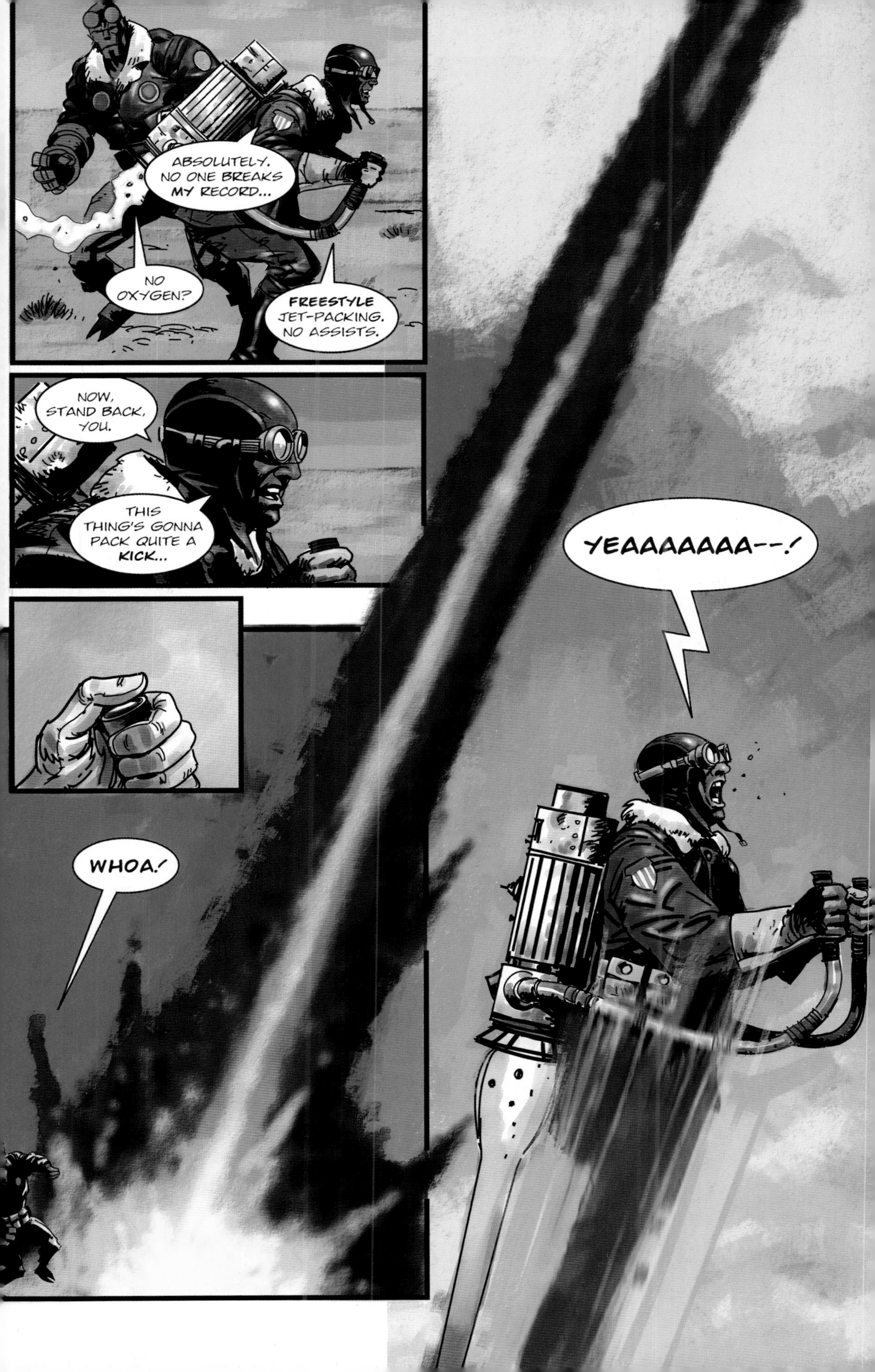
ABSOLUTELY. NO ONE BREAKS MY RECORD...
NO OXYGEN?
FREESTYLE JET-PACKING. NO ASSISTS.
NOW, STAND BACK, YOU.
THIS THING'S GONNA PACK QUITE A KICK...
WHOA!
YEAAAAAAA--!

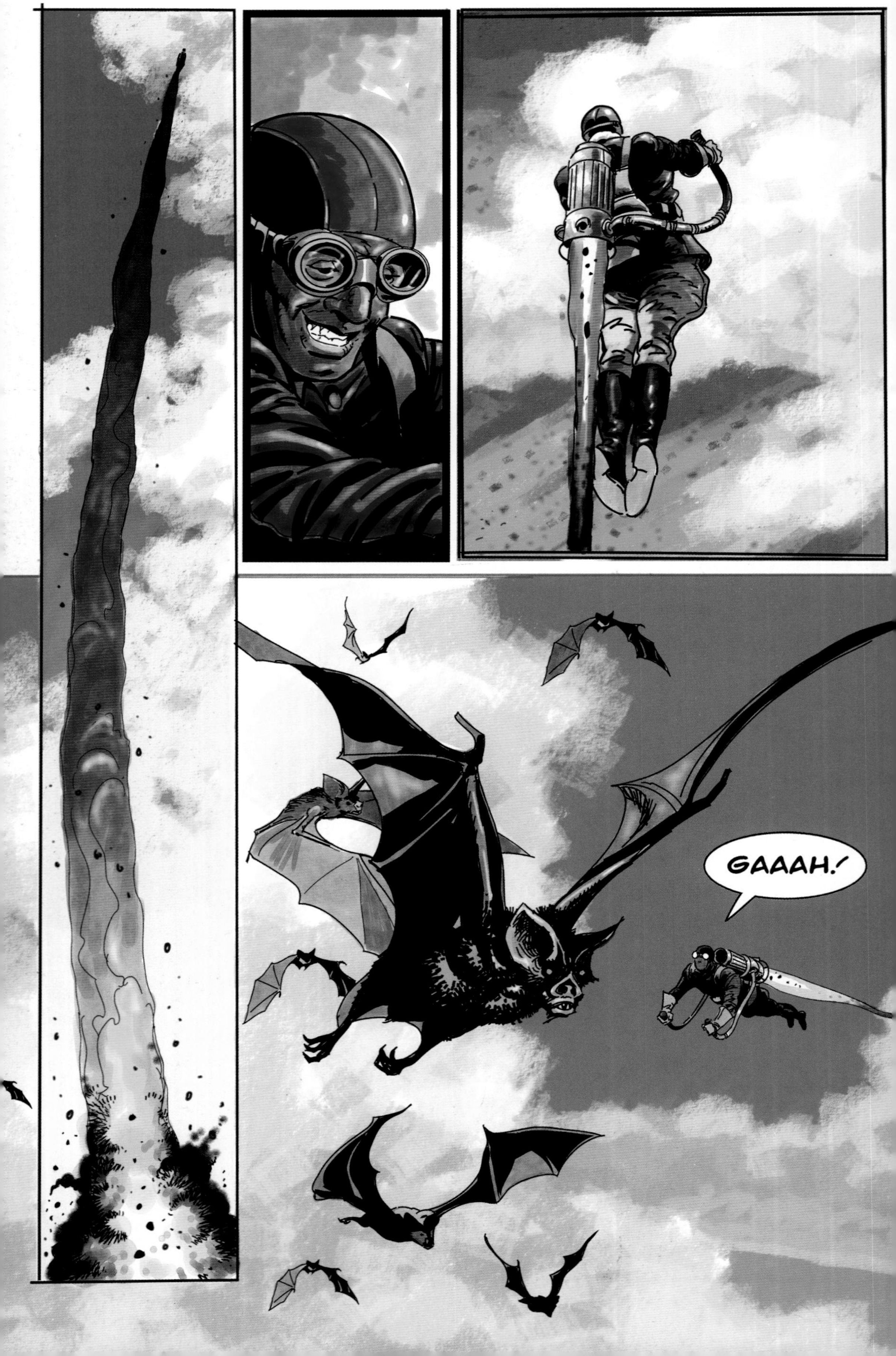
GAAAH!

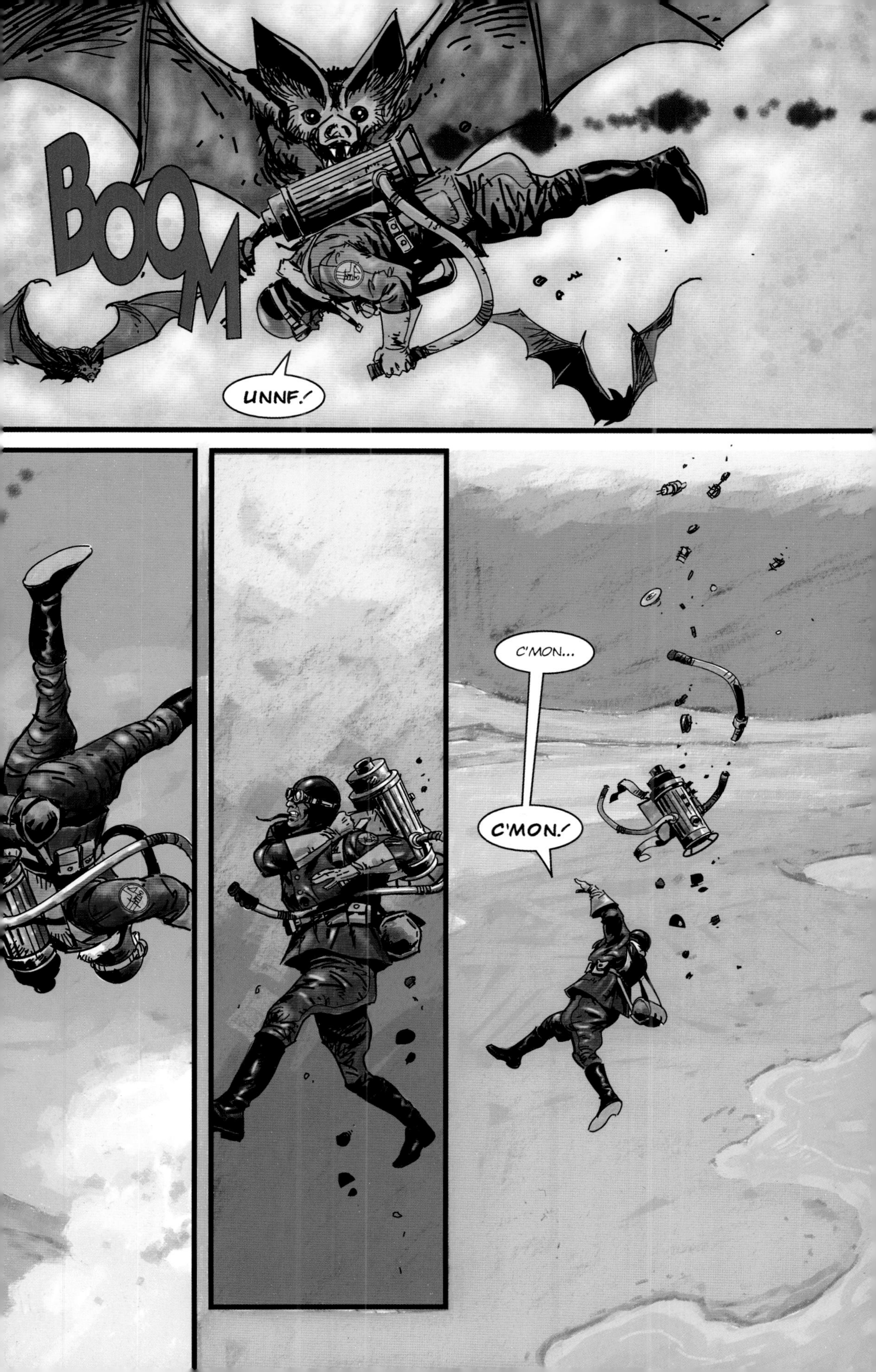
BOOM
UNNF.!
C'MON...
C'MON.!

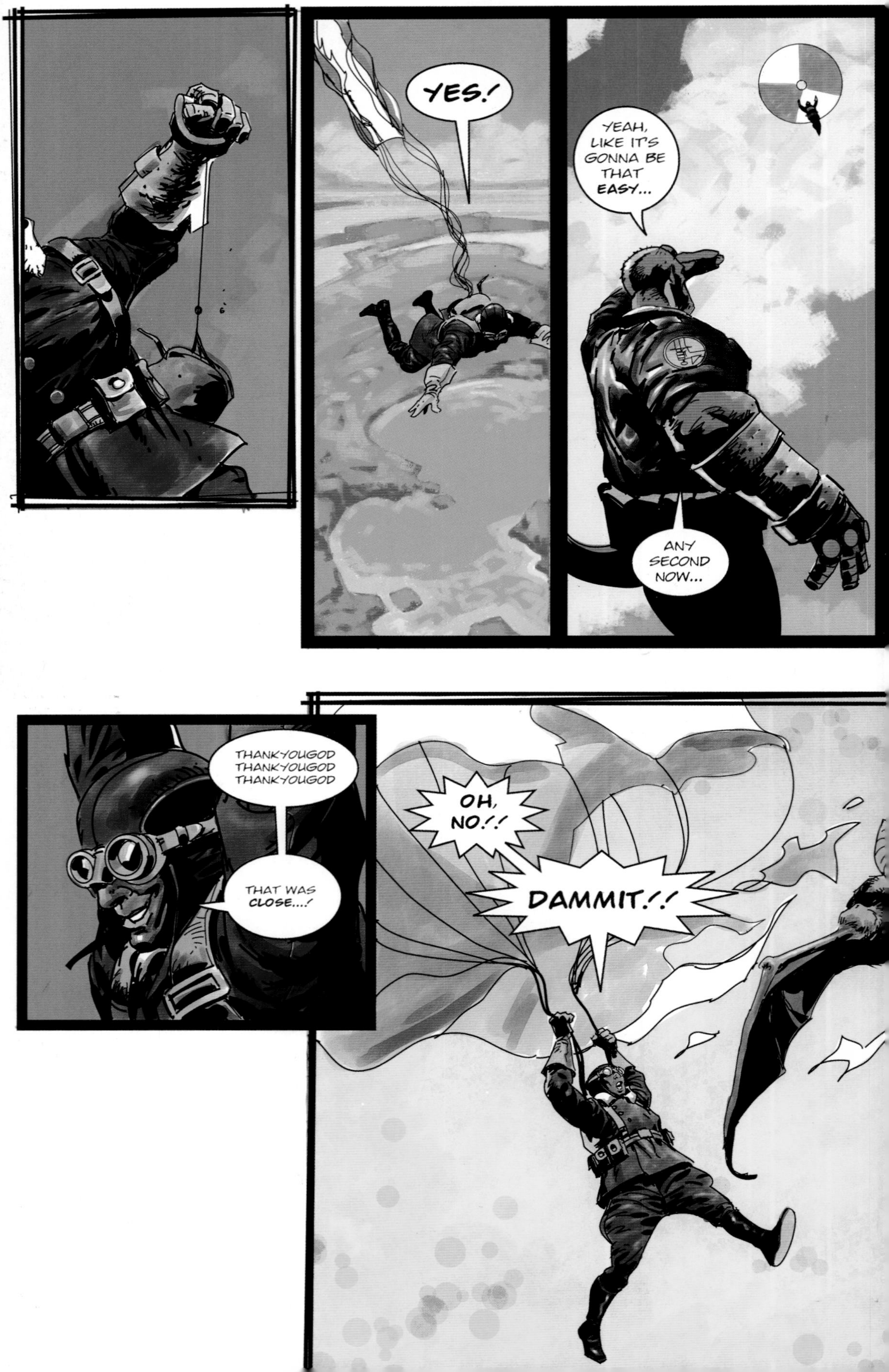
YES!
YEAH, LIKE IT'S GONNA BE THAT EASY...
ANY SECOND NOW...
THANKYOUGOD THANKYOUGOD THANKYOUGOD
THAT WAS CLOSE...!
OH, NO!!
DAMMIT!!

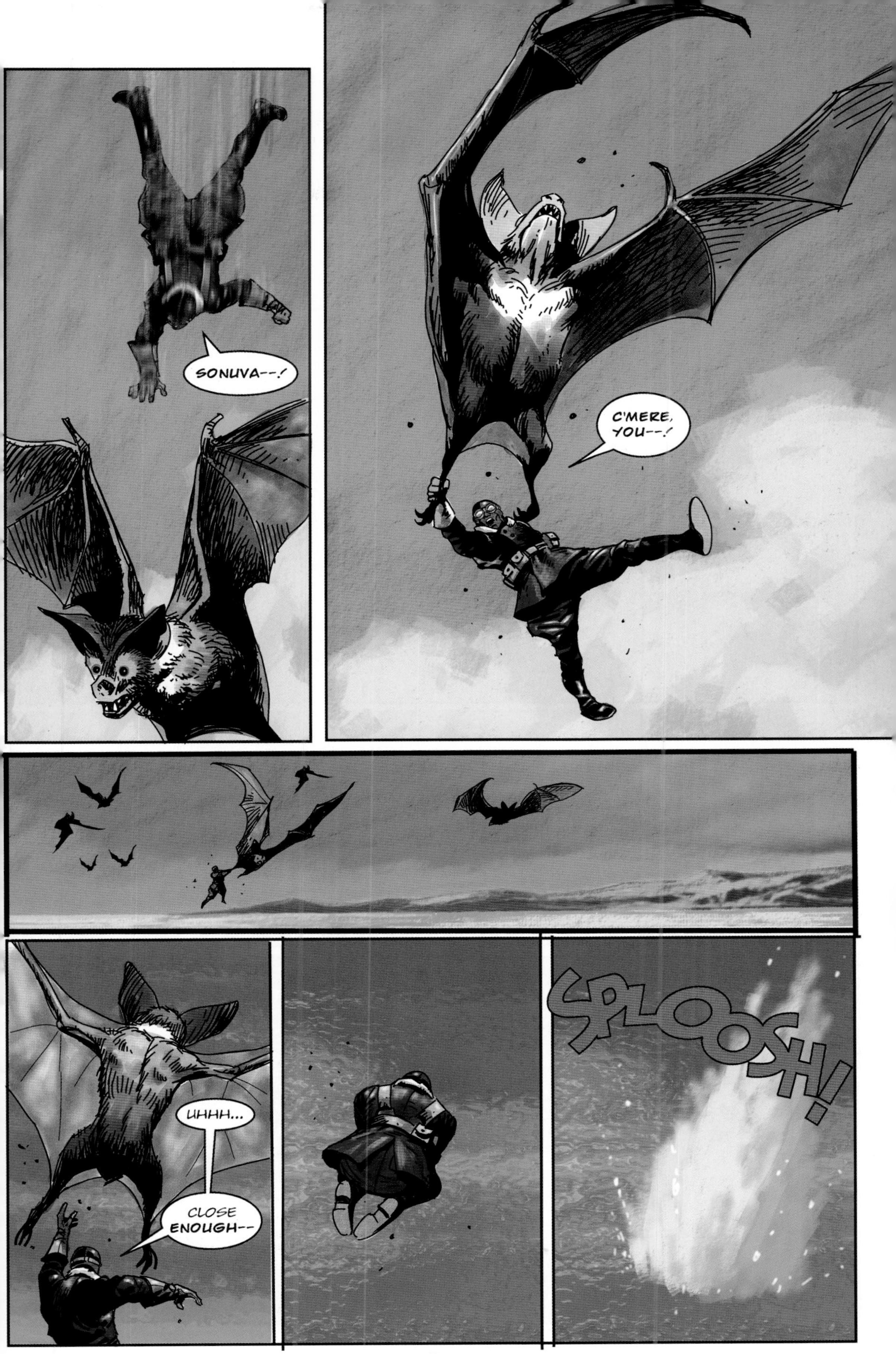
SONUVA--!
C'MERE, YOU--!
UHHH...
CLOSE ENOUGH--
SPLOOSH!!

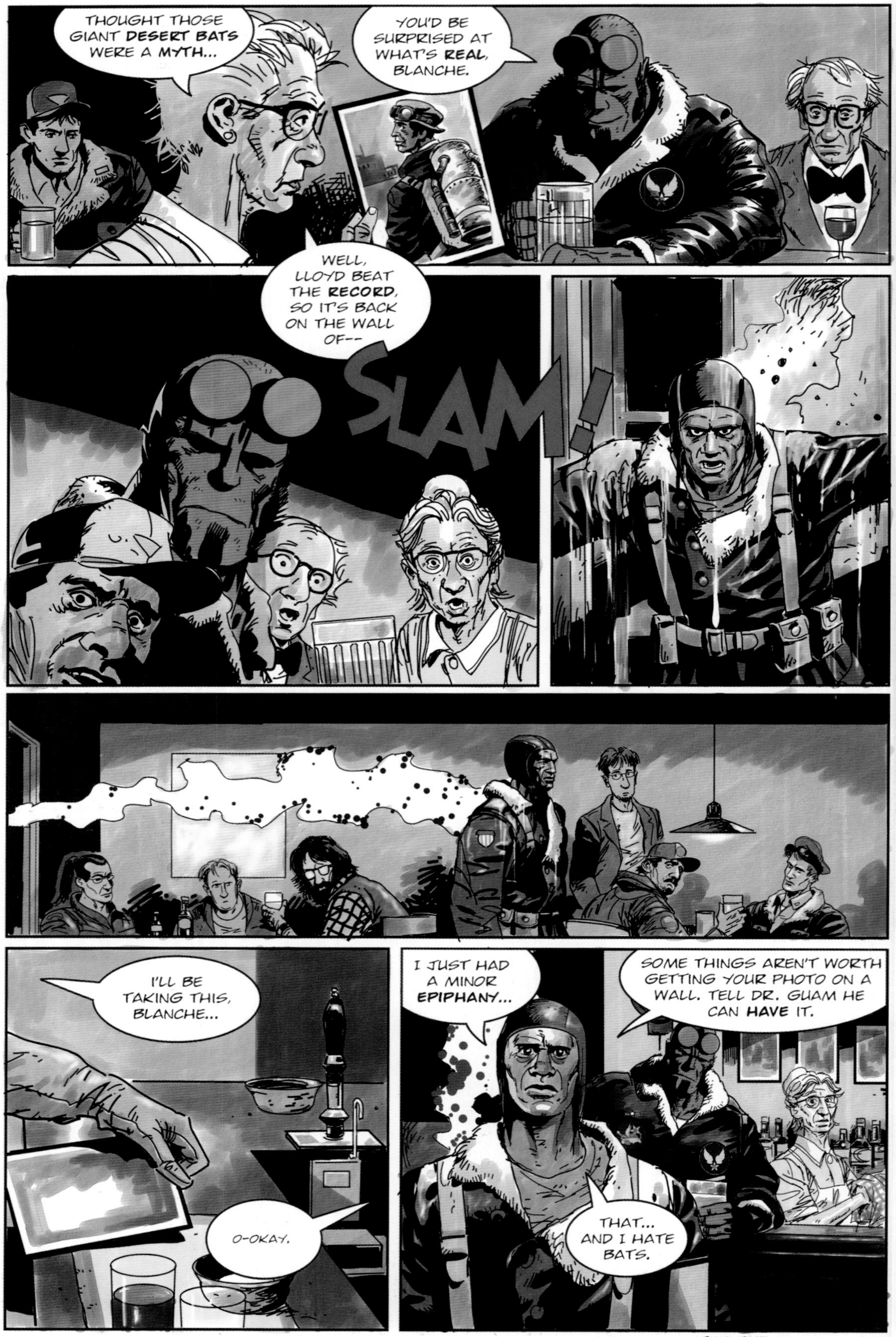
THOUGHT THOSE GIANT DESERT BATS WERE A MYTH...
YOU'D BE SURPRISED AT WHAT'S REAL, BLANCHE.
WELL, LLOYD BEAT THE RECORD, SO IT'S BACK ON THE WALL OF--
SLAM!
I'LL BE TAKING THIS, BLANCHE...
O-OKAY.
I JUST HAD A MINOR EPIPHANY...
SOME THINGS AREN'T WORTH GETTING YOUR PHOTO ON A WALL. TELL DR. GUAM HE CAN HAVE IT.
THAT... AND I HATE BATS.
THE END

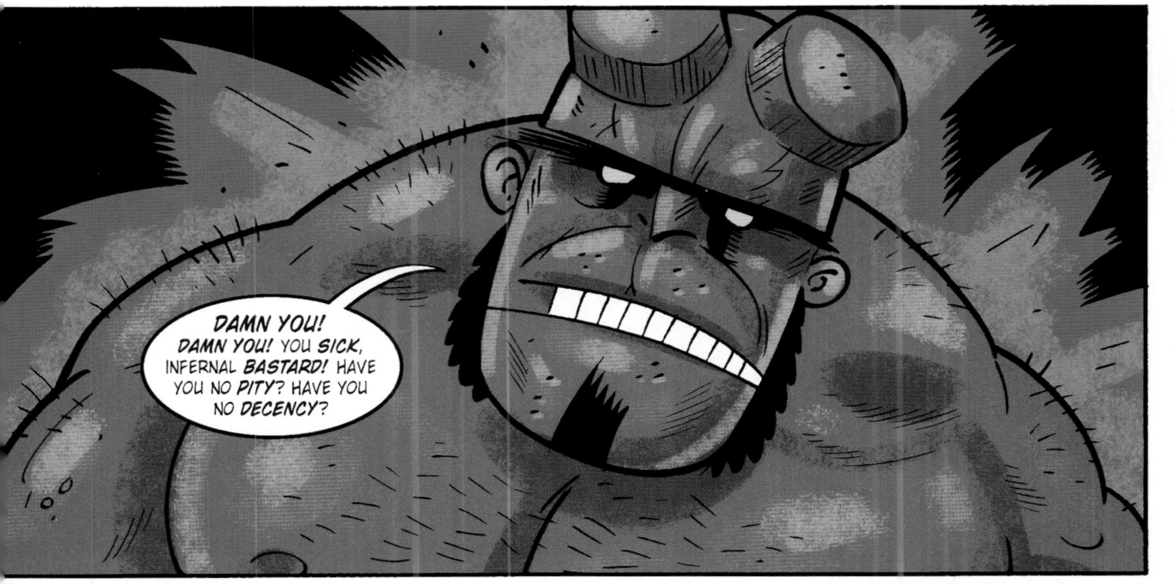
DAMN YOU! DAMN YOU! YOU SICK, INFERNAL BASTARD! HAVE YOU NO PITY? HAVE YOU NO DECENCY?

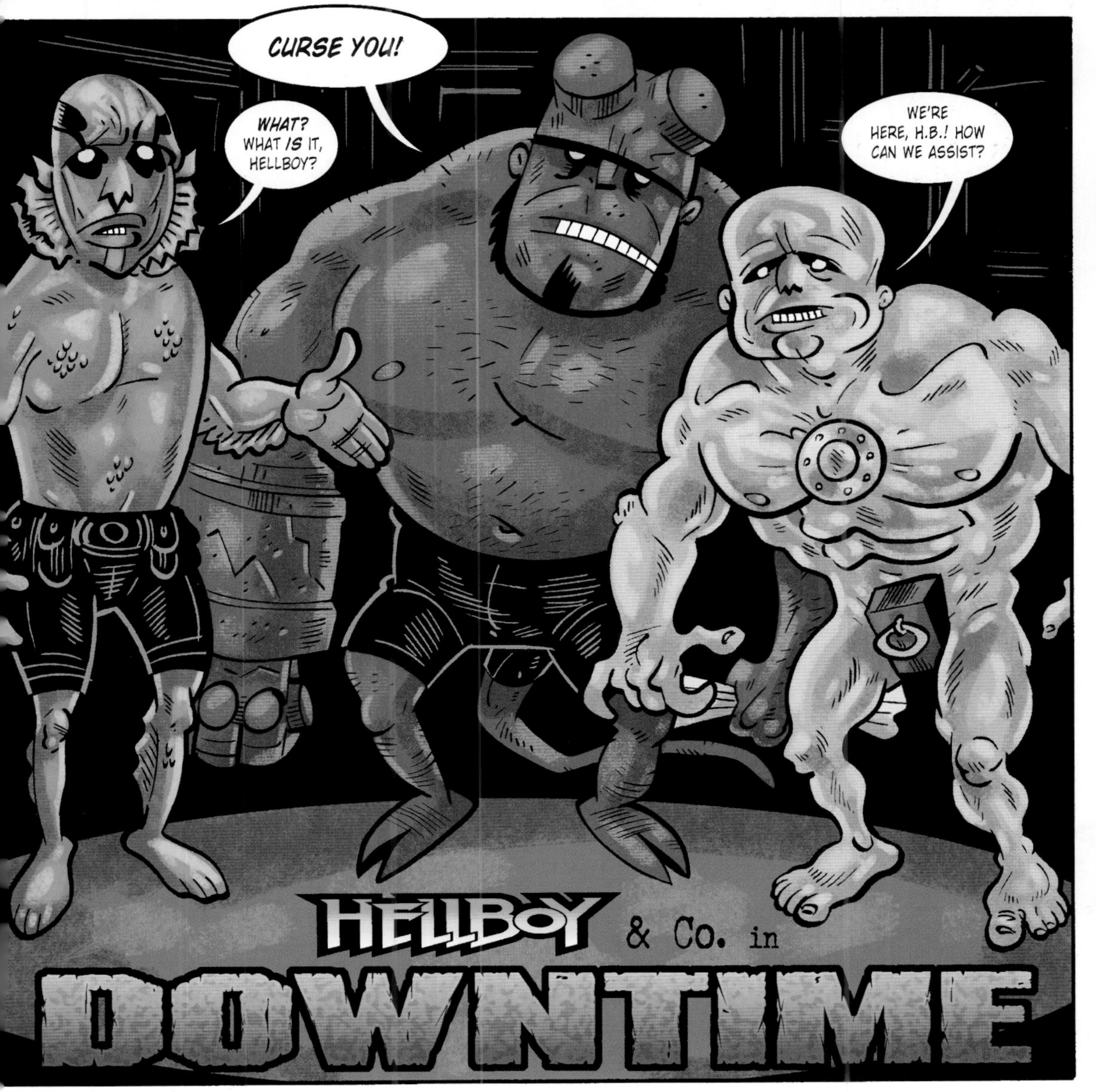
CURSE YOU!
WHAT? WHAT IS IT, HELLBOY?
WE'RE HERE, H.B.! HOW CAN WE ASSIST?
HELLBOY & Co. in
DOWNTIME

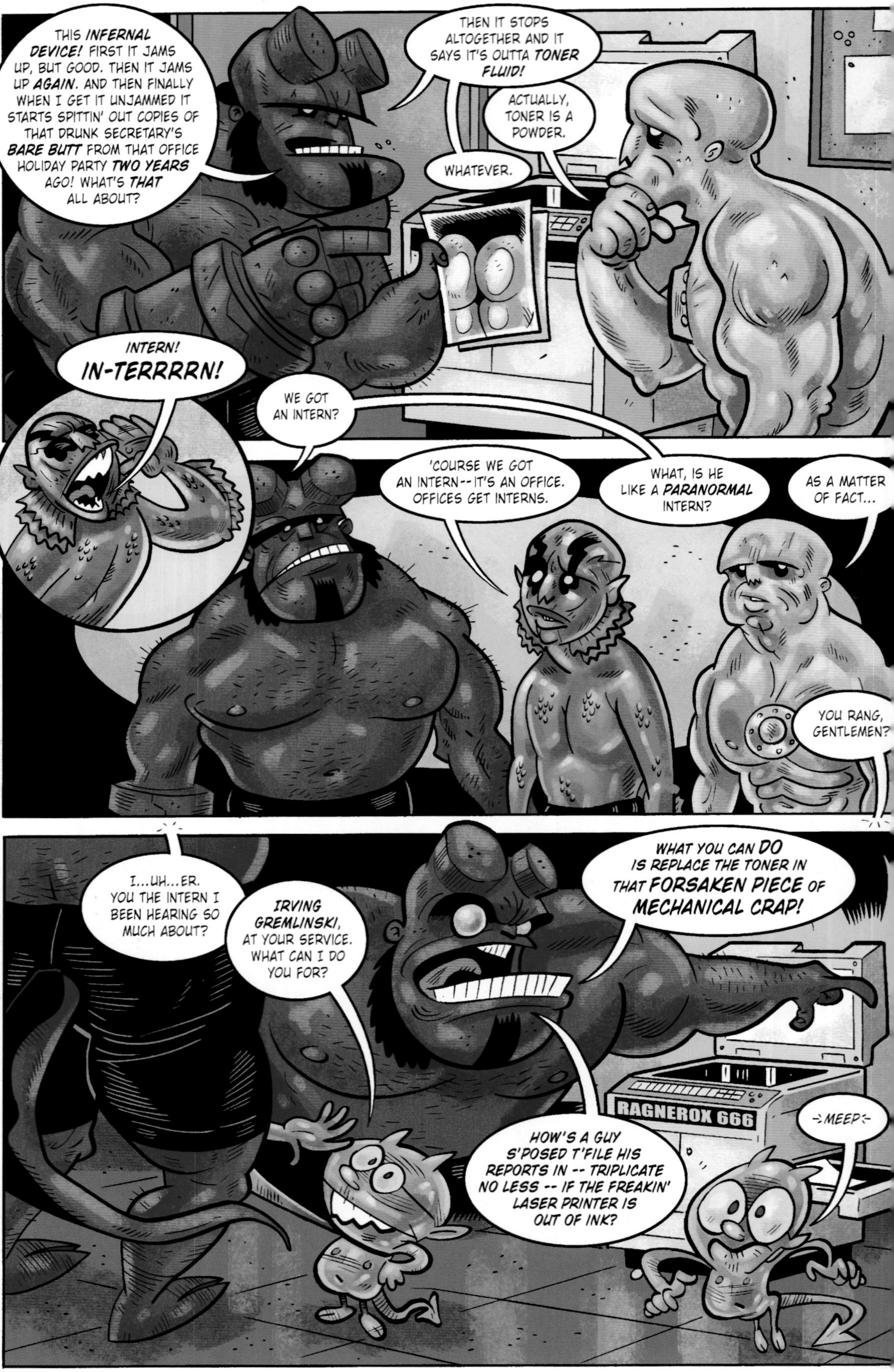
THIS INFERNAL DEVICE! FIRST IT JAMS UP, BUT GOOD. THEN IT JAMS UP AGAIN. AND THEN FINALLY WHEN I GET IT UNJAMMED IT STARTS SPITTIN' OUT COPIES OF THAT DRUNK SECRETARY'S BARE BUTT FROM THAT OFFICE HOLIDAY PARTY TWO YEARS AGO! WHAT'S THAT ALL ABOUT?
THEN IT STOPS ALTOGETHER AND IT SAYS IT'S OUTTA TONER FLUID!
ACTUALLY, TONER IS A POWDER.
WHATEVER.
INTERN! IN-TERRRRN!
WE GOT AN INTERN?
'COURSE WE GOT AN INTERN--IT'S AN OFFICE. OFFICES GET INTERNS.
WHAT, IS HE LIKE A PARANORMAL INTERN?
AS A MATTER OF FACT...
YOU RANG, GENTLEMEN?
I...UH...ER. YOU THE INTERN I BEEN HEARING SO MUCH ABOUT?
IRVING GREMLINSKI, AT YOUR SERVICE. WHAT CAN I DO YOU FOR?
WHAT YOU CAN DO IS REPLACE THE TONER IN THAT FORSAKEN PIECE OF MECHANICAL CRAP!
RAGNEROX 666
HOW'S A GUY S'POSED T'FILE HIS REPORTS IN -- TRIPLICATE NO LESS -- IF THE FREAKIN' LASER PRINTER IS OUT OF INK?
MEEP

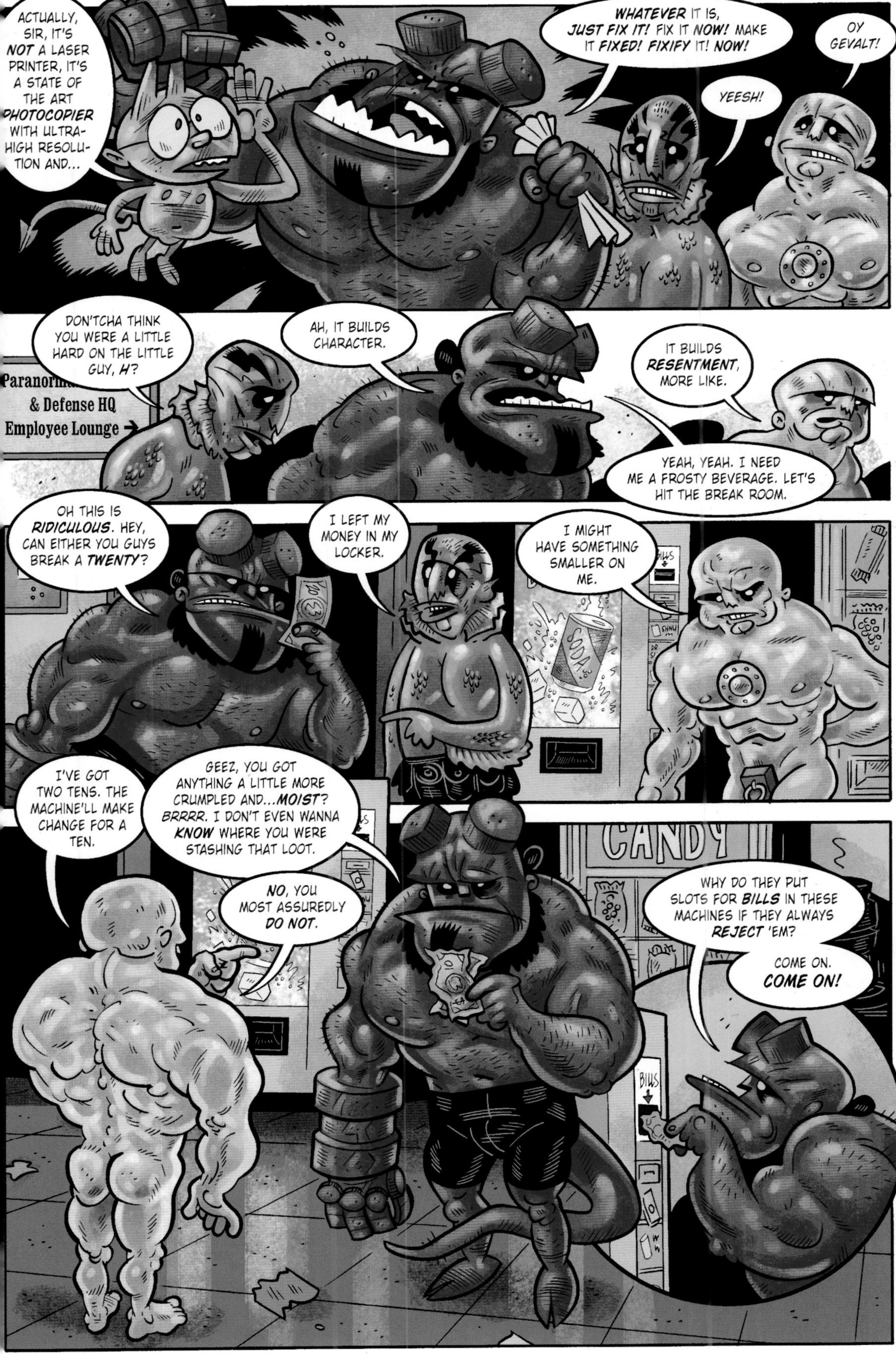
ACTUALLY, SIR, IT'S NOT A LASER PRINTER, IT'S A STATE OF THE ART PHOTOCOPIER WITH ULTRA-HIGH RESOLUTION AND...
WHATEVER IT IS, JUST FIX IT! FIX IT NOW! MAKE IT FIXED! FIXIFY IT! NOW!
YEESH!
OY GEVALT!
DON'TCHA THINK YOU WERE A LITTLE HARD ON THE LITTLE GUY, H?
AH, IT BUILDS CHARACTER.
IT BUILDS RESENTMENT, MORE LIKE.
Paranormal
& Defense HQ
Employee Lounge
YEAH, YEAH. I NEED ME A FROSTY BEVERAGE. LET'S HIT THE BREAK ROOM.
OH THIS IS RIDICULOUS. HEY, CAN EITHER YOU GUYS BREAK A TWENTY?
I LEFT MY MONEY IN MY LOCKER.
I MIGHT HAVE SOMETHING SMALLER ON ME.
SODA
I'VE GOT TWO TENS. THE MACHINE'LL MAKE CHANGE FOR A TEN.
GEEZ, YOU GOT ANYTHING A LITTLE MORE CRUMPLED AND...MOIST? BRRRR. I DON'T EVEN WANNA KNOW WHERE YOU WERE STASHING THAT LOOT.
NO, YOU MOST ASSUREDLY DO NOT.
CANDY
WHY DO THEY PUT SLOTS FOR BILLS IN THESE MACHINES IF THEY ALWAYS REJECT 'EM?
COME ON. COME ON!
BILLS

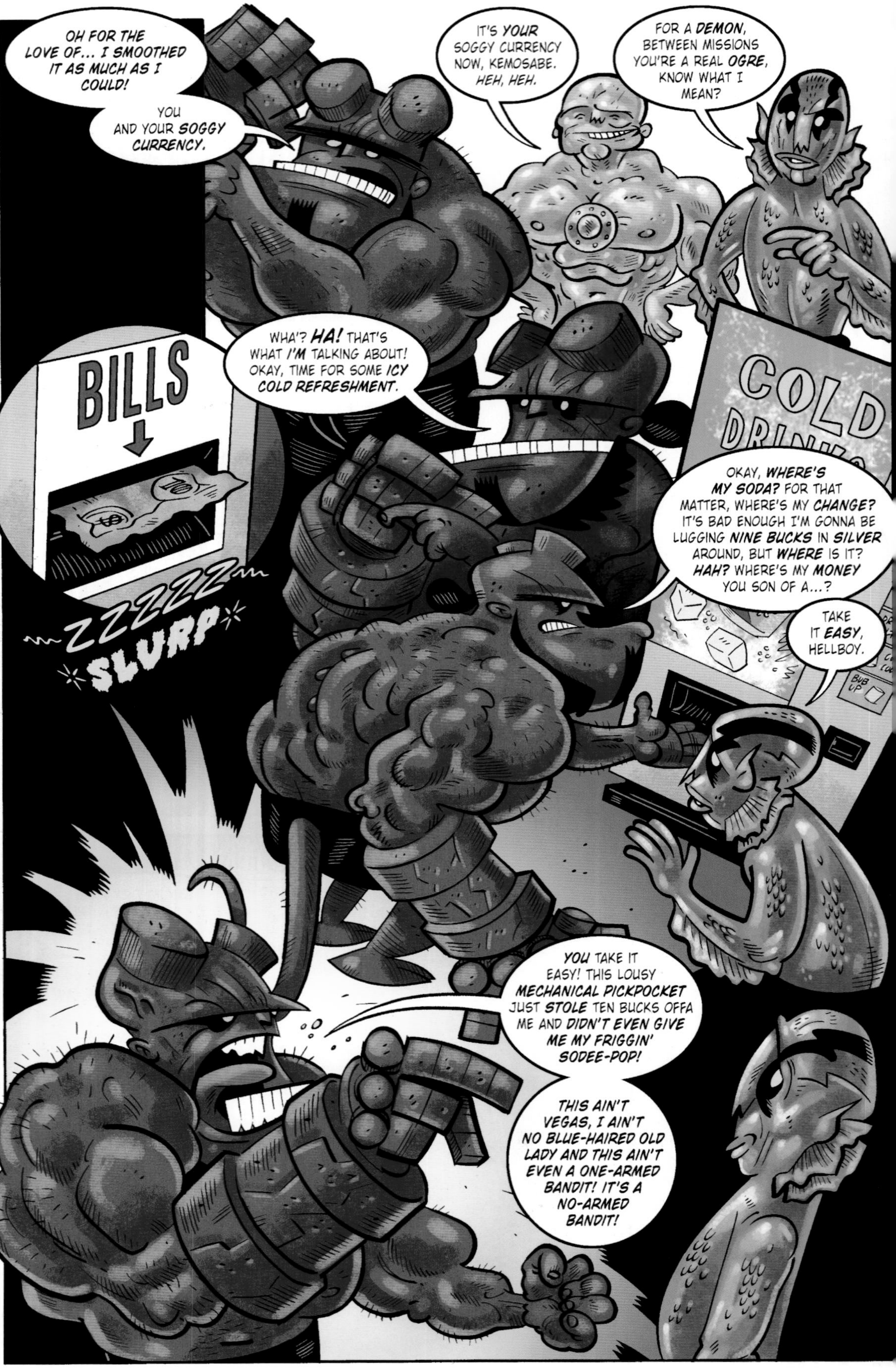
OH FOR THE LOVE OF... I SMOOTHED IT AS MUCH AS I COULD!
YOU AND YOUR SOGGY CURRENCY.
IT'S YOUR SOGGY CURRENCY NOW, KEMOSABE. HEH, HEH.
FOR A DEMON, BETWEEN MISSIONS YOU'RE A REAL OGRE, KNOW WHAT I MEAN?
BILLS
WHA'? HA! THAT'S WHAT I'M TALKING ABOUT! OKAY, TIME FOR SOME ICY COLD REFRESHMENT.
ZZZZZZ
SLURP
COLD
OKAY, WHERE'S MY SODA? FOR THAT MATTER, WHERE'S MY CHANGE? IT'S BAD ENOUGH I'M GONNA BE LUGGING NINE BUCKS IN SILVER AROUND, BUT WHERE IS IT? HAH? WHERE'S MY MONEY YOU SON OF A...?
TAKE IT EASY, HELLBOY.
YOU TAKE IT EASY! THIS LOUSY MECHANICAL PICKPOCKET JUST STOLE TEN BUCKS OFFA ME AND DIDN'T EVEN GIVE ME MY FRIGGIN' SODEE-POP!
THIS AIN'T VEGAS, I AIN'T NO BLUE-HAIRED OLD LADY AND THIS AIN'T EVEN A ONE-ARMED BANDIT! IT'S A NO-ARMED BANDIT!

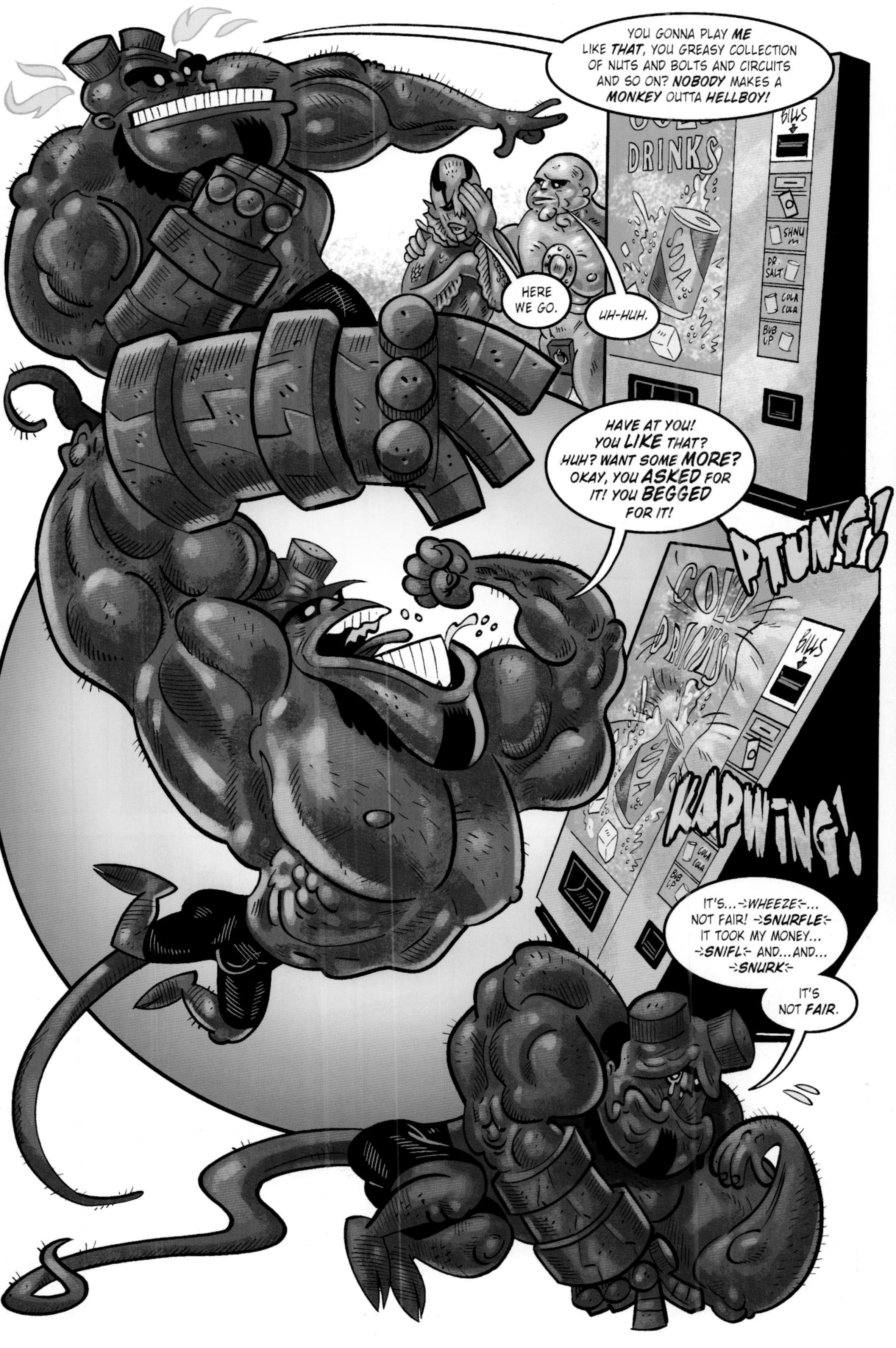
YOU GONNA PLAY ME LIKE THAT, YOU GREASY COLLECTION OF NUTS AND BOLTS AND CIRCUITS AND SO ON? NOBODY MAKES A MONKEY OUTTA HELLBOY!
COLD DRINKS
BILLS
SODA
SHNUM
DR. SALT
COLA COLA
BUB UP
HERE WE GO.
UH-HUH.
HAVE AT YOU! YOU LIKE THAT? HUH? WANT SOME MORE? OKAY, YOU ASKED FOR IT! YOU BEGGED FOR IT!
PTUNG!
KAPWING!
IT'S... -WHEEZE-... NOT FAIR! -SNURFLE- IT TOOK MY MONEY... -SNIFL- AND...AND... -SNURK-
IT'S NOT FAIR.

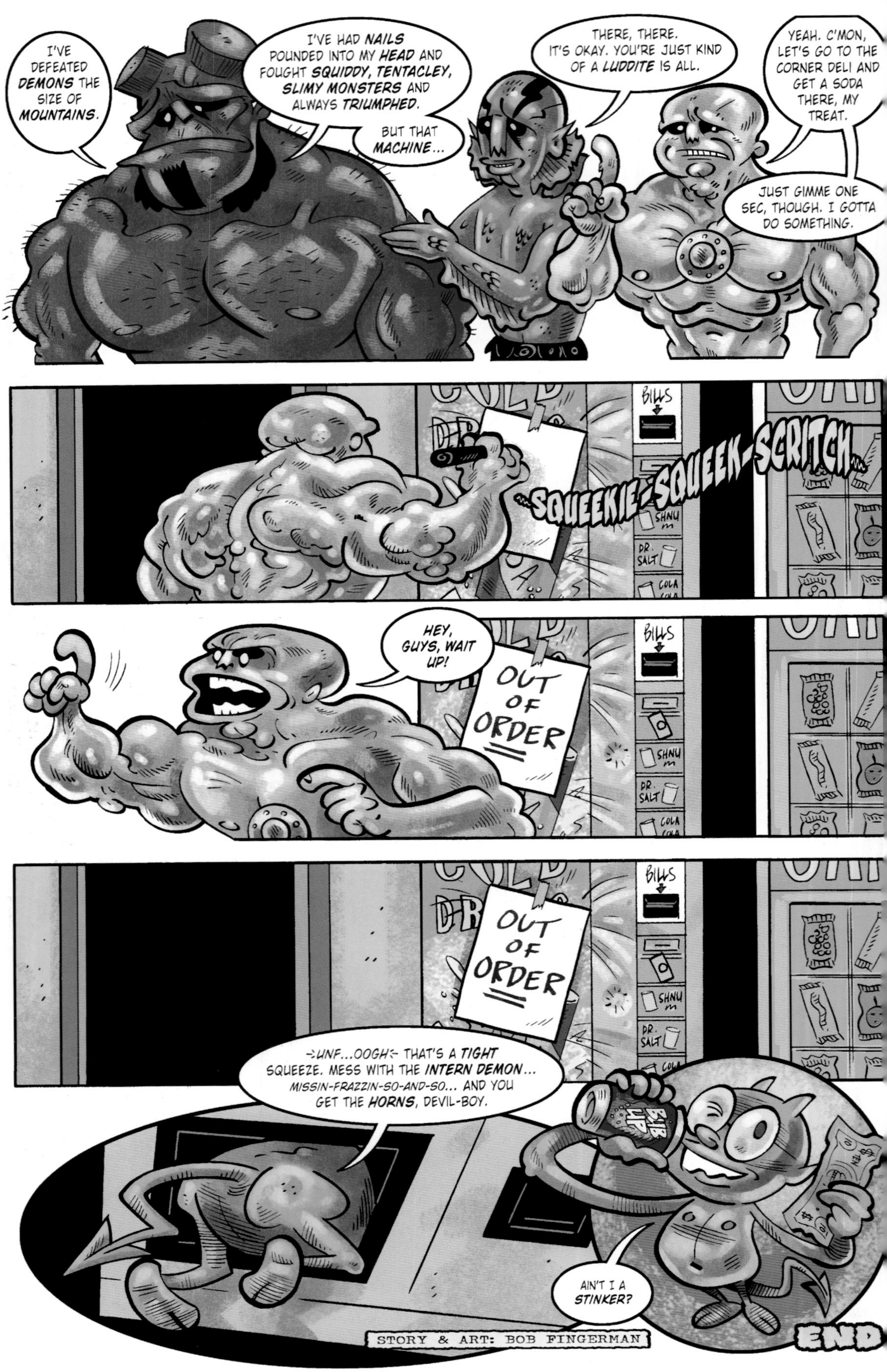
I'VE DEFEATED DEMONS THE SIZE OF MOUNTAINS.
I'VE HAD NAILS POUNDED INTO MY HEAD AND FOUGHT SQUIDDY, TENTACLEY, SLIMY MONSTERS AND ALWAYS TRIUMPHED.
BUT THAT MACHINE...
THERE, THERE. IT'S OKAY. YOU'RE JUST KIND OF A LUDDITE IS ALL.
YEAH. C'MON, LET'S GO TO THE CORNER DELI AND GET A SODA THERE, MY TREAT.
JUST GIMME ONE SEC, THOUGH. I GOTTA DO SOMETHING.
BILLS
SQUEEKIE-SQUEEK-SCRITCH
SHNU m
DR. SALT
COLA
HEY, GUYS, WAIT UP!
OUT OF ORDER
BILLS
OUT OF ORDER
BILLS
UNF...OOGH THAT'S A TIGHT SQUEEZE. MESS WITH THE INTERN DEMON... MISSIN-FRAZZIN-SO-AND-SO... AND YOU GET THE HORNS, DEVIL-BOY.
AIN'T I A STINKER?
STORY & ART: BOB FINGERMAN
END

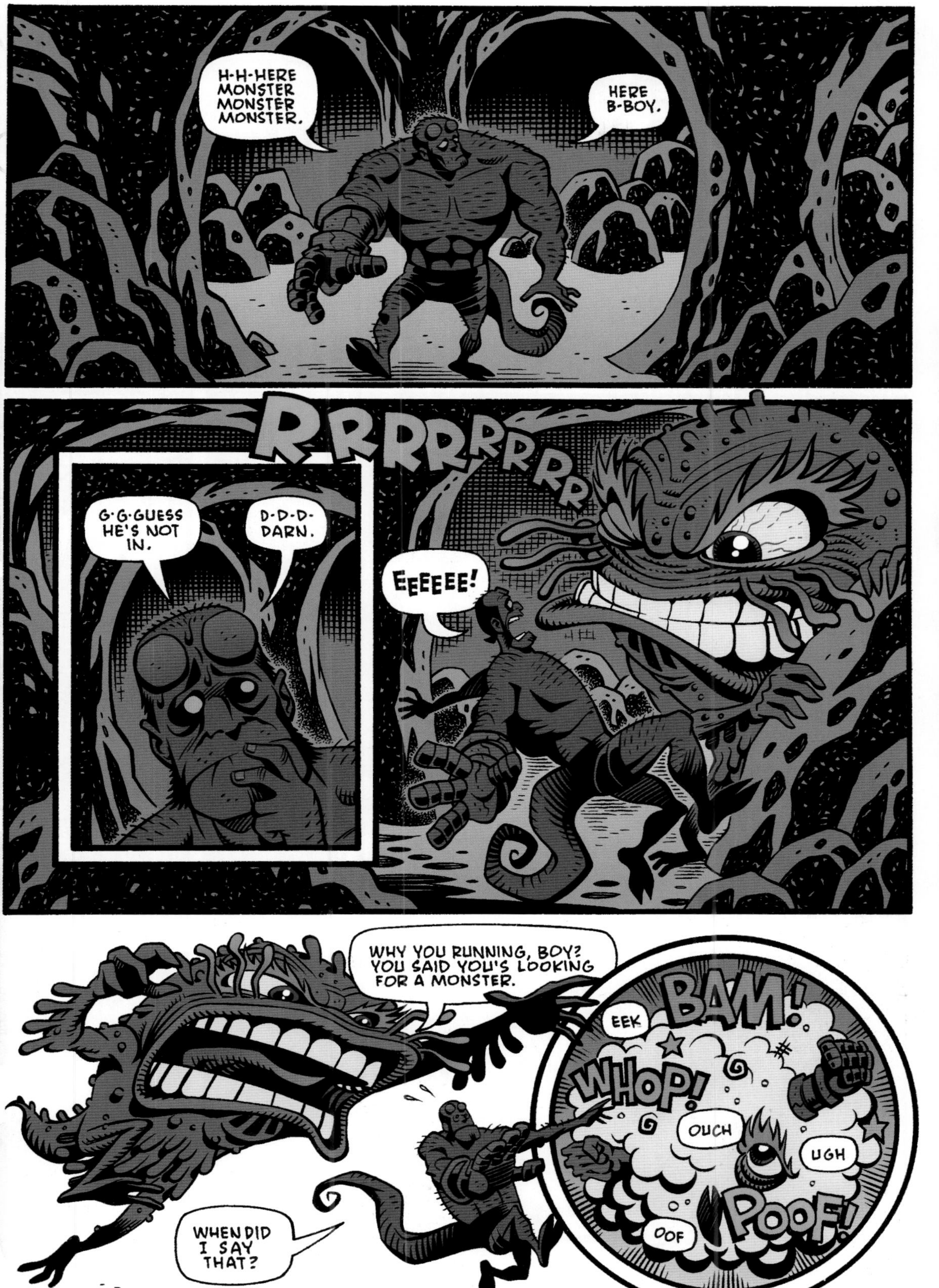
H-H-HERE MONSTER MONSTER MONSTER.
HERE B-BOY.
RRRRRRRRR
G-G-GUESS HE'S NOT IN.
D-D-D-DARN.
EEEEEE!
WHY YOU RUNNING, BOY? YOU SAID YOU'S LOOKING FOR A MONSTER.
EEK
BAM!
WHOP!
OUCH
UGH
OOF
POOF!
WHEN DID I SAY THAT?

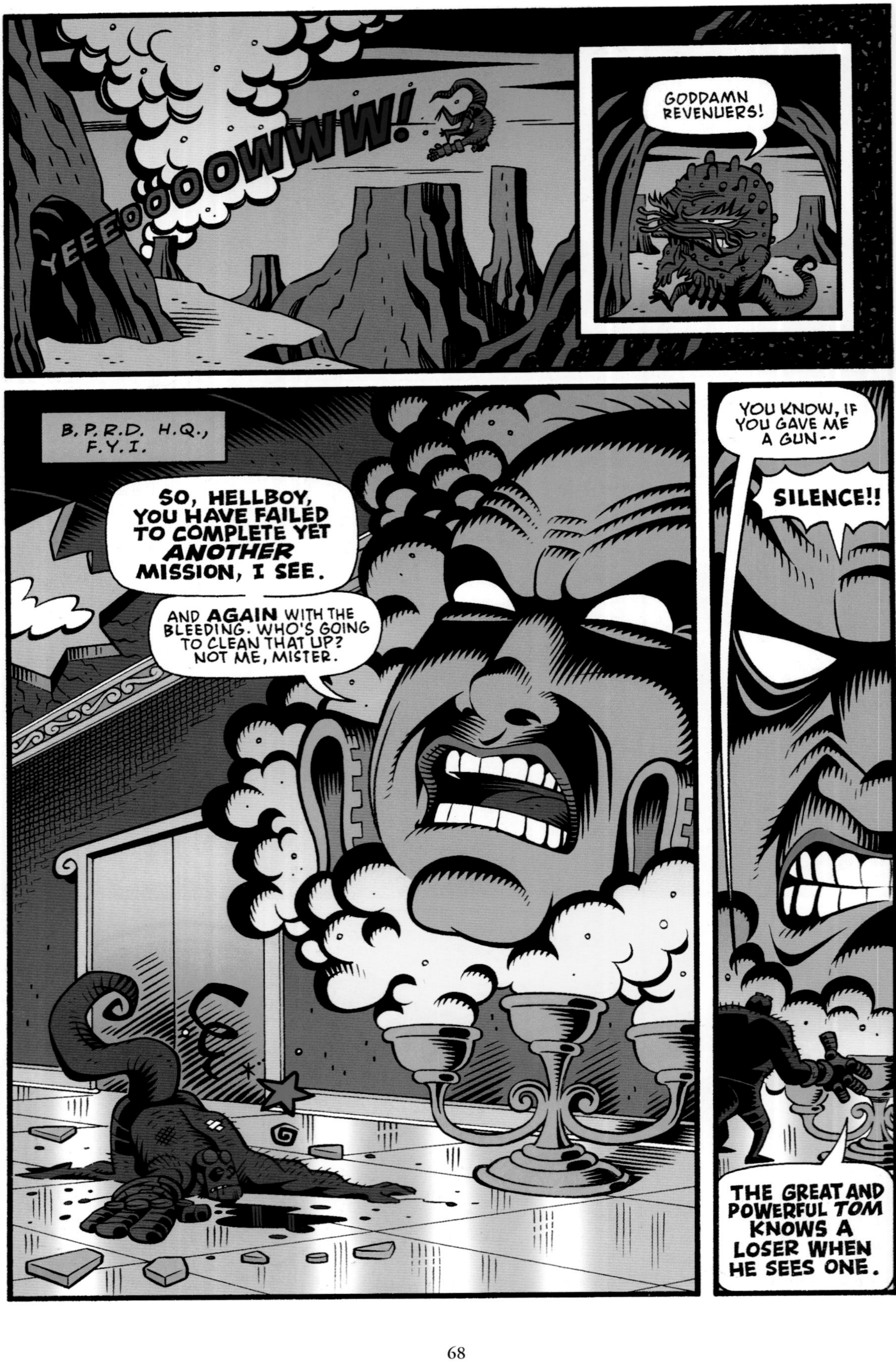
YEEEOOOOOWWWW!
GODDAMN REVENUERS!
B.P.R.D. H.Q., F.Y.I.
SO, HELLBOY, YOU HAVE FAILED TO COMPLETE YET ANOTHER MISSION, I SEE.
AND AGAIN WITH THE BLEEDING. WHO'S GOING TO CLEAN THAT UP? NOT ME, MISTER.
YOU KNOW, IF YOU GAVE ME A GUN--
SILENCE!!
THE GREAT AND POWERFUL TOM KNOWS A LOSER WHEN HE SEES ONE.

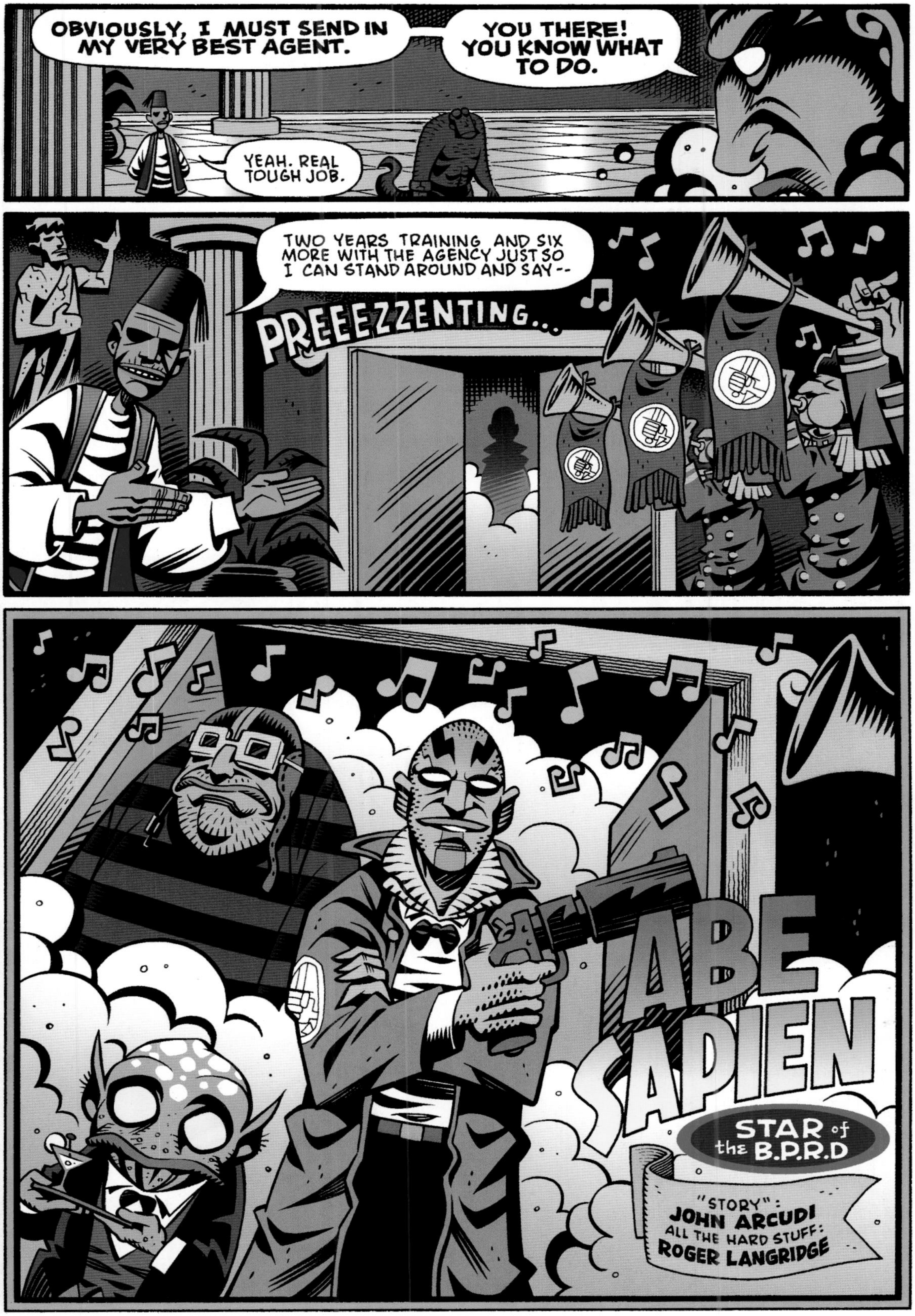
OBVIOUSLY, I MUST SEND IN MY VERY BEST AGENT.
YOU THERE! YOU KNOW WHAT TO DO.
YEAH. REAL TOUGH JOB.
TWO YEARS TRAINING AND SIX MORE WITH THE AGENCY JUST SO I CAN STAND AROUND AND SAY --
PREEEZZENTING...
ABE SAPIEN
STAR of the B.P.R.D
"STORY": JOHN ARCUDI
ALL THE HARD STUFF: ROGER LANGRIDGE

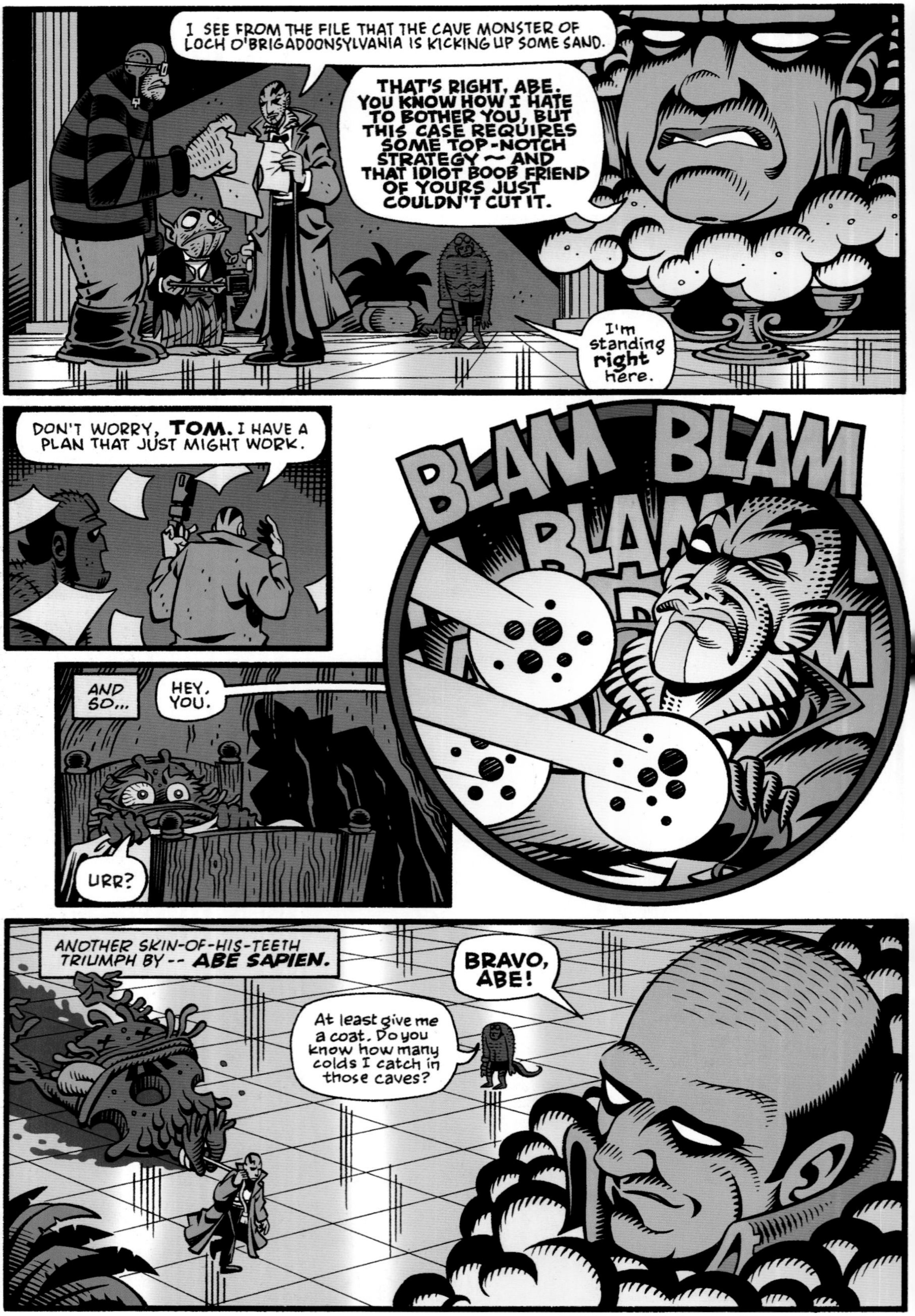
I SEE FROM THE FILE THAT THE CAVE MONSTER OF LOCH O'BRIGADOONSYLVANIA IS KICKING UP SOME SAND.
THAT'S RIGHT, ABE. YOU KNOW HOW I HATE TO BOTHER YOU, BUT THIS CASE REQUIRES SOME TOP-NOTCH STRATEGY ~ AND THAT IDIOT BOOB FRIEND OF YOURS JUST COULDN'T CUT IT.
I'm standing right here.
DON'T WORRY, TOM. I HAVE A PLAN THAT JUST MIGHT WORK.
BLAM BLAM
BLAM
AND SO...
HEY, YOU.
URR?
ANOTHER SKIN-OF-HIS-TEETH TRIUMPH BY -- ABE SAPIEN.
BRAVO, ABE!
At least give me a coat. Do you know how many colds I catch in those caves?

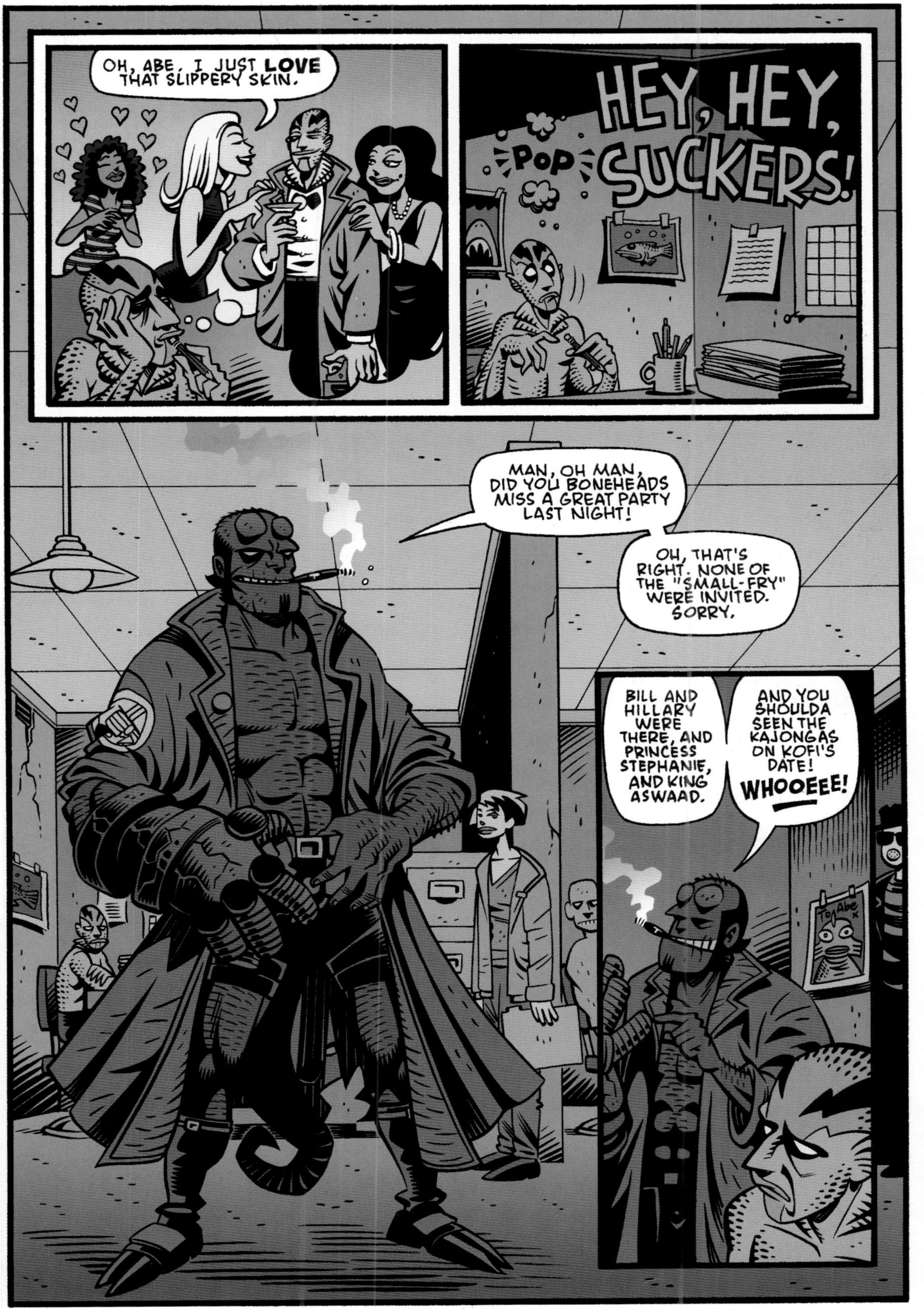
OH, ABE, I JUST LOVE THAT SLIPPERY SKIN.
POP
HEY, HEY, SUCKERS!
MAN, OH MAN, DID YOU BONEHEADS MISS A GREAT PARTY LAST NIGHT!
OH, THAT'S RIGHT. NONE OF THE "SMALL-FRY" WERE INVITED. SORRY.
BILL AND HILLARY WERE THERE, AND PRINCESS STEPHANIE, AND KING ASWAAD.
AND YOU SHOULDA SEEN THE KAJONGAS ON KOFI'S DATE! WHOOEEE!
To Abe

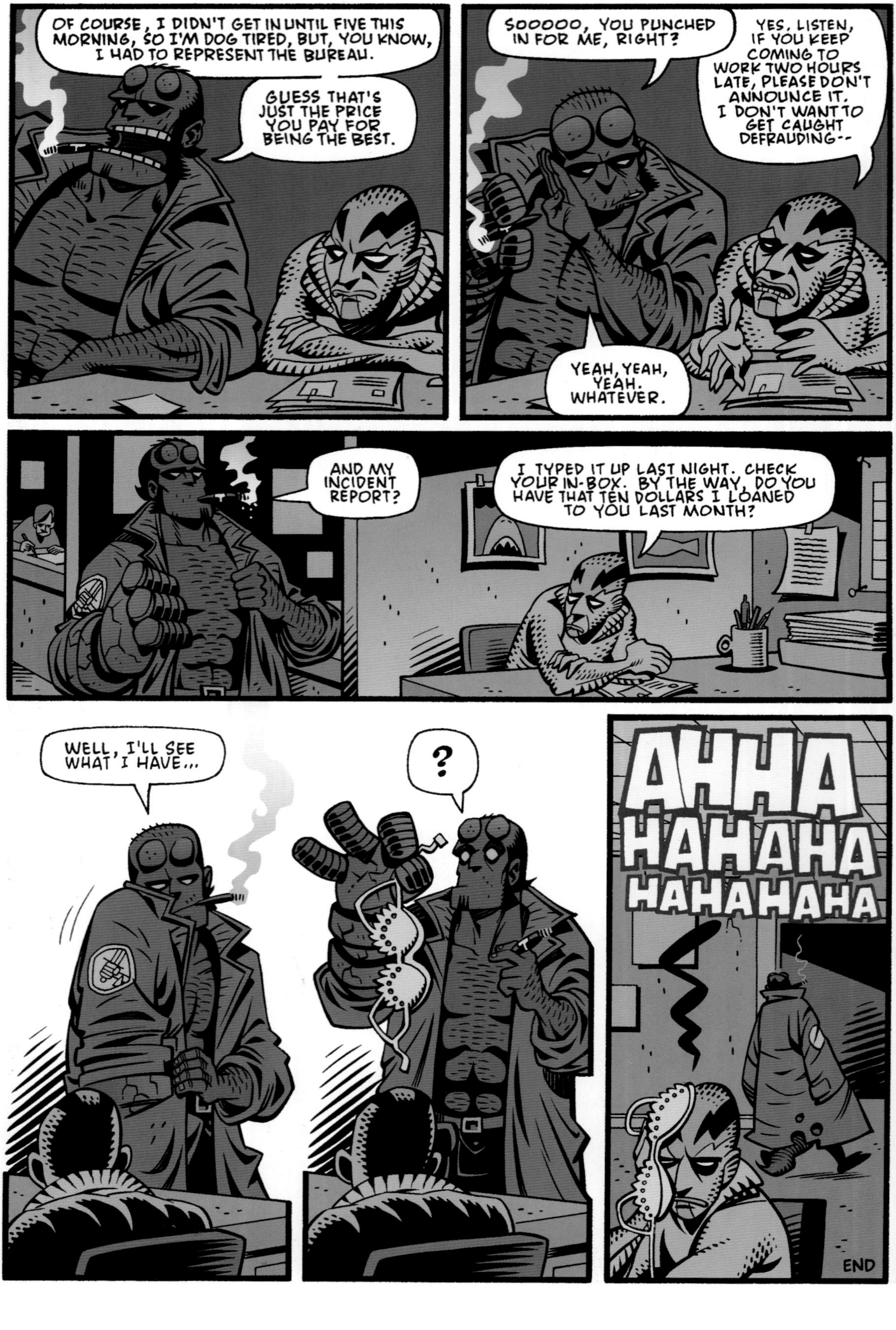
OF COURSE, I DIDN'T GET IN UNTIL FIVE THIS MORNING, SO I'M DOG TIRED, BUT, YOU KNOW, I HAD TO REPRESENT THE BUREAU.
GUESS THAT'S JUST THE PRICE YOU PAY FOR BEING THE BEST.
SOOOOO, YOU PUNCHED IN FOR ME, RIGHT?
YES, LISTEN, IF YOU KEEP COMING TO WORK TWO HOURS LATE, PLEASE DON'T ANNOUNCE IT. I DON'T WANT TO GET CAUGHT DEFRAUDING--
YEAH, YEAH, YEAH. WHATEVER.
AND MY INCIDENT REPORT?
I TYPED IT UP LAST NIGHT. CHECK YOUR IN-BOX. BY THE WAY, DO YOU HAVE THAT TEN DOLLARS I LOANED TO YOU LAST MONTH?
WELL, I'LL SEE WHAT I HAVE...
?
AHHA
HAHAHA
HAHAHAHA
END

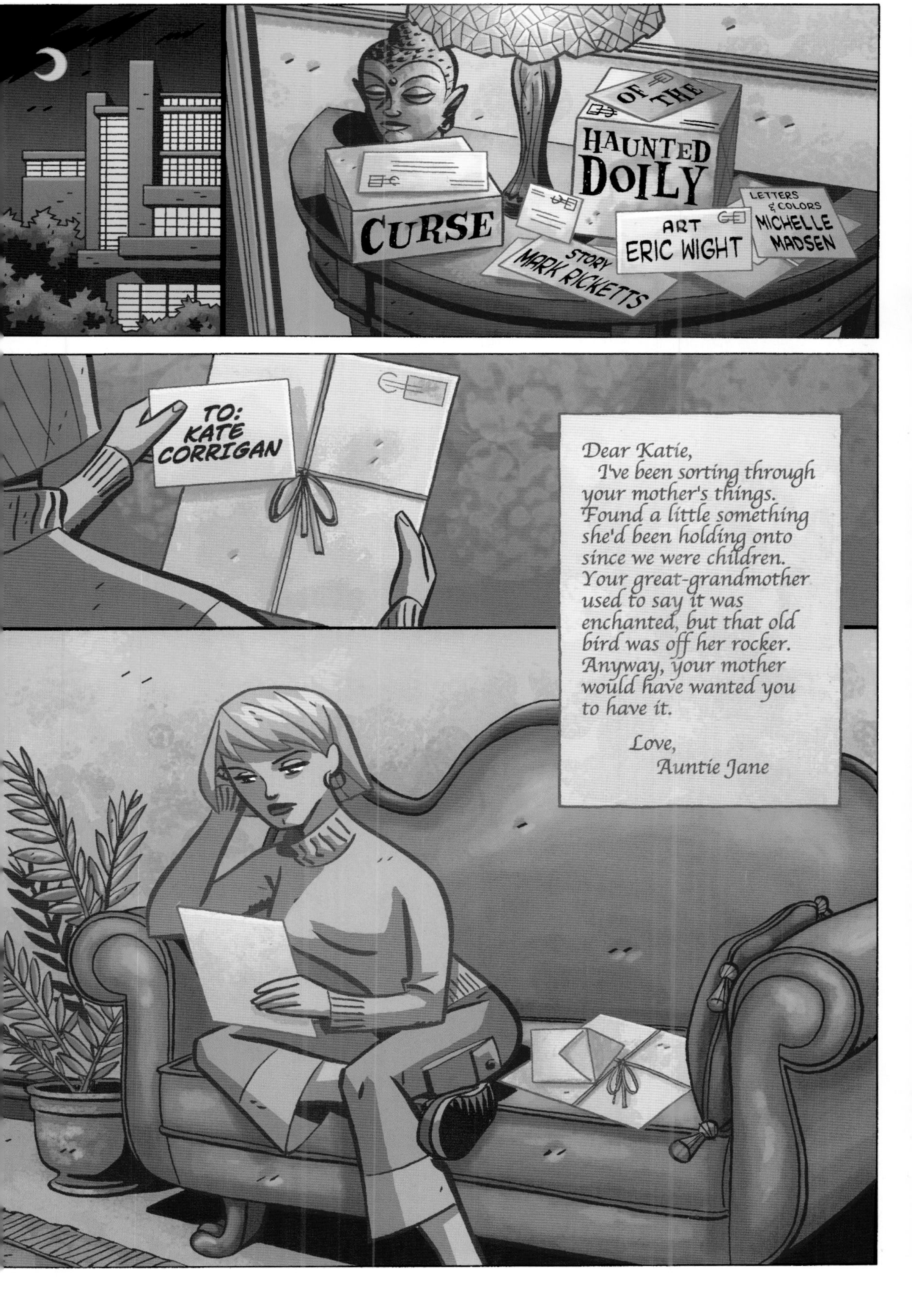
CURSE
OF THE
HAUNTED
DOILY
STORY
MARK RICKETTS
ART
ERIC WIGHT
LETTERS & COLORS
MICHELLE MADSEN
TO:
KATE
CORRIGAN
Dear Katie,
I've been sorting through your mother's things. Found a little something she'd been holding onto since we were children. Your great-grandmother used to say it was enchanted, but that old bird was off her rocker. Anyway, your mother would have wanted you to have it.
Love,
Auntie Jane

ELECTROLYSIS, A ROOT CANAL ... ANYTHING BUT A PAPER CUT.

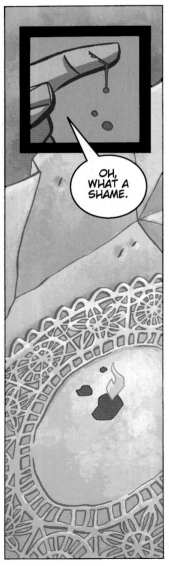

OH, WHAT A SHAME.

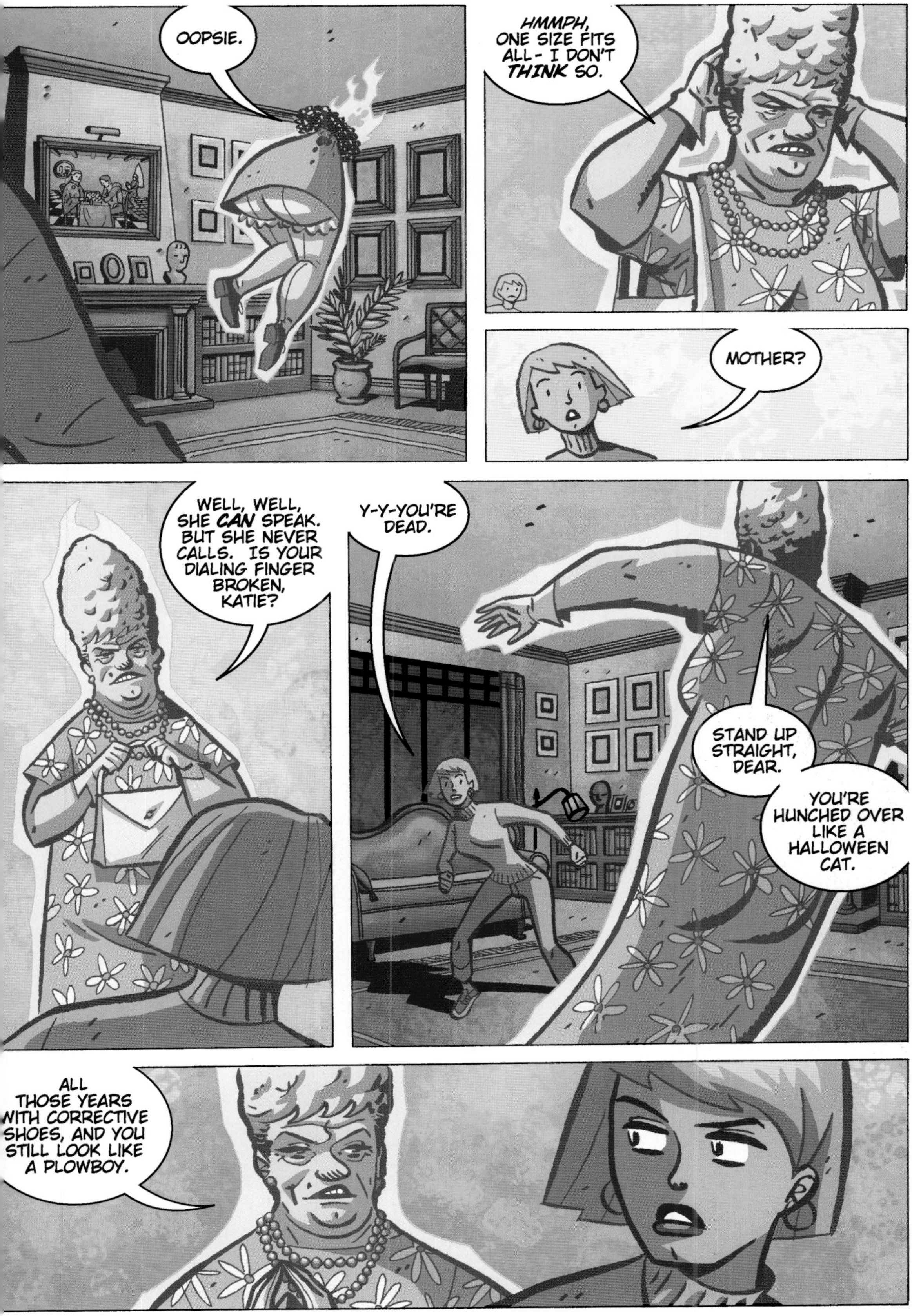
OOPSIE.
HMMPH, ONE SIZE FITS ALL- I DON'T THINK SO.
MOTHER?
WELL, WELL, SHE CAN SPEAK. BUT SHE NEVER CALLS. IS YOUR DIALING FINGER BROKEN, KATIE?
Y-Y-YOU'RE DEAD.
STAND UP STRAIGHT, DEAR.
YOU'RE HUNCHED OVER LIKE A HALLOWEEN CAT.
ALL THOSE YEARS WITH CORRECTIVE SHOES, AND YOU STILL LOOK LIKE A PLOWBOY.

HOW DID YOU G-GET HERE?

GABRIEL CALLED MY NUMBERS, I YELLED, **"BINGO!"** A TRAP DOOR OPENED AND, WELL, HERE I AM.

RIGHT ON TIME, TOO.

RAISING DUST BUNNIES FOR FUN AND PROFIT, ARE WE?

TSK. TSK. FILTH EVERYWHERE, BUT NOT ONE GRANDBABY IN SIGHT.

HONEY, YOUR BIOLOGICAL CLOCK NEEDS REWINDING.

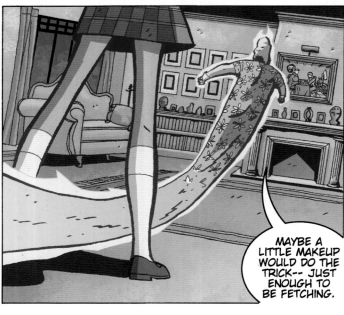

MAYBE A LITTLE MAKEUP WOULD DO THE TRICK-- JUST ENOUGH TO BE FETCHING.

OH, WHO ARE WE KIDDING? YOU'RE A LITTLE TOO LONG IN THE TOOTH TO BE SUBTLE. CAKE IT ON LIKE A SAIGON WHORE AND HOPE FOR THE BEST.

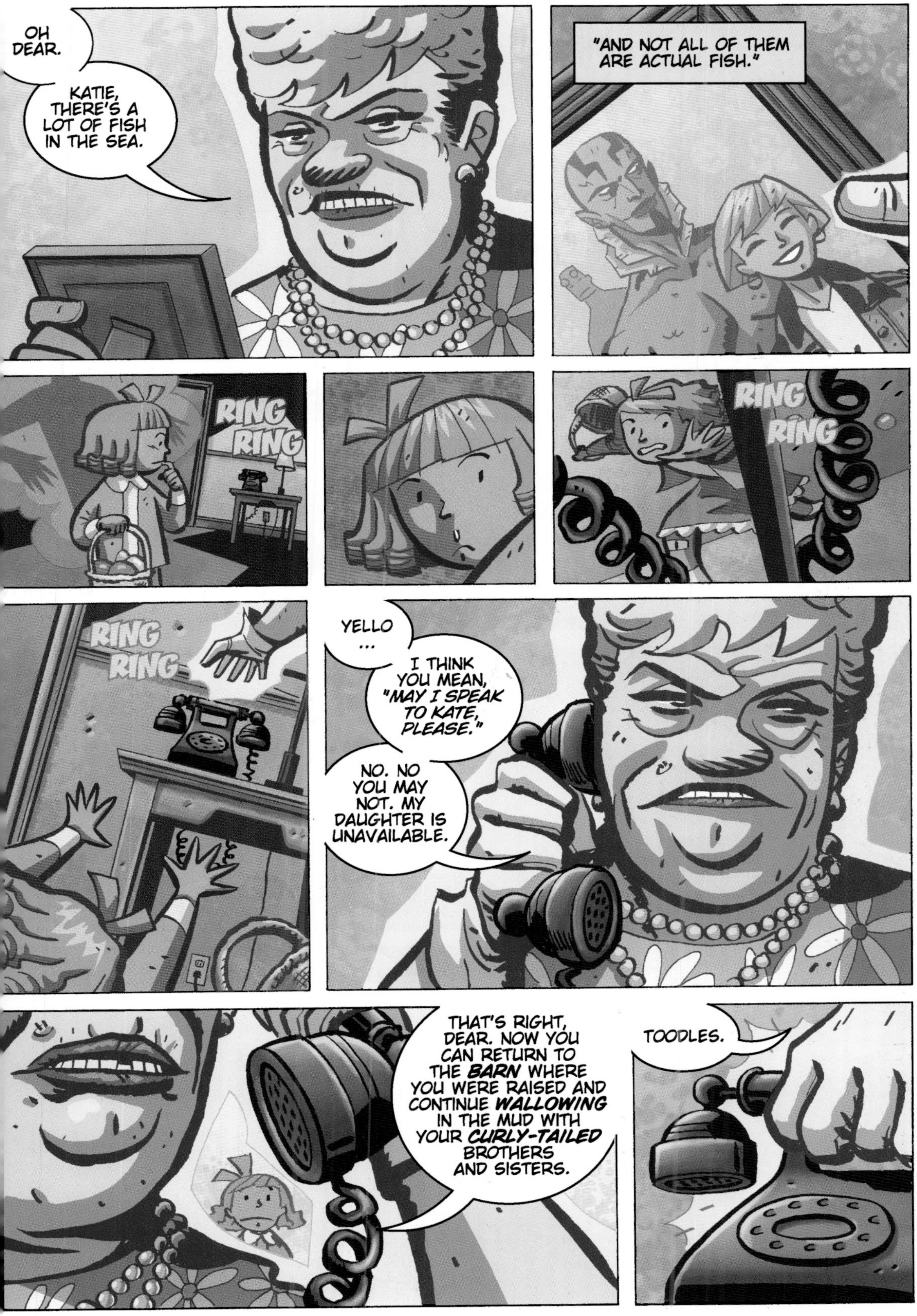
OH DEAR.
KATIE, THERE'S A LOT OF FISH IN THE SEA.
"AND NOT ALL OF THEM ARE ACTUAL FISH."
RING RING
RING RING
RING RING
YELLO ...
I THINK YOU MEAN, "MAY I SPEAK TO KATE, PLEASE."
NO. NO YOU MAY NOT. MY DAUGHTER IS UNAVAILABLE.
THAT'S RIGHT, DEAR. NOW YOU CAN RETURN TO THE BARN WHERE YOU WERE RAISED AND CONTINUE WALLOWING IN THE MUD WITH YOUR CURLY-TAILED BROTHERS AND SISTERS.
TOODLES.

DID YOU REACH HER?

THERE ARE *DARKER FORCES* AT WORK HERE THAN I FIRST THOUGHT.

NO, MOMMY, NO!! PLEASE, NO!!!

SO, HOW'D YOU GET RID OF HER?

I TOLD HER I'D MARRY A DOCTOR, MOVE TO THE SUBURBS, AND HAVE A BUNCH OF KIDS.

I'M A DOCTOR.

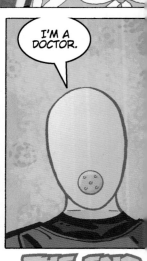

THE END

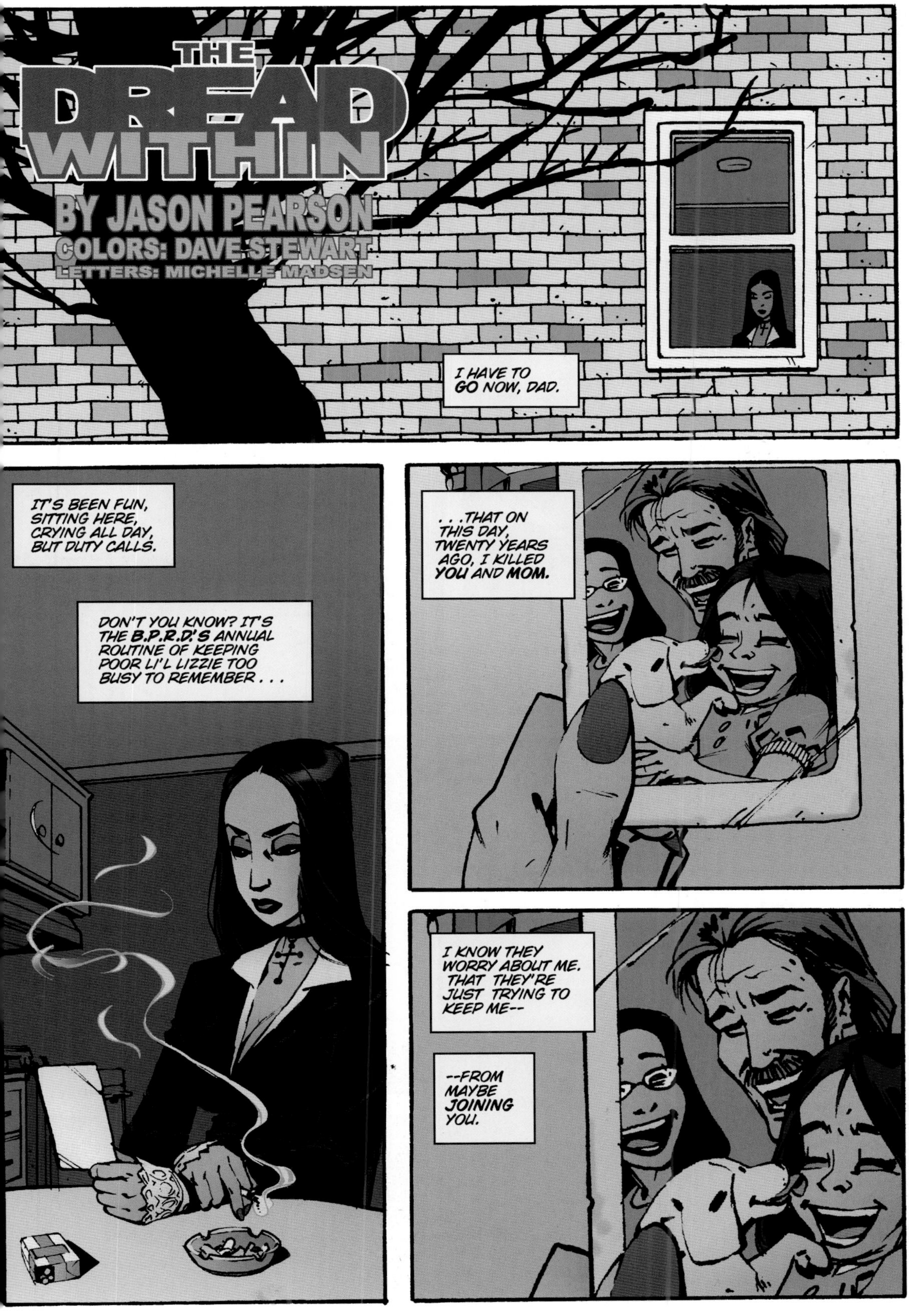
THE DREAD WITHIN
BY JASON PEARSON
COLORS: DAVE STEWART
LETTERS: MICHELLE MADSEN
I HAVE TO GO NOW, DAD.
IT'S BEEN FUN, SITTING HERE, CRYING ALL DAY, BUT DUTY CALLS.
DON'T YOU KNOW? IT'S THE B.P.R.D.'S ANNUAL ROUTINE OF KEEPING POOR LI'L LIZZIE TOO BUSY TO REMEMBER . . .
. . .THAT ON THIS DAY, TWENTY YEARS AGO, I KILLED YOU AND MOM.
I KNOW THEY WORRY ABOUT ME. THAT THEY'RE JUST TRYING TO KEEP ME--
--FROM MAYBE JOINING YOU.

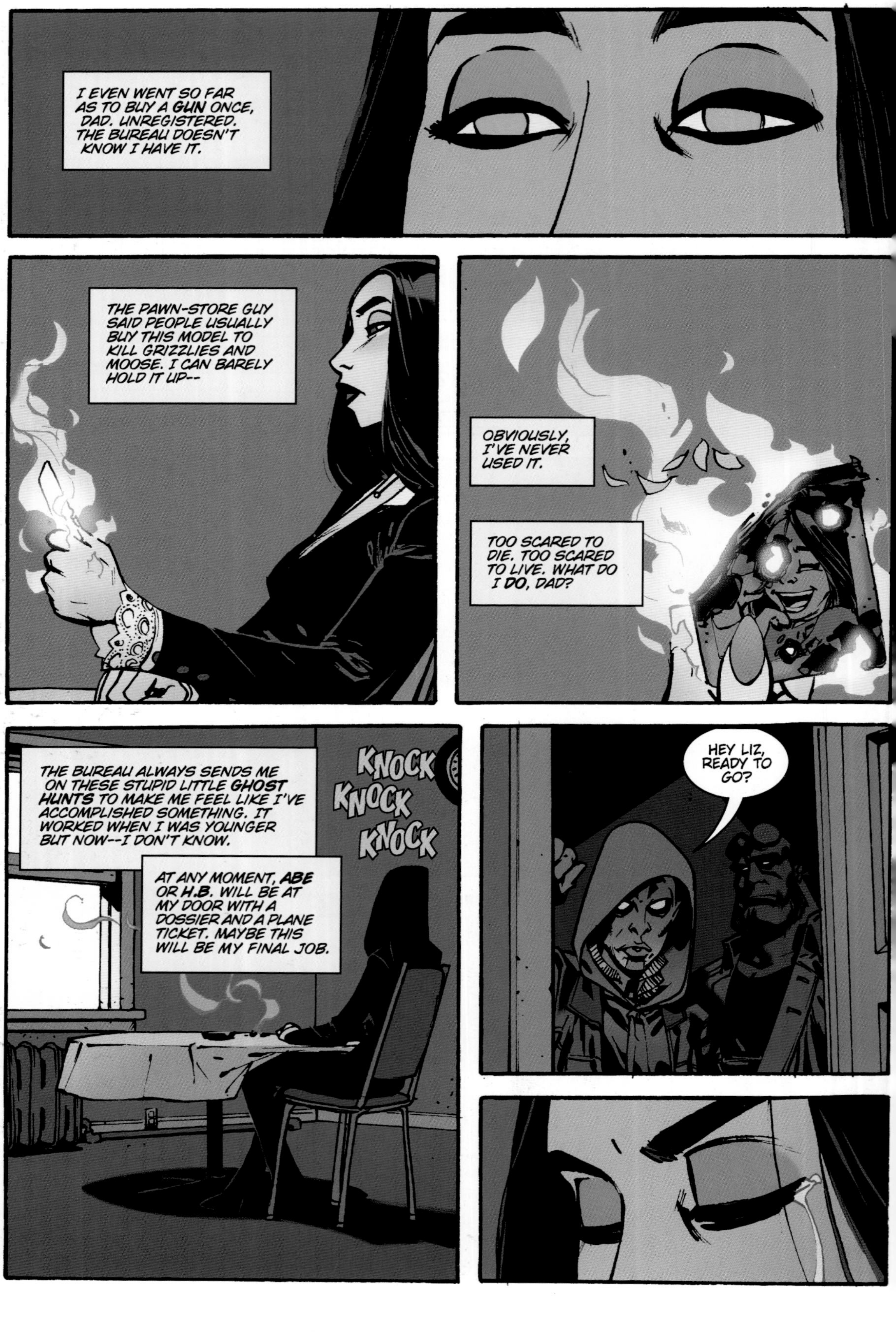
I EVEN WENT SO FAR AS TO BUY A GUN ONCE, DAD. UNREGISTERED. THE BUREAU DOESN'T KNOW I HAVE IT.
THE PAWN-STORE GUY SAID PEOPLE USUALLY BUY THIS MODEL TO KILL GRIZZLIES AND MOOSE. I CAN BARELY HOLD IT UP--
OBVIOUSLY, I'VE NEVER USED IT.
TOO SCARED TO DIE. TOO SCARED TO LIVE. WHAT DO I DO, DAD?
THE BUREAU ALWAYS SENDS ME ON THESE STUPID LITTLE GHOST HUNTS TO MAKE ME FEEL LIKE I'VE ACCOMPLISHED SOMETHING. IT WORKED WHEN I WAS YOUNGER BUT NOW--I DON'T KNOW.
KNOCK
KNOCK
KNOCK
AT ANY MOMENT, ABE OR H.B. WILL BE AT MY DOOR WITH A DOSSIER AND A PLANE TICKET. MAYBE THIS WILL BE MY FINAL JOB.
HEY LIZ, READY TO GO?

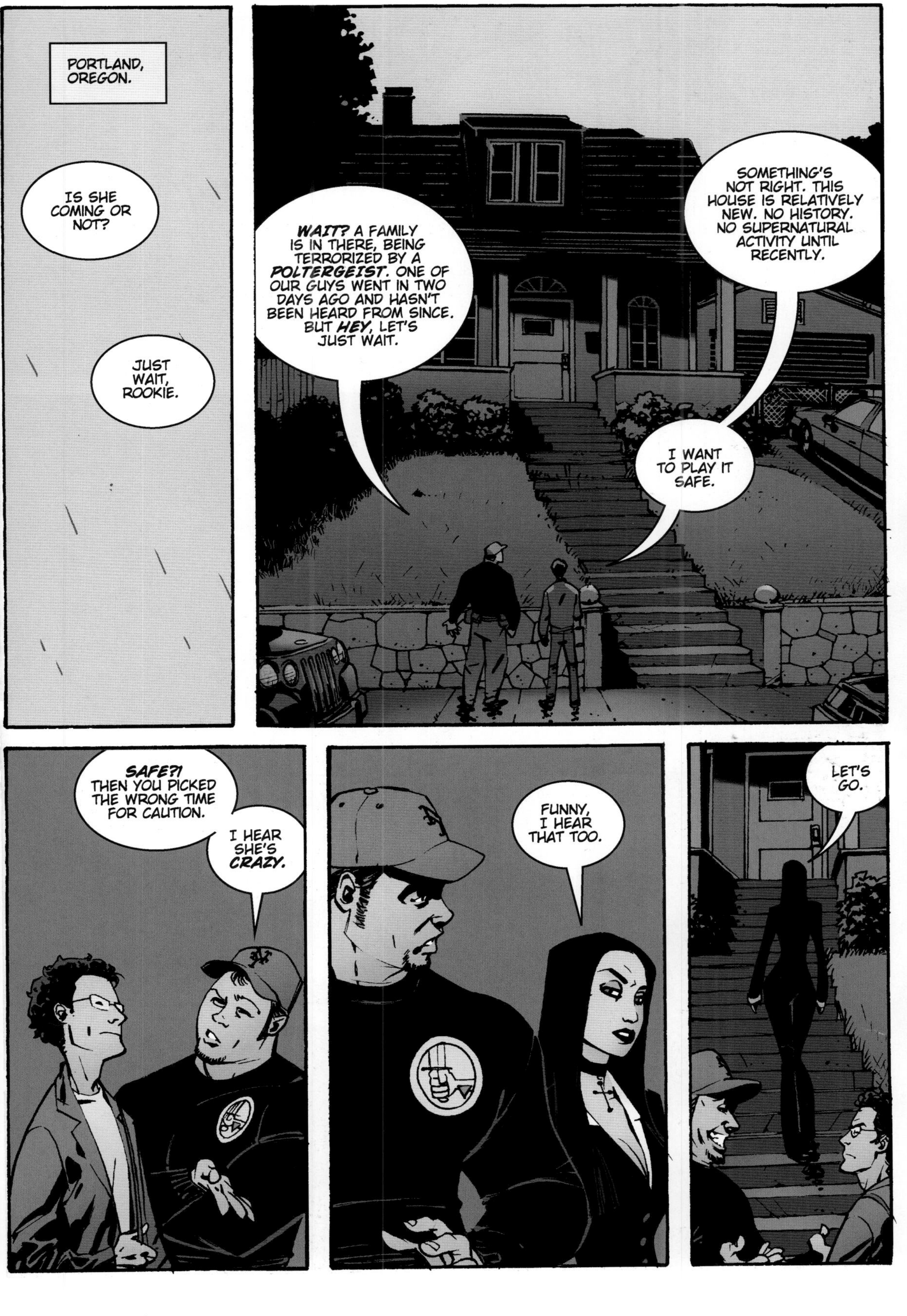

PORTLAND, OREGON.
IS SHE COMING OR NOT?
JUST WAIT, ROOKIE.
WAIT? A FAMILY IS IN THERE, BEING TERRORIZED BY A POLTERGEIST. ONE OF OUR GUYS WENT IN TWO DAYS AGO AND HASN'T BEEN HEARD FROM SINCE. BUT HEY, LET'S JUST WAIT.
SOMETHING'S NOT RIGHT. THIS HOUSE IS RELATIVELY NEW. NO HISTORY. NO SUPERNATURAL ACTIVITY UNTIL RECENTLY.
I WANT TO PLAY IT SAFE.
SAFE?! THEN YOU PICKED THE WRONG TIME FOR CAUTION.
I HEAR SHE'S CRAZY.
FUNNY, I HEAR THAT TOO.
LET'S GO.

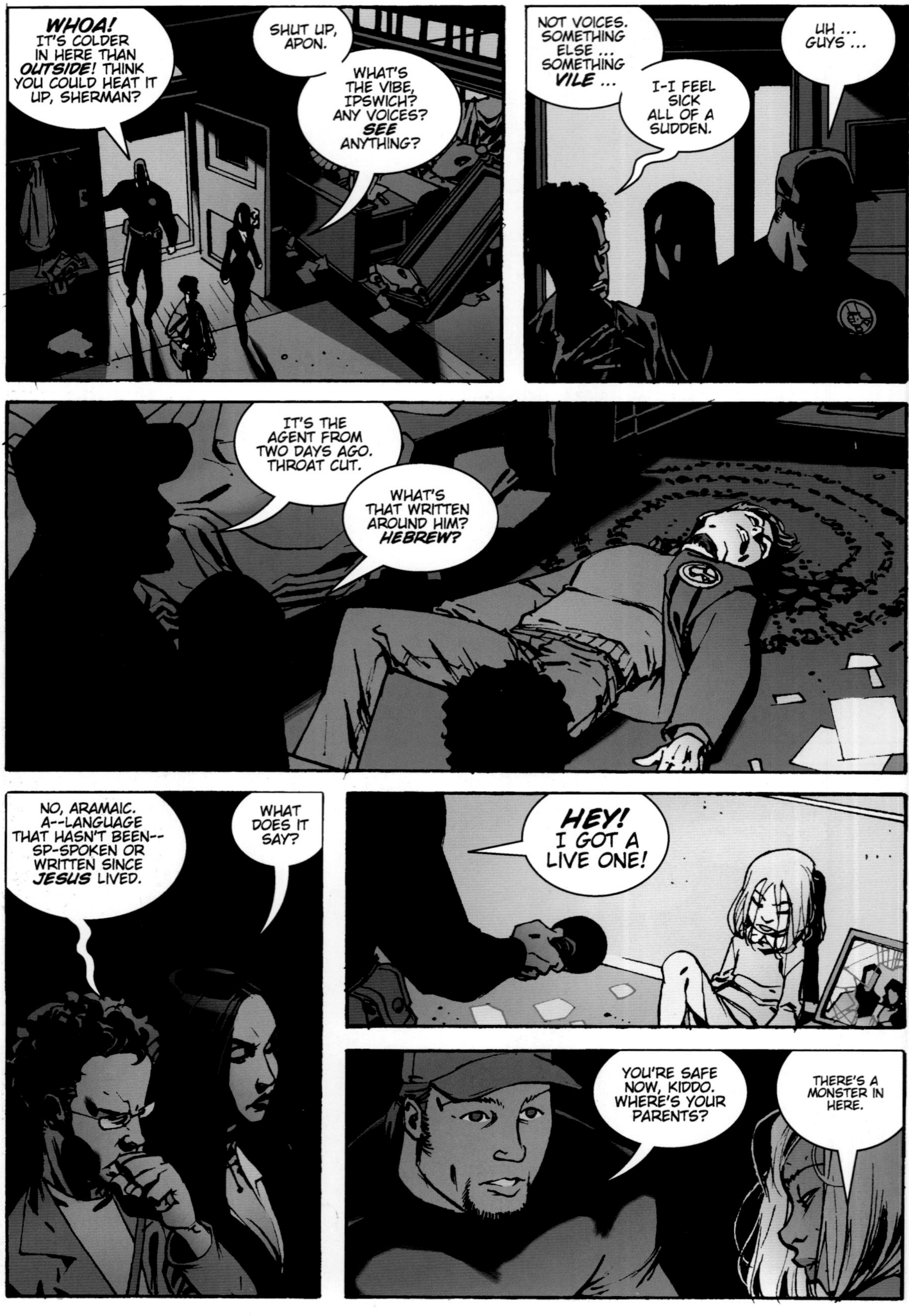
WHOA! IT'S COLDER IN HERE THAN OUTSIDE! THINK YOU COULD HEAT IT UP, SHERMAN?
SHUT UP, APON.
WHAT'S THE VIBE, IPSWICH? ANY VOICES? SEE ANYTHING?
NOT VOICES. SOMETHING ELSE ... SOMETHING VILE ...
I-I FEEL SICK ALL OF A SUDDEN.
UH ... GUYS ...
IT'S THE AGENT FROM TWO DAYS AGO. THROAT CUT.
WHAT'S THAT WRITTEN AROUND HIM? HEBREW?
NO, ARAMAIC. A--LANGUAGE THAT HASN'T BEEN--SP-SPOKEN OR WRITTEN SINCE JESUS LIVED.
WHAT DOES IT SAY?
HEY! I GOT A LIVE ONE!
YOU'RE SAFE NOW, KIDDO. WHERE'S YOUR PARENTS?
THERE'S A MONSTER IN HERE.

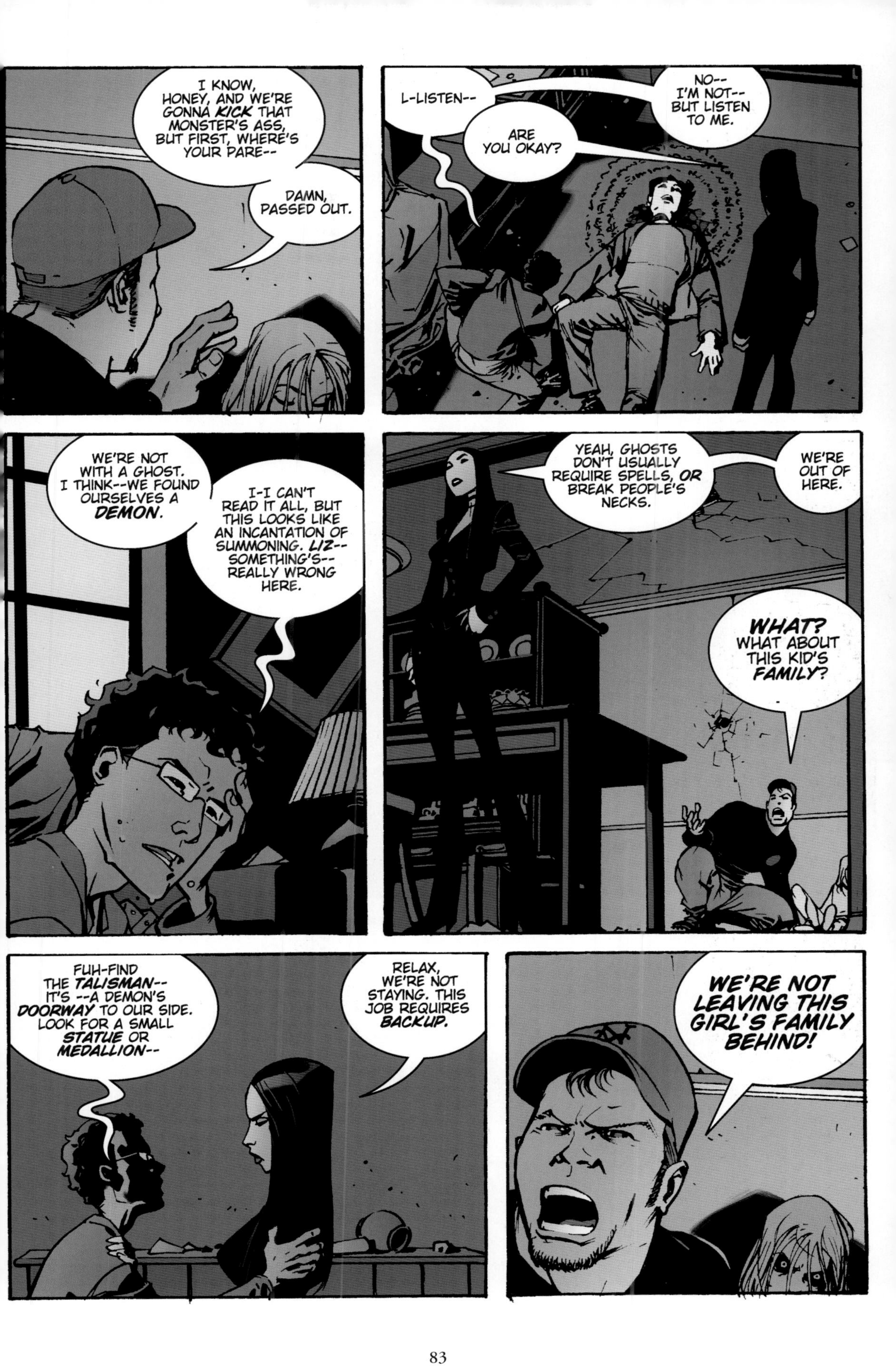
I KNOW, HONEY, AND WE'RE GONNA KICK THAT MONSTER'S ASS, BUT FIRST, WHERE'S YOUR PARE--
DAMN, PASSED OUT.
L-LISTEN--
ARE YOU OKAY?
NO-- I'M NOT-- BUT LISTEN TO ME.
WE'RE NOT WITH A GHOST. I THINK--WE FOUND OURSELVES A DEMON.
I-I CAN'T READ IT ALL, BUT THIS LOOKS LIKE AN INCANTATION OF SUMMONING. LIZ-- SOMETHING'S-- REALLY WRONG HERE.
YEAH, GHOSTS DON'T USUALLY REQUIRE SPELLS, OR BREAK PEOPLE'S NECKS.
WE'RE OUT OF HERE.
WHAT? WHAT ABOUT THIS KID'S FAMILY?
FUH-FIND THE TALISMAN-- IT'S --A DEMON'S DOORWAY TO OUR SIDE. LOOK FOR A SMALL STATUE OR MEDALLION--
RELAX, WE'RE NOT STAYING. THIS JOB REQUIRES BACKUP.
WE'RE NOT LEAVING THIS GIRL'S FAMILY BEHIND!

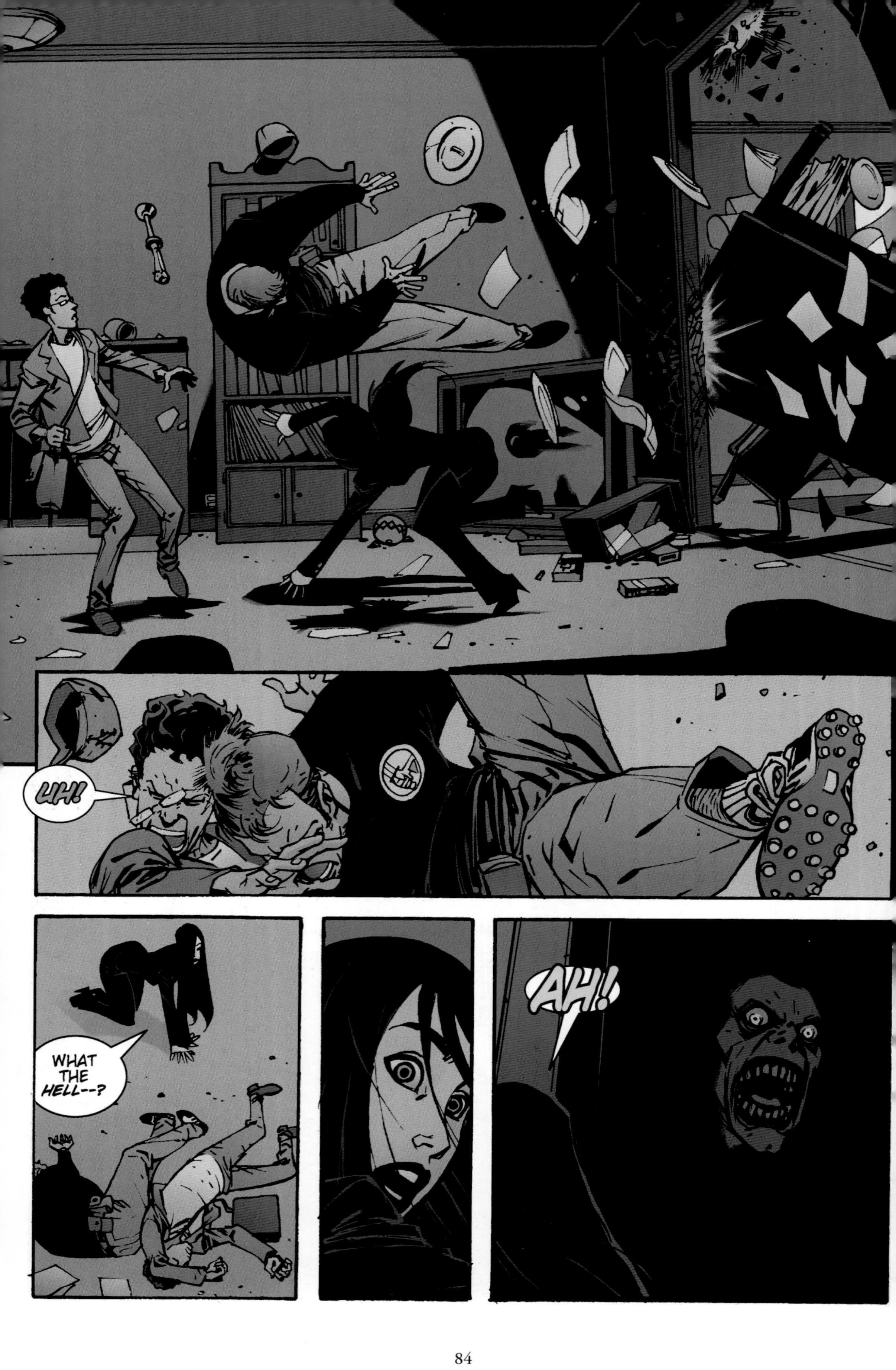
UH!
WHAT THE HELL--?
AH!

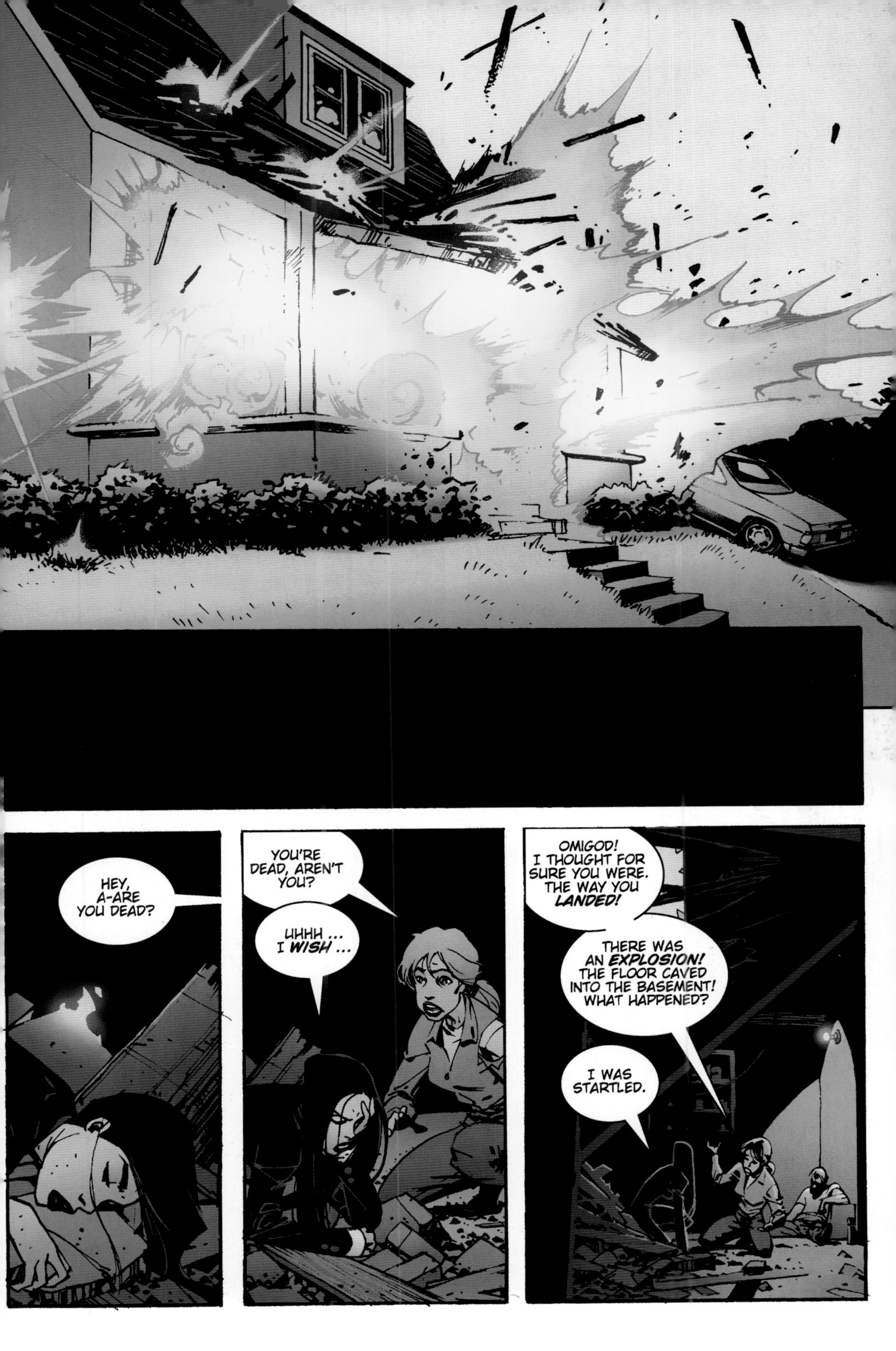
HEY, A-ARE YOU DEAD?
YOU'RE DEAD, AREN'T YOU?
UHHH ... I **WISH** ...
OMIGOD! I THOUGHT FOR SURE YOU WERE. THE WAY YOU **LANDED!**
THERE WAS AN **EXPLOSION!** THE FLOOR CAVED INTO THE BASEMENT! WHAT HAPPENED?
I WAS STARTLED.

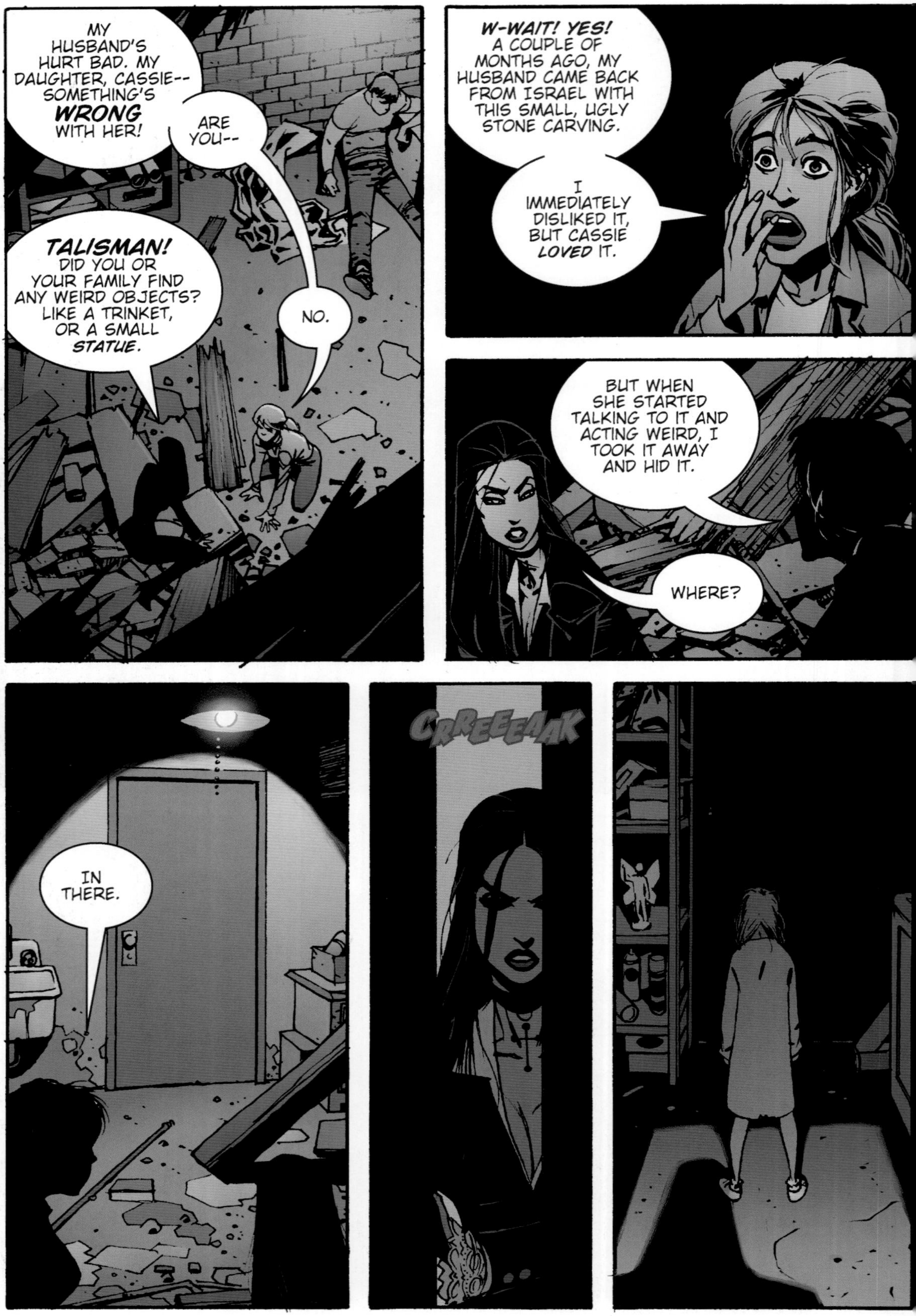
MY HUSBAND'S HURT BAD. MY DAUGHTER, CASSIE-- SOMETHING'S **WRONG** WITH HER!
ARE YOU--
TALISMAN! DID YOU OR YOUR FAMILY FIND ANY WEIRD OBJECTS? LIKE A TRINKET, OR A SMALL *STATUE*.
NO.
W-WAIT! YES! A COUPLE OF MONTHS AGO, MY HUSBAND CAME BACK FROM ISRAEL WITH THIS SMALL, UGLY STONE CARVING.
I IMMEDIATELY DISLIKED IT, BUT CASSIE *LOVED* IT.
BUT WHEN SHE STARTED TALKING TO IT AND ACTING WEIRD, I TOOK IT AWAY AND HID IT.
WHERE?
IN THERE.
CRREEEAAK

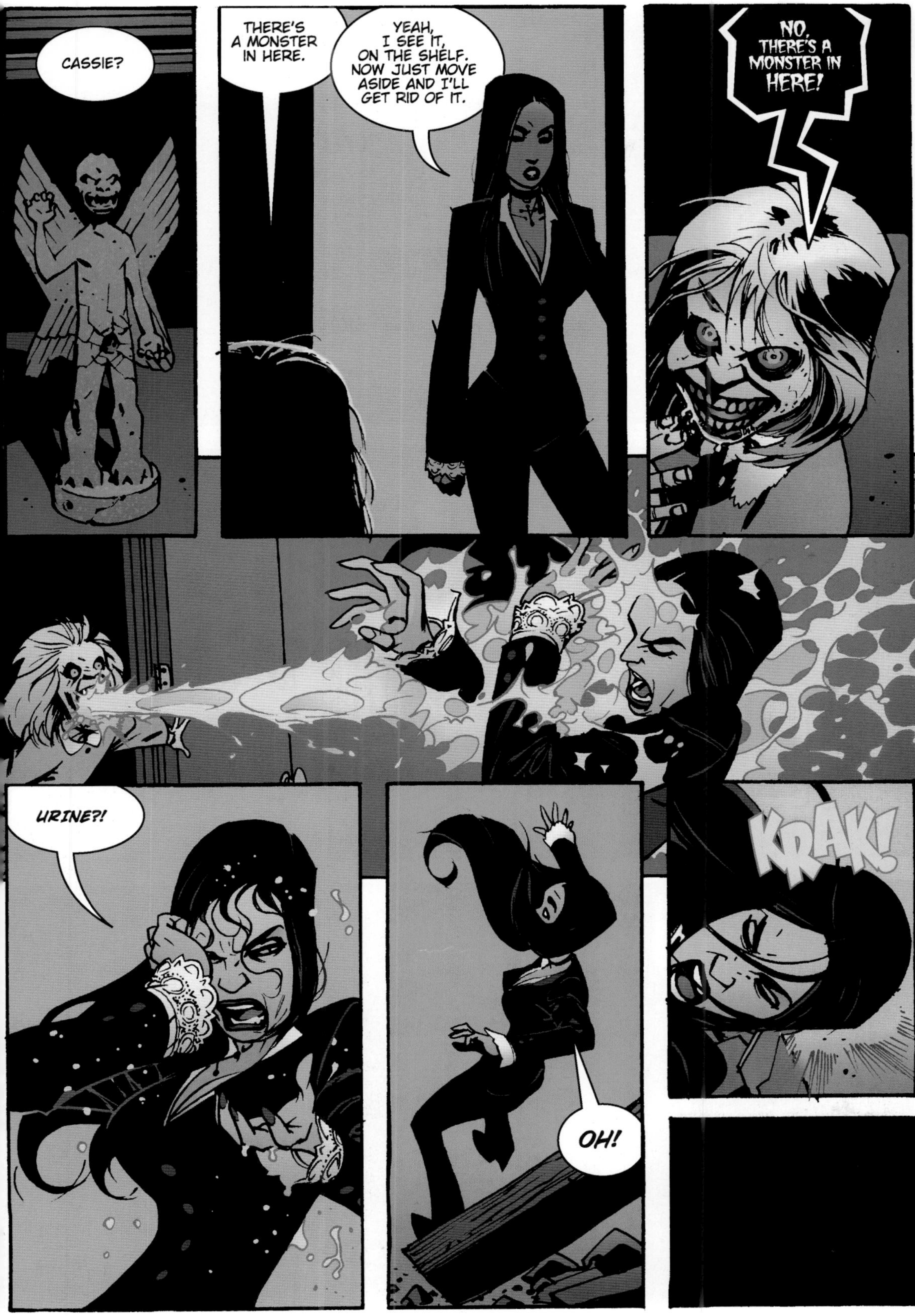
CASSIE?
THERE'S A MONSTER IN HERE.
YEAH, I SEE IT, ON THE SHELF. NOW JUST MOVE ASIDE AND I'LL GET RID OF IT.
NO, THERE'S A MONSTER IN HERE!
URINE?!
OH!
KRAK!

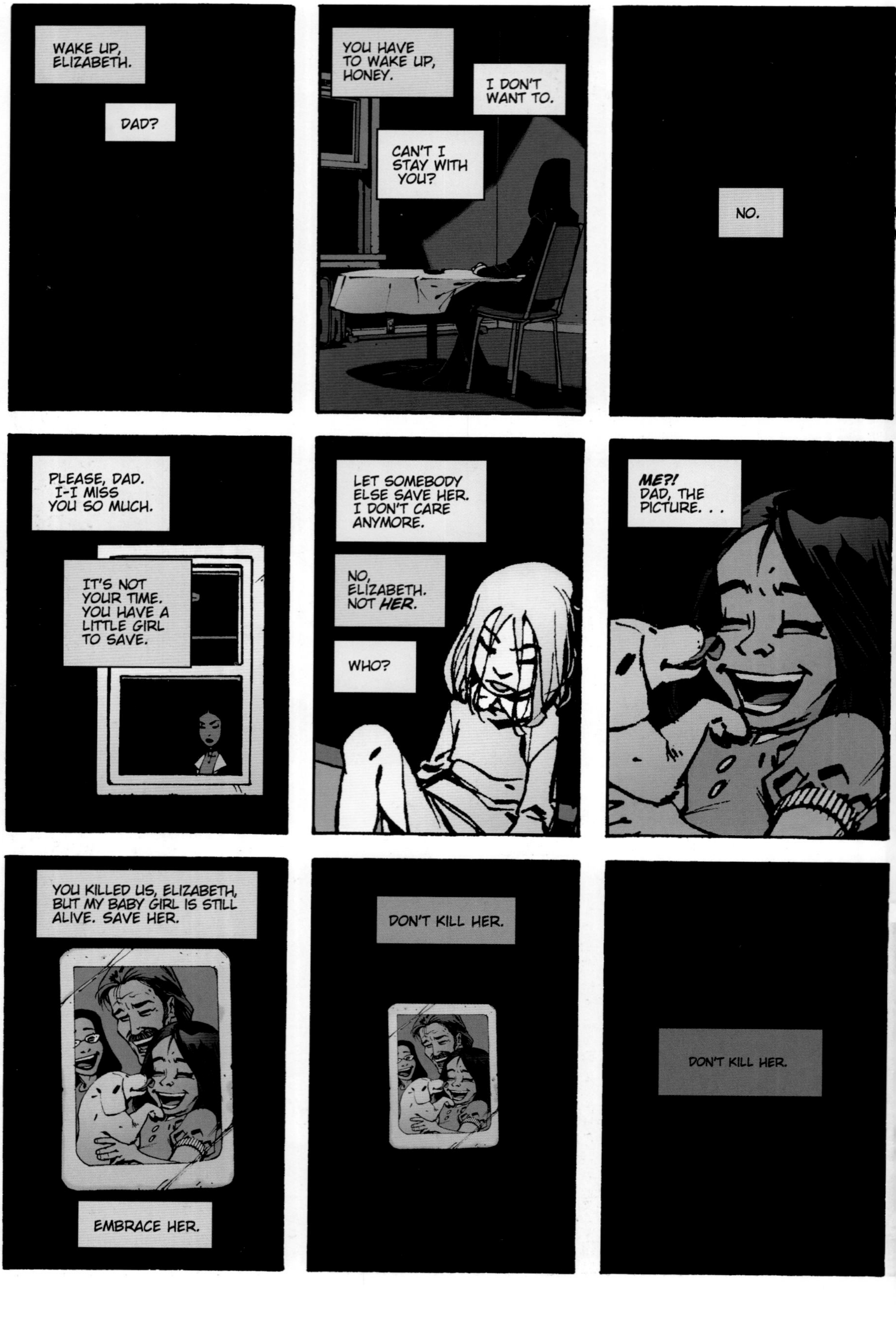
WAKE UP, ELIZABETH.
DAD?
YOU HAVE TO WAKE UP, HONEY.
I DON'T WANT TO.
CAN'T I STAY WITH YOU?
NO.
PLEASE, DAD. I-I MISS YOU SO MUCH.
IT'S NOT YOUR TIME. YOU HAVE A LITTLE GIRL TO SAVE.
LET SOMEBODY ELSE SAVE HER. I DON'T CARE ANYMORE.
NO, ELIZABETH. NOT *HER*.
WHO?
ME?! DAD, THE PICTURE. . .
YOU KILLED US, ELIZABETH, BUT MY BABY GIRL IS STILL ALIVE. SAVE HER.
EMBRACE HER.
DON'T KILL HER.
DON'T KILL HER.

DON'T KILL HER!

PLEASE, BABY, DON'T KILL HER!

GET OFF OF ME, WHORE! THE FIRE WITCH WILL DIE!

DIE!

TOO STRONG. . .

WAIT. . .

THE TALISMAN . . .

AAHR

RR

IS IT OVER?

IT BETTER BE.

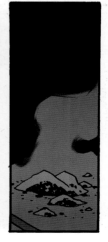

89

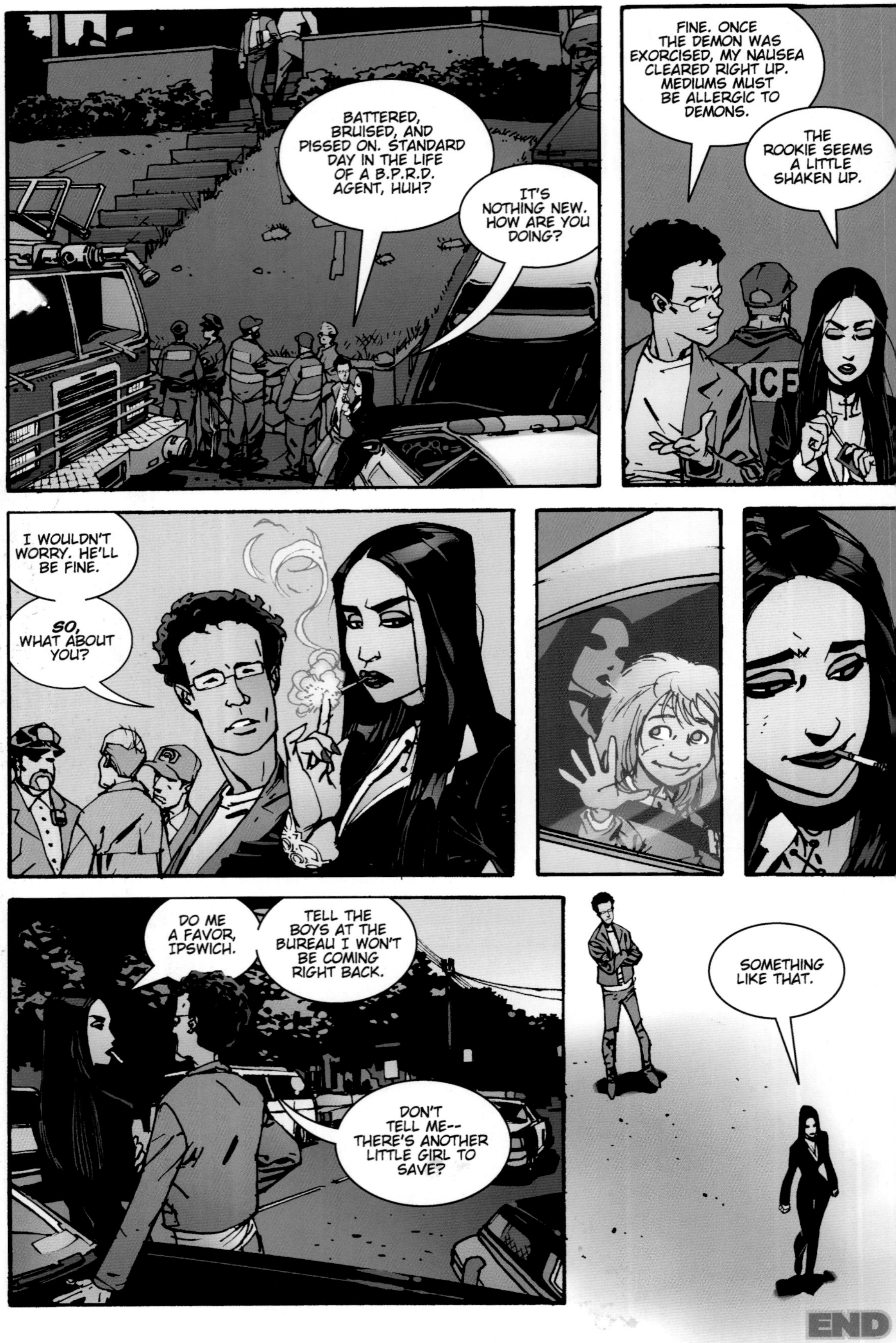
BATTERED, BRUISED, AND PISSED ON. STANDARD DAY IN THE LIFE OF A B.P.R.D. AGENT, HUH?
IT'S NOTHING NEW. HOW ARE YOU DOING?
FINE. ONCE THE DEMON WAS EXORCISED, MY NAUSEA CLEARED RIGHT UP. MEDIUMS MUST BE ALLERGIC TO DEMONS.
THE ROOKIE SEEMS A LITTLE SHAKEN UP.
I WOULDN'T WORRY. HE'LL BE FINE.
SO, WHAT ABOUT YOU?
DO ME A FAVOR, IPSWICH.
TELL THE BOYS AT THE BUREAU I WON'T BE COMING RIGHT BACK.
DON'T TELL ME-- THERE'S ANOTHER LITTLE GIRL TO SAVE?
SOMETHING LIKE THAT.
END

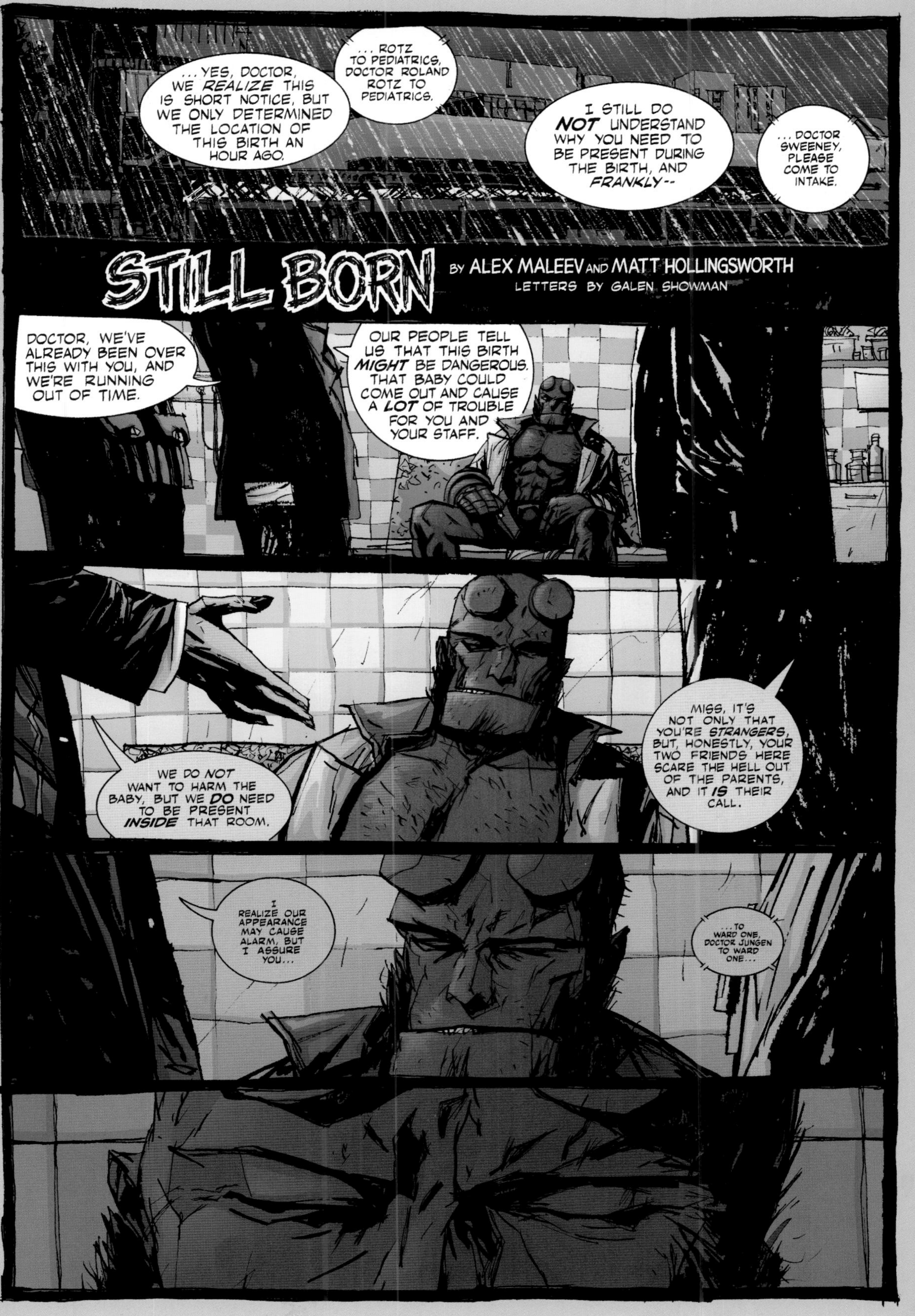
...YES, DOCTOR, WE REALIZE THIS IS SHORT NOTICE, BUT WE ONLY DETERMINED THE LOCATION OF THIS BIRTH AN HOUR AGO.
...ROTZ TO PEDIATRICS, DOCTOR ROLAND ROTZ TO PEDIATRICS.
I STILL DO NOT UNDERSTAND WHY YOU NEED TO BE PRESENT DURING THE BIRTH, AND FRANKLY--
...DOCTOR SWEENEY, PLEASE COME TO INTAKE.
STILL BORN
BY ALEX MALEEV AND MATT HOLLINGSWORTH
LETTERS BY GALEN SHOWMAN
DOCTOR, WE'VE ALREADY BEEN OVER THIS WITH YOU, AND WE'RE RUNNING OUT OF TIME.
OUR PEOPLE TELL US THAT THIS BIRTH MIGHT BE DANGEROUS. THAT BABY COULD COME OUT AND CAUSE A LOT OF TROUBLE FOR YOU AND YOUR STAFF.
WE DO NOT WANT TO HARM THE BABY, BUT WE DO NEED TO BE PRESENT INSIDE THAT ROOM.
MISS, IT'S NOT ONLY THAT YOU'RE STRANGERS, BUT, HONESTLY, YOUR TWO FRIENDS HERE SCARE THE HELL OUT OF THE PARENTS, AND IT IS THEIR CALL.
I REALIZE OUR APPEARANCE MAY CAUSE ALARM, BUT I ASSURE YOU...
...TO WARD ONE, DOCTOR JUNGEN TO WARD ONE...

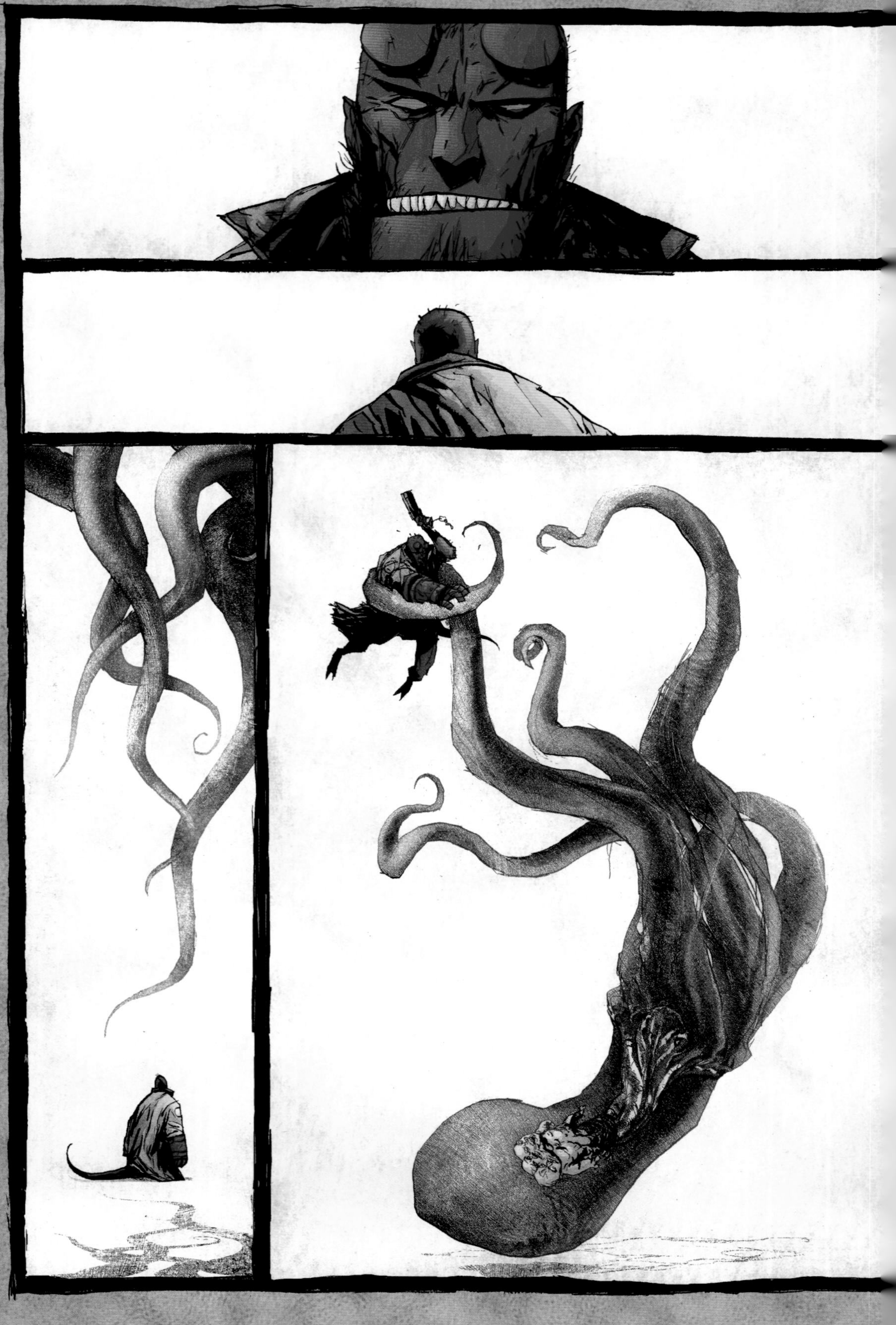

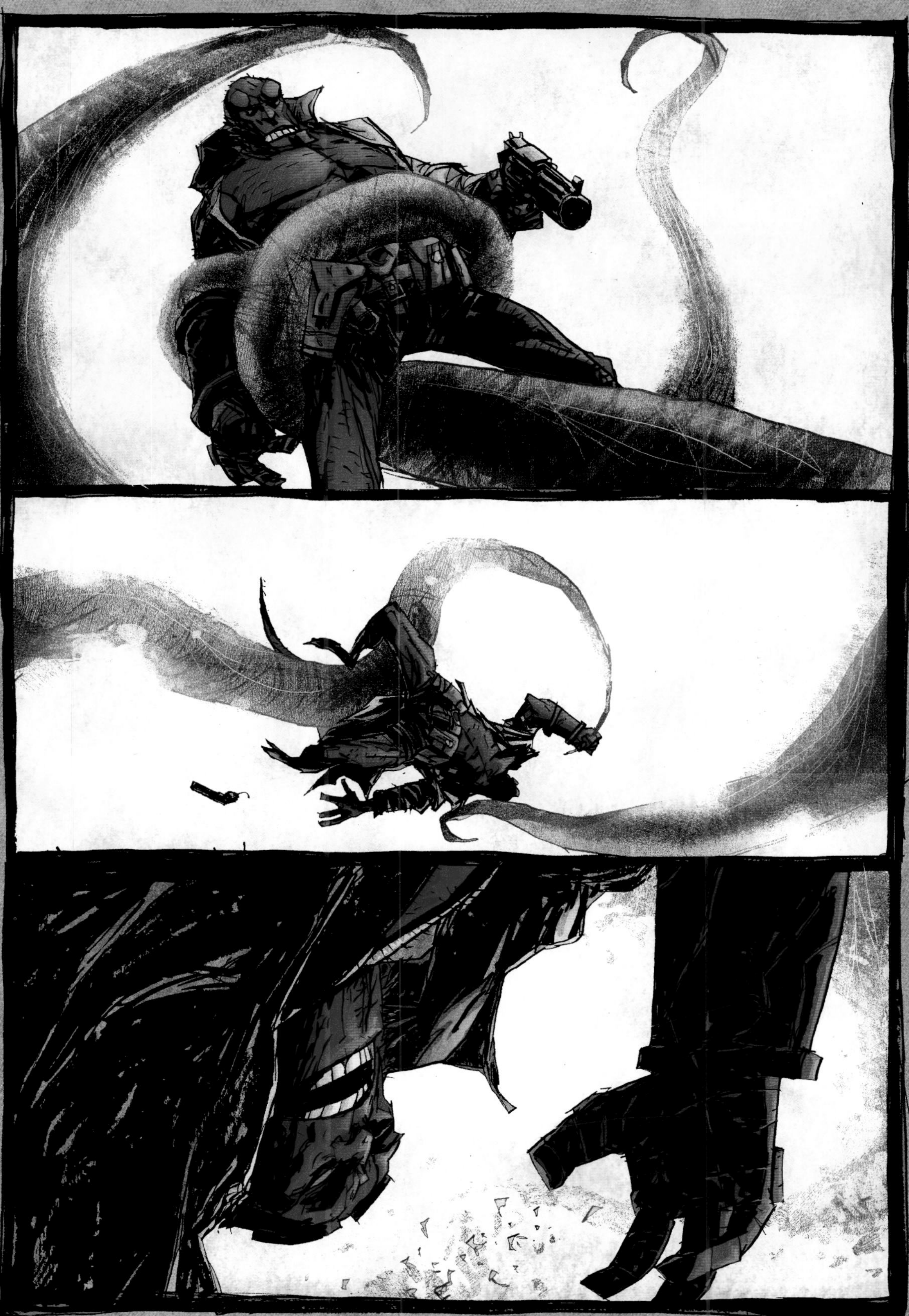

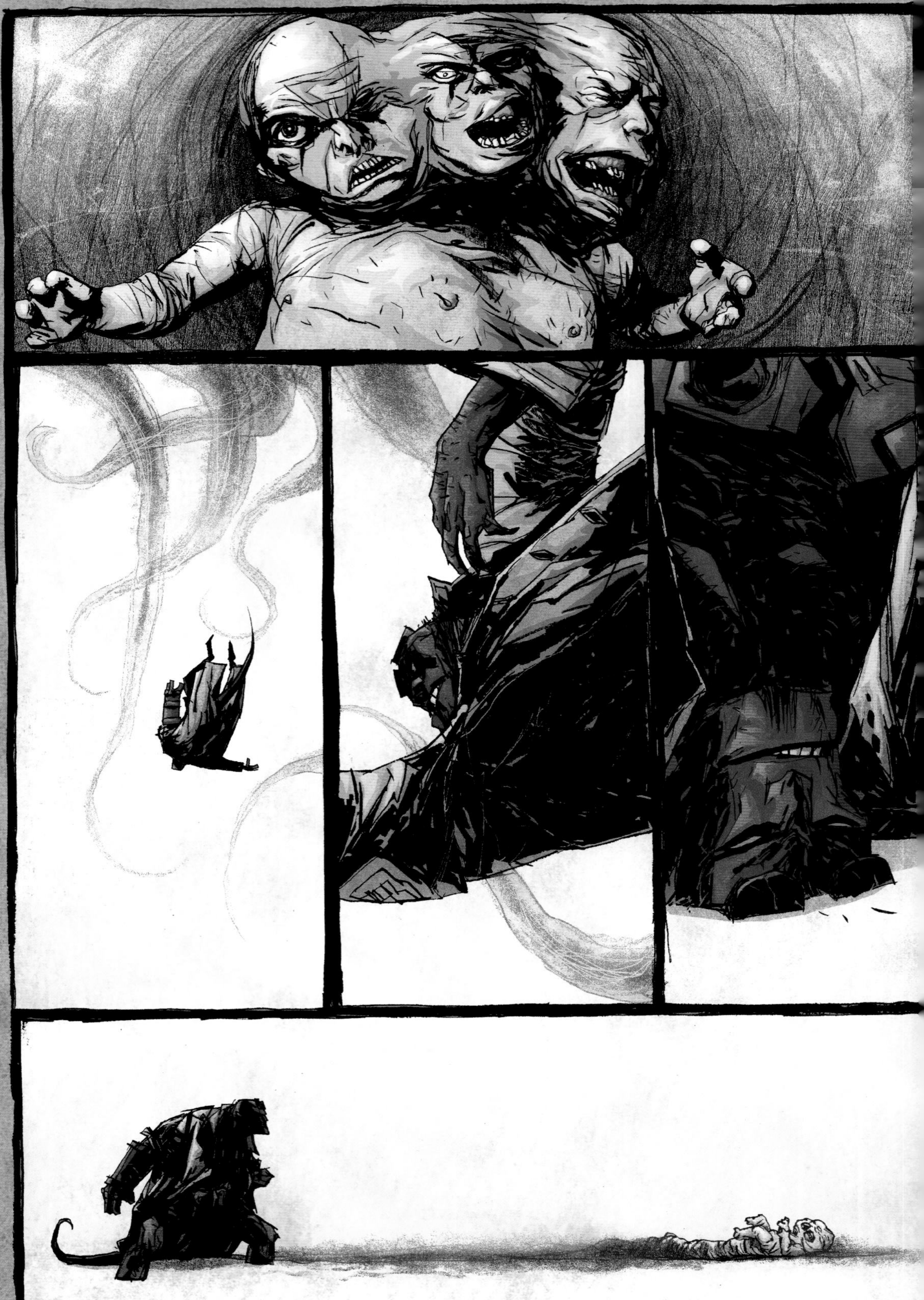

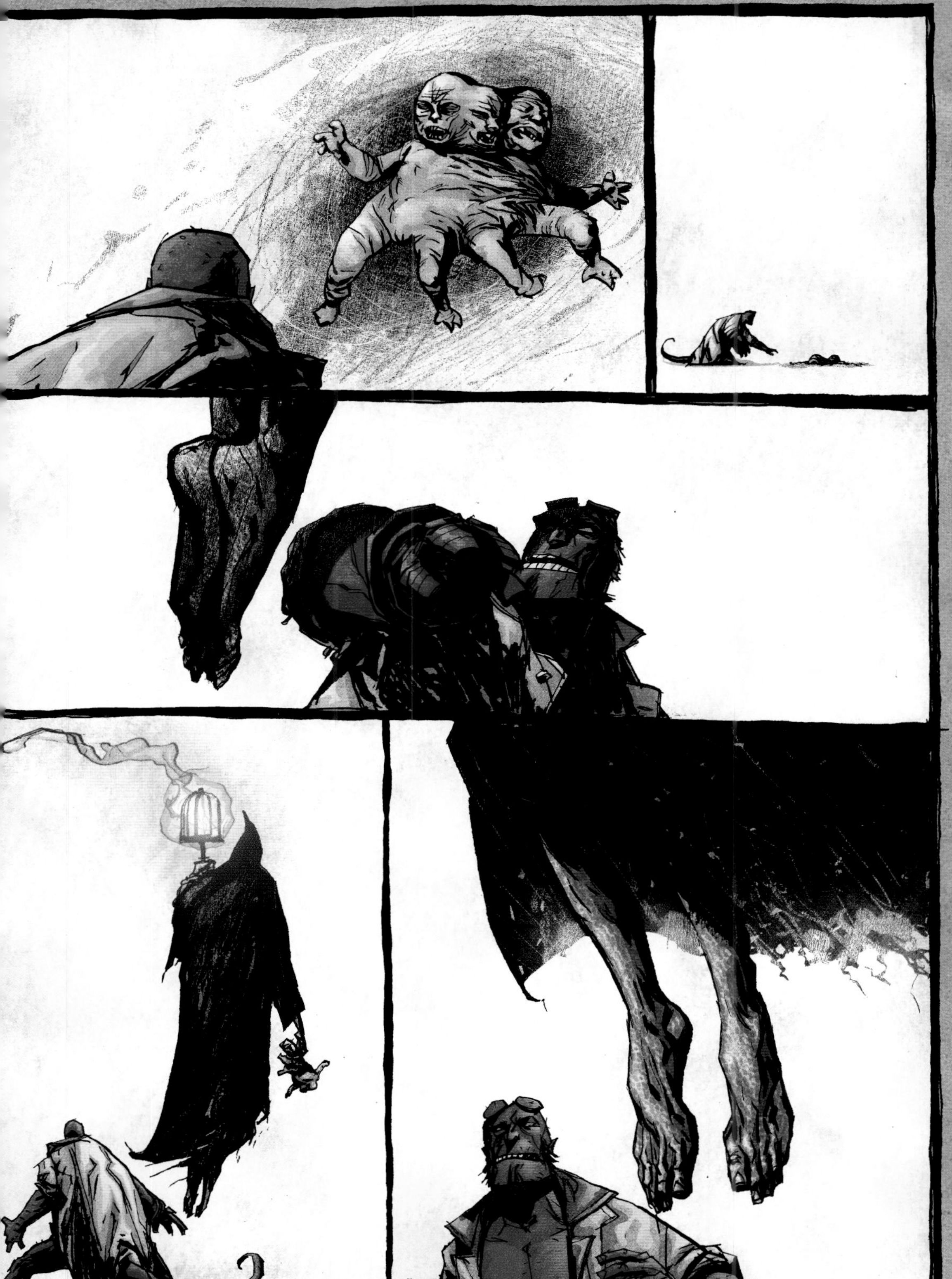

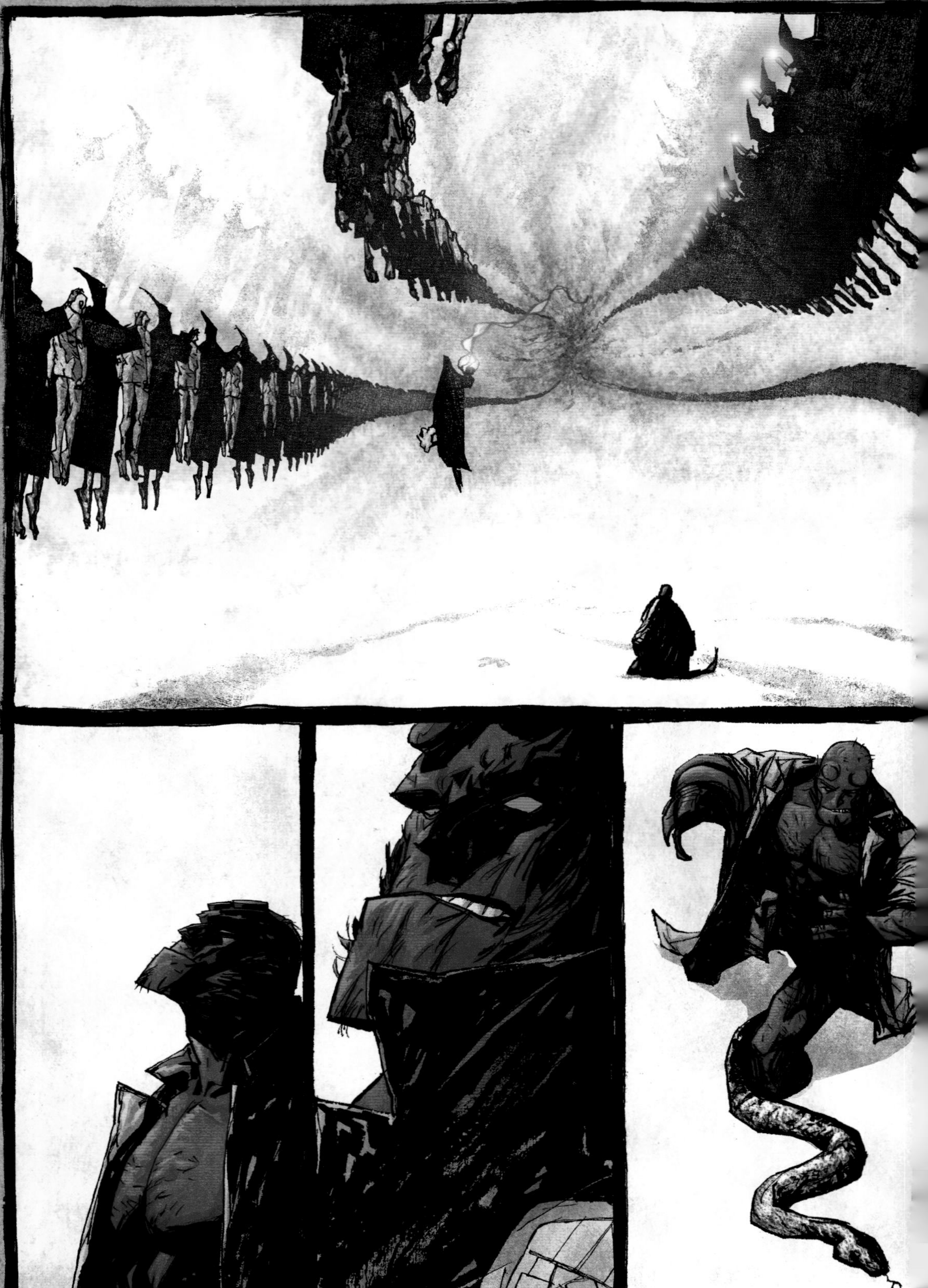

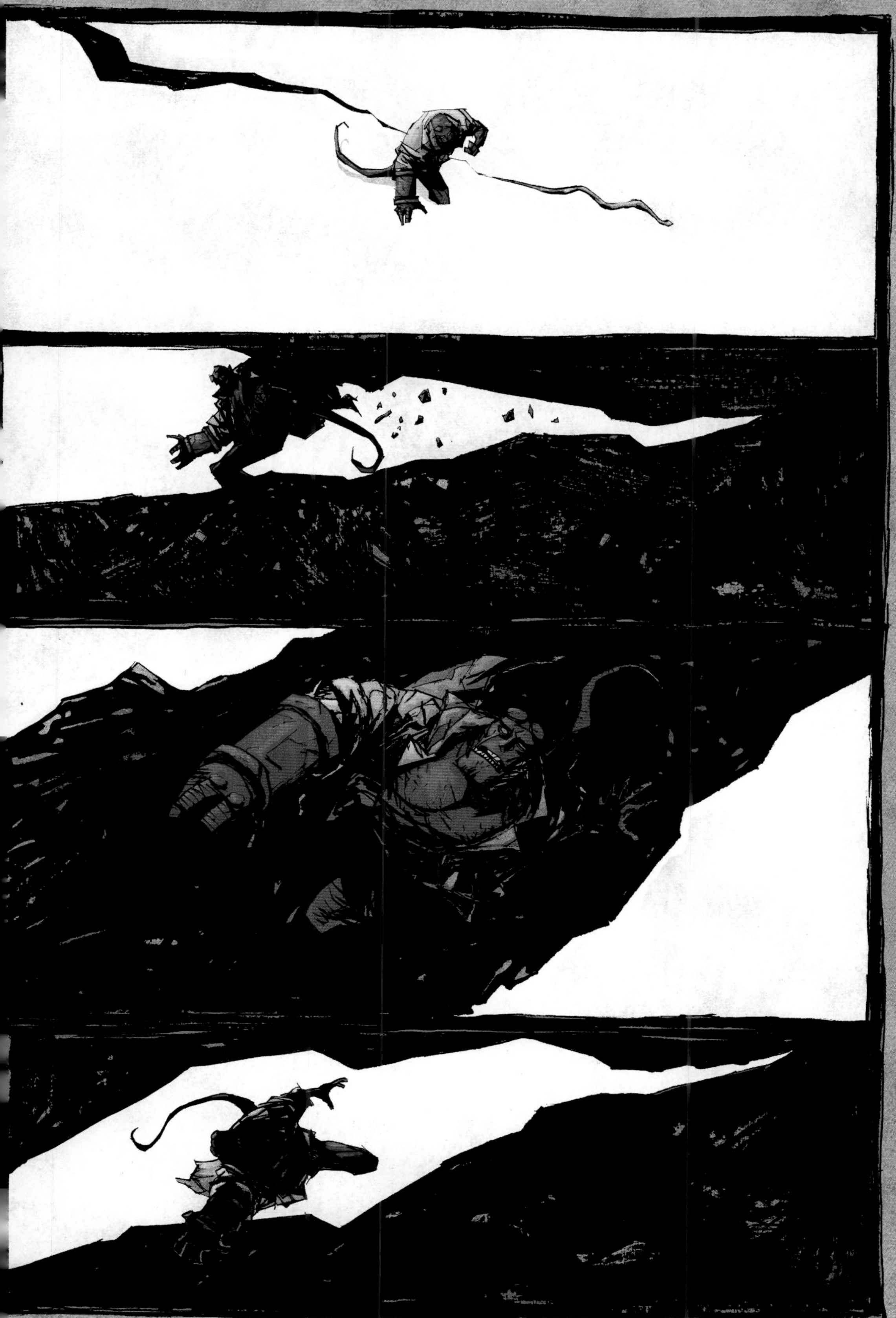

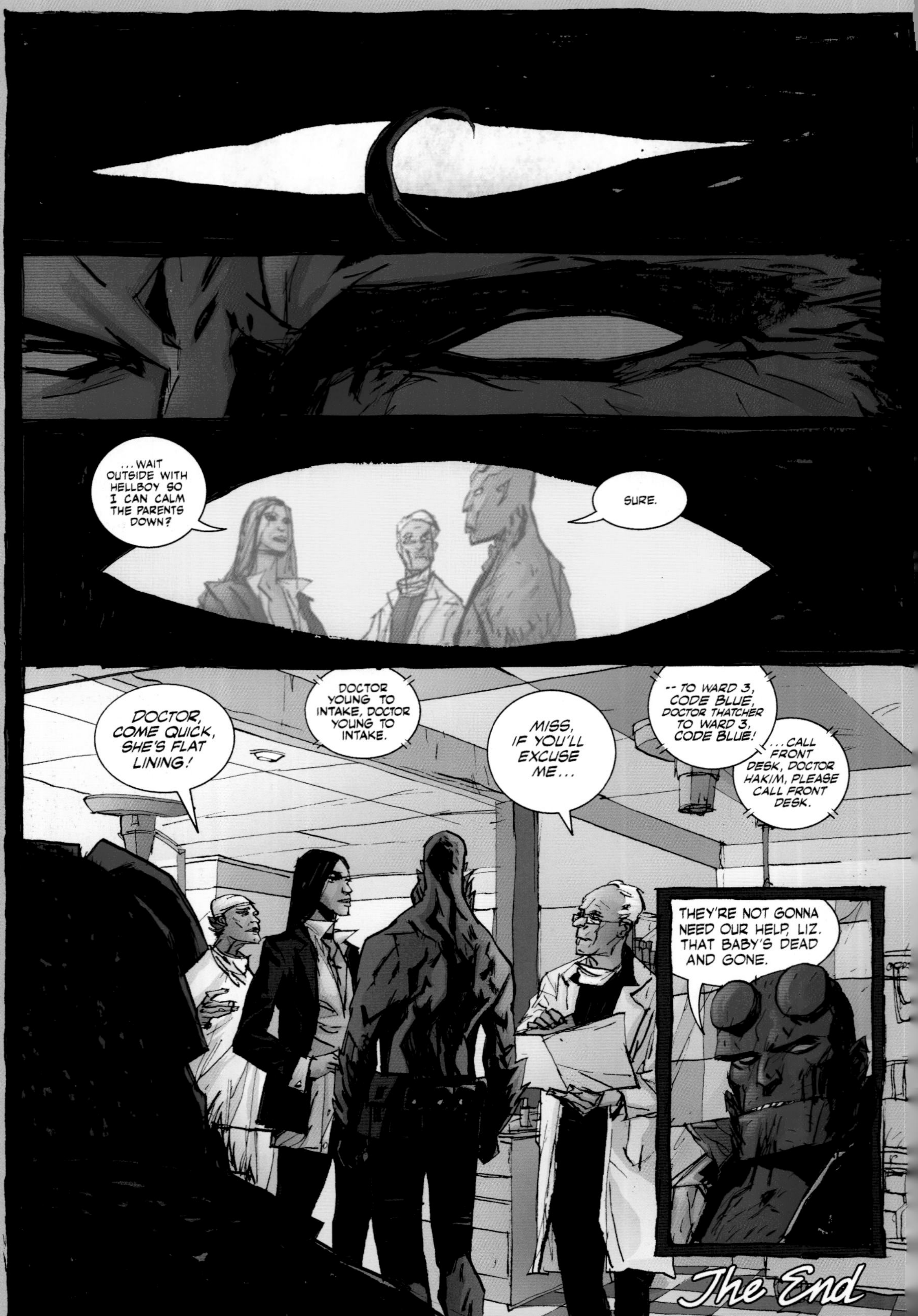

...WAIT OUTSIDE WITH HELLBOY SO I CAN CALM THE PARENTS DOWN?
SURE.
DOCTOR, COME QUICK, SHE'S FLAT LINING!
DOCTOR YOUNG TO INTAKE, DOCTOR YOUNG TO INTAKE.
MISS, IF YOU'LL EXCUSE ME...
-- TO WARD 3, CODE BLUE, DOCTOR THATCHER TO WARD 3, CODE BLUE!
...CALL FRONT DESK, DOCTOR HAKIM, PLEASE CALL FRONT DESK.
THEY'RE NOT GONNA NEED OUR HELP, LIZ. THAT BABY'S DEAD AND GONE.
The End

Party Pooper

andi '02

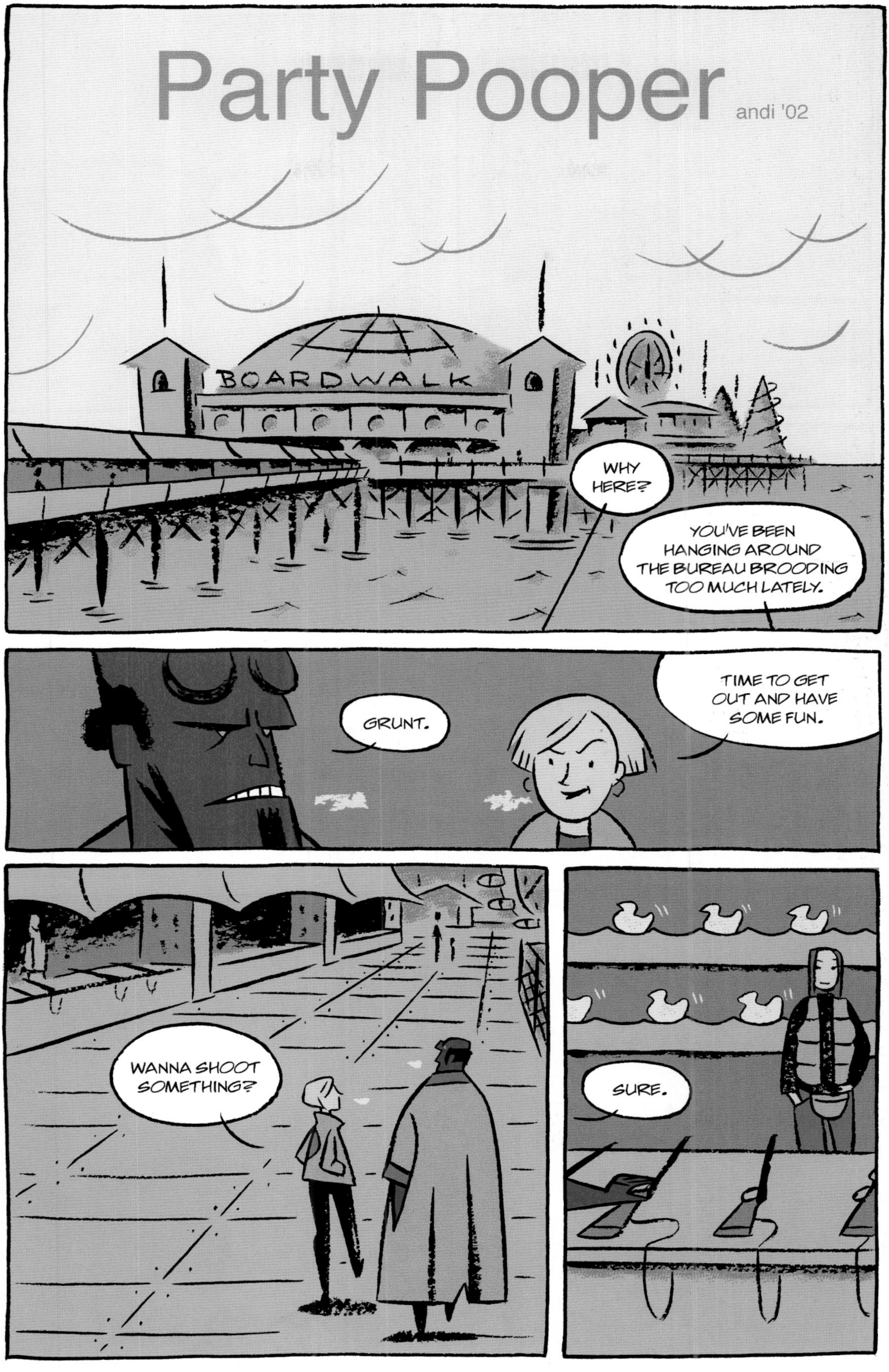
BOARDWALK
WHY HERE?
YOU'VE BEEN HANGING AROUND THE BUREAU BROODING TOO MUCH LATELY.
GRUNT.
TIME TO GET OUT AND HAVE SOME FUN.
WANNA SHOOT SOMETHING?
SURE.

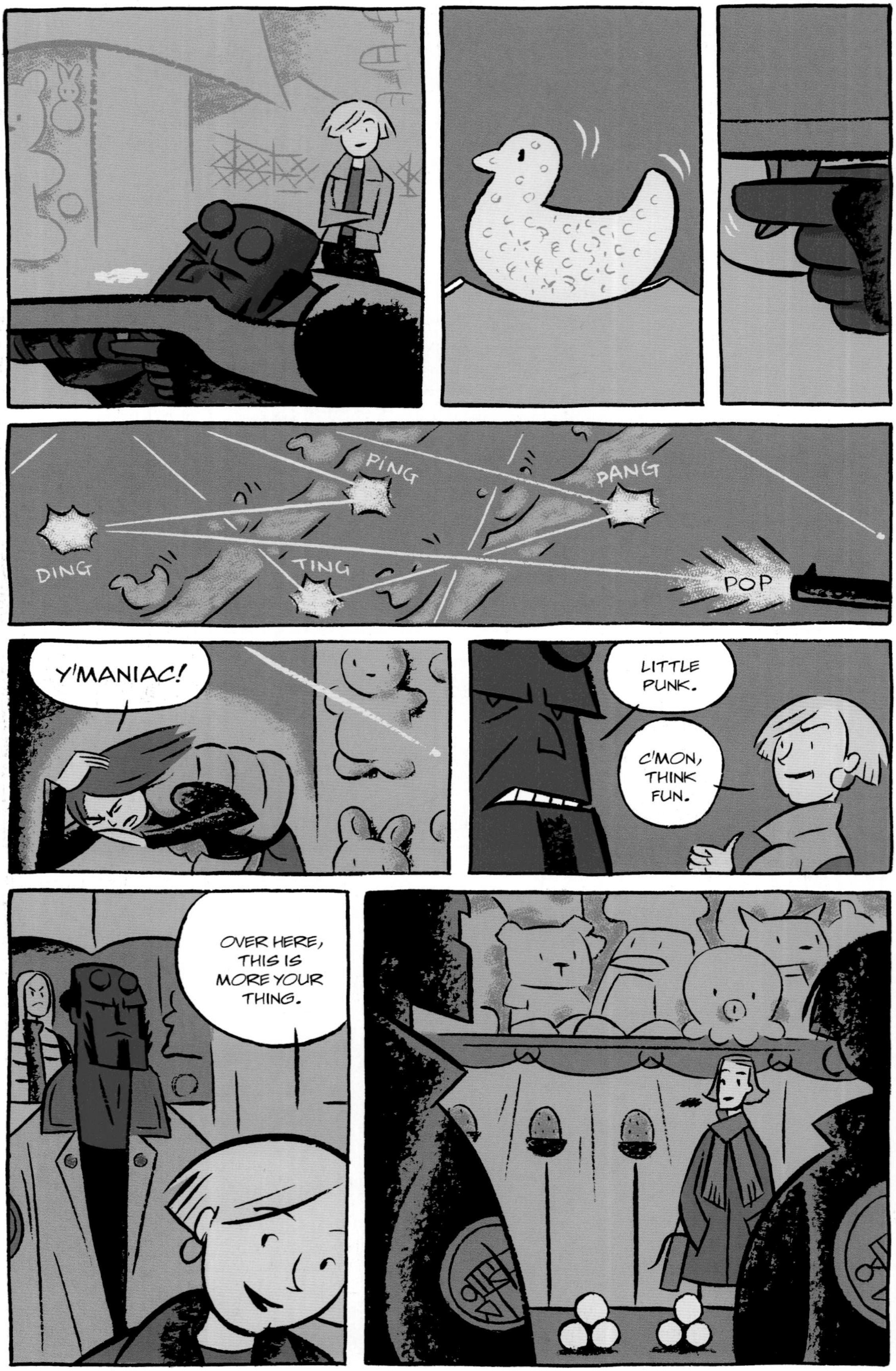
PING
PANG
DING
TING
POP
Y'MANIAC!
LITTLE PUNK.
C'MON, THINK FUN.
OVER HERE, THIS IS MORE YOUR THING.

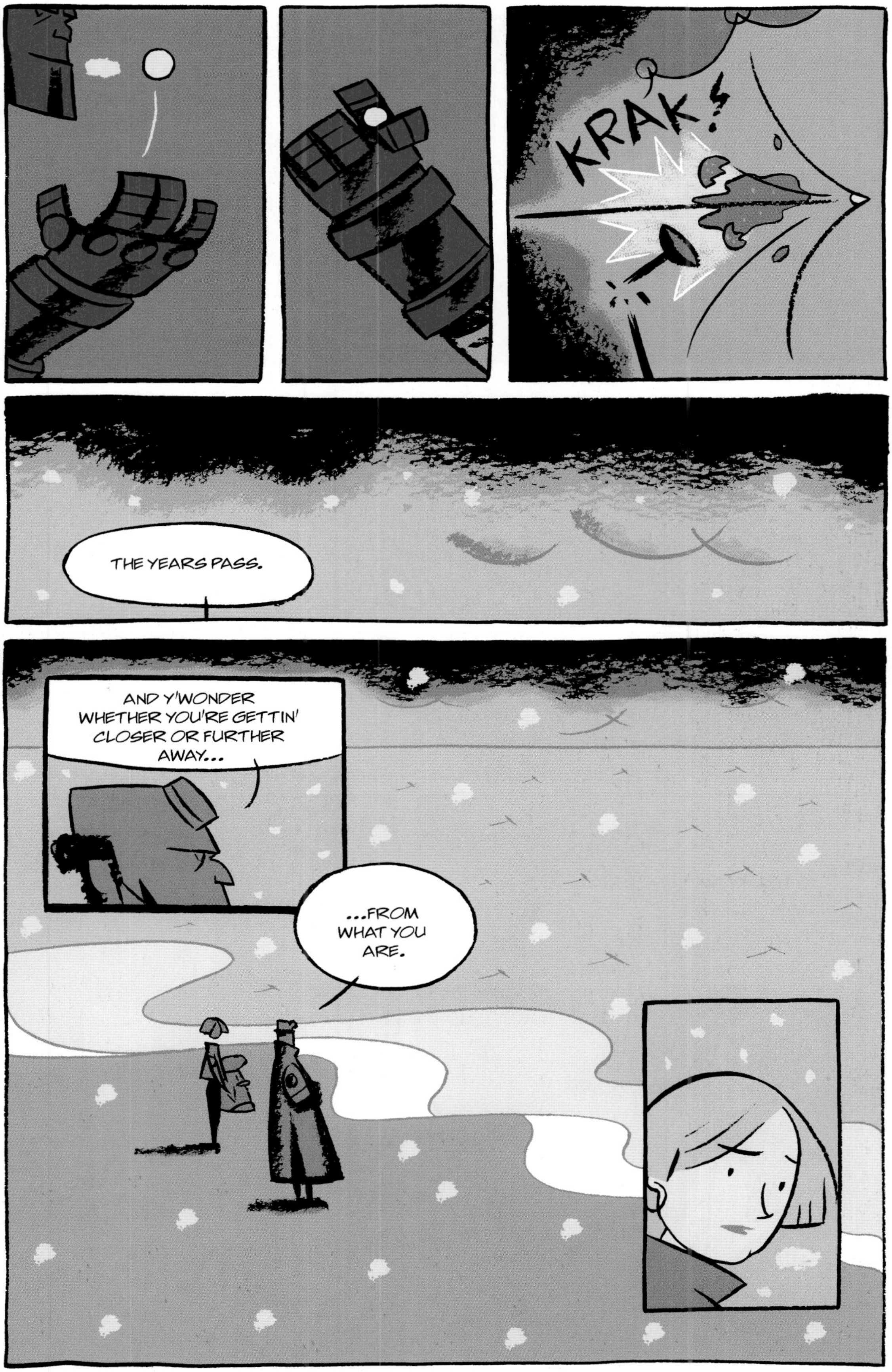
KRAK!
THE YEARS PASS.
AND Y'WONDER WHETHER YOU'RE GETTIN' CLOSER OR FURTHER AWAY...
...FROM WHAT YOU ARE.

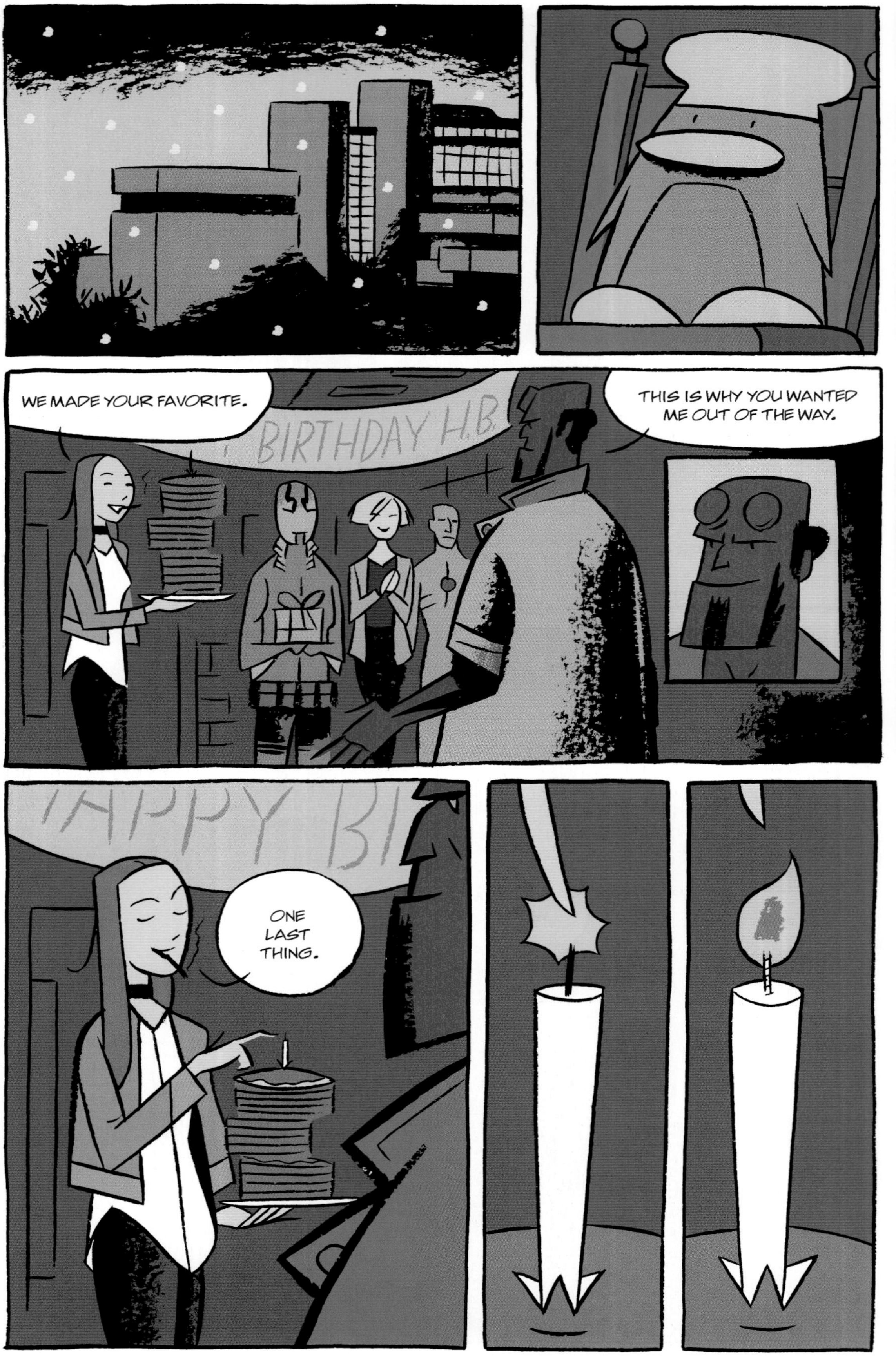
WE MADE YOUR FAVORITE.
BIRTHDAY H.B.
THIS IS WHY YOU WANTED ME OUT OF THE WAY.
APPY BI
ONE LAST THING.

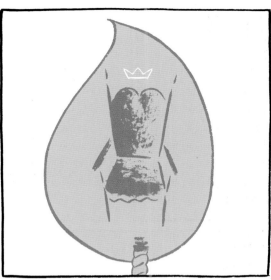

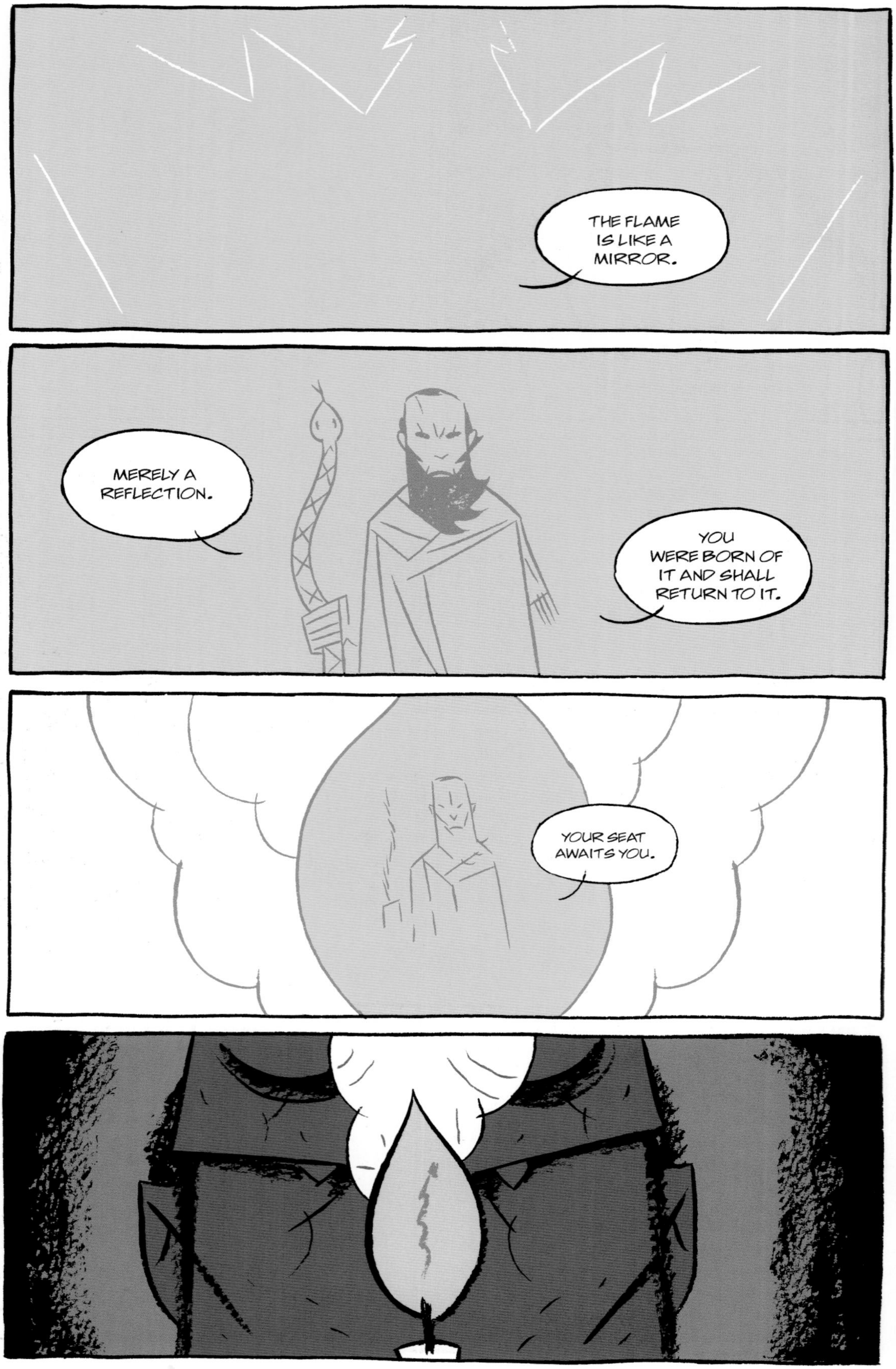
THE FLAME IS LIKE A MIRROR.
MERELY A REFLECTION.
YOU WERE BORN OF IT AND SHALL RETURN TO IT.
YOUR SEAT AWAITS YOU.

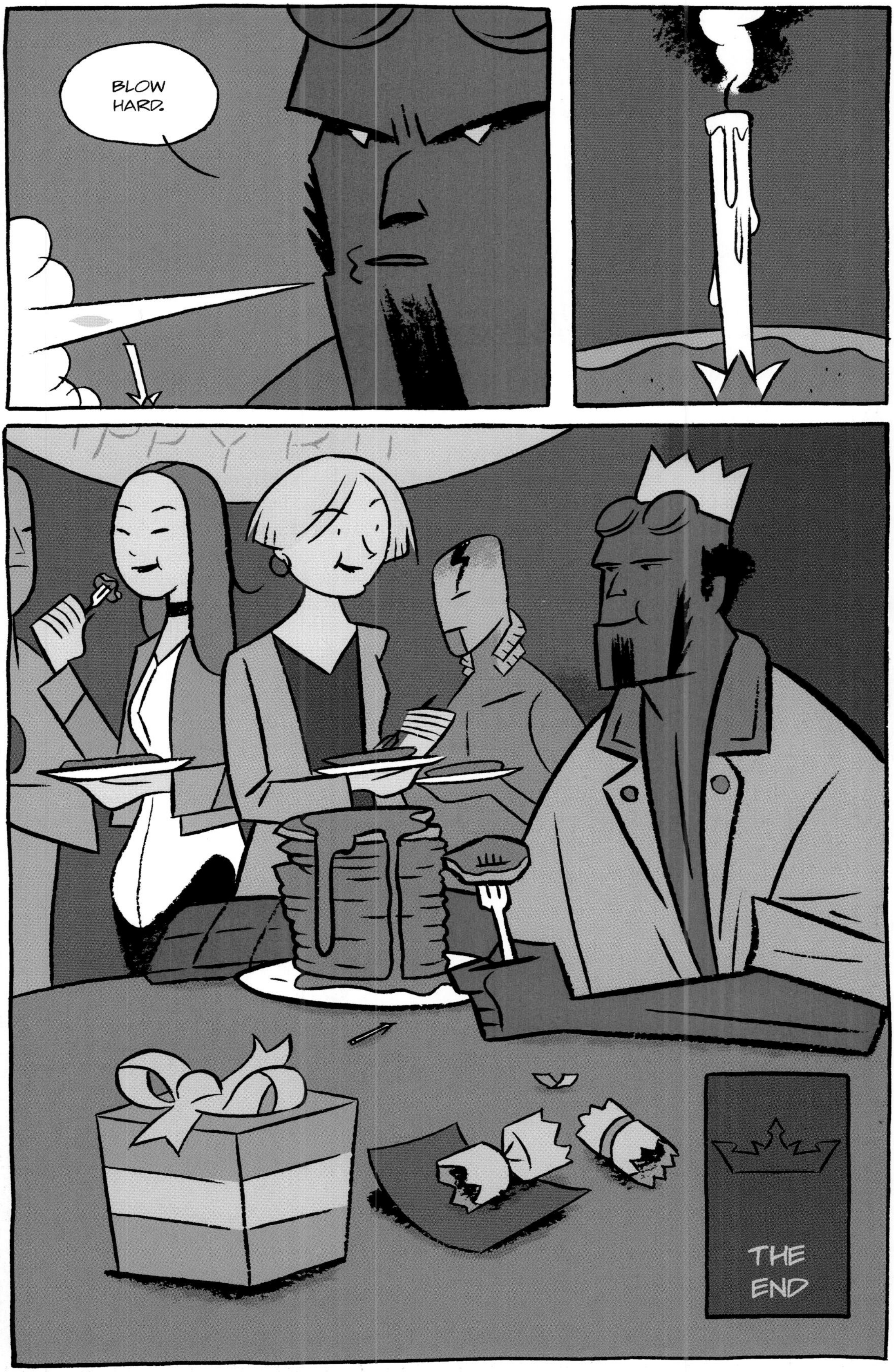
BLOW HARD.
THE END

Afterword

TOWARD THE END OF 1992, having spent almost ten years drawing other peoples' comic-book characters, I decided to create one of my own. I didn't try to come up with something particularly commercial—I wouldn't know how to do that even now. No, my main concern was taking all the stuff I like—spooky old buildings, creepy frog people, ghosts, statues, skeletons, mad scientists, Jack Kirby monsters, and giant Lovecraftian horrors—and cramming them into one thing. That's *Hellboy*. I never thought it would go beyond one miniseries . . . and here we are, more than ten years later. Guess I did something right.

That so many of my fellow cartoonists have been wanting to draw and/or write this funny little character of mine—that's the nicest compliment there is.

When my long-suffering editor Scott Allie and I began seriously discussing this project, I gave him just one suggestion—get people who know what they're doing and let them do what they do. Simple as that. I didn't want to be involved, I just wanted to sit back and enjoy the results. And I have.

I want to thank everyone who contributed to *Weird Tales, Volume I*, and I can't wait for *Volume II.*

There you go.

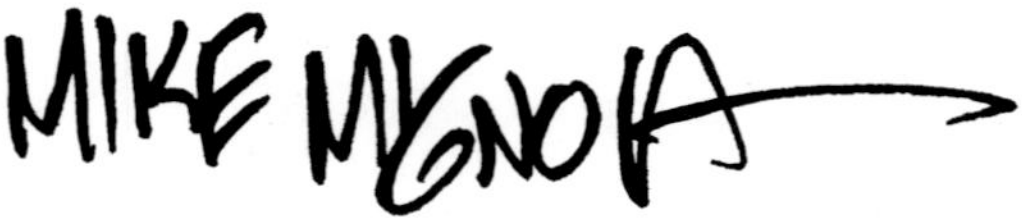

Mike Mignola
New York City

HELLBOY™

GALLERY

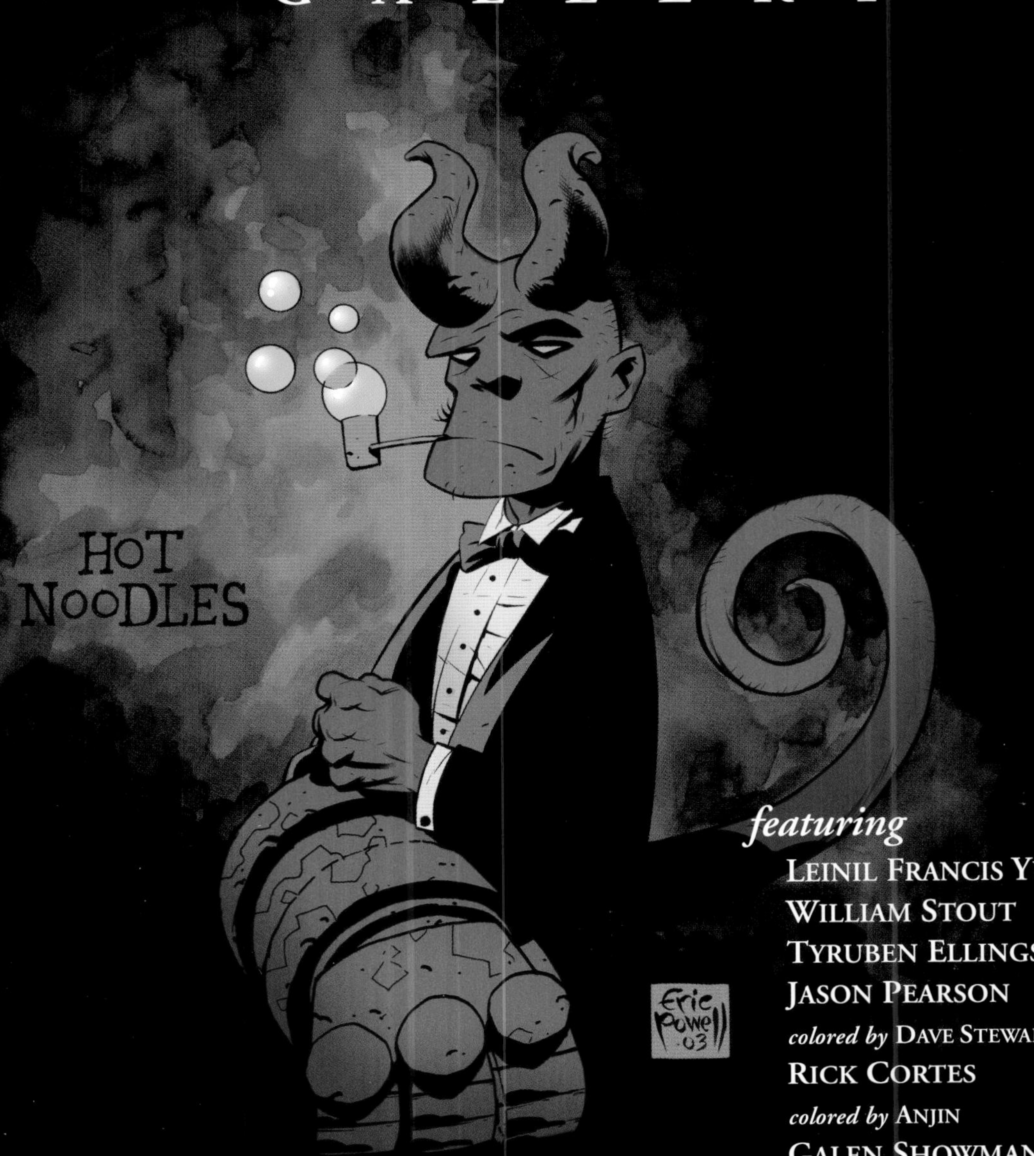
HOT NOODLES
Eric Powell 03

featuring

LEINIL FRANCIS YU

WILLIAM STOUT

TYRUBEN ELLINGSON

JASON PEARSON

colored by DAVE STEWART

RICK CORTES

colored by ANJIN

GALEN SHOWMAN

colored by MICHELLE MADSEN

and

ALEX MALEEV

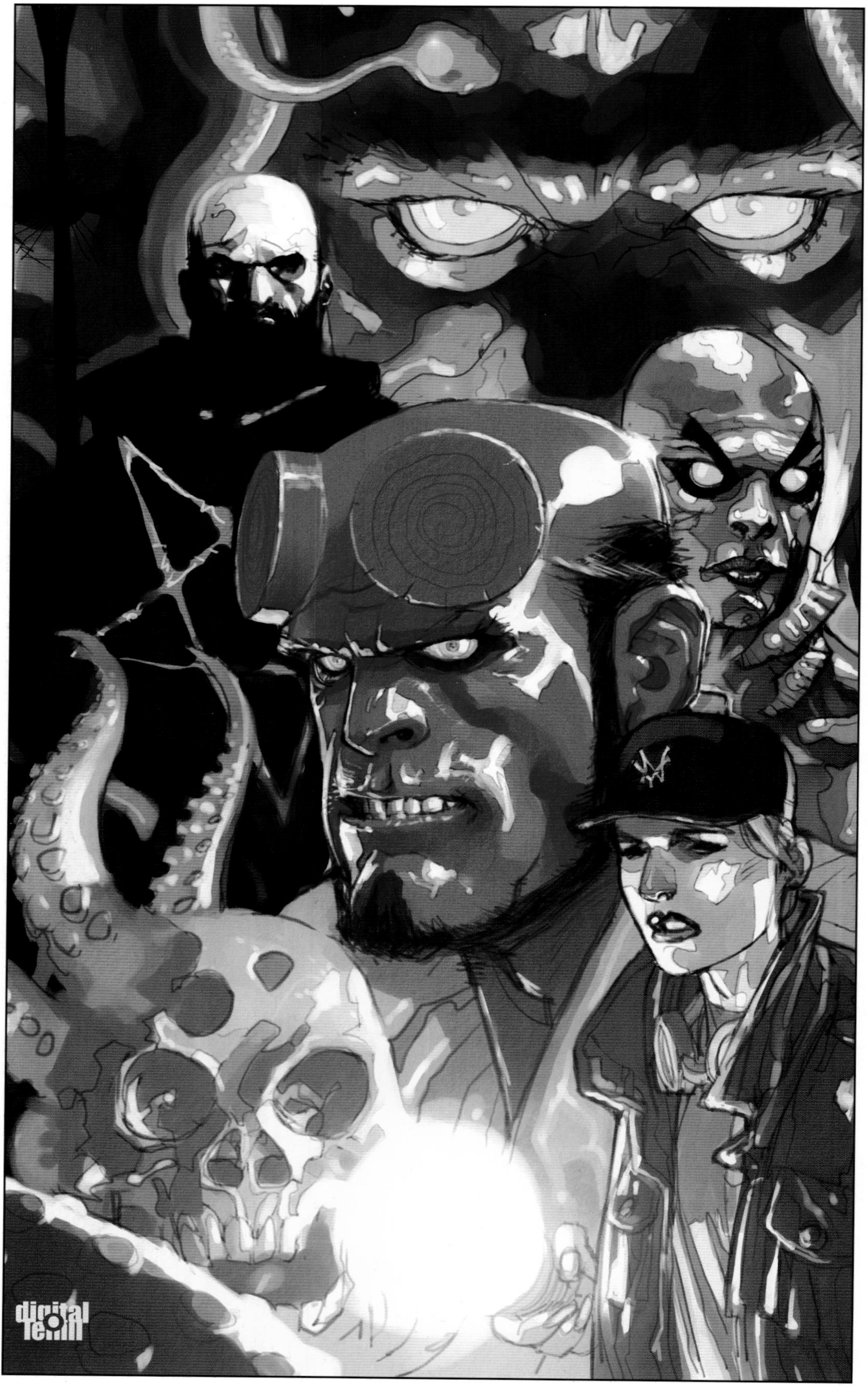

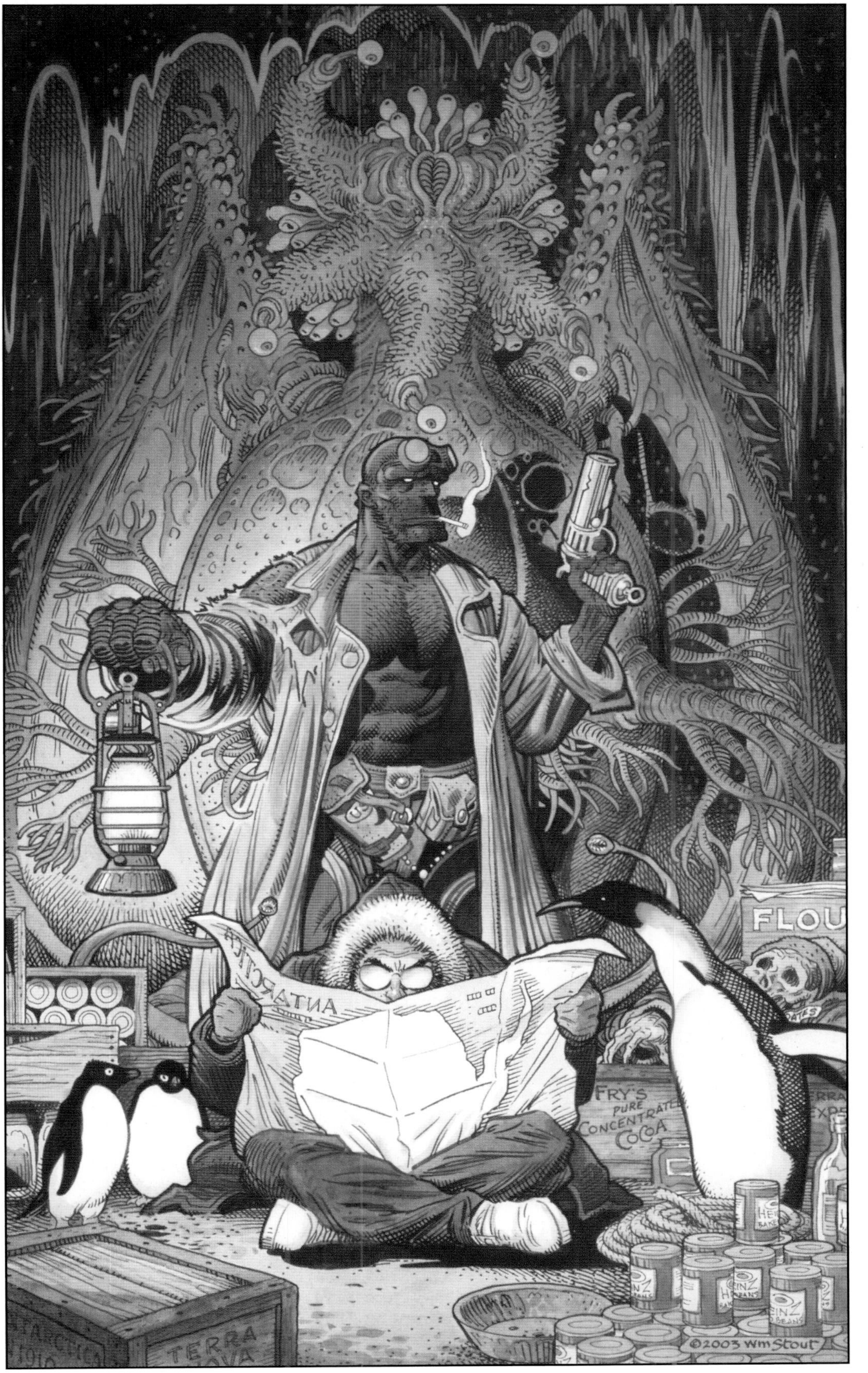
FLOU
FRY'S
PURE
CONCENTRATE
COCOA
TERRA
NOVA
©2003 Wm Stout

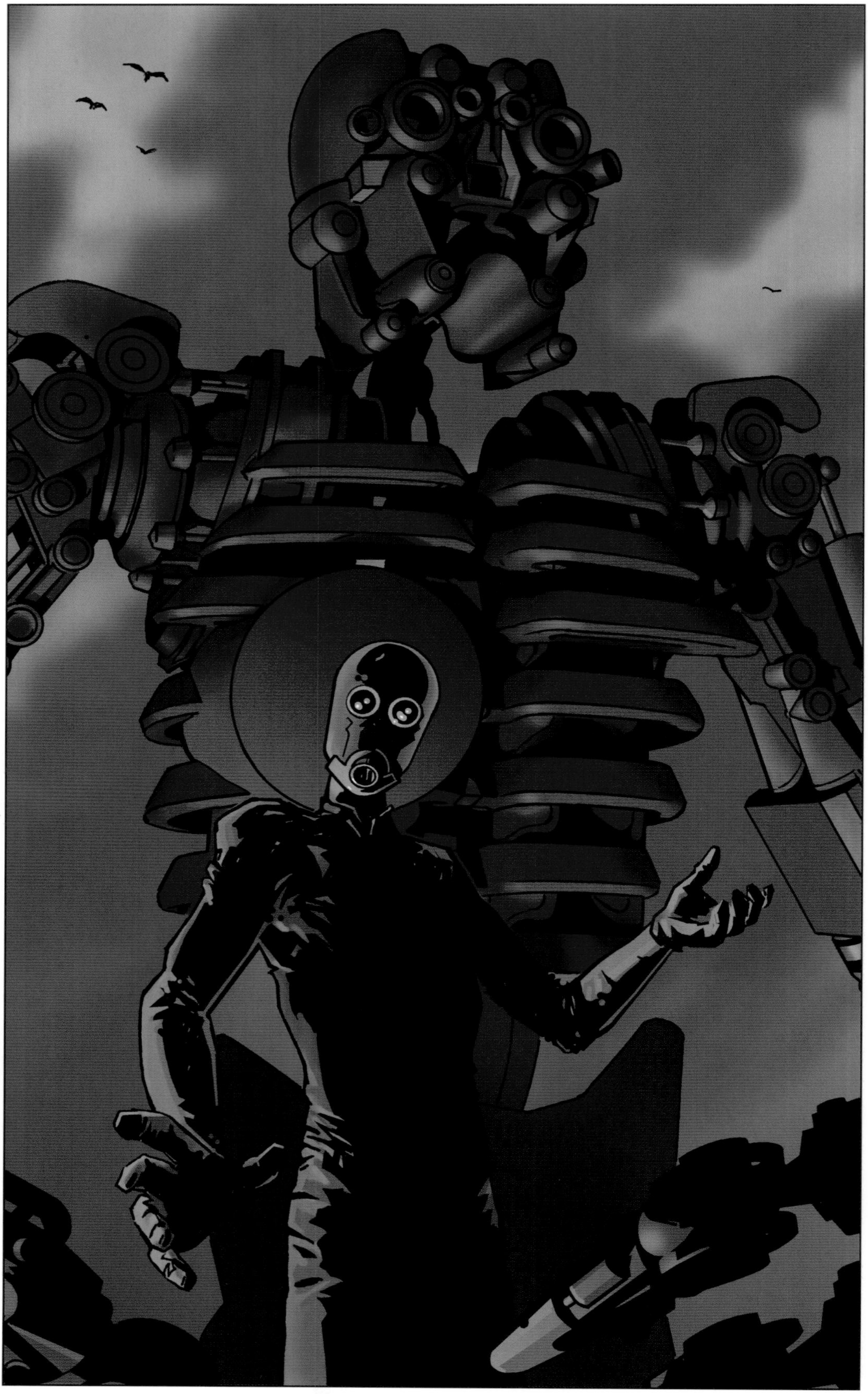

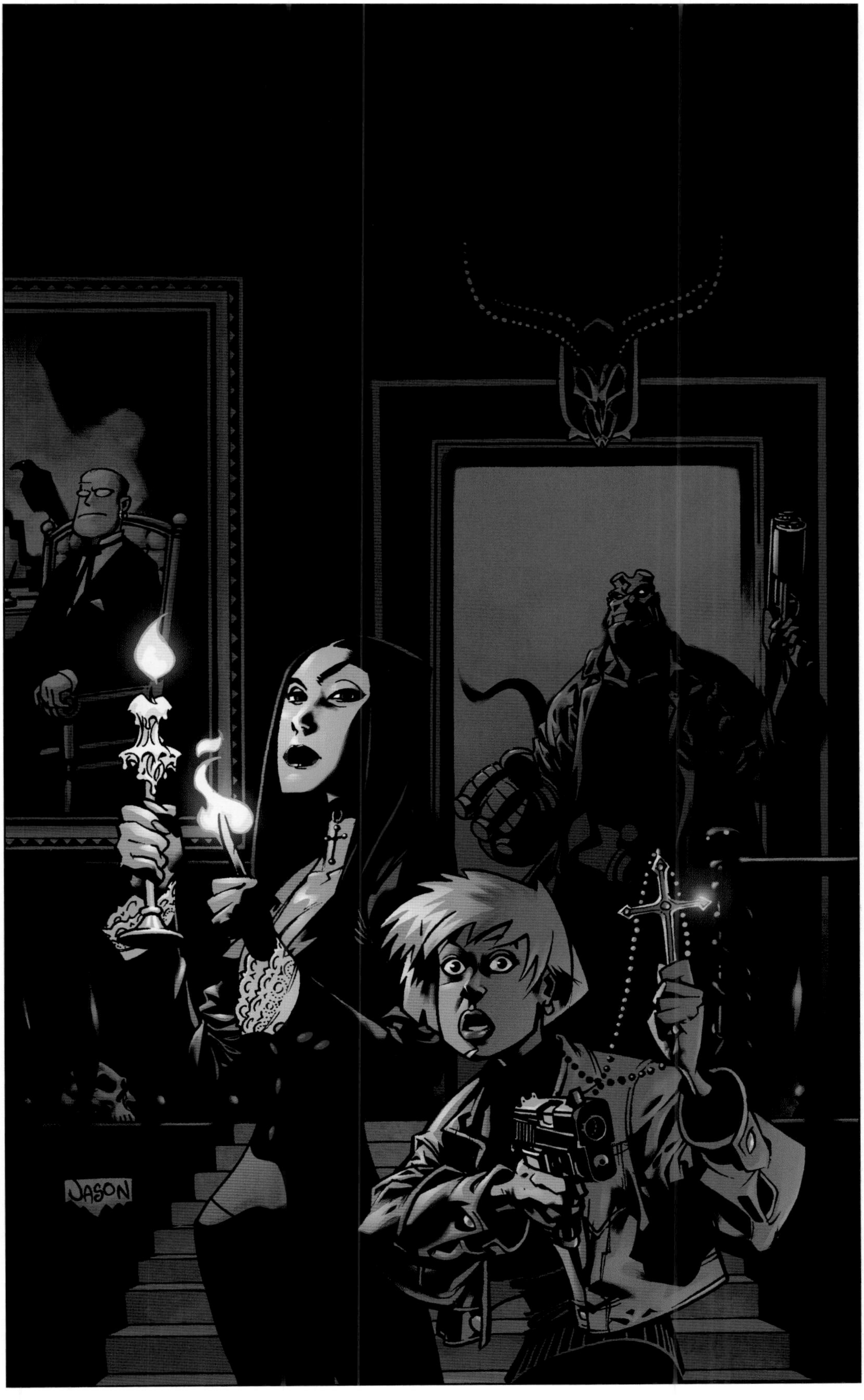
JASON

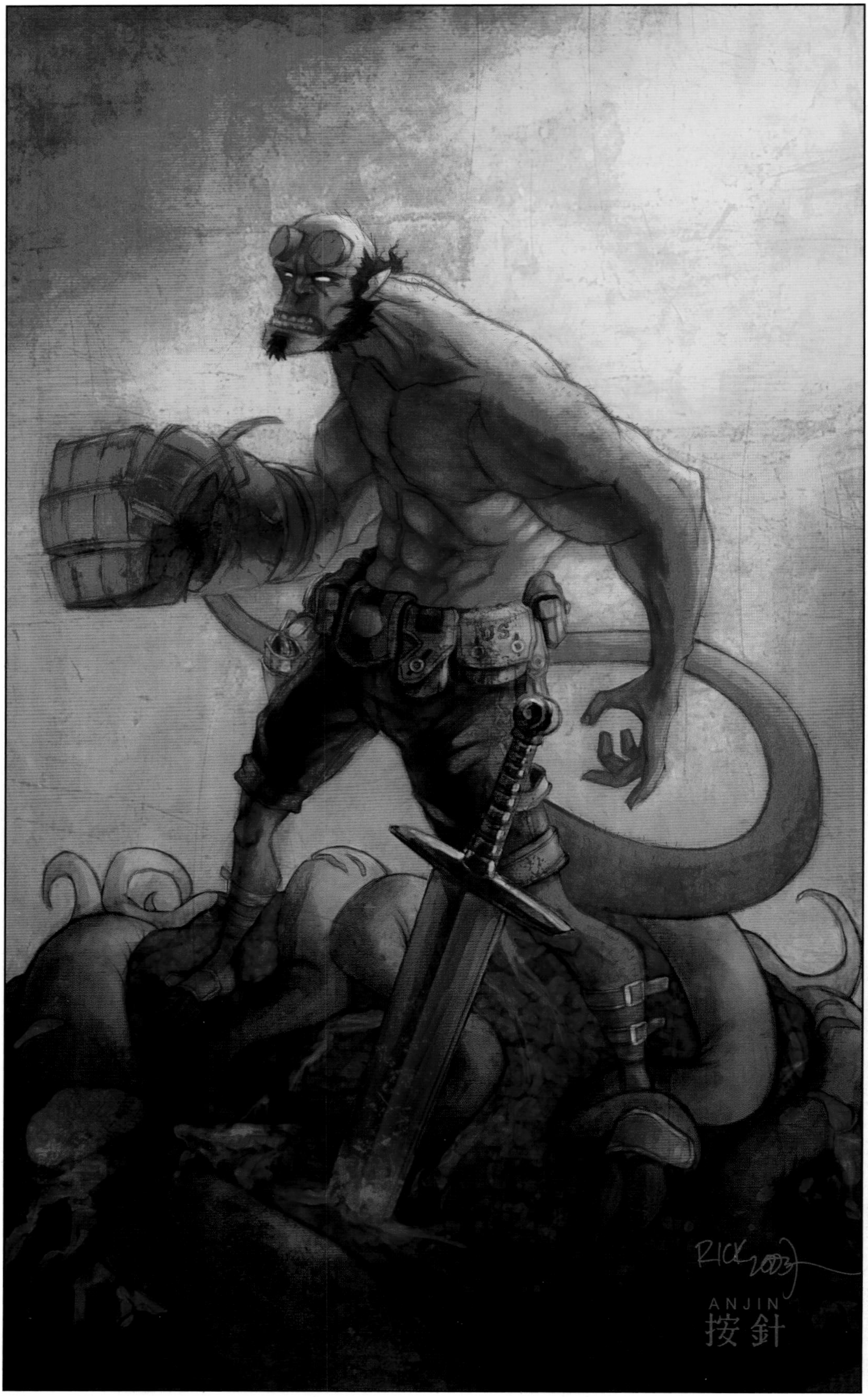
RICK 2003
ANJIN
按針

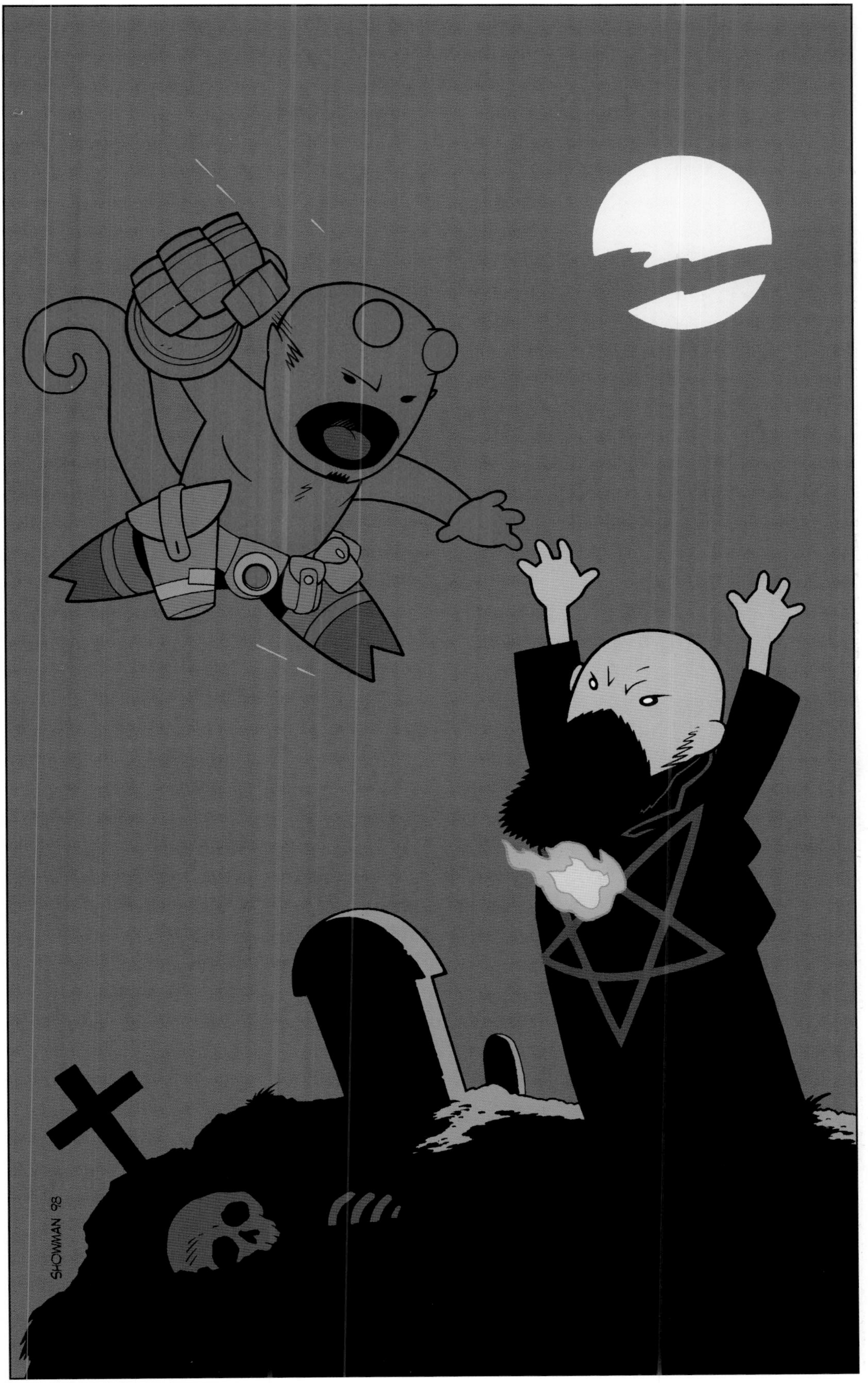

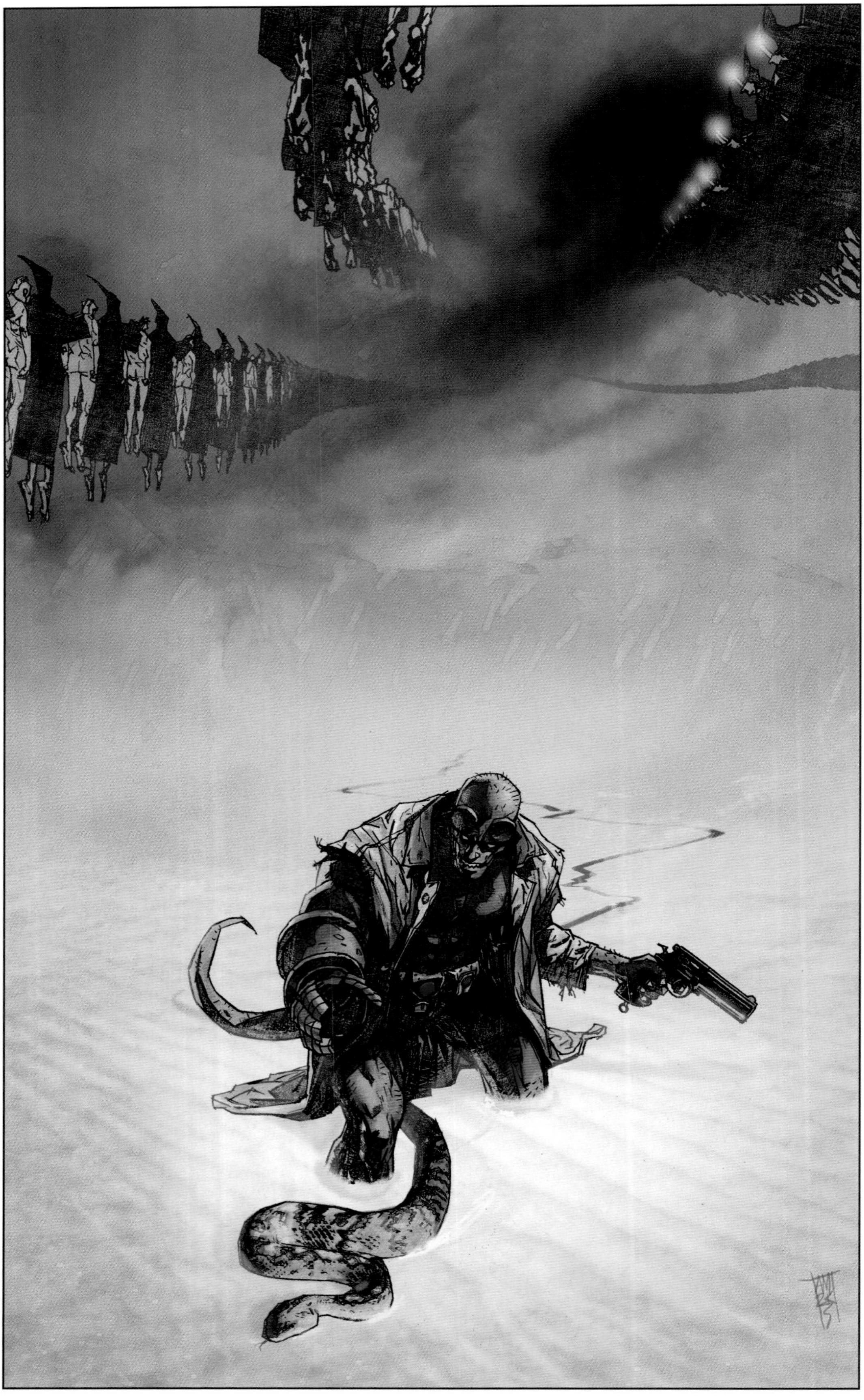

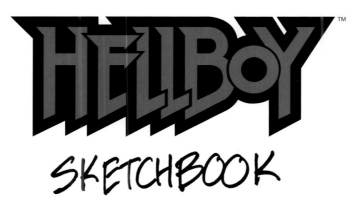

SKETCHBOOK

The following pages feature a sampling of warm-up and design art from some of the artists featured in Volume I.

This page,
Alex Maleev.

115

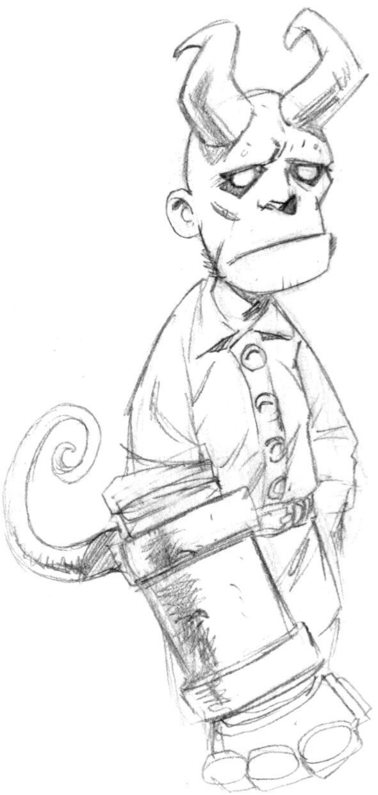

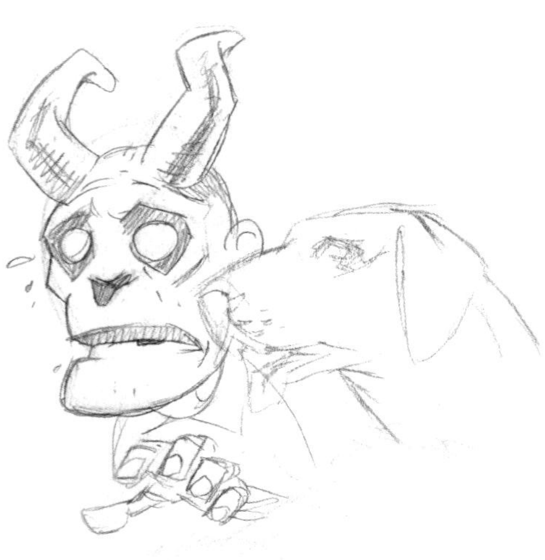

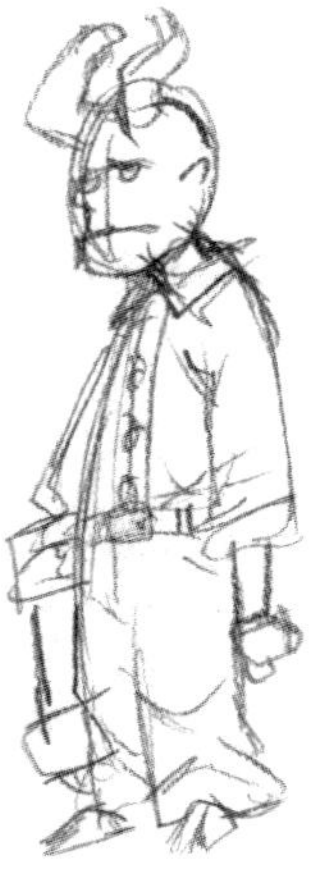

Eric Powell.

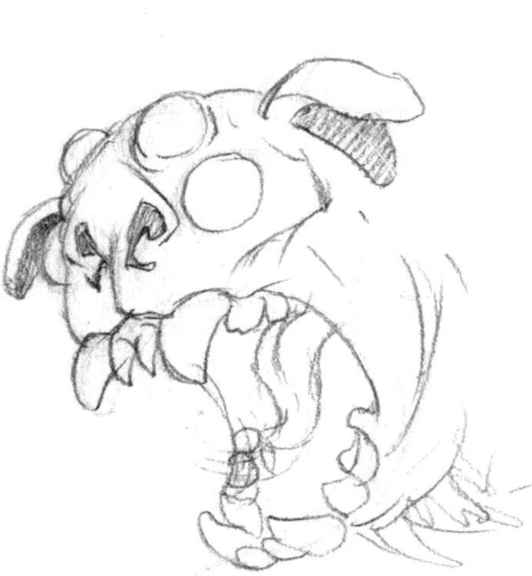

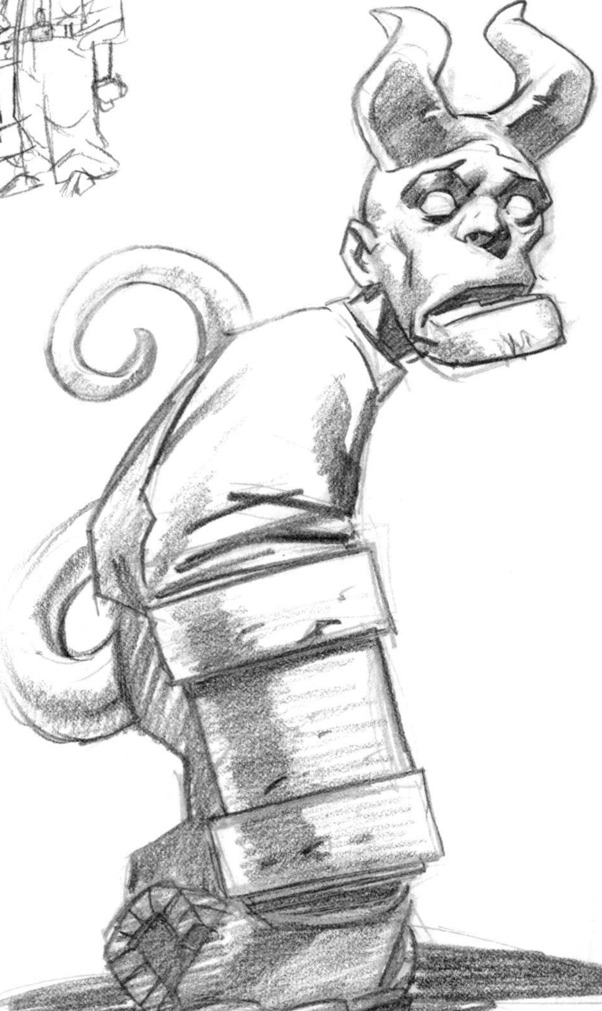

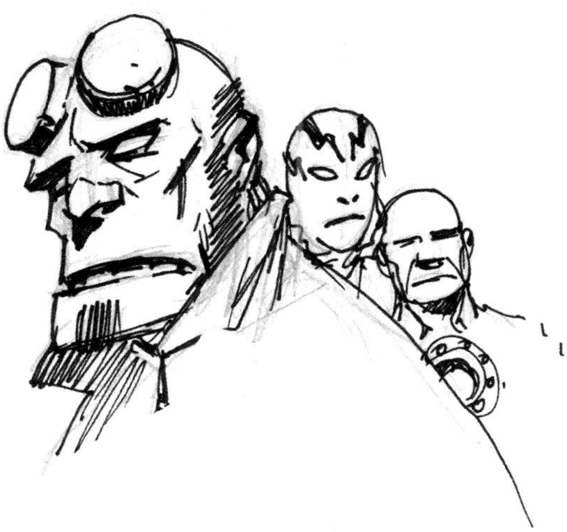

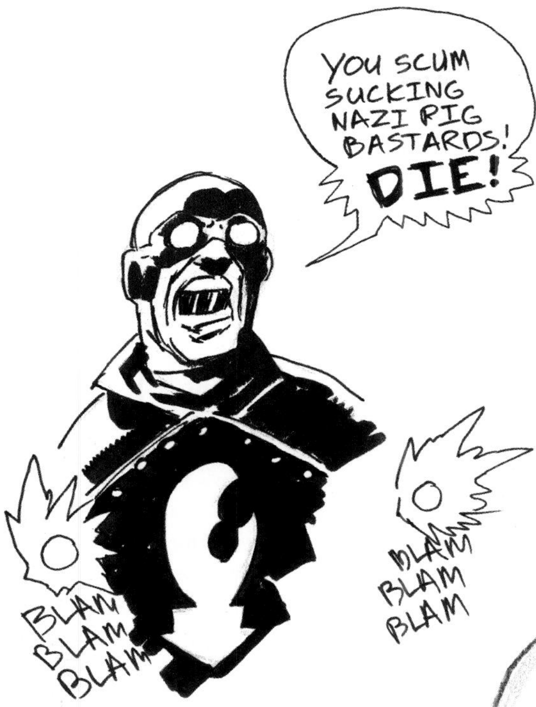
YOU SCUM SUCKING NAZI PIG BASTARDS! DIE!
BLAM BLAM BLAM
BLAM BLAM BLAM

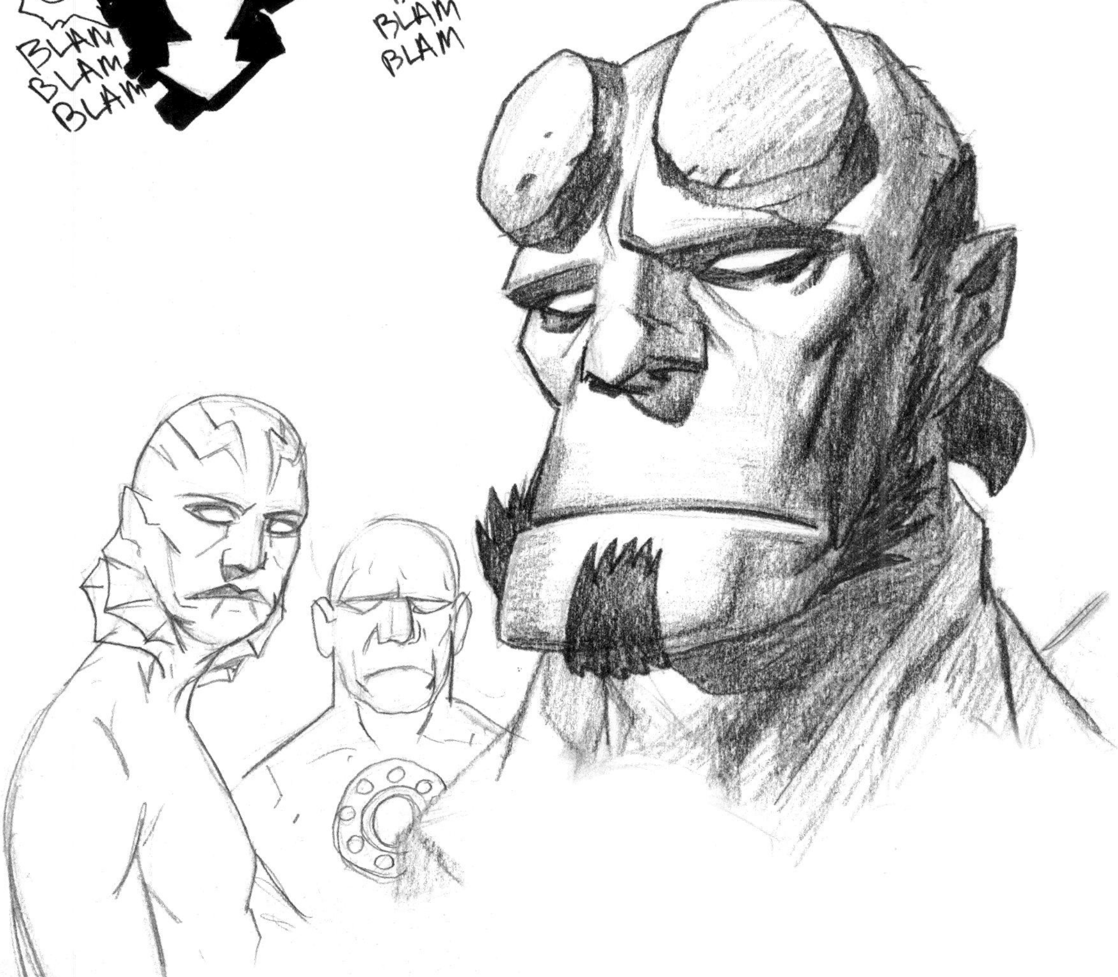

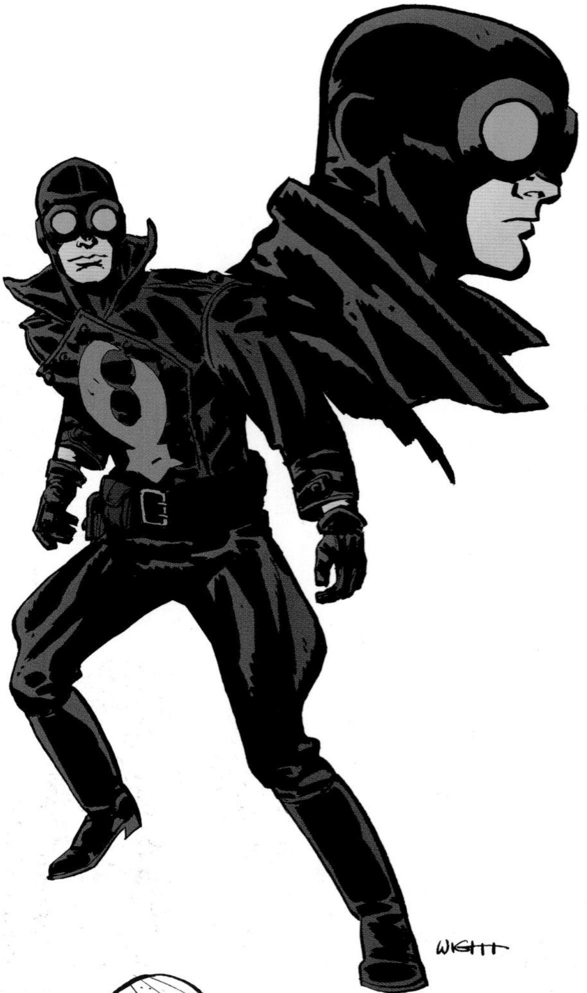
WIGHT

Animation art-director Eric Wight wanted to do a Lobster Johnson story, and got our attention with the facing page. After he drew the Kate Corrigan story in this volume with Mark Ricketts, Wight's Lobster Johnson sample earned him a job working on Pulitzer Prize-winning author Michael Chabon's *The Escapist.*

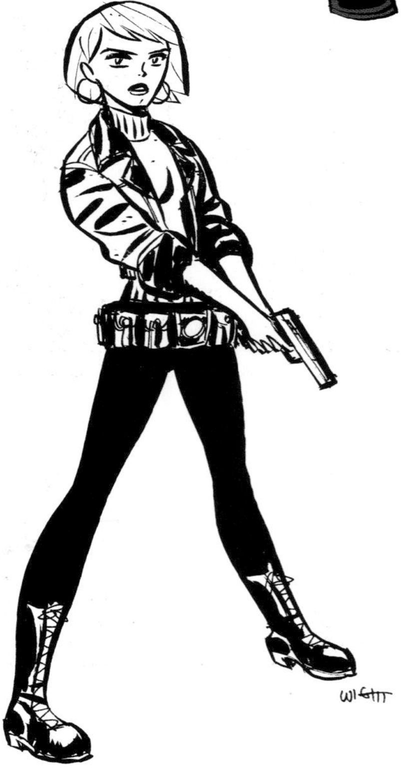
WIGHT

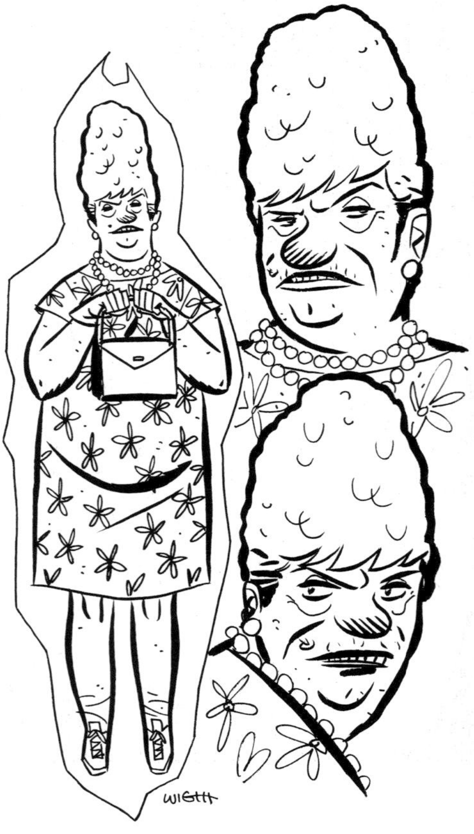
WIGHT

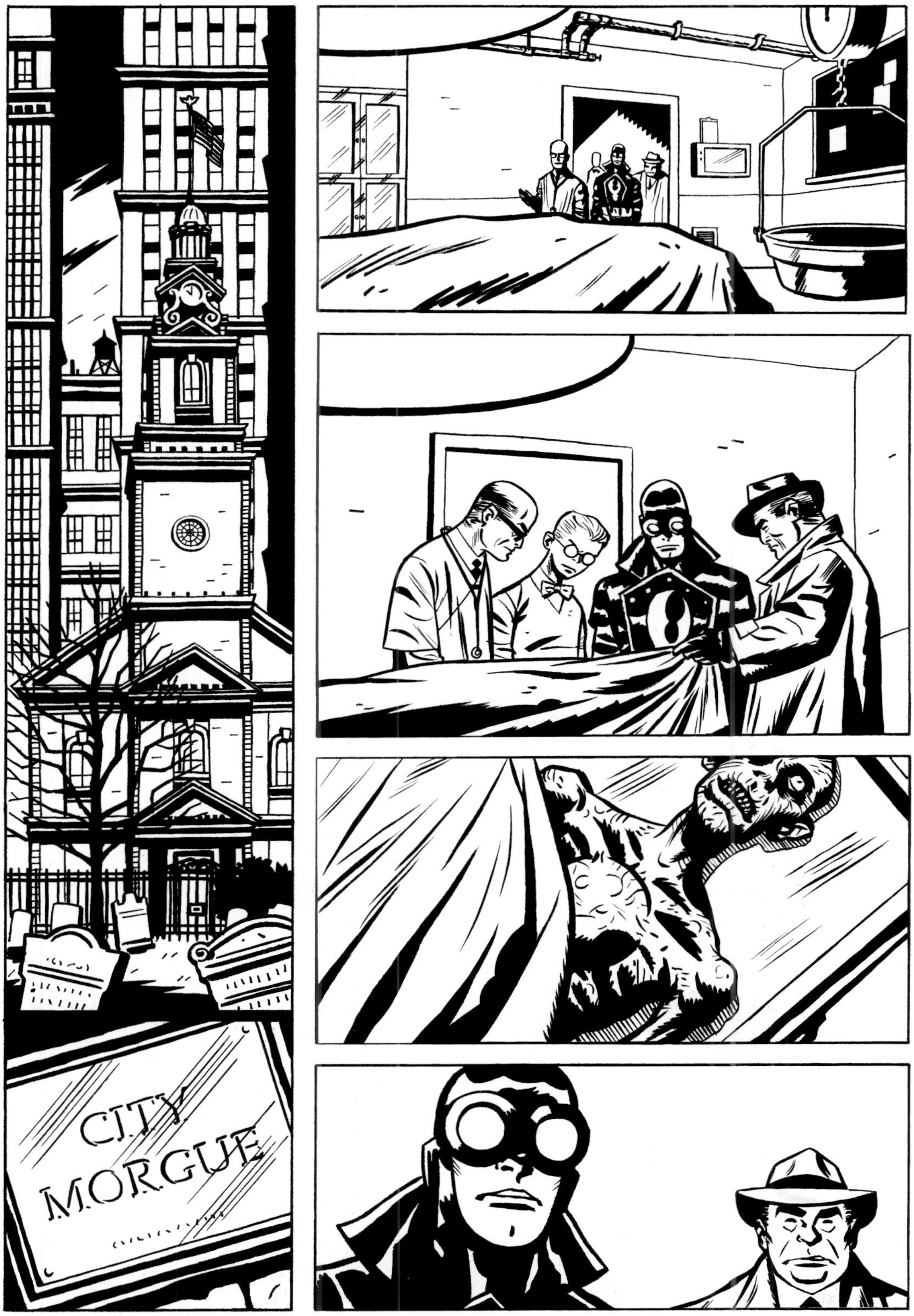
CITY
MORGUE

Roger Langridge.

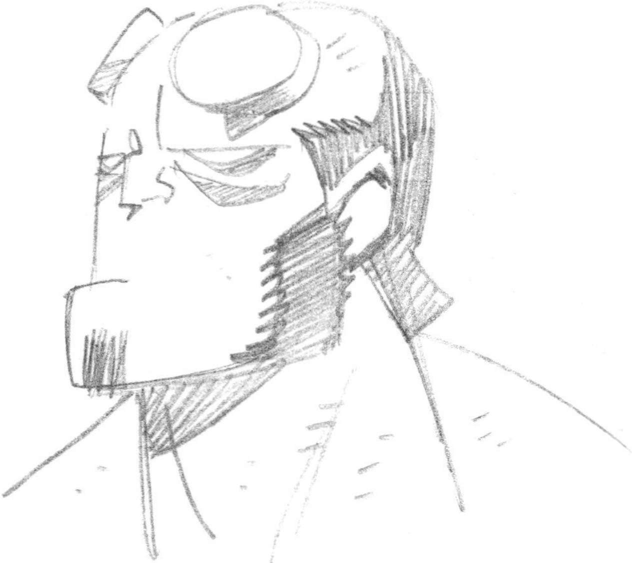

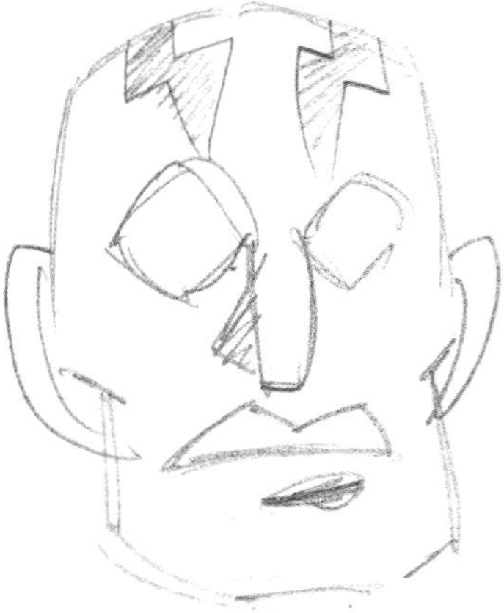

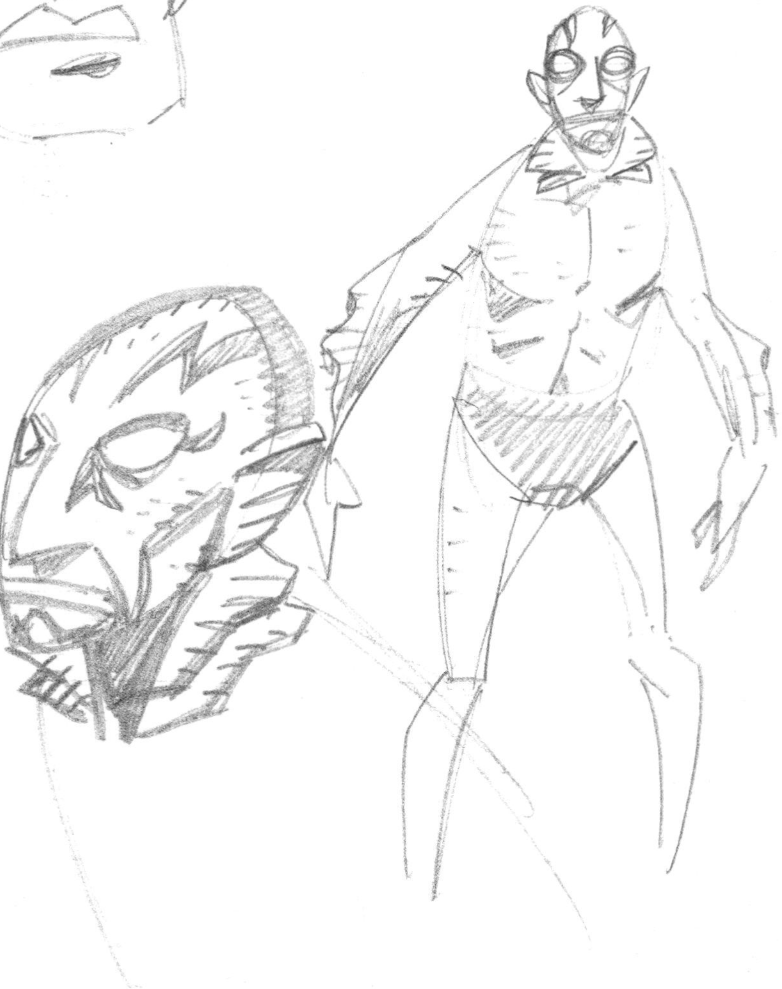

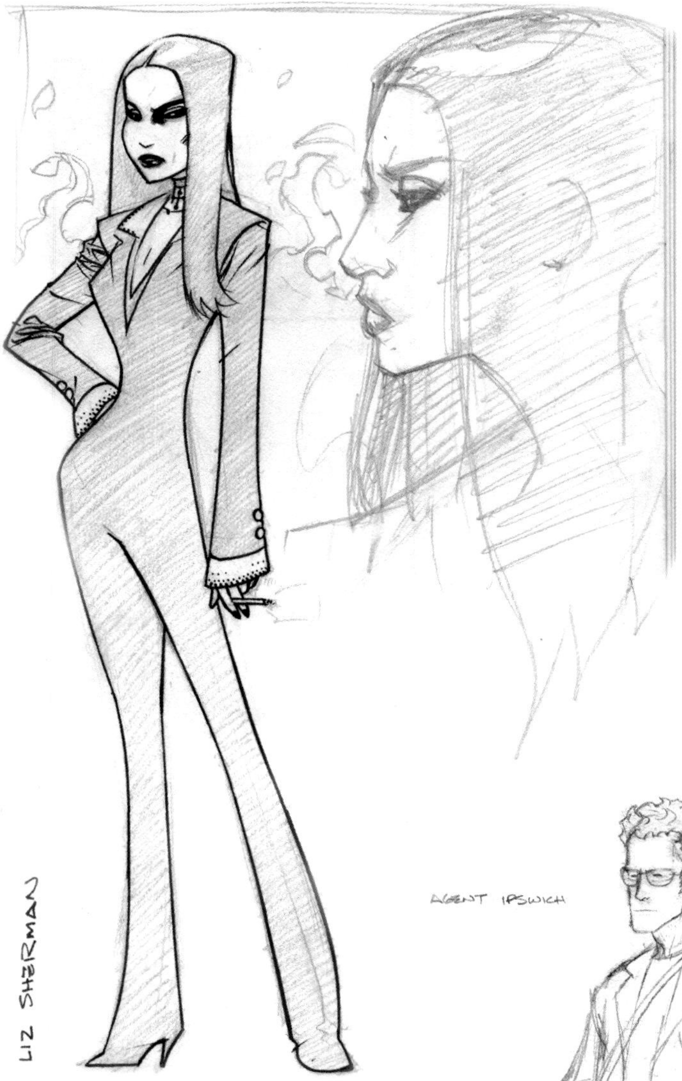
LIZ SHERMAN

Jason Pearson.

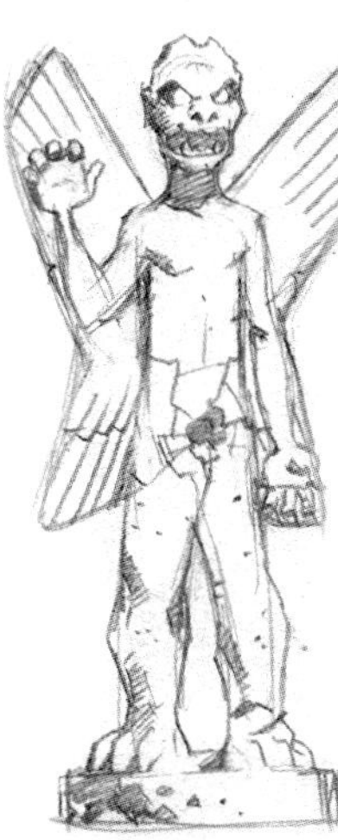
PAZUZU

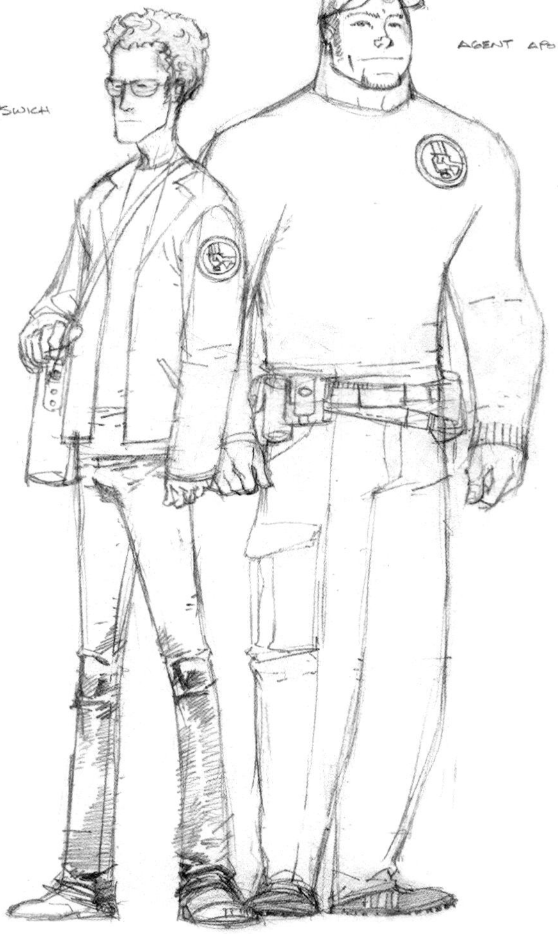
AGENT IPSWICH
AGENT APON

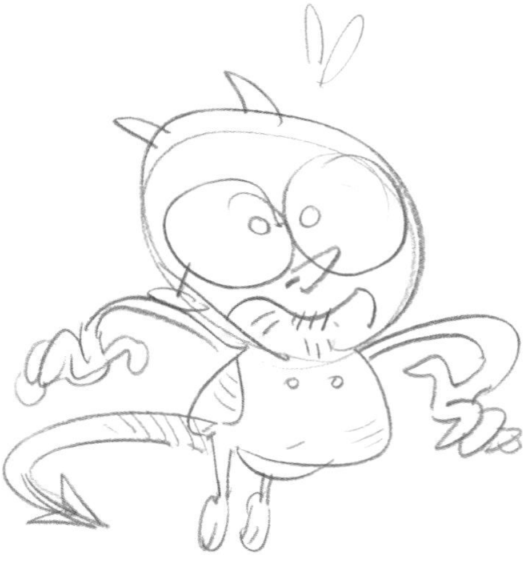

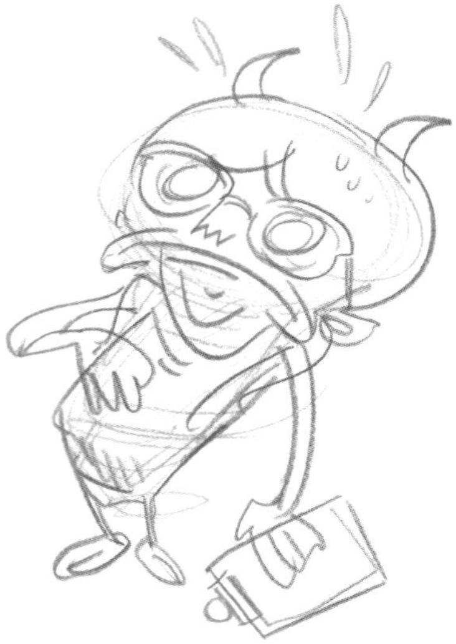

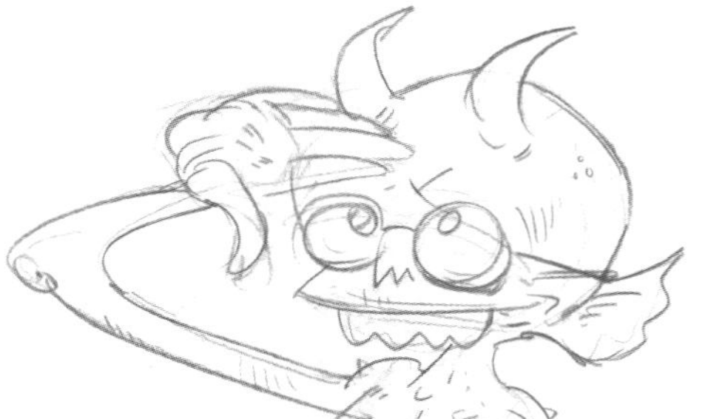

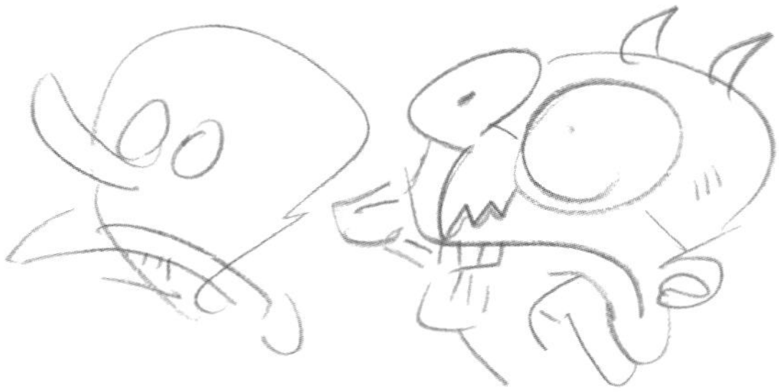

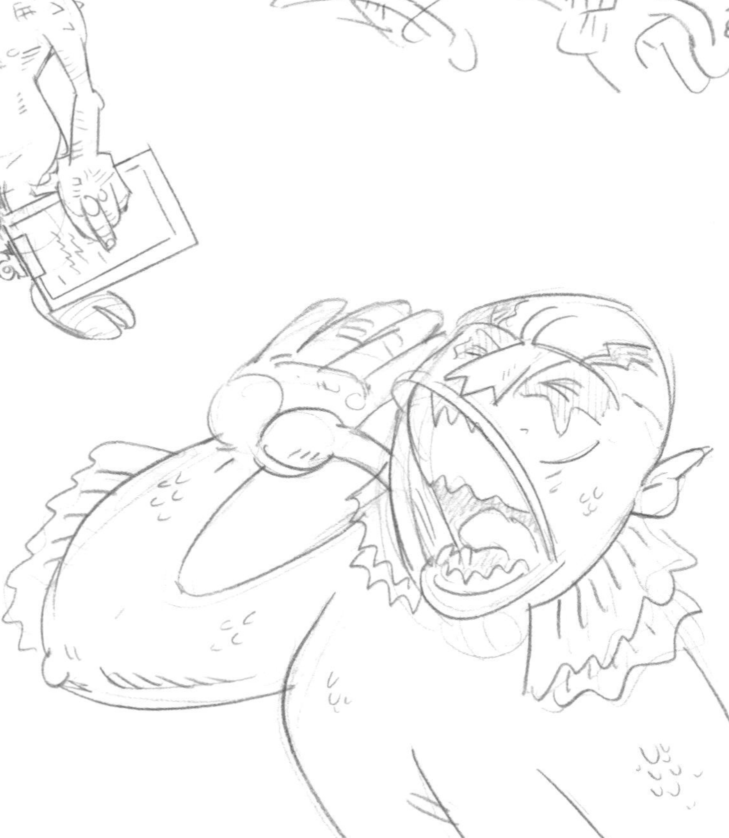

Bob Fingerman.

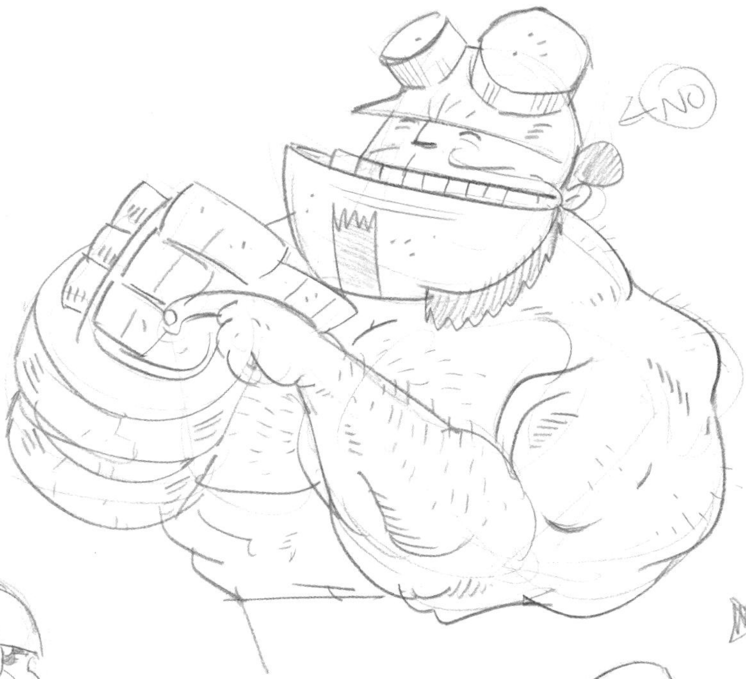
NO

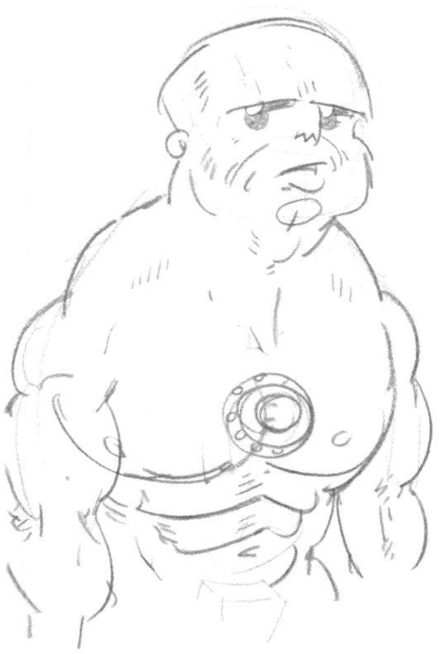

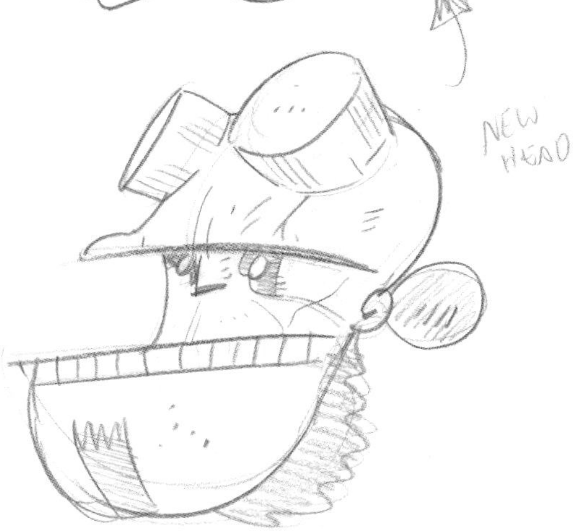
NEW HEAD

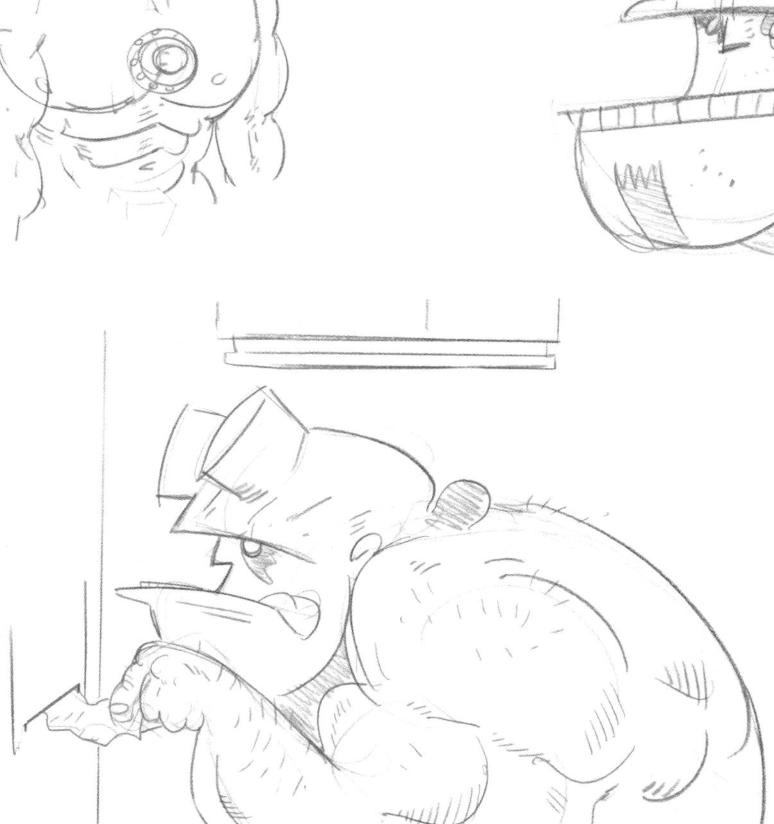

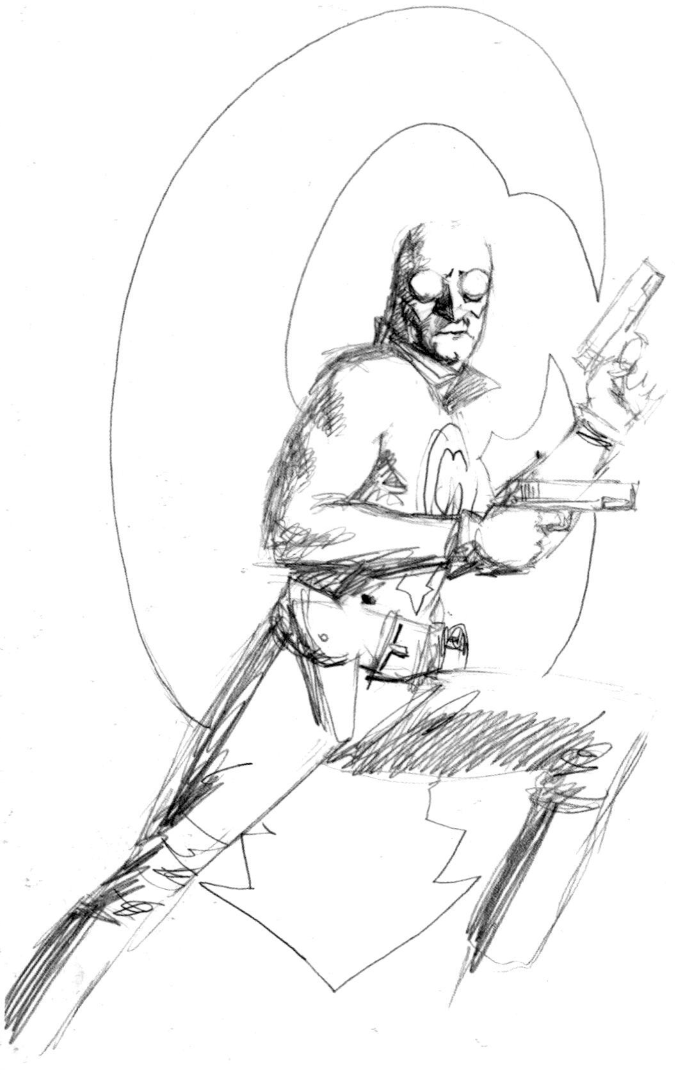

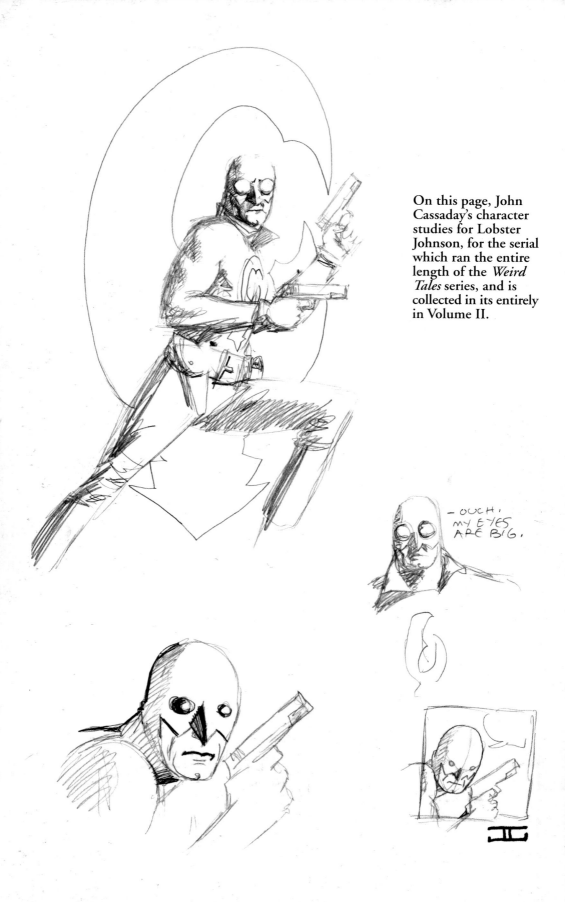

On this page, John Cassaday's character studies for Lobster Johnson, for the serial which ran the entire length of the *Weird Tales* series, and is collected in its entirely in Volume II.

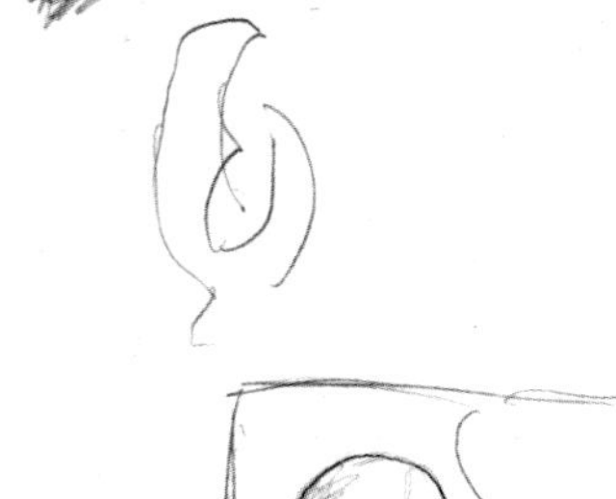
- OUCH, MY EYES ARE BIG.

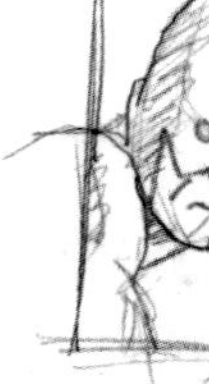

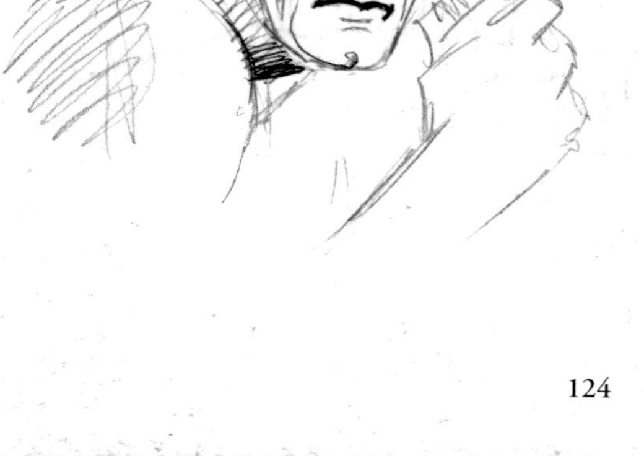

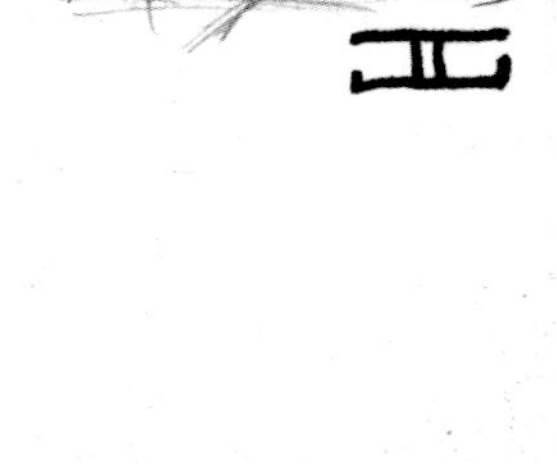

CREATORS

JOHN ARCUDI has written more comic books than his parole officer even knows about. He rocketed to comics stardom with his early work on *The Mask*, *Aliens*, and *Predator* comics for Dark Horse, and has since alienated thousands of fans with his more recent writing stints on *Gen 13*, *Doom Patrol*, and *Thunderbolts*.

JOE CASEY writes comic books, from the big franchise characters to creator-owned properties. He writes other things, too. He plays big, loud rock 'n' roll. He lives and works in Los Angeles, California.

JOHN CASSADAY never got to live his dream of replacing Slayer guitarist Kerry King. Still, he did become a highly respected professional comic book artist, and that's not so bad for a long-haired kid from Texas. His works to date include acclaimed stints on *Desperadoes*, *Captain America*, and *Planetary*.

RICK CORTES is a nearly ten-year veteran of the visual effects and illustration industries, having worked on dozens of films, television shows, videos, and the odd comic book or two. Past projects include the films *The League of Extraordinary Gentlemen* and *The House on Haunted Hill*. This summer, Rick executive produced the film *Here Comes Dr. Tran*, now touring North America as part of Spike & Mike's Sick and Twisted Festival of Animation.

TYRUBEN ELLINGSON is a long standing veteran of the film industry. He was a concept designer on the *Hellboy* movie as well as such films as *Blade 2*, *Men in Black*, and *Wolf*. He was also the effects art director on *Star Wars* (Special Edition), *Twister*, *Jurassic Park*, *Star Trek VI*, and many others.

BOB FINGERMAN created the critically acclaimed graphic novel, *Beg the Question*. He's also written several prose novels, some of which might actually see print someday. His latest offering is *Guilty Pancake*, a collection of drawings of hot chicks and demons. For more info visit www.bobfingerman.com.

MATT HOLLINGSWORTH is great at brewing his own beer, but he makes a living as one of the most prolific and talented colorists working in comics today. He attended the Joe Kubert School of Art before moving on to color such books as *Preacher*, *Legends of the Dark Knight*, *Catwoman*, *Grendel: Devils and Deaths*, and *The Punisher*. He lives in Santa Monica, California.

SEUNG KIM's first job in comics was *Hellboy Weird Tales*, and now he is very happy.

ROGER LANGRIDGE has worked for Marvel, DC, 2000AD, Fantagraphics, and many others over the last 15 years. His self-published comic, *Fred the Clown*, has been nominated for two Eisner Awards and one Ignatz Award.

STEVE LIEBER is best known for his art on *Whiteout* for Oni Press. He's illustrated everything from self-published young-adult minis to top-20 mainstream superhero titles.

ALEX MALEEV was asked to leave the famous Joe Kubert School of Cartooning after completing only half the program. Not because he wasn't good; he was so good his teachers told him he didn't need to be there. A native of Bulgaria, Maleev's dark scratchy style blossomed on *The Crow*. Credits include *Batman: No Man's Land* for DC and *Aliens vs. Predator* for Dark Horse. He is the regular artist on Marvel's *Daredevil*.

OVI NEDELCU, as well as being a talented writer and artist, enjoys schooling friend and fellow artist, Jeff Matsuda on the basketball court. His artistic career has taken him from animation to illustration, comics, and back again. To learn more or view his portfolio go to www.ovinedelcu.com.

FABIAN NICIEZA has written lots of comics. Many of them sold a lot of copies. Some of them were even good. He has also been an Advertising Manager, an Editor, an Editor-in-Chief, and a President/Publisher. He is now bald and tired. His latest work is *The Blackburne Covenant* with his *Weird Tales* collaborator Stefano Raffaele.

STEVE PARKHOUSE is British but not proud of it. He would rather be Icelandic, Swedish, or Navajo. He is quite old, but would rather be ancient. That should tell you everything.

JASON PEARSON lives and works in Portland, Oregon. When he's not protecting the home turf of the notorious Portland street gang The Jefferson Dragons, he's sure to be hard at work pencilling comics for companies like Dark Horse, Wildstorm, and Marvel. Pearson's recent work can be seen on such titles as *Body Bags* and *Global Frequency* #11.

ERIC POWELL is a hermit who lives in the Tennessee woods with his wife Robin and his two sons Gage and Cade. After realizing he could be a cartoonist without ever having to leave his house, he opted for the comic book industry rather than a lucrative career in the janitorial arts. He is best known for his critically acclaimed black comedy *The Goon* published bi-monthly from Dark Horse Comics.

STEFANO RAFFAELE was born in Milan in 1970. He began working in the Italian comics industry in 1994, breaking in to the U.S. market in 1996 with Valiant, and then DC and Marvel, on *New Gods*, *Legends of the Dark Knight*, and *X-Men*. After five years of drawing superheroes, he took a break from comics, returning with a style more suited to horror books. He's recently completed *Fragile* for Humanoids Publishing, and the Dark Horse miniseries *The Blackburne Covenant*, with Fabian Nicieza. He and Nicieza are now working on the monthly series *Hawkeye* for Marvel Comics.

MARK RICKETTS is dead. However, he continues to annoy the living by producing graphic novels like *Nowheresville* and *Whiskey Dickel, Int'l Cowgirl* from the grave. He is also working on the graphic novel, *Lazarus Jack* with artist Horacio Domingues. Can no one stop this monster?

SARA RYAN is the author of *Empress Of The World*, a winner of the Oregon Book Award. She was nominated for an Eisner Award for her first comic, *Me And Edith Head*. This Hellboy story was her second.